Tradition and Change
in the Asian Family

 EAST-WEST CENTER

Tradition and Change in the Asian Family

**Edited by Lee-Jay Cho
and Motō Yada**

East-West Center
Honolulu

Published in cooperation
with University Research
Center, Nihon University,
Tokyo

©1994 by the East-West Center
All rights reserved
Manufactured in the United States of America

LIBRARY OF CONGRESS
CATALOGING-IN-PUBLICATION DATA

Tradition and change in the Asian family / edited by Lee-Jay Cho and Motō [Motoo] Yada.
  p. cm.
  "Published in cooperation with University Research Center, Nihon University."
  Includes bibliographical references and index.
  ISBN 0-86638-161-9 (alk. paper) : $48.00
  1. Family—Asia. I. Cho, Lee-Jay. II. Yada, Motō, 1931– .
  HQ663.T73 1994
  306.85'095—dc20   94-21867
                                                    CIP

This book was printed on acid-free paper and meets the guidelines for permanence and durability of the Council on Library Resources.

Published in 1994 by the
East-West Center
1777 East-West Road,
Honolulu, Hawaii 96848

Distributed by the
University of Hawaii Press
2840 Kolowalu Street,
Honolulu, Hawaii 96822

Photographs on dust jacket:

Left: Family of Kensuke Akimoto (child in center), taken in the ninth year of the Taishō Era (1920). Kensuke Akimoto was the father of Mitsuko Katayama, program officer at the University Research Center of Nihon University. Photographer: unknown.

Right: Dr. Toshio Kuroda, author of Chapter 4 in this volume, and his wife (kneeling), surrounded by their two daughters, son-in-law, and granddaughter. Photographer: Katsumi Tanaka of Sankogeisha, Inc.

CONTENTS

List of Figures and Exhibits   ix

List of Tables   xi

Contributors   xxiii

Preface   xxix

PART I   INTRODUCTION AND BACKGROUND

1. Introduction   3
   by Lee-Jay Cho and Motō Yada

2. Families in Developing Countries: Idealized Morality and Theories of Family Change   19
   by Peter McDonald

3. A Cultural Approach to the Family in Japan and the United States   29
   by Patricia G. Steinhoff

4. Family Structure and Social Change: Implications of Fertility Changes in Japan and China   45
   by Toshio Kuroda

PART II   THE JAPANESE FAMILY IN COMPARATIVE AND HISTORICAL PERSPECTIVE

5. Tradition and Change in the Japanese Family and Community Life of Japan   59
   by Noriaki Gotō

Contents

6. Changing Attitudes toward Marriage and the Family in Japan 91
   by Noriko O. Tsuya

7. Japanese Perceptions of the Family and Living Arrangements: The Trend toward Nuclearization 121
   by Hiroshi Kawabe and Hiroaki Shimizu

8. A Structural Study of Spouse Selection in Japan 135
   by Yasuo Natsukari

9. Middle-Aged Japanese and Their Parents: Coresidence and Contact 153
   by Linda G. Martin and Noriko O. Tsuya

10. Who Lives in the Extended Family and Why? The Case of Japan 179
    by Satomi Kurosu

11. Contact with Parents in Japan: Effects on Attitudes toward Gender and Intergenerational Roles 199
    by Ronald R. Rindfuss, Tim Futing Liao, and Noriko O. Tsuya

12. A Comparative Analysis of Coresidence and Contact with Parents in Japan and the United States 221
    by Larry L. Bumpass

13. Industry Restructuring and Family Migration Decisions: A Community Study in Japan 247
    by Suzanne Culter

PART III FAMILY CHANGE IN OTHER ASIAN SOCIETIES

14. Rural Family and Community Life in South Korea: Changes in Family Attitudes and Living Arrangements for the Elderly 273
    by Nam-Il Kim, Soon Choi, and Insook Han Park

15. Changes in Intergenerational Relations in the Chinese Family: Taiwan's Experience 319
    by Te-Hsiung Sun and Yin Hsing Liu

16. Coresidence and the Transition to Adulthood in the Rural Thai Family 363
    by Chai Podhisita

17. Family Formation in Rural Thailand: Evidence from the 1989–90 Family and Household Survey 383
    by Bhassorn Limanonda

18. Attitudes toward Family Values in Rural Thailand 401
    by Malinee Wongsith

Contents

PART IV   CONCLUSION

19. The Japanese Family in   421
    Comparative Perspective
      by Andrew Cherlin

    Appendix
    Origin and Design of   435
    Japan's 1988 National
    Family Survey
      by Michio Ozaki

    Index   449

LIST OF FIGURES AND EXHIBITS

Figures

5.1. Location of Uenohara Town   65

5.2. Location of Ōgaito in Uenohara Town and the municipalities around Uenohara Town   66

5.3. Settlements in Ōgaito, 1989   72

5.4. Settlements in Ōgaito, 1938   73

5.5. Settlements in Ōgaito, 1961   74

5.6. Related households in Ōgaito, 1989   77

6.1. Total fertility rates: Japan, 1947–89   94

8.1. Trend in marriage rate: Japan, 1947–88   137

8.2. Trends in the percentage of women single, by age group: Japan, 1955–85   138

8.3. Trends in the percentage of men single, by age group: Japan, 1955–85   140

8.4. Prevalence of marriage type among married men and women, by age group: Japan, 1988   143

11.1. Model of the effect of contact with husband's and wife's parents on family attitudes   204

12.1. Age differences in seeing parents weekly: married persons with living, non-coresiding parents   235

List of Figures and Exhibits

12.2. Age differences in seeing parents weekly: all married persons (including those with no living parents)   244

14.1. The three study areas   275

14.2. Age and sex distributions of the population: South Korea and the study areas, 1959 and 1990   279

15.1. The 15 dependent variables and their arrangement in the model of intergenerational relations: Taiwan   323

Exhibits

10.A. Index of variables   190

15.A. The 38 independent variables representing background characteristics of KAP respondent families: Taiwan   324

LIST OF TABLES

4.1. Percentage distribution of households, by type: Japan, selected years, 1920–90   46

4.2. Percentages of small and large households and average number of household members: Japan, selected years, 1920–90   47

4.3. Number of households, population size, and average number of household members: China, selected years, 1911–47   48

4.4. Average number of household members in urban, rural, and all areas: China, 1953, 1964, and 1982   49

4.5. Percentages of small and large households: China, selected years, 1930–82   49

4.6. Percentage distribution of households, by generation: China, 1930, 1982, and 1987   50

4.7. Fertility, mortality, and family size: Japan, selected years, 1920–90   51

4.8. Percentage distribution of households, by type of settlement and number of household members: China, 1987   52

5.1. Changes in percentages of the employed population, by industry: Japan, 1800–1985   60

5.2. Urban population as percentage of total population: Japan, 1920–85   61

5.3. Population trends in Yuzurihara, Japan, 1900–85   67

5.4. Number of related households in Ōgaito, Japan, 1938   69

5.5. Numbers of households in the surveys of 1938, 1961, and 1989: Ōgaito   75

5.6. Birthplace of marriage partners in Ōgaito, by year of marriage: 1961   78

5.7. Birthplace of wives in Ōgaito, by year of birth: 1984   78

5.8. Place where mothers and wives of current household heads spent their early childhood years: Ōgaito, 1989   79

5.9. Number of households, by type of household: Ōgaito, 1984 and 1989   82

5.10. Number of households, by number of persons per household: Ōgaito, 1984 and 1989   82

5.11. Population of working ages and employed persons, by sex: Ōgaito, 1984 and 1989   83

5.12. Occupations and places of work, excluding agriculture: Ōgaito, 1984   84

5.13. Areas for shopping and daily life for residents: Ōgaito, 1989   85

5.14. Household affiliations with social and administrative groups (*kumi*): Ōgaito, 1989   86

6.1. Age-specific fertility rates and percentage changes in rate: Japan, 1950–90   95

6.2. Age-specific proportions ever married, by sex and the singulate mean age at marriage (SMAM): Japan, 1950–90   96

6.3. Divorce rates, marriage rates, and ratios of divorces to 100 marriages: Japan, 1950–90   97

6.4. Life-table estimates of the proportion of marriages disrupted by divorce within selected marriage durations: Japan, 1955–85   98

6.5. Effects of changes in marital composition and marital fertility rates on the total fertility rate with interaction components allocated equally: Japan, 1950–90   99

6.6. Variables used in the analysis of attitudes toward marriage and the family among never-married Japanese, ages 20–34: National Family Survey, 1988   101

6.7. Variables used in the analysis of attitudes toward marriage and the family among currently married Japanese, ages 30 and above: National Family Survey, 1988   102

6.8. Coefficients (Betas) and standard errors estimated from the logit regression analyses of approval of singlehood, expected functions of the home, and reasons for having children: never-

List of Tables

married Japanese, ages 20–34, 1988   110

6.9. Coefficients (Betas) and standard errors estimated from the logit regression analyses of approval of singlehood, positive attitudes toward remarriage in old age, and expected functions of the home: currently married Japanese, ages 30 and above, 1988   112

6.10. Estimated coefficients and standard errors from the multinomial logit analysis of reasons for having children: currently married Japanese, ages 30 and above, 1988   113

7.1. Four perceptions of the basic structure of the Japanese family and how it has been changing in recent decades   122

7.2. Japanese family structure, living arrangements, and intentions   123

7.3. Percentage distribution of households, by household type and by sex and age group of elderly household heads: United States, England, France, and Japan: 1981   125

7.4. Percentage distribution of the elderly Japanese population, by household type, sex, and age group: 1985   127

7.5. Parents' attitudes about living with married children (%): United States, England, France, and Japan, 1980   128

7.6. Opinions about the living arrangements of elderly people, by age group (%): Japan, 1986   129

7.7. Preferred living arrangements of adult Japanese, by actual living arrangements (%): 1986   130

8.1. Numbers of marriages and the marriage rate: Japan, selected years, 1935–88   136

8.2. Percentage of single women, by age group: Japan, 1955–85   139

8.3. Percentage of single men, by age group: Japan, 1955–85   139

8.4. Intentions to marry, by sex and age group (%): single Japanese, 1982 and 1987   142

8.5. How married women met their husbands (%): Japan, 1988   145

8.6. Criteria for spouse selection, by age and sex: Japan, 1988   147

8.7. Criteria for spouse selection, by educational level and sex: Japan, 1988   147

9.1. Definitions and means of variables for coresidence analysis: Japan, 1988   159

9.2. Coefficients and standard errors from the logit estimation of coresidence with one or more of the index person's own parents: Japan, 1988   163

9.3. Coresidence arrangements of middle-aged men and women coresiding with their parents (%): Japan, 1988   165

9.4. Timing of coresidence among middle-aged men and women coresiding with their parents (%): Japan, 1988   165

9.5. Who moved in with whom among men and women coresiding with their parents (%): Japan, 1988   166

9.6. Persons responsible for the household expenses among men and women coresiding with their parents (%): Japan, 1988   166

9.7. Main reason for coresidence among men and women coresiding with their parents (%): Japan, 1988   166

9.8. Frequency of seeing and phoning their own parents among men and women not coresiding with their parents (%): Japan, 1988   168

9.9. Coefficients and standard errors from the ordered probit analysis of frequency of seeing and phoning non-coresident parents: Japan, 1988   172

App. 9.1. Coefficients and standard errors from the logit estimation of nonresponse to questions about seeing and phoning non-coresident parents: Japan, 1988   176

10.1 Number and percentage of minimal household units (MHUs), by age group of respondent: Japan, 1979   188

10.2. Pearson correlation coefficients among variables: ages 60 and above   191

10.3. Pearson correlation coefficients among variables: ages 30–59   191

10.4 Effects of individual-level and contextual variables on the extended family: ages 60 and above   192

10.5 Effects of individual-level and contextual variables on the extended family: ages 30–59   193

11.1. Percentages of respondents choosing a specified trait as one of the three characteristics they would like for their son or daughter: Japan, 1988 National Family Survey   207

11.2. Means and percentage distributions for the independent variables in the multivariate analyses   209

11.3. Logistic regression model estimates (Betas) of whether it is the eldest son's duty to look after his parents, for the visiting and telephoning parents variables   211

11.4. Logistic regression model estimates (Betas) of whether the family name must be succeeded even by adopting a child, for the visiting and telephoning parents variables   212

11.5. Logistic regression model estimates (Betas) of whether it is a good thing for men to work in the kitchen at home, for the visiting and telephoning parents variables   214

List of Tables

11.6. Number of significant coefficients in logistic regression analyses of socialization traits   215

12.1. Percentages with living parents, by age: Japan and United States, married persons, ages 25–64   223

12.2. Percentages coresiding with own or spouse's parents, by sex and age group: Japan and United States, married persons, ages 25–64   224

12.3. Percentages whose parents or parents-in-law ever lived with them, by selected respondent characteristics: United States, persons 55–64 in an intact first marriage   225

12.4. Coresidence with own parents, by selected respondent characteristics: Japan, married persons ages 25–64, with a living parent   227

12.5. Percentage distribution of frequency of seeing own parents, by sex: Japan and United States, married persons, ages 25–64, with a living parent   229

12.6. Percentages seeing own parents at least weekly, by selected respondent characteristics: Japan and United States, married persons, ages 25–64, with at least one living parent but not coresiding   231

12.7. Logit analysis of seeing own parents at least weekly, by respondent characteristics: Japan and United States, married males, ages 25–64, with at least one living parent but not coresiding   232

12.8. Logit analysis of seeing own parents at least weekly, by respondent characteristics: Japan and United States, married females, ages 25–64, with at least one living parent but not coresiding   233

12.9. Percentages having weekly contact with own parents, by respondent characteristics: Japan and United States, married persons, ages 25–64, with at least one living parent but not coresiding   238

12.10. Logit analysis of weekly contact with own parents, by respondent characteristics: Japan and United States, married males, ages 25–64, with at least one living parent but not coresiding   239

12.11. Logit analysis of weekly contact with own parents, by respondent characteristics: Japan and United States, married females, ages 25–64, with at least one living parent but not coresiding   240

12.12. Weekly contact with own parents in total population (including those with no living parents), by age: Japan and United States, married persons, ages 25–64   244

13.1. Total population of Yūbari City and percentage change: five-year periods, 1900–90   251

List of Tables

13.2. Age distribution of sample and of Yūbari City population: mid-1980s 254

13.3. Age distribution of sample and of Yūbari City, by five-year age group: mid-1980s 254

13.4. Descriptive statistics for the determinants of leaving Yūbari 256

13.5. Coefficients and standard errors from the logit estimation of intentions to leave Yūbari 257

13.6. Adjusted probability of leaving Yūbari, by selected determinants (values of the other determinants controlled at their means) 259

13.7. Intention to leave Yūbari, by home ownership: 1986 260

14.1. Age distributions: 1959 and 1990 278

14.2. Attitudes toward children's obedience to parents: 1959 and 1990 282

14.3. Attitudes toward continuing the family lineage in the case of having no sons: 1959 and 1990 282

14.4. Parents' aspirations for sons' education: 1959 and 1990 283

14.5. Parents' aspirations for daughters' education: 1959 and 1990 283

14.6. Parents' aspirations for eldest son's occupation: 1959 and 1990 284

14.7. Responsibility for arranging sons' marriages: 1959 and 1990 285

14.8. Responsiblity for arranging daughters' marriages: 1959 and 1990 285

14.9. Attitudes toward divorce: 1959 and 1990 286

14.10. Attitudes toward widows' remarriage: 1959 and 1990 286

14.11. Percentages of respondents observing traditional family events: 1990 287

14.12. Households involved in *kye* meetings: 1959 and 1990 288

14.13. Households involved in *kye* meetings, by purpose of meeting: 1959 and 1990 288

14.14. Summary data on households, by family types, from various studies: Korea, 1630–1975 290

14.15. Households, by family type: South Korea, 1966–85 291

14.16. Households, by family type: 1959 and 1990 291

14.17. Households including one or both parents of the husband or wife, by husband's age: respondents with one or both parents living, 1990 293

14.18. Definitions and means of variables used in the analysis of data on living with any parents 295

List of Tables

14.19. Results of the logistic regression on living with parent or not, based on the sample of sons with one or both parents alive   296

14.20. Unadjusted and adjusted proportions of respondents living with any parents, controlling for other predictor variables by holding them at their mean values   297

14.21. Summary data on living arrangements of the elderly, from various surveys: South Korea, 1972–88   298

14.22. Living arrangements of the elderly, by sex and marital status: 1990   301

14.23. Definitions and means of variables used in the analysis of the elderly, living alone or with spouse only   302

14.24. Results of the logistic regression on living alone or with spouse only, based on the sample of the elderly   303

14.25. Unadjusted and adjusted proportions of elderly persons living alone or with spouse only, controlling for other predictor variables by holding them at their mean values   304

App. 14.1. Summary results of the survey, by region and administrative district: 1990   307

App. 14.2. Age-sex distribution of respondents: study areas, 1990   308

App. 14.3. Distribution of households, by size of household: study areas, 1959 and 1990   309

App. 14.4. Distribution of households, by generational composition: study areas, 1959 and 1990   309

App. 14.5. Distribution of households, by the size of farmland owned: study areas, 1959 and 1990   309

App. 14.6. Age distribution of the heads of household: study areas, 1959 and 1990   310

App. 14.7. Educational attainment of the heads of household: study areas, 1959 and 1960   310

App. 14.8. Religion of the respondents and their spouses: study areas, 1959 and 1990   311

App. 14.9. Patterns of respondents' residence, current versus childhood residence: study areas, 1990   311

App. 14.10. Percentage distribution of preferred care-givers in case of becoming old and ill: study areas, 1990   312

App. 14.11. Percentages of respondents who would consider specified relatives as members of their own family, by sex and coresidence: study areas, 1990   313

App. 14.12. Percentage of respondents living with any parents, by age of parents and survivorship of parents: study areas, 1990   314

App. 14.13. Percentage of respondents living with parents, by age and birth order of respondents: study areas, 1990   314

App. 14.14. Percentage of respondents living with parents, by birth order and father's status as a member of the head family for at least two generations: study areas, 1990   314

App. 14.15. Percentage of respondents living with parents, by educational attainment and father's status as a member of the head family for at least two generations: study areas, 1990   315

App. 14.16. Percentage of respondents living with parents, by age and type of marriage: study areas, 1990   315

App. 14.17. Percentage of elderly persons, by sex, marital status, and age: study areas, 1990   315

App. 14.18. Working status of elderly persons, by sex and living arrangements (%): study areas, 1990   316

15.1. Sample size for each KAP survey: Taiwan, 1967–86   322

15.2. Newly married couples living with the husband's parents immediately after marriage, by marriage cohort (%): Taiwan 1952–86   326

15.3. Newly married couples living with the husband's parents immediately after marriage, by survey year and selected characteristics (%): Taiwan 1973–86   327

15.4. Couples living with the husband's parents at the time of the survey and the results of MCA for those whose husband's parents were available in Taiwan at the time of the survey, by survey year and selected variables (%): Taiwan, 1967–86   329

15.5. Relative importance of selected independent variables in explaining the proportion living with husband's parents at the time of the survey, by survey year, expressed in Eta and Beta values in an MCA: Taiwan, 1967–86   331

15.6. Husband's parents living alone, by survey year and selected variables (%): Taiwan, 1973–86   335

15.7. Couples living with the wife's parents at the time of the survey, among those with the wife's parents living in Taiwan and who were not living with the husband's parents, by survey year and selected variables (%): Taiwan, 1967–86   337

15.8. Couples wanting and not wanting to live with their married sons in the future, by survey year and selected variables (%): Taiwan, 1967–86   339

15.9. Couples believing that newlywed couples should live alone immediately after marriage, by survey year and selected variables: Taiwan, 1973–86   341

List of Tables

15.10. Changes in four types of money flow between married children and their parents, by survey year: Taiwan, 1973–86   344

15.11. Couples frequently giving money to the husband's parents or sharing meals with them, by selected variables and survey year (%): Taiwan, 1973–86   346

15.12. Couples ever giving money to the wife's parents or sharing meals with them, by selected variables and survey year (%): Taiwan, 1973–86   347

15.13. Wives expecting their sons to contribute to the family economy before marriage by working in the family business or on the family farm, by selected variables and survey year (%): Taiwan, 1973–86   348

15.14. Wives wanting to depend on their sons economically in old age, by selected variables and survey year: Taiwan, 1973–86   349

15.15. Wives' educational aspirations for the first and second child, by survey year (%): Taiwan, 1973–86   352

15.16. Wives expecting their first child to receive a college or better education, by selected variables and survey year (%): Taiwan, 1973–86   353

15.17. Marriages decided by the couple alone, by parents alone, or collaboratively, by selected variables and survey year (%): Taiwan, 1973–86   354

15.18. Frequency of mutual visiting between the couple and the husband's parents, by survey year (%): Taiwan, 1973–86   356

16.1. Respondents who had specified family members living in the same residence or in the same community with them when they were about 10 years old, by sex of respondents (%): rural Thailand, 1989   368

16.2. Respondents who had specified family members sharing the same residence with them when they were about 10 years old, by current age of respondents (%): rural Thailand, 1989   369

16.3. Ever-married respondents who had specified family members living in the same residence or in the same community with them during the first year of their marriage, by sex of respondents (%): rural Thailand, 1989   370

16.4. Ever-married respondents who had specified family members sharing the same residence with them during the first year of their marriage, by current age of respondents (%): rural Thailand, 1989   370

16.5. Respondents whose family property had been divided, by the method of division: rural Thailand, 1989   371

16.6. Responses to the question about the age or stage of their lives when respondents realized that they had

List of Tables

become adults: rural Thailand, 1989   374

16.7. Timing and prevalence of important life-course events experienced by respondents between ages 10 and 30, by sex: rural Thailand, 1989   375

17.1. Percentage distribution of respondents by region, method of spouse selection, and sex: Thai Family and Household Survey, 1989–90   386

17.2. Percentage distribution of respondents by age at marriage, sex, and region: Thailand, 1989–90   387

17.3. Percentage distribution of respondents' age at first marriage by sex and spouse's age at same marriage: Thai Family and Household Survey, 1989–90   388

17.4. Percentage distribution of respondents by attitudes toward marriage, divorce, and remarriage and by sex: Thai Family and Household Survey, 1989–90   389

17.5. Percentage distribution of respondents by sex and type of relatives who resided in the same house or same locality during the first year of their first marriage: Thai Family and Household Survey, 1989–90   391

17.6. Percentage distribution of respondents by region and type of relatives who resided in the same house or same locality during the first year of their first marriage: Thai Family and Household Survey, 1989–90   392

17.7. Percentage distribution of respondents by region, amount of time after marriage before establishing their own household, and current age: Thai Family and Household Survey, 1989–90   393

17.8. Percentage distribution of respondents by region, amount of time after marriage before establishing their own household, and sex: Thai Family and Household Survey, 1989–90   394

17.9. Percentage distribution of respondents by sex and source of assistance received in buying or building a house, moving, and purchasing household appliances and furniture: Thai Family and Household Survey, 1989–90   395

17.10. Percentage distribution of female respondents by place where the first child was born and current age: Thai Family and Household Survey, 1989–90   396

17.11. Percentage distribution of respondents by region, whether assistance was received, and source of assistance during the first months after the first child was born: Thai Family and Household Survey, 1989–90   397

18.1. Percentages agreeing with family-value items: Thai Family Survey, 1989   405

18.2. Percentages agreeing with family-value items, by age and sex: Thai Family Survey, 1989   408

18.3. Percentages agreeing with family-value items, by education, occupation, and region: Thai Family Survey, 1989   410

18.4. Scoring scheme for the 10 family-value items selected for the modernity index   412

18.5. Correlation matrix of the 10 modernity-index items   413

18.6. Frequency of scores on modernity-index items: Thai Family Survey, 1989   414

18.7. Multiple classification analysis of the mean of the modernity index, by selected characteristics of respondents: Thai Family Survey, 1989   415

18.8. Respondents' choice of caretaker in old age or long-term illness (%): Thai Family Survey, 1989   416

18.9. Person with whom respondents expected to live when old (%): Thai Family Survey, 1989   416

18.10. Person to inherit the parents' properties after their demise (%): Thai Family Survey, 1989   416

CONTRIBUTORS

Editors

Lee-Jay CHO is vice president for program development at the East-West Center and former director of the Center's Population Institute (now the Program on Population). He holds a Ph.D. in sociology from the University of Chicago, a doctorate in economics from Keio University, and a doctorate in demography from Tokyo University. His publications include numerous books and articles on Asian demography and economic development, including *Economic Development in the Republic of Korea: A Policy Perspective* (edited with Yoon Hyung Kim, East-West Center, 1991) and *Korea's Political Economy: An Institutional Perspective* (edited with Yoon Kyung Kim, Westview Press, 1994).

Motō YADA is professor of sociology, anthropology, and anatomy at the College of Humanities and Sciences of Nihon University, Tokyo, and is in charge of a comprehensive study of Japanese culture at the university's Culture Institute. He holds a doctorate in medicine from Nihon University. His primary research focus is on the comparative study of cultures, particularly those of the United States, Korea, and Japan.

Authors

BHASSORN Limanonda is associate professor and former director (1989–92) of the Institute of Population Studies, Chulalongkorn University, Bangkok. Since 1975 her research on population issues has focused on marriage and the family, and currently she is investigating the AIDS problem in Thailand. Dr. Limanonda has a Ph.D. in sociology-demography from Brown University.

Larry L. BUMPASS is the N. B. Ryder Professor of Sociology, University of Wisconsin–Madison, and co-director of the (U.S.) National Survey of Families and Households. He is a former president of the Population Association of America. His research interests lie in the social demography of the family, including fertility, cohabitation, marriage, union stability, children's family experiences and the life-course consequences of those, and intergenerational relationships. He has a Ph.D. in sociology from the University of Michigan.

CHAI Podhisita is an assistant professor at the Institute for Population and Social Research, Mahidol University, Bangkok. He served as deputy director of the institute from 1990 to 1992, and since 1991 he has been a member of the Steering Committee of the World Health Organization's Task Force for Social Science Research on Reproductive Health. Since 1985 Dr. Chai has taught demography and conducted several research studies in population and related fields. His research interests include family and youth in transitional societies, social and behavioral aspects of reproductive health, and the social dimension of AIDS transmission in Thailand. He has a Ph.D. in anthropology from the University of Hawaii.

Andrew CHERLIN is Griswold Professor of Public Policy in the Department of Sociology at Johns Hopkins University, Baltimore. He conducts research on a number of issues concerning families and households and is the author (with Frank Furstenberg) of *Divided Families: What Happens to Children when Parents Part* (Harvard University Press, 1991). He holds a Ph.D. in sociology from the University of California at Los Angeles.

Soon CHOI is associate professor of sociology at the College of Social Science and research associate at the Population Research Center, Dong-A University, in Pusan, Republic of Korea. He received his undergraduate education at Seoul National University in Korea and his graduate education in sociology from the University of Hawaii.

Suzanne CULTER is assistant professor in the Department of East Asian Studies, McGill University, Montreal. She has a Ph.D. in sociology from the University of Hawaii.

Noriaki GOTŌ is assistant professor of sociology at Nihon University in Tokyo. He is a specialist in rural and regional sociology and a member of the Asian Rural Sociology Working Group, among other professional associations.

Contributors

Hiroshi KAWABE is professor of geography at Senshu University in Tokyo. During 1986–91 he held a professorship at the Population Research Institute of Nihon University. He holds a Ph.D. in geography from the University of Tokyo.

Nam-Il KIM is professor of applied statistics at Dong-A University in Pusan, Republic of Korea. He was director of the Population Research Center of the university during 1985–93 and a member of the Bureau of Statistics between 1967 and 1982. Since 1985 he has been a member of the Statistical Advisory Committee for the National Statistical Office. He holds a doctorate in public health (biostatistics) from the University of Hawaii.

Toshio KURODA is director emeritus of the Population Research Institute, Nihon University, Tokyo, and special advisor to the University Research Center of Nihon University. He served as the Population Research Institute's first director between June 1979 and March 1980. Prior to that assignment, he served for 30 years at the Institute of Population Problems, Ministry of Health and Welfare, respectively as a technical research officer, chief of the Migration Section and the Migration Division, chief of the Population Policy Division, and director of the institute. Dr. Kuroda holds a doctorate of economics from Keiō University.

Satomi KUROSU is research associate at International Research Center for Japanese Studies, Kyoto, Japan. She is currently a visiting researcher at the Max-Planck Institute for Human Development and Education, Berlin, Germany. Dr. Kurosu has a Ph.D. in sociology from the University of Washington.

Tim Futing LIAO is assistant professor of sociology at the University of Illinois, Urbana-Champaign. Dr. Liao has also taught at the University of Georgia in Athens. He has a Ph.D. in sociology from the University of North Carolina–Chapel Hill.

Yin-Hsing LIU is associate professor of statistics at National Cheng-Kung University in Taiwan. He was a research associate and then senior specialist at Taiwan Provincial Institute of Family Planning from 1981 to 1990. He holds a Ph.D. in statistics from National Central University in Taiwan.

Peter MCDONALD is deputy director (research) of the Australian Institute of Family Studies in Melbourne. During 1994 he is on secondment to the Australian Urban and Regional Development Review, a major initiative of the Australian Government. Dr. McDonald is an internationally known population expert with research interests focusing on changing marriage, divorce, and family trends in both developed and developing nations. He has advised a number of overseas governments on census and population measuring. He has a Ph.D. in demography from The Australian National University.

MALINEE Wongsith is associate professor at the Institute of Population Studies, Chulalongkorn University, in Bangkok. Her research interests include aging and related matters. She has published articles on family care of the elderly in Thailand, the social and economic effects of aging in Thailand, and the impact of living arrangements for the elderly on government programs in that country.

Linda G. MARTIN is director of the Domestic Research Division and vice president of RAND in Santa Monica, California. From 1989 to 1993 she was director of the Committee on Population of the U.S. National Research Council in Washington, D.C. Prior to that for 10 years she was a research associate at the East-West Center's Population Institute and successively assistant, associate, and full professor of economics at the University of Hawaii. Dr. Martin has a Ph.D. in economics from Princeton University.

Yasuo NATSUKARI is associate professor of sociology at Nihon University in Tokyo and research fellow at the university's Population Research Institute.

Michio OZAKI is executive director of The Population Problems Research Council of the Mainichi Newspapers Company, Tokyo, and executive senior writer of the Mainichi Newspapers. He is also a lecturer at Tokai University in Kanagawa Prefecture. During 1993–94 he is serving as assistant attaché to Japan's Permanent Mission to the United Nations. Between 1985 and 1989, while managing the Opinion Poll Department of the Mainichi Newspapers, Mr. Ozaki oversaw the conduct of the Japanese National Family Survey. He is an experienced journalist specializing in political affairs.

Insook Han PARK is associate professor of sociology at Konkuk University, Seoul. Dr. Park is a member of the Korean Sociological Association and the Korean Association of Women's Study. She has a Ph.D. in sociology from the University of Hawaii.

Ronald R. RINDFUSS is director of the Carolina Population Center and professor of sociology at the University of North Carolina at Chapel Hill. He is currently a member of the Committee on Population and the Committee on Human Dimensions of Global Change, U.S. National Research Council. He has a Ph.D. in sociology from Princeton University.

Hiroaki SHIMIZU is professor of sociology at Nihon University in Tokyo. He has a Ph.D. in sociology from Tōyō University.

Patricia G. STEINHOFF is professor of sociology at the University of Hawaii. She served as director of the university's Center for Japanese Studies from 1986 to 1994. She has published five books and nearly fifty articles and reviews concerning Japan and Japanese studies. A member of the American Advisory Committee of The Japan Foundation since 1987, she has also served as chair of the Northeast Asia Council of the Association for Asian Studies and as a member of the Social Science Research Council–American Council of Learned Societies Joint Committee on Japanese Studies. Dr. Steinhoff has a B.A. in Japanese language and literature from the University of Michigan and a Ph.D. in sociology from Harvard University.

Te-Hsiung SUN holds the minister-rank position of chairman of the Research, Development and Evaluation Commission, Executive Yuan (Cabinet), Taiwan. He is also an adjunct professor at National Taiwan University. He directed Taiwan's family planning program during 1969–87 and received a national award as the Outstanding Specialist of Applied Science and Technology in 1985. He has a Ph.D. in sociology from the University of Michigan.

Noriko O. TSUYA is associate professor at the College of Economics, Nihon University, and concurrently adjunct research fellow at the Population Research Institute, Nihon University. Formerly a research fellow at the Program on Population, East-West Center, she has a Ph.D. in sociology from the University of Chicago.

PREFACE

Nihon University in Tokyo marked its centennial in 1989 by publishing preliminary research findings related to a wide-ranging project on the globalization of human society that had commenced three years earlier. A major component of this decade-long venture sponsored by the university's Office of the President is a comparative study of the changing family in five Asian countries—Japan, the Republic of Korea, China (Taiwan), the Philippines, and Thailand—and in the United States. The study involves sociologists, demographers, psychologists, economists, anthropologists, public-health experts, and journalists.

The Japanese segment of the study was launched in April 1988 when the University Research Center of Nihon University, in collaboration with Mainichi Newspapers, conducted a national survey of the contemporary Japanese family based on multistage random samples. Over a period of four days, members of the Mainichi survey network distributed questionnaires to 3,400 men and women of ages 20 and over throughout Japan. Recovered responses totaled 2,406, or 71 percent; participants 60 years and older comprised 20 percent. A survey team from the Sociology Department of Nihon University followed up with related inquiries in three communities selected for study. The purpose of the survey was to collect and analyze data that would indicate changes in the internal structure of the Japanese family and in its relationship to outside communities. The survey also sought to investigate how the modern Japanese family differs from the traditional family in its functions, life style, solution of family problems, and perceptions of traditional values.

The results of the survey have important implications for other Asian countries. When Japan began to adopt Western technology and aspects of Western culture more than a hundred years ago, many of its Asian neighbors looked on with disapproval, assuming that Japan would forfeit its own national traditions and values. But after a century of economic development and modernization, Japan has demonstrated that it can selectively apply Western technology and absorb Western culture during the process of modernization while retaining, to a large degree, its East Asian culture and values.

After analyzing the data from the Japanese National Family Survey and comparable survey data from the Republic of Korea, Thailand, and the United States, staff members of Nihon University organized in 1990 an international symposium entitled "The Family and Contemporary Culture: An International Perspective." Cosponsors were the Mainichi Newspapers and the East-West Center's Population Institute (now called the Program on Population) in Honolulu. The symposium focused on family institutions and structural change within the original five Asian countries and compared the findings with similar data from the United States. Selected conference papers and several additional papers written specifically for inclusion in this volume present the current views of the contributors on the modern family in Asia and America.

A note is in order about the romanization of Japanese words and the way bibliographic references are formatted in the citations and lists of references in this volume. Except for well-known place names, such as Tokyo, we have followed the Hepburn method of romanizing Japanese words, substituting macrons over long vowels. We have also used the Hepburn method to romanize Japanese authors' names unless the works cited were published in English and the authors' names were romanized differently there. Western authors are cited and listed in the usual way, by surname followed, in the case of references, with the given name or first initials; a comma separates the surname from the given name, indicating the inversion of the normal name order. In the case of Chinese, Japanese, and Korean authors' surnames, however, the normal name order is surname first, followed by given name or initials; and therefore no comma follows the surname. In Thailand the custom is to cite authors by their given names, which (as in the West) precede the family name. We have followed that custom here, and therefore in the reference lists Thai authors' names are alphabetized in their normal order: first name followed by given name with-

Preface

out a comma. The point to bear in mind is that, regardless of the nationality of an author, the first name listed in every reference is the name by which the author is cited in the text.

Nihon University's leadership in designing, funding, and implementing this important study on Japanese culture and the changing family is to be commended. We wish particularly to express our appreciation to Mr. Fukuji Kawarazaki, executive director of the University Research Center, and his staff for their expert coordination of the project in Japan. The Office of Population Research at Mainichi Newspapers deserves special recognition for its valuable contribution; Mr. Michio Ozaki of that institution provided able supervision of the national survey. We offer our gratitude to those researchers at the Program on Population of the East-West Center who collaborated with Nihon University and Mainichi Newspapers on this ambitious project. We also express our thanks to Korean and Thai colleagues who collected and analyzed data from their respective surveys and to the researchers at the University of Wisconsin and the University of North Carolina whose collaboration on the American survey analysis made an important contribution to the comparative analyses of the modern family.

To Sandra Ward, senior editor in the Program on Population, East-West Center, we express our sincere thanks for her invaluable technical editing of the manuscript, and to the staff of the Program's Publications Unit and the Center's Graphics and Production Services Unit—in particular, Steven Swapp, Connie Kawamoto, Clifford Takara, Russell Fujita, and Lois Bender—we extend our appreciation for their follow-through on all the cumbersome steps required for the successful completion of this volume.

CHAPTER 1

Introduction

by Lee-Jay Cho and Motō Yada

Almost all members of human societies throughout the world have been raised in some kind of family. The form and structure of the family have varied over a long historical period from one culture to another. Despite the widespread existence of such forms as the extended family and the stem family, in the last several centuries the predominant form has been the conjugal, or nuclear, family. Furthermore, monogamy has been the most common type of marriage in most cultures. Despite cultural differences, the principal functions of the family include procreation, child socialization, the preservation of lineage, and physical, emotional, and economic security. Over time, the social and economic functions of the family and its relationship to society have changed, along with other social and economic changes, especially in the modern era, in both the West and the East.

During Biblical times, polygamy and concubines were allowed and women were accorded a lower status than men. Family law of ancient Rome gave absolute power to the father, who represented the family in the community; he even had the right to kill his own sons. The father's primary duties were to guard his children and to create a home for his extended family. Family lineage was emphasized, and the dowry system practiced. Roman family law influenced all parts of the Roman Empire, and the extended family continued to be the prevalent form for many centuries, throughout medieval times and until the onset of industrialization and urbanization.

The Industrial Revolution and consequent widespread migration from villages to towns and cities began to have major effects on the form, structure, and functions of the family. Most notable of these effects were, first, the transformation of the family's function from production to consumption as work became separated from the family and its domicile, and second, the transition from high to low fertility, which led to the dissolution of the traditional, extended Western family and the emergence of a nuclear family as a predominant form.

In both the East and the West, the family has been the basic unit of society as well as the basic demographic institution. In Confucian cultures, also known as the Chinese cultural sphere—in particular China, Japan, Korea, and Vietnam—the family is the foundation upon which the nation and the society rest. In his writings, Confucius (551–479? B.C.) placed the greatest emphasis on familial values; filial piety predicated the relationship between parents and children, ensuring family cohesion. Characteristic of Confucian family cultures are the patrilineal family system and male dominance. In Japan, Korea, and China, the government and the political system were molded after the Confucian family system, and thus filial piety was equated with loyalty to the sovereign. The function, structure, composition, and values of the East Asian family type continued for many centuries. The numerous dynasties of China, the Yi Dynasty in Korea, and the Japanese Meiji government (1868–1912), all of which placed the imperial family at the top of their societies, exemplified the Confucian family system and its values.

The importance placed on family cohesion and integration has been manifested demographically in universal marriage and childbearing. As evidenced by census data for China, Japan, Korea, Taiwan, and the Chinese ethnic populations of Southeast Asia, the proportions of women remaining single by age 35 have been extremely small, around 2 percent. This indicates a strong desire to form a family through marriage. Moreover, high proportions of married women in those societies, nearly all, give birth to at least one child. In contrast, in the United States and Europe the proportions of women remaining single have been substantially higher. For example, in the United States about 10 percent of the cohort of women of reproductive age during the Great Depression of the 1930s remained single, and of those ever married about one-quarter remained childless. Among American and European women who are currently in the childbearing ages, about 15–20 percent will remain childless. About one-half of young adults cohabit with a partner before marriage, and one-half of all mar-

Introduction

riages are projected to end in divorce (Cherlin 1992:24). In contrast, divorce rates in East Asia are extremely low.

In both the East and the West, major demographic and economic changes have occurred in recent times, but the pace of change has been much greater in the East. In the case of Europe and the United States, industrial development and the demographic transition from high to low mortality and fertility took one or two centuries. Japan, which started its demographic transition shortly after World War II, and Korea, Taiwan, and mainland China, which began theirs more recently, completed their transitions much more rapidly. Coinciding with these demographic transitions have been rapid industrial transitions in East Asia. The big question is, with the impact of these social and economic changes, will the family in East Asian cultures retain its function, structure, composition, and values?

Interestingly, almost the same question was raised by intellectuals during the Han Dynasty of China, in the great debate over salt and steel in 150 B.C. (Zhi Gong, 1983). The intellectuals were critical of the government's monopoly of the production of salt, steel, and farm tools. They scorned the corruption and extravagance of government officials and the upper class. The amount of resources spent on funerals and weddings, for example, had become ostentatious, demoralizing the common people. The critics advanced the following argument:

The traditional conjugal family system is based on the principle of monogamy. But the system has gradually changed to allow one concubine for scholars, two concubines for government ministers, and nine concubines for provincial governors. The current situation has deteriorated to the extent that the governors enjoy more than a hundred, ministers have scores of concubines, and even merchants' residences are filled with them. Under this kind of marriage system, many women will never receive family love and care, while many men will be left with no wives. (Zhi Gong, 1983:203–204)

Today, more than 2,100 years later, we are asking the same basic question: whether or not the family system can survive in the face of the dramatic social and economic changes that are taking place.

A leading family sociologist, William Goode (1963), proposed the family convergence theory, which posits that families of all societies will evolve into a uniform nuclear family system. The majority of family sociologists support the application of the theory to Western societies, but there has been much discussion about its applicability to the East Asian countries.

In recent years a great deal of research and discussion has taken place on the subject of the contemporary family as a result of increased attention to demographic and family planning issues. Much of the research has been based on census and survey data on the family. This work has contributed to the understanding of the relationship between population dynamics and the family in both developed and developing countries. Over the years a wealth of empirical data and analysis has been accumulated—for example, through a series of World Fertility Surveys focusing on the family, fertility, and the changing position of women in the family. Less work has been done, and therefore fewer sets of data have been available, on the effects of migration and urbanization on the family, partly because of the difficulty of conducting such research.

THE GENESIS OF THIS VOLUME

Most of the chapters in this volume are based on selected papers from the International Symposium on Family and Contemporary Japanese Culture in International Perspective, held in Tokyo in October 1990 and sponsored by Nihon University in cooperation with the East-West Center's Program on Population (formerly the East-West Population Institute) and the Mainichi Newspapers. The purpose of the symposium was to compare family institutions in Asia and the West by reviewing research on the family in Japan, Korea, Taiwan, Thailand, and the Philippines on the one hand, and in the United States on the other.

Since 1950, when the Mainichi Newspapers began conducting what has generally been known as the National Opinion Survey on Family Planning in Japan, their surveys have enjoyed an excellent reputation. In 1988, in collaboration with the University Research Center of Nihon University, the Mainichi Newspapers conducted a national survey on the family to investigate various aspects of family life in Japan. Family sociologists at Nihon University conducted several in-depth community studies of the Japanese family to complement data from the survey. The survey data and the community studies provided valuable material on which a number of the papers presented at the 1990 symposium were based.

Also contributing to an understanding of the Asian family have been analyses based on data sets generated by family surveys conducted in South Korea and Thailand with support from Nihon University. Fascinating comparisons with the United States were made possible at the symposium because a few of the participants—in particular Larry L. Bumpass, Ronald R. Rindfuss, Linda G. Martin, and Noriko O. Tsuya—analyzed U.S. survey data on the family. During the meeting a great deal of mutual understanding was gained about the Japanese and other East Asian families, and in what ways they are similar to, and differ from, Western families. The main issues explored at the symposium were (1) the relationship between demographic and socioeconomic changes and the family, (2) arrangements for caring for the ever-growing elderly populations in Asia and the West, and (3) likely relations among older and younger generations in the future.

This volume is an attempt to present both the selected symposium papers and several others written for inclusion in the volume in such a way as to bring together views on the contemporary family, particularly the Asian family, from Eastern and Western perspectives. Compared with earlier literature on the family, we have made a greater effort to present the cultural dimensions of family institutions, especially those related to residence, intergenerational issues, and status and power within the family, in the demographically aging societies of East Asia. Questions about "spiritual culture" and ethos were frequently raised during the symposium in discussions of cultural differences between Asian and Western family relationships—for example, in discussions of the obligations, functional roles, and behavior of family members. Such cultural differences account, among other things, for the varying degrees of government and private care for the elderly members of a society. Cultural dimensions are difficult to operationalize but are nevertheless very important. Empirical knowledge about families is critical to gaining an understanding of their cultural dimension.

Several more basic questions must be answered before the question about the continuity of existing family systems can be broached. The first is: What is the family? The family is usually defined as the basic social unit, composed of members who are related by blood and who share a livelihood. The household, by contrast, is usually defined as a group of persons, including family members, who dwell in the same home but are not necessarily related by blood. The family may be classified into several types, according to their composition. The *nuclear family* is commonly defined as a family unit composed of only a husband and wife and their children. The *stem family* is one in which three generations live together. The *extended family* includes not only the parents and their unwed children, but also married children and their spouses and offspring. The *conjugal family* is one organized around the marriage of the husband and wife and their offspring, in which consanguine bonds are emphasized; in the modern literature this term has tended to be replaced by *nuclear family*.

FAMILY TRADITIONS IN EAST ASIA

The general perception of the traditional family in East Asia has been that of a large extended family. Until recently the Chinese family, for example, was stereotyped as a large extended family with the grandparents at the head and scores of children (cousins, nephews, and nieces) living together. Historical data on Chinese families and households indicate, however, that extended families were not the most prevalent type. Fei HsiaoTung, who conducted field studies before World War II, found that only about 20 percent of Chinese families were extended; the remainder fitted more closely the definition of a nuclear family (Fei, 1983:25). An interesting example is found in a well-known classic of Chinese literature, *A Dream of Red Mansions* (Tsao and Kao, 1980), first published in 1791, in which a score of families related by blood reside in an enclosed clan community where the servants outnumber the family members. But the upper-class Chinese family, even in Tsao and Kao's time, was more likely to be a nuclear family, in which the husband and wife and their children lived in a separate house from that of the grandmother, who was treated as having the ultimate authority over the extended family and dwelled in a central pavilion. Therefore, what may have appeared to be a clan, or extended family, in actuality consisted of basic units of conjugal families, living together with their children, and with most of the household work done by servants. What is noteworthy about such families is the structure of the relationships and the patterns of interaction between the conjugal units, which were based on the Confucian ideals of filial piety, benevolence, and family harmony.

Many scholars argue that in Japan, which has experienced major socioeconomic changes during the process of modernization over the past century, the conjugal family has been in essence sustained and not substantially changed. Some Japanese scholars even argue that the conjugal family is the basic foundation of human society and therefore it cannot be easily dissolved. Their view is understandable, given the demographic evidence of universal marriage in East Asia. But the situation is quite different in some other societies, for example, among African Americans in the United States. Some 25 to 30 percent of African American children under age 10 do not live with their own mothers (Cho, Grabill, and Bogue, 1970: 318–319), and this would seem to contribute to the instability characteristic of many African American families. The corresponding figures for South Korea and Japan are 3.3 percent and 2.3 percent, respectively (Republic of Korea, Statistics Bureau, 1980; Japan, Bureau of Statistics, 1989; Cho, 1974:270).

In Japan, the postwar influence of American culture and the mass media has led to the common misperception that the Japanese family has undergone a rapid transition or "nuclearization" from a traditional extended family type to the nuclear family. Japanese census data for households dating back several generations indicate, however, that the proportion of three-generation households, consisting mostly of the stem family type, has remained at about one-quarter over the years. It is not possible to have a majority of stem-type families because the stem family, as defined, requires coresidence of parents and their married sons; in such families other siblings separate from the stem and form separate conjugal families (what the Japanese call "family separation"). In traditional societies, such as those of premodern China, Japan, and Korea, fertility and mortality levels are the most important factors influencing the composition of the family. In cases of high fertility, the eldest children marry and live with their parents, whereas younger children move out upon marrying. If the siblings remain unmarried and continue to live with their parents, their family is referred to as a complex family.

To preserve Japanese cultural values and the traditional family system, the Meiji government in 1898 legislated the civil code, defining the obligations and rights of the head of the family and household in such matters as property, marriage, authority to determine the location of the family residence, and the naming of new family members. The code gave authoritarian rights to the household heads and reaffirmed patrilineal authority, "family virtues," and filial piety. The purpose of this family law was to dampen the speed of urbanization, which was occurring as a consequence of industrialization as younger workers left their families' homes to take jobs in cities, most intending ultimately to return. The Japanese authorities knew that the process of industrialization in Western countries had been accompanied by a dissolution of traditional families. They also knew that it created conflicts between the integrity of the family system, with its values, and the secularization and individualism born of industrialization and capitalist development.

To coincide with the civil code's reinforcement of the vertical authority structure of the family, the Meiji regime codified a hierarchical system of families, in which the imperial family became the ultimate object of loyalty at the summit of the new structure. The Confucian precept of filial piety became synonymous with loyalty to the imperial head of state.

To enforce the family law, the Meiji leadership issued an imperial edict establishing a new creed for public education, drawing primarily on Confucian values and ethics. The creed placed emphasis on the emperor's ancestry, loyalty to the nation, filial piety toward one's parents, trust among friends, harmony among community members, diligence in one's studies, and the development of skills and abilities. The government took these measures to mobilize the spiritual and psychological support of the populace for maintaining the family.

A family creed typical of turn-of-the-century Japan is that of the Katakawa family and its textile firm, established during the Meiji period (Mito, 1992:264–265). The creed had 10 basic precepts: first, pay homage to the Buddha or worship some deity, and honor your ancestors; second, never forget the path of loyalty and filial piety; third, work hard and avoid extravagance; fourth, within your family maintain a simple and tranquil household, but at your work place perform actively and vigorously; fifth, always carry out duties at work to conform with national goals and the public good; sixth, perform your duties as best you can, as though nature had given them to you to perform, and receive whatever compensation naturally comes to you; seventh, never be lazy; eighth, always treat others better than you treat yourself; ninth, always try to help others who are in need; and tenth, treat your employees as you treat members of your family. This creed, which was deeply imbued with Confucian ideals, provided an ethical system for the textile firm's managers and employees alike.

After World War II, a new system of family laws replaced the Meiji family code. The new laws incorporated more democratic values, such as equal treatment of female members of the family in matters of succession and inheritance. In addition to these legal changes, major social and economic changes, including the rapid pace of urbanization, affected the Japanese family system. Nevertheless, most scholars agree that traditional Japanese family values have remained essentially unchanged.

The Korean traditional family was a patrilineal institution, in which the family as an entity was given preference over its individual members and the family group was inseparably identified with the clan. Its most important function was to maintain and preserve the household within the Confucian system. Accordingly, the central familial relationship was not that between husband and wife, but rather that between parent and child, particularly between father and son. As in Japan, these Confucian principles of family relationships were projected onto the community and national life and given important social value.

During the premodern period, the Korean family remained essentially Confucian. The family registration law established by the Japanese colonial government was therefore readily accepted by the Koreans. Even after national liberation in 1945, Korean family law continued to emphasize the importance of blood relations and the authority of the male household head.

Because women had no right to inherit the position of head of the household, they were often prevented from inheriting property. The share of inheritance due to unmarried daughters was always given to the eldest son, who would pay for the daughters' weddings when they married. In practice, then, women were given a share of the family property upon their marriage, but their share was much smaller than the sons' share. This practice was the same as the inheritance system of China, and it continued during the Japanese occupation of Korea.

A Korean law enacted in 1991 provides that, in the case of there being no will, the spouse of the deceased is to receive one-half of the property and the other half is to be distributed equally among the children, regardless of their sex or marital status. A properly executed will takes precedence over the law, however.

The deeply rooted preference for patrilineal succession remains dominant in South Korea today. Regardless of whether the parents and the eldest son maintain separate households, the relationship between parents and their grown children is one of mutual reliance, and most children plan to rejoin their parents when the parents become too old to care for themselves. This custom of mutual dependence persists even though industrialization has caused urban families to evolve into the nuclear type. Although there are signs that in urban areas family ties and the importance attached to kinship are gradually weakening, the Confucian influence on the Korean family is still strong, as evidenced by close kinship bonds, wives' deference to their husbands, and son preference.

COMPARISONS BETWEEN ASIA AND THE WEST

Changes in family composition due to modernization and urbanization may cause relationships among family members to change as well, but family relationships in different societies evolve in different ways. There appears to be a sharp contrast between family relationships in the East and the West. The differences are evident in the living arrangements, attitudes, and behavior of family members.

A consistent trend in both Asia and the West is for adult married children to reside separately from their parents, but this practice is largely determined by a family's economic situation. In well-to-do Asian families, married children tend to have residences separate from but near those of their parents, whereas members of low-income families, unable to afford separate housing, tend to live together. Various types of living arrangements have been found in Japan and South Korea, and these have implications for family composition, function, and structure.

Family surveys have revealed striking contrasts in the attitudes and behavior of families in East Asia—notably Japan, South Korea, and Taiwan—and those in the West. The 1988 National Family Survey in Japan, for example, found that more than 70 percent of respondents desired to live with their parents when their parents became old or ill and needed help; and the proportion would likely be even larger in South Korea and Taiwan. Recent family surveys in the United States, however, have indicated that fewer than 5 percent of Americans have such a desire.

Another striking contrast between families steeped in Confucian values and those in the West is in attitudes toward ancestors. The 1988 Japanese survey found strong evidence of ancestor worship: a large majority of Japanese respondents regularly visited their ancestors' graves. Questions about ancestor worship, however, are unlikely to be part of a survey of Europeans or Americans.

OVERVIEW OF THE FOLLOWING CHAPTERS AND COMMENT

In Chapter 2 of this volume, Peter McDonald points out that early Western social scientists, influenced by social Darwinism—that is, the notion that the strongest societies survive the weakest—believed that social systems evolved toward higher forms and regarded the European model as the pinnacle of social development. They were surprised to discover the diversity of social systems that existed in other cultures, and they manifested a missionary zeal in trying to change the social systems of those cultures to promote the economic development of their societies. The structural-functionalists held somewhat different views from those of the social Darwinists. As McDonald notes, they argued that the composition and structure of the modern nuclear family, as compared with the traditional extended family, can better endure the process of functional differentiation in modernizing societies. The nuclear family appeared compact in form and could maintain its stability through structural isolation, the intensive nature of its family life, and a rigid role segregation of husband and wife. The breadwinner model of the nuclear family, with its clear delineation of the husband's role as income earner and of the wife's domestic role as the provider of childcare, was thought to be more compatible with such prevailing characteristics of modern society as individual achievement and social and geographic mobility.

Neither social Darwinism nor structural-functionalism has succeeded in accounting for the economic and social changes that have occurred in East Asia during the last few decades. Many of the Western economies have been growing at a much slower pace than those of Japan and other newly industrializing countries of the region. The hypothesis that economic development leads to a corresponding change in family systems has therefore been weakened. It is not an overstatement to say that family theory is now "in a state of flux" (McDonald, Chapter 2, p. 21). As McDonald cogently proposes (pp. 22–23), "societies vary in the degree to which deviation [from an idealized family morality] is considered permissible.... Changes in the family systems of these societies cannot be predicted from changes in the characteristics of individuals, such as improvements in education, occupational changes, or increases in economic well-being."

We believe that the study of family systems and change not only must include the analysis of cross-sectional survey data on the individual characteristics of families, but also must be approached from a cultural and institutional perspective. Of paramount importance is a society's value system, expressed as its morality or, as we prefer to call it, its spiritual culture. That spiritual culture is normally maintained and nurtured by leadership groups, in particular by political leaders. Added to these perspectives is the historical perspective. The cultural and institutional dimensions of family systems and changes within them cannot be easily operationalized and quantified for rigorous scientific analysis; nevertheless, they deserve greater attention in family studies.

In Chapter 3, Patricia G. Steinhoff compares the Japanese with the American family. The Japanese family is predicated on family cohesion, continuity, and the priority of the collectivity, whereas the American family is characterized by the development, protection, and welfare of the family's individual members. Steinhoff's insightful analysis relates these differences in family values and behavior to the sociocultural and economic structures of the two countries.

Toshio Kuroda (Chapter 4) compares Japanese and Chinese families and households, relating the data on household composition to such demographic factors as fertility and mortality. He argues that the perceived traditional predominance of the extended family type in Japan and China was illusionary and that the nuclear family has always been more prevalent in the two countries.

Several of the chapters in Part II, focusing on the Japanese family, draw upon data from the 1988 National Family Survey. An outline of the survey design and the questionnaire are presented in the Appendix to this volume.

In Chapter 5, Noriaki Gotō reveals some fascinating historical data on the Japanese *ie*, or extended family, in the context of a village community (*mura*). Rapid economic changes and urban transformation adjacent to the community under observation have had a major impact on the community's economic life; but the process of community interactions, though weakened in intensity, appears to have persisted over the decades— for example, through the activities of the neighborhood association (*tonari kumi*).

Analyzing data from the 1988 National Family Survey, Noriko O. Tsuya (Chapter 6) finds that, despite Japan's rapid social and economic development and urbanization, Japanese attitudes toward marriage and the family appear not to have undergone a fundamental change. Young, unmarried, college-educated Japanese living in cities tend to have practical and conservative expectations regarding the functions of the family. Moreover, working wives and their husbands perceive the traditional reproductive and economic functions of the family to be its primary purpose. Tsuya's findings thus indicate the continued existence of traditional attitudes and family norms.

Hiroshi Kawabe and Hiroaki Shimizu (Chapter 7) reveal remarkable differences in family attitudes and actual living arrangements in Japan on one hand and the United States, England, and France on the other. They maintain that the traditional stem-family system continues to be the fundamental unit of Japanese society.

Yasuo Natsukari (Chapter 8) argues that universal marriage remains the norm in Japan, as evidenced by survey data from an in-depth follow-up survey that fewer than 3 percent of Japanese want to remain single. Although those under age 40 indicated a preference for a love match, as opposed to an arranged marriage, most young women (nine-tenths of those in their 20s) considered a man's income to be an important factor in mate selection, whereas a substantially smaller proportion of men regarded a woman's income as an important criterion. The findings suggest the persistence of Japan's traditional gender roles and authority structure.

Again, analyzing data from the 1988 National Family Survey, Linda G. Martin and Noriko O. Tsuya (Chapter 9) find that among middle-aged Japanese, firstborn children assume most of the responsibility for contact and coresidence with elderly parents. A continued decline in multigenerational living arrangements may not necessarily mean that intergenerational relations will deteriorate. Instead, the authors speculate that the Japanese will move toward the Western model of "intimacy at a distance."

Satomi Kurosu (Chapter 10) presents interesting evidence based on his analysis of Japanese survey data that such economic factors as income, land ownership, and living space significantly increase individuals' propensity to live in extended families. The Japanese *ie* ideology, he concludes, still exerts a significant normative influence on family extension, particularly among older Japanese.

Examining 1988 National Family Survey data on adult children's contact with parents in Japan, Ronald R. Rindfuss, Tim Futing Liao, and Noriko O. Tsuya (Chapter 11) find that firstborn male children still have a strong tendency to observe traditional family values and practices. Even so, higher education, particularly university education, tends to weaken traditional attitudes toward the family. Comparing respondents' preferred traits in sons and daughters, the authors find a traditional differentiation of sex roles. For example, 51 percent of respondents preferred their sons to be independent, but only 20 percent wanted their daughters to be so; and 59 percent mentioned responsibility as a desirable trait in sons, but only 30 percent mentioned that as a desirable trait in daughters.

Larry L. Bumpass (Chapter 12), who compares patterns of coresidence and contact with parents in Japan and the United States, reports that it is common in Japan for eldest sons and their wives to live with elderly parents, whereas such coresidence is almost nonexistent in the United States. But on the question of how parental survival affects the structure of intergenerational contact over the life course, Bumpass makes the interesting observation that trends in life-course experience in the levels of contact with parents are similar in direction to those in the United States.

Suzanne Culter (Chapter 13) presents a fascinating set of survey data on a Japanese coal-mining city that is dying under the impact of industrial restructuring. Family cohesion appears to be a key factor in the decision to remain in the city or migrate. For example, owners of family-run shops, stores, and small businesses indicated their desire to remain.

Part III examines evidence of family change in three other Asian societies.

Introduction

The first two, Korea and Taiwan, are steeped in Confucian tradition. The third, Thailand, has been influenced by Buddhism.

Nam-Il Kim, Soon Choi, and Insook Han Park (Chapter 14) report dramatic changes in Korean family size, composition, and attitudes in the face of South Korea's rapid industrialization and urbanization. Their findings are based on a 1990 family survey in three village communities that follows up on a 1960 survey by Hwang-Kyeong Ko, Man-Gap Lee, and Hyo-Chae Lee. The authors conclude that family cohesion persists in the form of intergenerational coresidence, care for elderly parents by their adult children, ancestor worship, and other traditional values.

Analyzing data from Taiwan, Te-Hsiung Sun and Yin-Hsing Liu (Chapter 15) note interesting tradeoffs in intergenerational relations within the Chinese family. Although the proportion of couples living with the husbands' parents is still very high compared with that in Western societies, it is declining. The decline, however, is matched by increasing monetary flows from married children to their parents and greater frequency of mutual visits and telephone communication. This tradeoff implies the existence of a social force to preserve traditional Chinese family values in a modernizing society.

The three chapters on Thailand (Chapter 16, by Chai Podhisita; Chapter 17, by Bhassorn Limanonda; and Chapter 18, by Malinee Wongsith) reveal interesting differences between the Thai family system and the family systems of countries influenced by Confucianism. Chai discusses the important role and position of the youngest daughter in the Thai family as caretaker of elderly parents and recipient of the largest share of the children's inheritance. Bhassorn reveals remarkable differences in family residence patterns between the Northeastern Region of Thailand, where a majority of couples reside permanently with the wife's parents, and the South, where couples tend to reside temporarily with the husband's parents. These differences are attributed to cultural differences between ethnic Thai in the Northeast and ethnic Chinese in the South. Malinee presents survey data from rural Thailand indicating the persistence of traditional values that emphasize husbands' authority in family matters, the domestic role of wives, and respect for elderly family members.

PRINCIPAL FINDINGS AND REMAINING QUESTIONS

To summarize, a number of basic issues and questions are explored in this volume. Although the main focus is on East Asia and Thailand, several chapters draw comparisons with the United States and Europe. First, dramatic demographic changes—in particular, rapid fertility and mortality declines that have resulted in smaller families and greater life expectancy for family members—have had major effects on families both in East Asia and in the West. Second, the increasing rate of divorce among younger couples in the United States is having a severe impact on the composition of the American family. Third, the decline of old industries and the rise of new ones have led to family dislocations and consequent migration, which in turn have produced significant changes in family systems and in community structures—not just in physical settlements but also in interpersonal community relationships. Even so, de-industrialization and the increasing divorce rate can actually strengthen intergenerational relationships and bonds. Fourth, economic development and rising income are certain to influence the structure of the family and families' living arrangements. Fifth, traditional social, religious, and cultural values have played an important role of barricading family systems against the forces of modernization and uniformity.

In both Eastern and Western societies the nuclear family type appears to have been more prevalent than the extended family, at least in modern times. The conditional nature of the extended family residence in East Asia is an interesting phenomenon because higher-income families can afford more spacious homes (and extended-family living arrangements), but lower-income families live separately until the parents are too old to care for themselves.

Overriding cultural differences between Eastern and Western societies is the difference in emphasis on individual versus collective family values. East Asian societies place emphasis on the family as a collective unit, whereas in the West, especially in the United States, the emphasis is on the individual. Consequently, economic development has followed a substantially different pattern in East Asia, where there is much greater reliance on the private provision of social services, such as support for children and the elderly, than is the case in the United States and Europe.

Will the traditional family in East Asia, particularly in Japan, remain intact, or will it break up or change in some other way? More specifically, what kinds of relationships will exist among family members in the future? Who will care for the large, and growing, elderly population? Will the amount of care provided by family members decline?

The conclusion drawn from the chapters presented in this volume is that the Japanese family, and East Asian families in general, will not evolve toward the American, or Western, family type. Both East and West will be faced with the inexorable processes of further population aging, migration, and urbanization. Family institutional responses to those changes may share some common characteristics, but they will nevertheless manifest substantial cultural differences.

REFERENCES

Cherlin, Andrew J. 1992. *Marriage, Divorce, Remarriage.* Revised ed. Cambridge, Mass.: Harvard University Press.

Cho, Lee-Jay. 1974. "The Own-Children Approach to Fertility Estimation." In International Union for the Scientific Study of Population, *International Population Conference, Liège, 1973*, Vol. 2, pp. 263–278. Liège: IUSSP.

Cho, Lee-Jay, Wilson H. Grabill, and Donald Bogue. 1970. *Differential Current Fertility in the United States.* Chicago: University of Chicago Press.

Fei Hsiao-Tung. 1983. *Chinese Village Close-up.* Beijing: New World Press.

Goode, William. 1963. *World Revolution and Family Patterns.* New York: Free Press.

Japan, Bureau of Statistics, Management and Coordinating Agency. 1989. *1985 Census Report, Population Census of Japan*, Vol. 5, Sect. 1–3.

Mito Tadashi. 1992. *Ie No Ronri* (Formation of the Japanese management system), Vol. 2. Tokyo: Bunshito Co.

Tsao Hsueh-Chin and Kao Ngo. 1980. *A Dream of Red Mansions.* Translated by Yang Hsien-Yi and Gladys Yang. Beijing: Foreign Language Press.

Zhi Gong. 1983. *Yentierun* (Salt and steel debate). Taipei: Shibao Wenhwa Chubanchiye.

CHAPTER 2

Families in Developing Countries: Idealized Morality and Theories of Family Change

by Peter McDonald

THE DEVELOPMENT OF THEORIES RELATED TO FAMILY FORMS IN DEVELOPING COUNTRIES

Upon closer contact with social systems in developing countries and the birth of anthropology, social scientists in the latter half of the nineteenth century viewed social change as evolutionary. Building upon theories of physical evolution at the time, those scientists regarded social systems as evolving toward higher forms, with the strongest surviving the weakest (Spencer, 1972). The social scientists to whom I refer were Western, although they would not have described themselves in this way. They saw the European world as the pinnacle of social development, they were surprised at the diversity of social systems that existed in other cultures, and they concluded that the low level of economic development of those societies was related to their low level of social development. Following in the wake of centuries of religious missions, some of those social scientists had a missionary zeal to change the social systems of those cultures in order to promote the development of their peoples.

The viewpoints of structural-functionalists in the 1950s and 1960s were similar but different. These writers had moved away from the notion of a natural process of the evolution of social systems to a process of differentiation in modernizing societies. In regard to the family, they saw the modern, nuclear family as being better structured to accommodate this process of differentiation. They characterized the nuclear family by its structural isolation, the intensive nature of family life, and a rigid role segregation of husband and wife. This has been referred to as the breadwinner model of the nuclear family, in which the wife stays at home to mind the children while the husband goes out to earn the income. These characteristics of the breadwinner model of the nuclear family were seen as better equipped than other family forms to operate in the modern world, which revolves around individual achievement and social and geographic mobility (Parsons and Bales, 1955; Goode, 1963). There was a certain sense of confidence in the 1960s that economic development could be achieved rapidly in almost all societies. In 1962 Walt Rostow provided a model of a universal path to economic development for all societies, and international aid was seen as a means by which societies could be brought to the take-off point (Rostow, 1962). Family sociologists at the time saw the family changing along with economic development so that as all world cultures moved toward industrialization, their family systems would approach some variant of the nuclear or conjugal type (Goode, 1963).

This has not happened, and we are now all wiser in hindsight. Economic downturns at various times during the past 20 years, not least of all the present downturn, have led the developed countries to focus much more upon their own economic survival. Economic aid to developing countries is promoted less for reasons of altruism or self-satisfaction than to prop up ailing economies so that they can continue to pay back at least part of their massive debts. Many economies are poorer and arguably less developed now than they were in the 1960s. The process of industrialization, with several exceptions, has not occurred, and social systems have remained more or less unscathed. A prominent view at the present time is that economic development, rather than leading to or moving simultaneously with changes in social systems, is in fact dependent upon prior changes in social systems. This idea has been the driving force behind the remarkable political changes that have occurred in the former Soviet Union and Eastern Europe in the past few years. It is the reason, also, that many developed nations that are feeling the pinch look to the models of other countries (Japan on one hand, Sweden on the other, depending upon social perspective), to see how they can improve their own economic and social security performance. But social rules are often difficult to change, particularly when new rules are seen as being "imported." It has even been argued that family systems determine social systems and that family systems are so rigid, so unamenable to change, and so all-encompassing that the social and economic systems we see now will change only very slowly (Todd, 1985).

THE CONSTRUCTION AND DECONSTRUCTION OF FAMILY THEORY

Theory about change in family systems in developing countries or, for that matter, in developed countries as well, is now in a state of flux. Several writers in recent years have argued against theories of social change that are based on dichotomies or are linear in nature. Yanagisako and Collier (1987) argue that the use of dichotomies in social theory is often associated with tautological arguments. With regard to family systems, the tautology takes the form of associating a particular family structure with the process of being developed; thus, as countries develop, they take on this family form. In unraveling metaphors or theories to reveal the underlying logic, deconstructionists claim that this logic conventionally consists of a simple dichotomy according to which one side is always superior to the other side (Derrida, 1976). These elements of linearity and superiority are evident in the nineteenth century evolutionary theories and in the structural-functional theories of the 1950s discussed above. Those theories have been deconstructed.

Given the ease with which theories of family change are deconstructed and overthrown, it is easier to be on the side of the deconstructors. It might even be argued that family change is so specific to culture that theorizing across cultures is pointless. If linear theories of change are simplistic and driven by the values of the theorist, multidimensional theories may be so specific as merely to describe one culture. Indeed, the success rate for predicting family change even within one culture is abysmally low. To give an example from the field of family studies, the vast swings in age at first marriage that have occurred in Western countries in the twentieth century were largely unpredicted by theorists. Even in retrospect, we have some difficulty in explaining these swings, yet they occurred rapidly in numerous countries at approximately the same time. And what will be the pattern of marriage in the United States or Australia in 20 years' time?

Other examples can be provided of present-day circumstances: the position of women in Iran as predicted from the mid-1970s, the fertility rates of educated Malay women as predicted from the late 1970s, the work-force participation rates of married women in Japan as predicted from the 1970s, divorce rates in the West as predicted from the early 1960s. These examples indicate that substantial changes in family patterns do occur but that our capacity to predict those changes is very limited indeed. Nevertheless, numerous counter examples can be offered of no change having been predicted and no change having in fact occurred. Throughout the past 40 years, we would have predicted little change in family systems in Saudi Arabia, despite changes in the wealth of the society, and we would have been right.

Perhaps we can better construct family theory by assessing the characteristics of instances of change that were not predicted and the characteristics of change (or stability) that were predicted. By asking ourselves why we were not able to predict particular changes, we can move closer to a somewhat more generalized theory.

An important aspect of the development of theories of family change is the level of emphasis that a prevailing social system places on the well-being of individuals relative to the emphasis that it places upon the well-being of groups within the society. In respect of the family specifically, how much weight is attached to the well-being of individuals within the family as compared with the well-being of the family as a whole? Depending upon the social system, so-called group well-being may in fact be more correctly expressed as the well-being of those holding power and status within the group. It is quite evident that changes in family systems in Western countries in the past 30 years have reflected a shift in society toward the promotion of the rights of individuals within families over those of the family as a whole (McDonald, 1988). The most evident manifestation of this has been the shift to easy and unilateral divorce, which has been accompanied by a sizable increase in the rate of divorce on the part of individuals.

The general theme of the rights of the individual versus the rights of the group needs to be considered in all discussions of family change, but shifts in the balance of rights do not simply happen in some kind of natural, linear progression. They take place within a social system and within a prevailing power structure. They take place also within a belief structure about what is proper family behavior. This belief structure will have developed over a long period of the society's history. With regard to families, I refer to this belief structure as idealized family morality.

FAMILY SYSTEMS, CULTURE, AND MORALITY

I would postulate that an idealized family morality is a fundamental component of the culture of all societies, but that societies vary in the degree to which deviation from that ideal is considered permissable. There will be little variation from the ideal where the family system is reinforced by the morality of the society; that is, variation from the ideal will be illegal, antisocial, or contrary to the teachings of the prevailing religion, and this morality will be policed by the strong, formal institutions of the society.

In societies in which the ideal is rigidly enforced, changes in family systems will occur only through changes in the control of formal institutions, that is, through the redefining of morality by formal institutions. Thus, in such societies, prediction is difficult because changes in institutions occur through changes in the viewpoints of a small number of persons who control those institutions or through the overthrow of those persons. Changes in the family systems of these societies cannot be predicted from changes in the characteristics of individuals, such as improvements in education, occupational changes, or increases in economic well-being. Thus, prediction of social change falls more in the field of the political scientist than in that of the sociologist or economist.

A structural-functional interpretation of these societies would show how the particular family system meshed with other features of the society, such as its level of development and its political and religious institutions. In contrast, the interpretation taken in this chapter is that the prevailing family system is simply taken to be morally correct and enforceable from that perspective alone. This is not to say that changes in the family system would not have implications for other areas of life, merely that there is not a necessary functional relationship between the various components of a culture such that change in one area necessarily leads to a particular change in another area.

The Middle East offers examples of societies in which political and religious institutions rigidly enforce the morality of the existing family system. The prediction referred to above of stability in the family system in Saudi Arabia is based, then, on a prediction about the stability of political and religious institutions. In this regard, it has been argued that the endogamous family system in the Middle East tends to promote stability of the region's political and religious institutions (Patai, 1971). In these circumstances, one might predict with confidence that family systems will remain unchanged despite increases in wealth and education of the population. One might not predict the invasion of Saudi Arabia, however, or any social changes that ensued from such an invasion.

It might be argued that the stability of patrilineal family systems in Sub-Saharan Africa is similarly determined by strong, prevailing moralities backed by the force of formal institutions. Those formal institutions in turn derive their power from family systems—not endogamous systems, but rather tribal or clan-based systems.

It is common in developing countries for the state to take a position on an issue that is counter to the idealized family morality prevailing in the culture of that society. Usually the state takes this approach because its leaders have become convinced that some aspect of the family system is impeding economic development or the development of a modern-thinking society. Examples include policies to restrict birth rates, to improve the status of women, or to redistribute wealth among families. Such endeavors of the state frequently fail, even to the extent of leading to the fall of the government, as happened in Iran and India. Failure rates are high in Africa and the Middle East and, in those regions the experience itself of the state attempting to modify prevailing family systems is uncommon. With few exceptions, success has been rare in South Asia, somewhat better in Latin America, much better in Southeast Asia, and spectacular in East Asia. Variables in the success of such endeavors include the level of commitment of the state to the change, the organizational capacity of the state, the power of the state to counter opposition, the strength of the prevailing morality, the existence of institutionalized power bases promoting that morality, and levels of social and economic development.

A commitment to democracy was the undoing of the Indian government of Indira Gandhi during the 1975 Emergency, whereas the Shah of Iran fell afoul of the power of institutionalized religion. The strength of the prevailing morality has been instrumental in the success of governmental attempts to increase the birth rates of Malays in Malaysia and in the failure of the Marcos government to reduce birth rates substantially in the Philippines. The power and organization of the state were crucial elements in the success of policies to reduce birth rates and improve the status of women in China and in Singapore, but with reinforcement, at least in Singapore, by rapid social and economic development. In Indonesia and Thailand, institutionalized opposition to governmental initiatives is weak.

These examples imply a multidimensional approach to the prediction of family change in developing countries. But political upheaval, which can radically alter the position of the state and hence the course of family change, is relatively unpredictable.

In other instances of movement away from the idealized family morality, the driving force for the change lies outside the state. It may come from other institutions such as organized religion, the armed forces, the political opposition, or labor unions, or it may come directly from changes in the behavior of groups within the society in response to a variety of sources of influence (educational, economic, technological, cross-cultural). The state may resist the change, act as an agent for the change, or be indifferent to the change.

In acting as an agent for change, the state may provide protection to those adopting new modes of behavior through amendment of the law or may seek to turn a blind eye to breaches of the law. For example, in 1974 the Indonesian government adopted a new marriage law that restricted child marriage, polygamy, and divorce. There was a degree of commitment to the changes on the part of the state, but the changes owed more to the commitment of some opposition groups and to women's groups. Nevertheless, the government saw the changes as desirable for the promotion of certain of its aims, particularly family planning, as well as the promotion of Indonesia internationally as a modern-thinking country. Furthermore, a considerable shift had already occurred in the general population away from the old morality toward the practices enacted in the new law. At the same time, the government recognized that strict enforcement of the law would be a dangerous venture in certain areas of the country; it viewed the law as a desirable target to be achieved as the people became more enlightened through educational and media influences. In this instance, therefore, change in the prevailing morality of marriage was the result of a complex combination of forces: a commitment of organized groups outside the state, general social development, the agency of the state, and weakness of the forces supporting the old morality.

At yet another level, with the advance of pluralism and liberalism, the idealized family morality may be ill-defined or flexible. This is the situation that prevails in many instances in the West. The society is often seeking morality through social experimentation. In such instances, the role of "experts" becomes paramount. If we are liberal and pluralistic, then we shall consider various points of view and tend to opt for the "scientific" solution (Wolfe, 1989). The experience of the West is that these conditions can lead to wide swings in what is considered to be acceptable behavior. Instances include the shift to early and nearly universal marriage in the years following World War II and the complete abandonment of that norm beginning in the mid-1970s. Another instance, related to the former, was the shift to "living together" relationships in the 1970s; recent evidence is beginning to suggest a movement away from this form of behavior among young couples (McDonald, 1990). A weak idealized family morality also permits the promotion of pluralism per se. For example, much effort has been directed toward the acceptance in Western countries of one-parent families as legitimate families. The evidence of experts is strong that it is often in the best interests of children and the partners themselves to live apart rather than to continue to live in a highly conflictual situation. But, as a consequence of this revision of morality and another change, the acceptance of exnuptial births, we now have high levels of noncontact by noncustodial fathers with their children (40–50 per cent in the United States and Australia). Experts would again suggest that this situation is not generally in the best interests of children, and so we seek a new morality to accommodate this opinion.

CONCLUDING REMARKS

A conventional approach to explaining social change is to conduct a survey of individuals and to apply multivariate statistical techniques to the sample of individuals as if each person or family were an autonomous unit whose actions could be determined by measurable, individual characteristics such as education, occupation, and income. An advance on this approach is to incorporate community-level variables, such as the size of the local community, into a multilevel, multivariate approach. Another, quite different, appoach is the microlevel or anthropological approach, which relies upon finding the answers from intensive interviewing and discussion with the actors about their behavior. Both of these broad approaches, the statistical and the anthropological, contribute to our understanding of social change. Both approaches, however, place considerable emphasis upon assessment of or by individuals. The arguments in this chapter suggest that the development of theories of family change and of social change more broadly require macrolevel, political studies—studies that examine the strength of ideologies within the society and examine the prevailing structures of power and influence.

Theoretical explanations of family change have focused upon social and economic development or upon institutional factors. This chapter argues for greater attention to be directed toward the nature of, the strength of, and the institutional support for an idealized family morality in addressing changes in family systems. It is suggested that morality has a force of its own and does not need to be seen as serving a functional purpose that closely complements other aspects of the society. Nor should morality be seen purely from a political perspective, that is, as a mechanism used by powerful groups to retain their position. This view is consistent with a complex approach to family change in which outcomes may differ in various societies because only one of several preconditions for change is not met. As some of these preconditions revolve around the attitudes and personalities of persons in powerful positions or upon the changing opinions of experts, one can expect a low degree of success in predicting change in family systems upon the basis of theoretical frameworks.

REFERENCES

Derrida. 1976. *Of Grammatology*, G. Spivak, (trans.) Baltimore: Johns Hopkins University Press.

Goode, William. 1963. *World Revolution and Family Patterns*. New York: Free Press.

McDonald, Peter. 1988. "Families in the Future: The Pursuit of Personal Autonomy," *Family Matters*, No. 22, December.

———. 1990. "The 1980s: Social and Economic Changes Affecting Families," *Family Matters*, No. 26, April.

Parsons, Talcott, and Robert Bales. 1955. *The Family: Socialization and Interaction Process*. New York: Free Press.

Patai, Raphael. 1971. *Society, Culture and Change in the Middle East*. Philadelphia: University of Pennsylvania Press.

Rostow, Walter. 1962. *The Stages of Economic Growth*. Cambridge: Cambridge University Press.

Spencer, Herbert. 1972. *On Social Evolution: Selected Writings*. Chicago: University of Chicago Press.

Todd, Emmanuel. 1985. *The Explanation of Ideology: Family Structures and Social Systems*. New York: B. Blackwell.

Wolfe, Arthur. 1989. *Whose Keeper? Social Science and Moral Obligation*. Berkeley: University of California Press.

Yanagisako, Sylvia, and Janet Collier. 1987. "Toward a Unified Analysis of Gender and Kinship," in J. Collier and S. Yanagisako (eds.), *Gender and Kinship: Essays Toward a Unified Analysis*. Stanford: Stanford University Press.

CHAPTER 3

A Cultural Approach to the Family in Japan and the United States

by Patricia G. Steinhoff

The term culture means many different things in contemporary social science, each implying different assumptions and research questions. One type of cultural analysis focuses on the description of social institutions and the cultural ideals that inform them, and then explains the stability of a society as a result of those institutions. In such analyses, the American family is usually described as a nuclear living unit of married parents and their minor children, with strong horizontal bonds between the married partners and between siblings. This living unit maintains ties of mutual aid and intimacy with a wider kinship network extending one or two degrees of kinship on both the husband's and the wife's side, through all living generations. Invoking the pioneer family image of a small independent unit struggling against the wilderness, this cultural ideal of family is often credited with producing the independent and self-reliant American character.

The Japanese family is usually described as a strongly patrilineal unit, a line of first sons who live together with their wives and minor children, and who maintain ties of mutual aid and intimacy with a wider kinship network on the husband's side. The wider kin network extends beyond living generations to include reverence for family ancestors and a sense of responsibility toward succeeding generations not yet born. This cultural ideal of the traditional Japanese family invokes images of devotion, loyalty, and self-sacrifice for the good of the larger collectivity, offered in partial repayment for limitless parental benevolence.

I do not think that this approach is very useful anymore for the comparative cultural analysis of the family in American and Japanese societies. For one thing, the descriptions of family structure no longer match the data for either society. The best place to find such stereotypical families is on television, but even television is beginning to change its presentation of families in both Japan and the United States. Second, although it is important for scholars to understand the nature and power of cultural images, this sort of research sometimes ends up believing and perpetuating these myths, rather than analyzing them. Cultural images and myths do have a certain power, but they do not explain social institutions. Analysis must unpack the images and myths to find out how and why they have a social effect.

I also think there are some methodological problems with using the traditional cultural approach, which is derived from functionalist theory. The functionalist institutional approach to cultural analysis is static and oriented toward explaining the stability of societies, when the contemporary reality is rapid change. We need to use an approach that helps us understand that change and predict where it is headed. The functionalist approach also emphasizes the successful functioning of existing institutions and tends to ignore the problems that are created by those institutions, which in turn are one important source of social change. And finally, the functionalist approach to culture tends to reify cultural ideals as if they were the universal reality, and thus it does not pay sufficient attention to variations within a society. Some of the variation within a society may represent emerging new patterns; whereas some of it may have been there all the time but was ignored because it did not fit the prevailing research paradigm. In either case, the failure to take serious account of internal variations weakens our capacity to understand and predict change.

Many things may be wrong with our old methods of studying culture, yet culture itself is certainly a real phenomenon. Whenever we step outside our own culture we can see it clearly, even if we are not able to recognize its traces in our own behavior at home. To capture that essential reality and use it effectively to understand how families are changing, we must begin with a more fluid and dynamic concept of culture.

If our aim is to understand changing families, then we must focus on how culture affects the precise points at which change occurs: the microlevel choices that individual families and their members make in response to situations they confront in their own lives. Rather than viewing culture as embodied in certain idealized institutional forms, I prefer to see it as a loose but identifiable set of assumptions and preferences that people use to make the critical decisions in their lives. Children absorb these preferences as they grow up in a family, but they also may resist them, or rethink them when they are exposed to wider social influences and changing historical circumstances. And always, they apply their assumptions and preferences to real problems that arise in the form of a unique and personal human situation. Through the choices people make in a myriad of specific situations, using similar cultural assumptions and preferences, they create and re-create the institutions of their society.

Of course culture alone does not produce institutions. Human choices take into consideration a whole range of economic, political, social, and interpersonal factors as they arise in particular historical moments. Cultural preferences help us understand why these choices, and the resulting institutions, come out differently in what appear to be objectively similar circumstances. Consequently, it is dangerous to try to use only a cultural approach to understand a situation without first taking these other elements into account. As a research strategy, I believe culture should be applied last, after we have explained everything we can in terms of more universal factors.

Nevertheless, because my task is to present a comparative cultural analysis of Japanese and American families, I am going to reverse the order a bit. I will first discuss some basic cultural assumptions and preferences in Japanese and American societies, and show how they apply to situations that arise in contemporary families. Then I will look at the structure of the larger society in each case and try to see how families fit into that structure, by identifying the broader social factors that impinge on families and frame the decisions they must make. Finally, I will try to draw out some key problems that in the near future may change families, or other parts of the social structure, or even the cultural ideas themselves.

CULTURAL ASSUMPTIONS IN JAPAN AND THE UNITED STATES

When we compare Japanese and American cultures from this perspective, three differences in basic assumptions stand out, which produce cultural preferences for certain kinds of decisions. The areas of difference concern the nature and goals of the family, its internal organization, and cultural attitudes toward conflict.

Family Goals

The first assumptions concern the nature and goals of the family. They affect the way family issues are formulated and thus the preference for various options when problems arise. These assumptions also affect the capacity of individual family members to resist the demands of other family members.

In Japan there is a general cultural assumption that the family exists of and for itself, as a collectivity. The corollary to this is the assumption that individual family members can be called upon to make personal sacrifices for the sake of the family as a collectivity. This idea has been described by Nakamura (1964) as a basic, ancient Japanese cultural idea about the fundamental reality and priority of social groups. Bellah (1964) has discussed its implications for individuals' sense of identity, which tends to be realized in and through membership in groups such as the family. The concept of membership in a family line that extends through generations past, present, and future is an embodiment of this assumption, as is the institution of the three-generational family. But the fundamental assumption about the priority of groups is more general and flexible, and I think it is a more useful device for understanding the present and future of the Japanese family.

By contrast, in the United States there is a general assumption that the family exists for the development and protection of individual family members, rather than as an enduring entity above and beyond those individuals (Gecas, 1987; Winch, 1971). This more contractual orientation implies that the family is a purposeful creation of its members, who can dissolve it or leave it if it does not accomplish its goals (Spanier, 1989:6). This view of the family is of course deeply connected to the strong individual sense of identity that Americans have, which they believe to be somehow prior to and independent of any group affiliations they may hold (Bellah et al., 1985).

An extensive body of research documents this difference in cultural assumptions between the two societies, but I want to emphasize that it is certainly not an absolute difference. Many individuals in both societies actively resist these assumptions or do not activate them in making critical decisions. I am pointing to tendencies, preferences, and probabilities.

Internal Family Structure

A second set of basic assumptions has to do with the relative positions of the members within a family. These assumptions affect the weighting of options when there is a family problem, by specifying the relative burden of sacrifice that each family member is expected to bear. They also affect the dynamics of the decision-making process, by specifying the relative weight of each family member's opinion.

In Japan there is a relatively strong and clear set of assumptions about the hierarchical order of things. There is both an assumption that it is important and natural to rank people or things hierarchically and broad agreement about the appropriate criteria for such ranking

(Lebra, 1976). Within families, differences of generation, birth order, and sex are assumed to be fair and reasonable criteria for rank ordering. The position of head of the family takes on special significance as the pinnacle of this overall hierarchy.

By contrast, in American families there is a stronger assumption of equality among family members and a correspondingly greater obligation to justify ranking by generation, sex, or birth order. Hierarchical ranking can sometimes be justified as "fair" on the basis of some other criterion, or it can be compensated by another transaction that restores the basic balance among family members (Bernard, 1973). This assumption of equality is greatest among white, middle-class American families, but it is probably more characteristic of American families than of Japanese families, regardless of internal cultural variations. The position of head of the family also varies in its significance among American families, but generally it is seen less as an inviolate structural property of the group and more as a status earned by individual performance.

Both Americans and Japanese have larger cultural conceptions about the nature of fairness or mutual obligation, within which these assumptions are embedded. I want to emphasize again that the assumptions I am describing constitute relative differences that are likely to help tip the balance in critical decisions. I do not intend them as absolute statements about the daily life of families in the two cultures because one could certainly find many examples of the opposite behavior in each society.

Family Conflict

The third area of difference involves basic assumptions about conflict. Within the family, these differences affect family communication, with two rather large implications. First, they can affect whether certain alternatives are raised for consideration and who will pay attention to them. And second, they can affect how the family and its members deal with the consequences of a decision.

In Japan there is an assumption that open conflict is dangerous to the continuation of the group, and because the group itself has heightened significance, conflict is profoundly dangerous. The cultural preference is to avoid conflict by anticipating and managing it in advance, and if that fails, to suppress its expression in the group and let individuals deal with it as an internal, private, personal problem. Within families conflict is frequently managed by role segregation, indirect communication, and polite inattention. The strong hierarchy within the family defines who may express conflict and who must suppress it (Krauss, Rohlen, and Steinhoff, 1984; Lebra, 1984).

By contrast, the American assumption is that open expression of conflict is a relatively normal part of group life and communication. It may be unpleasant, but it can lead to constructive solutions that meet the needs of individual family members (Rafaelli, 1992:660). A corollary assumption is that it is healthier for individuals to express their anger than to keep it bottled up, which in turn is related to the priority given to individual satisfaction as a family goal. The relative equality of family members means that any family member is free to express conflict, although there may be constraints on what forms of expression are acceptable for particular members. And since Americans tend to have a more contractual orientation toward families in the first place, leaving the family remains a viable option if the conflict becomes too protracted and severe for individuals to bear.

Because conflict has such profoundly different meaning in the two cultures, it is difficult to study cross-culturally in a systematic way; yet I do not think we can understand what is going on in either Japanese or American families unless we look carefully at the sources, expressions, and management of conflict. For example, the decline in Japan of coresidence of young married couples with the husband's family is clearly an attempt to reduce the major source of conflict in the three-generational family, that between mother-in-law and daughter-in-law. The inability to resolve a structural problem in one generation can lead the next generation to rethink its priorities and make new choices that apply cultural preferences in a different way.

These systematic differences are important not only because they affect the decisions that families make about a wide variety of issues, but also because the family itself is the first place where children become oriented to these cultural assumptions. The process begins in infancy and early childhood, through the daily interactions of parents and children.

Japanese children experience the continual, attentive presence of their mothers, who anticipate their needs by responding to tiny, often nonverbal cues (Caudill and Weinstein, 1969). By paying such close attention, mothers are able to avoid direct confrontations with their children and to guide them flexibly into desired kinds of behavior. The effect of this child-rearing strategy is to emphasize the child's interdependence with other people, the capacity of others to know what is best for the child, and the child's own need to cooperate within the family for mutual satisfaction (Vogel, 1991). In addition, the child learns the social skills of communicating ambiguous personal needs to others by tiny social cues, and learns to read and respond to the equally subtle cues of the others upon whom he depends. In effect, the child learns the importance of the group for his own well-being, the dangers of open conflict, and the need to orient his behavior to the requirements of those around him.

By contrast, American infants and small children experience less constant attention from their mothers. They learn very early to recognize their own needs clearly and to express them verbally (Caudill and Weinstein, 1969). In the process they learn to take risks, to make choices, and to meet their own needs. American parents take seriously the choices and opinions of two-year-olds, thereby making the children personally responsible for their own satisfaction. Parents willingly engage in direct confrontation with a small child because they attribute an independent will to the child and respect it. The effect of this child-rearing strategy is to give the child a strong sense of personal independence, a feeling of equality with other people, and a high tolerance for conflict and risk.

In both Japan and the United States, these outcomes result from the cultural assumptions that parents bring to their daily interactions with infants and small children. It is through these minute daily interactions that the cultural aspects of a child's personality and sense of identity are formed and he "becomes" Japanese or American.

CONTEMPORARY SOCIAL STRUCTURE AND FAMILIES

We must now look more closely at the larger social structures of the United States and Japan, and at how families interact with those structures. The same cultural assumptions that we see in families have helped to produce those social arrangements, but this does not mean the connections between them are smooth or trouble-free.

Contemporary Japan

Contemporary Japan has a highly developed dual, or stratified, economy. At the top are a few large corporate groups that offer long-term economic and social security, career advancement, and high social status to a select corps of male permanent employees. These privileges are supported in two main ways: through an elaborate hierarchy of subsidiary and subcontracting firms that offer correspondingly lower levels of economic and social security, career advancement, and social status to their employees; and through the heavy use of both male and female workers under various kinds of contractual statuses that offer no long-term economic or social security and no career advancement.

Entry into the Japanese corporate elite is determined by a meritocratic educational competition that culminates in entrance to institutions of higher education that are themselves hierarchically ranked. In a quite circular process, college rankings are determined largely on the basis of their capacity to place graduates in the corporate elite, which affects the number of applicants, hence the difficulty of entry and the selectivity of the schools, thus self-validating the top corporations' preference for recruiting from only a limited number of highly ranked schools. The rank of a college therefore correlates closely with the rank of the companies where its graduates find employment. The heavy use of internal promotion for positions above the entry levels means that lifetime opportunity for male career advancement is more or less determined by college entrance examinations (Tsukada, 1988). Companies make a substantial investment in employee training, but the resulting skills and talents are regarded essentially as the property of the company rather than of the individual. Company loyalty and dedication are assiduously cultivated, often by calling upon traditional cultural images of the family (Rohlen, 1974). Government employment is also highly regarded for its economic and social security and its high prestige; it is entered through the same route as the top corporations.

Most young men do not enter the elite universities and do not get hired by the top companies or the national government. Nevertheless, their lifetime career opportunities, economic and social security, and status are also heavily determined by educational performance unless the family happens to own a business that offers better opportunities (Rosenbaum and Kariya, 1989). Most interfirm mobility is lateral or to smaller and lower-ranking companies. It occurs under three circumstances: retirement, when most men seek a second position for a few years; voluntary severance due to mid-career dissatisfaction, which is still a relatively rare phenomenon; and, at smaller companies, involuntary severance due to layoffs, industrial restructuring, or bankruptcy of the firm.

Young women face less severe academic competition than men because they are generally discouraged from seeking career credentials. They do, however, compete with other women for entry-level positions in large corporations. These positions are usually gender-linked and excluded from opportunities for career advancement, but they offer enhanced marriage opportunities. Women are encouraged to retire into marriage and child rearing after a few years of employment, but nowadays they are likely to return to the labor force as part-time workers in much lower status positions after a few years at home (Brinton, 1993; Roberts, 1994). In addition to substantial numbers of women in traditionally female careers, such as nursing and teaching, a small but growing number of women hold managerial positions. In general, the smaller the firm, the more likely there will be women in management. Women are active participants in the management of small family businesses; and the number of companies headed by women, though still modest, is growing by about 10 percent each year (Steinhoff and Tanaka, 1994).

Owing to low birth rates, high educational levels, and long-term economic growth, Japan has a chronic labor shortage that is most acute at the low skill level but is also affecting white-collar positions. Despite Japan's current economic difficulties, the labor shortage is expected to become more severe over the next two decades. The labor shortage has drawn many married women into part-time positions and has attracted many foreign workers, most of whom have a precarious visa status. Japanese immigration policy not only discourages new foreign workers; it also perpetuates the resident-alien status of about half a million Koreans, many of them second- and third-generation residents of Japan, who have restricted employment and welfare rights and limited opportunity to obtain Japanese citizenship.

This brief account of the social structure of contemporary Japan reflects the cultural preferences for long-term group affiliation and hierarchical ranking, as well as the tendency to manage conflict by segregation of roles and statuses. We now need to see how the contemporary Japanese family relates to this structure.

The Japanese economy is oriented to providing employment security to male heads of households through long-term affiliation with a single employer. Families, in turn, are expected to provide extensive personal support for the employed male head, who devotes most of his waking hours to work-related demands (which may include a substantial amount of work-related leisure activity). In addition, families are expected to support married women during their child-rearing years and to continue to support them so that they may return to the labor force at wages well below subsistence level. The family is also expected to support household members and extended kin during illness and old age; hence other social institutions to perform these functions are not well developed. Because of the husband's absence, this burden falls almost entirely on the wife.

In response to the current employment system, families generally provide for the future economic and social security of their children by investing heavily in education. This same investment also serves to ensure economic and social security for their own old age. Although some state-supported daycare now exists for working mothers, the presumption remains that childcare is the full-time responsibility of mothers because the customary mode of interaction between Japanese young children and their caretakers demands a high degree of focused attention on the part of the caretaker. In addition, both preschools and elementary schools make heavy demands on mothers, and mothers also provide a high level of support to older children, who are expected to devote their full energies to studying.

Children remain at least partially economically dependent upon their parents until they complete their education, and they often live at home until marriage; but they are not usually expected to contribute much labor or income to the household unless they participate in a family business. They are, however, expected to meet parental expectations for educational performance, employment, and marriage. If they have left home, they may be called back to assume family responsibilities.

Cultural assumptions can also be seen quite clearly in the Japanese family's transactions with the larger social structure. The family unit has a wide range of economic and social responsibilities, which fall unevenly on family members according to the internal hierarchy. The collective needs of the family take precedence over individual desires in the resolution of many kinds of problems.

The fact that there are cultural preferences for resolving problems in certain ways does not necessarily mean that Japanese family members meet those demands spontaneously or happily. They may be quite unhappy but simply see no way out. In addition to the cultural expectation that members will make such sacrifices for the family's welfare, the internal hierarchy of the family limits the capacity of affected members to express resistance or press for alternate solutions, and cultural attitudes toward conflict add to their difficulty.

Contemporary America

Traces of basic cultural assumptions can also be seen in the social structure of the contemporary United States. The United States, too, has a somewhat stratified labor market, but it is less rigidly structured than the Japanese and certainly less hierarchical. Considerably more interfirm mobility occurs among employees of large corporations, although there is also substantial internal promotion. American companies invest much less than Japanese firms in the direct training of their employees, for fear of losing their investment when an employee moves to another firm. Instead, individuals cultivate their own portable collection of skills through a combination of formal education and work experience, and companies hire individuals specifically to gain access to those skills. Interfirm mobility, additional formal education, and even complete career changes can occur at any time in the working life of an American.

Consequently, opportunities for career success are spread out much more broadly throughout one's working lifetime, rather than being determined by college entrance. Higher education does make a substantial difference in lifetime earnings, and postgraduate training at one's own expense is a prerequisite for entry to many high-income, high-status occupations. Although quality distinctions among colleges and universities also make some difference, the rankings are much looser, more variable, and subject to debate. There is also a much weaker correlation between the rank of a college and the rank of a graduate's employer, in part because the ranks themselves are less clearly defined. In addition, independent professions such as law and medicine offer higher status and income potential in the United States than they do in Japan, and thus employment in large corporations is less central to status and success in the United States than it is in Japan. Government employment, like corporate employment, can be entered at mid-career in the United States. It does not have particularly high economic or prestige value.

For blue-collar employment, there is virtually no relationship between school performance and employment, except that some positions nominally require a high school diploma. The restructuring of the American economy has reduced the number of high-paying skilled and semi-skilled blue-collar jobs and replaced them primarily with low-paying, low-level service jobs. Employment opportunities have shifted from "rust-belt" cities in the North to "sun-belt" cities in the South and West, but there has been little corresponding migration of displaced workers or retraining of industrial workers for new forms of skilled employment. Unemployment levels for minority workers with minimal job skills and education are chronically high (Wilson, 1987).

Yet America remains an immigrant society, absorbing large numbers of new immigrants annually despite continuing problems of unemployment and industrial restructuring. Citizenship is a birthright of anyone born on American soil, and immigration laws give preference to family members. Thus U.S. immigration laws generally encourage the eventual permanent migration of whole families into American society. Most new immigrants begin at the lower levels of the economy, with many family members employed. Although they may experience some discrimination, the family's subsequent movement upward is primarily dependent upon the education and skills they acquire.

Over the past 25 years there has been strong and steady movement of women into the American labor force at all levels. Most married women now work, and those with higher education or special skills generally are oriented to a full-time, long-term career. Women still earn less than men on average, but many barriers to career advancement have fallen and women are now found at all levels in virtually all occupations and professions.

Although they provide some support for spouses, both private and public old-age security programs in the United States are heavily geared to the work history of the individual, male or female. American companies do not offer long-term employment security to employees, and they view reduction of their labor force as a primary means of cutting costs. Except in heavily unionized industries such as the automobile industry, government-sponsored unemployment insurance is the employee's main economic protection during layoffs. Unemployment insurance is paid directly to the individual unemployed worker. The state also pays a variety of other welfare benefits directly to individuals who are outside the labor force, such as disabled workers and women with dependent children who have no other source of support.

The United States does not yet have a national health insurance system to supplement that provided by employers to employees and their families, but minimal health care is provided through the welfare system and directly by public and charitable hospitals. The family is not expected to provide supplemental nursing care for hospitalized family members, as is the case in Japan.

As this brief overview suggests, the contemporary American social and economic structure reflects the strong emphasis on individualism in American culture and the relative independence of individuals from permanent group affiliations. Hierarchical ranking is much less prominent than in Japanese society and much less related to long-term economic and social security. Opportunities for success and failure are spread throughout the working years in the United States.

The connections between the family and the larger social structure are also much looser. In the contemporary United States there is little direct connection between the family and the workplace, and the presumption that a nonworking wife is available to provide full support to a corporate employee has all but disappeared. The corporate employee may be a woman, may have a spouse who is also working in a career position, or may be divorced. Companies hire individuals and pay them on the basis of their personal credentials, regardless of their family status. Only mass employee benefit plans, such as health and life insurance, extend to the families of employees. In general, the American social structure has lower expectations of family support for individuals, and the state provides more social welfare directly to the individual than is the case in Japan.

Yet American families remain a primary source of economic and social support for their members across three or four generations (Bengtson and Dannefer, 1987). Although the majority of families now survive on multiple incomes, families also absorb persons who are out of work or unable to afford independent living, regardless of age or generation. Both adult children and the elderly strongly prefer to live independently but may return to live with family members if necessary. In addition, family wealth and emotional support flow toward those in need, regardless of generation or living arrangements. All these features reflect the general egalitarianism and lack of hierarchy in American families, as well as the strong independence of individual family members.

Since American childrearing practices emphasize the independence and self-reliance of the child at a very young age, the movement of mothers of young children into the workplace does not alter socialization strategies fundamentally, and it tends to reinforce basic cultural assumptions rather than to undermine them. American families also invest in their children's education, but not with the intensity of families in Japan, since the child's future and the family's old-age security rest less heavily on one critical point of educational achievement. In fact,

American families are more apt to invest in the education of any family member, at any point in the life cycle, because of the perceived benefits to that individual. Moreover, because of the higher levels of postgraduate training required for entry into high-income, high-status professions in the United States, middle-class and upper middle-class American families often provide partial support for the education of children into their late 20s.

At the same time, Americans place high demands on their families for the satisfaction of personal needs, and they feel increasingly free to dissolve family relationships if their needs are not being met. Employment instability and the inability of many men to support other family members has increased family conflict, while the increased participation of women in the labor force has made them correspondingly less dependent upon marriage for economic support. The resulting proliferation of new living arrangements and family configurations has kept the demographers busy recoding and the lexicographers busy inventing new terms.

It is clear that there is more open expression of conflict in American families and also less family stability than in Japan, but as an American I am reluctant to infer the cause-and-effect relationship that Japanese culture would assume. Americans begin by assigning less importance to the permanence of group relationships, and in general they have a greater tolerance than Japanese for both conflict and uncertainty. The whole cultural package surrounding these issues is simply different in the two societies. That is indeed what culture is about, and why we need to include it in our analyses.

CONFLICT AND CHANGE

I began this chapter by criticizing the traditional style of analyzing the family as a cultural institution for its lack of utility in understanding and predicting social change in the contemporary Japanese and American family. It behooves me, therefore, to conclude by pointing to the implications for future social change that derive from my analysis.

In keeping with an orientation to culture as a set of preferences that affect the choices people make under specific economic, social, and political circumstances, I do not think we can point to a single direction of change for all families in either Japan or the United States. Rather, it is necessary to examine the major alternatives that families face and then consider the broad social implications of these choices.

The Future of American Families

In the United States, the assumption that the family exists to maximize the development and security of individuals, combined with strong egalitarianism within the family, has led over the past few decades to greater awareness of the needs of each family member. But because this assumption has been combined with a contractual attitude toward the family as a creation of its members, and with the willingness of American family members to engage in open conflict, the result has been both more family dissolution and increased experimentation with new forms of family and family-like small groups.

When this combination of factors works effectively, it produces flexible, participatory family arrangements that facilitate individual development while providing emotional and economic security for family members. When it does not work effectively, it produces family divisions that are destructive to children, economically detrimental to women and children, and emotionally destabilizing for young and old.

I think this division is increasingly playing out in the United States as a class division, in which the upper levels of the society benefit from increased individual opportunity and the affluence of dual-career families, while an underclass of unmarried mothers and children lives in economically and socially deprived conditions. These contrasts are not the direct and simple result of cultural preferences, but rather reflect the application of those cultural preferences to personal situations constrained by political, economic, and social conditions. To some extent they also reflect cultural variations within American society that lie outside the scope of this chapter.

I think the notion of family is still very real in American society, but if we look only for the old stereotypes of family structure we will fail to recognize the cultural persistence of American assumptions about the family, operating in a new and complex environment. In fact, some of our current family problems in the United States stem precisely from terrible social policy that was hidden in a lot of rhetoric about stereotyped family structures and values.

The Future of Japanese Families

The situation in Japan is different in its details, but I think it poses equally difficult problems for the future. The emphasis in Japan on the collective goals of the family, combined with a well-defined internal family hierarchy and a strong desire to avoid conflict, means that families have clear long-term goals, plan for the future, and deploy resources rationally for the long-term security of family members. When the system works, it supports the education of children and provides security for old age. At a larger social level, the family absorbs a great deal of responsibility for social security, supports the male career work force at relatively low cost, and provides additional cheap, flexible labor from married women.

When the package does not work, the hierarchical preferences of the Japanese family, combined with strong assumptions about the need to sacrifice individual desires for collective family goals, place very heavy burdens on Japanese married women and adult children. The preference for avoiding conflict adds to this burden, keeping the problems from being dealt with effectively either by families or by the society as a whole.

I see a growing gender gap in the middle and upper-middle class, where the lives of married Japanese men and women are most separate. Men are isolated by heavy work demands and corporate expectations of family support, while women are caught by these same expectations, plus the burden of caring for the elderly, which conflict with their own increasing desire to work outside the home for personal rewards even if it is not necessary for economic reasons. In this situation, difficulties in expressing conflict, hierarchies of sacrifice, and the general orientation to collective family goals rather than individual needs all translate into real problems for Japanese women in the coming decade.

As in American society, these problems are not a simple and direct reflection of culture, but rather result from the interaction of cultural preferences with the social, economic, and political context of family decisions. And as in the American case, part of the difficulty lies in deliberate social policies that are cloaked in a lot of rhetoric based on stereotyped views of family structure and family values, but that in fact exacerbate certain family problems.

I do not think the Japanese family as an institution is in serious trouble, but I do think that a number of problems are going to become more critical in the coming decade. And although the economic and social environment is certainly more favorable to the resolution of problems than is the case in the United States, the Japanese family problems I see on the horizon may turn out to be difficult to resolve because they are more intimately connected to the basic assumptions I have outlined.

I think it is inevitable that Japanese women will continue to experiment with new solutions to their dilemma. It is equally inevitable that the changes they achieve in their individual lives will alter a wide range of Japanese social arrangements. The ripple effect of these changes, in turn, will alter socialization practices and eventually begin to change some of the most basic cultural assumptions of Japanese society. In fact, this may already be happening.

In some ways, the problems of contemporary American families would be lessened if we had a somewhat more Japanese set of cultural assumptions about the family. Likewise, the problems of contemporary Japanese families would be alleviated if Japan had more American cultural assumptions about the family. It is in times of crisis that people in any culture rely most heavily on their basic assumptions and cultural preferences to make decisions. Yet even basic cultural orientations do change over time, as people reevaluate their applicability to immediate situations and reinterpret them to fit their needs. In the process, they alter the environment in which the next generation acquires its cultural assumptions.

REFERENCES

Bellah, Robert. 1964. "Values and Social Change in Modern Japan." *Studies in Modernization of Japan by Western Scholars. Asian Cultural Studies*, Vol. III. Tokyo: International Christian University.

Bellah, Robert, Richard Madsen, William M. Sullivan, Ann Swidler, and Steven M. Tipton. 1985. *Habits of the Heart*. Berkeley: University of California Press.

Bengtson, Vern L., and Dale Dannefer. 1987. "Families, Work, and Aging: Implications of Disordered Cohort Flow for the Twenty-first Century." In Russell A. Ward and Sheldon S. Tobin (eds.), *Health in Aging: Sociological Issues and Policy Direction*. New York: Springer.

Bernard, Jessie. 1973. *The Future of Marriage*. New York: Bantam Books.

Brinton, Mary. 1993 *Women and the Economic Miracle: Gender and Work in Postwar Japan*. Berkeley: University of California Press.

Caudill, William, and Helen Weinstein. 1969. "Maternal Care and Infant Behavior in Japan and America." *Psychiatry* 32:12–43.

Gecas, Victor. 1987. "Born in the USA in the 1980's: Growing up in Difficult Times." *Journal of Family Issues* 8:434–436.

Krauss, Ellis S., Thomas P. Rohlen, and Patricia G. Steinhoff. 1984. "Conflict and Its Resolution in Postwar Japan." In Ellis S. Krauss, Thomas P. Rohlen, and Patricia G. Steinhoff (eds.) *Conflict in Japan*. Honolulu: University of Hawaii Press.

Lebra, Takie S. 1976. *Japanese Patterns of Behavior*. Honolulu: University Press of Hawaii.

———. 1984. "Non-confrontational Strategies for Management of Interpersonal Conflicts." In Ellis S. Krauss, Thomas P. Rohlen, and Patricia G. Steinhoff (eds.) *Conflict in Japan*. Honolulu: University of Hawaii Press.

Nakamura Hajime. 1964. *The Ways of Thinking of Eastern Peoples: India, China, Tibet, Japan*, ed. by Philip P. Wiener. Honolulu: East-West Center Press.

Raffaelli, Marcela. 1992. "Sibling Conflict in Early Adolescence." *Journal of Marriage and the Family* 54(Aug.):652–663.

Roberts, Glenda. 1994. *Staying on the Line: Blue-Collar Women in Contemporary Japan*. Honolulu: University of Hawaii Press.

Rohlen, Thomas P. 1974. *For Harmony and Strength: Japanese White-Collar Organization in Anthropological Perspective*. Berkeley: University of California Press.

Rosenbaum, James E., and Takehiko Kariya. 1989. "High School to Work: Market and Institutional Mechanisms in Japan." *American Journal of Sociology* 94(6):1334–1365.

Spanier, Graham. 1989. "Bequeathing Family Continuity." *Journal of Marriage and the Family* 51(Feb.):3–13.

Steinhoff, Patricia G., and Kazuko Tanaka. 1994. "Women Managers in Japan." In Nancy J. Adler and Dafna Izraeli, eds., *Competitive Frontiers: Women Managers in the Global Economy*. Cambridge, Mass. and London: Blackwell Publishers.

Tsukada Mamoru. 1988. "Institutionalized Supplementary Education in Japan: The *Yobiko* and *Ronin* Student Adaptations" *Comparative Education* 24(3):285–303.

Vogel, Ezra F. 1991. *Japan's New Middle Class*, rev. ed. Berkeley: University of California Press.

Wilson, William J. 1987. *The Truly Disadvantaged: The Inner City, the Underclass, and Public Policy*. Chicago: The University of Chicago Press.

Winch, Robert F. 1971. *The Modern Family*. 3d ed. New York: Holt, Rinehart, and Winston.

CHAPTER 4

Family Structure and Social Change: Implications of Fertility Changes in Japan and China

by Toshio Kuroda

Evolutionary stage theory, which argues that family structure changes over time from the clan to the large extended family and then to the so-called nuclear family, has received wide support from sociologists and social anthropologists. Goode's (1963) convergence theory, positing the universal convergence of family types to the nuclear family, has drawn particular attention. My own view is that these theories are not necessarily applicable to the cases of China and Japan, and I wish to take issue with the general proposition that the large extended family type was dominant in China and Japan in the past.

My argument is based on demographic evidence. Demographic variables are often overlooked or inappropriately interpreted in studies of family structure. The result of high fertility, in particular, may be families with many children, and such large families may be mistaken for extended families. Granted, under conditions of early marriage and high fertility, the extended family—that is, a family consisting of three generations of members who share the same household—may be common, at least temporarily. Under conditions of high fertility and falling mortality, large families, whether nuclear or extended, will be the norm. Another factor that affects the average size of family households is population mobility, and changes in the family life cycle caused by sharp declines in fertility and mortality affect the incidence of various types of families. This chapter attempts to demonstrate the dominance of the conjugal family type in China and Japan prior to World War II, relying mostly on demographic variables and in particular fertility.

CONTINUITY OF THE NUCLEAR FAMILY SYSTEM IN JAPAN

It is commonly argued that the Japanese family system changed dramatically after World War II from an extended-family system of the prewar period to a nuclear-family system centered around the husband and wife with children. I do not deny that major changes have occurred in the status and functions of the husband, wife, and children and in the Japanese family life cycle since the war. As far as family type is concerned, however, no essential change can be recognized. Statistical data from Japanese censuses clearly indicate continuity of the nuclear family system (Table 4.1). Even in 1920, nuclear families accounted for more than half, 54 percent, of all families, a figure only slightly below that of recent years, whereas the proportion of three-generation families in 1920 was only 29 percent. The proportion of couples with children, who make up the typical nuclear family, has remained nearly constant between 1920 and 1990, around 40 percent. The proportions of other types of nuclear families have also remained fairly stable, although the proportion of couples without children has risen from 10 to nearly 16 percent, showing a steadily increasing trend after World War II.

Table 4.1. Percentage distribution of households, by type: Japan, selected years, 1920–90

Household type	1920	1975	1980	1985	1990
All households	100.0	100.0	100.0	100.0	100.0
Nuclear-family households	54.0	59.5	60.3	60.0	59.5
Couples with children	38.3	42.5	42.1	40.0	37.3
Fathers with children	} 5.4	0.8	0.8	0.9	1.0
Mothers with children		4.6	4.9	5.4	5.7
Couples only	10.3	11.6	12.5	13.7	15.5
Three-generation family households	29.1	14.8	14.6	13.9	12.1
Others	16.9	25.7	25.1	26.1	28.4

Sources: 1920: Toda (1937), based on 1,000 sample tabulations from the 1920 census. 1975–90: derived from population census results reported by Japan, Statistics Bureau (1992).

Family Structure and Social Change: Implications of Fertility Changes in Japan and China

On the other hand, household size has undergone substantial changes since World War II (Table 4.2). First, slightly less than one-half (49 percent) of all households had fewer than four members in 1920, and the share of small households fell until 1955. After 1960, however, the proportion of such households rose, reaching 71 percent in 1970, 79 percent in 1980, and 83 percent in 1990. Second, the proportion of large families (defined as those with more than six members) decreased remarkably over the same period, from nearly 37 percent in 1920 to 21 percent in 1965, 9.5 percent in 1980, and 7.3 percent in 1990. Third, the average number of household members also declined rapidly, from 4.89 persons in 1920 to 3.33 persons in 1980 and 2.99 persons in 1990.

These findings demonstrate that the nuclear-family system has been very stable throughout the pre- and postwar periods and only the size of the family has undergone major change. This point is very important. The sizable proportion of large-family households before the war was a major cause for the mistaken view that the dominant family type was the large extended family. Although very large households, those with more than 10 members, constituted only 4.5 percent of all families in 1920 and by 1980 had practically disappeared (at 0.1 percent), they helped to create the illusion of extended-family dominance. In reality, a sharp decline in fertility occurred in the postwar period, making the predominance of the nuclear family more evident. The fertility decline was the major cause of the dramatic change in the distribution of households by size, but it did not cause a change in the distribution of family types.

Table 4.2. Percentages of small and large households and average number of household members: Japan, selected years, 1920–90

Year	Small households < 4 members (%)	Large households > 6 members (%)	Average number of household members (persons)
1920	48.8	36.7	4.89
1950	46.3	38.4	4.97
1955	45.4	38.0	4.97
1960	52.5	28.5	4.54
1965	62.8	21.2	4.05
1970	71.4	14.2	3.69
1975	76.8	10.5	3.45
1980	79.0	9.5	3.33
1985	80.8	8.1	3.14
1990	83.4	7.3	2.99

Sources: Population censuses (Japan, Statistics Bureau, 1990).
Note: Households with five members are not shown.

CHINA'S ILLUSORY EXTENDED-FAMILY SYSTEM

It is generally believed that the large extended family was traditionally the dominant family type in China. Nevertheless, a famous Chinese scholar, Fei Hsiao-Tung (1947), has argued that this perception is wrong and that the large extended family has not been historically the dominant form of the Chinese family. He speculates that this mistaken notion may be due to the popularity of such novels as Ba Jin's *Jia* (Family) and Cao Xue-qin's *Hong Lou Meng*, which chronicle the experiences of multigenerational families. On the basis of his own sample surveys made in 1936 and 1981, Professor Fei has concluded that even in rural areas of China, large extended families accounted for only 10 percent and 21 percent of all families respectively in 1936 and 1981. The nuclear family was the most prevalent type, representing 39 percent of the total in 1981, although extended families were more common in 1981 than they had been when he conducted his earlier survey.

Some idea of the average size of households in China before the founding of the People's Republic of China in 1949 is given in Table 4.3, which is based on official statistics of the prerevolutionary Chinese government. It shows that during the first half of the century the average size of households was quite stable at around five persons. Of course, the official statistics contained errors and omissions. Compared with the results obtained from small sample surveys, however, they were reasonably accurate.

National censuses and large sample surveys provide more detailed information that confirms the dominance of the nuclear-family pattern in China. Table 4.4 shows very stable household size over the period from 1953 to 1982, at between 4.29 and 4.43 persons on average, and also interesting trends in the average size of households in urban and rural areas. Although the average size of households in

Table 4.3. Number of households, population size, and average number of household members: China, selected years, 1911–47

Year	Number of households	Population	Average number of household members	Source of data
1911	71,268,651	368,146,520	5.17	*1934 Economic Yearbook of China*
1912	76,366,074	405,810,967	5.31	Statistics of former Ministry of Internal Affairs
1928	83,855,901	441,849,148	5.27	Statistics of former Ministry of Internal Affairs
1933	83,960,443	444,486,537	5.29	*Statistical Abstracts*
1936	85,827,345	479,084,651	5.38	Reports of former Ministry of Internal Affairs
1947	86,637,312	463,198,093	5.35	Statistics of former Bureau of Population, Ministry of Internal Affairs

Source: Ma (1984:Table 1, p. 453).

Family Structure and Social Change: Implications of Fertility Changes in Japan and China

urban areas declined continuously during the three decades, it rose in rural areas. This finding suggests that China's fertility decline has been more remarkable in urban than in rural areas.

Table 4.5, which parallels Table 4.2 on Japan, presents the percentages of small households (those with fewer than four members) and large households (those with more than six members) in China between 1930 and 1982, based on data from various sources. Over the 1930–40 decade the proportion of large families was slightly larger than that of small families, 43 percent versus 41 percent; but by 1982, small-family households greatly outnumbered large families, 54 percent versus 28 percent. As in Japan, however, a large family is not necessarily equated with an extended family. When fertility is high, the number of nuclear families with many children tends to increase. High fertility is thus one cause of expanding proportions of large-family households.

Nuclear-family households can be divided into those consisting of couples only (one-generation families) and couples with children (two-generation families). In 1982, according to the Chinese census of that year, two-generation households were dominant, representing 65 percent of all Chinese households (Table 4.6). With couple-only households added, the proportion of nuclear-family households rises to 70 percent for that year. Multigenerational households represented only 17 percent of the total, and one-person households only 8 percent. Even in 1930, two-generation households accounted for as much as 49 percent of

Table 4.4. Average number of household members in urban, rural, and all areas: China, 1953, 1964, and 1982

Year	Urban	Rural	All areas
1953	4.66	4.26	4.30
1964	4.11	4.35	4.29
1982	3.95	4.57	4.43

Source: Ma (1984).

Table 4.5. Percentages of small and large households: China, selected years, 1930–82

Year	Small households, < 4 members (%)	Large households, > 6 members (%)	Source of data
1930	40.3	44.8	Survey by Jin-Ghan Li in Ding County, Hebei Province
1931	45.2	36.9	Survey by Buck of 22 provinces
1930–40	40.8	43.5	Survey of birth histories by the Population Research Center, Chinese Academy of Social Sciences, in 7 areas
1982	53.6	28.0	1982 Census

Source: Ma (1984), based on various sources.
Note: Households with five members are not shown.

all households. If one- and two-generation households are combined, the percentage of nuclear-family households in that year was nearly 52 percent, compared with nearly 49 percent for those with three or more generations (Ma, 1984:463). According to a survey of 10,842 households conducted in the mid-1980s in Jilin Province (Jilin Provincial Commission on Family Planning, 1985), 78 percent of the households consisted of two generations.

Prior to World War II, therefore, the proportion of small families in China was roughly equal to that of large families, although at times large families may have been more prevalent. Nevertheless, the nuclear family, and specifically the two-generation household, seems to have been the dominant type of family structure in China even before the war. In the postwar period, the Chinese economic and social system has undergone remarkable change. Today, 71 percent of all households consist of nuclear families, compared with 60 percent in Japan. The fertility level is closely associated with household size and its distribution. Reduced mortality has also affected family structure.

JAPAN'S FERTILITY TRANSITION

High fertility prevailed in Japan for a long time before World War II. The crude birth rate was above 30 per thousand with some fluctuation. The total fertility rate (TFR) was also high, at more than 4 births per woman. These high fertility rates were reflected in the average number of household members, which remained at approximately five persons from 1920 to 1955.

A sharp decline in fertility began in 1950, immediately after the postwar baby boom. Between 1947 and 1957 the crude birth rate fell from 34.3 to 17.2. After vacillating slightly, it reached 19.4 in 1973, when a new declining trend started, resulting in a record low of 10.0 in 1990. The total fertility rate displayed a similar trend. After fluctuating around the replacement level of 2.1 births per woman, it finally dipped below it and has been much lower since 1975. It reached 1.75 in 1980 and 1.54 in 1990.

Table 4.7 shows the relationship among fertility, mortality, and average household size in Japan over the period between 1920 and 1990. Although fertility began a rapid decline around 1950, the decline in the size of Japanese households

Table 4.6. Percentage distribution of households, by generation: China, 1930, 1982, and 1987

Generation	1930	1982	1987
One generation	2.6	12.8	11.0
One-person households		8.0	5.5
Couple-only households		4.8	5.5
Two generations	48.9	64.7	65.9
Three generations	} 48.5	17.2	{ 17.8
Four generations			0.7
Others		5.3	4.6
Total		100.0 100.0	100.0

Sources: 1930: Ma (1984:463). 1982: Ma, (1984:Table 6, p. 461). 1987: China, Department of Population Statistics (1988:512–513).

was delayed by one decade. Japan's rapid decline in mortality can be assumed to have contributed to the delay by increasing the number of surviving family members, particularly children.

These major changes in fertility and mortality—and also in migration patterns, which are not discussed here but are also important—are closely associated with changes in family structure. For example, a rapid decline in fertility is inevitably associated with the aging of family households. Japan is a typical case. Households containing persons 65 years old and over increased by 51 percent during the 15 years from 1962 to 1977. In the same period, one-person households consisting of elderly persons grew 2.4 times, and households containing elderly couples grew by 2.5 times, while three-generation households grew by only 19 percent. Whereas the percentage of elderly people coresiding with their children was 80 percent and higher around 1960, by 1987 it had declined to 63 percent—which is still extremely high when compared with Western countries. In addition, changes in the family life cycle caused by fertility decline, the remarkable extension of average life expectancy due to lower mortality, delayed marriage, and so on, are related to changes in family structure.

The nuclear family will continue to be the dominant family type in Japan. It is likely, however, that in the future the nuclear family will be characterized by a dual structure consisting, on the one hand, of relatively young couples (those 30–40 years old) and, on the other, of elderly couples and individuals (65 and older) without children. The proportion of persons 65 and over living with their married children has been decreasing since World War II, from 86.8 percent in 1960 to 65.5 percent in 1985 (Japan, Ministry

Table 4.7. Fertility, mortality, and family size: Japan, selected years, 1920–90

Year	Crude birth rate	Total fertility rate	Crude death rate	Average number of household members
1920	36.2	5.20	25.4	4.89
1930	32.4	4.71	18.2	4.98
1950	28.1	3.66	10.9	4.97
1955	19.4	2.37	7.8	4.97
1960	17.2	2.00	7.6	4.54
1965	18.6	2.14	7.1	4.05
1970	18.8	2.14	6.9	3.69
1975	17.1	1.91	6.3	3.45
1980	13.6	1.75	6.2	3.33
1985	11.9	1.76	6.3	3.14
1990	10.0	1.54	6.7	2.99

Sources: Crude birth rates, crude death rates, and total fertility rates (TFRs) are from the Ministry of Health and Welfare. The TFR for 1920 is estimated. Average numbers of household members are based on population censuses.

of Health and Welfare, IPP, 1993:Tables 7–19, p. 96). This trend is expected to continue for some time because the majority of middle-aged Japanese wish to live independently from their children in old age. But coresidence of the elderly with their children may increase as the elderly become the very old (80 years and older) and require care. The Japanese government plans to encourage families to take care of their elderly relatives at home by increasing assistance to them.

CHINA'S FERTILITY TRANSITION

Chinese population statistics predating the founding of the People's Republic in 1949 are not accurate. This is particularly the case with vital statistics. From sample surveys conducted by scholars, however, it is generally known that Chinese birth and death rates were very high. In the early years of the new government, the crude birth rate is estimated to have been about 37 per thousand. For about 10 years after the establishment of the republic, the birth rate remained high, at more than 30 per thousand. The total fertility rate was also very high, around six births per woman, during 1949–57. These high fertility rates suggest that family size was large. Large families were in the minority in some areas, however, because mortality was also high and many children did not survive.

Fertility and mortality conditions may have differed considerably from region to region. For example, in 1947, just before the formation of the new government, it was reported that the average number of household members was very high, 9.43 persons, in Heilongjiang Province but only 4.72 in Shanxi Province (Ministry of the Interior, 1947 household statistics, reported by Ma, 1984:459).

High fertility continued until 1971, except for the years 1958–61. The crude birth rate remained above 30, reaching a peak of 43.4 in 1963. The TFR was around 6 births per woman (7.5 in 1963). It was only after 1972 that fertility began a rapid decline in China. The TFR fell to 2.69 in 1978 and the crude birth rate dropped to 17 per thousand the following year.

Table 4.8. Percentage distribution of households, by type of settlement and number of household members: China, 1987

Settlement type	Number of persons per household (%)			
	1–4	5	6+	Total
All settlements	59.8	19.1	21.1	100.0
Cities	71.7	15.2	13.1	100.0
Zhen (towns)	62.3	18.6	19.0	100.0
Xian (villages)	54.6	20.6	24.7	100.0

Source: China, Department of Population Statistics (1988:504–505).
Note: Percentages may not sum exactly to 100.0 because of rounding.

Family Structure and Social Change: Implications of Fertility Changes in Japan and China

In recent years, Chinese fertility has increased slightly, probably because of the increasing number of young people of marriage age, who were born in the years of high fertility. The most recent information on the distribution of households by number of members and by generation is from a 1 percent population sample survey conducted in 1987 (Tables 4.6 and 4.8).

Small families (those with one to four members) are most prevalent in every type of settlement, accounting for 60 percent of households for the country as a whole, 72 percent in cities, 62 percent in towns, and 55 percent in villages. Nevertheless, one-fifth of Chinese families are large, with six or more members. Large families are nearly twice as common in villages as in cities, representing one-fourth of the total, because fertility remains much higher in rural than in urban areas. (See Table 4.8.)

As for household composition by generation (Table 4.6), two-generation households are by far the most prevalent, representing two-thirds of all households by 1987. If couple-only households are added to two-generation households, the percentage of nuclear-family households in that year is 71. Households with three and more generations account for only 19 percent of the total.

The results of a 1 percent population sample survey in 1987 indicate that the average size of Chinese households is about 4.23 persons, down from 4.43 persons in 1982. The decrease over the five-year period seems to reflect China's declining fertility in the 1970s. This more recent household size is close to that of Japan in 1960 (4.45 persons). Despite China's remarkable decline in fertility overall, rural fertility has remained higher than urban fertility, with TFRs of 2.91 and 1.39, respectively, in 1981.

The rural population, which constitutes about 80 percent of total population, naturally raises the national average size of households. A factor having a contrary influence on both the number of households and household size is migration, which particularly involves the youthful population. Many young, unmarried people leave the rural areas for the cities and sooner or later marry. Their migration reduces the size of rural families and increases the number of households.

THE *IE* SYSTEM IN JAPAN AND THE *JIA* SYSTEM IN CHINA

The traditional Japanese *ie* system was a fundamental system for regulating people's daily lives. The central value of the *ie* (literally "house") was the continuity of the family line through male descendants. High fertility was necessary for that purpose. When couples were unable to have children, they had to adopt a male heir from a close relative. This *ie* system, which was legally abolished after World War II, did not have a substantial effect on average family size, however. Owing to the effect of the baby boom of the late 1940s, the average number of household members in 1950 and 1955 was about the same as in 1920, at approximately five, as we have seen in Table 4.2. A rapid decline in fertility and heavy migration, which have occurred since 1950, were major factors in reducing average household size.

The words *jia* in Chinese and *ie* in Japanese are written with the same Chinese character and have more or less the same meaning. But there are some differences. According to Fei (1947), *jia* does not correspond to the English word *family* but rather to a kind of extended family based on the nuclear family. In contrast, the Japanese word *ie* came to represent a large extended family whose function was to maintain the family line in times of high fertility.

Since the abolition of the *ie* system, a conjugal family system based on marriage has been established in Japan. The new conjugal family system is characterized by individualistic values and activities, in contrast with the familistic values of the old system (Taeuber, 1958:100–103). It is another factor that has led to an increase in the number of households. It should be noted, however, that although the *ie* system was legally abolished, the lineal family system continues to be observed by many Japanese.

CONCLUSION

The family is a universal system and a basic unit of all societies, but its forms and functions are influenced by the social, economic, cultural, and political systems of particular countries, and even vary within local areas of individual countries. Within countries sharing the Confucian culture, family structures may vary considerably. In South Korea and Singapore the direct stem family system is generally the norm, whereas in China and Japan the dominant family structure is the conjugal family system known as the nuclear family. The influence of Confucian values is still strong in both China and Japan, but the political and economic systems of the two countries are completely different.

With regard to the question of whether the Japanese family system has changed since World War II, some observers argue that no change has occurred, whereas others contend that there was a drastic change, from the extended family system to the nuclear family centered around the husband, wife, and children. My view is that the extended family norm, which was thought to be dominant in Japan and China prior to World War II, was an illusion. I do not deny the existence of several types of family, including the extended family, but it was not the dominant type in either country. A major reason for the misperception that the extended family was characteristic of the majority of Japanese and Chinese households until after the war has been the failure to consider changes in demographic and sociodemographic variables, in particular fertility and the life cycle, which has been affected by the dramatic decline in fertility and mortality in recent decades.

The so-called nuclear family, consisting of one or two generations, was more or less the dominant type even before the war, but until fairly recently fertility has been high even in nuclear families—making them difficult to distinguish from extended families of three or more generations. Moreover, extended families, although they were not the most prevalent family type, were very common; and even today such families, in which grown children reside with their elderly parents, are numerous in Japan, especially in some northeastern prefectures.

Finally, I suggest that the family is one of the Japanese institutions to which both Confucian and Western cultural values have been grafted. A better understanding of this phenomenon can be reached through research comparing Japan with other countries sharing the Confucian tradition and also with Western countries such as the United States.

REFERENCES

China, Department of Population Statistics (ed.), 1988. *Tabulations of China 1% Population Sample Survey, 1987: National Volume.* Beijing: State Statistical Bureau.

China Population Information Center. 1984. *Analysis of China's National One-per-Thousand Population Fertility Sample Survey.* Beijing.

Fei Hsiao-Tung. 1947. *Seiiku Seido Chūgoku no Kazoku to Shakai* (Family and society in China in 1985), trans. from Chinese into Japanese by Yokoyama Kiroko. Tokyo: Tokyo Daigaku Shuppankai.

Goode, William J. 1963. *World Revolution and Family Patterns.* New York: Free Press of Glencoe.

Hajnal, John. 1980. "Two Kinds of Preindustrial Household Formation Systems." *Population and Development Review* 8(3):449–494.

Japan, Ministry of Health and Welfare, Institute of Population Problems (IPP). 1993. *Latest Demographic Statistics, 1993.* Tokyo.

Japan, Statistics Bureau. 1990. *Final Report of the 1985 Population Census of Japan (Statistical Tables.* Tokyo, Management and Coordination Agency.

——. 1992. *Wagakuni Jinkō no Gaikan* (Major aspects of population in Japan). 1990 Population Census of Japan Abridged Report Series, No. 1. Tokyo: Management and Coordination Agency.

Jilin Provincial Commission on Family Planning. 1985. *Family Planning and Level of Living Standards in Jilin Province* (in Chinese). Changchum, China.

Ma Xia. 1984. "An Analysis of the Size of Domestic Households and the Family Structures in China," in Li Chengrui (ed.), *A Census of One Billion People: Papers for the International Seminar on China's 1982 Population Census, March 26–31, Beijing, China.* Beijing: Population Census Office under the State Council Department of Population Statistics, State Statistical Bureau.

Taeuber, Irene B. 1958. *The Population of Japan.* Princeton: Princeton University Press.

Toda Teizō. 1937. *Kazoku-Kōsei* (Family composition). Tokyo: Kobundo (reprinted by Shinsensha, Tokyo, 1982).

PART II

The Japanese Family in Comparative and Historical Perspective

CHAPTER 5

Tradition and Change in the Japanese Family and Community Life of Japan

by Noriaki Gotō

In studying the history of social science in Japan, researchers who examined the basic structure of Japanese society or the fundamentals of Japanese culture focused for a long time almost invariably on village life. This approach still exists today, particularly in international comparative studies, where there is a strong tendency to look for explanations of the basic features and principles of Japanese society, those elements that change the least, in traditional village society.

Although village society still retains a few of those deeply rooted social features, drastic changes have taken place in recent decades. Urbanization has spread throughout the country, blurring the boundaries between cities and villages. As a result, the great differences between urban and rural life styles, on which explanations of the dual nature of Japanese society were based, have largely disappeared, making it all but meaningless to think of a dichotomy between cities and villages. Given this situation, one can no longer discuss the unique social and cultural features of Japan by emphasizing its formal rural traditions.[1]

---

1. In an analysis of data from the National Opinion

It is therefore important to analyze the process and the results of change in traditional families and village communities to understand the contemporary features of Japanese culture. This is because the current state of village society can be considered either premodern or modern, and because it shares a contemporary existence in common with cities.

THE *IE* AND THE *MURA* AS PROTOTYPES OF RURAL JAPAN

When the Japanese economy began its rapid growth around 1955, typical urban life styles gradually began to penetrate into the country's villages. As these life styles became commonplace, the dividing line between cities and villages broke down and the "age of the city" replaced the "age of the village" as representative of community life.[2]

Table 5.1, which shows the changes in the proportions of the employed population, by industry, from the Meiji period (1868–1912), when Japan became a modern state, to the present, reveals that less than 10 percent of Japan's employed population is working in the primary sector today. In 1880, however, 82 percent of the working population worked in the primary sector, mainly agriculture. This proportion decreased gradually as Japanese capitalism developed, but until 1950 about half the population still worked in that sector.

Table 5.2, showing changes in the urban proportion of the population, uses densely inhabited districts (DIDs), or areas with 4,000 or more inhabitants per square kilometer, to represent the urban population. According to these figures, the urban population, which accounted for about one-third of Japan's population from 1920 to 1950, began growing quickly

Table 5.1. Changes in percentages of the employed population, by industry: Japan, 1800–1985

Year	Primary industry	Secondary industry	Tertiary industry
1880	82.3	5.7	12.1
1885	79.2	7.3	13.5
1890	76.2	8.9	14.9
1895	73.1	10.4	16.5
1900	70.0	11.8	18.2
1905	66.6	13.2	20.3
1910	63.0	14.9	22.1
1915	59.2	16.3	24.5
1920	53.8	20.5	25.6
1930	49.7	20.3	30.1
1940	44.3	26.0	29.7
1950	48.3	21.9	29.8
1955	41.0	23.5	35.5
1960	32.6	29.2	38.2
1965	24.6	32.0	43.4
1970	19.4	34.0	46.7
1975	13.9	34.0	52.1
1980	10.9	33.6	55.4
1985	9.3	33.1	57.3

Source: Kadowaki et al. (1985:302–303).

Survey of the Family in Japan, in which I examined the two parameters of urbanity-rurality and mobility-fixity, I concluded that "traditionality in families is connected to urbanity and mobility. However, the difference between the two parameters is only relative" (Gotō, 1989:33).

2. What I refer to as the "age of the city" in this chapter is the contemporary age, in which the city represents Japanese society and culture.

thereafter. By 1985, around 61 percent of the population lived in urban areas, even though urban areas accounted for only 2.8 percent of the country's total land area.

Together, the statistics presented in Tables 5.1 and 5.2 indicate that a restructuring of Japanese industry took place during a scant 30 years, ushering in the "age of the city" and a period of high economic growth. Because farming villages and agriculture had characterized Japanese society and controlled the lives of most Japanese until then, Japanese sociologists conducted numerous studies of farming villages and families prior to World War II.

Before the 1950s, when rural sociologists began to adopt U.S. statistical methods involving mass observation, they employed a different method, the homological approach, to establish a sociological theory of fixed residence that reflected the realities of Japanese society. The homological approach consists of modeling the characteristics of a society by observing changes within that society over time. It was advanced by Kazuko Tsurumi and Saburo Ichii, who argued that the heterological approach to studying the modernization of Japan, which applied Western standards of modernization to Japan, was inappropriate (Tsurumi and Ichii, 1974).

It is generally believed that the culmination of prewar Japanese rural sociology came with Eitaro Suzuki (1940) and his "natural village" (*mura*) theory, and with Kizaemon Aruga (1943) and his theory of "family (*ie*) associations." Their findings continued to be influential even after World War II. These two men considered *mura* (primary rural communities, called "natural villages" by Suzuki) to be the prototype of Japanese rural society and focused on various social phenomena there. For example, they identified the basic organizational units of the villages to be not individuals, but rather families (*ie*) whose lineage continued over generations; and they focused on how, to ensure the continuation of both the *ie* and the *mura*, the various *ie* had to enter into cooperative relationships (forming what Aruga called "extended family associations"). Along with Seiichi Kitano and

Table 5.2. Urban population as percentage of total population: Japan, 1920–85

Year	DID as % of population
1920	30.2
1930	33.7
1940	36.4
1950	33.8
1955	38.5
1960	43.7
1965	48.1
1970	53.5
1975	57.0
1980	59.7
1985	60.6

Sources: 1920–55: Ōtomo (1982:216); 1960–85: Japan, Statistics Bureau (1987:2–3).
DID—densely inhabited districts, defined as "survey areas within cities, towns, or villages with a high population density (4,000 or more inhabitants per km^2) which adjoin each other to form areas with a total population of 5,000 people or over" (Japan, Statistics Bureau, 1987:I–IV).

others,[3] Suzuki and Aruga conducted numerous studies of the *ie* and the *mura* before and after World War II.

The main features of the *ie* and the *mura* that emerged from those studies were the following:

1. The *mura* constitutes the framework for community life in a specific area.

2. The constituent elements of the *mura* are the *ie*. The *ie* differs in concept from the family, household, and home because it has a supragenerational permanence—encompassing the past, present, and future—within the same community.

3. The *ie* is controlled and directed by the household head, has a physical base in the family business or enterprise, and is responsible for the worship of ancestors.

4. The *ie* is the unit of consumption as well as of production and is based generally on small-scale, family-run farming. Because the *ie*'s economic base is so weak, each *ie*, to ensure its survival, forms a close relationship of mutual assistance with other *ie*, and that relationship is typified by extended-family groupings centering on a main household.

5. Since it is impossible for *ie* to exist independently, people establish settlements that constitute a communal material base; and villages (*mura*), with communality and solidarity as their main elements, are formed in a common defense of the inhabitants' livelihood.

6. For the *mura* and the *ie* to continue to have a means of production, they need a material base of jointly owned land or wooded slopes, which they protect (communal land ownership); communal labor, with which they supplement their weak productivity (communal assistance); and laws (communal rules), with which they control the behavior of members of the community.

7. Therefore, individuals are absorbed into the *ie* and the *mura*. They are not permitted to pursue their own gain or to act on an individual basis.

8. The *mura* is the site of both production (labor) and consumption, and in economic terms it is highly self-sufficient.

9. Relations between the families (*ie*) in the *mura* continue over generations, forming various multilayered social groups. Marriage partners also come from a restricted area; and as traditional ceremonies and living customs are maintained, the *mura* is also highly self-contained in social and cultural terms. Generally speaking, the *mura* offers a well-rounded social life.

10. These factors mean that the *mura* is a feudalistic and closed "microcosm" (Gotō, 1993b).

---

3. Other studies besides those of Kitano (1940), Suzuki (1940), and Aruga (1943) include those of Fukutake (1949, 1959), Sonraku Shakai Kenkyūkai (1956, 1959), Kawashima (1946), and Hisao Ōtsuka (1955). Among the books in English that discuss the *ie* and *mura* and are based on field surveys are those by Embree (1939), Dore (1958, 1959), Beardsley, Hall, and Ward (1959), and Smith (1958). The work by Beardsley et al. (pp. 269–272) outlines and summarizes the studies of Aruga mentioned above.

THE PROCESS OF CHANGE AND THE CURRENT STATE OF THE *IE* AND THE *MURA*

The *ie* and the *mura* began to change drastically after 1955 with the advent of rapid economic growth. Around that time, industrialization, led by heavy and chemical industries, began to flourish and the industrial structure of Japan shifted from a primary to a secondary and tertiary industry-based pattern. Secondary and tertiary industries were concentrated primarily in the cities, so that the more the country became industrialized, the more demand grew for an urban labor force. As a result, there was a large outflow of the farming population from the rural areas to the cities. Because the population shift from villages to cities was so rapid, large cities like Tokyo and Osaka became overcrowded, while local villages suffered from depopulation. This phenomenon continues to make living conditions worse in both cases; the concentration of people, goods, capital, and information in cities exacerbates the problem of regional imbalances.

Rectifying regional imbalances continues to be a priority on the agenda of the National Land Development Plan, with huge investments in public works being made to this end. The result, however, is that the transportation and communication networks that are being built enable industrialization and urbanization to spread throughout the country. Not only has regional specialization become more entrenched, it has spread everywhere, sprouting networks and building an ever more tenaciously entrenched hierarchy of cities and towns that places Tokyo at the top. The densely interwoven transportation and telecommunications networks contribute to the expansion of the outlying areas of the cities, which are the nerve centers of these networks. They increase the concentration in Tokyo, the transportation and communications hub, and place all areas of the country under its influence.

From the viewpoint of local areas (Gotō, 1987, 1993a), the development of transportation and communications networks shortens the time and social distance between cities and regions, filling in the geographical and spatial distance between them. Social contacts become closer through the intermediaries of transportation and communications. Regional links are strengthened, facilitating the penetration of typical urban life styles and attitudes, and expanding people's areas of daily life by giving them a wider range of movement. As a result, the borders between separate regions and their unique regional characteristics begin to blur as they merge with urban areas, until the family and community life represented by the *ie* and the *mura* are also forced to change.

Even in villages in remote areas, household heads and their eldest sons take up seasonal work in the cities during the winter, while others move to the cities in large numbers. The resulting

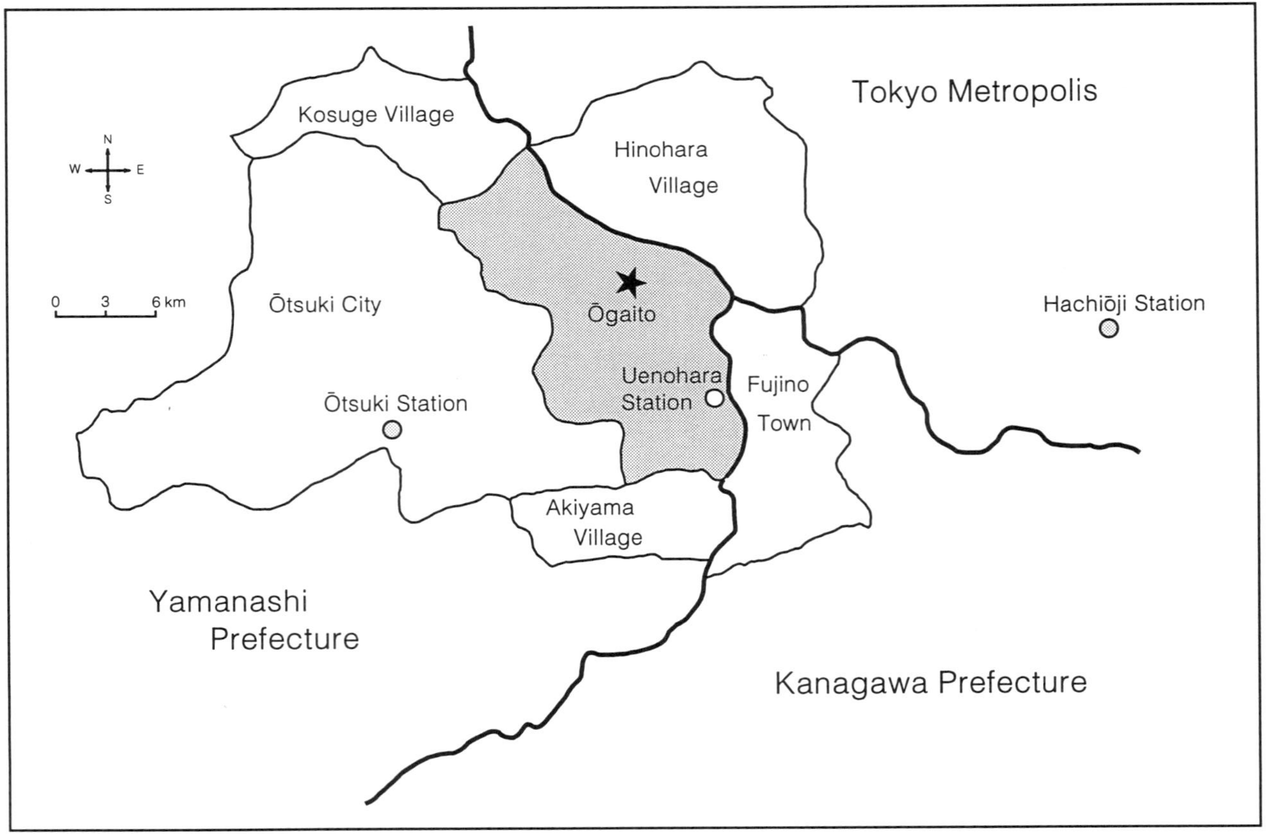

Figure 5.2. Location of Ōgaito in Uenohara Town and the municipalities around Uenohara Town

Source: Based on map from Uenohara Town (1975:25, Figure 4).

Tradition and Change in the Japanese Family
and Community Life of Japan

worked in Tokyo. Most of those people worked in Hachiōji or Hino, areas of Tokyo that are close to Uenohara; but 467, or 4 percent, worked in the 23 central wards of Tokyo.

Nevertheless, ties to the daily life of Tokyo are strong only in the urban center of Uenohara, which has convenient transportation links to Tokyo. In the rural areas farther away from the center of town, daily ties with Tokyo are weaker. The same can be said for Yuzurihara, which has been virtually unaffected by the suburbanization of Tokyo.

Yuzurihara occupies a stretch of land along the Tsurukawa Gorge. It is a typical mountain village consisting of the eight independent settlements ("natural villages") of Ozuku, Yōtake, Ido, Kobushi, Imari, Hibara, Ōgaito, and Sawatari, which have existed since at least the fourteenth century. The villages are situated at an altitude of 400–500 meters on gentle mountain slopes, surrounded by fields on the steeper mountainsides. The national census of 1985 recorded a population of 1,983 persons and 492 households in Yuzurihara, an average of 4.03 persons per household.

Changes recorded by the census in the population and number of households since 1900 are shown in Table 5.3. The population peaked in 1947, with 3,638 people and 610 households, and has declined steadily since then. Depopulation is not an easy trend to halt. According to the 1985 agriculture and forestry census, altogether 73.5 hectares of land were under cultivation in the area (fields, 52.3 hectares; tree farms, 19.7 hecatres; paddies, 1.4 hectares). The number of farm households was 354, accounting for 72 percent of all households, but only 30 of them were engaged exclusively in farming activities whereas the other 324 combined farming with other occupations. Of the latter group, 315 households engaged in farming as a secondary occupation, receiving their main income from nonagricultural activities. Farming is thus no longer the sole means of livelihood.

Before World War II, when transportation and communications were still undeveloped and mountain villages continued to be microcosms, agriculture was virtually the only family occupation. For

Table 5.3. Population trends in Yuzurihara, Japan, 1900–85

Year	No. of households	Population	Persons per household
1900	461	2,915	6.32
1910	548	3,065	5.59
1920	575	3,146	5.47
1930	545	2,941	5.40
1940	518	2,976	5.75
1947	610	3,638	5.96
1950	590	3,535	5.99
1955	570	3,366	5.84
1960	557	2,990	5.37
1965	543	2,771	5.10
1970	526	2,447	4.65
1975	513	2,281	4.45
1980	505	2,093	4.14
1985	492	1,983	4.03

Sources: 1900–70: Uenohara Town (1975:48–49); 1975–85: Uenohara Town Office, unpublished data.
a. Up to 1940, "houses" were counted; after 1947, "households" were counted.

a long time, the farms in Yuzurihara grew mostly barley, other cereals, and yams, with silkworm-raising and charcoal-making as side occupations. Since only a small area could be cultivated in the steeply graded fields, and only field crops were grown, agricultural productivity was low. The farms had always been marginal at best, so that the practice of combining farming with other occupations appeared quite early.[4] Nonetheless, farming was the foundation of the village, and in order to have a community with individual families continue, the main families controlled the branch families. The families helped each other to compensate for their low productivity and kept up the living patterns of the *ie* and the *mura*.

Village life changed after World War II. A bus service was begun in 1952 that ran from the center of Uenohara to Yuzurihara in 40 minutes. Construction of roads also began around that time to accommodate motor vehicles. These links stimulated social contact with the outside world, greatly expanded the range of daily activities and movement, and made inroads into the microcosm that had existed until then.

As Japan's economy began gaining strength in the 1960s, the demand for labor in the cities increased. The younger generation of Yuzurihara, made up mostly of second and third sons, left the area, or household heads took nonagricultural jobs elsewhere. Today, as a result of the village's depopulation and diversified occupations, few men and women in their prime are to be seen in Yuzurihara in the daytime. Farming is left to the elderly and has declined to such an extent that it now produces just enough food to supply household needs.

The *Ie* and the *Mura* in Ōgaito prior to World War II

Before World War II, the eight settlements in Yuzurihara were independent villages (*mura*). Each was a microcosm of Yuzurihara and had more or less the same characteristics as those just described, but Ōgaito had the best-established system of mutual assistance. This was described by Seiichi Kitano, who studied basic attitudes of Japanese rural societies toward social relationships between families of the same line, and between master and followers, and whose case study of Ōgaito in 1938 was published in a famous paper entitled "Extended Family Structure and Master-Follower Relationships in a Kōshū Mountain Village" (Kitano, 1940). The main points of that study can be summarized as follows.

---

4. For example, a farm survey taken in the Yuzurihara area (then Ōgaito) in September 1938 showed that of the 60 households in the hamlet, 16 conducted farming exclusively, 34 combined farming as the main occupation with other occupations, and 10 had other occupations, with farming as a secondary occupation (Kitano, 1940:48). Although the practice of combining farming with other occupations was spreading, all of the households in the hamlet farmed, and the majority farmed exclusively or engaged in farming as the main occupation along with other occupations. From this example one can understand that villagers were forced to depend on farming—which explains the high proportion of households that farmed.

Three categories of family lines (families with the same ancestors) are found in Ōgaito. Category I consists of the family lines that have resided there for the longest time; these are the Takahashi, Kido, Ishii, Shiratori, Okabe, and Itō families. Category II, consisting of family lines that came to Ōgaito after the sixteenth century, includes the Sado, Tsurukiri, Ōkubo, Shimizu, and Morita families. Category III consists of outsiders who settled in Ōgaito after 1868. Table 5.4 shows which family lines the 60 households belonged to in 1938. In category I were 41 households, including those of six main families; in category II were 10 households, including those of five main families; and in category III were nine households, all consisting of unrelated families.

The 11 family lines in the first and second categories formed strong extended families (branch families linked to the main families). In addition, the branch families lived in houses that stood around each main family house. Therefore, the *kumi* (neighborhood association), which consisted mainly of the extended family, also had strong overtones of a mutual assistance group, and neighboring groups were absorbed into this extended family group.

The *mura*'s leaders had always been the families in the first category of family lines. In 1938 these families still enjoyed a high position, prestige, and power.

Table 5.4. Number of related households in Ōgaito, Japan, 1938

Family line	Main family	Directly-descended branch family	Third-generation family	Total
I				
Takahashi	1	3	12	16
Kido	1	2	4	7
Ishii	1	1	0	2
Shiratori	1	3	3	7
Okabe	1	1	6	8
Itō	1	0	0	1
II				
Sado	1	0	0	1
Tsurukiri	1	2	1	4
Ōkubo	1	1	0	2
Shimizu	1	1	0	2
Morita	1	0	0	1
Subtotal	11	14	26	51
III	0	9		9
Total	11	49		60

Source: Kitano (1940:56, Table 2).

The main family of the Takahashi family in particular was called the ōkata—the most powerful politically, economically, and socially—and had control over the village leaders.

As to customs relating to the master-follower (oyabun-kobun) relationship in this area, the master sponsored the follower socially and offered him financial support, thus protecting his follower. For example, in the case of marriage the master acted as a go-between in arranging the follower's marriage. The follower, in turn, served the master by providing labor during the busy farming season. The master-follower relationship among families was hereditary, joining the families together over generations.

The family pattern of master-follower relationships was as follows: the main family assumed the role of master, and the branch families of the same family constituted the main body of followers. Other followers were servant branch families and completely unrelated families (those of mixed composition). This was the case with the Takahashi and Shiratori families studied by Kitano, whereas the Kido and Okabe families followed the pattern of the simplest type of family group organization, with the main family as the master.

In Ōgaito the masters came from main families or powerful, directly descended branch families belonging to the first category of families. Branch families from the same extended family occupied the position of followers, but main families of the first category might have ōkata as masters while simultaneously having their own branch families as followers. Therefore, the ōkata acted as the overall master for the entire hamlet.

Six of the nine late-arriving households (those in the third category) settled in the hamlet by turning for help to powerful families of the first category—four had ōkata as sponsors—and had master-follower relationships with those families because of that connection. But the remaining three households that settled in Ōgaito were sponsored by masters in a nearby hamlet and did not participate in the communal life of the *mura*.

Although the fixed hereditary relations of the families in the master-follower relationship are normally based on extended-family relations, this was not the case for the Takahashi, Shiratori, Kido, and Okabe families in the first category of families, which gave little organized assistance to their extended families.

Kitano concluded that extended family groups formed the basis for the structure and function of the master-follower relationship and that the function of mutual assistance in daily life in the extended group family was maintained through this practice.

Changes in the *Ie* and the *Mura* of Ōgaito

Kitano's paper not only was a culmination of research in the field of Japanese rural sociology during the pre-World War

Tradition and Change in the Japanese Family
and Community Life of Japan

II stage, it also provided topics for discussion that continued to be read after 1945. Similar research was conducted by various scholars on Ōgaito's sociology or folklore.

In 1961, 20 years after Kitano's survey, the Society for the Study of Folklore of the Tokyo Liberal Arts University conducted another survey of Ōgaito (Tokyo Liberal Arts University, 1962). In 1984 the sociology department of Waseda University surveyed the village (Waseda University, 1985), and in 1989 the University Research Center of Nihon University conducted personal interviews with all of Ōgaito's households (Nihon University, 1991). Although the subjects and methods of these surveys differed, they all bore in mind Kitano's findings. They also have historical value as sources on the conditions that existed in Ōgaito at the time of the studies.

The Nihon University survey was conducted during the first week of November 1989. According to the register of residents as of November 1, the village had 57 households and 216 residents (109 men, 107 women). All 57 households were visited, and the household heads (52 men, 5 women) were interviewed as the main respondents. Valid replies were received from 54 households.

Figure 5.3, which is based on an aerial survey of the hamlet, shows the location of each household in Ōgaito at the time of the survey. The houses are represented by uniformly-sized rectangles numbered from 1 to 57. This map represents fairly accurately the contours of the river and the road and the position of the houses relative to one another.

Figure 5.4 is based on a map of Ōgaito from Kitano's 1938 survey, and Figure 5.5 is based on a map of Ōgaito prepared at the time of the Tokyo Liberal Arts University's 1961 survey. Kitano's map shows 61 houses, and the Tokyo Liberal Arts University's map shows 73. Neither of these maps is accurate from the standpoint of topography or distance; but taken together, the three maps show that although the number of houses in Ōgaito has varied over the past 50 years, there has been little change in the position of the houses or of the roads and rivers, which form the framework for the hamlet.

Table 5.5, which is based on estimates obtained in the 1989 survey, matches the households in the three surveys of 1938, 1961, and 1989. It gives a rough indication of when each household was established or disappeared. For example, in 1989 it was found that only seven of the 57 households had been established between 1938 and 1961, and that one had been established after 1961. The majority of the households in present-day Ōgaito thus date from more than 50 years ago, continuing over multiple generations. In addition, of the eight households established in the past 50 years, six were branch families of Ōgaito families and only two were from outside the hamlet. Thus, most of the current households have existed for a number of

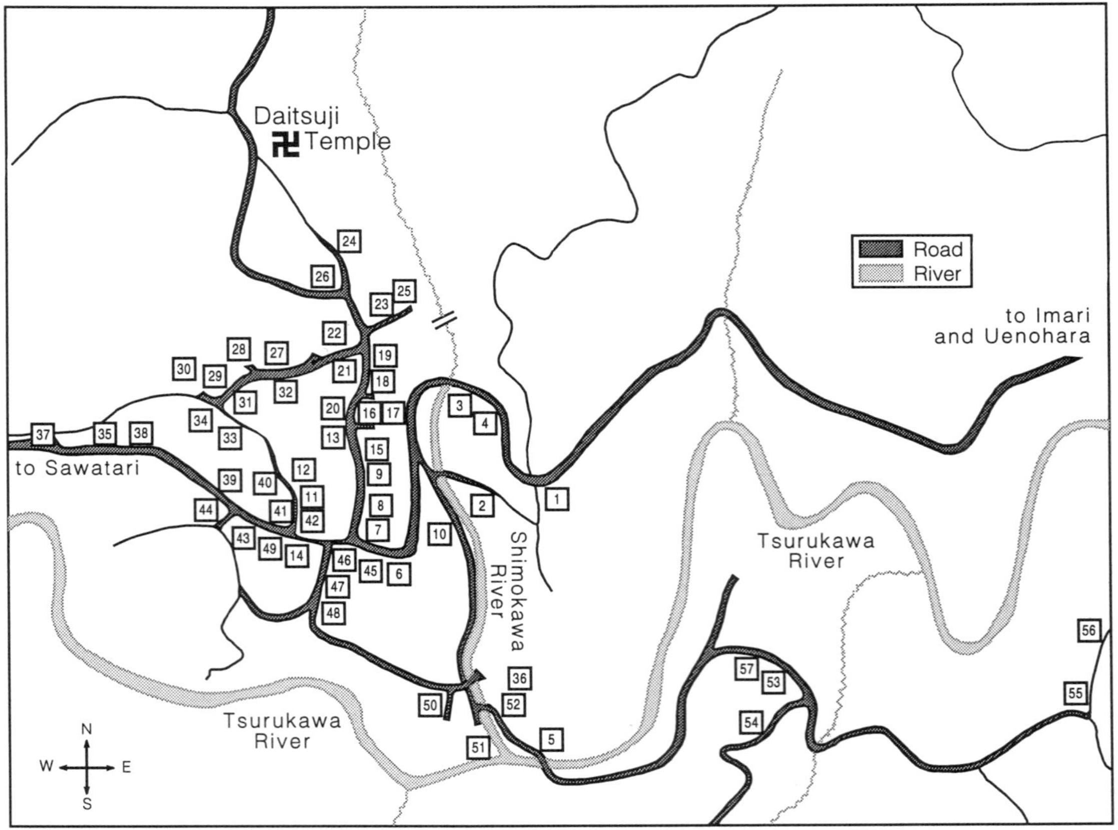

Figure 5.3. Settlements in Ōgaito, 1989

Source: Based on map from Nihon University (1991:38, Figure 2-2).

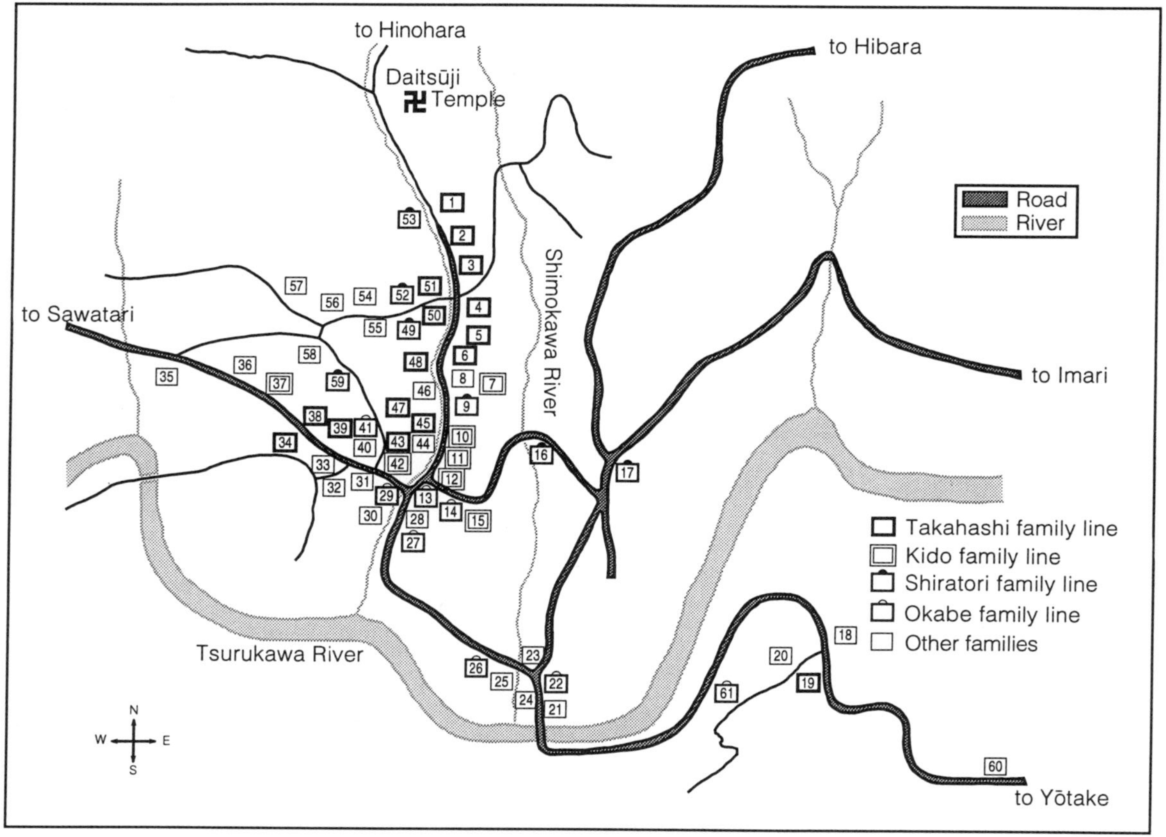

Figure 5.4. Settlements in Ōgaito, 1938

Source: Based on map from Kitano (1940:49).

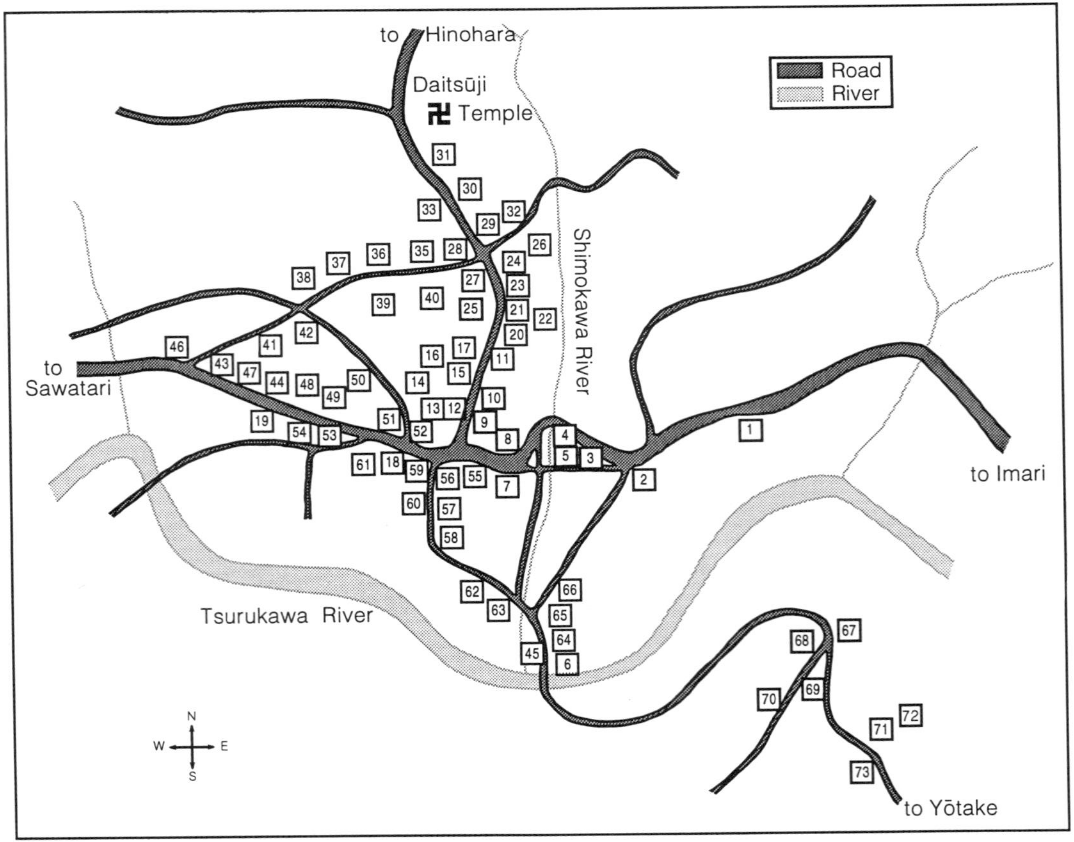

Figure 5.5 Settlements in Ōgaito, 1961

Source: Based on map from Tokyo Liberal Arts University (1962:frontispiece).

Tradition and Change in the Japanese Family
and Community Life of Japan

Table 5.5. Numbers of households in the surveys of 1938, 1961, and 1989: Ōgaito

1938	1961	1989	1938	1961	1989
17	2	1	40	51	41
16	3	2	42	52	42
—	4	3	33	53	43
—	5	4	34	54	44
21	6	5	14	55	45
15	7	6	13	56	46
12	8	7	28	5	47
11	9	8	27	58	48
10	10	9	32*	61*	49
—	13	10	26	62	50
43	14	11	—	63	51
47	16	12	—	65*	52
46	17	13	20	68	53
31	18	14	61	70	54
9	20	15	60	71	55
8	21	16	—	72	56
7	22	17	—	—	57
6	23	18			
5	24	19	4	—	—
48	25	20	23	—	—
50	27	21	24	—	—
51	28	22	—	—	—
3	29	23	—	1	—
1	31	24	44	11	—
—	32	25	45	12	—
53	33	26	—	15	—
52	35	27	—	19	—
54	36	28	2	26	—
56	37	29	—	30	—
57	38	30	—	34	—
55	39	31	39	44	—
49	40	32	29	49	—
59	41	33	30	59	—
58	42	34	22	60	—
36	43	35	—	64	—
25	45	36	18	66	—
35*	46*	37	19	67	—
37	47	38	—	69	—
38	48	39	—	73	—
41	50	40			

Source: Nihon University (1991:41, Table 2-2).
Note: Dash indicates that there is no corresponding household.
* Estimated number.

generations, and the number of new households is unexpectedly small.

This being the case, one can assume that relations among the households are very close. Figure 5.6 is a schematic representation of respondents' answers to the question, "Please tell us which of the households in the hamlet are your relatives." The households (numbered from 1 to 57 on the right-hand side) that respondents (numbered from 1 to 57 on the left-hand side) indicated were those of relatives (blood relatives or persons related by marriage) are connected by lines. Only seven households on the left-hand side have no lines extending from them: households 17, 18, and 37, which could not be surveyed; households 10, 20, and 57, whose respondents answered that they did not have any relatives in Ōgaito; and household 6, whose respondent did not answer this question. The other households were linked by a total of 220 lines to other households in the village.

This figure is visually effective in illustrating the dense network of family relationships in one hamlet. A closer and more objective analysis reveals a somewhat different pattern, however. Here, three points will be examined.

First, the patterns of naming other households as relatives and being named as such do not necessarily correspond. For example, respondents in households 16, 44, 45, 46, and 56 (numbers on the left-hand side) named a great many relatives (numbers on the right-hand side). Households that were often identified as being related to respondents were 16, 17, 34, and 49 (numbers on the right-hand side). Households 44, 45, 46, and 56, however, were not named as relatives as often as they named other households as relatives, whereas households 34 and 49 were named as relatives more often than the other way around (household 17 could not be interviewed). There were also discrepancies in the frequency of naming and being named as a relative in the case of households 1, 7, 8, 13, 15, 22, 27, 36, 39, and 47.

Second, as can be inferred from the first point, the correspondence ratio between naming and being named as a relative was not that high when the sample was examined as a whole. Of 220 pairs named, the relationship was mutual (i.e., both households had named each other as relatives) in 114 cases (a correspondence ratio of 51.8 percent). In 106 cases (48.2 percent), one party named the other as a relative while the other did not.

Third, the average number of related families per household was not as high as expected. When the 220 replies were divided by the 53 households that could be interviewed and answered the question, the result was an average of 4.15 related families per household. This correspondence is by no means high, given the fact that a great many of the households have continued for generations and that close relations between families have been forged over the years.

Tables 5.6–5.8 show changes in the areas from which marriage partners come.

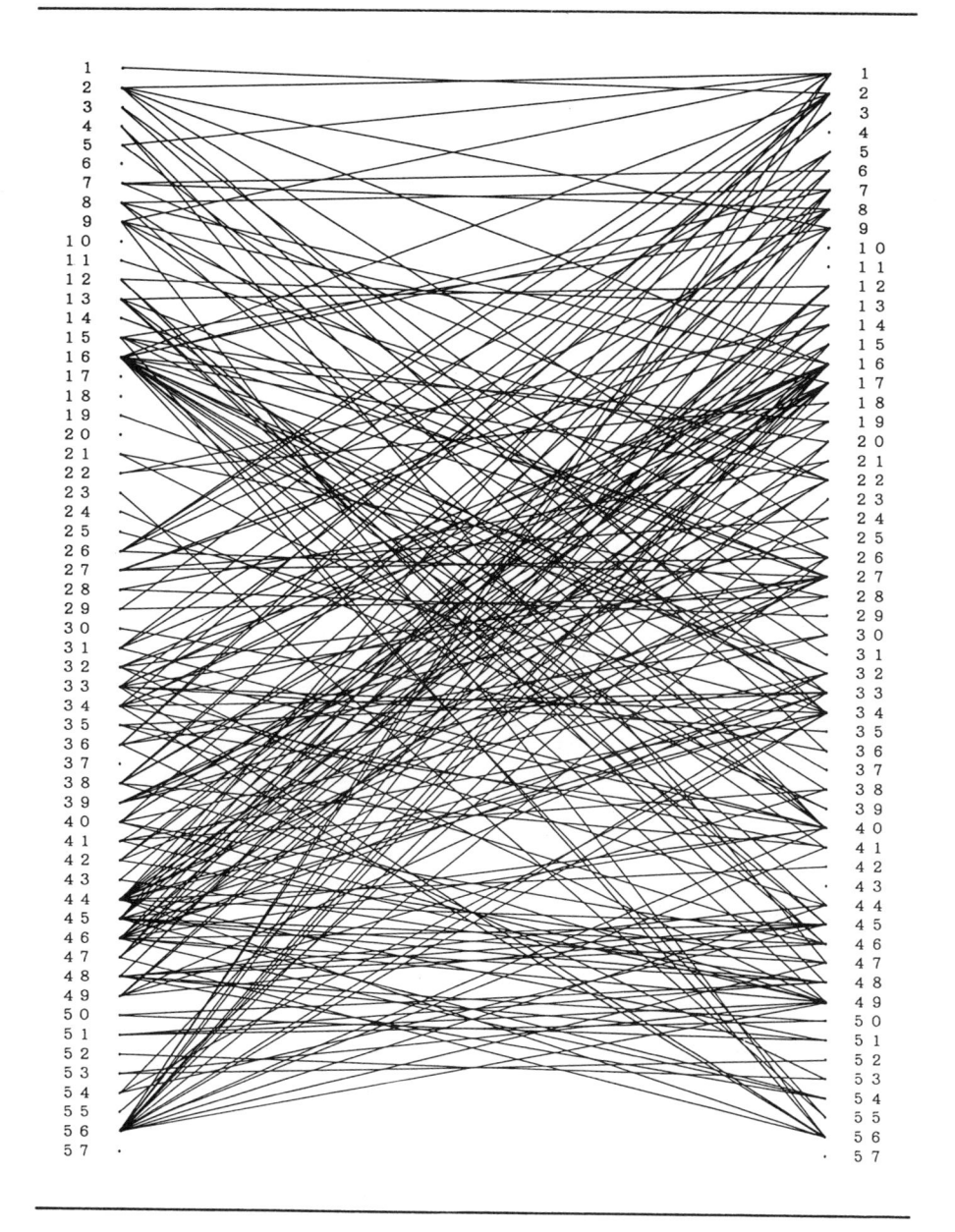

Figure 5.6. Related households in Ōgaito, 1989

Source: Nihon University (1991:42, Figure 2-5).

A simple comparison is difficult because data collection methods and categories vary, but a few points of interest will be mentioned.

Table 5.6 shows that until the end of the nineteenth century and into the beginning of the twentieth, more than 80 percent of marriage partners came only from the Yuzurihara area, including Ōgaito, an extremely small region. For more than 100 years until 1961, the number of marriage partners coming from the hamlet remained more or less constant at slightly more than 40 percent. In contrast, the proportion of marriage partners from Yuzurihara, excluding Ōgaito, decreased steadily, whereas the number of partners coming from the Uenohara district or from outside the prefecture increased correspondingly.

Table 5.6. Birthplace of marriage partners in Ōgaito, by year of marriage: 1961

	Number and percentage of partners from specified birthplace					
Year of marriage	Ōgaito No. (%)	Yuzurihara No. (%)	Uenohara No. (%)	Yamanashi No. (%)	Outside Yamanashi Prefecture No. (%)	All places No. (%)
Before 1872	24 (40)	26 (43)	3 (5)	2 (3)	5 (8)	60 (100)
1873–98	34 (56)	19 (31)	4 (7)	1 (2)	3 (5)	61 (100)
1899–1923	26 (44)	16 (28)	9 (16)	0 (0)	7 (12)	58 (100)
1924–40	25 (46)	9 (17)	3 (6)	0 (0)	17 (31)	54 (100)
1941–61	8 (42)	1 (5)	6 (32)	1 (5)	3 (16)	19 (100)
All years	117 (46)	71 (28)	25 (10)	4 (2)	34 (13)	252 (100)

Source: Based on Tokyo Liberal Arts University (1962: 8; Table 7).
Notes: "Marriage partners" refer to persons entered in the family registers of households in Ōgaito through marriage. Figures for Yuzurihara exclude Ōgaito, figures for Uenohara exclude Yuzurihara, and figures for Yamanashi Prefecture exclude Uenohara.

Table 5.7. Birthplace of wives in Ōgaito, by year of birth: 1984

	Number and percentage of wives from specified birthplace					
Year of birth	Ōgaito No. (%)	Yuzurihara No. (%)	Uenohara No. (%)	Yamanashi No. (%)	Outside Yamanashi Prefecture No. (%)	All places No. (%)
1867–1913	26 (41)	25 (40)	5 (8)	4 (6)	3 (5)	63 (100)
1914–45	10 (22)	18 (39)	10 (22)	2 (4)	6 (13)	46 (100)
After 1946	1 (6)	6 (35)	7 (41)	0 (0)	3 (18)	17 (100)
All years	37 (29)	49 (39)	22 (17)	6 (5)	12 (10)	126 (100)

Source: Based on Waseda University (1985:42; Figure III–6).
Note: Wives are the wives of heir couples.

Tradition and Change in the Japanese Family
and Community Life of Japan

Table 5.7 (based on the 1984 survey conducted by Waseda University) shows the reverse. In other words, the proportion of wives from Yuzurihara remained constant at around 40 percent, while that of wives from within the village fell steadily, with a correspondingly larger share of partners coming from Uenohara or from outside the prefecture. Table 5.8 (based on the 1989 survey) shows similar patterns.

Together, these survey data indicate that although the proportion of marriage partners from Yuzurihara, including Ōgaito, dropped considerably over the past century, a certain minimum ratio has been maintained. Nevertheless, the area from which marriage partners have come has definitely been broadening.

With this increasing exogamy as the basic assumption, it is of interest to examine in some detail what has happened to the family lines and groups and to the master-follower relations described by Kitano, for it is probably through changing marriage patterns that most of the changes in the *ie* and the *mura* of Ōgaito have occurred. To explore this question, we analyze information obtained from the 1961 Tokyo Liberal Arts University survey and the 1989 Nihon University survey about which families served as go-betweens (*nakodo-oya*) when marriages took place, and compare it with Kitano's findings from his 1938 survey.

In the 1961 survey, 63 of the 73 households in the hamlet at the time named go-betweens. Of those, we focus on the four families—Takahashi, Shiratori, Kido, and Okabe—of the first category of families that Kitano, when he examined master-follower relations, said had not formed family groups.

The main family of the Takahashi (ōkata) had served as the go-between for 29 families (39.7 percent of the total), including 12 families that were branches of the Takahashi family; five branch fami-

Table 5.8. Place where mothers and wives of current household heads spent their early childhood years: Ōgaito, 1989

Mother or wife	Number and percentage from specified birthplace					
	Ōgaito No. (%)	Yuzurihara No. (%)	Uenohara No. (%)	Yamanishi Prefecture No. (%)	Outside Yamanishi No. (%)	All places No. (%)
Mother	13 (27)	20 (42)	10 (21)	2 (4)	3 (6)	48 (100)
Wife	10 (23)	17 (39)	12 (27)	0 (0)	5 (11)	44 (100)
Both	23 (25)	37 (40)	22 (24)	2 (2)	8 (9)	92 (100)

Source: Nihon University. (1991:43, Table 2–3–c).
Notes: "Place of early childhood years" refers to the place where the mother or wife lived the longest until the age of 12 (the age of graduation from elementary school). Table includes five women who were household heads. Women for whom data were missing are excluded.

lies of the Shiratori family, which also belonged to the first category; all the families of the Ishii family, also of the first category; the main family of the first-category Itō family; and the main families of the Tsurukiri and Morita families, which belonged to the second category. Another Takahashi family, directly descended from the main Takahashi family (followers of the ōkata), served as the go-between for five families in four family lines, including two branches of their own family. This points to the overwhelming superiority and strong family grouping that the Takahashi family, which was the ōkata, maintained.

In the case of the other three families, the main Okabe family was the go-between for five families of three family lines, including three branches of its own family. A directly descended Okabe branch family was the go-between for three families, however, so that the power of the main and branch families was about equal.

In the Kido family, the main family was the go-between for only one family, its direct branch, but that direct branch family was the go-between for five families, including the main family and others in the Kido family line. In this case, the directly descended branch family was more powerful than the main family.

In the Shiratori family, the main family was the go-between only to a direct branch of the main Ōkubo family, which belonged to the second category. For most of the other families in the Shiratori line, ōkata served as go-betweens.

In the above three families (Okabe, Kido, and Shiratori), the main-branch family and master-follower relationships were starting to break down. Although the situation that has been evolving is quite different from the master-follower relationship formed with the go-between when marriage took place as described by Kitano, in general this practice survives and serves its function.

In the 1989 survey, the go-betweens in the marriages of 54 heads of the hamlet's 57 households (excluding three not available for the survey) were examined. The main family (ōkata) of the Takahashi family line, a first-category family, had been the go-between for 17 households (31.5 percent of those surveyed), including five of its own branch families, four families of the first-category Shiratori family (including the main family), and the main families of the second-category Tsurukiri, Ōkubo, and Morita families. This family had undeniably experienced a decline in its position as the "overall leader of the hamlet," but the ōkata still had considerable power and status.

On the other hand, in the Kido family, a direct branch of the main Kido family was the go-between for six families, three from the Kido family line (including the main family), and three other families. This family, called the Kido-kumi (group), was at the head of a group composed of related families, but the internal connection between households had weakened greatly. The same trend was evident in the Okabe and Shiratori families. In the Okabe family, the branch family directly descended from the main family was named as go-between by only two families, including the main family. In the Shiratori family, only four families, including the main family, had the Takahashi main family for a go-between. No information on go-betweens was available from any other families.

According to Kitano, in such a situation the extended family relationships that form the basis for the master-follower relationship would tend to decline systematically. That is what has happened in Ōgaito, as described above, but the process needs to be examined in more detail.

One question in the 1989 survey asked respondents, "Are you a main family or a branch family?" A follow-up question asked those who answered "main family" to identify their branch families, and those who answered "branch family" to identify their main family. The answers revealed the existence of 26 main families and 20 branch families. (Eight respondents either did not know the answer to the question or did not answer.) Given that Kitano identified only 11 main families in Ōgaito, 26 represents a large increase. However, in quite a few cases the respondents in the 1989 survey based their answers on whether their families had branches or not, rather than on whether their family was the main family or a branch of a particular family. Kitano considered family lines to be the basic element of the Ōgaito community, but the fact that some respondents answered the question as they did in 1989 may indicate that family lines (extended family groups) no longer functioned as Kitano had observed, having already fallen apart.

Another noteworthy point is that of the 20 respondents answering that their households were branch families, five did not know who their main families were. Moreover, the eight respondents who did not answer this question gave such responses as "I cannot tell the difference between main and branch families," "I don't think in terms of main and branch families," "Ours is not a branch family but not a main family either," "Ours is something like a branch family and something like a main family," "I don't really know," and "I don't want to talk about this." All but one of those households had been in the hamlet for a long time. Grouped according to Kitano's classification, they included two families of the Takahashi family and one each of the Kido, Shiratori, Ishii, and Itō families, all first-category families, and one family of the second-category Tsurukiri family.

The above analysis indicates that family lines or extended family groups and master-follower relationships no longer function as they did in the past. Other data support this finding, both directly and indirectly; but instead of presenting the data, we will quote the words of the household head of a leading family to conclude this section.

A group of families composed mainly of an extended-family group had held a festival each year at the family home; but according to the household head, "The main-branch family relationship is growing steadily weaker, and holding the festival is a bother too, so we decided not to hold it anymore last year." He continued: " In the past, if a house had to be dismantled or a roof thatched, all the households worked together to help each other, but when we rethatched the roof of this house last year, we asked people not to come and help because they would get in the way, now that the work is so specialized." These words are an apt illustration of the changes that have taken place place in the *ie* and the *mura* of Ōgaito.

The Current State of Family and Community Life in Ōgaito

In this section, data obtained from the 1989 survey conducted by Nihon University, along with findings from the 1984 survey conducted by Waseda University, are used to document the features of present-day family and community life in Ōgaito.

Tables 5.9 and 5.10 show the number of households by type of household and the number of persons per household, using figures from the 1984 and 1989 surveys. They indicate a trend toward small, nuclear families.

Table 5.11 shows, again from the

Table 5.9. Number of households, by type of household: Ōgaito, 1984 and 1989

Household type	1984	1989
Single-person households	6	4
Households consisting of only a married couple	8	8
Households consisting of a married couple and unmarried children	18	22
Households including two married couples	9	8
Households including a married couple and father or mother	13	12
Total	54	54

Sources: 1984: Waseda University (1985:15, Table II-2); 1989: Nihon University (1991:45, Table 2–4)

Table 5.10. Number of households, by number of persons per household: Ōgaito, 1984 and 1989

	Number of persons per household							
Year	1	2	3	4	5	6	7	8	Total no. of households (average no. per household)
1984	6	10	6	13	4	8	6	1	54 (3.96 persons)
1989	4	14	12	5	5	6	7	1	54 (3.81 persons)

Sources: 1984: Waseda University (1985:15, Table II-1); 1989: Nihon University (1991:46, Table 2–5).

1984 and the 1989 surveys, the number of employed persons between the ages of 20 and 64. It is obvious that the percentage of women working is also high.

Table 5.12, based on the 1984 survey data, lists the occupations of the 100 working household members, including 35 women, who were not engaged in farming and indicates the locations of their jobs. It shows that people worked in jobs other than farming and outside Ōgaito but that nearly two-thirds of the workers held jobs in the Uenohara area. These findings suggest that Ōgaito families are combining farming with other occupations.

Table 5.13, based on responses to questions in the 1989 survey, shows the extent of the area in which people did their shopping and conducted the activities of their daily lives. It reveals that people in Ōgaito depended a great deal on Uenohara district and Hachiōji City for shopping, and that while most of them conducted their daily activities within the Uenohara area, approximately 20 percent of the respondents considered their daily activities to range over the wider area of neighboring towns and cities surrounding Hachiōji. The data suggest that the range of daily activities and movement of people in Ōgaito is broadening, that more social exchanges are taking place with other areas, and that Ōgaito and Yuzurihara no longer suffice for daily life. In other words, Ōgaito has collapsed as a microcosm.

Nonetheless, other data obtained from the 1989 survey indicate the existence of little social mobility in Ōgaito. For example, 80 percent of the household heads spent all or most of their early childhood years (until age 12) in Ōgaito, and nearly 80 percent of the couples heading households had not moved since marriage. This is an extremely important point because the changes observed in Ōgaito reflect the gradual shift in attitudes of people as they have adjusted to the process of change. If the change had been due only to outside forces—for example, to suburbanization caused by new arrivals outnumbering the original residents—the transformation would probably have been more extreme.

The data presented in Table 5.14, which belie the breakdown of the *ie* and the *mura*, are related to this point. The

Table 5.11. Population of working ages and employed persons, by sex: Ōgaito, 1984 and 1989

Population	1984 Males	1984 Females	1984 Total	1989 Males	1989 Females	1989 Total
Population, ages 20–64	62	55	117	60	51	111
Employed persons, ages 20–64	61	36	97	56	34	90
Percentage of employed persons	98.4	65.5	82.9	93.3	66.7	81.1

Sources: 1984: Waseda University (1985:13, Figure II–1); 1989: Nihon University (1991:46, Table 2–6).

Table 5.12. Occupations and places of work, excluding agriculture: Ōgaito, 1984

Occupation	Ōgaito	Yuzurihara	Uenohara	Yamanashi	Western Tokyo area	Tokyo ward area	Kanagawa	Wide area, no specific location	Unknown	All places
Production										
Men	4	3	10	1	4	4	4	16	0	46
Women	11	1	3	0	1	0	0	0	0	16
Sales and service										
Men	5	1	1	0	0	0	0	1	1	9
Women	7	1	2	0	1	0	0	0	0	11
Clerical, technical, and managerial										
Men	0	3	3	0	2	0	0	0	1	9
Women	0	2	5	0	0	0	0	0	0	7
Other occupations										
Men	0	0	0	0	1	0	0	0	0	1
Women	0	0	0	0	0	0	0	0	1	1
All occupations										
Men	9	7	14	1	7	4	4	17	2	65
Women	18	4	10	0	2	0	0	0	1	35

Source: Based on Waseda University (1985:20, Table II–4).

Table 5.13. Areas for shopping and daily life for residents: Ōgaito, 1989

Number and percentage of respondents identifying specific place

Question	Ōgaito No.	Ōgaito %	Yuzurihara No.	Yuzurihara %	Uenohara No.	Uenohara %	Hachiōji No.	Hachiōji %	Other No.	Other %	All places No.	All places %
Where do your household members usually shop for the following items?												
Daily goods	9	17	7	13	31	57	0	0	7	13	54	100
Seasonal gifts	3	6	10	19	26	48	5	9	10	19	54	100
High-quality clothing	0	0	0	0	16	30	31	57	7	13	54	100
Durable goods	2	4	0	0	30	56	9	17	13	24	54	100
What is the area where most of your daily life takes place	6	11	7	13	20	37	10[a]	19	11	20	54	100

Source: Based on Nihon University (1991:48, Tables 2–8 and 2–9).
a. Area includes the whole region around Hachiōji City, Tokyo.

table shows households in Ōgaito as part of both social and administrative *kumi* (groups). The administrative *kumi* were established a number of years ago as the smallest administrative units, having the function of distributing and circulating public information and messages from the Uenohara town office. As Figure 5.3 shows, the households in these *kumi* are located close to each other. The social *kumi*, on the other hand, are *tonari-kumi* (neighborhood groups) that have existed since the old days. They are the smallest local community organization, whose aim is mutual aid and fostering solidarity, and families' daily contact with them is frequent. By comparing the social with the administrative *kumi* shown side by side in Table 5.14, one sees that they do not correspond for households 5, 36, 50, 51, and 52. The administrative *kumi* for those households are located quite far away from their social *kumi*. In our survey, we discovered that those households were, without exception, branches of other families in the same *kumi* or new settlers whose sponsors (*waraji-oya*) belonged to that *kumi*, indicating a main-branch family or master-follower relationship.

Thus, it appears that *tonari-kumi* in Ōgaito are formed according to both geographical proximity and social proximity, and that *kumi* that are formed according to both principles are main-branch family relationships or master-follower relationships. This finding agrees with Kitano's observation that *kumi* were the basic unit of mutual assistance formed by extended families.

An additional important point is

Table 5.14. Household affiliations with social and administrative groups (*kumi*): Ōgaito, 1989

Social group			Administrative group		
I.	1 . 2		I.	1 . 2	
	3 . 4			3 . 4	
	5 . 6			6 . 7	
	7 . 8			8 . 9	
	9				
II.	10 . 11		II.	10 . 11	
	12 . 13			12 . 13	
	14			14	
III.	15 . 16		III.	15 . 16	
	17 . 18			17 . 18	
	19 . 20			19 . 20	
IV.	21 . 22		IV.	21 . 22	
	23 . 24			23 . 24	
	25 . 26			25 . 26	
V.	27 . 28		V.	27 . 28	
	29 . 30			29 . 30	
	31 . 32			31 . 32	
	33 . 34			33 . 34	
	35 . 36			35	
VI.	37 . 38		VI.	37 . 38	
	39 . 40			39 . 40	
	41 . 42			41 . 42	
	43 . 44			43 . 44	
VII.	45 . 46		VII.	45 . 46	
	47 . 48			47 . 48	
	49 . 50			49	
	51				
VIII.	52 . 53		VIII.	5 . 36	
	54 . 55			50 . 51	
	56 . 57			52	
			IX.	53 . 54	
				55 . 56	
				57	

Source: Nihon University (1991:49, Table 2–10).

that, according to information gathered from numerous respondents, until some years ago Ōgaito had only one type of *kumi*, that corresponding to today's social *kumi*, and that it functioned also as an administrative *kumi*. However, because people began to feel that it was too much trouble to distribute information frequently issued by the town office, after much discussion, new administrative *kumi* were formed, based on the eight existing *kumi*, to cover nine assigned areas. At the time, some people suggested that the new *kumi* should incorporate social functions, so that the initial plan was to establish nine social *kumi*; but in the end, separate sets of social and administrative *kumi* were formed. The respondents said that it had taken four or five years to reach that conclusion.

This interesting finding shows that old-style *kumi*, though on the point of collapse, still survive. According to comments made by various respondents, once people started working outside the hamlet, they were always busy and so they started to feel that the circulars from the town office were a bother. It was exactly because everyone felt the same way that they were able to reorganize the *kumi*. They did not, however, feel a pressing need to incorporate the social *kumi* into the new administrative *kumi* because relations within the social *kumi* had not weakened to the same extent. Many regarded the administrative *kumi* as simply a formality. A typical comment was that "it's very difficult to do away with the *kumi* you've always associated with."

The foregoing analysis indicates that Ōgaito's main-branch family and master-follower relationships have eroded or disappeared. Nevertheless, it must be acknowledged that the tradition of such relationships has restricted the direction and framework of certain changes in the social life of Ōgaito residents.

SUMMARY AND CONCLUSION

Using the example of Ōgaito, this chapter has focused on the shift in Japan from village life and agriculture, the long-term model for Japanese society and culture, to life in the "age of the city." A prototype for family and community life was postulated in the *ie* (family group or line) and the *mura* (primary rural community). Ten characteristics of the *ie* and the *mura* were presented and a model was advanced to describe the process of change in villages. To verify the model, the results of a case study of Ōgaito hamlet, located in the district of Yuzurihara, Yamanashi Prefecture, were described. Findings from previous surveys confirmed that Ōgaito's characteristics, particularly those of the *ie* and the *mura*, matched those of the prototype.

Ōgaito had a weak agricultural base. For the *ie* and the *mura* to survive there, the villagers adopted a strategy of mutual assistance according to which main families (or masters) controlled branch families (or followers) and families continued to help each other, thus offsetting the low productivity of individual households. Strong links among families, marriage between partners from a restricted area, and social interaction confined almost exclusively to the village fostered communality and solidarity, made the hamlet economically self-sufficient, and created a highly self-contained social environment, or microcosm.

Today, however, this type of traditional family and community life is disappearing and individual households are relying less on the mutual-assistance system. This change encourages independence on the part of households and family members and makes it difficult for the communality and solidarity of the *ie* and the *mura* to exist in the old form. These developments are due to the fact that, as Japan has undergone an economic and technological transformation, villagers have escaped from subsistence farming as a livelihood, and what also made that possible was the breakdown of the spatial and social barriers supporting the microcosm.

Many respondents to our survey commented that life in Ōgaito began to change quickly once regular bus service was introduced. This was in 1954, when a bus route started running from the center of Uenohara to Ōgaito. This was also the time when the Japanese economy was starting to expand. Roads inside and outside the area were widened and paved, the use of motor vehicles spread, and television was introduced. All these changes, especially the development of transportation and communications, exposed Ōgaito to the transformations taking place in all of Japanese society.

As the spatial and social barriers broke down, social contacts with outside society became more frequent, broadening the range of villagers' daily lives and activities. More people from Ōgaito began to work outside the hamlet in jobs other than agriculture, and farming decreased markedly. When husbands and wives both started working outside the hamlet in nonfarming jobs, the daytime population declined, opportunities for gathering, talking, and having an enjoyable time dwindled, and traditional ceremonies could no longer be held as in the past. Once it became possible for households to support themselves without having to depend on powerful families, main- versus branch-family, or master-follower, relationships weakened or broke down, and the mutual-assistance system that supported the entire hamlet disappeared.

It can thus be said that Ōgaito has lost the foundation enabling it to continue the *ie* and the *mura*. Nevertheless, the social *kumi* (groups) continue to be connected through extended-family or master-follower relationships. If one thinks schematically of a pure form of family and community structure, this phenomenon is truly "the contemporaneity of the non-contemporaneous" (Mannheim, 1940:41). On the other hand, it could also be viewed as a special feature of a period of transition, as part of the Japanese psychological character, or as a characteristic of modern Japanese culture.

I prefer to withhold an interpretation and instead focus on the fact that households in Ōgaito remain intact and family and community life has been maintained. In other words, in Ōgaito the present does not represent a break with the past. Rather, it reflects the inhabitants' way of carrying out family and community life in contemporary Japan despite the weight of tradition represented by the *ie* and the *mura*.

Although the *ie* and the *mura* no longer exist as they once did, the long history of the community's structure and an accumulation of main-branch and master-follower relationships continue to restrict certain aspects of people's social lives, for example their decision frameworks and ideas. The residents of Ōgaito, therefore, cannot move away completely from the *ie* and the *mura* in their attitudes or in their relationships among households. However, if outsiders were to become the majority of residents or living patterns changed more radically, perhaps through increased mobility, the continuity of family and community life would be threatened and Ōgaito would be forced to dismantle its *ie* and *mura* structure. In any case, future developments are worth watching.

REFERENCES

Aruga Kizaemon. 1943. *Nihon Kazoku Seido to Kosaku Seido* (Japanese family systems and tenant farming systems). Collected Works of Kizaemon Aruga, Vols. I, II. Tokyo: Miraisha, 1966.

Beardsley, R. K., J. W. Hall, and R. E. Ward. 1959. *Village Japan*. Chicago: University of Chicago Press.

Dore, Ronald Philip. 1958. *City Life in Japan*. London: Routledge & Kegan Paul.

———. 1959. *Land Reform in Japan*. Oxford: Oxford University Press.

Embree, John Fee. 1939. *Suye Mura: A Japanese Village*. New York: Black Star Publishing Co.

Fukutake Tadashi. 1949. *Nihon Nōson no Shakaiteki Seikaku* (The social character of Japanese rural societies). Collected Works of Tadashi Fukutake, Vol. 4. Tokyo: Tokyo University Press, 1976.

———. 1959. *Nihon Sonraku no Shakai Kōzō* (Social structure of Japanese villages). Collected Works of Tadashi Fukutake, Vol. 5. Tokyo: Tokyo University Press, 1976.

Gotō Noriaki. 1987. "Kōtsū Nettowāku no Hen'yō to Chiiki Shakai Kōzō Hendō" (Changes in local community structures resulting from changes in transportation networks), *Shakaigaku Ronsō* (The journal of sociology) 99:72–99. Sociological Society of Nihon University.

———. 1989. "Analysis of the Japanese Family by Regional-Residential Factors." In University Research Center (ed.), *Summary of the National Opinion Survey of the Family in Japan*, pp. 29–36. Tokyo: Nihon University.

———. 1993a. "Metropolitanization and Transport-Communication Networks: The Cases of Tokyo and Paris." In University Research Center (ed.), *Trends and Prospects of World Urbanization*, pp. 317–339. Tokyo: Nihon University.

———. 1993b. "Sankan Shūraku Niokeru Kyokuchi-teki Shōuchūsei to Sonraku Ketsugō" (Microcosmic local cohesion in Japanese villages in the past half-century). In Japanese Association for Rural Studies (ed.), *Sonraku Shakai Kenkyū* (Annual bulletin of rural studies) 29:103–135. Tokyo: Nōsan Gyoson Bunka Kyōkai.

Japan, Statistics Bureau. 1987. *Wagakuni no Jinkō Shūchū Chiku* (Densely inhabited districts). Tokyo.

Kadowaki A., Yano M., and Imada T. 1985. *Seikatsu Suijun no Rekishiteki Suii* (Historical Trends in living standards). Tokyo: Sōgō Kenkyū Kaihatsu Kikō (NIRA).

Kawashima, Takeya. 1946. *Nihon Shakai no Kazokuteki Kōsei* (The family-like structure of Japanese society). Tokyo: Gakusei Shobō.

Kitano, Seiichi. 1940. "Kōshū Sanson no Dōzoku Soshiki to Oyakata-Kokata Kankō" (Extended family structure and master-follower relationships in a Kōshū mountain village), *Minzokugaku Nenpō* (The annual review of ethnology) 2:41–95. Tokyo: Sanseidō.

Mannheim, Karl. 1940. *Man and Society in an Age of Reconstruction*. London: Routledge & Kegan Paul.

Nihon University, University Research Center. 1991. *Gendai Kazoku no Seikatsu Kōdō ni Kansuru Kobetsu Chōsa Houkokusho* (Case studies of the patterns of behavior in modern family life). Tokyo.

Ōtomo Atsushi. 1982. *Chiiki Bunseki Nyūmon* (Introduction to regional analysis). Tokyo: Tokyo Keizai Shinpōsha.

Ōtsuka, Hisao. 1955. *Kyōdotai no Kiso Riron* (Basic theory of the community). Tokyo: Iwanami Shoten.

Sonraku Shakai Kenkyūkai. 1956. *Sonraku Kyōdōtai no Kōzō Bunseki* (Analysis of the structure of village community). Tokyo: Zichōsha.

———. 1959. *Sonraku Kyōdotairon no Tenkai* (Development of the theory of village community). Tokyo: Zichōsha.

Smith, T. C. 1958. *The Agrarian Origins of Modern Japan*. Palo Alto: Stanford University Press.

Suzuki, Eitarō. 1940. *Nihon Nōson Shakaigaku Genri* (The principles of Japanese rural sociology). Collected Works of Eitaro Suzuki, Vols. I, II. Tokyo: Miraisha, 1968.

Tokyo Liberal Arts University, Society for the Study of Folklore. 1962. *Ōgaito no Minzoku* (The folk of Ōgaito). Tokyo.

Tsurumi K. and Ichii S. 1974. *Shisō no Bōken* (An adventure in thought: New paradigm for society and change). Tokyo: Chikuma Shobō.

Uenohara Town. 1975. *Uenohara Chōshi, Jō* (Topography of Uenohara Town), Vol. 1. Tokyo: Kōyō Shobō.

Waseda University, Department of Sociology. 1985. *Ōgaito no Rekishi to Jinsei* (History and lives of Ōgaito). Tokyo.

CHAPTER 6

Changing Attitudes toward Marriage and the Family in Japan

by Noriko O. Tsuya

> If we are to understand social change, the things at work inside people's heads, whether they are called ideas or social values or habits of thought, need analysis as much as the objective conditions that lie outside.
>
> Samuel H. Preston (1987:189)

This study seeks to analyze determinants and correlates of attitudes toward marriage and the family among the contemporary Japanese. Through the analysis, it also attempts to account, indirectly, for attitudinal changes underlying Japan's recent fertility decline. Since the mid-1970s, Japan's birth rates have been on a gradual but clear decline to a below-replacement level, achieving in 1990 the lowest total fertility rate (TFR) ever recorded in its modern history—1.54 children per woman (Japan, Ministry of Health and Welfare, Institute of Population Problems [IPP], 1992:49). Because this rate was even lower than that in 1966, the astrological Year of the Fire Horse, or *Hinoeuma* (which is thought to be an unpropitious year for having daughters), it stirred the concern of not only policymakers but also the mass media, thus attracting a great deal of public attention.

As Bumpass (1990) argues, because fertility cannot be isolated theoretically from the larger social context in which it is embedded, an explanation of Japan's fertility decline has to be sought in the realm of changes in the social institutions of marriage and the family. Since these institutional changes tend to accompany changes in value systems and norms, one way to account for reproductive behavioral change is to examine changes in people's attitudes toward and normative expectations of marriage and the family. More specifically, as in the case of Western Europe's fertility decline (Lesthaeghe, 1983; Lesthaeghe and Surkyn, 1988; van de Kaa, 1987), the recent Japanese fertility decline can be seen as a reflection, and probably a consequence, of increasing acceptance in the Japanese society of the principle of individual (especially women's) freedom of choice in decisions about marriage and family building. This progressive emphasis on individual interests may lead to a further step away from the traditionally strong group orientation of Japanese society (Nakane, 1973; Yamamura and Hanley, 1975). Because normative changes often lag behind behavioral changes (Lesthaeghe, 1983; Bumpass, 1990), it may also be the case that Japanese attitudes and normative expectations have finally come to accommodate below-replacement fertility—the behavioral reality of the past 15 years.

In East Asia a strong traditional value has been attached to marriage and family formation (Cho, 1989), and Japan is no exception. Marriage and procreation were (and, to a certain extent, still are) viewed as social and economic "necessities," and the sociocultural pressure to comply with these imperatives has been applied more strictly to women than to men (Tsuya and Choe, 1991). Until quite recently, many Japanese did not even doubt the legitimacy of such normative statements as "One does not become a full-fledged member of society until he or she marries" or "Women's happiness lies solely in marriage" (Kojima, 1990).

Viewed as an inevitable outcome of marriage, procreation also served an important purpose of marriage because children ensured the succession and continuance of the family, and also because women's social status depended heavily on their role as wife and mother (Morioka, 1988; Tsuya and Choe, 1991). This situation was facilitated and perpetuated by the social structure under which men assumed the major role of decision maker within the family and women were mostly confined to the home so that their activities were not worth much outside the household (Smith, 1987; Vogel, 1971:181–182). Today, however, Japanese attitudes toward the normative primacy of marriage and reproduction seem to be changing, as manifested in the popularity of writings and media programs dealing with "single life," marital disruption, and childless marriages of "career women" (Ebisaka, 1986; Sugawara, 1987).

The actual patterns of fertility and family building appear to be generally in accordance with these attitudinal changes, with behavioral changes preceding normative shifts. Characteristics of Japanese marriage and reproductive behavior during the earlier postwar fertility transition were "universal" marriage occurring within a narrow age band of the mid-20s and bunched births, i.e., concentration of childbearing within a brief period shortly after marriage (Taeuber, 1960; Yamamura and Hanley, 1975). Although these characteristics are still strong in Japan, the proportions of never-married men and women in their 20s (and, to a lesser extent, of those in their early 30s) started to increase rapidly in the mid-1970s; and evidence from a simulation analysis of the reproductive process suggests the possibility that after 1970, young Japanese women may have started to space their births or delay childbearing within marriage (Tsuya, 1986). Consequently, Japanese fertility fell to a below-replacement level in 1974 and has not risen to a replacement level again since then.

Japan's current low fertility appears to be associated to some degree with women's (couples') calculations of the utilities and disutilities involved in marriage and family formation. Studies have shown that such economic mechanisms were indeed working in the postwar Japanese fertility transition (Hashimoto, 1974; Osawa, 1988; Yamamura and Hanley, 1975). I believe, however, that changes in the Japanese value system—in particular, the loosening of normative expectations about the necessity and importance of marriage and reproduction—due to rapid postwar socioeconomic changes also have had a great deal to do with the recent low fertility because, to use Lesthaeghe's (1983) terminology, "ideational systems" give meaning to econodemographic behavior.

The relationship between attitudinal or normative factors and behavior is extremely complex, and this study is not meant to do full justice to untangling the threads of this complexity. Rather, as an attempt to understand the forces behind the recent low fertility, it explores Japanese attitudes toward marriage and family life by examining their socioeconomic and demographic covariates. In the case of modern Japan, this approach seems to be especially appropriate because since the 1970s socioeconomic differentials in fertility have been disappearing despite the increasing heterogeneity of socioeconomic characteristics of the Japanese population (Atoh, 1985; Hodge and Ogawa, 1987).

Specifically, I first examine aggregate trends of fertility and nuptiality in postwar Japan, using census data and vital-registration statistics. Then, using data from the 1988 Japanese National Family Survey conducted by the Mainichi Newspapers and Nihon University, I investigate socioeconomic and demographic correlates of attitudes of never-married young Japanese adults concerning singlehood, functions of the home, and reasons for having children. Next, I examine covariates of attitudes of currently married Japanese aged 30 and above toward such family-related issues as singlehood, remarriage, functions of the home, and reasons for having children. These multivariate analyses are done with binary or multinomial logit models. The study concludes with a summary of findings and a discussion of their implications.

AGGREGATE TRENDS OF FERTILITY AND NUPTIALITY IN POSTWAR JAPAN

From shortly after World War II to the late 1950s, Japan experienced a sharp downturn in fertility. The fertility rate fell by half in the span of a decade from 4.5 children per woman in 1947 to 2.0 in 1957. After that dramatic decline, which was more rapid than any that had preceded it in the West, Japan's fertility stabilized at the TFR level of 2.0 to 2.2 until 1974, when it began to decline again. Since the mid-1970s the rate has been at a below-replacement level, showing a trend of gradual but further decline, and in 1990 the rate reached a low of 1.54 (Figure 6.1). Although the tempo of the post-1974 decline was not as dramatic as the earlier postwar decline, it was substantial in percentage terms, the TFR declining by 21 percent between 1975 and 1990.

Examining changes in the age-specific fertility rates shown in Table 6.1, we notice that the earlier dramatic decline in overall fertility was associated not only with decreases in fertility of women in

Figure 6.1. Total fertility rates: Japan, 1947–89

their prime reproductive years (ages 20–34) but also with sharp declines in fertility among women over age 34, indicating a rapid shift from a pattern of prolonged childbearing to deliberate curtailment of marital fertility before the onset of natural sterility. On the other hand, the decline after the mid-1970s was due to considerable decreases in the birth rates of women in their 20s but accompanied by a slight upturn of the rate for women in their early 30s, implying the effects of delayed marriage and, possibly, delayed childbearing.

An examination of changes in age-specific proportions of women ever married supports these findings (Table 6.2, upper panel). After some declines in the ever-married proportions among women in their 20s during the earlier postwar fertility transition, the proportions were relatively stable until the rates for these young women started to decrease again in the mid-1970s.

The declines in the proportion ever married for women of ages 20–24 have been especially substantial, indicating increasing postponement of first marriage

Table 6.1. Age-specific fertility rates and percentage changes in rate: Japan, 1950–90

Year/period	15–19	20–24	25–29	30–34	35–39	40–44	45–49	TFR[a] (per 1000 women)
Fertility rates
1950	13	161	236	174	104	36	2	3,630
1955	6	112	181	112	49	13	1	2,370
1960	4	106	181	80	24	5	0	2,000
1965	3	112	203	86	19	3	0	2,130
1970	4	96	208	85	20	3	0	2,080
1975	4	106	188	69	15	2	0	1,920
1980	4	77	182	73	13	2	0	1,755
1985	4	62	178	85	18	2	0	1,745
1990	4	45	140	93	21	2	0	1,525
Percentage changes
1950–55	−54	−30	−23	−36	−53	−64	*	−35
1955–60	*	−5	0	−29	−51	−62	*	−16
1960–65	*	6	12	8	−21	*	*	7
1965–70	*	−14	2	−1	5	*	*	−2
1970–75	*	10	−10	−19	−25	*	*	−4
1975–80	*	−27	−3	6	−13	*	*	−9
1980–85	*	−19	−2	16	38	*	*	−1
1985–90	*	−27	−21	9	17	*	*	−13

Sources: Japan, Ministry of Health and Welfare, Statistics and Information Department, *Vital Statistics of Japan* (various years).
* Base figure is too small to compute percentage change.
a. TFRs are calculated from rates for five-year age groups.

among young Japanese women beginning in the mid-1970s. From the singulate mean ages at marriage (SMAM) shown in Table 6.2, we can also see that the timing of first marriage has been postponed substantially since the mid-1970s, reaching a mean of 26.9 years of age for women and 29.9 years of age for men in 1990. Although some Scandinavian countries, such as Sweden and Denmark, have comparably high or even higher mean ages at first marriage (UN, DIESA, Statistical Office, 1983), Japan's age at first marriage can be considered to be one of the world's highest. Furthermore, in contrast with many Northern and Western European countries, in which the incidence of out-of-wedlock fertility is considerable (van de Kaa, 1987), Japan's illegitimate fertility has been extremely low, around 1 percent of total births, since 1960. Given the traditionally low incidence of childbearing outside marriage, changes in marriage behavior in Japan have had profound fertility effects because delayed marriage has meant the delayed beginning of women's

Table 6.2. Age-specific proportions ever married, by sex and the singulate mean age at marriage (SMAM): Japan, 1950–90

	Age group							
Year	15–19	20–24	25–29	30–34	35–39	40–44	45–49	SMAM[a]
Females								
1950	3.4	44.7	84.8	94.3	97.0	98.0	98.5	23.6
1955	1.7	33.5	79.4	92.1	96.1	97.7	98.3	24.6
1960	1.3	31.6	78.8	90.4	94.4	96.9	98.1	25.0
1965	1.5	31.9	81.8	90.9	93.2	95.3	97.0	24.7
1970	2.2	28.4	81.9	92.8	94.2	94.7	96.0	24.6
1975	1.4	30.8	79.1	92.3	94.7	95.0	95.1	24.4
1980	1.0	22.3	76.0	90.9	94.5	95.6	95.6	25.1
1985	1.1	18.6	69.4	89.6	93.4	95.1	95.7	25.8
1990	1.8	15.0	59.8	86.1	92.5	94.2	95.4	26.9
Males								
1950	0.5	17.1	65.5	92.0	96.8	98.1	98.5	26.2
1955	0.1	9.8	58.9	90.9	96.9	98.3	98.7	27.0
1960	0.2	8.4	53.8	90.1	96.3	98.0	98.7	27.4
1965	0.4	9.7	54.3	89.0	95.8	97.6	98.3	27.4
1970	0.7	10.0	53.5	88.3	95.3	97.2	98.1	27.4
1975	0.5	12.0	51.7	85.7	93.9	96.3	97.5	27.6
1980	0.4	8.5	44.9	78.5	91.5	95.3	96.9	28.5
1985	0.6	7.9	39.6	71.9	85.8	92.6	95.3	29.3
1990	1.5	7.8	35.6	67.4	81.0	88.3	93.3	29.9

Sources: Japan, Management and Coordination Agency, Bureau of Statistics, Population Census of Japan (various years).
a. SMAM is calculated from the percentages ever married in each five-year age interval from 15–19 through 45–49.

Changing Attitudes toward Marriage and the Family in Japan

(couples') reproductive careers.

In addition to the increasing postponement of first marriage among young Japanese, there is another phenomenon that calls into question the primacy of the institution of marriage in Japan in recent years: an increasing rate of divorce. From Table 6.3, we can see that the divorce rate (the number of divorces per 1,000 population) steadily increased from the mid-1960s until the mid-1980s, and that the ratio of divorces to 100 marriages started to increase substantially in the 1970s.

Life-table estimation (based on synthetic cohorts) of the probability of marital disruption confirms this trend. Table 6.4 reveals that while the probability of marital disruption due to divorce has been increasing for all selected marital durations since 1960, the probability of disruption started to increase noticeably in the mid-1970s in accordance with marital duration: the longer-lasting the marriages, the higher the rate of increase in the probability of divorce. Although the overall level of marital disruption in Japan is still much lower than that in many Western countries such as the United States, where well over half of first marriages are estimated to be dissolved

Table 6.3. Divorce rates, marriage rates, and ratios of divorces to 100 marriages: Japan, 1950–90

Year	Divorces per 1,000 population	Marriages per 1,000 population	Ratio of divorces to 100 marriages
1950	1.01	8.6	11.7
1955	0.84	8.0	10.5
1960	0.74	9.3	8.0
1965	0.79	9.7	8.1
1970	0.93	10.0	9.3
1975	1.07	8.5	12.7
1976	1.11	7.8	14.3
1977	1.14	7.2	15.8
1978	1.15	6.9	16.7
1979	1.17	6.8	17.2
1980	1.22	6.7	18.3
1981	1.32	6.6	19.9
1982	1.39	6.6	21.0
1983	1.51	6.4	23.5
1984	1.50	6.2	24.2
1985	1.39	6.1	22.7
1986	1.37	5.9	23.4
1987	1.30	5.7	22.7
1988	1.25	5.8	21.7
1989	1.29	5.8	22.4
1990	1.28	5.9	21.8

Sources: Japan, Ministry of Health and Welfare, Statistics and Information Department, *Vital Statistics of Japan* (various years).

(Bumpass, 1990) the increasing trend of marital disruption in Japan seems to imply significant changes in people's attitudes toward the primacy of marriage as well as the meaning of family life.

To examine directly the fertility effects of these changes in marital behavior, I have also analyzed the components of change in total fertility, specifically the effects of changes in the female age pattern of marriage and changes in age-specific marital fertility rates. (For an explanation of the general concept, logic, and mathematical procedure of the component analysis, see Kitagawa, 1955, and Das Gupta, 1978. For applications to studies of fertility change, see Blake and Das Gupta, 1975, and Gibson, 1976.) From Table 6.5 we can see that whereas the rapid fertility decline in earlier postwar years was due primarily to a decline in marital fertility, the decline to the below-replacement level since the mid-1970s has been due solely to decreases in the proportions of women currently married. In other words, the earlier postwar fertility decline was brought about primarily by family limitation practiced by married couples, whereas the recent decline was produced by the postponement of first marriages.

Do these findings imply that, as in the earlier case of Western Europe, the two postwar fertility transitions in Japan have been driven by different sets of norms and attitudes? According to van de Kaa (1987), the first fertility transition in Western Europe, which took place during the nineteenth and the early twentieth centuries, was dominated by "altruistic" attitudes, i.e., concerns for family and offspring, whereas the second transition to below-replacement fertility since the mid-1960s has been characterized by increasing "individualistic" concerns. Is this characterization of altruistic versus individualistic value systems underlying the two European fertility transitions also applicable to postwar Japan's first and second fertility transitions? Later in this

Table 6.4. Life-table estimates of the proportion of marriages disrupted by divorce within selected marriage durations: Japan, 1955–85

Year	1 year	5 years	10 years	15 years	20 years	30 years
1955	0.0157	0.0599	0.0859	0.0976	0.1050	0.1105
1960	0.0155	0.0499	0.0709	0.0837	0.0910	0.0976
1965	0.0159	0.0517	0.0743	0.0874	0.0947	0.1014
1970	0.0185	0.0591	0.0865	0.1025	0.1113	0.1186
1975	0.0186	0.0654	0.0981	0.1177	0.1287	0.1382
1980	0.0193	0.0710	0.1113	0.1402	0.1584	0.1771
1985	0.0193	0.0794	0.1253	0.1603	0.1867	0.2191

Source: Japan, Ministry of Health and Welfare, IPP (1989).

Changing Attitudes toward Marriage and the Family in Japan

chapter, I will attempt to identify clues for answering this question by examining covariates of recent attitudes toward marriage and the family in Japan.

DATA AND DEFINITIONS OF VARIABLES

As I have already mentioned, the data for the microlevel analysis used in this study have been drawn from the 1988 National Family Survey in Japan, conducted by the Mainichi Newspapers and Nihon University. Details of the survey design and data-collection procedure are given by Ozaki (1989). The survey used a stratified multistage random-sampling technique to collect nationally representative data on family issues in contemporary Japan. Of the 3,400 adults aged 20 and above who were sampled, 2,406 returned a self-administered questionnaire, thus making the response rate approximately 71 percent. The coverage across standard demographic groups appears to have been generally good, although compared with the 1985 census data, the survey somewhat underrepresented unmarried persons younger than 40 (Martin and Tsuya, Chapter 9 in this volume; Tsuya, 1989). Nevertheless, it has provided valuable national-level information on various aspects of the family-related behavior and attitudes of men and women of every marital status in Japan, where most of the data on the family come from the national

Table 6.5. Effects of changes in marital composition and marital fertility rates on the total fertility rate with interaction components allocated equally: Japan, 1950–90

				Change in TFR due to changes in:		
Period	TFR beginning	TFR end	Amount of change in TFR	Marital fertility (%)	Marital composition (%)	Total (%)
1950–55	3,630	2,370	−1,260	81.4	18.6	100.0
1955–60	2,370	2,000	−370	95.0	5.0	100.0
1960–65	2,000	2,130	130	55.7	44.3	100.0
1965–70	2,130	2,080	−50	35.9	64.1	100.0
1970–75	2,080	1,920	−160	102.1	−2.1	100.0
1975–80	1,920	1,755	−165	−24.0	124.0	100.0
1980–85	1,755	1,745	−10	−1,568.8	1,668.8	100.0
1985–90	1,745	1,525	−220	−4.6	104.6	100.0
1950–75	3,630	1,920	−1,710	88.8	11.2	100.0
1975–90	1,920	1,525	−395	−48.8	148.8	100.0

Sources: The same as in Tables 6.1 and 6.2.
Note: Interaction term in the decomposition has been allocated equally to marital fertility and marital composition.

fertility surveys of currently married women in reproductive ages.[1]

Here, my analysis focuses on the 278 never-married respondents of ages 20–34 and the 1,725 currently married respondents 30 and older. I have imposed the upper age limit on the never-married subsample because, given that the mean age at first marriage in Japan ranges between 25 and 29 (Japan, Ministry of Health and Welfare, IPP, 1992:68), never-married persons 35 and older are thought to be "outliers," whose inclusion in the analysis might distort the results. Bivariate analysis of the attitudes of never-married Japanese over age 34 toward singlehood, together with the importance of age as a criterion of mate selection, indicated a strong tendency among this age group to rationalize their unmarried status and other family-related attitudes. Correspondingly, it was necessary to impose the lower age limit on the currently married subsample to avoid the effects of bias toward very young ages at marriage. Since a large majority of Japanese marriages take place in a narrow age span from the mid- to late 20s, I decided to restrict my analysis of the currently married Japanese to those aged 30 and above.

Dependent Variables

The 1988 National Family Survey included a number of attitudinal, or normative, questions on family issues (Nihon University, University Research Center, 1989: supplement). Among those questions, as an important aspect of attitudes toward marriage, I focus first on a question about the acceptability of singlehood as an alternative to married life. As I have already mentioned, "universal" marriage has long been the norm and behavioral reality in Japanese society. The normative expectation of marriage used to be so strong that if a person had not married by the age of 30 or 35, his or her physiological as well as emotional normality was sometimes doubted (Ebisaka, 1986; Sugawara, 1987). It was not until the late 1970s or the early 1980s that singlehood came to be accepted as a life-style, although it is still not clear how legitimate and prevalent its acceptance has become in the society as a whole (Koshitani, 1989).

The survey question on attitudes toward singlehood asked whether respondents approved or disapproved of the recent trend among an increasing number of young people to remain single, rather than marry. Because the response category was dichotomous, this independent variable was coded as 1 if a respondent approved and 0 if he or she disapproved.

---

1. As a notable exception, the Institute of Population Problems, Ministry of Health and Welfare, collected data on attitudes and behavior related to marriage and the family among never-married Japanese first as part of its 8th National Fertility Survey in 1982 and again in the 9th National Fertility Survey in 1987. These surveys have an advantage over the 1988 National Family Survey, that of larger sample sizes (more than 8,000 cases). Unlike the National Family Survey, however, the National Fertility Surveys exclude currently married men as well as those who have been married but currently have no spouse.

Changing Attitudes toward Marriage and the Family in Japan

The proportion approving of singlehood was approximately 69 percent among never-married respondents of ages 20–34 (Table 6.6), and the corresponding figure was 49 percent among those currently married who were aged 30 and older (Table 6.7).

Among the currently married, I examined another item related to marriage, their attitudes toward remarriage in old

Table 6.6. Variables used in the analysis of attitudes toward marriage and the family among never-married Japanese, ages 20–34: National Family Survey, 1988 (Proportions and means)

Variable	Singlehood	Functions of the home	Reasons for having children
Attitude toward singlehood			
Approve	0.689		
(Disapprove)	0.311		
Functions associated with the home			
Emotional only		0.744	
(Other)		0.256	
Reasons for having children			
Emotional only			0.426
(Other)			0.574
Age	24.6	24.6	24.6
Sex			
(Male)	0.502	0.508	0.506
Female	0.498	0.492	0.494
Birth order			
(1)	0.680	0.678	0.681
Not 1	0.320	0.322	0.319
Education			
(High school or less)	0.386	0.384	0.387
Junior college or higher	0.614	0.616	0.613
Upbringing			
Urban	0.747	0.740	0.732
(Rural)	0.253	0.260	0.268
Current residence			
Big city	0.216	0.219	0.217
(Other)	0.784	0.781	0.783
Father's education			
(Junior high school or less)	0.382	0.376	0.374
High school	0.407	0.413	0.413
Junior college or higher	0.212	0.211	0.213
No. of cases	241	242	235

Notes: Means are based on the number of observations actually used in the analysis. Omitted (reference) categories are shown in parentheses.

Table 6.7. Variables used in the analysis of attitudes toward marriage and the family among currently married Japanese, ages 30 and above: National Family Survey, 1988 (Proportions and means)

Variable	Singlehood	Remarriage	Functions of the home	Reasons for having children
Attitude toward singlehood				
Approve	0.490			
(Disapprove)	0.510			
Attitude toward remarriage in old age				
Would like to remarry		0.324		
(Would not like to remarry)		0.674		
Functions associated with the home				
Emotional only			0.632	
(Pragmatic as well as emotional)			0.368	
Reasons for having children				
Emotional gratification only				0.327
Emotional gratification and succession				0.536
(Succession only)				0.137
Age	48.5	48.6	48.5	48.5
Age at marriage	25.9	25.9	26.0	26.0
Sex				
(Male)	0.513	0.504	0.507	0.504
Female	0.487	0.496	0.493	0.496
Husband's birth order				
1	0.439	0.440	0.441	0.440
(Not 1)	0.561	0.560	0.559	0.560
Wife's birth order				
1	0.444	0.444	0.445	0.447
(Not 1)	0.556	0.556	0.555	0.553
Education				
(Junior high school or less)	0.285	0.284	0.282	0.280
High school	0.456	0.458	0.459	0.461
Junior college or higher	0.259	0.258	0.259	0.259
Husband's occupation				
Professional or business proprietor	0.433	0.433	0.434	0.436
(Other)	0.567	0.567	0.566	0.564
Wife's work status				
(Not working)[a]	0.478	0.479	0.478	0.476
Working outside the home in the paid sector				
Part-time	0.146	0.147	0.146	0.144
Full-time	0.174	0.170	0.172	0.174
Working at home[b]	0.202	0.204	0.204	0.206
Upbringing				
Urban	0.484	0.487	0.487	0.485
(Rural)	0.516	0.513	0.513	0.515

Changing Attitudes toward Marriage and the
Family in Japan

Table 6.7. *(continued)*

Variable	Singlehood	Remarriage	Functions of the home	Reasons for having children
Current residence				
(Traditional agricultural region)	0.297	0.298	0.297	0.294
Not a traditional agricultural region	0.703	0.702	0.703	0.706
Type of marriage				
Not arranged[c]	0.515	0.512	0.514	0.512
(Arranged)	0.485	0.488	0.486	0.488
No. of cases	1,470	1,498	1,504	1,469

Notes: Means are based on the number of observations actually used in the analysis. Omitted (reference) categories are shown in parentheses.
a. Includes full-time homemakers, students, and the unemployed.
b. Includes family workers (e.g., those in agriculture) and the self-employed.
c. Includes those whose marriages were love matches.

age.[2] Although little statistical information is available in Japan on rates of remarriage by previous marital status (divorced or widowed), it is safe to assume that until the mid-1970s the likelihood of remarriage was very low because the possibility of remarriage was low. That is, as discussed in the previous section, the divorce rate was low and even declining during the 1950s and 1960s; moreover, the probability of widowhood had become low owing to rapid increases in life expectancy in postwar Japan (Japan, Ministry of Health and Welfare, Institute of Population Problems, 1989). True to these behavioral realities, norms against remarriage, especially remarriage of divorced women, seem to be strong in Japan—at least until recently. Unlike the contemporary situation in the United States, where divorce is generally treated as a temporary hiatus in the marital career (Thornton and Freedman, 1983), divorce in Japan has traditionally been regarded as a failure or a "selfish act" that especially stigmatized women (Hardacre, 1984:119–120; Lebra, 1984:152–162).

The survey question on attitudes toward remarriage asked whether respondents would like to remarry if they were

2. Among the young never-married Japanese, I also examined, both bivariately and multivariately, two items designed to shed light on their attitudes toward the timing of marriage, their preferred age at marriage and the importance of age as a criterion for mate selection. The results revealed both that an overwhelming majority of men and women chose ages 25–29 (and a considerable proportion of men chose ages 30–34) as their preferred age at marriage, and also that university-level education was the only covariate significantly (and negatively) associated with importance of age as a criterion for mate selection. Consequently, I decided to exclude attitudes toward the timing of marriage from the analysis presented in this chapter. In addition, the survey included a question asking currently married respondents whether they had ever thought about divorcing their current spouse. I decided not to deal with that question in this study because it inquired about respondent's personal contemplation of divorce, rather than their general attitudes toward it.

to become single in old age. The four response categories were ordered as follows: (1) definitely want to remarry, (2) would like to remarry if one could find a suitable partner; (3) prefer to stay unmarried; and (4) absolutely do not want to remarry. After conducting preliminary cross-tabulational analysis as well as some multinomial analyses, I decided to dichotomize this dependent variable by assigning a value of 1 for those who would like to remarry (that is, those who chose one of the first two responses) and a value of 0 for those who would not like to remarry (those who chose one of the remaining two categories). Among currently married Japanese of ages 30 and above, approximately one-third expressed positive attitudes toward remarriage in old age (Table 6.7).

To measure respondents' attitudes toward the family, the survey included two questions, one about the functions of the home and the other about the perceived benefits of having children. The first question was worded as follows: "The home has various functions and roles; which do you think is the most important among the following?" Respondents had the option of choosing one or two of six responses (five precoded and one open-ended). The precoded response categories were: (1) a place for economic support, (2) a place for marital affection between husband and wife, (3) a place for rest and comfort, (4) a place to produce and raise children, and (5) a place for mutual (mental) growth among family members. Among those categories, the first and the fourth responses are thought to be more pragmatic and traditional, whereas the remaining three lean more toward emotional, and less traditional, functions. Marital roles in Japan have historically been strictly segregated along gender lines (Smith, 1987; Tsuya and Choe, 1991; Vogel, 1971:181–207); and the normative view of the husband as the breadwinner and of the wife as the homemaker responsible for caring for children has been strong and pervasive. The notion that a married couple might consist of equal lifetime partners having a strong emotional bond is relatively new and considered to be less traditional.

A vast majority of the respondents chose at least one precoded emotional response. Among respondents who chose two precoded responses, the proportion of the never-married who chose two pragmatic, or traditional, functions of marriage was almost nil (less than 1 percent), and the corresponding proportion of those who were currently married was less than 7 percent. Therefore, I again decided to dichotomize this dependent variable, coding the responses as 1 if they included only emotional functions of the home, and as 0 if they included at least one pragmatic (traditional) function. Around 74 percent of the never-married respondents regarded the functions of the home to be entirely emotional (Table 6.6), whereas among currently married respondents the corresponding figure was 63 percent.

Another family-related attitudinal

issue examined by this study is reasons for having children. The questionnaire asked: "What do you think are the major benefits of having children?" Respondents were allowed to select two of eight responses, one of which was open-ended. The seven precoded responses were: (1) children brighten family life, (2) child rearing is a joy, (3) children are necessary because they become wage-earners, (4) parents can depend on children in old age, (5) children can inherit the family business, (6) children can inherit the family name and property, and (7) children ensure succession of the family line to posterity. The first two responses express the emotional gratification gained from having children, whereas the remaining five emphasize the pragmatic benefits of children.

In prewar Japan, great importance was attached to having children for the purpose of continuing the family and as a means of providing old-age security to their parents (Mosk, 1979; Dore, 1953). Having children for succession purposes may be considered to reflect traditional attitudes toward childbearing, although children must have been sources of great emotional gratification for many parents, especially for mothers, even in prewar Japanese society (Morioka, 1988). Less traditional attitudes toward children (that is, expectations of more emotional benefits from having children) do not necessarily have a detrimental effect on fertility. However, detachment from the family as the primary unit for the family's succession and continuation is thought to affect fertility negatively.

Only about 6 percent of never-married respondents chose succession-related responses to the question about reasons for having children, whereas 57 percent chose reasons associated with emotional gratification (Table 6.6). Therefore, for analysis of the never-married respondents, I dichotomized the dependent variable, scoring it as 1 if the selected reasons were entirely for emotional gratification and 0 if otherwise. Among the currently married respondents, 33 percent chose answers associated with emotional gratification, 14 percent chose succession-oriented answers, and the remaining 54 percent chose both emotional and succession-oriented answers (Table 6.7). Therefore, for the analysis of currently married respondents, I trichotomized this dependent variable, scoring it as 1 if the reasons for having children were solely emotional, 2 if the reasons were both emotional and succession-related, and 3 if they were only for succession.

Covariates

Because attitudes toward singlehood, remarriage, the home, and children are known to be associated with a variety of demographic and socioeconomic factors, I decided to investigate the relationship of these attitudinal variables with selected demographic and socioeconomic covariates, employing a binary or multinomial logit model. Tables 6.6 and 6.7

show the definitions and means of the covariates included in the logit analysis of attitudes among never-married and currently married respondents, respectively. As shown in Table 6.6, the model for the never-married Japanese includes three demographic variables (age, sex, and birth order) and four socioeconomic variables (education, rural or urban upbringing until graduation from elementary school, current residence in a big city or other location, and father's education). The first demographic variable, respondent's age, is included not only to measure the effects of physical age, but also to capture, at least in part, the possible effects of birth cohort. Although the age range of the never-married subsample was narrow, because recent changes in Japanese-life styles have been so rapid I still expected older respondents to be more traditional than younger ones in their attitudes toward singlehood and especially toward the home and children.

Within Japan's tradition of the stem family and primogeniture, the eldest son (and, to a lesser extent, the eldest daughter) plays an important role, having many privileges but also extra responsibilities for the family (Matsumoto, 1962; Martin, 1990; Tsuya and Choe, 1991). I therefore expected respondents who were eldest sons and daughters to have more traditional attitudes toward marriage and the family than other respondents. Since I also expected to encounter large gender differences in attitudes and normative expectations toward marriage and the family, I introduced gender as a covariate.

As for socioeconomic covariates, higher education is generally considered to be associated with increased individualism and less traditional attitudes. Reflecting the extremely high educational attainment of the postwar Japanese population, more than 61 percent of the young, never-married subsample had a university-level education and most of the remaining 39 percent had a high school education (Table 6.6).

Also reflecting the rapid urbanization of postwar Japan, approximately 74 percent of the never-married respondents reported that they had had an urban upbringing (that is, had lived mostly in an urban area until completing elementary school). I hypothesized that an urban upbringing would be negatively associated with more traditional attitudes toward marriage and the family because such an upbringing is generally thought to exert less traditional socialization effects than a rural upbringing on the early formation of values.

The analysis included a dichotomous variable indicating current residence in a big city or elsewhere. Residence in a large metropolitan area is commonly thought to be associated with more individualistic and less traditional attitudes toward marriage and the family.

The last socioeconomic variable, father's education, was included to measure (and control for) the effects of the respondent's socioeconomic background.

In this case, I regarded the respondent's occupation as inappropriate for such a measure because a considerable proportion (around 10 percent) of the never-married respondents, being students, were not yet in the labor market and because, among those who were in the labor market, a majority were thought to have had a relatively short occupational career. Therefore, I decided to rely on the father's education instead of the respondent's occupation as a measure of respondent's social status. Father's occupation was not used in the model because of a large number of missing cases.

Table 6.7 presents the definitions and means of the covariates for analysis of attitudes toward marriage and the family among the currently married Japanese. Among the 11 covariates listed, respondent's age, sex, education, and upbringing had the same definitions, and were expected to have similar effects, as those included in the model for the never-married.[3] Since, for currently married respondents, data on birth order were available for both the respondent and his or her spouse, the analysis includes the variables of husband's birth order (being the eldest son or not) as well as wife's birth order (being the eldest daughter or not).

Similarly, since data on occupation (work status) were available for both husband and wife, I decided to include variables to measure the attitudinal effects of both husband's and wife's work. The variable of husband's occupation was dichotomous: 1 if his occupation was professional or business proprietor, and 0 otherwise. Professionals or business proprietors were chosen because of their high status, and a husband's high-status occupation was expected to be associated with less traditional attitudes toward marriage and the family.

The variable of wife's work status was recoded to have four categories: (1) not working (i.e., full-time homemaker, student, or unemployed), (2) working full time outside the home, (3) working part-time outside the home, and (4) working at home (i.e., family worker in agriculture or a family business, or self-employed). From these four categories, I selected "not working" as the reference category and constructed three dummy variables. It is widely accepted that a wife's labor force participation tends to lower her fertility. Assuming that a wife's experience in the labor market would make her, and probably her husband as well, more inclined to form individualistic attitudes, I hypothesized that women's work would be associated with less traditional attitudes toward marriage and the family. I assumed, furthermore, that not only the experience of participating in the labor force per se, but also working outside the home, would make women's

---

3. Because the survey obtained information on education for both the respondent and his or her spouse, I also experimented with using the husband's education and wife's education, instead of the respondent's education, in the analyses of currently married respondents. Doing so produced little difference in the results, and I therefore decided to exclude the spouse's education from the analysis.

attitudes toward marriage and family issues less traditional, and that their husbands would similarly have less traditional attitudes.[4] In other words, if wives worked outside the home (and husbands let their wives do so), I hypothesized that both the wives and their husbands would acquire more independent attitudes toward marriage and the family than would wives who either did not work or who worked at home, engaging in a family business or in household-centered production. In addition, since part-time employment outside the home (called *pāto* in Japanese) has become increasingly typical of female employment in Japan (Japan, Ministry of Health and Welfare, IPP, 1985), I further divided women's work outside the home into two categories, part-time and full-time, hypothesizing that full-time work would be associated with more modern attitudes than would part-time work.

A dichotomous variable of current residence in a traditionally agricultural region was also included in the analysis of currently married respondents. Given the rapid urbanization and industrialization of postwar Japan, I speculated that some regions of Japan that appear today to be urban and modern may have been more rural, agricultural, and traditional just a few decades ago, when many of the currently married respondents were adolescents or young adults. I constructed the variable first by ranking the 12 constituent regions of Japan by the percentage of population aged 15 and over employed in the primary sector at the censal years of 1950, 1960, 1970, and 1980, and then by grouping the five regions with the highest average rankings to form the omitted category, coded as 0. The five regions were Tohoku, Hokuriku-Tosan, Kita-Kanto, Shikoku, and Minami-Kyushu. The category coded as 1 included the remaining seven regions of Hokkaido, Minami-Kanto, Tokai, Nishi-Kinki, Higashi-Kinki, Chugoku, and Kita-Kyushu.

I did not include this variable of not living in a traditionally agricultural region in the analysis of never-married respondents because, as most of the never-married were still young adults at the time of the survey, I assumed that their urban or rural upbringing would capture most of the effects of this variable. Moreover, I could not include another residential variable, residence in a big city, in the analysis of currently married respondents because none of the respondents living in a big city lived in a traditionally agricultural region. (As stated earlier, for analysis of never-married respondents, I included the variable of residence in a big city because the variable of not living in a traditionally agricultural region was excluded.)

---

4. Analyzing the effects of rising female labor force participation on the postwar fertility decline in Japan, Osawa (1988) found that the expected negative relationship between women's time (opportunity) cost and fertility was significant only among those working outside the home in the paid sector, and also that such a negative association was insignificant among women engaged in a family business or in household-centered production.

Finally, the analysis included the type of marriage, whether it had been arranged or not, as a covariate. In present-day Japan an arranged marriage (*miai*) is not strictly the type of marriage prevalent under the prewar *ie* system, in which parents (especially a father) and other male relatives exerted absolute control over mate selection of young men and women (Taeuber, 1958:207–209). Rather, it now commonly means a marriage between two people who were first introduced by their parents, relatives, or superiors at a workplace. Such introductions are a traditional form of initiating a courtship leading to marriage in Japan, although a series of national fertility surveys indicates that the proportion of arranged marriages has been declining among younger marriage cohorts (Japan, Ministry of Health and Welfare, IPP, 1988:26–27). I therefore hypothesized that an arranged marriage would be positively associated with more traditional attitudes toward marriage and the family.

RESULTS OF LOGIT ANALYSIS OF THE NEVER-MARRIED JAPANESE

Coefficients presented in Table 6.8 indicate the effect of each covariate on the log odds that never-married Japanese would approve of singlehood, choose entirely emotional functions of the home, and select only emotional reasons for having children. As hypothesized, being female was significantly and positively associated with less traditional attitudes toward all three attitudinal variables; that is, young, single women were much more likely than young, single men to approve of singlehood, to have more emotional expectations about home life, and to desire children solely for emotional gratification. Also as hypothesized, an urban upbringing was associated positively with less traditional attitudes toward singlehood, indicating that young unmarried Japanese who had had an urban upbringing were more likely to have positive attitudes toward singlehood than their counterparts who had grown up in a rural setting.

With respect to attitudes toward (functions of) the home, the respondent's gender had a significant effect on the expected direction; but contrary to my hypothesis, university education was negatively associated with the expectation of totally emotional functions of the home. Similarly, residence in a big city was inversely related to such an attitude. These findings indicate therefore that young, unmarried Japanese who had a university education or were living in a large metropolis were likely to have less emotional and more pragmatic or traditional expectations toward home life. One possible interpretation of these unexpected findings is that young, single people with high education have more monetary resources and skills for expanding their human contacts than their less educated counterparts, so that they can obtain some of their emotional support from nonfamilial sources. It is also possible that the high cost of urban residence makes single people more aware of the financial (utilitarian) value of marriage, or that bachelor living makes them nostalgic for the stability associated with traditional marriages. Likewise, residents in a big city are likely to be exposed to a wider variety of human contacts so that they may have more opportunities, besides home life, to have their emotional needs met.

Turning to results of the analysis of reasons for having children, we see in Table 6.8 that the variables with statistically significant effects were, besides being female, father's university education and residence in a big city. Compared with residents in a medium-sized city, small town, or village, residents in a big city were, as expected, more likely to cite entirely emotional reasons for having children, and less likely to choose a combination of emotional and succession-oriented reasons. Although this finding appears to contradict the negative association found between big-city residence and emotional expectations of home life, the two findings are not really in conflict.

Table 6.8. Coefficients (Betas) and standard errors estimated from the logit regression analyses of approval of singlehood, expected functions of the home, and reasons for having children: never-married Japanese, ages 20–34, 1988

Covariate	Singlehood	Functions of the home	Reasons for having children
Constant	1.29 (1.20)	1.13 (1.33)	−2.05 (1.20)
Age	−0.02 (0.04)	0.05 (0.05)	0.06 (0.04)
Female	0.70* (0.30)	0.68* (0.33)	0.57* (0.29)
Birth order not 1	−0.38 (0.31)	0.11 (0.35)	−0.33 (0.30)
University education	0.32 (0.33)	−1.14** (0.39)	0.10 (0.31)
Father's high school education	0.35 (0.34)	0.57 (0.38)	0.49 (0.32)
Father's university education	−0.18 (0.43)	0.31 (0.45)	0.76* (0.43)
Urban upbringing	−0.68* (0.36)	0.23 (0.37)	0.14 (0.32)
Living in a big city	0.60 (0.39)	−0.82* (0.37)	0.96** (0.39)
Log-likelihood	−141.4	−125.5	−149.7

Note: Standard errors are shown in parentheses.
* Significant at the .05 level with a one- or two-tail test used as appropriate to the hypothesis.
** Significant at the .01 level with a one- or two-tail test used as appropriate to the hypothesis.

Changing Attitudes toward Marriage and the Family in Japan

While residents in a big city are less likely than others to seek emotional comfort and support solely from the home, and more likely to expect the home to be a place for procreation and economic provision in addition to emotional support, if they are to have children, their reasons tend to be solely for emotional gratification. Because these young respondents had not yet married and none of them actually had children, there is a possibility that the question about reasons for having children was too unrealistic and too unspecific to elicit their true attitudes toward family formation.

Compared with young, unmarried Japanese whose fathers had low (junior high school or less) education, those whose fathers had high (university or higher) education were more likely to indicate emotional reasons for having children, whereas there was no significant difference between those whose fathers had low education and intermediate (high school) education. This finding suggests that, as expected, young Japanese from affluent backgrounds are more likely to attach emotional value to family formation.

In addition, Table 6.8 indicates that the effect of respondents' birth order was insignificant in all of the three logit regression analyses conducted. This means that men and women of second- and higher-order births were not significantly different from their firstborn counterparts in their attitudes toward singlehood, expected fuctions of the home, and reasons for having children.

RESULTS OF THE LOGIT ANALYSIS OF CURRENTLY MARRIED JAPANESE

Table 6.9 presents the results of the logit analysis of currently married Japanese aged 30 and over concerning their attitudes toward singlehood, remarriage in old age, and exclusively emotional functions of the home. Results of the multinomial analysis of reasons for having children are shown in Table 6.10.[5] From these tables, we first notice that the respondent's age had a consistently strong negative association with all four attitudinal variables, indicating that (as hypothesized) the younger the respondents were, the less likely they were to have traditional attitudes toward marriage and the family. To the extent that these age effects were actually cohort effects, this finding in turn implies that Japanese attitudes about marriage and the family have become less traditional in recent years.

In addition to age, we can see from Table 6.9 that being female, having had an urban upbringing, not living in a traditionally agricultural region, and not having had an in arranged marriage were all significantly and positively related to

---

5. The multinomial logit model is a generalization of the binary logit model, which can be used to estimate covariates of a categorical dependent variable with more than two mutually exclusive and exhaustive outcomes. See Maddala (1983:41–46) for a general description and explanation of the model.

approval of singlehood. These findings, which are in complete accordance with my expectation, indicate that Japanese wives are less traditional and more liberal than their husbands in their attitudes toward singlehood as an alternative lifestyle, and that urbanization has also had profound effects in forming more flexible attitudes toward the primacy of marriage.

With regard to attitudes toward re-

Table 6.9. Coefficients (Betas) and standard errors estimated from the logit regression analyses of approval of singlehood, positive attitudes toward remarriage in old age, and expected functions of the home: currently married Japanese, ages 30 and above, 1988

Covariate	Singlehood	Remarriage in old age	Functions of the home
Constant	0.62 (0.49)	2.28** (0.53)	1.17* (0.47)
Age	−0.4** (0.006)	−0.05** (0.006)	−0.02** (0.005)
Age at marriage	0.01 (0.01)	0.003 (0.01)	0.01 (0.01)
Female	0.58** (0.12)	−1.06** (0.13)	0.10 (0.12)
Husband's birth order 1	−0.08 (0.11)	−0.12 (0.12)	−0.10 (0.11)
Wife's birth order 1	0.05 (0.11)	0.09 (0.12)	−0.03 (0.11)
High school education	0.18 (0.16)	−0.32 (0.16)	0.20 (0.14)
University education	0.28 (0.17)	−0.04 (0.18)	0.10 (0.17)
Husband in higher-status occupation	−0.06 (0.12)	0.08 (0.12)	0.01 (0.12)
Wife working part-time outside the home	0.07 (0.17)	0.32* (0.17)	−0.42** (0.17)
Wife working full-time outside the home	−0.07 (0.16)	0.28* (0.16)	−0.26* (0.16)
Wife working at home	0.02 (0.15)	−0.06 (0.17)	−0.31* (0.15)
Urban upbringing	0.23* (0.12)	0.14 (0.12)	0.23* (0.12)
Not living in a traditional agricultural region	0.36** (0.13)	−0.10 (0.13)	0.11 (0.12)
Marriage not arranged	0.30** (0.12)	−0.04 (0.13)	0.13 (0.12)
Log-likelihood	−933.9	−855.6	−961.5

Note: Standard errors are shown in parentheses.
* Significant at the .05 level with a one- or two-tail test used as appropriate to the hypothesis.
** Significant at the .01 level with a one- or two-tail test used as appropriate to the hypothesis.

Changing Attitudes toward Marriage and the Family in Japan

marriage in old age, we note from Table 6.9 that female respondents were much less likely than their male counterparts to have positive attitudes toward remarriage in old age. Since remarriage was not an abstract issue for many of these currently married respondents (in the sense that there was a possibility for this to happen to all of them), this result may be a reflection of women's own unwilling-

Table 6.10. Estimated coefficients and standard errors from the multinomial logit analysis of reasons for having children: currently married Japanese, ages 30 and above, 1988

Covariate	Emotional only vs. (mixed)	Emotional only vs. (succession)	Mixed vs. (succession)
Constant	−0.24 (0.54)	4.12** (0.77)	4.37** (0.71)
Age	−0.05** (0.007)	−0.10** (0.01)	0.05** (0.008)
Age at marriage	0.04** (0.01)	0.04* (0.02)	−0.01 (0.02)
Female	0.35** (0.13)	0.29 (0.20)	−0.06 (0.18)
Husband's birth order 1	0.04 (0.12)	0.06 (0.19)	0.02 (0.17)
Wife's birth order 1	0.13 (0.12)	0.07 (0.19)	−0.05 (0.17)
High school education	−0.01 (0.17)	0.008 (0.23)	0.02 (0.20)
University education	0.01 (0.19)	−0.16 (0.28)	−0.16 (0.25)
Husband in higher-status occupation	0.01 (0.13)	0.07 (0.20)	0.06 (0.18)
Wife working part-time outside the home	0.05 (0.18)	0.28 (0.32)	0.23 (0.30)
Wife working full-time outside the home	−0.27 (0.17)	0.09 (0.28)	0.36 (0.26)
Wife working at home	0.12 (0.17)	−0.10 (0.23)	−0.23 (0.20)
Urban upbringing	0.27* (0.13)	0.46* (0.19)	0.20 (0.18)
Not living in a traditional agricultural region	0.30* (0.14)	0.58** (0.20)	0.28 (0.18)
Marriage not arranged	0.32** (0.13)	−0.04 (0.19)	−0.36* (0.18)

Note: Omitted (reference) categories and standard errors are shown in parentheses.

* Significant at the .05 level with a one- or two-tail test used as appropriate to the hypothesis.
** Significant at the .01 level with a one- or two-tail test used as appropriate to the hypothesis.

ness to remarry (assuming that the opportunity were to arise) rather than as disapproval of others who remarry. Cornell (1989) found that Japanese women were actually less likely to remarry than men.[6] Studies of the remarriage intentions of widows and divorcees have also indicated that, in addition to anticipating a lack of opportunity, women were uninterested in remarriage, reporting that they were "fed up with" marriage (Lebra, 1984:257; Smith, 1987; Japan, Ministry of Health and Welfare, Statistics and Information Department, 1978:44–46).

My own analysis also indicates that married women's work outside the home, whether part-time or full-time, was positively associated with more favorable attitudes toward remarriage in old age, as expected. My interpretation of this finding is that married women's experiences of working outside the home make them (and their husbands) less traditional, thus making the notion of remarriage in old age more acceptable to them.

Turning to attitudes toward the family, the analysis of expected functions of the home reveals that, contrary to my hypothesis, women's work, regardless of employment status (part-time or full-time) or whether outside or inside the home, was associated with more traditional expectations of the home life, indicating that working women and their husbands were more likely to regard the home as a place for procreation and economic provision, rather than as a place solely for mutual emotional support. This finding in turn implies that women's experiences in the labor market make them and their husbands less inclined to seek emotional comfort and support exclusively from the home, possibly because working women can divert their attention from the home more easily than their nonworking counterparts, and also because their husbands learn not to expect too much from a home in which wives are not always present to "take care of their needs." Consequently, Japanese working wives and their husbands may come to regard more traditional (reproductive and economic) functions as the primary functions of the home.

As in the case of never-married respondents, married respondents' urban upbringing was found to be significantly and positively associated with entirely emotional expectations of the functions of the home, suggesting that urbanization significantly contributes to the formation of less traditional attitudes toward marriage through socialization.

Turning to the results of the multinomial analysis of perceived benefits of having children, we can see from Table 6.10 that, although their effects were neither as consistent nor as pervasive as the effect of age, nevertheless higher age at

---

6. Cornell (1989) also found that women in the United States, like their Japanese counterparts, were less likely to remarry than American men. Nonetheless, the likelihood of remarriage for American women after age 30 seems to be substantially higher than that for Japanese women.

marriage, an urban upbringing, and not residing in a traditionally agricultural region were all significantly and positively associated with less traditional attitudes toward children—that is, citing only emotional reasons rather than succession-oriented or a mixture of emotional and succession-oriented reasons for having children. Being female was also significantly and positively associated with solely emotional reasons for having children. It may be the case that because women's responses heavily favored emotional reasons (i.e., only a small number of women chose entirely succession-oriented reasons), there was not much variation to be accounted for in the case of the other two combinations.

The multinomial logit analysis also revealed that not having had an arranged marriage was positively associated with solely emotional reasons for having children in the contrast between emotional only and mixed reasons. It was also positively associated with succession-oriented responses in the combination of succession-oriented and mixed responses. I interpret these findings to indicate that the effects of nonarranged marriage are polarized, with spouses in such marriages being likely to choose either entirely emotional benefits or entirely succession-oriented reasons for having children.

Finally, contrary to my expectation, the effects of husbands' and wives' birth order were found to be insignificant in all the analyses under consideration—that is, approval of singlehood, attitudes toward remarriage in old age, expected functions of the home, and reasons for having children. This complete lack of significance of respondents' eldest-child status means that when the effects of other covariates in the model were controlled, the attitudes of firstborn men and women toward marriage and the family were not significantly different from those of second- and later-born men and women.

SUMMARY AND IMPLICATIONS

To the extent that respondents' ages reflect cohort effects, the results of this study suggest that attitudes toward marriage and the family in Japan have been changing in recent years. Although it is not possible to confirm this hypothesis with the cross-sectional data available from the 1988 National Family Survey, Japanese attitudes toward marriage and family formation seem to have become less traditional as the society has grown more urbanized and developed socioeconomically. Because younger individuals who took part in the survey expressed much less traditional attitudes than older respondents, it seems likely that Japan's recent fertility decline has been due in large measure to the individualistic attitudes of the younger Japanese.

Although the evidence is not conclusive, women, both those who were unmarried and those who were currently married, tended to have less traditional attitudes toward marriage and the family than did men. However, whereas currently married women viewed singlehood more favorably than did men, they were less favorable than men toward remarriage in old age. I interpret these findings to imply that married women were not interested in remarrying themselves, were the opportunity to do so to arise, rather than to imply that they disapproved of remarriage as an alternative lifestyle. If my interpretation is correct, these findings indicate that Japanese women are not only more ambivalent than men about the primacy of marriage, but also more disenchanted with the institution of marriage, probably because of their firsthand experiences. At any rate, given that the attitudes and behavior of young Japanese women with respect to the institutions of marriage and the family are less traditional than in the past, the negative implications of these changes for fertility cannot be ignored.

Having had an urban upbringing was also found to be associated with less traditional attitudes toward singlehood and procreation among the currently married Japanese. Likewise, not currently living in a traditionally agricultural region was associated with more flexible attitudes toward singlehood and emotional as opposed to utilitarian reasons for having children. Given the rapid and continuous urbanization of Japanese society, one may well ask whether these findings prefigure a further relaxation of the normative primacy of marriage as a social institution and a decline in the importance of children as a means of ensuring a family's succession. Although one must be careful when inferring future trends from cross-sectional results, the effects of urbanization on Japanese attitudes toward marriage and the family seem to be heading in less traditional directions.

Interestingly, married women's work, especially work outside the home, was found to make women and their husbands more receptive to the idea of remarriage in old age, but it also made them more traditional in their expectations toward the home and in their reasons for having children. Does this finding imply that labor force participation causes women to adopt "masculine" attitudes, as is often alleged in the mass media? This is a topic that needs further systematic analysis.

Having had a nonarranged marriage was found to be associated with favorable attitudes toward singlehood. With respect to attitudes toward family building, however, nonarranged marriages appeared to have polarized effects; that is, people in nonarranged marriages had either totally emotion-oriented or totally succession-oriented reasons for desiring children. Therefore, the fertility implications of different types of marriage appear to be mixed. Nonetheless, the positive association between nonarranged marriages and approval of singlehood suggests, given an increasing trend toward nonarranged marriages, the decreasing primacy of marriage and thus a negative fertility effect.

Another piece of evidence suggesting the declining primacy of marriage and the decreasing importance of children as a means of ensuring family succession was the lack of statistical significance for the effects of respondents' eldest-child status. Contrary to my expectation, eldest-child status had no significant effects on any of the attitudinal variables under consideration, and this was the case for both never-married and currently married respondents. Whereas birth order (being the firstborn) has been shown to be a significant correlate of many family-related behaviors, such as coresidence with parents (Kojima, 1989; Martin and Tsuya, Chapter 9 in this volume), its insignificant effect on attitudes of contemporary Japanese toward marriage and the family seems to indicate that another support for traditional Japanese attitudes toward the primacy of marriage and family building has been disappearing.

Taken together, the findings from this study suggest that forces of socioeconomic change are causing attitudes of contemporary Japanese toward marriage and the family to become less traditional, although forces tending to preserve traditional attitudes and norms are also present. The attitudinal changes can be expected not only to affect the actual pattern of family building but also to alter the basic meaning of primary relationships between husband and wife, and between parents and children, in the Japanese society.

ACKNOWLEDGMENTS

I wish to thank Andrew Cherlin, Minja Kim Choe, Karen Oppenheim Mason, and Ronald Rindfuss for their comments on an earlier version of this chapter.

REFERENCES

Atoh Makoto. 1985. "Changes in Fertility and Fertility Control Behavior in Japan." In Minoru Muramatsu and Tameyoshi Katagiri (eds.), *Basic Readings on Population and Family Planning in Japan*, pp. 40–60. 3d ed. Tokyo: Japanese Organization for International Cooperation in Family Planning.

Blake, Judith, and Prithwis Das Gupta. 1975. "Reproductive Motivation Versus Contraceptive Technology: Is Recent American Experience an Exception?" *Population and Development Review* 1:229–249.

Bumpass, Larry L. 1990. "What's Happening to the Family? Interactions between Demographic and Institutional Change." *Demography* 27(4): 483–498.

Cho, Lee-Jay. 1989. *China's Population: Recent Trends and Future Challenges*. NUPRI Research Paper Series, No. 50. Tokyo: Population Research Institute, Nihon University.

Cornell, Laurel L. 1989. "Gender Differences in Remarriage after Divorce in Japan and the United States." *Journal of Marriage and the Family* 51(May):457–463.

Das Gupta, Prithwis. 1978. "A General Method of Decomposing a Difference between Two Rates into Several Components." *Demography* 15(1):99–112.

Dore, R. P. 1953. "Japanese Rural Fertility: Some Social and Economic Factors." *Population Studies* 7:62–88.

Ebisaka Takeshi. 1986. *Single Life* (in Japanese). Tokyo: Chūō Kōron Sha.

Gibson, Campbell. 1976. "The U.S. Fertility Decline, 1961–1975: The Contribution of Changes in Marital Status and Marital Fertility." *Family Planning Perspectives* 8:249–252.

Hardacre, Helen. 1984. *Lay Buddhism in Contemporary Japan*. Princeton: Princeton University Press.

Hashimoto Masanori. 1974. "Economics of Postwar Fertility in Japan." In Theodore W. Schultz (ed.), *Economics of the Family: Marriage, Children, and Human Capital*, pp. 225–249. Chicago: University of Chicago Press.

Hodge, Robert W., and Naohiro Ogawa. 1987. *On the Homogenization of Fertility Experiences.* NUPRI Research Paper Series, No. 38. Tokyo: Population Research Institute, Nihon University.

Japan, Management and Coordination Agency, Bureau of Statistics. Various years. *Population Census of Japan* (in Japanese). Tokyo.

Japan, Ministry of Health and Welfare, Institute of Population Problems (IPP). 1985. *The Demographic Survey on Married Women's Labor Force Participation*. Tokyo.

———. 1988. *Shōwa 62-nen Nihonjin no Kekkon to Shussan: Dai-9 Ji Shussan-Ryoku Chōsa* (Marriage and fertility of the Japanese in 1987: Results of the 9th National Fertility Survey). Tokyo: Kōsei Tōkei Kyōkai.

———. 1989. *Marriage Dissolution Tables for Japanese Couples, 1935–1985* (in Japanese). Tokyo.

———. 1992. *Latest Demographic Statistics, 1992* (in Japanese). Tokyo.

Japan, Ministry of Health and Welfare, Statistics and Information Department. 1978. *Jinkō Dōtai Shakai Keizaimen Chōsa Hōkoku: Rikon* (Survey report on vital statistics from a socioeconomic viewpoint: Divorce). Tokyo.

———. Various years. *Vital Statistics of Japan* (in Japanese). Tokyo.

Kitagawa, Evelyn M. 1955. "Components of a Difference between Two Rates." *Journal of the American Statistical Association* 50:1168–1194.

Kojima Hiroshi. 1989. "Intergenerational Household Extension in Japan." In Frances K. Goldscheider and Calvin Goldscheider (eds.), *Ethnicity and the New Family Economy: Living Arrangements and Intergenerational Financial Flows*, pp. 163–184. Boulder: Westview Press.

———. 1990. "Bankonka no Keiko/Singuruzu no Zōka: Naze Kekkon o Tamerau no ka?" (The trend toward later marriage and increases in the unmarried: Why do people hesitate to marry?). *Kazoku Shakaigaku Kenkyū* 2:10–23.

Koshitani Kazuko. 1989. "Awareness of Problems Concerning Marriage and Divorce." In University Research Center (ed.), *Summary of the National Opinion Survey of the Family in Japan*, pp. 79–83. Tokyo: University Research Center, Nihon University.

Lebra, Takie Sugiyama. 1984. *Japanese Women: Constraint and Fulfillment*. Honolulu: University of Hawaii Press.

Lesthaeghe, Ron. 1983. "A Century of Demographic and Cultural Change in Western Europe: An Exploration of Underlying Dimensions." *Population and Development Review* 9(3):411–435.

Lesthaeghe, Ron, and Johan Surkyn. 1988. "Cultural Dynamics and Economic Theories of Fertility Change." *Population and Development Review* 14(1):1–45.

Maddala, G. S. 1983. *Limited-Dependent and Qualitative Variables in Econometrics*. Cambridge: Cambridge University Press.

Martin, Linda G. 1990. "Changing Intergenerational Family Relations in East Asia." *Annals of the American Academy of Political and Social Sciences* 510(July):102–114.

Martin, Linda G., and Noriko O. Tsuya. 1991. "Interactions of Middle-aged Japanese with Their Parents." *Population Studies* 45(2):299–311.

Matsumoto, Y. Scott. 1962. "Notes on Primogeniture in Postwar Japan." In Robert J. Smith and Richard K. Beardsley (eds.), *Japanese Culture: Its Development and Characteristics*, pp. 55–69. Chicago: Aldine.

Morioka Kiyomi. 1988. "Changing Family Background for Children in Contemporary Japan." *Seijō Bungei* 123:63–76.

Mosk, Carl. 1979. "The Decline of Marital Fertility in Japan." *Population Studies* 33(1):19–38.

Nakane Chie. 1973. *Japanese Society*. Harmondsworth: Penguin.

Nihon University, University Research Center. 1989. *Summary of the National Opinion Survey of the the Family in Japan*. Tokyo.

Osawa Machiko. 1988. "Working Mothers: Changing Patterns of Employment and Fertility in Japan." *Economic Development and Cultural Change* 36(4):623–650.

Ozaki Michio. 1989. "Introduction and Summary of the Survey on the Family." In University Research Center (ed.), *Summary of the National Opinion Survey of the Family in Japan*, pp. 1–21. Tokyo: University Research Center, Nihon University.

Preston, Samuel H. 1987. "Changing Values and Falling Birth Rates." In Kingsley Davis, Mikhail S. Bernstam, and Rita Ricardo-Campbell (eds.), *Below-Replacement Fertility in Industrial Societies: Causes, Consequences, Policies*, pp. 176–195. New York: Population Council.

Smith, Robert J. 1987. "Gender Inequality in Contemporary Japan." *Journal of Japanese Studies* 13(1):1–25.

Sugawara Mariko. 1987. *Shin Kazoku-no-Jidai* (The new family era) Chuko Shinsho, No. 858. Tokyo: Chūō Kōron Sha.

Taeuber, Irene B. 1958. *The Population of Japan*. Princeton: Princeton University Press.

———. 1960. "Continuities in the Declining Fertility of the Japanese." *Milbank Memorial Fund Quarterly* 38:264–283.

Thornton, Arland, and Deborah Freedman. 1983. "Changing Attitudes toward Marriage and Single Life." *Family Planning Perspectives* 14(6):297–303.

Tsuya, Noriko O. 1986. Proximate Determinants of Fertility Decline in Japan after World War II. Ph.D. dissertation. University of Chicago.

———. 1989. "Changes in Marriage and Family Formation among Contemporary Japanese Women." In University Research Center (ed.), *Summary of the National Opinion Survey of the Family in Japan*, pp. 65–77. Tokyo: University Research Center, Nihon University.

Tsuya, Noriko O., and Minja Kim Choe. 1991. *Changes in Intrafamilial Relationships and the Roles of Women in Japan and Korea*. NUPRI Research Paper Series, No. 58. Tokyo: Population Research Institute, Nihon University.

United Nations (UN), Department of International Economic and Social Affairs (DIESA), Statistical Office. 1983. *Demographic Yearbook, 1982*. New York.

van de Kaa, Dirk J. 1987. "Europe's Second Demographic Transition." *Population Bulletin* 42(1):1–57.

Vogel, Ezra F. 1971. *Japan's New Middle Class: The Salary Man and His Family in a Tokyo Suburb*. Berkeley: University of California Press.

Yamamura Kozo, and Susan B. Hanley. 1975. "*Ichi Hime, Ni Taro*: Educational Aspirations and the Decline in Fertility in Postwar Japan." *Journal of Japanese Studies* 2(1):83–125.

CHAPTER 7

Japanese Perceptions of the Family and Living Arrangements: The Trend toward Nuclearization

by Hiroshi Kawabe and Hiroaki Shimizu

Changes in Japanese attitudes about family life after World War II, the phenomenal increase in population mobility, and the aging of the Japanese population since the 1960s have led to the general view that family structure in Japan has shifted from the stem-family system to one based on the conjugal family. It is also generally thought that living arrangements have begun changing from a traditional pattern, in which parents reside with their married children, to a conjugal family pattern, in which grown children establish separate households from those of their parents—in short, that family nuclearization is becoming more common in Japan. Data from various surveys, however, do not indicate a clear trend away from the stem-family structure to the conjugal-family structure, nor do they unequivocally indicate that living arrangements are shifting from three-generation households toward the two-generation, or conjugal, model. In fact, the reverse may be true. Drawing upon survey and census data, this chapter analyzes Japanese family living arrangements from an international perspective and attempts to clarify the formative process of Japanese coresidence in order to determine whether a noticeable shift toward the conjugal-family system is actually occurring in Japan.

THE INTERRELATIONSHIP BETWEEN LIVING ARRANGEMENTS AND PERCEPTIONS OF THE FAMILY

Scholars disagree about the structure of the Japanese family and the basis of living arrangements that support daily life in Japan. Their theories about the fundamental structure of family organization fall primarily into two opposing categories. One posits that the traditional stem-family system is the fundamental family structure (e.g., Nakane, 1970:11, 35). The other holds that both the traditional stem-family system and the conjugal-family system have always coexisted (e.g., Gamō, 1978:330-331). Furthermore, both theories can be divided into two lines of argument. The first line of argument of the theory supporting the stem family as the fundamental family structure emphasizes the structural continuity of the traditional Japanese family since World War II and asserts that the stem-family system continues to be maintained and supported. The second argues that the traditional stem-family system is being transformed into a conjugal- or nuclear-family system. As for the second theory supporting two coexistent family systems, one argument holds that both the stem family and the conjugal family are continuing to be maintained and that their relative numbers vary only from region to region (e.g., Morioka, 1980:31-32). The other view is that the coexistence of the two types of living arrangements may be dissolving, and that the conjugal family may be undergoing a structural transformation to the stem-family type (e.g., Emori, 1976:53 ff.). Table 7.1 diagrams these conflicting positions.

On the basis of these views of the Japanese family, its structure can be divided into four types corresponding to the living arrangements of parents and children and their attitudes toward living together: (1) the stem family continuing from the traditional stem-family system, (2) the conjugal family emerging from the traditional stem-family system, (3) the stem family emerging from the conjugal-family system, and (4) the conjugal family continuing from the conjugal-family system.

Among them, the first type, the stem family continuing from the traditional stem-family system, is one of the basic forms of family organization ob-

Table 7.1. Four perceptions of the basic structure of the Japanese family and how it has been changing in recent decades

Basic structure	Direction of change
Stem family	No change
Stem family	Becoming predominantly conjugal
Stem and conjugal families	No change
Stem and conjugal families	Becoming predominantly stem

Japanese Perceptions of the Family and Living Arrangements

served in Japan. In this type of family, the link between generations in the *ie*, or extended-family household, system is given particular weight. The ideal type of living arrangement for this family type is permanent coresidence, which means that even after grown children marry, they continue to live with their parents. Complete coresidence means that they live under the same roof, share all household expenses, and share meals. This type of family is therefore one that is defined as having the intention to coreside permanently, based on the belief that it is always best to live together, regardless of whether the parents are in good or ill health (Table 7.2).

The second type, the conjugal family emerging from the traditional stem family, which adheres to the social norms of the *ie* system, is somewhat weak. Members of this type of family consider coresidence to be desirable, but the older and younger generations tend to live separately as long as the parents remain healthy. They do not hesitate to resume coresidence, however, if the parents fall ill or if one of the parents dies. Also included in this type is the family whose members are forced to have separate residences. In such families the parents would like to coreside with their grown children but are unable to do so because their children have jobs in other locations.

The third type, the stem family emerging from the conjugal-family system, is a family whose members coreside temporarily under certain conditions but for whom the norm is to live separately. It, too, is a rather weak type. For such a family it is desirable to have a semi-coresident dwelling arrangement, in which married children live in separate dwellings located near their parents' home so that they can share daily activities with them. This type of family is considered to have a conditional intent to coreside. Such families are more likely to share daily activities than are families of the second type, for whom physical distance often precludes interaction between the generations on a daily basis.

Table 7.2. Japanese family structure, living arrangements, and intentions

Family structure	Living arrangement	Intention
Stem family continuing from the stem family system	Permanent coresidence	To coreside permanently
Conjugal family emerging from the stem family system	Temporarily separate residences under certain conditions	Conditionally to live separately
Stem family emerging from the conjugal family system	Temporary coresidence under certain conditions	Conditionally to coreside
Conjugal family continuing from the conjugal family system	Permanently separate residences	To reside separately on a permanent basis

For the fourth family type, the conjugal family continuing from the conjugal-family system, the ideal is for the two generations of married couples to live apart in permanently separate dwellings, and for parents not to live with any of their married children. This family type is therefore defined as one having the permanent intention to live separately, or voluntarily having separate residences. Members of such families are of the opinion that it is best or more pleasant for the older and younger generations to live separately.

ACTUAL LIVING ARRANGEMENTS AND ATTITUDES TOWARD LIVING ARRANGEMENTS

Actual Living Arrangements

To clarify the prevalence of various living arrangements in Japan, it is useful to compare data on living arrangements there with data on living arrangements in the West. For this purpose, we draw primarily upon data from the 1981 International Comparative Survey on the Lives and Attitudes of Elderly People (Japan, Policy Office of the Aged, 1982); 1985 population census data (Japan, Bureau of Statistics, 1985); a 1979 survey on human values conducted in 13 countries, including Japan, the United States, England, and France (Secretariat, 1980 International Conference on Human Values, 1980); a 1986 opinion survey on the family (Japan, Public Relations Office, 1986); and the 1988 National Family Survey, conducted by the University Research Center of Nihon University and Mainichi Newspapers (University Research Center, 1989). For comparison with the recent past, we have also used data from two surveys on the elderly conducted by the Policy Office of the Aged in the mid-1970s, one on support for the elderly (Japan, Policy Office of the Aged, 1975) and the other on perspectives about old age (Japan, Policy Office of the Aged, 1977).

The International Comparative Survey on the Lives and Attitudes of Elderly People had samples of approximately 1,000 men and women of ages 60 and over in each country. The households of the respondents were classified into three categories: (1) those consisting of married couples only, (2) those consisting of parents and their married and unmarried children (that is, both two- and three-generation households), and (3) single-member households. Respondents were also divided into three age groups—the "young-old" (ages 60–69), an intermediate group (ages 70–79), and the "old-old" (ages 80+). (See Table 7.3.)

Among the Americans surveyed, approximately two-thirds of men in the "young-old" age group were living in households consisting only of married couples. Next in order of prevalence were households consisting of parents and their children (21 percent), followed by single-member households (16 percent). Among men in the "old-old" age group, the larg-

Japanese Perceptions of the Family and Living Arrangements

est proportion (50 percent) comprised those living in single-member households.

As for American women, in all three elderly age groups the largest proportions were living in single-member households (47 percent, 62 percent, and 66 percent, respectively, among the young-old, the intermediate age group, and the old-old). These differences be-tween men and women seem to reflect the two sexes' differential longevity and ages at marriage.

The pattern among English respondents was similar to that of the Americans. Most men in the 60–69 and 70–79 age groups were living in households consisting only of married couples (73 percent and 67 percent, respectively), whereas the majority of men in the old-

Table 7.3. Percentage distribution of households, by household type and by sex and age group of elderly household heads: United States, England, France, and Japan: 1981

Country and household type	Men 60–69	Men 70–79	Men 80+	Women 60–69	Women 70–79	Women 80+
United States						
One-person	15.7	25.2	50.0	46.5	62.2	66.3
Couple-only	63.8	61.3	33.3	33.5	20.9	9.8
Parents & children	20.5	13.5	16.7	20.0	16.9	23.9
All types	100.0	100.0	100.0	100.0	100.0	100.0
(No.)	(229)	(155)	(48)	(226)	(237)	(92)
England						
One-person	13.1	25.1	51.2	41.4	64.0	70.0
Couple-only	72.9	66.5	32.6	44.1	26.8	15.0
Parents & children	14.1	8.4	16.3	14.5	9.2	15.0
All types	100.0	100.0	100.0	100.0	100.0	100.0
(No.)	(199)	(167)	(43)	(297)	(261)	(43)
France						
One-person	9.9	16.7	21.3	27.8	46.0	59.8
Couple-only	63.4	72.0	61.7	45.7	30.4	7.8
Parents & children	26.7	11.3	17.0	26.5	23.6	32.4
All types	100.0	100.0	100.0	100.0	100.0	100.0
(No.)	(302)	(150)	(47)	(245)	(250)	(102)
Japan						
One-person	.1.5	3.5	4.0	9.3	9.6	4.8
Couple-only	34.2	35.3	28.0	19.6	13.6	2.4
Parents & children	64.3	61.3	68.0	71.1	76.8	92.9
Total	100.0	100.0	100.0	100.0	100.0	100.0
(No.)	(395)	(173)	(25)	(388)	(198)	(42)

Source: Japan, Policy Office of the Aged (1982: Table 4 of pp. 302, 406, 458, and 510).
Notes: Percentages may not sum exactly to 100.0 because of rounding. Households consisting of parents and children are a residual category that includes three-generation households and other types of household.

old age group (51 percent) were living alone.

Among English women in the 60–69 age group, the largest proportion (44 percent) was living in households consisting of married couples only, and nearly as many (41 percent) were living in single-member households. Among the 70–79 and 80+ age groups, however, more than half of the women (64 percent and 70 percent, respectively) were living alone.

In France, well over half (63 percent) of the men surveyed in the young-old age group were living in couple-only households; the next most common living arrangement for them was to live with their children (27 percent). Even among the oldest men (ages 80+), the majority (62 percent) were living in couple-only households, but a somewhat larger percentage lived alone than lived with their children (21 percent versus 17 percent).

Among French women, slightly fewer than half of the young-old (46 percent) were living in couple-only households (although this was the most prevalent living arrangement for them as well as for men), and about equal percentages of them were living alone and with children (28 percent and 27 percent, respectively). Among the oldest women, the largest proportion (60 percent) was living alone.

Considering these findings for the United States, England, and France, we can see that the conjugal family continuing from the conjugal-family system is the basic living arrangement for at least half of the elderly. Moving from the young-old category to the oldest age category in each country, we can infer that the death of a spouse leads to the noticeable increase in single-member households; and in the oldest age category the percentages of both men and women living with adult children are higher than in the intermediate age group even in these societies, where the conjugal family is the traditional type. It is particularly noteworthy that among women 80 years old and older, 15 percent in England, 24 percent in the United States, and more than 32 percent in France were living with their children.

In Japan, by comparison, sizable majorities of men and women in all three elderly age groups were living with their offspring. Among the oldest age group, 68 percent of men and 93 percent of women had such a living arrangement. In every age group slightly larger percentages of women than men lived with their children. The next most common pattern was for men and women to live in couple-only households, the single exception being among the oldest women, many of whom, it can be supposed, had outlived their spouses and therefore either lived with children or lived alone. Living alone was the least popular arrangement for both sexes, however, particularly for men; in no age group did it reach 10 percent.

It is apparent from the foregoing discussion that the living arrangements for elderly people in Japan are substantially different from those found in Western Europe and the United States, where the conjugal-family system prevails. In Japan, as most parents approach old age, they are encouraged to reside with their children if coresidence is a viable option.

Although it is widely believed that Japan's traditional stem-family system is in transition to the conjugal-family system, the survey data presented in Table 7.3 indicate that even in 1981 the traditional stem-family system was being maintained, particularly among women. Among the three Western populations included in the survey, the French appear to be closest to the Japanese in their attitudes toward living arrangements for the elderly.

Results from the 1985 census lend support to the view that elderly Japanese parents are being reabsorbed into family households. Table 7.4, which presents a distribution of the Japanese population by sex and type of living arrangement for four elderly age groups, shows that conjugal family households containing only married couples accounted for only approximately one-third of men and about one-fourth of women in their 60s. Among those aged 75 and over, however, the percentages living with only a spouse were slightly lower for men (26 percent) and much lower for women (5.7 percent), again probably reflecting in part the greater longevity of women. About 10 percent of both men and women in the 75 and over age group were living with children, but by far the largest proportions—58 percent among men, 73 percent among women—were residing with other family members. Single-member households were the choice (or necessity) of only 5.5 percent of men and 12 percent of women in the oldest age group.

Table 7.4. Percentage distribution of the elderly Japanese population, by household type, sex, and age group: 1985

	Men				Women			
Household (HH) type	60–64	65–69	70–74	75+	60–64	65–69	70–74	75+
Conjugal family HH								
Married couple only	32.9	36.7	35.1	26.1	27.4	21.8	14.8	5.7
Married couple & children	26.2	18.4	13.1	7.7	14.2	8.1	4.4	1.6
Father & children	1.4	1.4	1.6	2.4	0.1	0.0	0.0	0.0
Mother & children	0.3	0.1	0.1	0.0	6.6	6.7	6.9	8.0
Subtotal	60.8	56.7	49.9	36.3	48.3	36.7	26.1	15.3
HH with other family members	35.1	39.2	45.5	58.0	40.2	49.0	58.9	72.5
Single-member HH	4.0	4.1	4.6	5.5	11.3	14.0	14.9	12.0
Nonrelative-member HH	0.1	0.1	0.1	0.2	0.2	0.2	0.2	0.1
Total								
%	100.0	100.0	100.0	100.0	100.0	100.0	100.0	100.0
(No. in 10,000s)	(299)	(237)	(200)	(266)	(299)	(237)	(200)	(266)

Source: Japan, Bureau of Statistics (1985: Table 4, pp. 18–19, and Table 10, pp. 202–209).
Note: Percentages may not sum exactly to 100.0 because of rounding.

Attitudes toward Living Arrangements

Using data from the 1979 survey on human values in 13 countries (Secretariat, 1980 International Conference on Human Values, 1980), we next compare parents' attitudes toward various living arrangements in the four countries examined in the previous section for their actual living arrangements for the elderly. In response to a question about their preferences for living arrangements, respondents were given three choices of response, each beginning with the normative statement "It is best . . . ." The choices were for parents to live with one of their married children, for parents to avoid living with their married children, and for a widowed parent to live with one of his or her married children. (Because marriage is virtually universal in Japan, living with an unmarried child would not be an option for most parents.)

Solid majorities of the elderly Americans, English, and French responded that it was best for parents to live separately from their married children, whereas the overwhelming majority (89 percent) of the Japanese favored living with their married children either unconditionally or if they themselves were widowed (Table 7.5). A fifth of French respondents had an unconditional preference for living with their married children, compared with much smaller percentages of Americans (5.9 percent) and English respondents (9.3 percent). Thus, elderly persons in the United States and England clearly favor the conjugal-family system and elderly Japanese clearly favor the traditional stem-family system, whereas attitudes of elderly French lie somewhere between the two extremes but closer to the conjugal pattern.

Taking a closer look at the Japanese responses to this question about their preferred living arrangement in old age, we note that in addition to the more than half of the elderly Japanese who preferred to live with their married children under any circumstances, one-third had a conditional preference for coresidence. Thus it is possible to state that the preference for coresidence is overwhelming in Japan.

Table 7.5. Parents' attitudes about living with married children (%): United States, England, France, and Japan, 1980

Opinion	United States	England	France	Japan
It's best not to live with married children	59.4	61.0	57.6	9.5
It's best for parents to live with married children	5.9	9.3	20.5	55.4
It's best for widowed parents to live with married children	19.4	22.4	19.5	33.4
Unknown	15.4	7.3	2.3	1.7
All opinions	100.0	100.0	100.0	100.0

Source: Secretariat, 1980 International Conferences on Human Values (1980).
Note: Percentages may not sum exactly to 100.0 because of rounding.

Japanese Perceptions of the Family and Living Arrangements

A survey of adult Japanese respondents' preferences for coresidence versus separate living arrangements, conducted in 1986 by the Public Relations Office of the Prime Minister's Office, posed the question: "Generally speaking, what do you think about elderly people living with their married children?" More than half (62 percent) favored coresidence with a married son or married daughter, whereas only one-fifth thought that parents should live separately from their married children (Table 7.6). Interestingly, it was not only the elderly and middle-aged respondents who favored coresidence, but also the majority of those in their 20s and 30s.

As shown in Table 7.7, when asked about their own preferred living arrangements, a substantially greater proportion of respondents living in nuclear-family households (33 percent of those in couple-only households and 20 percent of those in two-generation households) expressed a preference for residing separately than did those coresiding in three-generation households (12 percent). It should be noted, however, that even among respondents in nuclear households, larger proportions (47 percent of those in couple-only households and 61 percent of those in two-generation households) preferred to live with a married son or daughter than to live separately. Among respondents in three-generation households, three-quarters preferred a coresidential arrangement. Thus, although a large number of respondents resided in nuclear-family households, we cannot immediately conclude that Japan's traditional stem-family system will necessarily be transformed into a conjugal-family system.

Namihira (1986:36) has made some interesting observations on the current trends in Japanese living arrangements:

The nuclear family household is the modal Japanese family structure, and people tend to regard such households as typical. Nevertheless, when they are asked about their preferred

Table 7.6. Opinions about the living arrangements of elderly people, by age group (%): Japan, 1986

Opinion	20–29	30–39	40–49	50–59	60–69	60+	70+	All ages
Elderly should live with married son and daughter-in-law	38.3	39.9	41.5	51.0	53.0	53.1	53.5	45.1
Elderly should live with married daughter and son-in-law	18.7	20.5	16.6	16.3	10.3	10.2	10.1	16.4
Elderly should live separately	16.2	20.5	20.4	17.2	23.2	21.3	17.6	19.5
Other arrangements	18.3	16.4	18.8	12.5	11.3	11.9	13.2	15.4
Don't know	8.5	2.7	2.8	2.9	2.3	3.5	5.7	3.5
All responses (%)	100.0	100.0	100.0	100.0	100.0	100.0	100.0	100.0
(No.)	(235)	(561)	(506)	(447)	(302)	(461)	(159)	(2,210)

Source: Japan, Public Relations Office (1986: Table 4, p. 118).
Note: Percentages may not sum exactly to 100.0 because of rounding.

living arrangements, the proportion of people who hope to live with their grown children increases dramatically with age.

To understand such attitudes, one should bear in mind the public's uneasiness over the current social situation. Social welfare programs are underdeveloped in Japan and the aged population is increasing at an unprecedented rate, with the result that existing programs are likely to be overcrowded and their quality to deteriorate in the near future as the impact of population aging on the society is felt more keenly.

Although people may not know explicitly what the *ie* system was like, they prefer to live out the remainder of their lives with their own children. In other words, when they imagine an ideal living situation, they seem to long for the family system enjoyed by their ancestors, even though the nuclear family has been glorified during the 30 years since the end of World War II.

On the other hand, it is plausible that current attitudes toward family formation are in transition from the traditional (inheritance) family system. The most typical preference nowadays seems to be "in youth, a nuclear family; and in old age, if it is impossible to maintain an independent lifestyle, a three-generation family."

This view seems to sum up the prevalent attitude toward family structure in Japan. If that is the case, how can there be a serious claim that the traditional stem-family system is being maintained?

Table 7.7. Preferred living arrangements of adult Japanese, by actual living arrangements (%): 1986

Preferred arrangement	Married couple only (1-generation HH)	Married couple with unmarried children (2-generation HH)	Parents with married child and spouse, plus grandchildren (3-generation HH)	Living alone	All actual living arrangements
Living with married son and daughter-in-law	35.7	41.6	61.2	31.5	45.1
Living with married daughter and son-in-law	11.2	19.3	12.7	15.2	16.1
Living separately	32.7	20.0	12.1	15.2	19.5
Other	16.7	15.8	11.5	27.2	15.4
Don't know	3.7	3.2	2.5	10.5	3.5
Total	100.0	100.0	100.0	100.0	100.0
(No.)	(294)	(1,268)	(487)	(92)	(2,141)

Source: Japan, Public Relations Office (1986: Table 4, p. 119)
Note: Percentages may not sum exactly to 100.0 because of rounding.
HH—household.

THE PROCESS OF FORMING A CORESIDENT FAMILY

Whereas the surveys examined thus far in this chapter focused on specific geographic areas of Japan or on specific household types, such as three-generation households, the 1988 National Family Survey collected information on residential patterns and attitudes from a nationally representative sample of 3,400 men and women of ages 20 and above. In 91 percent of the cases, one or both of the respondents' parents were living, and 22 percent of those parents were living with respondents. Seventy-eight percent of respondents' parents were living separately from the respondents—32 percent of them with a sibling of the respondent-household's head, 27 percent with other relatives or persons, and 19 percent alone. Thus, more than half (54 percent) of the parents were living with their own children.

In comparison, the Policy Office of the Aged's 1975 survey found that about 38 percent of respondents were living with their parents and that, among the 62 percent who reported living separately from their parents, about half were doing so to avoid living with siblings. It may be assumed from these findings that a large proportion of the respondents' parents were living with adult children. The findings from the 1988 National Family Survey therefore do not represent a major change in the prevalence of coresidence.

When respondents in the 1988 survey who were coresiding were asked with whom they coresided, 52 percent named one or both of their own parents, and 47 percent named one or both of their spouse's parents. But whereas only 10 percent reported living with their own or their spouse's father, 46 percent reported living with their own or their spouse's mother. These findings are related to the differential ages at marriage and life expectancy of men and women, which make it much more likely that a grown child will coreside with his or her mother than with the father.

When asked how long they had been coresiding, two-thirds of coresiding respondents in the 1988 survey said they had done so since the beginning of their marriage, implying lifelong coresidence. Only one-fourth responded that they had lived separately at the time of marriage and began coresidence later. Thus, lifelong coresidence is the more prevalent pattern. It is possible, however, that an increasing proportion of Japanese families will opt for eventual coresidence in the future. According to the 1977 survey conducted by the Policy Office of the Aged, for example, a large proportion of respondents favored eventual coresidence. Although only 44 percent desired to live with their parents even while the parents remained healthy, 64 percent and 71 percent, respectively, preferred to coreside when their parents' condition weakened or when the parents were alone (Policy Office of the Aged, 1977).

Finally, when coresiding respondents to the 1988 survey were asked about their main reason for coresiding with their parents, 51 percent responded that it was the first son or daughter's duty. The second most common response (given by 16 percent) was that it was the parents' desire to coreside. Other reasons cited were the desire to live near parents (8.9 percent), to support parents economically (6.2 percent), and to take care of ill parents (3.7 percent).

Taken together, these survey data indicate that coresidence is the fundamental family system in Japan. Among those Japanese who opt for eventual rather than lifelong coresidence, the most typical pattern is for adult children to move in with their parents rather than vice versa. In this type of coresident family, the eldest son's or daughter's sense of duty is the prevailing reason for coresidence. Although conjugal families exist in Japan, they are not the norm—in contrast with Western Europe and America, where the predominant family structure is conjugal rather than coresidential.

CONCLUSION

We have attempted to analyze the concepts related to living arrangements found in Japan, the actual family living arrangements in Japan and three Western societies (England, France, and the United States), and the process by which Japanese coresident families are formed. Survey and census data indicate that the conjugal-family system, in which parents live separately from their married children, is predominant in the Western societies, whereas family formation and living arrangements of the Japanese are governed by the norm of the stem family, or coresidence of parents with their married children. In the future, however, as Japan's population continues to age, increased longevity and the growing burden of providing care for the aged can be expected to lead to a structural change in the Japanese family system and living arrangements. In the past, when life expectancy was lower, the duration of the ideal three-generation family was much shorter than it is today. In the near future, the length of time that Japanese actually live in stem families is likely to increase dramatically. It is reasonable to expect that the much longer duration of the stem family will alter the concept of that family type as an ideal.

REFERENCES

Emori Itsuo. 1976. *Nihon Sonrakushakai no Kōzō* (Structure of the Japanese village community). Tokyo: Kōbundo Publishing Company.

Gamō Masao. 1978. *Nihonjin no Seikatsu Kōzō Josetsu* (An introduction to the life structure of Japanese). Tokyo: Pelican Publishing Company.

Japan, Bureau of Statistics. 1985. *Shōwa 62-nen Kokuseichōsa Daigokan (20% Chūshutsu Shūkeikekka* (1985 Population Census [20% sample tabulation]). Tokyo: Management and Co-ordination Agency.

Japan, Policy Office of the Aged. 1975. *Rōfuyō ni Kansuru Chōsa (Survey on support of the elderly).* Tokyo: Management and Coordination Agency.

———. 1977. *Rōgo Seikatsu e no Tenbō ni Kansuru Chōsa* (Survey of perspectives on old age). Tokyo: Management and Coordination Agency.

———. 1982. *Rōjin no Seikatsu to Ishiki— Kokusai Hikaku Chōsa Hōkokusho* (Report on the international comparative survey on the lives and attitudes of elderly people). Tokyo: Management and Coordination Agency.

Japan, Public Relations Office. 1986. *Kazoku-Katei ni Kansuru Yoron Chōsa* (Opinion Survey on the Family). Tokyo: Prime Minister's Office.

Morioka Kiyomi. 1980. "Kazoku to Shinzoku" (Family and kinship). In Fukutake T. (ed.), *Shakaigaku* (Sociology). Tokyo: Yūshindō-Kōbun Publishing Company.

Nakane Chie. 1970. *Kazoku no Kōzō—Shakai-jinruigakuteki Bunseki* (Family structure—Social anthropological analysis). Tokyo: Tokyo University Press.

Namihira Emiko. 1986. *Kurashi no Naka no Bunkajinruigaku* (Cultural anthropology in daily life). Tokyo: Fukutake Publishing Company.

Secretariat, 1980 International Conference on Human Values. 1980. *13 Kakoku Kachikan Chōsa Deitā-Bukku* (Data book on human values in 13 countries). Tokyo: The Leisure Development Center.

University Research Center. 1989. *Gendai Kazoku no Seikatsukōdō ni Kansuru Zenkokuchōsa Hōkokusho* (Report of the national opinion survey of contemporary family life in Japan). Tokyo: Nihon University.

CHAPTER 8

A Structural Study of Spouse Selection in Japan

by Yasuo Natsukari

One can examine the conditions for spouse selection from the vantage point of demography, examining the balance of men and women in a population; in terms of economic and social conditions, by considering economic trends, changes in legal systems, social streams, and values; or from the psychological or physiological viewpoint, taking into account such personal characteristics of prospective spouses as disposition and appearance. In this chapter I approach the issue of spouse selection from the social viewpoint and use structural analysis to examine it within the context of social relationships, which form the foundation of the Japanese social structure. By structural analysis I refer to the distribution of marriage within the population and the differences and similarities in the social backgrounds of men and women who meet, get to know each other, and marry (Blau, 1975).

I begin by examining trends in the Japanese marriage pattern. Rather than focusing solely on the criteria for spouse selection or the circumstances in which individuals meet and form spousal relationships, this portion of the chapter focuses on differences in the social positions of Japanese men and women and on whether social position helps or hinders spouse selection. The analysis is based primarily on results from the 1988 National Family Survey. Next, I consider the conditions in which people meet and form spousal relationships, and on criteria that men and women consider important in a spouse. I also discuss differences in the social positions of men and women, the relationship between marital status and social acceptance, whether social status helps or hinders spouse selection, and differences and similarities in social backgrounds of men and women who meet, get to know each other, and marry. The analysis will identify various forms of Japanese social differentiation—in other words, describe the state of the social structure.

MARRIAGE PATTERNS AND ATTITUDES TOWARD MARRIAGE

Before analyzing the conditions and factors affecting spouse selection, it is useful to consider Japanese marriage patterns and trends. Vital statistics, census data, and the results of several surveys shed light on recent changes in the pattern of universal marriage.

Continuity and Change in the Marriage Pattern

Table 8.1 and Figure 8.1, which present trends in Japan's postwar marriage rate, show that the rate fell from 12.0 marriages per 1,000 population in 1947 to the prewar (1935) rate of 8.0 by 1955, then rose gradually to 10.0 in 1970. After 1970, however, the rate dropped steadily, reaching 5.8 in 1988. Overall, the marriage rate was cut almost in half in just 18 years.

The rise and fall in the number of marriages over the same period corresponded to the changes in the marriage rate. In 1947 that number was approximately 930,000. It fell to approximately 710,000 in 1955, topped 1 million in 1970, dropped back down to around 711,000 in 1986, and then plunged to around 700,000 in 1987, to mark an all-time low. It would be rash to conclude from these trends that the Japanese pattern of universal marriage has been destroyed and is being replaced by a trend toward single life. Nevertheless, the downward trend in both the marriage rate and the number of mar-

Table 8.1. Numbers of marriages and the marriage rate: Japan, selected years, 1935–88

Year	Marriages	Marriage rate per 1,000 population
1935	556,730	8.0
1947	934,170	12.0
1950	715,081	8.6
1955	714,861	8.0
1960	866,115	9.3
1965	954,852	9.7
1970	1,029,405	10.0
1975	941,628	8.5
1980	774,702	6.7
1985	735,850	6.1
1986	710,962	5.9
1987	696,173	5.7
1988	707,716	5.8

Source: Japan, Ministry of Health and Welfare, Statistics and Information Department (various years).

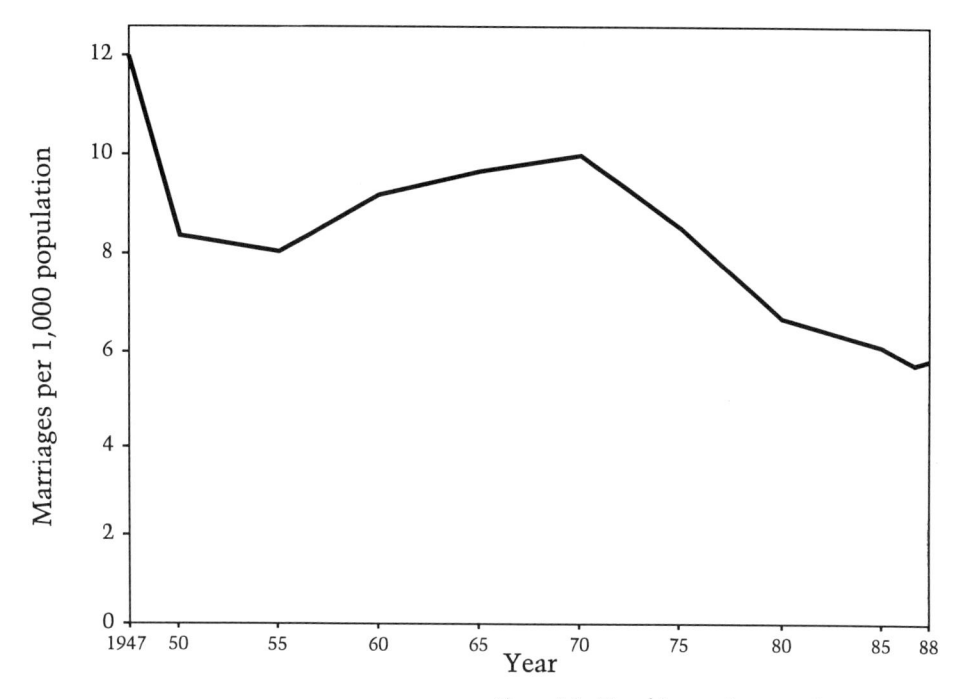

A Structural Study of Spouse Selection in Japan

Figure 8.1. Trend in marriage rate: Japan, 1947–88
Source: Japan, Ministry of Health and Welfare, Statistics and Information Department (various years).

riages since 1980 indicates a rise in the number of single persons as well as a change in the timing of marriage.

These changes in the marriage pattern can be clarified by observing changes in the percentages of single (never-married) men and women by age group. The percentage of women single in the 20–24 age group fluctuated around 68 percent from 1955 to 1975; then in 1980 it increased to 77 percent and in 1985 jumped to 81 percent (Figure 8.2 and Table 8.2). The percentage single in the 25–29 age group was around 21 percent in 1955. After rising and then dipping slightly between 1960 and 1970, it began a steady rise, reaching 24 percent in 1980 and nearly 31 percent in 1985. The proportion single in the 30–34 age group, which was hovering around 7–9 percent until 1980, passed the 10 percent mark in 1985. The proportion of women single in their 40s has remained at around 4–5 percent since 1970. The proportion of women remaining single throughout their lives (the average percentage of those over age 50) remained at around 1–2 percent between 1955 and 1970, increased to around 2.5 percent in 1975 and 1980, and then rose to 3.1 percent in 1985.

The increase in the proportion of single women is quite apparent among

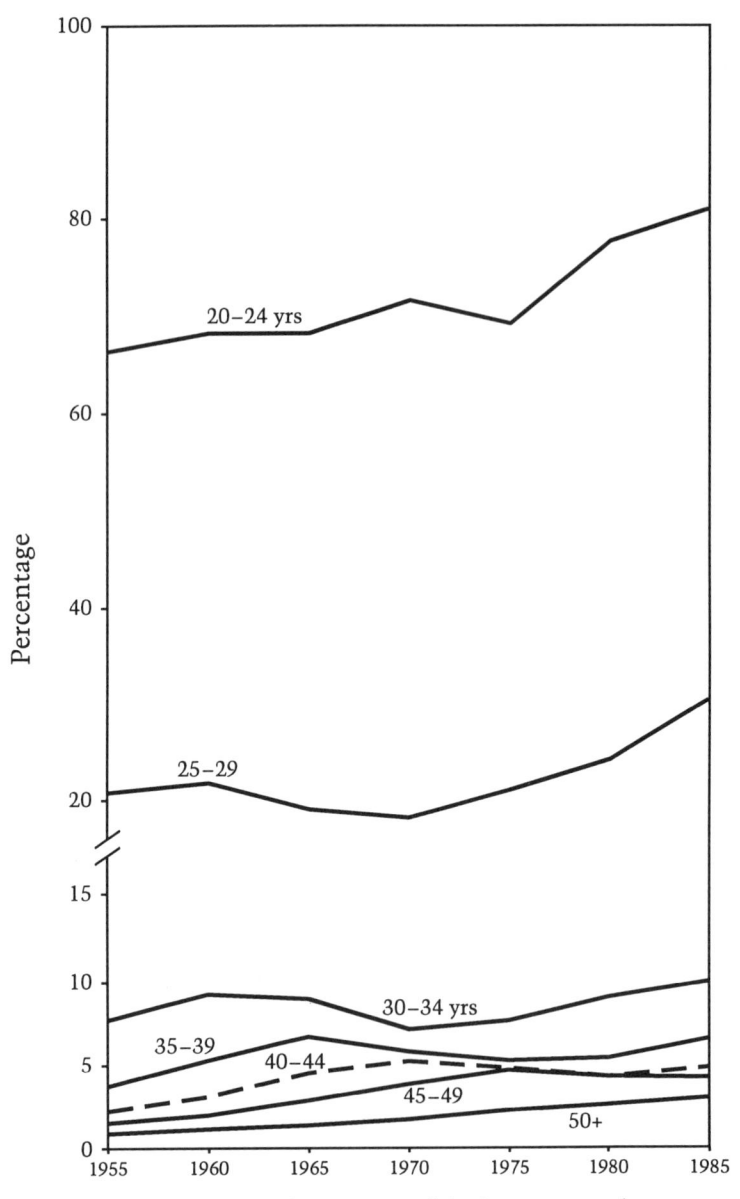

Figure 8.2. Trends in the percentage of women single, by age group: Japan, 1955–85
Source: Japan, Management and Coordination Agency, Bureau of Statistics (various years).

the younger age groups. This change is related to a rising average age at marriage among Japanese women, and it is partly responsible for the decline in Japan's birth rate. The gradual increase in the proportion of single women who remain single suggests that growing numbers of Japanese women prefer not to marry, thus leading to an increase in the number of one-person households occupied by older single women.

In contrast with women, men of all age groups except those 20–24 and those 50 and over experienced major increases in the percentage single between 1975 and 1985. Notably, the proportions single rose from 48 to 61 percent in the 25–29 age group, doubled (rising from 14 to 28 percent) in the 30–34 age group, and more than doubled (rising from 6.1 to 14.2 percent) in the 35–39 age group (Table 8.3 and Figure 8.3). Although the proportion of men remaining single throughout their lives rose slightly between 1980 and 1985, it was still only about 2 percent. The proportions of single men, excluding the percentage of men remaining single throughout their lives, were higher than those of women in all age groups in 1985. The rise in the proportions of single men at various ages indicates an accelerating pace of delayed marriage.

The data on proportions single at various ages reveal a difference in mar-

Table 8.2. Percentage of single women, by age group: Japan, 1955–85

Year	20–24	25–29	30–34	35–39	40–44	45–49	50+
1955	66.5	20.6	7.9	3.9	2.3	1.7	1.0
1960	68.3	21.6	9.4	5.5	3.2	2.1	1.3
1965	68.1	19.0	9.0	6.8	4.7	3.0	1.5
1970	71.6	18.1	7.2	5.8	5.3	4.0	1.8
1975	69.2	20.9	7.7	5.3	5.0	4.9	2.4
1980	77.0	24.0	9.1	5.5	4.4	4.4	2.7
1985	81.4	30.6	10.4	6.6	4.9	4.4	3.1

Source: Japan, Management and Coordination Agency, Bureau of Statistics (various years).

Table 8.3. Percentage of single men, by age group: Japan, 1955–85

Year	20–24	25–29	30–34	35–39	40–44	45–49	50+
1955	90.2	41.1	9.1	3.1	1.7	1.3	0.9
1960	91.6	46.1	9.9	3.6	2.0	1.4	1.0
1965	90.3	45.7	11.1	4.2	2.4	1.7	1.1
1970	90.0	46.5	11.7	4.7	2.8	1.9	1.1
1975	88.0	48.3	14.3	6.1	3.7	2.5	1.3
1980	91.5	55.1	21.5	8.5	4.7	3.1	1.4
1985	92.1	60.4	28.1	14.2	7.4	4.7	1.9

Source: Japan, Management and Coordination Agency, Bureau of Statistics (various years).

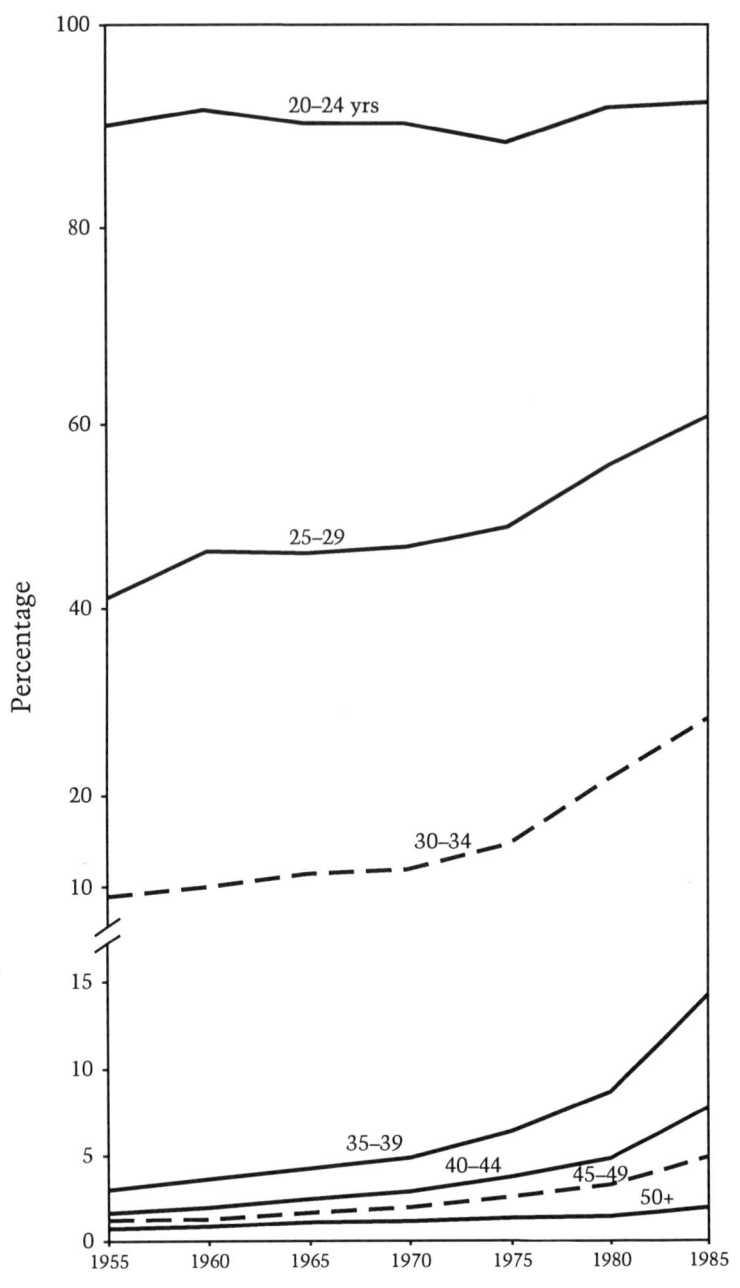

Figure 8.3. Trends in the percentage of men single, by age group: Japan, 1955–85
Source: Japan, Management and Coordination Agency, Bureau of Statistics (various years).

riage trends between men and women. In the case of women, the increase in proportions single has been greatest for those in their 20s, among whom the rise has been sharpest since 1980. In the case of men, the rise in proportions single has been most significant between the ages of 25 and 39 and the upward trend has been most apparent since 1975. Thus, 1975 for men and 1980 for women marked a significant shift toward delayed marriage among younger Japanese. The extremely low proportions of single men and women in the 50 and older age group indicate that the Japanese custom of universal marriage has been maintained.

Given the rise in the proportions single, it is interesting to speculate whether single people between the ages of 20 and 30 today—those in the age groups most likely to undermine Japan's universal marriage pattern—intend to marry. In the next section, we turn to a review of survey results indicating single men and women's future marriage intentions.

Intention of Marrying

The National Family Survey, conducted by the University Research Center of Nihon University and the Mainichi Newspapers in 1988, collected, along with other data, information about the intentions of single persons to marry. Among men and women who were currently single, only 1 percent of those in their 20s and none of those in their 30s said that they wanted to remain single throughout their lives. This result indicates a universal intention to marry. Among single men in their 20s, 77 percent wanted to marry by the age of 29 and 11 percent wanted to do so by the age of 34. Among women in their 20s, 81 percent wanted to marry by age 29 and 5 percent wanted to do so by age 34. Thus, large majorities of both young men and young women wanted to marry before turning 30.

Among single men in their 30s, 50 percent wanted to marry before age 34 and 19 percent by age 39. Twenty-two percent wanted to marry "at any age" (compared with only 3 percent of men in their 20s). Among women in their 30s, 25 percent wanted to marry by age 34, 19 percent by age 39, and 56 percent at any time (compared with 9 percent of single women in their 20s). It therefore appears that whereas men prefer to marry by a specific age (e.g., by age 34), women are more willing to marry at any age. The survey results also showed that single people in their 30s continued to have a strong desire to marry. Thus, the increase in the proportions of men and women single does not appear to be due to a decision to refuse marriage altogether but rather to a decision to postpone marriage or to a lack of opportunity.

Data on intentions to marry were also collected in the Ninth Fertility Survey of 1987 and in the Eighth Fertility Survey of 1982, conducted by the Institute of Population Problems (Japan, Ministry of Health and Welfare, IPP, 1989). Respondents to those surveys were unmarried Japanese men and women between the ages of 18 and 34. Valid responses were obtained from 4,987 respondents (86 percent of those randomly selected) in 1982 and from 6,074 respondents (84 percent) in 1987.

Table 8.4, which compares responses of three age groups of single Japanese to a question about whether they intended to marry eventually or never to marry, shows that in each age group, except for women between ages 30 and 34, the percentage of respondents who intended eventually to marry declined between 1982 and 1987, whereas the percentage who said they would never marry increased slightly. The drop in percentages intending to marry was statistically significant among men in the 20–24 and 30–34 age groups. In 1987, 93–94 percent of men and 92–95 percent of women in their 20s said they would marry eventually, whereas only 3.6 percent of men and 3–6 percent of women under 30 said that they would never marry. In the 30–34 age group, however, 87 percent of the men and 76 percent of the women surveyed said they intended to marry eventually, whereas 8 percent of the men and nearly 17 percent of the women responded that they would never marry. The figures for those who said they would never marry indicate a realistic assessment of their chances of ever marrying, which did not surface in the 1988 National Family Survey. The expectation of remaining single represented a minority of respondents in the 1987 Fertility Survey, however, and one can therefore assume that Japan's pattern of universal marriage will not change radically in the future.

Changes in Marriage Types and Opportunities for Marriage

Using data from the 1988 National Family Survey and the Ninth Fertility Survey, in this section I first examine evidence

Table 8.4. Intentions to marry, by sex and age group (%): single Japanese, 1982 and 1987

	Ages 20–24		Ages 25–29		Ages 30–34	
Sex and intention	1982	1987	1982	1987	1982	1987
Men						
Will marry eventually	97.1	92.6	95.8	93.9	92.4	86.9
Will never marry	1.2	3.6	2.9	3.6	5.1	8.3
Don't know	1.7	3.8	1.4	2.5	2.4	4.8
Women						
Will marry eventually	97.5	95.1	92.5	91.8	72.7	75.6
Will never marry	1.9	2.8	4.0	5.6	23.6	16.9
Don't know	0.6	2.2	3.5	2.6	3.6	7.5

Source: Japan, Ministry of Health and Welfare, IPP (1989:9).
Note: Percentages may not sum exactly to 100.0 because of rounding.

that arranged (*miai*) marriages have become less frequent and love (*ren'ai*) matches more frequent among the Japanese. Then I consider the opportunities for prospective partners to meet and turn my attention to a segment of the population having difficulty finding spouses.

In the National Family Survey conducted by Nihon University, among married people of both sexes the proportion of love marriages was inversely related to age. For example, among married people in their 20s, 82 percent of men and 84 percent of women had married for love, whereas the respective figures for those who had arranged marriages were 18 percent and 11 percent (Figure 8.4). Conversely, in the age group of 60 and over,

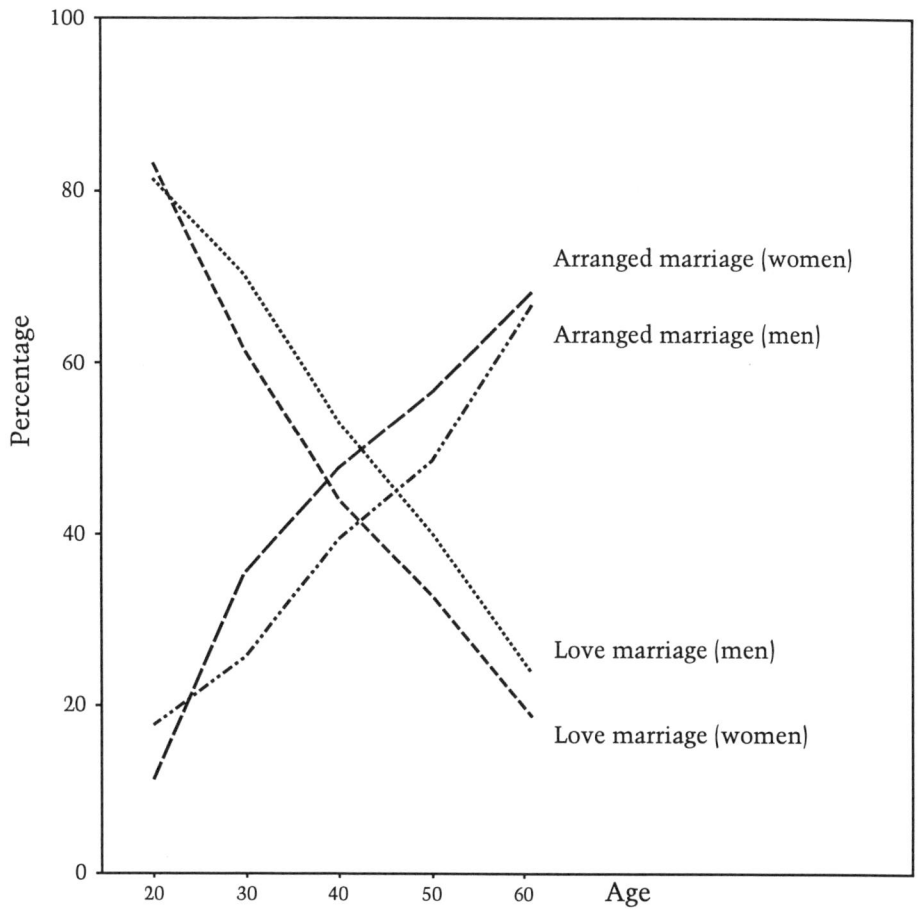

Figure 8.4. Prevalence of marriage type among married men and women, by age group: Japan, 1988
Source: Unpublished National Family Survey data.

70 percent of both men and women had arranged marriages, whereas roughly 20 percent had married for love. Among those in their 50s, approximately 50 percent of the men and 60 percent of the women had arranged marriages, while 40 and 30 percent, respectively, had love matches. Thus, for those in the 50 and over age groups, arranged marriages were clearly the prevalent form of marriage. Among men in their 40s, love marriages were more prevalent than arranged marriages (about 50 and 40 percent, respectively); but for women in their 40s, arranged marriages were still more prevalent (the same percentages being reversed). The shift to a preponderance of love matches occurred for women in the 30–39 age group.

A similar trend toward more love marriages among younger people is evident in the findings from the Ninth Fertility Survey conducted by the Institute of Population Problems in 1987. Thus, it is safe to conclude that a large-scale shift from arranged to love marriages has been occurring in Japan.

The new pattern of marriages raises questions about the process of spouse selection in contemporary Japan and in particular how men and women who wish to form love matches meet one another. Marriages based on the feelings and free choice of individuals differ from those in which a spouse is selected by parents in accordance with the tradition of maintaining the family (or *ie*) lineage. Love marriages are also perceived as unions based on egalitarian social intercourse and extensive social mobility characteristic of an open and elastic social structure. Even in such social structures, however, some young people may find it difficult to marry for love precisely because of their social position.

The fact is that not all people have equal opportunities to meet members of the opposite sex and form relationships leading to marriage. One tends to assume that everyone has an equal chance of falling in love, but individual opportunities for social contacts vary, depending on a variety of circumstances, including a person's social position. In my own case, for example, my chances of marrying a Thai were zero because I had neither Thai friends nor opportunities to have social contact with them.

In Japan today, group affiliations have become increasingly important means for prospective spouses to meet (Japan, Ministry of Health and Welfare, IPP, 1988:25). Nearly one of every two women responding to the Ninth Fertility Survey had met her husband at their work place, and one in four had met through friends or siblings (Table 8.5). Overall, for nearly 90 percent of the respondents, belonging to some kind of group had afforded opportunities for meeting others.

The cross-sectional survey findings suggest some interesting trends in the circumstances in which people meet their spouses. Compared with couples married during the latter half of the 1960s, three times as many respondents married after

1985 said they had met their spouses at school, whereas the proportion who had known their spouses from childhood or had met through neighbors was sharply lower. This change occurred because social relations within the regional community have weakened and neighborhood relationships have become less close, whereas coeducation and the enrollment of larger numbers of women in institutions of higher learning in recent years have provided more opportunities for contact between men and women within school environments.

Given that the work place was by far the most frequently mentioned environment for contact leading to love marriages and that in all marriage cohorts the percentage of couples who had met through a group interest or club activity was stable, while the percentage who had met at school was growing, I decided to examine more closely the relationship between group affiliation and love marriages in Japan. I was interested in doing so because the notion that group affiliation leads to romantic marriage obscures a structural factor that may limit opportunities for marriage or even prevent it for some young people. By "structural factor" I refer to an unequal distribution of young men and women having similar social characteristics. That is, group affiliations based on occupational position, number of years of education, group interests and activities, and so on divide people into two groups, those who have plentiful opportunities for spouse selection and those with limited opportunities.

For example, a person may not work in a place (e.g., in an office or factory) that gives him or her opportunities to meet a prospective partner for a love marriage. Similarly, fewer years of schooling limit a person's chances of joining certain group activities. Thus, some individuals have more opportunities than others to meet people socially, and this leads to differences in their chances of meeting someone whom they might wish to marry. The more groups that a person belongs to, the more opportunities exist for social inter-

Table 8.5. How married women met their husbands (%): Japan, 1988

Year of marriage	In school	In work place	From childhood, through neighbors	Through group interest or club activity	Through friends or siblings	On the street, while traveling
1965–69	2.9	50.0	7.6	6.6	25.4	7.5
1970–74	6.0	53.7	4.5	6.9	22.0	6.9
1975–79	7.7	46.3	4.1	7.0	27.3	7.6
1980–84	9.0	43.0	3.4	5.6	29.5	9.5
After 1985	8.9	44.5	1.6	8.7	27.7	8.7
Mean	6.5	47.9	5.2	6.6	25.9	7.8

Source: Japan, Ministry of Health and Welfare, IPP (1988:25).

change. The work place, group social activities, and schools are settings that typically stimulate such interchange.

Among those whose social contacts are limited are men who work in relative isolation, such as farmers, fishermen, and foresters. Young men in these primary industries are especially likely to have had only the minimal required schooling and to work in villages that are cut off from major metropolitan areas. One of the most serious social problems today in such villages is the shortage of young unmarried women. Thus, many young Japanese men lack the opportunity to marry not only because of their personal attributes, but also because of demographic and structural factors. The recent increase in love marriages, because they are based on social relationships, may cause some young people to experience difficulty in marrying, in particular those with limited opportunities for meeting persons of the opposite sex having a similar position in the social structure. The lack of social mechanisms for encouraging contacts between the sexes at home, at school, or in the neighborhood has given rise to a group of young people who do not have an opportunity to fall in love.

A person's schooling and occupation not only provide opportunities and a setting for social contacts, they are extremely important yardsticks by which men and particularly women themselves choose a spouse. In the next section, I turn to an examination, based on data from the 1988 National Family Survey, of five social conditions related to marriage and possible obstacles to marriage inherent in those conditions. These are the criteria that men and women use to select marriage partners.

SOCIAL CRITERIA
FOR SPOUSE SELECTION

The 1988 National Family Survey included questions about the relative importance of five social criteria involved in spouse selection—educational level, occupation, income, religion, and family lineage. The degree of importance attached by respondents to each criterion indicated how limiting a factor it had been in the selection of their mates. Tables 8.6 and 8.7 show the percentages of men and women, by age and educational level respectively, who considered the criteria to be important or very important. Among all age groups (the youngest being 20–29), nearly one-fourth of men and one-third of women considered the educational level of their spouse to be an important or very important criterion (Table 8.6). In all age groups, fewer men than women considered their spouse's educational level to be important. The percentage regarding it as important was lowest (17 percent) among men in their

20s, but among women in that age group it was highest (36 percent). This indicates a major difference between men and women, even within the same age group, in their attitudes toward the importance of a spouse's educational level. Because people tend to be better educated now than in the past, a man with little education is at a disadvantage in the marriage market.

This becomes even more apparent when respondents are classified by educational level (Table 8.7). Whereas about one-fifth of male and female junior high school graduates and male graduates of senior high school and junior college considered the educational level of their spouse to be important, among female high school graduates and male university graduates the proportion was one-third. In addition, 43 percent of female junior college graduates and 70 percent of female university graduates regarded their spouse's educational level to be important. Thus, more women than men considered education to be an important criterion for a marriage partner, and

Table 8.6. Criteria for spouse selection, by age and sex: Japan, 1988
(% of those for whom a specified criterion was important or very important)

Age group	Education Men	Education Women	Occupation Men	Occupation Women	Income Men	Income Women	Religion Men	Religion Women	Family lineage Men	Family lineage Women
60+	25.7	30.4	35.7	64.5	32.9	66.0	24.1	20.5	26.5	25.8
50–59	27.9	30.2	37.4	67.9	41.1	72.8	25.6	18.5	20.1	19.7
40–49	20.8	32.3	40.8	75.0	35.6	84.3	27.8	21.7	15.5	20.6
30–39	23.6	32.6	28.9	69.9	28.9	81.6	25.3	25.8	14.6	14.6
20–29	17.4	36.2	27.4	75.8	21.3	87.0	23.3	21.7	12.0	17.3
Mean	23.3	32.5	34.6	70.6	32.9	78.3	25.4	22.0	18.2	19.6

Source: National Family Survey data.

Table 8.7. Criteria for spouse selection, by educational level and sex: Japan, 1988
(% of those for whom a specified criterion was important or very important)

Respondent's educational level	Education Men	Education Women	Occupation Men	Occupation Women	Income Men	Income Women	Religion Men	Religion Women	Family lineage Men	Family lineage Women
Junior high school graduate	18.6	21.2	37.7	60.8	41.1	70.3	25.6	18.2	18.3	18.0
Senior high school graduate	21.8	31.7	33.4	73.8	34.7	81.6	23.8	22.3	18.4	20.6
Junior college or technical school graduate	16.8	43.0	34.6	75.8	30.8	82.7	13.1	25.0	9.4	19.2
University graduate	34.5	69.9	34.0	76.2	20.1	77.8	34.1	31.1	21.3	23.8

Source: National Family Survey data.

highly educated women were the most likely to have that view. Differences in educational level therefore constitute a strong barrier to marriage between female university graduates and men with only a junior high school education.

Compared with those who thought educational level was important in a spouse, even more respondents to the National Family Survey—35 percent of men and 71 percent of women—held that occupation was an important criterion for choosing a wife or husband (Table 8.6). The proportion of men considering their wives' occupation to be important, however, was lowest among the younger age groups (27 and 29 percent, respectively, among those in their 20s and 30s), whereas the highest proportion of women (76 percent) who considered their husbands' occupation to be important was among those in their 20s. This figure was nearly three times as high as the equivalent figure for men in the same age group.

By educational level (Table 8.7), 38 percent of male junior high school graduates considered their wives' occupation to be important (this was the highest figure for men), whereas the proportions attaching importance to their wives' occupation among men of other educational levels were close to the average of 34 percent for men. Among women, 61 percent of junior high school graduates considered occupation to be important—the lowest proportion for women but still far above the proportions for men. As with the educational criterion, the proportion of women believing that occupation was an important criterion for their marriage partner rose in direct relation to their own educational level. This was particularly evident among women university graduates, 76 percent of whom considered their husbands' occupation to be important.

These survey results indicate that Japanese women consider a husband's occupation to be as important or even more so than his educational level. For men, this preference represents a barrier to marriage erected by women. The differences between the two sexes in the importance placed on the spouse's occupation indicates that women still rely on men to be the providers after marriage and points to a characteristic structural feature of Japanese society, namely, that women define the quality of family life in terms of their husbands' occupation. This tendency underscores the traditional relationship that continues to exist between men and women. The finding that the index of similarity in the educational backgrounds of husbands and wives rises in direct relation to women's educational level suggests that, for them, higher education is related to a desire to secure a high social and economic position through marriage.

What kinds of occupation make it difficult for men to marry? Our group did not directly investigate this topic; but, as I indicated earlier, farming, fishing, and forestry are occupations that do not usually afford opportunities for men to meet women.

For both men and women, income was an important attribute in a spouse. As Table 8.6 shows, 33 percent of men and 78 percent of women in the National Family Survey rated it as important. The age groups with the highest proportions considering it important were men in their 50s (41 percent) and women in their 20s (87 percent). The most pronounced difference in attitudes toward income for men was between those in their 50s and those in their 20s: only half as many men in their 20s as their older counterparts considered their wives' income to be important. Among women, the largest difference, around 20 percent, was between those in their 60s or older and those in their 20s; but the relationship with age was reversed. In other words, the smallest proportion of men (21 percent) who considered their spouses' income to be important was among those in their 20s, whereas the largest proportion (nearly 90 percent) of women in their 20s considered it an important criterion for spouse selection. This means that four times as many women as men in the age group most likely to be contemplating marriage rated a prospective spouse's income as important or very important.

Although it is natural for individuals to consider income, which provides the economic foundation for family life, important when considering a prospective marriage partner, how can a difference of more than 65 percent between men and women in the youngest age group be explained? Simply put, income, like occupation, reflects the central role assumed by men in the traditional Japanese marriage. The difference between men's and women's responses thus reflects women's dependence on men and their preference for economic stability derived from marriage. In structural terms, it means that both the men and the women surveyed realized, at least subconsciously, that the husband's social and economic status determines the couple's status after marriage. From that viewpoint, the survey results related to occupation and income indicate that the traditional gender roles and authority structure in Japanese households remain unchanged. If we interpret these results from the perspective of structuralism (Levi-Strauss, 1963), such acceptance of gender roles can be said to represent the "reality of an unconsciousness" or "the unconsciousness infrastructure" underlying the Japanese social structure.

Next, let us consider religion as a criterion for spouse selection. This variable, which classified respondents by religion or sect and according to the strength of their religious beliefs, can be regarded as an indicator of social position. Only one out of four or five respondents to the 1988 National Family Survey assigned importance to religion-based social position as a criterion for choosing a spouse (Table 8.6). By age group, the largest proportion of those who considered the religion of their spouse to be important were men in their 40s and women in their 30s, but differences among age groups were not substantial and no uniform trends were suggested by the results.

By educational level (Table 8.7), the largest proportion of those placing importance on religion was among university graduates, roughly one in three of whom considered it an important criterion for their spouse. Accordingly, in Japan a difference in religious affiliation does not generally constitute a serious barrier to spouse selection.

The last criterion to be examined is social standing or lineage. If a large proportion of respondents considered this to be an important factor in spouse selection, it would indicate the persistence of the traditional view of marriage as primarily a union of two families, or *ie*, and one that placed more importance on *ie* groups than on individuals. This view of marriage implies approval of a social structure ranked according to familial lineage. In such a structure, a family's pedigree restricts the freedom of offspring to have personal contact with persons outside their own class and is an impediment to intermarriage.

Viewed from this vantage point, family lineage is no longer a strong structural feature of Japanese society. Although one out of four respondents of ages 60 and over considered family lineage to be important in the selection of a spouse, in the younger age groups fewer than 20 percent rated it as important (Table 8.6). This was particularly the case among men, whose tendency to consider family lineage important showed a consistent inverse relationship to age. This finding indicates that the traditional practice of selecting a spouse on the basis of family lineage is weakening and that Japan's social structure is becoming more open and elastic. Nonetheless, among university graduates, nearly one-fourth of women and more than one-fifth of men considered family lineage to be important, so that it must be noted that highly educated Japanese care more about social position based on *ie* groups than do those of other educational levels (Table 8.7).

The analysis of respondents' attitudes toward the five criteria for spouse selection has revealed a consistent pattern among younger women and women with higher educational levels. More than others in the sample, such women attached importance to education, occupation, and income as criteria for choosing a spouse. This finding can be interpreted as evidence that Japanese women remain dependent on their husbands economically and socially. The findings also suggest, however, that, especially among younger Japanese, the choice of marriage partner is regarded as a personal decision and is no longer influenced by consideration of family connections, which traditionally dictated spouse selection.

SUMMARY AND CONCLUSION

A review of the postwar Japanese marriage pattern as indicated by marriage rates, proportions of women and men single at various ages, marriage intentions, and types of marriage indicate major changes in the pattern in recent years. Although marriage remains virtually universal, the marriage rate has declined since 1970 to the lowest level on record. This change is due to an older average age at marriage among both men and women. Most Japanese intend to marry eventually, but a significant percentage of women in their 30s say they will never marry—either because they reject marriage or because they may realize their chances of doing so are small at that age. These changes from traditionally early marriage and universal expectations of marriage, especially among women, are the subject of current interest in Japan.

The changes in marriage pattern are known to be related to the tendency of young women to place stricter conditions upon marriage today than in the past. Analysis of data from the National Family Survey of 1988 revealed that younger women considered three personal characteristics—education, occupation, and income—to be important in spouse selection, whereas as a group they placed less importance on the traditional value of family (*ie*) lineage (as did younger men). This marks a shift in social values from emphasis on the relationship between the families of the couple to emphasis on the personal attributes of the individuals who marry. Moreover, younger Japanese appear to seek a more equal partnership in married life.

The diminished importance that young Japanese women attach to the *ie* and its lineage can be understood as a result of their increased awareness of themselves as individuals and of their growing economic, social, and psychological independence. Nevertheless, women's desire to pursue personal goals tends to create obstacles to marriage. Considerably higher proportions of female than of male university graduates interviewed in the National Family Survey regarded educational level, occupation, and income as important criteria in a spouse, thus narrowing their choices of marriage partner. My colleagues and I have characterized this group of women as active and difficult to marry, and we describe the group of men who cannot live up to the women's high standards as passive and at a disadvantage in marrying.

In conclusion, Japanese society does not appear to have structural impediments to universal marriage. Differences in education, occupation, or ethnic background may limit opportunities for social contact between single men and women, however; and as the emphasis moves away from arranged marriages and marriages joining families (*ie*) to marriages based on love and the free choice of individuals, these structural factors may affect the pattern of universal marriage in Japan. The importance that young women are placing on social criteria (especially income, occupation, and education) in spouse selection is an indication of this changing pattern. On the one hand, the shift in emphasis from family groups to individuals threatens the traditional Japanese social structure. On the other, it may lead to the creation of new social relationships. The Japanese social and cultural systems can thus be said to be facing an era of major change.

REFERENCES

Blau, Peter M. 1975. "Parameters of Social Structure." In Peter M. Blau (ed.), *Approaches to the Study of Social Structure,* pp. 220–253. New York: Free Press.

Japan, Ministry of Health and Welfare, Institute of Population Problems (IPP). 1988. *Marriage and Fertility in Present-Day Japan: The Ninth Japanese National Fertility Survey,* Vol. 1. Tokyo.

———. 1989. *Attitudes toward Marriage and the Family among Unmarried Japanese Youth: The Ninth Japanese Fertility Survey,* Vol. 2. Tokyo.

Japan, Ministry of Health and Welfare, Statistics and Information Department. Various years. *Vital Statistics of Japan.* Tokyo: Minister's Secretariat.

Japan, Management and Coordination Agency, Bureau of Statistics. Various years. *Population Census of Japan.* Tokyo: Prime Minister's Office.

Levi-Strauss, Claude. 1963. *Structural Anthropology.* New York: Basic Books.

Morioka Kiyomi and Takashi Mochizuki. 1984. *Atarashii Kazokushakaigaku* (New family sociology). Tokyo: Baihukan.

CHAPTER 9

Middle-Aged Japanese and Their Parents: Coresidence and Contact

by Linda G. Martin and Noriko O. Tsuya

In the ideal Japanese stem family, the eldest son takes his bride into the home of his parents, with whom they live until the parents die. Other offspring form their own households upon marriage. When the parents do not have a son, the eldest daughter may bring her husband into the parental home, where he may be formally adopted as a son. Increasingly, however, these ideal arrangements are not achieved or, if they are, may involve tensions.

Research on the attitudes of the elderly about whom they want to have take care of them if they become unable to care for themselves indicates a departure from the ideal arrangement of living with the eldest son and his wife. Data from Japan's 1988 National Family Survey indicate that 36 percent of the Japanese over age 60 wanted to have their spouses take care of them, although there were differences by sex of the respondent. More than half of the men named their spouses, whereas less than one-fourth of the women did so. The first choice of the elderly women was a daughter-in-law or son (32 percent), but 21 percent named their own daughters. Younger women expressed an even greater preference for future care by daughters.

Such attitudes about relying on one's spouse rather than on one's children and about turning to a daughter for assistance rather than to a son or his wife are consistent with the observed change in coresidence behavior. Between 1975 and 1985, married elderly showed a declining tendency to live with their children. In 1975, for example, 68 percent of married men between the ages of 70 and 74 were living with their children, but by 1985 only 54 percent were doing so (Hirosima, 1987). Between 1980 and 1985 there was a decline in the extent to which Japanese men of ages 40–54 were living with their own parents but a slight increase in the incidence of such men living with their wives' parents. Of course, mutual support and interaction across the generations can occur without coresidence. It could be that increasing numbers of younger and older Japanese are opting for "intimacy at a distance," as Western elderly are thought to have done. With additional economic resources, they may be purchasing more privacy.

The issue of intergenerational family relations is of special concern in Japan, where the population is aging more rapidly than any other on earth. The government is concerned that the public sector will increasingly be expected to provide assistance to the elderly that was previously provided by the family (Martin, 1989a). In this chapter we use logit analysis to investigate the extent to which married Japanese men and women between the ages of 30 and 59 live with their parents and, in particular, how socioeconomic and demographic variables are associated with coresidence. Among the questions we address are: Are those with higher socioeconomic status more or less likely to coreside? Are urban and rural residence associated with different coresidence behaviors? Are firstborn offspring more likely to live with their parents than others? Does the birth order of the spouse and the survival of the spouse's parents affect the extent to which middle-aged Japanese live with their own parents? Does parents' marital status affect coresidence? Are couples in arranged marriages more or less likely than others to coreside with their parents? Finally, how do all these relations differ for sons and daughters?

For those who do coreside, we also present information on the stage of the life cycle at which coresidence began, who moved in with whom, the stated reason for coresidence, and who pays most of the household expenses. For those middle-aged Japanese who do not coreside, we use ordered probit analysis to look at how their frequencies of seeing and phoning their parents are associated with socioeconomic and demographic factors. The analysis is based on data from the 1988 National Family Survey.

In the next section we present a review of research on coresidence and intergenerational contact in Japan. It is followed by a description of the data set and methodology for the coresidence analysis and a section that presents the logit results, plus additional information about those who coreside. We then discuss the data set and methodology used in the analysis of seeing and phoning patterns and present the results of the ordered probit analysis. The chapter concludes with a summary of the findings and a discussion of possible future research directions.

RECENT RESEARCH ON CORESIDENCE AND CONTACT ACROSS GENERATIONS

Coresidence

Research on the determinants of intergenerational coresidence in Japan can be divided roughly into three categories: analysis of postnuptial coresidence, analysis of coresidence of the middle-aged with their parents, and analysis of the living arrangements of the elderly.

Postnuptial coresidence of eldest sons has declined since the early 1960s: 58 percent of eldest sons who married between 1960 and 1964 lived with their parents immediately after marriage, whereas only 41 percent of eldest sons married between 1980 and 1982 did so (Atoh, 1988:35). In recent years there has been a slight increase in the proportion of non-eldest sons living with their parents after marriage; about 15 percent of the 1980–82 marriage cohort who were not firstborn did so. Since the 1960s, only about 5 percent of newlywed couples have lived with the wife's parents. Altogether, from the late 1940s to the early 1970s the proportion of all newlyweds living with their parents decreased from 59 percent to 31 percent, and that proportion remained steady into the early 1980s (Atoh, 1988:35). Contributing to the stagnation of the decline in overall postnuptial coresidence is the increased probability that a given male newlywed is an eldest son.

Kojima (1987) found that postnuptial coresidence (with either the husband's or the wife's parents) was negatively associated with the year of marriage and the husband's education, but positively associated with the husband's being the eldest son, his premarital coresidence with parents, his marriage having been arranged, his current employment in agriculture or self-employment, his current residence in a rural area, and his wife's being the eldest daughter with no brothers. In a separate analysis of coresidence with the husband's parents, the wife's being the eldest had a negative effect, but in an analysis of coresidence with the wife's parents, the effect was positive.

The proportion of middle-aged men who live with their own or their wives' parents has changed since 1975, though not greatly, according to survey data collected by the Ministry of Health and Welfare. Hirosima (1987) examined the proportion by five-year age groups and found increases in coresidence with parents between 1975 and 1985 for the 30–34, 35–39, and 55–59 age groups, but declines for those between ages 40 and 54. He argued that, for the younger groups, parents had become more available as a result of the decline in the number of siblings and the improvement in parents' survival, even though the preference for coresidence had declined.

Kojima (1989) analyzed the coresidence with parents of married male household heads of unspecified ages, using logistic regression and data from a 1985 national household survey. He found that being the eldest son, employed in agriculture, and residing in a rural area increased the likelihood of coresidence with the household head's own parents. Education and age generally did not have effects. If the parent was widowed, the probability of coresidence was raised, but the health of the parent or parents had no effect. He also found that being a home owner had a positive effect, whereas being a migrant and having greater per capita household expenditures lowered coresidence, but there may have been simultaneity bias in these results. Kojima also analyzed the extent of coresidence with the wife's parents and found that the wife's being the eldest daughter and her having a widowed parent had positive effects.

From the perspective of the elderly, there has been a clear decline in coresidence with children, even though the probability of survival of the various family members has increased (Martin and Culter, 1983). Hirosima (1987) found that between 1975 and 1985 the proportion coresiding with their children declined for all age groups of the elderly, whether they were married or not. Nevertheless, Japanese elderly remain much more likely to live with their children than do elderly of the more developed countries of the West, such as the United States (Martin, 1989a).

Kojima (1989) also analyzed the coresidence of married male household heads with a married child. Although the household heads were not necessarily elderly, they most likely fell into the late middle-age to old-age categories. He found that the number of married children had a positive effect on coresidence, as did employment in agriculture. Tsuya and Martin (1992), using data from the 1988 National Family Survey, found that persons of ages 60 and over were more likely to be living with their married children if they had a junior high school education or less, were not living in a big city, and were women of ages 70 and over. Once again, coresidence was positively associated with the number of married children the elderly person had.

The analysis presented here will focus on the coresidence of middle-aged Japanese with their parents. Using many of the same explanatory variables but a different data set, we will first attempt to see the extent to which our results are consistent with those of Kojima (1989), which highlighted the importance of birth order and socioeconomic status of the younger generation, as well as parents' marital status. Given indications of changing attitudes toward the practice of coresidence with the eldest son, special attention will be paid to the coresidence of sons versus daughters; and we will further investigate the characteristics of multigenerational households.

Contact

Recent research on intergenerational contact in Japan is not so extensive as the work on coresidence and has usually been conducted on only a small scale. Analyzing data from a Tokyo suburb, Morioka (1968) found that eldest sons were not only more likely than other sons to live with their parents, but also more likely to contact them frequently, even when living separately. Morioka et al. (1985) analyzed family data collected in Shizuoka City in 1982 and 1983 and concluded that in the future, as coresidence declined, contact on formal or ritual occasions would remain frequent, but informal association would occur less often.

Koyama (1970) found that women living in cities were likely to have more frequent contact with their relatives than were men—the reverse of the rural pattern. On the basis of a review of a variety of studies published from 1966 to 1981, many of which were based on small samples, Long (1987:76) concluded that there was no clear pattern of differential contact by birth order, by education, by social class, or by husband's versus wife's parents. Palmore and Maeda (1985:42) reported that Okamura (1984) had found more contact between daughters and their relatives when they lived closer together, a result that is consistent with many studies in the West (see, for example, Cherlin and Furstenberg, 1986, and Dewit, Wister, and Burch, 1988).

Actual contact of Japanese elderly with their non-coresident adult children is, perhaps surprisingly, less than that of American elderly. A 1986 international survey conducted by the Japanese government of persons of ages 60 and over found that about 15 percent of Americans and Japanese saw their children every day, but that 36 percent of the Americans reported meetings of at least once a week, though not daily, whereas only 19 percent of the Japanese did so (Japan, Management Coordination Agency, 1987:268–269). These results are consistent with a small-scale comparative study of attitudes of women in the two countries that found that American women were more likely than Japanese women to disagree with the statement that children do not have an obligation to keep in touch with their parents once they have their own families (Campbell and Brody, 1985).

In the analysis here, for those middle-aged Japanese men and women not living with their parents, their frequency of seeing and telephoning their parents will be analyzed on the basis of the variables used in the coresidence analysis, plus variables indicating the distance separating them and their parents and whether or not their parents were living by themselves or with other relatives or nonrelatives. An additional factor that will be considered is whether or not the spouse's parents were living with the middle-aged couple.

DATA AND METHODOLOGY FOR ANALYSIS OF CORESIDENCE

The data used in this analysis are drawn from the 1988 National Family Survey. The sample used here is restricted to persons who were 30 to 59 years old at the time of the survey (1,532 respondents). The lower limit of the age range was selected because above age 30 most Japanese are married, and the upper limit was selected because above that age many persons would not have a surviving parent. Given our interest in the issue of coresidence or contact with the husband's versus the wife's parents, only married persons (about 90 percent of the relevant age groups, or approximately 1,379) were included in the analysis. Restricting the sample to persons with at least one surviving parent left just over 1,000 respondents, divided approximately equally between males and females.

Preliminary frequencies indicated that in about 35 percent of the cases the couples were living with one or both of the husband's parents and in around 9 percent of the cases they were living with one or both of the wife's parents. (Joint coresidence with parents from both sides was not common, as will be documented.) Because of the asymptotic properties of the maximum likelihood estimation procedures used, we decided essentially to double the sample size by creating for each male respondent an observation for his wife, as long as she fell into the appropriate age range and had a surviving parent, and for each female respondent an observation for her husband, once again, if he was between ages 30 and 59 and had a surviving parent. Because the analysis was done separately by sex, the problem of the two observations not being independent did not arise. This doubling of the sample was possible because a considerable amount of information was collected about the spouse of each respondent, as well as about coresidence with the spouse's parents.

The doubling procedure resulted in a sample of 938 men and 959 women. Some observations had to be discarded because of missing information for particular variables to be used in the analysis, so that the final sample sizes for the coresidence analysis were 889 men and 914 women, as shown in Table 9.1. Also shown in the table are the means of the variables used in the analysis. Categories of explanatory variables were selected on the basis of the previous research discussed above and a review of initial cross-tabulations of the variables with coresidence.

As with the initial frequencies, 35 percent of the men in our sample were living with one or both of their parents, whereas only 9.3 percent of the women were. More than half of each group were between ages 40 and 59 and a little fewer than half were in the 30–39 age group, the omitted category in the analysis. This asymmetry is due to the condition for inclusion in the analysis that at least one parent be alive. Besides indicating the age of the middle-aged person, the age variable roughly indicates the age of the parents—information that we do not have. Older people would on average have older parents, and if coresidence is based in part on the parents' need for care, which would be likely to increase with age, then the variable should have a positive effect on coresidence.

The age variable may also roughly indicate whether or not there might be children in the middle-aged couple's household. Younger couples would be more likely to have young children. Initially we considered including in the analysis a variable indicating the number of children of different ages in the household to see if the presence of children reduced coresidence, possibly through a crowding effect, as is the case in some Western populations (see, for example, Wolf, Burch, and Matthews, 1988). There was also the possibility, however, that coresidence would affect the number of children that the middle-aged couple had. It could be that fertility would be reduced if the household were already crowded or if substantial care of elderly parents were necessary. On the other hand, it could be that fertility would be increased by coresidence because po-

Table 9.1. Definitions and means of variables for coresidence analysis: Japan, 1988

Variable	Men	Women
Living with one or both of one's own parents	.348	.093
Ages 40–59	.614	.539
Birth order 1	.512	.509
Junior high school education or less	.178	.178
Lower-status occupation: not professional or business proprietor	.541	na
Husband in lower-status occupation: not professional or business proprietor	na	.520
Residence in a small town or rural area	.453	.444
Residence in a traditionally agricultural area	.308	.291
Spouse's age 40+	.470	.686
Spouse's education junior high school or less	.166	.194
Spouse has no living parents	.137	.240
Spouse not birth order 1	.512	.547
Arranged marriage	.440	.484
Parent has no spouse	.495	.474
Respondent	.492	.515
(No. of cases)	(889)	(914)

na—not applicable.

tential babysitters would be readily available (Morgan and Hirosima, 1983). Given the possibility of a simultaneity bias, we decided not to include the variable in the analysis. In short, we had no expectation about the effect of age on coresidence; there might be a negative effect because of the need for babysitting services at younger ages, or there might be a positive effect because of crowding at younger ages and the greater demands for elder care at older ages.

The next variable, birth order of 1, indicates whether or not the person was the eldest child in the family. Just over half of both men and women in our sample were the eldest. Unfortunately, we do not have any additional information about siblings, such as their number, sex, or age. So, for example, for a woman who had a birth order of 1, we do not know whether she had any brothers or not. In general, however, we would expect that being the eldest of either sex would have a positive effect on coresidence.

Only about 18 percent of each sex had only a junior high school education or less. We hypothesized that those with less education would be less exposed to modern ideas, would subscribe to more traditional practices, and might be more likely to coreside with their parents. To the extent that education indicates economic status and privacy is normally regarded as a good, we hypothesized that those with more education would be less likely to live with their parents. Thus, a positive effect of this variable was expected.

Just under half of the men in our sample were either professionals or business proprietors. Although we were interested in examining the effect on coresidence of self-employment and employment in agriculture, as suggested by the work of others, only 7 percent of the men fell into those categories. We chose to group professionals and business proprietors together because of their high status and because initial cross-tabulations with coresidence indicated that less coresidence was associated with those occupations. The variable used in the analysis, lower-status occupation, included all the other occupations (agriculture, self-employed, white-collar, blue-collar, family, part-time, female or male homemaker, and unemployed) and was expected to have a positive effect on coresidence for the same reasons as having a relatively low amount of education.

An occupational variable was not included for women because their labor force participation may have been influenced by their coresidence status. For example, Morgan and Hirosima (1983) argue that coresidence may increase female labor force participation by providing an affordable source of childcare. It could also be that if the elderly parents require care, female labor force participation could be discouraged. Accordingly, in the analysis of the coresidence of women with their parents, to control in part for the socioeconomic status of the household, we included their husbands' occupational status, instead of their own, as an explanatory variable, coded in the same way as was occupation for the men.[1] For the same reasons, we expected a positive effect.

The next variable listed in Table 9.1, residence in a small town or rural area, could have either a positive or a negative effect on coresidence. Residents in such areas, around 45 percent of each of the samples, would be more likely than others to be involved in agriculture and might be more likely to follow the practice of coresidence, both because of having more traditional attitudes and because of the need for family labor on the farm. Similarly, if the younger generation had moved to the city and left the older generation behind in the rural area, then residence of the younger generation in the city would be associated with less coresidence. Another reason to expect a positive effect of residence in a rural area on the probability of coresidence was the shortage of reasonably priced housing appropriate for multigenerational living in Japanese cities. In some Asian countries, however, living in urban areas is associated with more rather than less coresidence, perhaps because of the economic necessity of doubling up (Martin, 1989b), and so we had no firm prediction for the sign of the effect. We grouped rural areas and small towns together because many Japanese who are engaged in agriculture actually live in small towns and because initial cross-tabulations with coresidence indicated the similarity of the two categories in coresidence patterns.

A variable indicating residence in a traditionally agricultural area was also included in the analysis. Given the rapidity of urbanization and industrialization in Japan, we thought that some of the regions that today appear modern may have been more rural, agricultural, and traditional just a few decades ago, when the middle-aged in our sample were growing up and when their parents were middle-aged. Other research on family structure in Japan has noted that certain regions, Tohoku and Hokuriku in particular, have a high incidence of three-generation households (Shimizu, 1989). We ranked the 12 regions of Japan by the percentage of persons of ages 15 and over employed in the primary sector, as indicated by census data for 1950, 1960, 1970, and 1980. We then grouped the five regions with the highest average rankings to form our variable. The five regions were Tohoku, Minami-Kyushu, Kita-Kanto, Shikoku, and Hokuriku. The omitted category includes the other seven regions: Hokkaido, Minami-Kanto, Tokai, Nishi-Kinki, Higashi-Kinki, Chugoku, and Kita-Kyushu.

Next in Table 9.1 are several variables that indicate characteristics of the spouse: age, education, no living parents, and birth order not 1. The interpretations

---

1. Respondents were asked about their income, but there was a high rate of nonresponses and therefore we omitted this variable from the analysis.

of the spouse's age[2] and education are similar to those of the respondent's own age and education, although to the extent that husbands with less education were more traditional, there might be less coresidence with the wife's parents. If the spouse had no living parents, then he or she would have no responsibility to his or her own parents and the probability of coresidence with our index person's parents might be increased. We also had information on the birth order of the spouse and expected that the spouse not being the eldest offspring, i.e., not being of birth order 1, would increase coresidence with the index person's parents.

Almost half of the women and men in our samples were in marriages that had been arranged. On the basis of Kojima's (1987) research and bivariate analysis by Hodge and Ogawa (1986), we expected them to be more likely than those whose marriages had not been arranged to be coresiding with their parents. About half of each sample had a parent with no spouse (in most cases a parent who had been widowed). We expected that such persons would also be more likely to coreside with the parent. We had hoped to include in the analysis other information about the parents, such as the father's education or occupation, as indicators of the socioeconomic status of the parental generation. Unfortunately, these questions were left unanswered by many respondents, so that inclusion of those data in the analysis would have required a substantial reduction in sample size; and our preliminary work indicated that they did not have significant effects on coresidence. Therefore, they are not included in the models presented here.

Finally, to make sure that we had not introduced bias into our samples by the doubling procedure used, we included a variable indicating whether or not the observation represented an actual survey respondent or the respondent's spouse. We hoped and expected that this variable would have no effect on coresidence.

The analysis of coresidence presented below is based on a simple logit model in which the dependent variable is living with one or both of one's own parents or not—the first variable listed in Table 9.1—and the explanatory variables are the others listed there. For those who did live together, we present information on characteristics of their living arrangements.

RESULTS OF ANALYSIS OF CORESIDENCE

Table 9.2 presents the results of the logit analysis of coresidence with parents for men and women separately. Coefficients indicate the effect of the variable on the log odds of living with parents versus not

---

2. Given sex differentials in age at marriage, in a few cases the spouse's age might be less than 30 or greater than 59, even though the index person's age was within the 30–59 range. As in the case of the index person's age, we used 40 as the age of demarcation in forming the categories for spouse's age.

Middle-Aged Japanese and Their Parents:
Coresidence and Contact

doing so (the logarithm of the ratio of the probability of living with parents to the probability of not doing so). In parentheses below each coefficient is the standard error of the estimate. One and two asterisks indicate whether or not the coefficient is significantly different from zero at the 5 percent level when a one-tail or

Table 9.2. Coefficients and standard errors from the logit estimation of coresidence with one or more of the index person's own parents: Japan, 1988

Coefficient (standard error)	Men	Women
Constant	−3.18**	−3.69**
	(.27)	(.41)
Age 40–59	.22	−.10
	(.25)	(.35)
Birth order 1	1.99*	.78*
	(.18)	(.25)
Education junior high school or less	−.05	−.18
	(.26)	(.37)
Lower-status occupation	.46*	na
	(.17)	
Husband in lower-status occupation	na	−.12
		(.24)
Residence in a small town or rural area	.68**	.24
	(.17)	(.25)
Residence in a traditionally agricultural area	.19	.12
	(.18)	(.26)
Spouse's age 40+	−.25	−.42
	(.24)	(.37)
Spouse's education junior high school or less	.42	.36
	(.27)	(.34)
Spouse has no living parents	−.05	−.04
	(.25)	(.29)
Spouse not birth order 1	.25	.62*
	(.17)	(.25)
Arranged marriage	.49*	.40
	(.17)	(.25)
Parent has no spouse	.39*	.96*
	(.18)	(.26)
Respondent	.19	.10
	(.16)	(.24)
(No. of cases)	(889)	(914)
Log-likelihood	−460.2	−264.9
Chi-squared	228.0	35.8
(Degrees of freedom)	(13)	(13)

* and ** indicate a coefficient significantly different from zero at the 5% level, using a one-tail or two-tail test as appropriate to the hypothesis.

two-tail test, respectively, is used as appropriate to the hypothesis. In the previous section, for all variables but age, rural/small-town residence, spouse's age, husband's education, and respondent variables, hypotheses about the positive signs of coefficients were specified, so that one-tail tests are appropriate in most cases. As indicated by log-likelihood ratio tests based on the chi-squared distribution, for both men and women the variables as a group were found to contribute significantly to the explanation of coresidence.

For both men and women, being the firstborn and having a parent with no spouse had positive effects on the log-odds of coresidence, as expected. For women, having a spouse who was not the firstborn also had a positive effect.[3] For women, these three variables were the only ones that had significant effects,[4] so that only demographic factors—mortality and birth order—affected their coresidence with their own parents, a phenomenon that remains relatively uncommon in Japan. In the future, should fertility and mortality decline further, these factors might have opposite effects in changing coresidence, if this cross-sectional relationship held over time. With fertility decline in the postwar period, more middle-aged women would be likely to be firstborn, so that from their perspective coresidence would increase. In contrast, lower mortality might reduce the incidence of widowhood and thus reduce coresidence. With lower fertility, a woman's husband would be more likely to be the firstborn, and coresidence with her parents would also be reduced for that reason. Thus, no clear prediction is possible.

For men, several other variables had significant effects on coresidence. Being in a lower-status occupation or being in an arranged marriage raised the log-odds of coresidence, as expected. Another way

---

3. In preliminary work we included a variable, spouse having no traditional responsibility to parents, which we defined as either the spouse not being the firstborn or the spouse not having a surviving parent. Because the variable represented an interaction of the spouse's birth order and the spouse not having surviving parents, it could not be entered in a model that included those two variables. In a model from which we dropped the spouse's birth order, but in which we included the interaction variable, it was found to have a positive effect on coresidence for men, as well as for women.

4. To obtain more parsimonious models for both men and women, we dropped variables sequentially from the models in Table 9.2 according to their t-statistics from lowest to highest. Log-likelihood ratio tests were used to ensure that variables were not inappropriately dropped. With two exceptions, the resulting models contained only the variables that were initially found to have significant effects on the log-odds of coresidence, as indicated in Table 9.2. For women, being in an arranged marriage ultimately had a significantly positive effect on the log-odds of coresidence. For men, having a spouse with a junior high school education or less was positively associated with greater coresidence.

The age variables—age of oneself and spouse—had no effect on coresidence for either sex, although they were correlated. Nevertheless, models in which one was kept and the other was dropped did not result in significant effects, nor did dropping both variables from the models significantly affect the explanatory power of the variables as a group.

of saying the same thing is that those with more "modern" characteristics, i.e., having a higher-status occupation or being in a "love match," were less likely than other men to live with their parents. Similarly, living in a city rather than a small town or rural area had a negative effect on the log-odds, a result that could be due to different attitudes in urban areas toward coresidence, to the possibility that the parents were living in a rural area and not willing to join their offspring in the city, or to the unavailability of appropriate housing for coresidence in cities. Thus, for men in the future, the demographic factors that were highlighted for women (birth order and mortality) might work both to raise and to lower coresidence, whereas further socioeconomic development and an increasing prevalence of the more modern characteristics would reduce coresidence.

For those middle-aged persons who were actually living with their parents, the nature of the coresidence with parents also differed between men and women in several ways. Tables 9.3 through 9.7 present various characteristics of the living arrangements of the 309 middle-aged men and 85 middle-aged women in our samples who were married and living with their parents.

Table 9.3 shows that most of the men were living either with both parents or with their mothers only. For coresiding women, however, a much smaller percentage was living with both parents and a larger percentage was living with mothers only or in arrangements that combined coresidence with their mothers and one or both of their husbands' parents.

As shown in Table 9.4, men were more likely to have begun their coresidence with their parents at marriage than were women, who were more likely than the men to have lived separately after marriage but to have moved together later. Table 9.5 shows that men were also more likely than women to have settled in their parents' homes, whereas women

Table 9.3. Coresidence arrangements of middle-aged men and women coresiding with their parents (%): Japan, 1988

Coresidence arrangement	Men	Women
Both of own parents	45.6	27.1
Own mother only	44.0	55.3
Own father only	8.7	10.6
Own mother and spouse's mother	1.0	4.7
Own parents and spouse's mother	0.7	0.0
Own mother and spouse's parents	0.0	2.4
(No. of cases)	(309)	(85)

Table 9.4. Timing of coresidence among middle-aged men and women coresiding with their parents (%): Japan, 1988

Timing	Men	Women
Since marriage	74.8	47.1
Lived separately after marriage and began coresiding later	22.0	47.1
Lived together after marriage, then separately, and then together again	2.6	1.2
Other	0.7	3.5
No answer	0.0	1.2
(No. of cases)	(309)	(85)

were more likely than men to have had their parents move in with them. This latter type of move was especially common in the case of mothers living with their daughters (figures not shown), although there is some possibility that at the time of the move, both parents were alive.

There were also differences between men and women in the financial arrangements of the households. As shown in Table 9.6, coresidence with the daughter was associated with more sharing of expenses than was coresidence with the son. This outcome was especially

Table 9.5. Who moved in with whom among men and women coresiding with their parents (%): Japan, 1988

Mover	Men	Women
Parents moved in with us	7.8	21.2
We moved in with parents	71.2	51.8
We all moved to a new residence	11.7	16.5
Other	5.2	2.4
No answer	4.2	8.2
(No. of cases)	(309)	(85)

Table 9.6. Persons responsible for the household expenses among men and women coresiding with their parents (%): Japan, 1988

Persons responsible	Men	Women
Parents pay most	2.6	1.2
Parents pay more than we	9.4	2.4
We share almost equally	12.6	18.8
We pay more than parents	14.9	20.0
We pay most	55.7	52.9
We pay expenses separately	2.9	3.5
No answer	1.9	1.2
(No. of cases)	(309)	(85)

Table 9.7. Main reason for coresidence among men and women coresiding with their parents (%): Japan, 1988

Reason	Men	Women
To give parents financial assistance	6.8	7.1
To look after parents	3.9	5.9
Duty as eldest child	59.2	34.1
Parents' wish	15.9	14.1
To be close to parents	6.2	20.0
Parents help with house and children	1.6	9.4
Parents offered housing	1.3	4.7
Other	3.6	4.7
No answer	1.6	0.0
(No. of cases)	(309)	(85)

likely when coresidence was with both parents or with the father only (figures not shown). About one-fourth of the men residing with both parents had a sharing arrangement, whereas almost one-half of the women who resided with both parents had one. The percentages for coresidence with the father only and sharing were 7.4 percent for men and 22.2 percent for women, although the numbers of cases were quite small.

Finally, Table 9.7 presents the main reasons stated for coresidence. It should be recalled that some of the answers listed in the column for men were given by their wives, who were the actual respondents, whereas some of the answers listed in the column for women were given by their respondent husbands. Therefore, the differences should not reflect male-female differences in perceptions, but rather differences in reasons for living with a husband's parents versus a wife's parents.

For both sexes, duty as the eldest child was the number one reason, but it was more popular in the case of living with the husband's parents than with the wife's. The number two reason for coresidence with the wife's parents, to be close to parents, was given less frequently as a reason for living with the husband's parents. The answer that it was the parents' wish was about equally popular between the two groups. Not surprisingly, in the case of coresidence of mothers only with their daughters (figures not shown), the main reason of receiving help from the parent was cited more frequently than in other situations—in 12.8 percent of the cases—although it still came after duty, closeness, and parents' wish in frequency of mention.

Therefore, one obtains a different picture of coresidence with parents for men and women. Men were more likely than women to follow the ideal pattern of living with both parents in the parents' home from the onset of marriage. A large proportion of coresident women had had their mothers move in with them after a period of separate postnuptial residence. The reasons given for living with parents were also somewhat different; fulfillment of duty was associated with living with both the husband's and the wife's parents, but closeness and the exchange of services were more common in cases of living with the wife's parents. It appears that "contingent" coresidence, that is, coresidence undertaken for specific reasons that benefit either the adult child or the parent, is more common for women and their parents, who by living together are behaving in a way that is counter to the Japanese ideal.

DATA AND METHODOLOGY FOR ANALYSIS OF SEEING AND PHONING

Although coresidence is an important indicator of interaction between adult offspring and their parents, interaction can also take place through visits and telephone contact. Because a husband and a wife may have different frequencies of seeing and phoning their parents and parents-in-law, it was necessary to return to the original, undoubled sample of respondents for this stage of the analysis. Shown in Table 9.8 are the distributions of responses to questions of frequency of seeing and phoning their own parents for the 277 male and 424 female respondents in our samples who did not live with their parents.

If we combine the first two frequency categories in Table 9.8, contact almost every day and approximately once a week, it would appear that men saw their parents more often than did women, but women phoned their parents more often. These differentials remain even if the percentages are adjusted for the nonresponse rates, on the assumption that nonresponses should be evenly distributed across all the categories. A notable feature of this table is the high proportion of nonresponses. About 17–18 percent of men and 26–27 percent of

Linda G. Martin and Noriko O. Tsuya

Table 9.8. Frequency of seeing and phoning their own parents among men and women not coresiding with their parents (%): Japan, 1988

Frequency	Seeing Men	Seeing Women	Phoning Men	Phoning Women
Almost every day	6.5	6.1	2.2	7.3
Approximately once a week	15.2	11.8	18.1	25.0
Approximately once a month	19.9	24.1	30.7	23.3
A few times a year	24.9	22.9	16.6	10.8
Approximately once a year	10.8	7.1	4.0	0.9
Seldom	5.8	2.1	10.8	5.7
No answer	17.0	25.9	17.7	26.9
(No. of cases)	(277)	(424)	(277)	(424)

women did not answer the questions. One possible reason was that respondents became confused in the course of answering the self-administered questionnaire about whether they should answer the question or not. Before analyzing the responses, we carried out a logit analysis of nonresponses (see the Appendix to this chapter). We concluded that the responses were not choice-based; i.e., respondents did not choose to answer the questions about contact on the basis of how often they actually had contact with their parents. Instead, it appears that their education or occupation, distance from parent, and whether or not their spouse had a living parent and the couple was coresiding with the spouse's parent affected the response rate. These are variables that are controlled for in the analysis of frequency of contact, as will be discussed below, so that the coefficient estimates based on analysis of the behavior of only the individuals who answered the questions about frequency of contact should be unbiased.

To analyze multivariately the frequencies of seeing and phoning requires an ordered probit approach because the categories of frequencies reported are only a crude ordinal scale that represents the true, underlying, but unobserved frequency of contact.[5] We formed two dependent variables of seeing and phoning that each had three categories: 0, indicating contact approximately once a year or

---

5. For the development of the ordered probit model, see McKelvey and Zavoina (1975). Winship and Mare (1984) discuss applications of the model in sociology. The basic idea is that there is an underlying, continuous variable Y that, in this case, indicates frequency of contact, but that the variable is unobserved. Instead, what we observe is Y^*, which is represented by categories of contact frequency that are ordered but separated by unknown distances. $Y^* = 0$, if $Y \leq \mu(0)$; $Y^* = 1$, if $\mu(0) < Y \leq \mu(1)$; and $Y^* = 2$, if $Y > \mu(1)$. In the LIMDEP software used here, $\mu(0)$ is normalized to zero, and $\mu(1)$ is estimated by maximizing the likelihood function, as are the coefficients in the equation, $Y = B'X + e$, where e is normally distributed with mean 0 and variance 1.

seldom; 1, indicating contact approximately once a month or a few times a year; and 2, indicating contact almost every day or approximately once a week.

We expected that many of the explanatory variables used in the coresidence analysis would have effects on seeing and phoning but that the signs of the effects would not always be the same. For example, assuming that the responsibility of the firstborn children would be greatest, even if they were not coresiding with their parents, one would expect them to contact their parents more frequently than other children. If there were competition between parents and parents-in-law for the middle-aged couple's attention, then having a spouse who had no living parents or who was not a firstborn would be expected to be associated with increased contact with the respondent's parents. On the other hand, if the spouse was not the eldest and the spouse's parents lived with one of the spouse's siblings (not included in the model), then a non-eldest spouse might have greater contact with his or her own parent and reduce the contact with the respondent's parents. Thus, the sign on the effect of spouse's birth order could be either positive or negative.

As in the coresidence analysis, one might expect that individuals in an arranged marriage or living in a traditionally agricultural area might be more likely to be in contact with their parents, as would offspring whose parents had no spouse. The expected effects of age of the respondent and the respondent's spouse and the other socioeconomic variables were not clear. Older couples would have fewer obligations to small children and therefore might have more time for contacting their parents than would younger couples, but on the other hand they might be more likely to have adult children living apart whom they spent time seeing and phoning. Those with less education or lower-status occupations, or who lived in a small town or rural area—"traditional" characteristics discussed above—might be expected to have more contact with their parents, if having those characteristics were associated with stronger familial bonds. Another possibility, however, was that such people might be less inclined, have less time, and have fewer resources to phone or to travel to see their parents if they lived at a distance. Those with more modern characteristics might have greater financial resources to facilitate contact, although their time might also be restricted.

Besides the variables used in the coresidence analysis, we included several other variables in the analysis of seeing and phoning. We did not include women's occupational status in the coresidence analysis because of the possibility of simultaneity bias, but we decided to include in this analysis a variable indicating whether or not the woman was working. About half of the women in the sample were either unemployed or not in the labor force, and we expected that those women would have more time available for seeing or phoning their parents.[6]

We also added a variable indicating distance between the respondents' and their parents' homes. Distance was coded into six categories: next-door; within a 5–6 minutes' walk; within the same village, town, or ward of a city, but more than a 5–6 minutes' walk away; in a neighboring village, town, or ward of a city; within the same prefecture; and in another prefecture. We collapsed these responses by ordered pairs into three dummy variables called close, medium, and far, and included the first two in the analysis.[7] The proportions of the 277 men falling into the three groups were 19, 39, and 42 percent, respectively. The proportions of the 424 women were 8, 54, and 39 percent, respectively. Thus, men were more likely than women to live close to their parents, but about equal proportions of each sex lived far from them. We expected those who lived near their parents to see more of them than those who lived at a medium distance, and those who lived at a medium distance to see them more often than those who lived at a far distance. The expected effect of distance on phoning was not necessarily monotonic. Those living close together might not have a need to phone so often if they saw one another frequently, but phone calls might be associated with arranging visits. For those living far apart, the costs of phoning might have a negative effect on frequency of phoning. Accordingly, we expected those who lived at either a close or medium distance to phone more frequently than those who lived far away, but we had no expectation of differences of behavior between those who lived close and those who lived at a medium distance.

We included in the analysis a variable indicating whether or not the respondent was living with the spouse's parents, although the expected sign of its effect was not clear. Not living with the spouse's parents might make contact with one's own parents less awkward, thus increasing contact; but it might also reduce the amount of time available for that contact, if free time had to be spent in seeing or phoning the spouse's parents.

Finally, we wanted to take into consideration the living arrangements of the respondent's non-coresident parents. We had information on whether they were living by themselves (with or without a spouse), with a different child, with another relative, or with someone else. We hypothesized that there might be greater contact with the respondent if the parent were living alone or with just his or her

---

6. We considered adding a variable indicating the number of school-age children each woman had, but its inclusion would have reduced the sample size because not all women answered the relevant question.

7. Ideally we would have taken advantage of the ordinal nature of distance but were unable to employ any of the methods suggested by Winship and Mare (1984) for doing so. We were also concerned about the possible endogeneity of the distance variable but did not have appropriate instruments to deal with this issue.

spouse, as opposed to living in other arrangements, and so we formed a dummy variable accordingly.

RESULTS OF ANALYSIS OF SEEING AND PHONING

The results of the ordered probit analyses of seeing and phoning non-coresident parents are presented in Table 9.9. The coefficients represent the effects of the variables on the underlying, unobserved frequency of contact. μ(1) in the table represents an estimate of one of the two cut-off points in the underlying distribution (see footnote 5).

Men's frequency of seeing non-coresident parents was negatively affected by being in a lower-status occupation; that is, men who were professionals or business proprietors saw their non-coresident parents more frequently than did others. As expected, the frequency with which men saw their parents was positively affected by living close or at a medium distance rather than at a far distance, the omitted category. The coefficient for the close-distance variable appears to be significantly bigger than the one for the medium-distance variable, as was also expected.

Living in a traditionally agricultural area and having a spouse who was not firstborn had positive and negative effects, respectively, on how often men saw their parents, although the effects were not significant when we used the appropriate tests in the model presented in Table 9.9. In other models from which we sequentially dropped variables according to their t-statistics and for which we used log-likelihood ratio tests to ensure that the variables were not inappropriately dropped, these variables had significant effects of the signs indicated above. Also ultimately having an effect, though not of the expected positive sign, was parent's not having a spouse. It could be that seeing a parent, perhaps the father, who no longer had a spouse tended to be awkward or unpleasant for men, but we would not place too much weight on such an argument.

For women, the distance variables also had positive effects on the frequency of seeing parents, with living close having a greater effect than living at a medium distance. As expected, being the eldest also increased the frequency of seeing one's own parents. However, just as for men, having a spouse who was not the firstborn lowered the frequency of seeing parents. When insignificant variables were dropped sequentially from the model, we found that having a spouse with no surviving parents was associated with more frequent visits, as expected.

For males, the initial model of their frequency of phoning their parents, in which the same variables as in the analysis of visits were included, did not have a significant chi-squared statistic. Therefore, variables with t-statistics having absolute values of less than 1 were dropped from the model with no significant change in the chi-squared statistic,

Table 9.9. Coefficients and standard errors from the ordered probit analysis of frequency of seeing and phoning non-coresident parents: Japan, 1988

Coefficient (standard error)	Seeing Men	Seeing Women	Phoning Men	Phoning Women
Constant	1.00 (.52)	.74** (.35)	.86** (.21)	1.13** (.36)
Age 40–59	.3 (.28)	−.30 (.23)	na	−.12 (.20)
Birth order 1	.20 (.19)	.30* (.16)	na	.38* (.15)
Education junior high school or less	.37 (.29)	−.21 (.26)	na	−.05 (.25)
Lower-status occupation	−.39** (.19)	na	na	na
Husband in lower-status occupation	na	.03 (.16)	na	−.09 (.14)
Not working	na	−.26 (.16)	na	−.21 (.14)
Residence in small town or rural area	.21 (.20)	.04 (.17)	na	.04 (.15)
Residence in a traditionally agricultural area	.33 (.22)	.01 (.18)	na	.21 (.16)
Spouse's age 40+	−.12 (.28)	.09 (.23)	na	.08 (.20)
Spouse's education junior high school or less	−.62 (.38)	−.13 (.24)	na na	−.41 (.22)
Spouse has no living parent	−.10 (.29)	.33 (.22)	−.45** (.22)	−.12 (.18)
Spouse not birth order 1	−.34 (.19)	−.38** (.17)	na	−.19 (.16)
Arranged marriage	−.13 (.22)	−.19 (.17)	na	.17 (.15)
Parent has no spouse	−.37 (.21)	.7 (.18)	−.26 (.18)	.04 (.16)
Parent living alone or with spouse only	.16 (.20)	.07 (.18)	.32* (.17)	.40* (.17)
Close distance from parents	2.37* (.32)	3.79* (.60)	.17 (.20)	−.29 (.23)
Medium distance from parents	.95* (.21)	1.53* (.25)	.39* (.20)	.23 (.17)
Not living with spouse's parents	−.24 (.45)	.26 (.25)	na	.13 (.26)
μ(1)	2.14* (.18)	2.74* (.24)	1.70* (.12)	1.61* (.12)
(No. of cases)	(229)	(312)	(227)	(308)
Log-likelihood	−166.6	−196.5	−209.9	−269.4
Chi-squared	128.1	159.9	22.2	36.9
(Degrees of freedom)	(16)	(17)	(5)	(17)

* and ** indicate a coefficient significantly different from zero at the 5% level using a one-tail or two-tail test as appropriate to the hypothesis.

but fewer degrees of freedom, so that the remaining variables as a group had a significant effect on the frequency of phoning. The resulting model, shown in Table 9.9, included only five variables, three of which individually had significant effects. As expected, living at a medium distance from parents versus living at a far distance raised the frequency with which men phoned them. The effect of living at a close distance was not significantly different from the effect of living at a far distance.[8] If a parent was living alone or the parents lived by themselves, the frequency of phoning increased, as expected. It is difficult to understand, however, the negative effect of the wife having no surviving parent on phoning the man's parents, although one possible explanation is that if the wife had no surviving parent, she was not providing a role model to the husband by phoning her parent.

For women, being the firstborn and having one's parent live alone or one's parents live with only each other had positive effects on the frequency of phoning, as expected. In subsequent models with fewer variables, we also found that living in a traditionally agricultural region had a positive effect whereas having a spouse with a junior high school education or less had a negative effect—somewhat contradictory results, given the traditional versus modern dichotomy posed.

In summary, contact with parents, through either seeing or phoning, was influenced by distance separating the generations, except in the case of telephone contact by women. For both sexes, the shorter the distance, the greater the frequency of seeing the parents. For men, the effect of distance on phoning was nonmonotonic, those living at a medium distance phoning most frequently. Residence in a traditionally agricultural region increased visits by men and phoning by women, but having a lower-status occupation or having a spouse with little education reduced contact in the same two models, respectively. Having a parent who lived alone or parents who lived with only each other increased the frequency of phoning among both men and women. For women, being the eldest offspring increased the frequency of both seeing and phoning, and having a spouse who had no surviving parents increased the frequency of seeing one's own parents. For both men and women, having a spouse who was not the firstborn reduced the frequency of seeing one's own parents. All the above results are understandable, but the negative effect of a parent not having a spouse on the frequency with which men saw their parents and the negative effect of a spouse not having a living parent on the frequency with which men phoned their parents are curious.

---

8. In preliminary work, we estimated a similar model in which we excluded respondents who lived next door to their parents. The effect of living at a close distance (redefined as living at a 5–6 minutes' walk away) was positive and not significantly different from the effect of living at a medium distance.

CONCLUSION

Our analysis has shown that both socioeconomic and demographic factors affect the probability of middle-aged Japanese married men living with their parents, whereas only demographic factors appear to influence the coresidence of middle-aged Japanese married women with their parents. Further influences on kin availability of declines in fertility and mortality might have opposing effects on coresidence with elderly parents, as modeled here, but future socioeconomic change would be likely to reduce the coresidence of men with their parents.

In our sample from the 1988 National Family Survey, contact with noncoresident parents was affected by distance in most cases. Socioeconomic variables generally had few effects. For women, being the eldest child increased contact, and for both sexes, phone calls were made more frequently if a parent was living alone or the parents were living with each other only. To the extent that future migration further separates the generations, contact may be reduced if the cross-sectional relations estimated here hold over time. Our findings imply, however, that having a parent who lives alone or having parents who live with each other only—a phenomenon that is likely to increase in the future—may lead to greater telephone contact. Indeed, it may become increasingly important for firstborn children to avoid marrying other firstborns in order not to have overwhelming responsibility for contact and coresidence with both sets of parents.

We have not discussed in this chapter the quality of the interaction that occurs through coresidence with parents or through seeing or phoning them. As suggested at the outset, living together may have its concomitant tensions. For example, in 1978, elderly residents of Tokyo who were living with their children and grandchildren were more likely to kill themselves than those living alone (Ueno et al., 1981). Morioka et al. (1985) found that in Shizuoka City the degree of affection across the generations was the same whether they were living together or not. Therefore, the expected further decline in multigenerational living in Japan may not necessarily mean that intergenerational relations will deteriorate. It could be that the Japanese will move toward the Western model of intimacy at a distance.

Also not addressed here, but important for policy formulation in an aging society, is the extent to which financial assistance occurs between family members who do not coreside. As we have shown, a variety of financial arrangements exist among those who live together. Undoubtedly, the same would be true for those who do not. Although Japanese policymakers are especially concerned about assistance given by the young to the old and the implications of changing family relations for assistance to those elderly persons who cannot care for themselves, one should not assume that intergenerational support is only one way. Critical to future research will be socioeconomic and demographic information on all the parties potentially involved, both young and old, and data on how interactions change over the course of the life cycle.

APPENDIX: ANALYSIS OF NONRESPONSES TO QUESTIONS ABOUT CONTACT WITH PARENTS

Given the high rate of nonresponses to the questions about frequency of seeing and phoning parents (shown in Table 9.8 of the text), we decided before proceeding with the analysis of contact to investigate which respondents answered the questions and which did not. Accordingly, we did two logit analyses for each sex in which the dependent variables were "did not or did answer the question about frequency of seeing" and "did not or did answer the question about frequency of phoning." For explanatory variables, we used the same variables that we intended to use in the probit analysis of contact, except for the variable indicating whether the parents were living alone or not, which also had a high nonresponse rate. The results of the logit analysis are shown in Appendix Table 9.1. (The sample sizes for these logit models were 275 men and 419 women. Of those respondents not living with parents, two male and five female cases were not used because information on the residence of the spouses' parents was not available.)

For both of the equations for men, living at a medium distance increased the probability of not responding, whereas not living with the spouse's parents lowered it. In addition, for the equation estimating the probability of nonresponse of males to the question about seeing, being in a low-status occupation had a positive effect. For both of the models for women, having a junior high school education or less increased the probability of not responding, as did having a spouse with no living parent. As in the results for men, not living with the spouse's parents lowered the probability of not responding or, put another way, living with the spouse's parents raised the probability of not responding to the questions about seeing or phoning one's own parents.

Why distance, especially medium distance, should have an effect on the probability of responding for men is a mystery to us. We believe that all the other significant effects, however, can be attributed to difficulties that respondents had in understanding the questions and skip-instructions in the self-administered questionnaire. The positive effects on nonresponse of women's having less education and of men's being in lower-status occupations were certainly consistent with this interpretation. Furthermore, women whose spouses had no living parent may have mistakenly assumed that it was not necessary for them to answer questions about their contact with their own non-coresident living parents. Similarly, both men and women living with

Linda G. Martin and Noriko O. Tsuya

Appendix Table 9.1. Coefficients and standard errors from the logit estimation of nonresponse to questions about seeing and phoning non-coresident parents: Japan, 1988

Coefficient (standard error)	Nonresponse to question about seeing Men	Nonresponse to question about seeing Women	Nonresponse to question about phoning Men	Nonresponse to question about phoning Women
Constant	.58 (.68)	.64 (.50)	.47 (.67)	.61 (.49)
Age 40–59	−.72 (.66)	−.18 (.40)	−.44 (.61)	−.26 (.40)
Birth order 1	−.30 (.42)	.02 (.28)	−.15 (.41)	.03 (.28)
Education junior high school or less	.18 (.64)	1.21** (.42)	.02 (.64)	1.06** (.42)
Lower-status occupation	.82** (.42)	na	.61 (.40)	na
Husband in lower-status occupation	na	−.19 (.29)	na	−.09 (.28)
Not working	na	−.17 (.30)	na	−.22 (.29)
Residence in small town or rural area	.03 (.42)	.26 (.30)	−.04 (.41)	.26 (.30)
Residence in a traditionally agricultural area	.08 (.48)	.53 (.31)	.34 (.45)	.32 (.31)
Spouse's age 40+	.62 (.66)	−.17 (.42)	.33 (.61)	.15 (.42)
Spouse's education junior high school or less	.70 (.68)	−.35 (.41)	.82 (.68)	−.31 (.40)
Spouse has no living parent	.48 (.62)	1.08** (.39)	.30 (.61)	.95** (.38)
Spouse not birth order 1	−.21 (.42)	−.38 (.31)	−.30 (.41)	−.33 (.31)
Arranged marriage	−.36 (.46)	.24 (.29)	−.47 (.44)	.04 (.29)
Parent has no spouse	−.35 (.45)	−.32 (.30)	−.25 (.44)	−.26 (.29)
Close distance from parents	.20 (.62)	.47 (.53)	.91 (.57)	.70 (.52)
Medium distance from parents	.89** (.44)	−.17 (.32)	.97** (.45)	−.00 (.32)
Not living with spouse's parents	−3.27** (.57)	−2.85** (.36)	−3.18** (.56)	−2.89** (.35)
(No. of cases)	(275)	(419)	(275)	(419)
Log-likelihood	−93.2	−169.7	−97.8	−172.3
Chi-squared	61.9	134.5	59.2	137.7
(Degrees of freedom)	(15)	(16)	(15)	(16)

** indicates a coefficient significantly different from zero at the 5% level using a two-tail test.

their spouses' parents may have assumed that no response was necessary about contact with their own parents.

ACKNOWLEDGMENTS

An abridged version of this chapter appears under the title "Interactions of Middle-Aged Japanese with Their Parents" in *Population Studies* 45(2):299–311. We are grateful to Larry Bumpass, Andrew Mason, James A. Palmore, and Ronald Rindfuss for their comments and suggestions, and to the East-West Center's Program on Population and Nihon University for supporting this research. The views expressed here are our own and not of our respective organizations.

REFERENCES

Atoh Makoto. 1988. "Changes in Family Patterns in Japan." Paper presented at the IUSSP Seminar on Theories of Family Change, sponsored by the International Union for the Scientific Study of Population (IUSSP), Tokyo, November 29–December 2.

Campbell, Ruth, and Elaine M. Brody. 1985. "Women's Changing Roles and Help to the Elderly: Attitudes of Women in the United States and Japan." *The Gerontologist* 25(6):584–592.

Cherlin, Andrew J., and Frank F. Furstenberg, Jr. 1986. *The New American Grandparent*. New York: Basic Books.

Dewit, David J., Andrew V. Wister, and Thomas K. Burch. 1988. "Physical Distance and Social Contact between Elders and Their Adult Children." *Research on Aging* 10(1):56–80.

Hirosima Kiyosi. 1987. "Recent Change in Prevalence of Parent-Child Co-residence in Japan." *Journal of Population Research* (in Japanese) 10(May):33–40.

Hodge, Robert W., and Naohiro Ogawa. 1986. *Arranged Marriages, Assortative Mating and Achievement in Japan*. NUPRI Research Paper Series, No. 27. Tokyo: Population Research Institute, Nihon University.

Japan, Management and Coordination Agency. 1987. *Report on the International Comparative Survey on the Lives and Perceptions of the Elderly* (in Japanese). Tokyo.

Kojima Hiroshi. 1987. "Correlates of Postnuptial Coresidence in Japan." Paper presented at the IUSSP Seminar on New Forms of Familial Life in MDC's, Vaucresson, France, October 6–9.

———. 1989. "Intergenerational Household Extension in Japan," in Frances K. Goldscheider and Calvin Goldscheider (eds.), *Ethnicity and the New Family Economy: Living Arrangements and Intergenerational Financial Flows*, pp. 163–184. Boulder: Westview Press.

Koyama Takashi. 1970. "Rural-Urban Comparison of Kinship Relations in Japan," in R. Hill and R. Konig (eds.), *Families in East and West*. Paris: Mouton.

Long, Susan Orpett. 1987. *Family Change and the Life Course in Japan*. Ithaca, N.Y.: China-Japan Program, Cornell University.

Martin, Linda G. 1989a. "The Graying of Japan." *Population Bulletin* (Population Reference Bureau) 44(2):1–43.

———. 1989b. "Living Arrangements of the Elderly in Fiji, Korea, Malaysia, and the Philippines." *Demography* 26(4):627–643.

Martin, Linda G., and Suzanne Culter. 1983. "Mortality Decline and Japanese Family Structure." *Population and Development Review* 9(4):633–649.

McKelvey, Richard D., and William Zavoina. 1975. "A Statistical Model for the Analysis of Ordinal Level Dependent Variables." *Journal of Mathematical Sociology* 4:103–120.

Morgan, S. Philip, and Kiyosi Hirosima. 1983. "The Persistence of Extended Family Residence in Japan: Anachronism or Alternative Strategy?" *American Sociological Review* 48:269–281.

Morioka Kiyomi. 1968. "Life History and Social Participation of the Families Living in a Public Housing Project in a Tokyo Suburb." *Journal of Social Sciences* (International Christian University, Tokyo) 7:199–275 (in Japanese).

Morioka Kiyomi, Yoshiko Sugaya, Michiaki Okuma, Akiko Nagayama, and Hiromi Fujii. 1985. "Intergenerational Relations: Generational Differences and Changes," in Kiyomi Morioka (ed.), *Family and Life Course of Middle-Aged Men*. Tokyo: The Family and Life Course Study Group.

Okamura, K. 1984. "Reciprocities between Elderly Mothers and Their Middle Aged Daughters in Separated Households." *Social Gerontology* 19 (January):106–197.

Palmore, Erdman B., and Daisaku Maeda. 1985. *The Honorable Elders Revisited*. Durham, N.C.: Duke University Press.

Shimizu Hiroaki. 1989. "Family and Regional Development," in Asian Population and Development Association, *Population and the Family in Japan*. Tokyo.

Tsuya, Noriko O., and Linda G. Martin. 1992. "Living Arrangements of Elderly Japanese and Attitudes toward Inheritance." *Journal of Gerontology* 47(2):S45–S54.

Ueno Masahiko, Munesuke Shōji, Masahiro Asakawa, Masae Orui, Tōru Kogure, Kōichi Minekawa, Toshiji Maka, Setsuyo Nagasawa, Genichi Matsuzaki, and Masami Washino. 1981. "Suicide among Elderly People Based on Records of the Tokyo Medical Examiner's Office," *Nihon University Journal of Medicine* 40(10):1109–1119 (in Japanese).

Winship, Christopher, and Robert D. Mare. 1984. "Regression Models with Ordinal Variables." *American Sociological Review* 49:512–525.

Wolf, Douglas A., Thomas K. Burch, and Beverly J. Matthews. 1988. "Kin Availability and the Living Arrangements of Older Unmarried Women: Canada, 1985." IIASA Working Paper WP–88–044. Laxenburg, Austria: International Institute for Applied Systems Analysis.

CHAPTER 10

Who Lives in the Extended Family and Why? The Case of Japan

by Satomi Kurosu

The association between family structure and economic and social developments in societies at large has been studied by family researchers from various disciplines. Goode (1963) predicted that the forces of industrialization and urbanization would affect all known societies and move them in the direction of some type of conjugal family. More recent historical and comparative studies, however, indicate that the transformation of the extended family into the nuclear family has not been unidirectional or continuous, nor has it been a simple response to the development of industrial society (Levy, 1965; Laslett, 1972; Blumberg and Winch, 1972; Hareven, 1987). Additional research on family structures and behaviors across time and space can further an understanding of this topic. The prevalence of vertically extended households in Japan provides an opportunity to test which social features, as well as personal characteristics, shape the propensity of individuals to live in an extended family—a living arrangement that is thought to be declining in industrialized settings.

The structures and behaviors of the Japanese family have changed dramatically in this last century, paralleling Western family experiences; yet the extended family, or multigenerational household, still retains sociological significance as a living arrangement. For example, of all Japanese households (including family and nonfamily households) in 1980, 21 percent consisted of extended families. In contrast, the proportion of extended families in France and West Germany in 1982, if one allows for slight differences in the definitions used by the respective national censuses,[1] was less than 3 percent (Council on Population Problems, 1986). The contrast becomes more apparent among the elderly (Kurosu, 1992). In the 1980s, 65 percent of elderly Japanese people (those 60 years old and above) were still living with their children in extended families. Although this proportion has declined from 80 percent since the 1960s, the proportion of older people living with their younger kin is remarkably high compared with Western societies, which record only 10 to 30 percent of elderly living in extended families (Japan, Ministry of Health and Welfare, IPP, 1987). How can we explain the prevalence of the extended family in postindustrialized Japan? My purpose is to discover the underlying forces and systematic variations that determine family living arrangements in contemporary Japan. More precisely, this chapter has three objectives: (1) to identify and then apply the three determinants of extended-family residence—that is, demographic, economic, and ideological factors—to the case of Japan; (2) using data from a 1979 survey by the Ministry of Health and Welfare, Japan, to test statistically how demographic factors, the economic standing of the family, and the effect of *ie* ideology enhance the extensiveness of the living arrangement; and (3) to examine how regional variations in an economic and normative climate can shape the propensity of individuals to reside in multigenerational families.

APPROACHES TO STUDYING THE EXTENDED FAMILY

An extended family here refers to a family, including a nuclear family and its kin, whose members live together in the same household. Such a family can take many forms, or combinations of members. An important characteristic of the Japanese extended family is that in most cases it is vertically extended (Kamiko, 1976:33). Thus, in Japan the terms extended family and multigenerational family are virtually synonymous.

Studies focusing on one dimension of family change—living arrangements—tend to emphasize historical household composition or intergenerational exchanges in industrial settings. The extended family is not often found in contemporary industrialized nations, and therefore theories about it are usually based on observations of historical and

---

1. The categories were defined as "two or more couples" in France and "3-generation" and "non-stem family household" in Germany (Council on Population Problems, 1986).

industrializing settings. Although the time periods and societies examined in such studies vary, most emphasize some or all of the three factors that affect the frequency of the extended family—namely, demographic, economic, and normative determinants. In Ruggles's (1987) words, they are the "three suspects" that played a role in the rise of the extended family in nineteenth-century England and America. In Kojima's (1989) model, which builds on the framework developed by Kobrin and Goldscheider (1982) for studying the determinants of nonfamily households, they are the feasibility of coresidence, the availability of kin for coresidence, and the desirability of coresidence. I will identify the key factors in each approach, attempting to bridge observations across periods.

The prime focus of the demographic approach is availability, or demographic constraints on the formation of the family. The idea was first set forth in Levy's (1965) influential essay that a high frequency of extended families is impossible in premodern societies because of high mortality. Applied to modern societies, Levy's thesis suggests that the availability of extended kin is the direct determinant of an individual's membership in an extended family. An important determinant of demographic availability is the developmental cycle of the family (Berkner, 1972). Freedman, Chang, and Sun (1982), for example, report that, in 1980, 83 percent of Taiwanese couples had at some time lived in extended-family households. This figure was underestimated in cross-sectional data. Moreover, Nasu (1985) and Shimizu (1986:297–303) report cases among elderly Japanese in which coresidence was more prevalent during their later years, when many of them experienced an increase in physical problems.

The economic approach emphasizes the material conditions that give rise to a particular family pattern (e.g., the nuclear family or the extended family) as a survival strategy. In traditional peasant economies, the family was organized in a way that kept family property or land intact. Therefore, the size or type of family property mattered for the formation of the family. Even in the stem family, or households formed by the coresidence of the parents and one married child, the choice of heir—whether the eldest child (primogeniture) or the youngest (ultimogeniture)—varied by region and by the amount of family wealth (Berkner, 1976:89). In early industrialized societies and also in contemporary ones, family extension can be seen as a strategy for easing the economic demands of marriage. Anderson (1971), in his study of nineteenth-century England, argues that kinship provides the main form of assistance to a family during critical life situations such as unemployment, illness, a housing shortage, and old age. In industrialized societies, too, according to Smelser and Halpern (1978:290), "the extended family serves as a resource to the conjugal unit." Among working-class populations, for example, kin are often relied upon for aid in migrating, settling in, and obtaining information about jobs (Tilly and Brown, 1974). Morgan and Hirosima's (1983) study of the Japanese family delineates the persistence of the extended family as a "family strategy" for both young couples and their parents. They show that the incompatibility of the roles of mother and wage worker is greatly reduced by the childcare and housework provided by grandparents in extended residences.

Two clarifications are necessary in making a causal connection between economic demands and the extended family. The first point relates to a central criticism of Anderson's study made by Ruggles (1987): that the economic situation explains how Victorians were able to live in extended families (i.e., able to afford the luxury of supporting their dependent kin). The notion that extended kin typically impose an added economic burden holds true in the contemporary context. Whether it be a young couple or aged parents who need financial or physical support (specific needs varying, depending on the stage of the life-cycle), the extended family will not be formed without sufficient financial means and household space. In cases where living space is not available, young couples can aid or be aided by parents without necessarily living with them. For example, in Hong Kong it is a common practice for a young couple to leave their child with parents who live in a separate household. In Taiwan, young couples and their parents, who live in separate households, often eat together (Martin, 1990). The second point is that the availability of social care and welfare within the community and the society—the level of "functional differentiation in the social structure," in Goode's term (1963)—may provide alternative choices for the family. In some communities, wives can solve the incompatibility between their role as mother or care provider for aged parents and their working role by such mechanisms as professional childcare or homes for the aged.

Yet another important determinant of family structure is normative. Unless a normative inclination for the family extension is present along with demographic availability and economic needs and affordability, the formation of an extended family will not be actualized. Ruggles's study shows that the rise of the extended family in England and America coincided with a revolution in attitudes about family life during the Victorian era. The Victorians idealized the family. They had an acute sense of obligation to kin and were willing to support their relatives at great economic and psychic cost. Although economic and demographic factors can explain the increased opportunities for people to reside in extended families, they do not explain why people choose to take advantage of those opportunities (Ruggles, 1987).

For the Chinese family, Zeng (1986) predicts that the ethnic tradition of respect and care for the elderly will continue to play an important role in sustaining the extended family. He cites Fei's two models: the "feedback model," into which the Chinese family fits and in which each generation fosters the generation succeeding it and in turn receives financial support in old age from the children; and the "continued linear model"—that is, a Western model, in which children's support of their parents in old age is absent. Considering these differences, Zeng argues that in Taiwan Province, for example, where 80 percent of the elderly were still living alone with a married son in 1973 and 76 percent were still doing so in 1980, changes in living arrangements are unlikely to replicate the Western nuclear model.

An important lesson to learn from these studies is that there exist society- and period-specific ideals of the family that are brought about by its history and social environment. Furthermore, we know from recent fertility studies (e.g., Coale 1983; Lesthaeghe and Wilson, 1986; Knodel and van de Walle, 1979; Lesthaeghe and Surkyn, 1988; Rindfuss and Morgan, 1983) that those ideals may be specified and quantified. Just as scholars who investigate fertility behavior treat the "value" dimension in their frameworks and try to quantify it, more family sociologists should try to assess systematically what are called "ideal" or "traditional" family values. I will make this attempt in the following section.

HYPOTHESES ABOUT INDIVIDUAL-LEVEL AND CONTEXTUAL DETERMINANTS OF EXTENDED FAMILIES

In applying these determinants—demographic, economic and normative—to the case of contemporary Japan, it is necessary to pay attention to a characteristic of the Japanese family ideal, the *ie* ideology, which emphasizes family continuity, ancestor worship, and the family as an economic unit. The ideology was successfully institutionalized by the Meiji government (1868–89), not only in its civil code but also through mass propaganda and ideological indoctrination in the schools, as its national polity aimed at industrialization and prepared for the two world wars. Although the stem family system was not new in Japan, where the Confucian tradition of filial piety and Buddhist worship of family ancestors were part of its history, the Meiji government institutionalized the stem family, patriarchy, and the continuity of the family as a collective goal and ideal. Thus, the eldest son was expected to remain in his parents' household, and both the hierarchical relationship among family members and sex segregation were reinforced and codified.

Although these ideals were legally abolished by the Civil Code after World War II, the strongly inculcated *ie* ideology can still be observed in people's preference for living with their eldest sons and attempts to continue family lineages and businesses (Kurosu, 1990). These points will be stressed in the following hypotheses.

Individual-Level Determinants

Demographic variables are important predictors of individual household extension. The extended family will not be formed in a family group that does not have nonnuclear family members (i.e., grown children or elderly parents) to begin with. Therefore, among the elderly, both the availability of children and the presence of a spouse affects family extension. As for younger and middle-aged individuals, the availability of parents is necessary for forming an extended family. I hypothesize that younger adults are likely to reside in their parents' household, whereas elderly parents, especially those in their 70s and 80s, are likely either to remain in their home, where their children now compose the core nuclear unit of the household and have the primary role in taking care of them, or to move into their children's household to be taken care of.

The economic status of the family should have a strong influence on the probability of extended family formation in Japan. The family's economic status is indicated by its income and real property, such as a house, land, or farm. The higher the family income and the value of its properties, the more extended the family will be as it can afford to have extended kin. At the individual level, persons whose families have more income and property are more likely than others to live in an extended family. Landowners and homeowners are therefore more likely to extend the family than are nonowners. Similarly, the larger a house is, the more likely is the family to form an extended household because there is available space in which extended kin can reside. Family property and family income, which are usually treated as interchangeable indices of a family's socioeconomic status in sociological studies, need to be treated separately in Japan, where the custom of maintaining family properties (*kasan*) intact is still strong. I suspect that having family property does not necessarily indicate the possession of higher household income. Both factors, however, encourage individuals to live in an extended family by providing either the opportunity or an obligation for young couples to remain in the parents' household. The opportunity is there because having more income or more property generally means being able to feed more household members. The obligation arises from the property owners' assumption that their children will inherit the property. It is thus part of the *ie* ideology and at the same time consistent with a universal tendency for those with property or wealth to attempt to retain it.

The functional differences between the nuclear and the extended family are well known. A larger (extended) family is required to maintain a farm or business, for example. My hypothesis is that self-employed individuals are more likely than those who are employed by others to stay in the extended, or stem, family. Among self-employed families, the notions of "work" and "family" are not so clearly demarcated as in the case of employed families. The social and geographical mobility of self-employed farmers and owners of family businesses is low because these people tend to inherit family enterprises. Self-employed family members may provide more direct assistance to their children to ensure their occupational success than does the employed family, whose youth go out to seek their own jobs. Moreover, the *ie* ideology can be passed on to younger generations more easily by self-employed than by employed families through sharing daily and ritualistic family and business or farm experiences.

The ideology of the stem family will be strongest among older people who were socialized prior to World War II. The normative factor involves two on-going processes. One is the persistence of old values, which are expressed by the *ie* ideology, and the other is the spread of new values, which may be represented by individualism and a conjugal family orientation. The more people cling to the old values, that is, to the *ie* ideology, the more they will favor living in the extended family; whereas the more they accept the new values, in particular the conjugal family ideology, the less they will want to live in an extended family. On the assumption that behavior is consistent with attitudes, I hypothesize that those who still favor the *ie* ideology are more likely than those who favor conjugal ideology actually to live in an extended family.

Contextual Determinants

The above hypotheses apply to the individual level. I propose that these three determinants are complementary and have additive effects to explain the extended family. To further our understanding of the mechanism by which the extended family is formed, it is necessary to account for regional variations. Failure to do so is one of the weaknesses of most demographic studies that employ statistical data (Kurosu, 1992). Here I will attempt to bridge the macro and individual levels.

The normative climate of a region affects both directly and indirectly the propensity of individuals to live in extended families. Individuals perceive and often conform to the direct influence of social norms, such as a traditional value from the *ie* system or individual-oriented values from Western ideology. I hypothesize that individuals who reside in communities that value the *ie* ideology rather than conjugal or individually oriented values will be more inclined to form extended families than will individuals who reside in areas influenced by Western ideology.

A more direct contextual influence is the availability of alternatives for care of the elderly, children, and other members of the family who need assistance that regions or communities can provide to individuals residing in them. Access to public care offers an alternative to the extended family. An elderly widow, for example, may not feel that it is necessary to live with her children if she knows that community care is available. Actual use of public facilities, however, is likely to be strongly influenced by the social acceptability of those facilities. Until recently, going to a home for the aged was considered equivalent to being abandoned by one's children, but an increase in the number of care facilities seems to be altering such attitudes. Accessibility to the public care system reflects the economic standing of a region because regions without large budgets cannot afford to build such facilities. It may also reflect the community's level of "functional differentiation in the social structure," which is caused by industrialization and is thought to foster the conjugal family type (Goode, 1963).

Indirect influences on the formation of extended families, such as education and socioeconomic status, can alter the perception of traditional values and customs. Urbanization and crowding also have an indirect, rather than a direct, effect on the probability of family extension. Although crowded urban areas tend to have smaller houses than do rural areas, it is the space that an individual family has that directly affects the individual decision on coresidence. Even in urban areas, the size of individual houses varies, and so a young couple may choose to stay in the home of the husband's parents if the house is large enough, in order to save money and to avoid having to look for their own apartment. In such a case, the housing squeeze in the area indirectly affects their decision.

DATA AND MEASUREMENT

The data set used in this study is from the Survey of Changes in Life Structure of the Population in Relation to Aging, conducted in 1979 by the Institute of Population Problems, Ministry of Health and Welfare. A total of 8,729 households were randomly sampled within 10 wards, cities, and towns that were chosen as being typical of five prefectures that include three types of residence—large cities, medium-size localities, and agricultural areas. The survey employed three questionnaires. The first, a household questionnaire, was addressed to household heads or representatives of the sampled households. The other two questionnaires were designed for members of the sampled households and were used to interview 5,440 respondents who were 60 or older and 12,897 respondents between the ages of 30 and 59. To compare the effects of individual and contextual determinants on the living arrangements of individuals at different stages of the life cycle, these two age groups will be analyzed separately.

The method of measuring the extended-family variable at the individual level varies according to the data and study design. My own theoretical interest is in whether a person lives in an extended or a nuclear family and how extensive an extended family is. I therefore use the concept of minimal household unit (MHU) recommended by Ermisch and Overton (1985) for studies of household formation. Ermisch and Overton define four types of MHU: (1) single persons, (2) single parents with children, (3) married couples without children, and (4) married couples with children. Berge (1989:127–128) notes that this classification is similar to the United Nations' definition of the conjugal family, with the category of single persons added. Berge also notes that the UN definition makes a distinction between married and unmarried couples with children, which Ermisch and Overton do not recognize, and that Ermisch and Overton place an age limit on children, which the UN definition does not.

I know of no statistics on Japanese families that differentiate married from unmarried couples with children (the UN distinction), but that distinction does not seem necessary for using the data set I have. As for children's ages, the age limit used by Ermisch and Overton to distinguish nuclear from extended family members is arbitrary. I believe that as long as a child is unmarried, the exchange system that exists between the nuclear members (i.e., between the child and his or her parents) will be essentially the same regardless of whether the child passes an arbitrary age limit.

Thus, the extensiveness of a family can be measured by counting the number of MHUs in a household. It should be noted that a household with one MHU is not necessarily equivalent to a nuclear family, whereas a household with several MHUs is equivalent to an extended family. By my reckoning, a single MHU household can contain *other kin members*, for example, married couples with children and an unmarried sibling of the household head. As soon as another MHU is recognized, a household is considered to be a multi-MHU household. The emphasis is on the linear relationship of household members to the household head. Members will be recognized as an MHU as long as they are linearly related to the household head (i.e., they are either parents or children of the head). They will not be recognized as an MHU if they are not linearly related. Therefore, a widowed mother is counted as an MHU but an unmarried sibling of the household head is not. If the sibling is married and lives with the household head's MHU, then the household has two MHUs. This is equivalent to a joint family, which is rarely found in Japan. In practice, owing to a limitation of the survey data, information on the marital status of *siblings* of the household head is not available. This limitation would be problematic for societies in which joint families are common. In Japanese families, however, most extensions are vertical. I recoded answers to a question about the respondent's relationship to the household head into household types to construct the MHUs and then counted the number of MHUs. The dependent variable (the number of MHUs in a household), constructed in this manner, is used in the OLS regression.[2] The distribution of the dependent variables for the two age groups is shown in Table 10.1. Those households whose number of MHUs could not be determined were put into an "other" category and excluded from the following analysis.

Demographic indicators used in the analysis were the *respondent's* age, whether the respondent's spouse was alive, and whether they had living parents (in the case of the younger age group) or children (in the case of the older age group). Economic dimensions were measured by three indicators. One was the total household income over the previous year, including agricultural income, salaries, pension and welfare payments, and rental income from land and buildings owned. The second was a dichotomous variable based on answers to the question, "Do you have land that you are cultivating?" Household heads who own land are likely to be farmers but are not necessarily so. It is a common practice for a rural family whose members used to be farmers but whose head now works somewhere else to own land and cultivate vegetables and rice. (The practice is similar to having a home garden in the West, but the size of these rice paddies and fields can be quite large.) I assumed, therefore, that owning land (size not specified) represented both the type of property belonging to a family and the family's geographic immobility. I also assumed that this variable represented the availability of space for the family. The third variable, a dichotomous variable of being either employed by others or self-employed, was constructed from the individual's occupational code. This variable was used for the analysis of the 30–59 age group. The survey obtained occupational information for each individual in the family. I was interested in testing

---

2. I am well aware of the peculiar distribution of the dependent variable. That is, although there are three categories of household based on the number of MHUs per household, actual distributions are concentrated in the first two categories. Therefore, I also created a dummy variable for the extended family from the data set (1 = extended family, 2 = other family). Using this dichotomous dependent variable, I tested models using logistic regression, which other researchers are increasingly using in family studies to analyze nominal-level variables (e.g., Morgan and Teachman, 1988). When the number of cases is large, however, both logistic and OLS procedures give similar results (personal communication from Hubert M. Blalock, Jr.). Further, the general results of the logistic regression analyses agree with those from the OLS regression analyses. Therefore, my discussion focuses on the OLS regression, which gives a better interpretation of the relationship among variables.

Table 10.1. Number and percentage of minimal household units (MHUs), by age group of respondent: Japan, 1979

Household type	60 and over No.	%	30–59 No.	%
1 MHU	2,271	41.9	7,401	57.6
2 MHUs	2,720	50.1	4,822	37.5
3 MHUs	285	5.3	455	3.5
Other	150	2.8	175	1.4
Total	5,426	100.0	12,853	100.0

my hypothesis that if one of the family members (most likely the household head) owned a business, other members of the family would somehow be involved in running the business to a greater or lesser degree, even though they might have other occupations outside. For example, if a couple had a farm, I assumed that their children would help during the busy season; or if a couple had a small shop, I hypothesized that their retired parents would sit in a corner of the shop to prevent petty theft when the shop was crowded. For respondents of ages 60 and above, the majority of whom were retired by the time of the survey, such occupational variables were not appropriate. A more suitable measurement for their financial status was constructed from the question, "Do you receive economic support from your children?" This question was asked regardless of their living arrangements. The elderly who required financial support from their children were likely to live with them unless they had an alternative. This raises an important issue related to the social welfare system, which is that although the elderly may want to be independent, they cannot be so if they do not have the means of supporting themselves. Finally, respondents' educational achievement was used to measure their acceptance or integration of the new ideology. The persistence of the *ie* ideology was measured from responses to questions about their opinions of coresidence and inheritance.

To test further the contextual determinants of family extension, I used several measures based on respondents' prefecture of residence. These were the number of hospitals per 100,000 persons in the prefecture, to indicate alternative sources of care available to the family; the average number of tatami mats (the size of one tatami mat is approximately 1.65 m²) per household in the prefecture, to indicate the amount of space available; and the percentage of the prefecture's population with higher than a secondary education, to suggest the normative climate.

Exhibit 10.A presents an index of the variables used in the analysis. From the discussion above, the following six models are specified:

(1) MHU = a + b_1 Child (Parent) + b_2 Spouse + b_3 Age

(2) MHU = a + b_1 Income (Support) + b_2 Occupation + b_3 Land

(3) MHU = a + b_1 Education + b_2 Opcores

(4) MHU = a + b_1 Child (Parent) + b_2 Spouse + b_3 Age + b_4 Income + b_5 Occupation + b_6 Land + b_7 Education + b_8 Opcores

(5) MHU = a + b_1 Hospital + b_2 Space + b_3 %Hi educ

(6) MHU = a + b_1 Child (Parent) + b_2 Spouse + b_3 Age + b_4 Income + b_5 Occupation + b_6 Land + b_7 Education + b_8 Opcores + b_9 Hospital + b_{10} Space + b_{11} %Hi educ

Model 1, which is the baseline model, tests the effect of demographic availability. Models 2 and 3 specify the effects of

Satomi Kurosu

Exhibit 10.A. Index of variables

DEPENDENT VARIABLE
MHU (Minimum Household Unit): Number of nuclear families in a household

INDEPENDENT VARIABLES
Demographic
  Child: Have living child(ren) (dummy)
  Parent: Have living parent(s) (dummy)
  Spouse: Spouse present (dummy)
  Age: Older group (1 = 60–69; 2 = 70–79; 3 = 80 and above)
              Younger group (1 = 30–39; 2 = 40–49; 3 = 50–59)
Economic
  Income: Household income during the last year
              (1 = less than ¥2 million; 2 = ¥2–4 million; 3 = ¥4 million or more)
  Support: Financial support from children (dummy) (older group)
  Land: Land ownership (dummy)
  Occupation: Either self-employed or not (dummy) (younger group)
Normative
  Education: Level of education achieved
  Opcores: Opinion about coresidence (a higher score representing a stronger value placed on coresidence and therefore stronger *ie* ideology)
Context
  Hospital: Number of hospitals per 100,000 persons in the prefecture (availability of alternative care)
  Space: Average number of tatami mats per household in the prefecture (1 tatami mat ≅ 1.65 m^2)
  % Hi educ: Percentage of population in the prefecture with higher than a secondary education (normative climate)

economic and normative factors on the number of MHUs in households where individuals with those characteristics reside. Model 4 predicts the additive effect of the three dimensions. Model 5 predicts the number of MHUs from the contextual characteristics of the prefecture where household members reside. And Model 6 predicts the additive effects of all the variables in explaining whether the family is extended or nuclear.

FINDINGS

I first computed bivariate correlations for each pair of variables to assess the validity of my assumptions. Tables 10.2 and 10.3 present the correlation matrix for the variables for the two age groups. The correlation coefficients of the individual explanatory variables and the dependent variable were all in the predicted direction. It should be noted that the demographic variables worked in a different

Who Lives in the Extended Family and Why?
The Case of Japan

manner for the two age groups, reflecting the difference in their life stages. The availability of either parents or children was positive and significant. For the presence of a spouse, the directions of the signs were reversed for the two groups. This suggests that in the older group, if the spouse was not present (i.e., the index person was a widow or widower), the individual was more likely to be living with non-nuclear family members. That was not the case for the younger age group, however. The positive association of spouse and MHU indicated the forma-

Table 10.2. Pearson correlation coefficients among variables: ages 60 and above

Variable	MHU	Inc	Sup	Land	Edu	Opco	Child	Spo	Age	Hsp	Space
Income	.39**										
Support	.26**	.07**									
Land	.36**	−.04**	.13**								
Education	−.17**	.15**	−.17**	−.31**							
Opcores	.35**	.20**	.20**	.16**	−.14**						
Child	.15**	.13**	.18**	.02**	−.01	.10**					
Spouse	−.16**	.02*	−.16**	.03**	.08**	−.06**	.02				
Age	.08**	.05**	.07**	−.04**	.16**	−.03	.03**	−.18**			
Hospital	−.26**	−.47**	−.05**	.29**	−.19**	−.27**	−.06**	−.01	−.04**		
Space	.32**	.19**	.06**	.06**	−.08**	.28**	.03*	−.02**	−.20**	−.42**	
% Hi educ	−.32**	.14**	−.12**	−.65**	.35**	−.20**	.02	.01	.20**	−.33**	−.51**

* $p < .05$.
** $p < .01$.

Table 10.3. Pearson correlation coefficients among variables: ages 30–59

Variable	MHU	Inc	Occup	Land	Edu	Opco	Prnt	Spo	Age	Hsp	Space
Income	.18**										
Support	.18**	−.06**									
Land	.43**	−.13**	.38**								
Education	−.15**	.28**	−.26**	−.41**							
Opcores	.27**	.04**	.11**	.28**	−.24**						
Parent	.28**	.11*	−.04**	−.04**	.16**	−.03**					
Spouse	.06**	.13**	.06**	.06**	−.00	.01	.00				
Age	−.06**	−.04**	.10**	.11**	−.22**	.05**	−.33**	−.07**			
Hospital	−.12**	−.32**	.18**	.32**	−.17**	−.27**	−.11**	.01	.08**		
Space	.15**	.05**	−.08**	.01	−.05**	.26**	.05**	.08**	−.13**	−.33**	
% Hi educ	−.32**	.19**	−.23**	−.63**	.38**	−.31**	.04**	−.09**	.00	−.29**	−.58**

* $p < .05$.
** $p < .01$.

tion of a nuclear family and therefore the extension of the family of origin. Age also showed opposite associations with the two age groups. These relationships are further clarified in the following discussion.

I tested the six models using the OLS regression method. The results of the analyses are summarized in Tables 10.4 and 10.5.

The demographic variables in Model 1 were all significant in both groups. For the younger group, whether a person had a living parent or not strongly affected his or her probability of living in an extended family. For the older group, having a child and being widowed affected one's living arrangement.

Model 2 tested the effect of economic variables on family extension. Income and land showed a strong effect on the dependent variable in both age groups. Financial support from children was as good a predictor as the other two economic variables in the older group (Table 10.4). Whether a person was self-employed or not was significant; but when the standardized regression coefficient of this variable was compared with the coefficients of income and land, the effect was small (Table 10.5).

Model 3 examined the effect of normative factors. In both age groups, as predicted, education, which indicates a con-

Table 10.4. Effects of individual-level and contextual variables on the extended family: ages 60 and above

Variables	(1) b	(1) B	(2) b	(2) B	(3) b	(3) B	(4) b	(4) B	(5) b	(5) B	(6) b	(6) B
Demographic												
Child	.41**	.18					.13**	.11			.18**	.08
Spouse	−.20**	−.17					−.16**	−.14			−.15**	−.13
Age	.03**	.05					.04**	.06			.06**	.10
Economic												
Income			.28**	.39			.26**	.36			.21**	.29
Support			.23**	.20			.13**	.11			.12**	.10
Land			.39**	.34			.34**	.30			.26**	.22
Normative												
Education					−.12**	−.13	−.09**	−.09			−.08**	−.08
Opcores					.14**	.33	.08**	.18			.04**	.09
Context												
Hospital									−.08**	−.61	−.03**	−.28
Space									−.18**	−.28	−.02	−.02
% Hi educ									−.08**	−.67	−.04**	−.27
R^2	.07		.32		.14		.39		.27		.45	
(N = 4,422)												

Note: All six models are significant (**p < .01).

jugal or individual-oriented ideology, had a negative effect on family extension, whereas a favorable opinion about coresidence, which indicates an *ie* ideology, had a positive effect. Overall, all the variables in the three dimensions were significant.

When these variables were put together in Model 4, the hypothesis that they would have independent effects on family extension generally held true. For the older age group (Table 10.4), all the variables were significant. When the explanatory variables were compared with those in the previous three models, the magnitude of all their coefficients was reduced. This was expected, since some of the variables explained the same variation in the dependent variable. Even so, the total explained variance was greater than in the previous models. The same thing can be said for the younger age group (Table 10.5). For the demographic variables, the effects of the spouse's presence and age were attenuated. This result was expected, since those variables are important among the elderly but not among younger people.

Model 5 examined the effects of the contextual variables on individuals' propensity to live in an extended family. The effects of three variables—the availability of alternative care, the availability of space, and the prevalence of the conjugal norm in the prefecture—were all negative and significant. That is, all three contex-

Table 10.5. Effects of individual-level and contextual variables on the extended family: ages 30–59

Variables	(1) b	(1) B	(2) b	(2) B	(3) b	(3) B	(4) b	(4) B	(5) b	(5) B	(6) b	(6) B
Demographic												
Parent	.37**	.31					.36**	.30			.34**	.28
Spouse	.13**	.07					.02	.01			.01	.01
Age	.03**	.05					−.01**	−.02			−.00	−.00
Economic												
Income			.17**	.44			.15**	.20			.13**	.17
Occupation			.02*	.02			.02*	.02			.04**	.03
Land			.50**	.24			.44**	.39			.38**	.34
Normative												
Education					−.07**	−.09	−.04**	−.05			−.02**	−.03
Opcores					.17**	.25	.10**	.15			.03**	.05
Context												
Hospital									−.07**	−.46	−.04**	−.27
Space									−.25**	−.40	−.08**	−.13
% Hi educ									−.07**	−.70	−.03**	−.28
R²	.09		.23		.08		.34		.20		.37	
(N = 10,644)												

Note: All six models are significant (**p < .01, *p < .05).

tual variables worked against the extended family.

When relative effects of these variables are considered, the standardized coefficients suggest that the effects of the normative factor had the greatest negative effect in both age groups. The relative effect of the accessibility to alternative care was as strong as the normative factor only among the elderly group. Therefore, the care system in the community was relatively important for the elderly; and when the community provided alternative care, family extension was less likely. The negative association between the availability of space and family extension was unexpected. But family extension may be more affected by the actual amount of space available in the family household than by the average amount of space in the community. These contextual effects must now be examined with the individual-level variables.

Model 6 included all the variables I have discussed so far. In the older group, as anticipated, all variables except space availability had significant effects. This finding suggests that the space-availability factor was effective only through more proximate determinants. The model explained 45 percent of the variance in extended families among the older group and 37 percent of the variance in the younger group. Among the younger group, however, the effect of space availability was still significant and negative. This result could mean that the variable used to measure the proximate space availability in this model (land ownership) was not appropriate. Land ownership indicated the economic standing of a family very well, but not space availability.

In sum, the series of multiple regression analyses supported the hypotheses. Each determinant had a strong independent effect on the extensiveness of the family. The normative factor and the prevalence of alternative care systems added to the explanation contributed by the individual mechanisms. The effects of the economic factors may have been underrepresented owing to the lack of appropriate measures of proximate space availability and family property. There may also have been an age-cohort effect. That is, as can be observed in Tables 10.4 and 10.5, the magnitude of the effects of the individual-level normative factors (education, opinion about coresidence) appear to have been stronger among the older group than among the younger group.

DISCUSSION AND CONCLUSION

The effects of the demographic and normative factors were found to vary depending on the stage of an individual's life cycle. For those who were in the early to late middle age, whether or not they had surviving parents to live with was the single most important factor in predicting family extension. For those in the later life stage, having children and not having a surviving spouse, as well as possessing the *ie* ideology, were most important in explaining family extension. A conjugal orientation and the availability of a care system in the community directly reduced an individual's propensity to reside in a multigenerational household. Space availabililty exerted only an indirect effect through the individual-level factors.

The effect of economic factors played a relatively strong role in the overall explanation regardless of age. Available space in the residence, ownership of houses or land that had been passed down from previous generations, and higher household income significantly increased an individual's propensity to live in an extended family. It should be noted again that these economic attributes also suggested an individual's inclination to accept the *ie* ideology. It is safe to conclude that economic factors, which are particularly related to the maintenance of family succession, are important determinants of the extended family in Japan.

Thus, the contemporary Japanese family is a product not only of intertwined norms and economic conditions at both individual and societal levels, but also of the social care system. Overall, this study supports the framework developed by Kojima (1989) and Ruggles (1987). I conclude that the three determinants discussed in this chapter can be applied across time and space. Nonetheless, the specific social, political, and demographic context must be taken into consideration. For example, rising income, which leads to separate households in the United States today (Michael et al., 1980) may still work in Japan to extend households, just as it did in Victorian England and America owing to the normative inclination to coresidence. Only by being aware of the spatial and historical context will we be able to understand a phenomenon and to test our framework in a comparative manner. In the case of Japan, particular attention must be paid to the historical context, given the long period in which a strong stem-family ideology has been sustained. The fact that some contemporary Japanese prefer to live with their parents or with their younger children cannot be explained solely by a materialistic assessment or attributed solely to cultural lag.

This study also supports Goode's (1963) theory. The two forces explicated by Goode—conjugal ideology and economic correlates of industrialization (that is, social and geographic mobility, a decreasing family role in determining the occupations of the offspring, and the functional differentiation of the social structure)—play major roles in explaining the extended family. These two forces, which facilitate the conjugal family type, were found to work against the persistence of the extended family in Japan.

I observed attenuated effects of normative factors, specifically the *ie* ideology, on the extended family among the younger age group. In the near future, demographic and economic factors may exert more power in shaping living arrangements, with the disappearance of those who have been socialized in the *ie* ideology. We are now able to think about variations in living arrangements that are neither extended nor conjugal in the conventional sense. For example, the Japanese housing market has already introduced "two-generation housing" in which separate kitchens and bathrooms are constructed for two or more generations. These housing units may increasingly attract families who can afford to have such living arrangements. As Japan's population continues to age, we may find an increase in the proportion of nuclear households, especially single-person households, or instead the persistence of the extended-family household as a strategy for coping with economic and social conditions. In the latter case, it would not be the same extended-family system as found in the past, but rather a joint living arrangement of two or more conjugal units. A very different exchange system among family members is to be expected from such a living arrangement.

Finally, this study has attempted to measure the value dimension and to incorporate both macro- and microlevel variables into its framework. Similar attempts should be encouraged of others who are interested in how individual characteristics and larger social forces shape individual behavior.

ACKNOWLEDGMENTS

This chapter is based on part of my doctoral dissertation, prepared at the University of Washington, Seattle. I would like to express my gratitude to Mr. Hiroaki Shimizu, Dr. Makoto Atō, and Dr. Hiroshi Kojima of the Institute of Population Problems, Ministry of Health and Welfare, for allowing me to use the data set and providing help with data management.

REFERENCES

Anderson, Michael. 1971. *Family Structure in Nineteenth Century Lancashire*. Cambridge: Cambridge University Press.

Berge, Erling. 1989. "On the Study of Households: Some Methodological Considerations on the Use of Household Data." *International Sociology* 4(2):115–130.

Berkner, Lutz K. 1972. "The Stem Family and the Development Cycle of the Peasant Household." *American Historical Review* 77(2):398–418.

———. 1976. "Inheritance, Land Tenure and Peasant Family Structure: A German Regional Comparison." In Jack Goody, Joan Thirsk, and E. P. Thompson (eds.), *Family and Inheritance*, pp. 71–95. London: Cambridge University Press.

Blumberg, R. L., and R. F. Winch. 1972. "Societal Complexity and Familial Complexity: Evidence for the Curvilinear Hypothesis." *American Journal of Sociology* 77:898–920.

Coale, Ansley J. 1983. "Recent Trends in Fertility in Less Developed Countries." *Science* 211(4613, 26 August):828–832.

Council on Population Problems (Jinkō Mondai Shingikai). 1986. *Nihon no Jinkō Nihon no Shakai* (Japanese population, Japanese society). Tokyo: Toyokeizai Shinposha.

Ermisch, J., and E. Overton. 1985. "Minimal Household Units: A New Approach to the Analysis of Household Formations." *Population Studies* 39(1):33-54.

Freedman, R., M.-C. Chang, and T.-H. Sun. 1982. "Household Composition, Extended Kinship, and Reproduction in Taiwan: 1973-1980." *Population Studies* 36:395-411.

Goode, William J. 1963. *World Revolution and Family Patterns*. New York: Free Press.

Hareven, Tamara K. 1987. "Historical Analysis of the Family." In Marvin B. Sussman and Suzanne K. Steinmertz (eds.), *Handbook of Marriage and the Family*, pp. 37-57. New York: Plenum Press.

Japan, Ministry of Health and Welfare, Institute of Population Problems (IPP). 1987. *Household Statistics by Regions and Prefectures of Japan: A Demographic Study of Household Formation and Growth and Their Regional Differences in Japan, 1986-88*. Special Study Project, Vol. 1. Tokyo: Institute of Population Problems, Ministry of Health and Welfare.

Kamiko Takeji. 1976. "Fukugō Kazoku no Bunpu to Shōkai" (Introduction and distribution of the extended family). In Kamiko Takeji and Masuda Kokichi (eds.), *Sanseidai-Kazoku* (The three-generational family), pp. 9-36. Tokyo: Kakiuchishuppan.

Knodel, John, and Etienne van de Walle. 1979. "Lessons from the Past: Policy Implications of Historical Fertility Studies." *Population and Development Review* 5:217-245.

Kobrin, Frances E., and Calvin Goldscheider. 1982. "Family Extension or Nonfamily Living: Life Cycle, Economic, and Ethnic Factors." *Western Sociological Review* 13:103-118.

Kojima Hiroshi. 1989. "Living Arrangements and Intergenerational Financial Flows." In Frances K. Goldscheider and Calvin Goldscheider (eds.), *Ethnicity and the New Family Economy: Living Arrangements and Intergenerational Financial Flows*, pp. 163-184. Boulder, Colo.: Westview Press.

Kurosu Satomi. 1990. "Determinants of the Contemporary Japanese Extended Family." Doctoral dissertation, Department of Sociology, University of Washington, Seattle.

———. 1992. "The Ecology of the Extended Family in Japan." *Japan Review* 3:73-95.

Laslett, Peter. 1972. *Household and Family in Past Time*. London: Cambridge University Press.

Lesthaeghe, Ron, and Chris Wilson. 1986. "Modes of Production, Secularization, and the Pace of the Fertility Decline in Western Europe, 1870-1930." In Ansley J. Coale and Susan Watkins (eds.), *The Decline of Fertility in Europe*, pp. 261-292. Princeton: Princeton University Press.

Lesthaeghe, Ron, and John Surkyn. 1988. "Cultural Dynamics and Economic Theories of Fertility Change." *Population and Development Review* 14(1):1-45.

Levy, Marion J., Jr. 1965. "Aspects of the Analysis of Family Structure." In Ansley J. Coale, Lloyd A. Fallers, Marion J. Levy, Jr., David M. Schneider, and Silvan S. Tomkins, *Aspects of the Analysis of Family Structure*, pp. 1-63. Princeton: Princeton University Press.

Martin, Linda G. 1990. "Changing Intergenerational Family Relations in East Asia." In Samuel H. Preston (ed.), *The Annals of the American Academy of Political and Social Science*, Vol. 510, pp. 102-114. Newbury Park, Calif.: Sage Publications.

Michael, R. T., V. R. Fuchs, and S. R. Scott. 1980. "Changes in the Propensity to Live Alone, 1950-1979." *Demography* 17:39-56.

Morgan, S. Philip, and Kiyosi Hirosima. 1983. "The Persistence of Extended Family Residence in Japan: Anachronism or Alternative Strategy?" *American Sociological Review* 48(2):269-281.

Morgan, S. Philip, and Jay D. Teachman. 1988. "Logistic Regression: Description, Examples, and Comparisons." *Journal of Marriage and the Family* 50:928-936.

Nasu Sōichi. 1985. "Gendai Shakai no Rojin to Kazoku Hendō." (Aged people in contemporary society and family change). In Nasu Sōichi and Masuda Kokichi (eds.), *Rojin to Kazoku no Shakaigaku* (Sociology of the aged and the family), pp. 1–42. Tokyo: Kakiuchishuppan.

Rindfuss, Ronald R., and S. Philip Morgan. 1983. "Marriage, Sex, and the First Birth Interval: The Quiet Revolution in Asia." *Population and Development Review* 9:259–278.

Ruggles, Steven. 1987. *Prolonged Connections: The Rise of the Extended Family in Nineteenth-Century England and America*. Wisconsin: University of Wisconsin Press.

Shimizu Hiroaki. 1986. *Jinkō to Kazoku no Shakaigaku* (Sociology of population and the family). Tokyo: Sai-shobo.

Smelser, Neil J., and Sydney Halpern. 1978. "The Historical Triangulation of Family, Economy, and Education." In John Demos and Sarane Spence Boocock (eds.), *Turning Points*, Chicago: University of Chicago Press.

Tilly, Charles, and C. Harold Brown. 1974. "On Uprooting, Kinship, and the Auspices of Migration." In Charles Tilly (ed.), *An Urban World*, pp. 108–133. Boston: Little Brown.

Zeng Yi. 1986. "Changes in Family Structure in China: A Simulation Study." *Population and Development Review* 12(4):675–703.

CHAPTER 11

Contact with Parents in Japan: Effects on Attitudes toward Gender and Intergenerational Roles

by Ronald R. Rindfuss, Tim Futing Liao, and Noriko O. Tsuya

Virtually all family scholars would agree that one of the principal roles assigned to families is socialization, that is, the process whereby individuals learn and maintain the norms, values, and customs of a society. As socializers, families are a conservative force in the sense that they pass on from generation to generation core norms and values of the society (Mead, 1970; Lash, 1979). This socialization process has received widespread attention from sociological researchers, and the expectation of socialization theory is that families are the key social institution responsible for new generations learning social values.

Empirically, researchers have tended to concentrate on early childhood through early adulthood, and the empirical evidence is mixed (Kohn, Slomczynski, and Schoenbach, 1986; Bengston, 1975; Kandel and Lesser, 1972; Furstenberg, 1971). It is perhaps in the area of marital behavior that the strongest intergenerational linkages have been found (McLanahan and Bumpass, 1988); and

Thornton (1991) has recently suggested that intergenerational influences on attitudes may be the most promising theoretical explanation of how socialization affects subsequent family processes.

Almost all of this attention on intergenerational value transmission has focused on children, or at best, young adults. This is unfortunate because we now recognize that in contemporary developed societies socialization is a lifelong process, as individuals learn to cope with a changing social environment (Mortimer and Simmons, 1978). For example, Kohn and Schooler's (1983) work shows the clear effect of adult occupational experiences on attitudes and values.

To what extent do families and the broader kinship network influence the adult socialization process? Do parents of adult children exert a conservative and traditional influence on their children, particularly in shaping family norms and values? The major evidence in this area is the recent study by Rossi and Rossi (1990). They find that there seems to be more influence between mothers and their adult children than between fathers and their adult children; but, as they acknowledge, their ability to examine intergenerational dynamics was quite limited.

The concern with intergenerational influences is particularly of interest in times of rapid change. The cohort model of social change (Ryder, 1965) implies that younger generations adopt new values and attitudes, which in turn lead to changed behavior. This model fits well with the age differences typically found in various measures of family values and attitudes (Thornton, 1989). Yet family norms and values tend to change gradually, even in the face of markedly changed societal conditions, suggesting the existence of substantial conservative forces. In this chapter, we examine one likely possibility for the gradual pace of family change, namely parents and in-laws, in Japan, where there have been marked legal, economic, and migratory pressures on traditional family values and practices. Yet, in Japan, as Nakane (1973) argues, numerous traditional features of basic cultural components persist even in changing social circumstances.

Despite ample evidence of regional variation (e.g., Befu, 1963) the traditional Japanese family system, dating from at least the Meiji era (1868–1912), was based on patrilineal descent, patriarchal authority, and patrilocal residence (Matsumoto, 1962; Ishihara, 1981; Goode, 1963; Fukutake, 1989). The practice of primogeniture gave status to sons over daughters and firstborn children over others. The eldest son would inherit the family residence and assets, and in turn he would be responsible for his parents in their old age. Daughters would marry into other families and younger sons would attempt to establish branch families. The *yōshi* system allowed families to adopt a son or son-in-law if a male heir did not exist (Taeuber, 1958:101; Befu, 1963; Lebra,

1984:20–21). Yet even with the emphasis on the male line, bilateral kin continued to play a role in everyday household functions, in visiting patterns, and on such ceremonial occasions as weddings and funerals.

Because the daughter-in-law was expected to move into the groom's household, and because the marriage united the two families, rather than just two individuals, parents, especially fathers, traditionally arranged for the marriage of their sons and daughters, rather than leaving it to the whim of romance (Taeuber, 1958:207–208). In other words, the traditional family system in Japan almost mandated that parents or fathers control their children's marriages because the system's ultimate goal was to secure continuation of the patrilineal family line. While the arranging of marriages has changed substantially during the twentieth century, it is still the case that marriage unites two families in a myriad of ways.

After marriage, contact with the husband's and wife's parents is one of the foundations of kinship exchanges. Even if sons or daughters do not live with their parents, contact with parents is basically the mechanism that allows or facilitates the exchanges and influences that occur within the kinship system. Furthermore, such visiting patterns are important in their own right, and they have been part of the traditional family and kinship patterns in Japan (Befu, 1963).

The central issue in this chapter is the extent to which contact with a husband's and wife's parents affects the attitudes held by husbands and wives about intergenerational relations and socialization goals. Our general expectation is that, other things being equal, the senior generation serves the role of preserving traditional values and attitudes. The more contact that individuals have with the senior generation, the more likely they will hold traditional values and attitudes.

By arguing that kinship exchanges are the "energy" providing a traditional or conservative force in society, we are suggesting that this is a mechanism that allows the senior generation an opportunity to reinterpret traditional family values and customs in light of changing social circumstances. Clearly, members of the younger generation can do this for themselves by trying to imagine how their parents might have wanted them to react to changing circumstances. We doubt, however, that such mental exercises, if they occur, are as effective as actual discussions with the senior generation. Furthermore, frequent contact with the senior generation is likely to increase the probability that the younger generation interprets changing circumstances in light of traditional family values. Finally, we expect that the repeated retelling of important family stories, the type of oral history often found when grandparents, parents, and children are together, is likely to reinforce traditional family values. Sometimes this reinforcement may be intentional on the part of the senior generation, and at other times it may be quite inadvertent.

Japan is an ideal setting in which to examine this broad theoretical issue. In the past half-century, it has experienced a substantial amount of social, economic, and demographic change (Taeuber, 1958; Dore, 1959; Mosk, 1983; Otani, 1987). Today, it is unquestionably one of the world's most economically and technologically developed countries, and the forces of development have clearly impinged on the family. In line with this socioeconomic change has come change in a variety of family values (Kobayashi, 1977). Yet, because their development grew out of an East Asian culture, rather than a Western culture, and because the development process was so rapid, there are large differences between the Japanese and the Western family. For example, extended households are more common in Japan. In 1985, 64 percent of Japanese aged 65 and over were living in households that contained at least one of their children (Japan, Statistics Bureau, 1986:324-325). Family solutions, rather than governmental solutions, are typically sought for childcare and elderly care concerns (Morgan and Hirosima, 1983; Martin, 1989). Compared with the West, there are also broad differences in the structure of the labor market and gender stratification (Brinton, 1989; Rosenbaum and Kariya, 1989).

CONCEPTUAL AND CAUSAL ISSUES

Examining broader relations within kinship groups and linking these relationships with current attitudes raise complex conceptual, causal, and methodological issues. One category of issues revolves around the causal priority of attitudes versus behavior. A second set revolves around the fact that families and kinship groups are *groups*, whereas the standard methodology is to interview individuals and have them report on their relations with members of their family and kinship group. We address both sets of issues in the following sections.

Causal Ordering

Attitudes are important because they shape the way in which individuals and families behave. But from a scientific perspective, attitudes can be frustrating to examine because by definition they have the potential of being ephemeral. Attitudes can and do change in response to the ongoing experiences of individuals. Although radical shifts are rare, moderate shifts are common. In the case of the present topic, it is clear that the contact patterns that individuals have with their parents and their in-laws are likely to be shaped in part by their attitudes. Contact in turn can shape the attitudes that individuals hold about appropriate intergenerational relations.

To start to untangle the attitude versus contact nexus, we would ideally like attitudes to be measured periodically, as well as to have a history of contact patterns. In the present case, we do not have data from a longitudinal study. Rather, we have results from a cross-sectional survey. We treat current attitudes as a function of recent visiting patterns. This is a plausible inference, given the temporal ordering. Visiting patterns refer to behavior in the past year or two; attitudes are those at the moment of the survey.

We also have purchase on the underlying causal mechanisms because if both parents are deceased, ours comes close to being a natural experiment. No one would argue that the attitudes resulted in having two dead parents. Rather, the death of the parents is clearly exogenous. Thus, if individuals whose parents were deceased held attitudes different from those of others after we controlled for other relevant variables, then we would feel comfortable in concluding that the lack of contact with parents resulting from death had led to the current intergenerational family attitudes.

Finally, 20 percent of our sample lived with the husband's parents, and 6 percent lived with the wife's parents. In the typical situation, decisions about living with parents are made before or at the time of marriage. Because we are working with a cross-section of adults, the typical marriage took place many years in the past. Moreover, the decision to live with parents often rests on structural rather than preferential criteria. Is the groom the eldest son? Does the bride have any brothers? Is the groom's employment in the same locale? Given the changeability of the attitudes we examine, and given the rapid pace of social change in Japan, we feel comfortable that the causal direction is from living with parents to current attitudes.

Individuals versus Families

Conceptually we are interested in the process outlined in Figure 11.1, which is a complicated process. Consider just visiting patterns with respect to husband's and wife's parents. In both cases, one can visit the parents only if they are alive. If the husband or wife shares a residence with the respective parents, then by definition contact is frequent. Furthermore, contact with one set of parents is likely to affect the amount of contact with the other set of parents.

In addition, one would expect that the attitudes currently held by the husband are related in a variety of ways to the attitudes held by the wife, and vice versa. These are attitudes about topics that often come up in discussion, sometimes in subtle ways and at other times in ways that are not so subtle.

To analyze the husband's and wife's attitudes, we would ideally have reports from both, and then would estimate the determinants of their attitudes using a model that allows for correlation between them. In the present case, however, we do not have measures of both the husband's and the wife's attitudes; rather, we have measures of one or the other. Either the husband or the wife was randomly selected to be the respondent.

To begin examining this issue, we can look at the extent to which visiting patterns or contact patterns with the husband's and wife's parents are influenced by the existence of unmeasured variables that jointly determine both of them. We are in a position to do so, even though only the husband or the wife was interviewed, because the respondent reported on visiting patterns to both the husband's and the wife's parents. In addition, he or she reported on shared residence with the husband's and wife's parents, and whether the husband's and wife's parents were alive.

To explore the issue of joint determination, we treated the husband's and wife's visiting patterns as two dependent variables in two separate equations that were correlated, using a bivariate probit model (Maddala, 1983). The results from the model (not shown here) clearly indicated what we had expected: the patterns of visiting the husband's and wife's parents were related; that is, error terms were significantly correlated. Nevertheless, the estimates of the coefficients for a set of independent variables determining patterns of visiting the husband's or wife's parents were essentially unchanged

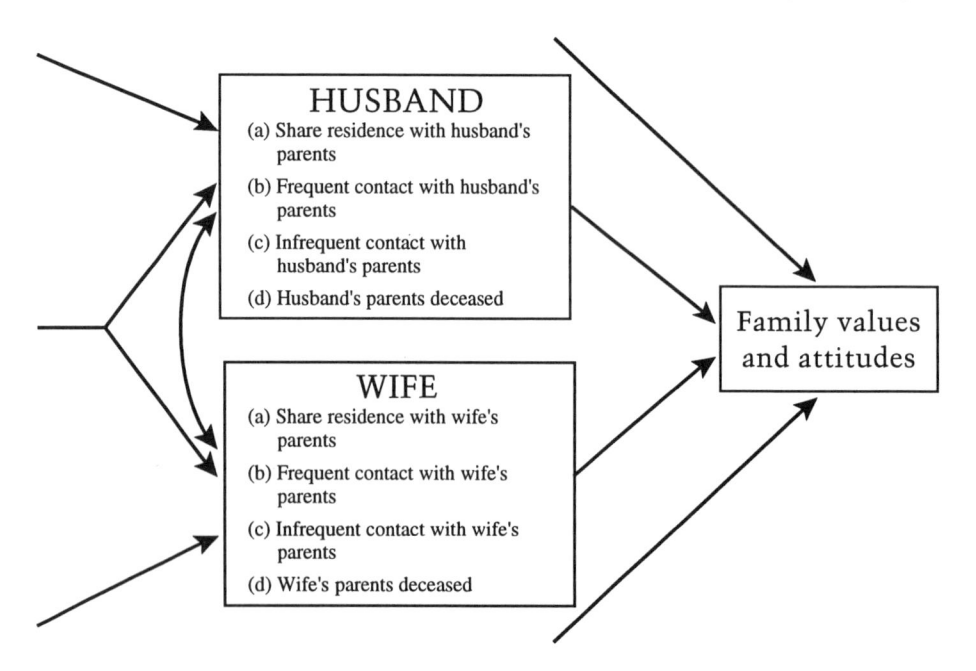

Figure 11.1. Model of the effect of contact with husband's and wife's parents on family attitudes

whether or not we used the bivariate or a simpler, univariate probit model. Put differently, complete understanding of the entire process required knowing something about the visiting patterns involving both the husband's parents and the wife's parents, but the effect of various independent variables was unbiased whether or not we took the broader structure into account.

On the basis of this knowledge, we proceeded to estimate the effect of a variety of factors (including contact with the husband's and the wife's parents) on the respondents' current attitudes without explicitly taking into account a parallel equation explaining the spouse's attitudes. In so doing, we assumed that the unaffected estimation, regardless of whether we used bivariate or univariate probit models, applied to attitudes as well as to visiting behavior. Although this was an untested assumption, we believe it was a reasonable one. A complete test of this assumption will have to wait until data from interviews of both husbands and wives are collected.

DATA AND METHODS

The data set was from the 1988 National Family Survey, sponsored by Mainichi Newspapers and Nihon University, and conducted by Mainichi Newspapers. Questionnaires were hand-delivered to 3,400 respondents who were selected throughout Japan by a stratified, multi-stage, random sampling technique (Ozaki, 1989). The questionnaires were self-administered and were picked up approximately one week after being left at the respondents' homes. The response rate was 71 percent and the coverage across standard demographic groups appears to have been excellent. On the basis of comparisons with census data, Martin and Tsuya (Chapter 9 in this volume) found that unmarried individuals were somewhat underrepresented. Since we restricted our attention to currently married individuals, this underrepresentation of single individuals was not a concern.

We limited our attention to currently married respondents because doing so allowed us to see the effects of contact with both the husband's and the wife's parents. (Otherwise we would have had to limit our attention to contact with the respondent's parents.) This had the effect of making marital status a constant, and thus its effect was not visible.

Since the analysis was restricted to currently married couples, it was necessary to impose a lower age cutoff to insure that the youngest age group was not biased toward a young age at marriage (Westoff and Ryder, 1977, Appendix C-2). Given that the overwhelming majority of Japanese marriages occur in a relatively narrow age band during the 20s (Rindfuss, Morgan, and Swicegood, 1988), we restricted our analysis to those aged 30 and above.

Ronald R. Rindfuss, Tim Futing Liao, and Noriko O. Tsuya

Dependent Variables

Our strategy was to examine a variety of attitudinal items tapping values toward intergenerational relations and gender roles. In so doing, we were looking for consistent patterns of effects of contact with the wife's and husband's parents across items. Our expectation was that frequent contact with the parents would lead to more traditional values.

The first two dependent variables tapped attitudes toward relationships between adult children and their parents. The first asked whether "it is the eldest son's duty to look after his parents," and the second asked whether "the name of the family must be succeeded even by adopting a child." The percentage of respondents who agreed with the first statement was 31; the percentage agreeing with the second was 26. It is worth noting that both items tapped traditional components of the Japanese family system, components that were widely agreed upon in prewar Japan (1868–1945). Although we know of no survey data on these items from the prewar years, qualitative evidence indicates that a substantially larger fraction would have responded affirmatively then (Tsuya and Choe, 1992). By 1988, however, only a minority of respondents agreed.

Both of these items presented respondents with an explicit "I don't know" choice. As expected, a significant minority gave this response (10 and 16 percent, respectively). In general, older respondents and those with less education were more likely than others to give "don't know" responses. In the analysis reported below, we estimated our models incorporating "I don't know" as a third choice, but we show only the results for the yes-no contrast. We also experimented with simply eliminating the "don't know" responses and treating the dependent variable as a dichotomy. In general, our substantive conclusions were the same no matter which procedure we used.

The next variable measured gender relations within the domestic household and was based on an initial question and its follow-up. The initial question was: "What do you think of a man doing kitchen work?" The three-quarters of the respondents who answered that "it is a good thing" were asked why. They were provided with four precoded responses and the option of writing in any other response. The follow-up responses tended to be practical reasons (such as women's employment outside the home is increasing and increasing numbers of men are living apart from their families owing to job transfers), except for one that was more normative: "The idea itself that housework is women's work is wrong." Expecting that those who chose this more normative response would be different from those who chose the practical ones, we created a three-category dependent variable: (1) good thing, practical reason (61 percent of respondents); (2) good thing, normative reason (14 percent); and (3) not a good thing (25 percent). Even though a majority considered it a good thing for a man to be involved in work around the house, particularly in the kitchen, this is not the behavioral reality in contemporary Japan (Nihon Hōsō Kyōkai, 1986; Tsuya and Choe, 1992). It remains to be seen if behavior will change to match the ideal.

The final set of dependent variables tapped the kinds of traits that parents would want in their sons and daughters. These variables were derived from the following question: "What kind of person would you like your child to become? Please choose three answers from the following, in case of a boy and girl, separately. If you do not have any children, give an answer on the assumption that you did have children." The questionnaire then listed 10 characteristics, shown in Table 11.1, and included spaces for up to three choices for a boy and three choices for a girl. Unfortunately, respondents were not asked, or allowed, to rank-order their choices (see Kohn, 1969, for a discussion of the importance of ranking). Thus, operationally, we can claim only that the items chosen ranked higher than the items not chosen.

Several aspects of the distributions shown in Table 11.1 are striking. First, as might be expected given the strong traditional differences in gender-role expectations, the traits chosen for sons were strikingly different from those for daughters. Moreover, respondents had less agreement on the traits preferred for sons than on the traits preferred for daughters.

Overwhelmingly, they wanted their daughters to be obedient and considerate. In contrast, the three top choices for sons were being responsible, independent, and considerate. For both sons and daughters, such characteristics as enjoying life, being a leader, or being popular were not highly valued. These results contrast sharply with gender-role expectations in the United States. Thornton (1989), for example, finds that sex-role attitudes have become considerably more egalitarian in the United States in the last few decades. These clear differentials in Japanese gender-role expectations may be due, at least in part, to the persistent and quite severe division of labor in the Japanese home along gender lines (Vogel, 1971: 181–193), although there are hints of recent change (Tsuya and Choe, 1992).

Table 11.1. Percentages of respondents choosing a specified trait as one of the three characteristics they would like for their son or daughter: Japan, 1988 National Family Survey

Characteristic	Son	Daughter
Enjoy life	13	19
Obedient	37	81
Independent	51	20
Successful	16	5
Leader	15	1
Popular	9	13
Considerate	51	87
Responsible	59	30
Vital	31	5
Dutiful	13	35
No. of cases	1,400	1,387

Note: Percentages shown do not sum to 300 in each column because a small percentage of respondents only gave one or two choices.

Because all of our dependent variables were categorical, without any obvious ordinal component, we used logistic regression to estimate the multivariate models. In most cases the dependent variable was a dichotomy, and in other cases it was a trichotomy.

Pattern of Contact with Parents

The independent variables of central interest were the patterns of contact with the wife's and husband's parents. Respondents were asked whether their own parents and their spouse's parents were alive. If the answers were affirmative, then respondents were asked if they lived with their own parents or with their spouse's parents. If they lived with neither, they were asked: (a) "How often did you see your parents during the last one or two years?" and (b) "How often did you telephone your own parents during the last one or two years?" Parallel questions were asked about contact with the spouse's parents. Given the traditional dominance of the male in the Japanese family system, we converted these variables into one set for the husband's parents and another set for the wife's parents (depending on who the respondent was) and created a dummy variable indicating whether the respondent was the husband or the wife. Thus, in addition to the sex of the respondent, we had four key predictor variables—two for the wife's parents, two for the husband's, two for visiting, and two for phoning. All were constructed the same way. Here we use visiting the husband's parents as an example:

(1) Both of the husband's parents are deceased
(2) Infrequently visit the husband's parents, once a month or less
(3) Frequently visit the husband's parents, once a week or more
(4) Living with one or both of the husband's parents

Because two of the four categories (both of the husband's parents are deceased, and living with one or both of the husband's parents) were identical for the visiting and telephoning variables, both sets of variables could not be included in the same model. We therefore ran separate analyses to gauge the effects of visiting and telephoning.

The distributions for these four contact variables are shown in the bottom panels of Table 11.2. As dictated by tradition, respondents were more likely to be living with the husband's parents than with the wife's parents. The husband's parents were also more likely to be deceased than the wife's parents, reflecting the age differences between spouses. If parents were alive but not living with the respondent, contact was more likely to be infrequent (once a month or less) than frequent. This was true for both the husband's parents and the wife's parents. Although this finding was somewhat surprising in light of the popular images of the elderly in Japan, it was consistent with results from other studies. For example, the proportion of elderly Japanese who reside with their children is about four times that of elderly Americans who reside with theirs, although Japanese not coresiding with their children see them less frequently than do their American counterparts (Japan, Management and Coordination Agency, 1987). Befu (1963) found that visits and telephone conversations were more likely to take place with the wife's parents than with the husband's parents—reflecting the sometimes overlooked role of female kinship patterns in Japan.

Other Control Variables

Since we knew that contact with parents was also related to a wide variety of other social and demographic variables, it was necessary to examine the effect of contact with parents, controlling for these other variables. Given the vast changes in family law and behavior in twentieth-century Japan, it was essential to control for the respondent's age. Controlling for age simultaneously controls for life-cycle stage and cohort membership, both of which are likely to be important in contemporary Japan. Even in the absence of these past changes, in most societies it is the eldest age groups that tend to hold the most traditional familial attitudes. It was also important to control for age at marriage. We expected that those who married at relatively old ages would have less conservative attitudes than those marrying at younger ages, even after educational attainment was controlled.

As noted earlier, the eldest daughter and especially the eldest son occupy a special place in Japanese family ideology. They receive extra privileges as well as added responsibilities. We expected that

Table 11.2. Means and percentage distributions for the independent variables in the multivariate analyses

Variable	Mean or %
Age (years)	48
Age at marriage (years)	26
Husband is eldest son (%)	44
Wife is eldest daughter (%)	44
Husband's education (%)	
Less than high school	28
High school	43
Junior college	9
University	20
Respondent is female (%)	51
Arranged or partially arranged marriage (%)	48
Pattern of visiting husband's parents (%)	
Both deceased	40
Infrequently visit	33
Frequently telephone	7
Live with	20
Pattern of telephoning husband's parents (%)	
Both deceased	40
Infrequently telephone	33
Frequently telephone	7
Live with	20
Pattern of visiting wife's parents (%)	
Both deceased	32
Infrequently visit	51
Frequently visit	11
Live with	6
Pattern of telephoning wife's parents (%)	
Both deceased	32
Infrequently telephone	44
Frequently telephone	18
Live with	6

the eldest child would have more traditional family attitudes than would other respondents; we also expected that the effect of being the eldest son would be stronger than the effect of being the eldest daughter.

In most societies, education is a force of change, and we expected the better educated to hold the least traditional family attitudes. Our data set has information on both the husband's and the wife's education. Even though husbands tended to be somewhat better educated than wives, the correlation between the two was sufficiently high that we did not want to enter both variables in the same equation. Given the patriarchal nature of Japanese society, we decided to use the husband's education. In the present context, education also stands as an indicator of various dimensions of social class.

Finally, we controlled for whether the marriage was arranged or not. Other things being equal, we anticipated that those with arranged marriages would hold more traditional family attitudes than those whose marriages had not been arranged. Close to one-half of the respondents had arranged marriages. The reader needs to be cautioned, however, that these were not arranged marriages in the strictest sense, whereby parents or others exercise complete power to choose a spouse for the young man or woman. The word used in the Japanese questionnaire, *miai*, also connotes a marriage resulting from an introduction made by the parents, senior relatives, or a professor or employer because the parents or person making the introduction thought that the young man and woman would make a suitable couple. Such formal introductions are still quite common in Japan and are an indication that marriage serves a broader social function than simply celebrating the love between a young man and a young woman.

RESULTS

Before we present our results in detail, it is useful to summarize the broader picture of the effect of contact with parents. In general, the variables of visiting and telephoning parents had remarkably little effect on any of the family variables examined here. Of the 300 contact-with-parents coefficients, only 30 (or 10 percent) were significant at the 5 percent level. Further, those that were significant tended to involve parents who were no longer alive or parents who lived with respondents, rather than the frequency-of-contact dimension. We discuss the implications of these findings in the conclusion. For now, as we go through the results, the remarkably few significant contact coefficients should be noted.

The effects of the various independent variables on whether respondents thought it was the eldest son's duty to look after his parents are shown in Table 11.3. For the visiting and telephoning variables, living with the husband's parents was significant. This effect was in the expected direction; that is, those who lived with the husband's parents tended to hold the most conservative position.

The other variables having significant effects were generally in the expected direction. Older respondents, those whose marriages had been arranged, and husbands who were the eldest son were more likely than others to agree that it was the eldest son's duty to look after his parents. Those with a high school diploma or more education were less likely to agree with that view.

Somewhat surprisingly, if the respondent was female, she was less likely to give the traditional response affirming the eldest son's duty to look after his parents. Perhaps women also want to take care of their parents, and the traditional

Table 11.3. Logistic regression model estimates (Betas) of whether it is the eldest son's duty to look after his parents, for the visiting and telephoning parents variables

Predictor variable	Model[a] Visiting	Model[a] Telephoning
Age	0.02*	0.03*
Age at marriage	−0.03	−0.03
Husband is eldest son[b]	0.50*	0.49*
Wife is eldest daughter[c]	−0.16	−0.16
Husband's education[d]		
High school	−0.58*	−0.58*
Junior college	−0.49*	−0.49*
University	−0.42*	−0.43*
Respondent is female[e]	−0.50*	−0.50*
Arranged or partially arranged marriage[f]	0.40*	0.39*
Pattern of visiting (telephoning) husband's parents[g]		
Both deceased	0.30	0.35*
Frequently visit (telephone)	0.02	0.31
Live with	0.50*	0.56*
Pattern of visiting (telephoning) wife's parents[h]		
Both deceased	−0.02	−0.03
Frequently visit (telephone)	0.10	0.01
Live with	0.21	0.22
Model χ^2	173.2	172.6

*Significant at 0.05 level.
a. Each model also has a third category on the dependent variable: missing data. To conserve space, the contrasts with missing data are not shown.
b. Omitted category: husband is not the eldest son.
c. Omitted category: wife is not the eldest daughter.
d. Omitted category: less than a high school diploma.
e. Omitted category: male.
f. Omitted category: love match.
g. Omitted category: infrequently visit husband's parents.
h. Omitted category: infrequently visit wife's parents.

assignment of this role to the eldest son conflicts with this desire. Along similar lines, we note that in another part of the questionnaire, respondents were asked: "By whom do you want to be looked after when you get old or are bedridden for a long time?" The respondent's spouse was the most common choice in response to this question, but a daughter, rather than a son or daughter-in-law, was next most common. This pattern again suggests a strong tie between parents and their daughters. Befu (1963) has argued that such ties have existed for a long time.

Table 11.4 shows the effects of the independent variables on attitudes about whether the couple must continue the family name even by adopting a child.

Table 11.4. Logistic regression model estimates (Betas) of whether the family name must be succeeded even by adopting a child, for the visiting and telephoning parents variables

	Model[a]	
Predictor variable	Visiting	Telephoning
Age	0.04*	0.04*
Age at marriage	−0.02	−0.02
Husband is eldest son[b]	0.14	0.12
Wife is eldest daughter[c]	−0.11	−0.11
Husband's education[d]		
High school	−0.23	−0.24
Junior college	−0.31	−0.32
University	−0.44*	−0.46*
Respondent is female[e]	−0.56*	−0.56*
Arranged or partially arranged marriage[f]	0.10	0.09
Pattern of visiting (telephoning) husband's parents[g]		
Both deceased	0.13	0.20
Frequently visit (telephone)	0.01	0.38
Live with	0.66*	0.76*
Pattern of visiting (telephoning) wife's parents[h]		
Both deceased	0.14	0.16
Frequently visit (telephone)	0.22	0.19
Live with	0.27	0.33
Model χ^2	150.5	153.8

*Significant at 0.05 level.
a. Each model also has a third category on the dependent variable: missing data. To conserve space, the contrasts with missing data are not shown.
b. Omitted category: husband is not the eldest son.
c. Omitted category: wife is not the eldest daughter.
d. Omitted category: less than a high school diploma.
e. Omitted category: male.
f. Omitted category: love match.
g. Omitted category: infrequently visit husband's parents.
h. Omitted category: infrequently visit wife's parents.

Among the parental-contact variables, only living with the husband's parents had a significant effect, and it was in the expected (i.e., traditional) direction. In contrast with the variable of caring for elderly parents, few of the other variables had significant effects. Age had the expected effect. Perhaps because most couples do not face the question of whether to adopt a son or a son-in-law, this issue proved to be less salient than others, and hence the types of structural variables controlled here were not as powerful.

The next dependent variable shifts our attention from relationships between parents and adult children to gender relationships within the household. Table 11.5 shows two logistic regression models—one for visiting and the other for telephoning—for the attitude toward whether it is a good thing for men to work in the kitchen at home. Of all the 36 coefficients involving patterns of parental contact, only one was significant. Because living with the wife's parents was significant only once, it is perhaps best not to overinterpret this coefficient.

For the other predictor variables, most of the effects were in the predicted direction. The female-respondent effect was particularly strong, women being far more likely than men to regard it as a good thing (for both reasons) for men to work in the kitchen. Older respondents either thought it was not a good idea for men to work in the kitchen or that there should be practical reasons for them to do so. They avoided saying that men should be in the kitchen for normative reasons—that is, because it was "wrong" for housework to be just women's work. Those who had married relatively late were the most likely to express the view that it was "wrong" for housework to be only women's work.

The final set of dependent variables includes the traits that respondents would prefer for their sons and daughters. We examined the determinants of all 10 traits for both sons and daughters. Since we had to run the models separately for the visiting and the telephoning variables, there was a total of 40 logistic regressions. Table 11.6 summarizes the results of these analyses by simply indicating the number of significant coefficients for each predictor variable.

We consider the effects of visiting and telephoning parents first. The simple count of significant coefficients tells most of the story. Only 26 out of a possible 240 coefficients (slightly over 10 percent) proved to be statistically significant at the 5 percent level. This result is little better than chance. The majority of those that were significant involved the husband's or wife's deceased parents. In short, the pattern of contact with living parents seems to have had little effect on the desired traits that parents would choose for their children.

The control variables that had the most consistent significant effects on the choice of traits for offspring were age, the husband being an eldest son, the hus-

Table 11.5. Logistic regression model estimates (Betas) of whether it is a good thing for men to work in the kitchen at home, for the visiting and telephoning parents variables

Predictor variable	Visiting model			Telephoning model		
	Good thing, practical vs. not a good thing	Good thing, normative vs. not a good thing	Good thing, practical vs. good thing, normative	Good thing, practical vs. not a good thing	Good thing, normative vs. not a good thing	Good thing, practical vs. good thing, normative
Age	−0.01	−0.05*	−0.04*	−0.01	−0.05*	−0.04*
Age at marriage	0.02	0.06*	−0.03	0.03	0.05*	−0.03
Husband is eldest son[a]	0.06	−0.34	0.40*	0.07	−0.32	0.39*
Wife is eldest daughter[b]	−0.10	−0.35	0.25	−0.08	−0.35	0.27
Husband's education[c]						
High school	0.02	−0.04	0.06	0.02	−0.04	0.06
Junior college	−0.18	−0.36	0.18	−0.18	−0.38	0.20
University	−0.07	0.37	−0.44	−0.04	0.39	−0.44
Respondent is female[d]	0.90*	0.81*	0.08	0.90*	0.81*	0.09
Arranged or partially arranged marriage[e]	−0.24	−0.01	−0.24	−0.24	0.01	−0.25
Pattern of visiting (telephoning) husband's parents[f]						
Both deceased	0.18	−0.06	0.24	0.12	−0.15	0.27
Frequently visit (telephone)	0.07	0.06	0.01	−0.24	−0.51	0.27
Live with	−0.19	−0.36	0.17	−0.32	−0.51	0.19
Pattern of visiting (telephoning) wife's parents[g]						
Both deceased	−0.18	0.09	−0.27	−0.25	0.06	−0.31
Frequently visit (telephone)	−0.06	0.07	−0.13	−0.32	−0.08	−0.25
Live with	−0.54*	−0.24	−0.30	−0.67*	−0.35	−0.32
Model χ^2	109.6			114.9		

* Significant at 0.05 level.
a. Omitted category: husband is not the eldest son.
b. Omitted category: wife is not the eldest daughter.
c. Omitted category: less than a high school diploma.
d. Omitted category: male.
e. Omitted category: love match.
f. Omitted category: infrequently visit husband's parents.
g. Omitted category: infrequently visit wife's parents.

band's education, and the respondent's being female. Both age and husbands who were eldest sons tended to operate in a conservative or traditional manner. For example, older respondents did not pre- fer their sons to enjoy life; rather, they wanted them to be responsible and independent. Higher levels of husband's education and being a female respondent tended to be forces of change. For ex-

Table 11.6. Number of significant coefficients in logistic regression analyses of socialization traits

Variable	Number of significant coefficients[a]
Age	12
Age at marriage	2
Husband is eldest son[b]	10
Wife is eldest daughter[c]	0
Husband's education[d]	
High school	12
Junior college	4
University	19
Respondent is female[e]	12
Arranged or partially arranged marriage[f]	0
Pattern of visiting husband's parents[g]	
Both deceased	3
Frequently visit	0
Live with	1
Pattern of telephoning husband's parents[g]	
Both deceased	2
Frequently telephone	1
Live with	2
Pattern of visiting wife's parents[h]	
Both deceased	5
Frequently visit	0
Live with	3
Pattern of telephoning wife's parents[h]	
Both deceased	4
Frequently telephone	3
Live with	2

*Significant at 0.05 level.
a. Maximum number is 40 for all but the visiting and telephoning variables, for which the maximum is 20.
b. Omitted category: husband is not the eldest son.
c. Omitted category: wife is not the eldest daughter.
d. Omitted category: less than a high school diploma.
e. Omitted category: male.
f. Omitted category: love match.
g. Omitted category: infrequently visit or telephone husband's parents.
h. Omitted category: infrequently visit or telephone wife's parents.

ample, university-educated parents wanted their daughters to enjoy life and be independent, rather than obedient.

SUMMARY AND CONCLUSION

We began this chapter with the underlying assumption that socialization of individuals to family norms, values, and customs is a lifelong process. Given the kinds of changes in other institutions that are occurring in modern, industrialized, and urbanized societies, such an assumption seemed almost tautological.

Perhaps nowhere is this clearer than in Japan. The legal foundation for its patriarchal family system was drastically and permanently changed during the Allied Occupation that immediately followed World War II (Taeuber, 1958:102–103). The dramatic economic changes of the postwar era have put pressures on most aspects of the Japanese family system. Living in a three-generational household is now more difficult. The rise in the importance of educational attainment for occupational achievement weakens the absolute power of the senior generation. Opportunities in the labor force are providing new roles for married women, roles that typically compete with traditional family obligations. The high cost of living in contemporary urban settings provides further impetus for changing female roles.

In light of these changes, we expected the parents of adults to be a conservative force in the ongoing process of reinterpreting family values and customs. Even though the senior generation might recognize the need for a certain amount of change in the face of the social transformations going on about them, we hypothesized that the pace of change in their thinking would be slower than among the younger generation. We further expected that the attitudes probed in the National Family Survey would be reflected in everyday topics of conversation and advice from parents to their adult children. Thus, other things being equal, we predicted that increased contact between adults and their parents would lead the younger generation to hold more traditional family attitudes.

Examining a variety of family attitudes, however, we found that the data did not support our expectations. For those not living with their parents, contact with parents had little, if any, effect on the attitudes held by our respondents. Why? One possibility is that the topics considered in the survey are not discussed when parents and their adult children are together. We think this is highly unlikely. These topics are so fundamental to the functioning of Japanese families that it is improbable that they do not arise in normal discourse between adults and their parents. Even if parents do not directly praise or criticize their offspring, the activities of relatives, common neighborhood gossip, or items in the news are bound to spark value-laden discussions of these topics.

From the data at hand, it is clear

that generational differences in attitude exist with respect to these family topics. Across the dependent variables examined, age proved to be one of the most consistent predictors. Typically, as expected, older respondents held the most traditional positions.

When respondents resided with their parents, there did seem to be an effect. Although it was not always the case, those living with their parents tended to have the most traditional or conservative attitudes. This finding was expected and presumably reflects the continual reinforcement that accompanies coresidence. Given the fairly consistent results for coresidence and the lack of consistent results for visiting (even if the visits were weekly), it would appear that contact with parents has to be extremely frequent before it affects attitudes.

Why was the effect of nonresident parental contact so limited? It may be that visits or telephone calls with nonresident parents have a formal or ceremonial character. Under such circumstances, even if a topic is discussed, the values of the senior generation may not have much influence on the junior generation. We note that our findings regarding coresidence are similar to those of Waite et al. (1986), who found that in the United States young women who lived outside the parental home acquired nontraditional gender attitudes. This result again points to the necessity of a critical density of interactions before the two generations appear similar. An alternative explanation may be that whatever conservative force nonresident parents may exert, it is simply overpowered by the changes that are occurring in the broader social context. When there is a major change in the economy, the legal system, or the educational system, it is likely to affect a broad cross-section of individuals.

Within the types of variables we have examined, what, then, are the forces tending to preserve traditional family values, and which propel change? The age effects are consistently strong: younger individuals hold less traditional attitudes than do older persons.

The earlier experiences of the traditional Japanese family system tend to be a conservative force. For example, if a marriage was arranged or partially arranged, the respondent was more likely to hold traditional values. Similarly, if the husband was an eldest son, a more traditional response was given.

The strongest force of change seems to be higher education, particularly a university education. Given that higher education is widely valued for its own sake within Japan (Reischauer, 1981:167–178), and given that occupations within the modern economy demand individuals with high levels of education, it is likely that the effects of education on changing family attitudes will be present in Japan for quite some time.

It would also appear that females will be a source of change in the Japanese family system, although our findings here were less consistent. The effects of gender showed up when we examined attitudes toward husbands' working in the kitchen and the socialization of daughters. Given the heavy responsibility of women in the day-to-day functioning of the family, their attitudes about the family are particularly important, even in a society that is traditionally patriarchal.

ACKNOWLEDGMENTS

The research reported here has benefited from the general support of the Carolina Population Center, the University of Georgia, the Program on Population of the East-West Center, and the Population Research Institute of Nihon University. Thanks go to Mainichi Newspapers and Nihon University Research Center for permission to use the National Family Survey data. Helpful comments on earlier drafts were received from Daishiro Nomiya and Chin-Chun Yi. A slightly revised version of this study appeared in the *Journal of Marriage and the Family*, Vol. 54, No. 4, pp. 812–822, in November 1992.

REFERENCES

Befu, H. 1963. "Patrilineal Descent and Personal Kindred in Japan." *American Anthropologist* 65:1328–1341.

Bengston, V. L. 1975. "Generation and Family Effects in Value Socialization." *American Sociological Review* 40:358–371.

Brinton, M. C. 1989. "Gender Stratification in Contemporary Urban Japan." *American Sociological Review* 54:549–564.

Dore, R. P. 1959. "Japan: Country of Accelerated Transition." *Population Studies* 13:103–111.

Fukutake T. 1989. *The Japanese Social Structure: Its Evolution in the Modern Century*, R. P. Dore, trans. 2d ed. Tokyo: University of Tokyo Press.

Furstenberg, F. F. 1971. "The Transmission of Mobility Orientation in the Family." *Social Forces* 49:595–603.

Goode, W. J. 1963. *World Revolution and Family Patterns*. New York: Free Press.

Ishihara K. 1981. "Trends in the Generational Continuity and Succession to Household Directorship." *Journal of Comparative Family Studies* 12:351–363.

Japan, Management and Coordination Agency. 1987. *Report on the International Comparative Survey on the Lives and Perceptions of the Elderly* (in Japanese). Tokyo.

Japan, Statistics Bureau. 1986. *1985 Population Census of Japan*, Vol. 2, *Results of the First Basic Complete Tabulation*, Part 1, *Japan*. Tokyo: Management and Coordination Agency.

Kandel, D. and G. Lesser. 1972. *Youth in Two Worlds*. San Francisco: Jossey-Bass.

Kobayashi K. 1977. "Attitudes Toward Children and Parents." In Japanese Organization for International Cooperation in Family Planning (JOICFP) and Population Problems Research Council of Mainichi Newspapers (eds.), *Fertility and Family Planning in Japan*, pp. 203–223. Tokyo: JOICFP.

Kohn, M. L. 1969. *Class and Conformity: A Study in Values*. Homewood, Ill.: Dorsey Press.

Kohn, M. L., and C. Schooler. 1983. *Work and Personality: An Inquiry into the Impact of Social Stratification*. Norwood, N.J.: Ablex.

Kohn, M. L., K. Slomczynski, and C. Schoenbach. 1986. "Social Stratification and the Transmission of Values in the Family: A Cross-national Assessment." *Sociological Forum* 1:73–102.

Lash, C. 1979. *Haven in a Heartless World: The Family Besieged*. New York: Basic Books.

Lebra, T. S. 1984. *Japanese Women: Constraints and Fulfillment*. Honolulu: University of Hawaii Press.

McLanahan, S., and L. L. Bumpass. 1988. "Intergenerational Consequences of Family Disruption." *American Journal of Sociology* 94:130–152.

Maddala, G. S. 1983. *Limited-Dependent and Qualitative Variables in Econometrics*. Cambridge: Cambridge University Press.

Martin, L. G. 1989. "The Graying of Japan." *Population Bulletin* 44:1–42.

Matsumoto, S. Y. 1962. "Notes on Primogeniture in Postwar Japan." In R. J. Smith and R. K. Beardsley (eds.), *Japanese Culture: Its Development and Characteristics*, pp. 55–60. Chicago: Aldine.

Mead, M. 1970. *Culture and Commitment: A Study of the Generation Gap*. New York: Natural History Press/Doubleday.

Morgan, S. P., and K. Hiroshima. 1983. "The Persistence of Extended Family Residence in Japan: Anachronism or Alternative Strategy?" *American Sociological Review* 48:269–281.

Mortimer, J. T., and R. G. Simmons. 1978. "Adult Socialization." *Annual Review of Sociology* 4:421–454.

Mosk, C. 1983. *Patriarchy and Fertility: The Evolution of Natality in Japan and Sweden, 1880–1960*. New York: Academic Press.

Nakane C. 1973. *Japanese Society*. Harmondsworth, England: Penguin.

Nihon Hōsō Kyōkai. 1986. *Shōwa 60-nendo Kokumin Seikatsu Jikan Kōsa* (Report of the survey on time allocation of daily life of the Japanese in 1985). Tokyo: Nihon Hōsō Kyōkai.

Otani K. 1987. "Determinants of the Tempo and Quantum of Japanese Cohort Marital Fertility Since the 1960s." Ph.D. dissertation, Australian National University.

Ozaki M. 1989. "Introduction and Summary of the Survey on the Family." In *Summary of the National Opinion Survey of the Family in Japan*, pp. 1–21. Tokyo: Nihon University, University Research Center.

Reischauer, E. O. 1981. *The Japanese*. Cambridge, Mass.: Harvard University Press.

Rindfuss, R. R., S. P. Morgan, and C. G. Swicegood. 1988. *First Births in America*. Berkeley: University of California Press.

Rosenbaum, J. E., and T. Kariya. 1989. "From High School to Work: Market and Institutional Mechanisms in Japan." *American Journal of Sociology* 94:1334–1365.

Rossi, A. S., and P. H. Rossi. 1990. *Of Human Bonding: Parent-Child Relationships across the Life Course*. New York: Aldine de Gruyter.

Ryder, N. B. 1965. "The Cohort as a Concept in the Study of Social Change." *American Sociological Review* 30:843–861.

Taeuber, I. B. 1958. *The Population of Japan*. Princeton: Princeton University Press.

Thornton, A. 1989. "Changing Attitudes toward Family Issues in the United States." *Journal of Marriage and the Family* 51:873–893.

———. 1991. "Influence of the Marital History of Parents on the Marital and Cohabitational Experiences of Children." *American Journal of Sociology* 96:868–894.

Tsuya N. O., and M. K. Choe. 1992. *Changes in Intrafamilial Relationships and the Roles of Women in Japan and Korea*. NUPRI Research Paper Series, No. 58. Tokyo: Nihon University, Population Research Institute.

Vogel, E. F. 1971. *Japan's New Middle Class: The Salary Man and His Family in a Tokyo Suburb*. Berkeley: University of California Press.

Waite, L. J., F. K. Goldscheider, and C. Witsberger. 1986. "Nonfamily Living and the Erosion of Traditional Family Orientations among Young Adults." *American Sociological Review* 51:541–554.

Westoff, C. F., and N. B. Ryder. 1977. *The Contraceptive Revolution*. Princeton: Princeton University Press.

CHAPTER 12

A Comparative Analysis of Coresidence and Contact with Parents in Japan and the United States

by Larry L. Bumpass

The international theme of this volume emphasizes that we have much to learn from examining similarities and differences between family patterns in markedly different cultural traditions. Few topics are likely to lead to greater contrasts than intergenerational relationships, when the comparison is between a society with a Confucian heritage, such as Japan, and the individualistically oriented United States. The present analysis is an attempt to compare Japan and the United States with respect to the coresidence of married persons with their parents and the extent to which those not living with their parents either see them weekly, or have any weekly contact.

This analysis builds on the excellent paper by Martin and Tsuya (1991) which includes a discussion of the relevant literature and an overview of trends. I will not repeat that material here, but will focus my attention on comparative results between the U.S. National Survey of Families and Households (NSFH) conducted with 13,017 respondents in 1987–88 and the National Family Survey of Japan conducted by the

Mainichi Newspapers and Nihon University in 1988. Comparisons can be only approximate in most cases because the studies available were designed for different purposes. Most technical details of differences between the surveys are discussed in the footnotes.

DATA AND METHODS

To increase comparability, this analysis is limited to married persons between the ages of 25 and 64. In addition, to reduce the confounding of comparisons due to racial and ethnic variation in family patterns in the United States, only non-Hispanic whites are included from the NSFH sample. Most of the analyses are also limited to respondents with living parents: 1,120 in Japan and 3,381 in the United States.

Initial comparative objectives seem better served by a description of actual levels of experience than by multivariate modeling of the independent effects of variables. Nonetheless, logit estimates of "net" effects will accompany observed differences, and these will be used in particular to examine the potential mediating role of distance in other observed differentials in seeing parents every week.

FINDINGS

Parental Survival

Age patterns of coresidence may be conditioned in several ways by age differences in the survival of parents. Most obviously, only those with at least one surviving parent can live with a parent, and differences in parental survival must be taken into account in considering levels and differentials in coresidence. In addition, however, ages at which increasing proportions experience parental loss are also likely ages during which higher proportions of adult offspring are likely to have parents in need of assistance because of poor health or functional limitations.

Table 12.1 documents the age patterns in Japan and the United States of having both or only one parent. Though Japanese life expectancy has exceeded that of the United States, the similarity of mortality conditions in the two countries would lead us to expect similar patterns in this table. The extremely high comparability is more a testimony to the quality of the two surveys than it is a surprising finding.

In both Japan and the United States, major transformations occur over adulthood in the potential for intergenerational relationships as this potential is structured by parental death. Virtually all persons of ages 25–34 have at least one surviving parent, compared with only one-third among those 55–64. Three-quarters of the youngest group, but only about one in 20 of the oldest group have both parents surviving. Middle age is a period in which about two-fifths of married persons in each country have a widowed parent.

Our understanding of intergenerational interaction must be set in the context of these marked differences by age in parental survival. Since interaction is possible only for those with surviving parents, we will proceed to examine rates of living with or interacting with parents, excluding those with no living parents. We will return in the conclusion, however, to observe life-course variation in the prevalence in each population, including those with no living parents.

Coresidence

On the face of it, there seems little to compare between Japan and the United States with respect to coresidence with parents. While we know that there have been marked changes in both attitudes and behavior in Japan (Martin and Tsuya, 1991; Kojima, 1989; Hirosima, 1987; Kendig, 1989), it remains extremely common for Japanese married couples to live with a parent. In the United States, however, such coresidence appears almost nonexistent.

Table 12.2 shows age patterns of coresidence with adults' own parents or with inlaws, both for the total population and for those with surviving parents. We see the well-known difference between Japan and the United States in the nature of kin relations: in the United States coresidence is bilateral—that is, similar for husbands' and wives' parents, whereas in Japan only 15 percent of coresident couples live with the wife's parents. The most important contrast in Table 12.2 is, of course, with respect to levels. Nearly two-fifths of married persons under age 45 in Japan live with a parent. This proportion declines with age because of the death of parents; among those with living parents it increases to nearly half among those 55–64 whose parents are in their late 70s and older. In the United States, on the other hand, only about 2 percent of married couples live with a parent, though coresidence also increases at the older ages, especially among those with living parents. It would be a mis-

Table 12.1. Percentages with living parents, by age: Japan and United States, married persons, ages 25–64

Age group	Japan				United States			
	Any	Both	Only mother	Only father	Any	Both	Only mother	Only father
25–34	96	76	18	3	97	77	15	5
35–44	89	52	32	6	90	53	28	9
45–54	65	25	31	9	67	22	37	8
55–64	31	6	20	4	32	4	25	3

Sources for this and all following tables in this chapter: Japan: National Family Survey, 1988, Mainichi Newspapers and Nihon University; United States: National Survey of Families and Households, 1987–88.

Note: U.S. sample is limited to white, non-Hispanic persons.

Larry L. Bumpass

Table 12.2. Percentages coresiding with own or spouse's parents, by sex and age group: Japan and United States, married persons, ages 25–64

Sex and age group	Japan Any	Japan Own	Japan In-law	United States Any	United States Own	United States In-law	Living with own parent/s, of those with a living parent Japan	Living with own parent/s, of those with a living parent U.S.
Males								
25–34	38	32	6	2	1	1	34	1
35–44	38	30	8	3	1	2	34	1
45–54	29	25	4	3	2	1	36	3
55–64	17	13	4	4	<1	4	42	<1
Total %	30	25	6	2	1	1	35	1
(No.)	(745)			(1,938)			(519)	(1,516)
Females								
25–34	38	6	32	2	1	1	6	1
35–44	36	8	28	1	1	<1	9	1
45–54	17	4	13	2	1	1	7	2
55–64	16	6	10	2	2	<1	20	4
Total %	27	6	21	1	1	1	9	1
(No.)	(821)			(2,352)			(601)	(1,865)

Note: Own parents plus in-laws may not sum to percentage for any parents because of rounding. Coresidence in the United States is too rare to estimate with any precision with samples of this size.

take, however, to conclude from this table that filial obligation and coresidence for the care of parents exist only in Japan and not in the individualistically oriented United States.

We see little coresidence between married couples and parents in the United States for several reasons. Obviously it is true that independent residence is preferred by both generations, and economic conditions (including the availability of housing) make it possible for most couples and their parents to maintain separate residences. What we miss in Table 12.2 is that coresidence is quite common when parents are less able to live on their own and need the intergenerational assistance. This type of coresidence is concentrated at the end of parents' lives and hence is not evident in cross-sectional measures. The proportion of NSFH respondents reporting that a parent had lived with them since they (the respondents) had been on their own increases steadily with age to about a quarter at ages 55–64 (Bumpass and Sweet, 1991). This measure[1] does not include

1. Question M86, "In the time that you have been on your own, have any of your parents (or parents-in-law) ever lived with you in your household? This does not include visits when your parents still had a household somewhere else."

those who returned to live with their parents, such as after a divorce, and hence may considerably understate lifetime experience of coresidence after adult children leave home by excluding those episodes occasioned by the needs of the younger generation.

Table 12.3 presents differences in having had a parent live with them for persons of ages 55–64. To avoid having the comparisons complicated by the high level of marital disruption in the United States, this table is restricted to continuously married couples in their first marriage. Three points in particular seem worth noting.

First, the association of coresidence with the final years of parents' lives is clearly indicated by the fact that over twice as many of those with no surviving

Table 12.3. Percentages whose parents or parents-in-law ever lived with them, by selected respondent characteristics: United States, persons 55–64 in an intact first marriage

Respondent characteristic	% Own	% Any	Observed effect[a] Own	Observed effect[a] Any	Net effect[a] Own	Net effect[a] Any
Living parents						
Yes	8	19				
No	18	28	2.43*	1.92*	3.04*	2.87*
Sex and birth order						
Eldest male	18	27				
Other male	6	21	.37*	.95	.25	.73
Eldest female	23	38	1.66	2.04†	1.83	2.14
Other female	19	29	1.29	1.42	.84	1.03
Father's education						
0–11 years	14	24				
12 years	14	23	.71	.80	.67	.80
College 1–3 years	4	20	.27†	.87	.22*	.78
Own education						
0–11 years	18	33				
12 years	15	27	.74	.74	.70	.77
College	13	24	.54†	.64†	.84	.87
Husband with low occupation?						
Yes	14	29				
No	15	27	.78	1.06	.82	1.12
Total %	15	27				
(No.)	(837)					

*Logit coefficient is at least twice its standard error.

†Logit coefficient is 1.5–1.99 times its standard error.

a. Exponent of the logit coefficient.

parents had had one of their parents live with them as did those with a surviving parent. As we saw in Table 12.1, only 6 percent of this age group had both parents surviving. Among that small group almost none had coresided (not shown in table). Because of the strong correlation between the survival of one's own and one's spouse's parents (which is associated with age variation within this range), I have not presented separate figures for the survival of spouses' parents. Twenty-eight percent of persons with no living parents had had a parent or parent-in-law live with them.

Second, the primary role of women in caring for kin is reflected in the second variable in this table. Men with older siblings were much less likely to have had their own parents live with them, though their wife's parents made up much of the difference. Parental coresidence was highest among women without older siblings, 38 percent of whom had had a parent or parent-in-law live with them. It is likely that this variable captures some of the effects of not having any female siblings (as in the level for eldest males, many of whom may not have had siblings), and this is a question that needs further exploration in the future.

Third, the respondent's education does not affect coresidence, whereas the father's education does. This is further evidence that the resources and well-being of the older generation are more important for this process than are those of their children.

Table 12.4 turns our attention to differentials in *current* coresidence in Japan among couples with a surviving parent. Since Martin and Tsuya (1991) have analyzed this much more fully already, I will keep my comments on this table brief, focusing on variations in observed levels rather than on the independent effects of variables.[2] It will be essential to keep in mind the levels and patterns of coresidence in this table when we turn to examining patterns of interaction between parents and children among those not coresiding.

In the Japanese cultural context, coresidence with the wife's parents should be much more dependent on parental need than living with the husband's parents. Martin and Tsuya report such a stronger effect, and the levels in Table 12.4 clearly illustrate it. Whereas only 5 percent of wives coresided with their own parents if both of their parents were living, 20 percent did so if only their mother was alive. The increase in coresidence at older ages among both men and women is likely to reflect increasing widowhood among parents as well as other aspects of increased dependence as parents become quite old.

The third variable in Table 12.4 combines the birth orders of husbands and wives. Coresidence between males and their parents seems to vary with the

---

2. Unlike the analysis by Martin and Tsuya, this table is restricted to the reports of respondents and does not include proxy records for their spouses.

Coresidence and Contact with Parents in Japan
and the United States

Table 12.4. Coresidence with own parents, by selected respondent characteristics: Japan, married persons ages 25–64, with a living parent

Respondent characteristic	% coresiding Males	% coresiding Females	Observed effect[a] Males	Observed effect[a] Females	Net effect[a] Males	Net effect[a] Females
Living parents						
Both	33	5				
Mother only	37	20	1.24	4.56*	1.31	4.65*
Father only	41	14	1.48*	3.04*	2.41*	3.01*
Marriage arranged (Japan)						
Yes	46	12				
No	30	7	.52*	.56*	.52*	.58†
Age group						
25–34	34	6				
35–44	35	10	1.05	1.59	.74	1.11
45–54	36	8	1.12	1.36	.72	1.12
55–64	43	22	1.51	4.17*	.86	2.09
Husband/wife the eldest sibling						
Husband yes, wife no	63	6				
Husband yes, wife yes	43	7	.44*	1.26	.53*	1.22
Husband no, wife no	20	7	.14*	1.26	.12*	1.12
Husband no, wife yes	14	16	.09*	3.34*	.08*	3.17*
Father's education						
< high school	40	11				
High school	28	8	.60*	.66	.59†	.66
College	24	6	.48*	.49	.59	.54
Husband professional or proprietor						
Yes	28	9				
No	42	10	1.93*	1.11	1.86*	1.16
Husband's education						
< high school	40	14				
High school	41	9	1.03	.62	1.69	.43†
College	27	7	.56*	.46†	1.36	.44†
Wife's education						
< high school	46	9				
High school	36	10	.65†	1.11	.54†	2.67*
College	28	7	.47*	.85	.59	2.44
City size						
Large	26	6				
Medium	31	9	1.33	1.48	2.00*	1.32
Small	43	14	2.16*	2.41†	2.45*	2.08
Rural	44	8	2.30*	1.18	2.30*	1.12
Total %	36	9				
(No.)	(520)	(601)				

*Logit coefficient is at least twice its standard error.

†Logit coefficient is 1.5–1.99 times its standard error.

a. Exponent of the logit coefficient

birth order of the wife—and perhaps also then with her responsibility for her own parents. The proportion of firstborn husbands living with their parents was 63 percent if the wife was not also an eldest child but only 43 percent if the wife was the eldest. If the wife was the eldest (or only) child and the husband was not, only 14 percent of couples were living with the husband's parents—a level comparable to coresidence with the wife's parents overall.

It is interesting that coresidence with a wife's parents does not represent a complete mirror image of the pattern of coresidence with the husband's parents. We see the expected effect of being the oldest sibling among women whose husbands are not the oldest. Being the oldest sibling, however, has no effect on a wife's coresidence with her parents if her husband is the oldest sibling in his family. I expected to see the reduction in male coresidence if the wife was the firstborn and the husband was not to be reflected in an increase in female coresidence, but it is not.

The negative effect of the father's education on coresidence most likely reflects the greatest retention of traditional expectations among the least educated in the older generation, but it means that it is harder for the elderly with little education to maintain an independent household. Although the education of neither the husband nor the wife has any effect on coresidence with other variables controlled, in the observed differences both education variables have a clear negative effect on living with the husband's parents, and the husband's education is negatively associated with living with the wife's parents. These effects are likely a consequence of parental education and whether the marriage was arranged.

Frequency of Seeing Parents

Measures of how often persons see their own parents are quite similar in the two surveys, though some differences are discussed in the Appendix. Table 12.5 presents the distributions on this variable in each country separately by sex, for all persons with a living parent, and for those with a living parent who were not coresiding with parents. The very large difference in coresidence between the United States and Japan is clearly the major factor affecting differences in intergenerational contact. If we assume, with likely some small error, that most people who live together see each other almost every day, then married Japanese males obviously have a much higher frequency of contact with their parents than married males in the United States. On the other hand, married women in the two countries have very similar levels of contact with their parents.

The first panel of Table 12.5 also reveals that infrequent contact with parents is rare for both sexes in both countries. Over 85 percent of married respondents with living parents reported seeing them more than once a year.

Coresidence and Contact with Parents in Japan
and the United States

Table 12.5. Percentage distribution of frequency of seeing own parents, by sex: Japan and United States, married persons, ages 25–64, with a living parent

	Males		Females	
Frequency	Japan	U.S.	Japan	U.S.
All married persons				
Less than yearly	4	4	3	4
Yearly	7	10	9	9
Several times/year	17	27	25	23
About every month	13	22	27	19
About every week	11	20	14	21
About every day	48	17	22	25
Total	100	100	100	100
Persons not coresiding with parents				
Less than yearly	7	4	3	4
Yearly	13	10	10	9
Several times/year	30	27	31	23
About every month	24	22	32	19
About every week	18	21	16	21
About every day	8	16	8	24
Total	100	100	100	100

Note: Percentages may not sum exactly to 100 because of rounding.

The second panel compares the two countries among persons who were not living with their parents. Focusing on this group may create a good deal of selection among Japanese men, for it excludes the 40 percent who may have had the most traditional values and may well include many who were not coresiding specifically because they had unusually difficult relationships with their parents. Whatever the reasons, the panel indicates that daily contact is more frequent among this group in the United States than in Japan: 16 percent versus 8 percent among husbands and 24 percent versus 8 percent among wives. Aside from the selection issues I have noted, the greater length of the Japanese work day may help account for this difference.

As indicated in the Appendix, these measures are most comparable at the break between at least weekly contact and less frequent contact. This is a sensible division in substantive terms, capturing a meaningful category of regular contact. Table 12.6 documents differentials in this measure as observed in the two countries, and Tables 12.7 and 12.8 present several logit models describing these patterns. The logit models present the odds ratios for seeing parents weekly for each variable as observed, for each variable once the effect of distance is controlled,[3] and finally for the full model.

---

3. Distance may sometimes be endogenous. Whether one interprets the role of distance as a mediating, or simply a correlated, variable will depend on the variable being considered.

This analysis is restricted to married persons with living parents who were not coresiding.

I will confine my discussion to a comparison of general patterns.

Distance Obviously, distance between children and their parents has to be the major factor affecting how often the children see them, and the interpretation of other differences should control for differences in how far away the parents live. Only approximate comparisons of distance categories are possible. Interaction falls off sharply with distance as measured in both countries, so that it is likely that comparisons of effects net of distance are more legitimate than any attempt to compare Japanese and U.S. married offspring within the same distance rings. Nonetheless, the U.S. response category of "less than 2 miles"[4] implies longer average distances than the Japanese response category of "less than a 5- or 6-minute walk," and within this first category, wives were equally likely in the two countries to see their parents weekly, whereas males were somewhat less likely to do so in Japan than in the United States. In the next ring, married persons in the United States who lived 2–24 miles from their parents were more than 1.5 times as likely to see their parents weekly as those in Japan who lived in the same town as their parents but not within a 5- or 6-minute walk.

In the multivariate models shown in Tables 12.7 and 12.8, distance is the dominant variable affecting interaction, with strong and significant effects in both countries, as expected.

Living parents Having both parents still living is generally associated with higher levels of seeing a parent than when only one is surviving (Table 12.7). This result was strongest among Japanese males, among whom 34 percent saw their parents weekly if both parents were living, but only half that many did so if just one parent was living. (These effects persist in the full model in Table 12.7, though they are no longer significant.) The major exception is for wives in the United States, who maintained greater interaction with their widowed mothers than with their widowed fathers. This pattern is strong and highly significant in Table 12.8.

Parents living with another child Having parents who are living with a sibling is a much more common occurrence in Japan than in the United States, reflecting the markedly different levels of coresidence we have already reviewed. Perhaps reflecting the differences in parental need, since parents are already being cared for, Japanese are much less likely than Americans to see their parents on a weekly basis if the parents are living with another child. The proportions were 17 percent versus 39 percent among men and 23 per-

---

4. A response of 1 mile may mean "1 but less than 2," or it may mean "closer to 1 than to 2" and therefore represents less than 1.5 miles.

Coresidence and Contact with Parents in Japan
and the United States

Table 12.6. Percentages seeing own parents at least weekly, by selected respondent characteristics: Japan and United States, married persons, ages 25–64, with at least one living parent but not coresiding

	Japan		United States	
Respondent characteristic	Males	Females	Males	Females
Distance				
< 6 min. (Japan), < 2 miles (U.S.)	74	93	86	93
Same town (Japan), 2–24 miles (U.S.)	41	40	63	77
Neighboring town (Japan), 25–49 miles (U.S.)	17	26	28	33
Same prefecture (Japan), 50–99 miles (U.S.)	9	5	16	11
Other prefecture (Japan), 100+ miles (U.S.)	2	1	1	3
Living parents				
Both	34	29	38	44
Father only	15	19	33	32
Mother only	18	21	34	46
Parents living with another child				
Yes	17	23	34	47
No	39	32	36	44
Age				
25–34	46	37	40	49
35–44	26	20	33	37
45–54	17	25	36	43
55–64	20	11	30	48
Father's education				
< high school	26	23	43	51
High school	33	28	35	43
College	14	36	27	32
Husband in low occupation				
Yes	26	25	40	49
No	27	26	22	26
Own education				
< high school	28	22	40	48
High school	29	23	47	52
College	24	32	29	35
City size[a]				
Large	19	16	28	39
Medium	19	26	36	40
Small	30	28	40	54
Rural/nonmetropolitan	44	31	43	50
Husband/wife the oldest sibling				
Husband yes, wife no (Japan), R eldest (U.S.)	31	25	33	43
Husband yes, wife yes (Japan)	37	31	38	44
Husband no, wife no (Japan), R other (U.S.)	18	22	na	na
Husband no, wife yes (Japan)	25	27	na	na
Marriage arranged (Japan)				
Yes	27	16	na	na
No	26	32	na	na
Total %	26	26	36	44
(No.)	(259)	(380)	(1,478)	(1,819)

na—not applicable.

a. For the United States, definitions are: large city = 1 million and over; medium city = 250,000–999,999; small city = 50,000–249,999; rural area = fewer than 50,000.

Larry L. Bumpass

Table 12.7. Logit analysis of seeing own parents at least weekly, by respondent characteristics: Japan and United States, married males, ages 25–64, with at least one living parent but not coresiding

	Japanese males			U.S. males		
Respondent characteristic	(1)	(2)	(3)	(1)	(2)	(3)
Distance						
< 6 min. (Japan), < 2 miles (U.S.)						
Same town (Japan), 2–24 miles (U.S.)	.24*		.23*	.30*		.31*
Neighboring town (Japan), 25–49 miles (U.S.)	.07*		.03*	.07*		.08*
Same prefecture (Japan), 50–99 miles (U.S.)	.04*		.04*	.03*		.03*
Other prefecture (Japan), 100+ miles (U.S.)	.01*		.01*	.00*		.00*
Living parents						
Both						
Father only	.34†	.17*	.41	.74	.68	.64
Mother only	.44*	.36*	.59	.89	.80	.75
Parents living with another child						
Yes						
No	3.18*	3.17*	2.46†	1.26	1.04	.95
Age						
25–34						
35–44	.40*	.19*	.25*	.74†	.81	.82
45–54	.24*	.11*	.13*	.82	1.19	1.22
55–64	.29†	.15*	.27*	.68†	.86	.90
Father's education						
< high school						
High school	1.41	1.63	1.19	.77†	.71†	.72†
College	.45†	.80	.67	.46*	.62*	.65†
Husband in low occupation						
Yes						
No	1.07	1.75†	2.16†	.37†	.66†	.76
Own education						
< high school						
High school	1.06	.84	.62	.96	1.20	1.25
College	.82	1.07	.40	.45*	.96	1.23
City size[a]						
Large						
Medium	1.08	.97	.78	1.32†	1.06	.99
Small	1.80	1.54	2.06	1.37	1.27	1.20
Rural/nonmetropolitan	3.36*	2.82†	2.29	2.13*	1.77*	2.26*
Husband/wife the oldest sibling						
Husband yes, wife no (Japan), R eldest (U.S.)						
Husband yes, wife yes (Japan)	1.33	2.01	2.26	1.14	1.04	1.02
Husband no, wife no (Japan), R other (U.S.)	.49†	.95	1.58	na	na	na
Husband no, wife yes (Japan)	.75	.53	1.10	na	na	na

Table 12.7. *(continued)*

	Exponent of logit estimate					
	Japanese males			U.S. males		
Respondent characteristic	(1)	(2)	(3)	(1)	(2)	(3)
Marriage arranged (Japan)						
Yes						
No	.98	1.94†	.87	na	na	na

Models: (1) variable alone, (2) variable + distance, (3) all variables.

na—not applicable.

*Logit coefficient is at least twice its standard error.

†Logit coefficient is 1.5–1.99 times its standard error.

a. For the United States, definitions are: large city = 1 million and over; medium city = 250,000–999,999; small city = 50,000–249,999; rural area = fewer than 50,000.

Table 12.8. Logit analysis of seeing own parents at least weekly, by respondent characteristics: Japan and United States, married females, ages 25–64, with at least one living parent but not coresiding

	Exponent of logit estimate					
	Japanese females			U.S. females		
Respondent characteristic	(1)	(2)	(3)	(1)	(2)	(3)
Distance						
< 6 min. (Japan), < 2 miles (U.S.)						
Same town (Japan), 2–24 miles (U.S.)	.05*		.03*	.27*		.26*
Neighboring town (Japan), 25–49 miles (U.S.)	.02*		.01*	.04*		.04*
Same prefecture (Japan), 50–99 miles (U.S.)	.00*		.00*	.01*		.01*
Other prefecture (Japan), 100+ miles (U.S.)	.00*		.00*	.00*		.00*
Living parents						
Both						
Father only	.57	.43	.81	.68†	.50*	.49*
Mother only	.63†	.99	1.26	1.35†	1.18	1.35†
Parents living with another child						
Yes						
No	1.58†	1.56	1.28	1.15	1.26	1.25
Age						
25–34						
35–44	.43*	.48*	.61	.62*	.69*	.66*
45–54	.57†	.58†	.88	.84	.93	.83
55–64	.21*	.18*	.31	.98	1.14	1.00
Father's education						
< high school						
High school	1.34	1.51	1.40	.71*	.95	1.02
College	1.87†	3.92*	3.24*	.46*	.70†	.88

Table 12.8. *(continued)*

	Exponent of logit estimate					
	Japanese females			U.S. females		
Respondent characteristic	(1)	(2)	(3)	(1)	(2)	(3)
Husband in low occupation						
Yes						
No	1.10	1.19	1.10	.42*	.60*	.65*
Own education						
< high school						
High school	1.03	1.36	.97	1.06	1.31	1.22
College	1.66	2.67*	1.43	.56*	.93	.95
City size[a]						
Large						
Medium	1.83†	1.19	2.20	1.05†	1.09	1.11
Small	1.93†	1.12	1.91	1.86*	1.68†	1.73†
Rural/nonmetropolitan	2.27*	1.24	2.32	1.44*	1.42†	1.40†
Husband/wife the oldest sibling						
Husband yes, wife no (Japan), R eldest (U.S.)						
Husband yes, wife yes (Japan)	1.34	1.37	1.23	1.00	.97	.96
Husband no, wife no (Japan), R other (U.S.)	1.10	.99	.91	na	na	na
Husband no, wife yes (Japan)	.82	.59	.57	na	na	na
Marriage arranged (Japan)						
Yes						
No	2.51*	2.57*	2.82*	na	na	na

Models: (1) variable alone, (2) variable + distance, (3) all variables.
na—not applicable.
*Logit coefficient is at least twice its standard error.
†Logit coefficient is 1.5–1.99 times its standard error.
a. For the United States, definitions are: large city = 1 million and over; medium city = 250,000–999,999; small city = 50,000– 249,999; rural area = fewer than 50,000.

cent versus 32 percent among women. The effect for men remains significant in the full multivariate model whereas that for women does not.

Age Age differences represent a major point of contrast between Japan and the United States, though several words of caution are in order. First, these cross-sectional patterns may or may not reflect actual life-course experience. Further, the youngest age group, 25–29, excludes those in this cohort who will marry at later ages.[5] Even so, there are marked national differences that warrant further attention.

Figure 12.1 graphs these patterns.

---

5. The extremes of this age distribution are represented by quite small samples in the Japanese data because of the marriage restriction at ages 25–29 and because of high parental mortality among respondents in the 55–64 age group. Recalculations using age groups that avoid these extremes, however, yield the same pattern.

In brief, interaction declines with age in Japan, perhaps as a consequence of care provided by another sibling, though the effect remains strong and significant in the full model for Japanese men. In the United States the declines are less strong for men and curvilinear for women. To the extent they would hold up in larger samples, these patterns suggest that interaction with parents is not all that different among (non-coresident) young married couples in the United States and Japan but that there may be increasing divergence between the two nations over the life course.

Father's education Father's education captures a number of possible factors related to intergenerational interactions. On the one hand, lower parental education is likely to be associated with more traditional family orientations on the part of the older generation, and perhaps also among the younger generation as an effect of social origin. On the other hand, parents are likely to have more resources to be independent when the father has more education.

We see the expected negative effects of father's education on seeing parents at least weekly among both men and women in the United States, though the effect remains significant in the full model only among men. Whereas 43 percent of U.S. men from the lowest educational origins saw their parents weekly, only 27 percent of those whose fathers attended college did so.

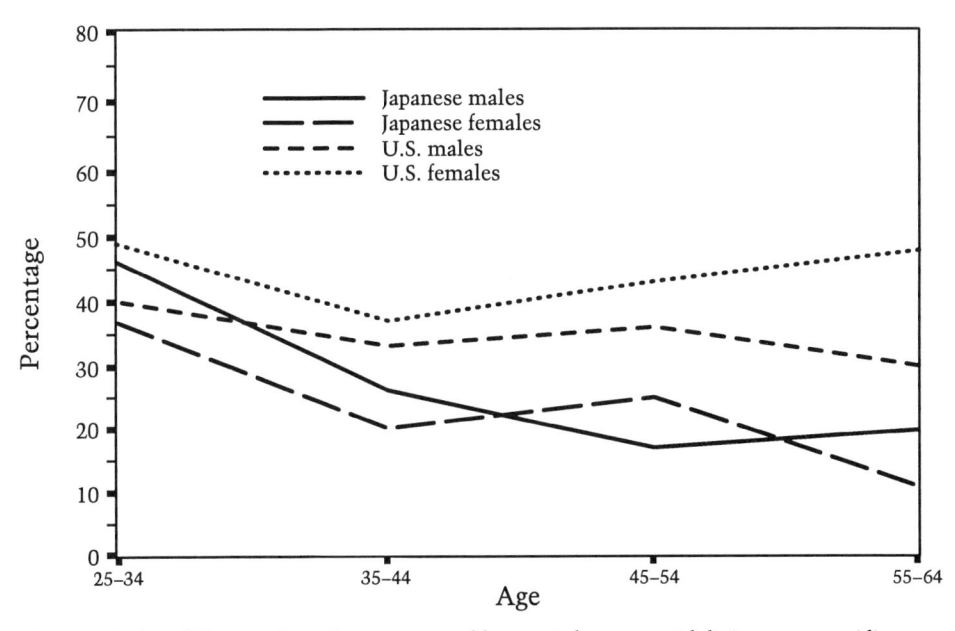

Figure 12.1. Age differences in seeing parents weekly: married persons with living, non-coresiding parents

Japanese sons of college-educated fathers are significantly less likely to see them than are those of less educated fathers, but the contrast is not significant in the full model. The most surprising finding is the positive effect of the father's education among Japanese women: a contrast of 23 percent versus 36 percent between the educational extremes and an effect that becomes even stronger when other variables are controlled. I can only speculate on this finding. Is it possible that intergenerational contrasts in values are felt most keenly by Japanese women and that such contrasts are felt least among daughters of college educated fathers?

Husband's occupation No differences by occupational status are apparent in the Japanese data for observed levels of seeing one's own parents weekly, though in the full models higher occupational status increases the amount of interaction with parents for Japanese husbands but not for Japanese wives. Surprisingly large differences are observed in the United States: women with higher-status husbands were barely half as likely to see their parents weekly as were those whose husbands are in the lower-status occupations. Similar differences are seen for U.S. men, though only the coefficient for females remains significant in the full model.

Perhaps quite different dimensions of occupation are relevant as resources facilitate meeting filial obligations (for males) in Japan, but social distance from parents reduces visiting in the United States. These issues can be examined further with the available data.

Education In the United States, frequency of seeing parents declines markedly with education. Comparing those without a high school diploma with those who had attended college, we find that the proportion seeing their parents at least weekly was 40 percent versus 29 percent among men and 48 percent versus 35 percent among women. These significant differences, however, are almost solely the result of the fact that the more educated are likely to live farther from their parents.

The major difference between the United States and Japan is that in Japan women who have attended college are *more* likely to see their parents every week than are those who did not complete high school. This result obtains despite the same correlation with distance noted for the United States. In fact, the effect increases and becomes significant when distance is controlled. The effect of education on contact with parents remains positive for Japanese women in the full model, and that for Japanese men becomes more negative; but neither is significant. Hence, descriptively more-educated men have lower amounts of direct contact with their parents whereas more-educated Japanese women have higher contact, but I am unable to demonstrate a direct effect attributable to education.

City size In both countries, weekly contact is much more frequent in small cities and rural areas than in large cities. Although this effect remains significant in the full model only in the United States, the coefficients remain large in this model in Japan as well and would likely be found significant in larger samples. Controlling for distance in the United States has little consequence for the size of these effects. This finding seems to support the interpretation that traditional values tend to be retained in less urban areas.

Birth order When presenting data on coresidence, I have used a combined husband-wife measure of birth order for Japan. This combination seems less appropriate for the United States, and therefore I have simply used a measure of whether or not the respondent was the eldest.[6]

Although we observed clear effects of birth order on wives' coresidence histories in the United States, being the eldest is unrelated to the frequency of seeing parents for either men or women in the United States. In Japan, weekly visiting between men and their parents was greatest when both spouses were the eldest children in their families (37 percent), and least when neither was (18 percent). A similar though somewhat weaker pattern is seen for visiting between Japanese wives and their parents. These birth-order effects would seem to support the assumption of greater filial obligations among the firstborn, but they do not remain significant in the full model.

Arranged marriage The variable of arranged marriage is obviously not suitable for comparative analysis. It was nonetheless retained in the equations for Japan because of its strong effects among Japanese wives. Wives not in arranged marriages were twice as likely to see their parents weekly as those whose marriages were arranged, 32 percent versus 16 percent. This effect, which remains significant in the full model, likely reflects the persistence of more traditional values in arranged marriages.

Weekly Contact with Parents

Table 12.9 and the associated logit models in Tables 12.10 and 12.11 present a parallel analysis of weekly contact. A major component of weekly contact consists of the patterns of seeing parents that we have just observed, but by including telephoning (and, in the United States, letters) the constraints of distance are markedly reduced. Table 12.9 provides a useful documentation of levels of contact by our variables of interest, but a parallel discussion of this table and then of the contrasts between the two measures

---

6. Although this measure includes in the category of eldest those who have no siblings ("only children"), such children are only a small minority of this group and are not likely to be responsible for the observed effects. To the extent possible, future work should separate out those with and without brothers.

Larry L. Bumpass

Table 12.9. Percentages having weekly contact with own parents, by respondent characteristics: Japan and United States, married persons, ages 25–64, with at least one living parent but not coresiding

Respondent characteristic	Japan Males	Japan Females	United States Males	United States Females
Distance				
< 6 min. (Japan), < 2 miles (U.S.)	77	97	88	98
Same town (Japan), 2–24 miles (U.S.)	51	58	76	90
Neighboring town (Japan), 25–49 miles (U.S.)	39	56	53	68
Same prefecture (Japan), 50–99 miles (U.S.)	16	45	45	58
Other prefecture (Japan), 100+ miles (U.S.)	10	29	26	44
Living parents				
Both	46	55	55	72
Father only	22	38	45	53
Mother only	24	46	55	71
Parents living with another child				
Yes	22	48	50	61
No	54	57	54	70
Age				
25–34	56	59	55	77
35–44	37	48	51	66
45–54	25	50	54	62
55–64	20	37	60	73
Father's education				
< high school	35	44	59	73
High school	43	54	52	70
College	28	67	51	67
Husband in low occupation				
Yes	38	46	56	73
No	33	56	50	64
Own education				
< high school	38	43	58	66
High school	35	47	60	72
College	35	58	50	69
City size[a]				
Large	28	49	50	68
Medium	30	51	57	70
Small	36	51	57	74
Rural/nonmetropolitan	53	52	55	72
Husband/wife the oldest sibling				
Husband yes, wife no (Japan), R eldest (U.S.)	51	48	55	70
Husband yes, wife yes (Japan)	45	63	54	70
Husband no, wife no (Japan), R other (U.S.)	26	40	na	na
Husband no, wife yes (Japan)	31	55	na	na

Coresidence and Contact with Parents in Japan and the United States

Table 12.9. *(continued)*

	Japan		United States	
Respondent characteristic	Males	Females	Males	Females
Marriage arranged (Japan)				
Yes	38	46	na	na
No	34	54	na	na
Total %	36	51	36	70
(No.)	(259)	(380)	(1,372)	(1,676)

na—not applicable.

a. For the United States, definitions are: large city = 1 million and over; medium city = 250,000–999,999; small city = 50,000–249,999; rural area = fewer than 50,000.

Table 12.10. Logit analysis of weekly contact with own parents, by respondent characteristics: Japan and United States, married males, ages 25–64, with at least one living parent but not coresiding

	Exponent of logit estimate						
	Japanese males			U.S. males		
Respondent characteristic	(1)	(2)	(3)	(1)	(2)	(3)
Distance						
< 6 min. (Japan), < 2 miles (U.S.)						
Same town (Japan), 2–24 miles (U.S.)	.32*		.34*	.48*		.45*
Neighboring town (Japan), 25–49 miles (U.S.)	.20*		.16*	.15*		.13*
Same prefecture (Japan), 50–99 miles (U.S.)	.06*		.06*	.10*		.09*
Other prefecture (Japan), 100+ miles (U.S.)	.04*		.03*	.05*		.05*
Living parents						
Both						
Father only	.34*	.18*	.34†	.62*	.56*	.50*
Mother only	.36*	.31*	.59	1.08	1.08	1.00
Parents living with another child						
Yes						
No	4.07*	4.21*	3.07*	1.16	.97	1.06
Age						
25–34						
35–44	.47*	.37*	.45†	.88	1.00	1.00
45–54	.27*	.19*	.24*	.99	1.27	1.21
55–64	.20*	.12*	.30	1.20	1.75*	1.78*
Father's education						
< high school						
High school	1.40	1.51	.86	.78	.78	.81
College	.69	1.19	.86	.66	.94	.90
Husband in low occupation						
Yes						
No	.78	.94	.91	.82	1.44†	1.38†

Larry L. Bumpass

Table 12.10. (continued)

	Exponent of logit estimate					
	Japanese males			U.S. males		
Respondent characteristic	(1)	(2)	(3)	(1)	(2)	(3)
Own education						
< high school						
High school	.91	.68	.58	.78	.85	.80
College	.90	1.12	.52	.56*	.99	.84
City size[a]						
Large						
Medium	1.06	1.09	1.24	1.24	1.08	1.07
Small	1.45	1.23	1.82	.95	.79	.79
Rural/nonmetropolitan	2.82*	2.12†	2.19	1.25	.92	.95
Husband/wife the oldest sibling						
Husband yes, wife no (Japan), R eldest (U.S.)						
Husband yes, wife yes (Japan)	.78	.79	.57	.94	.83	.84
Husband no, wife no (Japan), R other (U.S.)	.42*	.39*	.46	na	na	na
Husband no, wife yes (Japan)	.33*	.29*	.40	na	na	na
Marriage arranged (Japan)						
Yes						
No	.86	1.27	.71	na	na	na

Models: (1) variable alone, (2) variable + distance, (3) all variables.

na—not applicable.

*Logit coefficient is at least twice its standard error.

†Logit coefficient is 1.5–1.99 times its standard error.

a. For the United States, definitions are: large city = 1 million and over; medium city = 250,000–999,999; small city = 50,000–249,999; rural area = fewer than 50,000.

Table 12.11. Logit analysis of weekly contact with own parents, by respondent characteristics: Japan and United States, married females, ages 25–64, with at least one living parent but not coresiding

	Exponent of logit estimate					
	Japanese females			U.S. females		
Respondent characteristic	(1)	(2)	(3)	(1)	(2)	(3)
Distance						
< 6 min. (Japan), 0–1 mile (U.S.)						
Same town (Japan), 2–24 miles (U.S.)	.05*		.04*	.20		.19*
Neighboring town (Japan), 25–49 miles (U.S.)	.04*		.03*	.06		.05*
Same prefecture (Japan), 50–99 miles (U.S.)	.03*		.02*	.03		.03*
Other prefecture (Japan), 100+ miles (U.S.)	.01*		.01*	.02		.02*
Living parents						
Both						

Table 12.11. *(continued)*

| | \multicolumn{6}{c}{Exponent of logit estimate} |
Respondent characteristic	Japanese females (1)	(2)	(3)	U.S. females (1)	(2)	(3)
Father only	.51	.44†	.78	.44*	.35*	.39
Mother only	.71†	.92	1.10	.98	.98	1.22
Parents living with another child						
Yes						
No	1.34	1.34	1.17	2.21*	2.83*	2.92*
Age						
25–34						
35–44	.63†	.73	.84	.60*	.70*	.72*
45–54	.69	.73	.83	.61*	.61*	.61*
55–64	.40	.42†	.48	.88	1.00	1.00*
Father's education						
< high school						
High school	1.46†	1.63†	1.34	.84	1.08	.96
College	2.52*	3.34*	2.04†	.74*	1.20	1.03
Husband in low occupation						
Yes						
No	1.54*	1.61*	1.52†	1.08	.69*	.96
Own education						
< high school						
High school	2.34*	1.35	1.06	1.24	1.48†	1.39
College	1.32	2.99	1.71	1.04	1.84*	1.60†
City size[a]						
Large						
Medium	1.07	.80	.93	.96	.91	.95
Small	1.06	.69	.84	1.10	.79	.84
Rural/nonmetropolitan	1.10	.68	.91	1.00	.81	.89
Husband/wife the oldest sibling						
Husband yes, wife no (Japan), R eldest (U.S.)						
Husband yes, wife yes (Japan)	1.82†	1.88†	1.75	1.02	1.02	1.02
Husband no, wife no (Japan), R other (U.S.)	1.31	1.26	1.17	na	na	na
Husband no, wife yes (Japan)	.72	.63	.67	na	na	na
Marriage arranged (Japan)						
Yes						
No	1.37†	1.22		na	na	na

Models: (1) variable alone, (2) variable + distance, (3) all variables.

na—not applicable.

*Logit coefficient is at least twice its standard error.

†Logit coefficient is 1.5–1.99 its standard error.

a. For the United States, definitions are: large city = 1 million and over; medium city = 250,000–999,999; small city = 50,000– 249,999; rural area = fewer than 50,000.

would make this chapter far too long. I will just note for now that patterns of weekly contact do not necessarily mirror those of seeing parents weekly. The effects of some variables are even stronger in the contact measure, as the categories of people who are more likely to visit are also more likely to call when they cannot visit. For other variables, the observed effects on seeing parents are eliminated, or even reversed, as differences in visiting are compensated for by calling.

Differences between the two measures vary by sex and country. The most general difference is that, for all but Japanese husbands, the effects of city size disappear in the measure of total weekly contact. This result calls into question my interpretation of these differences as influenced by traditional values and suggests instead the difficulties associated with visiting in larger areas, including differences in distance not captured by the distance measure.

The contrast between seeing parents weekly and any weekly contact is notable for two other variables in each of the countries. For wives in the United States, those whose parents lived with another child were much less likely to have frequent contact with them than were those whose parents did not live with another child. Because women assume primary responsibility for parental care in the United States, having a sibling fully involved in such care may reduce this sense of obligation. Among U.S. husbands, the strong negative effect of the father's education on the frequency of seeing their parents disappears completely in the measure of any weekly contact. I do not have a ready explanation for this change. In Japan, the higher levels of weekly visiting with the husband's parents when both spouses were eldest siblings completely disappears when weekly contact is considered. Perhaps this should not be surprising since the filial obligations that increase a wife's visiting her husband's parents (as part of a couple) may be much less likely to result in a telephone call on her part. Finally, the strong negative effect of arranged marriage on visits between Japanese women and their parents is not significant in the full model for weekly contact. The fact that the differences remain in the observed levels of contact make me reluctant to try to interpret this contrast between the measures.

CONCLUSION

Although levels of intergenerational coresidence in Japan are so high as to be qualitatively different from those in the United States, the trends in Japan are similar in direction to those experienced in the United States and the persistence of filial obligation in the United States is expressed in surprisingly high degrees of life-course experience with intergenerational coresidence. With respect to the frequency of contact between adults and their parents who are not living with them, the findings for Japan and the

Coresidence and Contact with Parents in Japan and the United States

United States are quite parallel, even though many differences highlight the distinctive cultural traditions of each country. In both countries, differences between men and women reflect the patriarchal heritage of Japan, on the one hand, and, on the other, the more bilateral relations with parents in the United States, with an emphasis on women as the family caretakers. Differences by major variables, when they emerge, tend to be consistent (again with important exceptions).

Most obviously, distance strongly conditions interaction between adult children and their parents in both countries, and the effects of some variables are largely a consequence of their association with distance. In addition, however, significant effects were found in the observed levels of interaction for most of the variables for at least one sex in each of the countries, and these effects were usually in the same direction: negative for not having both parents surviving, negative if the parents live with another child, negative for father's education, and positive for less urban areas. Although a significant negative effect of education was found only for U.S. husbands, the differences were also in this direction among men in Japan, whereas the relationship was positive for Japanese women.

Whether one had older siblings was important for contact with parents only in Japan, even though an effect on coresidence histories emerged for women in the United States.

Husband's occupational level had contrasting effects in the two countries, tending to increase weekly visiting in Japan, especially among sons and fathers, and to decrease the proportion seeing their parents weekly in the United States, especially among daughters and their mothers.

A major contrast was found in age patterns, with a linear negative age effect in Japan but a curvilinear pattern in the United States. It seems likely that the response to additional needs as parents age seen in the U.S. patterns is dealt with by coresidence in Japan. This raises two important concluding points. The first concerns the flows into and out of coresidence in Japan. Martin and Tsuya (1991) document that a significant proportion of coresidence has not been continuous: a quarter among those living with the husband's parents and half among those living with the wife's. This finding suggests the importance for the future of obtaining life-history information on coresidence in Japan.

Finally, I return to my opening remarks about the need to keep in mind how parental survival affects the structure of intergenerational contact over the life course. Table 12.12 presents the proportions seeing a parent on a weekly basis and with any weekly contact by age for the total population, including those with no living parents. The first of these measures is displayed graphically in Figure 12.2. Here life-course experience in the two countries is remarkably similar,

Larry L. Bumpass

Table 12.12. Weekly contact with own parents in total population (including those with no living parents), by age: Japan and United States, married persons, ages 25–64

	See weekly (%)				Any weekly contact (%)			
	Japan		United States		Japan		United States	
Age group	Males	Females	Males	Females	Males	Females	Males	Females
25–34	63	41	38	47	69	61	54	75
35–44	48	26	28	33	54	47	46	60
45–54	34	19	23	26	38	31	37	40
55–64	17	10	9	15	17	15	17	24
Total %	38	23	26	32	42	38	40	53

and it becomes increasingly so with age. The higher levels of seeing parents weekly among Japanese men and among U.S. women rapidly converge toward their counterparts in the other country. By early middle age, fewer than a third in either country see parents weekly, and fewer than two-fifths have any weekly parental contact.

In both countries, of course, the cycles of generations begin to replace these relationships with interactions with couples' own adult children. In both countries, these family interactions up and down the generational ladder remain an important aspect of social life. It also

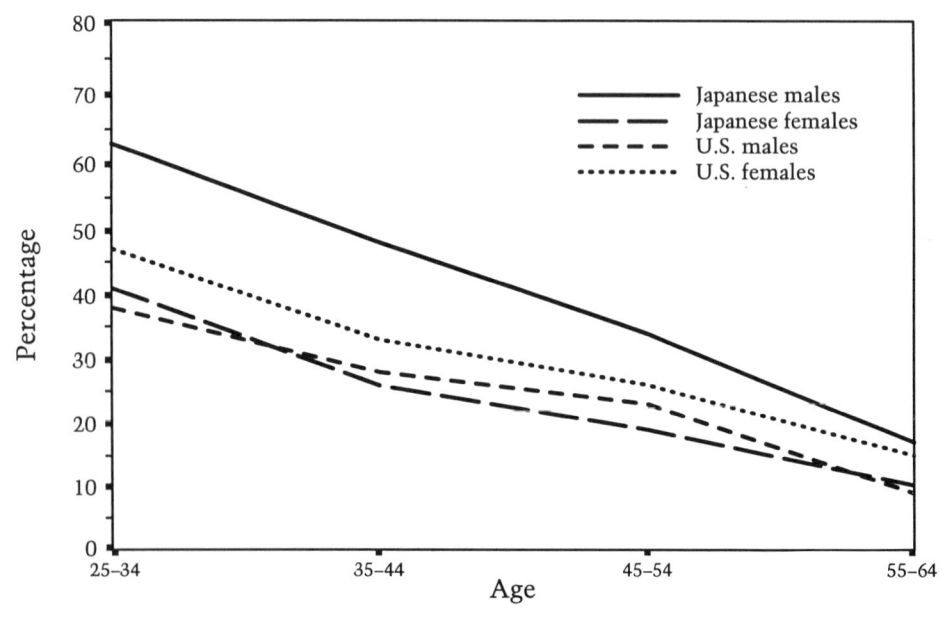

Figure 12.2. Age differences in seeing parents weekly: all married persons (including those with no living parents)

seems likely that in both countries, levels of intergenerational interaction are reduced with each turning of the generational wheel.

APPENDIX: CODING OF VARIABLES

Contact

In Japan the question was, "How often did you see your own parent(s) [your parents-in-law] during the last 1–2 years?" In the United States it was, "During the past 12 months, about how often did you see your mother [father, mother-in-law, father-in-law]?" Given that parents may be living apart in the United States because of divorce and the Japanese question refers to parents generically, I coded the variable for the United States to reflect the parent most frequently seen. Response categories were slightly different in the two countries and posed in reverse order: from most frequently to least frequently in Japan and the opposite in the United States. I reversed the scores on the variable in the Japanese data, obtaining the following approximate equivalence:

Japan	United States
1. Seldom see him/her/them	Not at all
2. Approximately once a year	About once a year
3. A few times a year	Several times a year
4. Approximately once a month	1–3 times a month
5. Approximately once a week	About once a week
6. Almost every day	Several times a week

I focused on weekly contact because of my substantive concern with frequent interaction, but it also appears to be the most comparable division for these two measures.

Martin and Tsuya noted the high level of missing data on parental contact measures and attributed it to respondents' difficulty with interpreting the questionnaire instructions. It seems that a major problem occurred for persons who were coresiding with their in-laws, most of whom did not continue to fill out the information on parents living elsewhere. More than half of the missing data on parental contact was left out by such respondents, and almost three-quarters of those who were coresiding did not complete the sections on contact. This omission had little effect on our estimates for men's relationships with their own parents, but probably biased somewhat our contact estimates for women. If living with her husband's parents was likely to reduce a wife's contact with her own parents, then our estimates for Japanese women may be somewhat too high.

The measure of seeing parents weekly was the most comparable. Both sources allowed us to use a broader measure, however. In Japan a similar question was asked: "How often do you phone your parents?" In the United States the additional question was: "How often do you communicate with your (mother/father) by letter or phone?" Hence, levels of contact with parents would be higher in the United States to the extent that respondents used letters but not the telephone. We have no evidence on this point but suspect that the response difference introduced by this wording difference was minor.

I found considerable overlap between visiting with parents and contact with them by telephone, though among women there was greater difference. I combined the two variables to create a measure of whether respondents had any contact on a weekly basis, either by visiting or by telephone or letter.

Occupation

I added a measure of occupation because of its importance in some of the equations examined by Martin and Tsuya. The coding distinguished proprietors and professionals from all others. In the United States, I examined quartiles of the husband's socioeconomic income (SEI) scores and found that the highest quartile stood out, so that was the distinction used here even though it was not as comparable a distinction as the upper half of the distribution would have been. My unfortunate decision to code this variable as "yes"/"no" resulted in an awkward structure of coefficients contrasting those who were not in the lowest quartile with those who were. For ease of presentation I simply refer to the effect of "higher" occupation rather than that of not being in the lowest occupations.

REFERENCES

Bumpass, Larry L., and James A. Sweet. 1991. "Family Experiences across the Life Course: Differences by Cohort, Education, and Race/Ethnicity." Center for Demography and Ecology NSFH Working Paper No. 42, University of Wisconsin, Madison.

Hirosima Kiyosi. 1987. "Recent Change in the Prevalence of Parent-Child Co-residence in Japan." *Journal of Population Problems* 10:33–41.

Kendig, Hal. 1989. "Social Change and Family Dependency in Old Age: Perceptions of Japanese Women in Middle Age." NUPRI Research Paper Series No. 54, Nihon University Population Research Institute, Tokyo.

Kojima Hiroshi. 1989. "Intergenerational Household Extension in Japan." In Frances K. Goldscheider and Calvin Goldscheider (eds.), *Ethnicity and the New Family Economy*, pp. 163–183. Boulder: Westview Press.

Martin, Linda G., and Noriko O. Tsuya. 1991. "Interactions of Middle-Aged Japanese with Their Parents." *Population Studies* 45:299–312.

Industry Restructuring and Family Migration Decisions: A Community Study in Japan

by Suzanne Culter

Japan is frequently referred to as a role model in discussions of industrial policy and industry restructuring. Whenever troubled industries in the United States restructure and unemployment increases, the debate volleys between those who reject government intervention and those who favor assistance, the latter citing Japan as an example of a nation with an efficient and humane approach to policies for declining industries. What has been missing, however, is any in-depth investigation of the impact of Japan's policies of industry restructuring at the microlevel. For example, do the macrolevel benefits of industry restructuring in Japan carry over to the local community? In other words, are the families in a community surrounding a restructured industry also benefiting from this industrial policy? What has generally been accepted as favorable at the macrolevel has remained ambiguous at the microlevel. This chapter therefore presents results from a study of households in a Japanese community that has been dealing with the decline and restructuring of its major industry of coal mining.

Japan's rapid postwar economic growth slowed for the first time with the

1973 oil shock. Within the next five years, corporate profits in many firms were reduced and the number of bankruptcies reached an unprecedented high (Saxonhouse, 1979). In response, legislation providing assistance to depressed industries was passed in 1978. The restructuring of major industries resulted in an increased level of unemployment, but the Japanese government also enacted laws to provide support programs and financial aid to workers and communities affected by the transition. Although first put into law in 1978, similar policies and measures had been used earlier in troubled industries such as the coal industry. It is this triple layer of guidance and support policies aimed at industry, the community, and the worker and formulated through the cooperation between government and business that has been lauded by those advocating industrial policy and plant-closure legislation in the United States. The expectation is that the restructuring process and accompanying policies not only are economically successful but also ensure adequate adjustment at all three levels. The industry maintains a profit, and a buffer system is put in place for the dependent community and the displaced workers.

In attempting to assess the validity of this assumption, it is fairly easy to find records of corporate profits, but it is far more difficult to determine if the affected communities and workers have fared as well. Although studies of the local-level effects of deindustrialization and plant closures have been conducted in the United States, similar studies have been lacking in Japan. Research in the United States has indicated that cities and towns affected by deindustrialization, industry restructuring, and plant closures lose major industries and economic stability. The impact of job loss and a shrinking tax base can affect nearly every social and economic organization within the surrounding community. The displaced workers are often unable to find new employment or, if reemployed, earn less and have fewer benefits. A pattern of long-term unemployment develops with an accompanying loss of family income and an increase of physical and mental health problems (Bluestone and Harrison, 1982; Flaim and Sehgal, 1985; Gordus, Jarley, and Ferman, 1981; Hammerman, 1987; Perrucci et al., 1988).

It would be anticipated that displaced workers needing jobs might move from their communities in search of employment. In a report on a U.S. Department of Labor survey, however, Flaim and Sehgal (1985) note that only a small minority of 5.1 million displaced workers who had been surveyed had moved to another city to look for work. They speculate that the reasons for not leaving included the following: (1) the workers had established community ties, (2) they may have owned homes that were hard to sell if located in a depressed area, and (3) they may have had family members who were still employed locally. If a closed plant has been the major employer in an area,

Industry Restructuring and Family Migration Decisions: A Community Study in Japan

however, opportunities for reemployment will be limited and workers may be forced to migrate from the community, taking their families with them. Shaw (1975:53) suggests that this type of out-migration, in turn, may "lead to increasing unemployment due to the multiplier effects of migrants taking their consumer expenditures elsewhere." In addition, if the repeated feedback cycle of unemployment, out-migration, and decline of social structure continues over a prolonged period, further out-migration may occur as a result of dissatisfaction with the community's quality of life.

These findings are from studies of communities and workers in the United States, a nation said to be lacking an industrial policy and legislated assistance for those suffering from the effects of industry restructuring. It is important to question whether similar effects of industry restructuring on communities of workers and their families would be found in Japan, a nation with a comprehensive set of policies for the process and consequences of industry restructuring. The study reported here therefore addressed the following questions: Will job loss lead to migration? Which family-related factors will determine the migration decision? And how does policy help or hinder this process?

An attempt to provide answers to these questions was made through an analysis of data collected during a two-year field study I conducted in the coal-mining city of Yūbari in Hokkaido Prefecture. Although the coal industry had been considered a structurally depressed industry long before the 1978 law went into effect, it became a major focus of the Maekawa report on economic structural adjustment for international harmony, issued in 1986, and was subsequently targeted for a nearly complete shutdown by 1992. Prime Minister Nakasone had appointed a former Bank of Japan official, Haruo Maekawa, to chair a commission of experts in an investigation of Japan's international economic relations and trade conflicts. The commission's final report emphasized the need for Japan to phase out declining industries, particularly the coal industry (Higashi and Lauter, 1987:99–138). During 1985 and 1986 I investigated the changes occurring in Yūbari as a result of the coal industry's decline through the use of participant observation and interviews with 212 households and 40 city officials.

In this chapter I present a brief review of the coal industry's transition and the role of Yūbari City as a coal producer, followed by a discussion of the consequences of the mine closures for Yūbari's social structure. A logit analysis of the household survey data is used to examine Yūbari residents' migration intentions in response to the city's transformation. To explain the effects on the migration decision of such sociocultural influences as community ties, family dynamics, and life-cycle patterns, I include a descriptive analysis of the surveyed households by major employment category.

Suzanne Culter

THE COAL INDUSTRY AND YŪBARI CITY: FROM BOOM TO BUST

Although commercial coal mining first began in Japan more than 200 years ago, it was the Meiji government (1868–1912) that pushed for the modernization of the coal-mining industry and the development of Hokkaido's rich coal resources. Coal continued to play an important role in Japan's industrial and economic growth and was a major pillar of the "priority production" method after World War II. However, a long history of labor-management problems, increasing production costs, and a switch by industrial consumers to cheaper imported oil resulted in rationalization and restructuring measures. The government produced the First Coal Plan to address these concerns in 1962. Even the oil shocks of 1973 and 1979 failed to slow the industry's decline. Rather than depend on imported oil or on increased production of domestic coal, Japan turned to imported coal. When the Eighth Coal Plan was announced in 1986, the domestic coal industry was virtually laid to rest. The plan called for a reduction in coal production that would guarantee the closure of most of Japan's coal mines by 1992. At the time it was presented, a total of 26 mines were operating in Japan—22 in Hokkaido, one in Honshu, and three in Kyushu. Only 11 were major collieries, however, eight in Hokkaido and the three in Kyushu. Only one mine in Hokkaido and two mines in Kyushu were expected to remain in operation.

Two of the 11 major collieries were in Yūbari City, Hokkaido. Coal was first discovered in Yūbari in 1888, and communities began to form there as coal development and production expanded. The population grew as coal miners, shopkeepers, and service workers flowed into the area seeking to partake of the benefits of a prosperous coal industry. By 1943 the population had reached about 65,000, and at least 29 communities stretching from the north mountain valley, curving into the two eastern mountain branches, and ending in the southern agricultural plain were designated as the city of Yūbari. The number of workers employed in mining in Yūbari reached a peak in 1953 at 19,555. But the nation's conversion to oil had begun in 1952, and toward the end of 1953 the city's coal industry began to adjust by reducing the number of mining employees. By 1960, 17 mines, the maximum number, were operating in Yūbari and employing 16,000 laborers, and the city's population had reached a peak of 107,972 residents (Yūbari City, 1985).

The climb to the top had taken nearly 70 years, but the fall would occur in half that time. In 1961 the national government liberalized oil imports. By 1962, Yūbari's descent had begun. From 1962 to 1982, 22 mines or major mining corridors were closed, taking jobs with them. In 1986, at the time I conducted my survey, only two mines remained open in Yūbari. By 1990, both had been shut down.

As Yūbari's mines closed, the city's population also began to decline (Table 13.1). A steady drop continued year after year until, by 1990, the population had declined by nearly 81 percent since the 1960 peak period. This loss in population has been attributed to the massive out-migration of residents that began with the loss of mining jobs. But the decline in mining employment was only the beginning. The reliance of the city's economy on the coal industry eventually led to the closure of affiliated industries and job layoffs for workers across a range of sectors in Yūbari. The long-awaited modernization of the area was soon offset by the lagging economy and deterioration of services. Thus, the feedback effects of the mine closures and outward flow of population precipitated even more out-migration. From 1960 to 1985, Yūbari's labor force declined overall by 60 percent and unemployment rose from 2.4 to 6.4 percent, more than double the national rate. By 1990, with the final mine closures, the percentage of unemployed had jumped to nearly 11.

During the 30 years of the city's population decline there was little migration into Yūbari and a very low rate of natural increase to balance the outflow. When I calculated the net out-migration of males from Yūbari using census data and life-table survivorship ratios, I found substantial out-migration among every five-year age group in every time interval from 1960 to 1975. Two broad age groups showed the greatest decrease in numbers, ages 10–34 and 50–59. Males of ages 10–19 in all likelihood included children leaving with their families, children sent to other cities for school, and those who left to find employment after graduating from junior high or high school. The drop in the number of those between the ages of 20 and 34 indicates the out-migration of the young adult labor force in search of jobs or in response to job transfers. Those aged 50–59 would include workers who left Yūbari after retiring from their jobs. The retirement age in Japan ranges generally from 55 to 60. But owing to the poor economic conditions

Table 13.1. Total population of Yūbari City and percentage change: five-year periods, 1900–90

Year	Population	% Change
1890	10,954	
1905	11,632	6.2
1910	21,462	84.5
1915	32,538	51.6
1920	51,064	56.9
1925	48,697	−4.6
1930	51,967	6.7
1935	42,508	−18.2
1940	64,998	52.9
1945	74,665	14.9
1950	99,530	33.3
1955	107,332	7.8
1960	107,972	0.6
1965	85,141	−21.1
1970	69,871	−17.9
1975	50,131	−28.3
1980	41,715	−16.8
1985	31,665	−24.1
1990	20,969	−33.8
1960–90		−80.6

Sources: Yūbari City (1987, Sect. 2, item 1; 1991, Sect. 2, item 1).

in Yūbari, many workers were asked to take early retirement in order to open positions up for the next younger cohort or so that mine operators and other employers throughout Yūbari could eliminate certain positions in job cutbacks. When a male head of household in Yūbari migrated from the city, he would take his family with him if it had not already preceded him.

Nearly every social institution within Yūbari has had to respond to the changes brought about by the mine closures and long-term out-migration of residents. Both government-supported and private facilities and services have been undergoing a constant process of readjustment that began in the 1960s.

Most of the city's factories were either interdependent, relying heavily on the coal industry, or were entirely dependent on the local economy; thus, when both bases declined, many factories were forced to close down or lay off employees. A site for an industrial complex was developed in the middle of the city in an attempt to bring in replacement industries, but many of the factories that were enticed in with special benefits and assistance from the city were unable to survive the depressed economy, transportation costs, and severe weather conditions. Most were bankrupt within three to five years.

Yūbari's commercial establishments were severely affected by both the population loss and the changing population composition. Much of the younger population was leaving while the elderly on lower incomes remained; this imbalance substantially affected consumer purchasing patterns and levels. From 1960 to 1985, the number of retail stores declined by 27 percent and the number of employees working in them decreased by 46 percent. During the same period, 57 percent of the small eating and drinking establishments closed down, resulting in a 70 percent drop in the number of employees. For those shops still in business, the decline in customers brought a decline in sales volume.

Finally, as the number of clients decreased, similar declines were seen in public services such as bus and train transportation, postal and telephone networks, school and educational facilities, medical establishments, and even the fire department. Only one public service grew. The steady loss of employment and income pushed more and more families into needing public assistance. In 1960 one measure of Yūbari's welfare rate indicated that the city was below that of the Hokkaido prefecture and the nation as a whole. By 1985, however, Yūbari was in the lead with a rate of 39.4 per thousand, nearly double that of Hokkaido and triple that of the nation.

In summary, unlike workers described in the results reported by Flaim and Sehgal (1985) for the United States, laid-off workers in Yūbari have tended to migrate out in search of employment. Policy has never been directed at trying to retain them in the city. The long-term consequence of this massive outward flow has been a steady wearing away of the city's basic social foundation. Employment opportunities across sectors have declined. Tax revenues from the coal industry and other businesses have decreased. The adjustments in a variety of public services to meet the demands of a shrinking population base have resulted not only in a reduction in the number of employees but also in a possible decrease in the quality of services.

Even the physical environment and social atmosphere of Yūbari changed during this restructuring. Neighborhoods disappeared as vacant housing was torn down and construction projects remodeled the landscape. Forests were cleared to become parks and man-made lakes became tourist spots; land was dug away, then filled in; neighborhoods were built up and torn down. But in the middle of the reconstruction, the loss of familiar neighborhoods, friends, coworkers, and family members left a *sabishii*, or lonely, feeling, throughout the city. Residents nostalgically recall the crowds of people who used to fill the shopping districts at the end of a work day, the excitement of the city's festivals when parades would line the streets for miles, and the security of knowing that their families and friends were living nearby. They miss the people and the former liveliness of the city, and they wish that more young people and children lived in their neighborhoods. Although Japan as a whole is graying, the exodus of the young labor force from Yūbari has increased the elderly proportion of the city's population. From 1960 to 1985, the proportion of the population 65 years of age or older grew from 3.1 percent to nearly 12 percent. Schools in the city are being torn down or consolidated while more emphasis is going into facilities and programs for senior citizens.

THE HOUSEHOLD SURVEY

With the vast transformation of their social structure, Yūbari residents were faced with deciding whether they had a future in this city. Whether they would be able to, or would want to, remain in Yūbari became a daily concern. To investigate the effects of the coal-mine closures and changes in the social structure on Yūbari's workers and residents, and particularly on their families' migration decisions, I conducted a household survey. With the assistance of officials in the branch district offices of City Hall, I selected a quota sample of 212 households. My interviews with respondents lasted one to two hours each, and the survey time period extended from January to September 1986. The following section presents characteristics of the survey sample and the results of a logit regression analysis of determinants related to respondents' migration intentions.

Sample Characteristics

A quota sample of 212 households from all seven administrative districts was selected based on the employment categories of household heads. Major employers in Yūbari were the coal mining companies and wholesale, retail, and service establishments; therefore, a larger number of household heads in these categories was sampled. To ensure the inclusion of white-collar permanent employees, I included public employees as the third largest group. Information on a total of 1,048 household members was recorded for the 212 households, including 351 members who had migrated out of the households. Forty-eight of the out-migrants had remained in Yūbari, whereas 303 had moved to areas primarily within Hokkaido.

Of the 697 household members who remained in Yūbari, excluding the 48 who had moved from their homes but remained in Yūbari, 49.5 percent were males and 50.5 percent were females. These figures correspond closely to the ratio of males to females in the city population for the same year (49.6 percent males to 50.4 percent females). The mean number of resident household members for the sample was 3.3, higher than the city average of 2.7 members per household. The fact that the sample was younger than the city population, as shown in Table 13.2, may account for this difference. Younger children had not yet left the households.

The age distributions of the sample and the city population are displayed in Table 13.3 by five-year age groups. Although the percentage of those in the 0–14 age group was higher for the sample, the breakdown by age groups shows that the proportions between ages 15 and 34

Table 13.2. Age distribution of sample and of Yūbari City population: mid-1980s

Age group	Sample (1986) No.	%	Yūbari (1985) No.	%
0–14	149	21.5	5,641	17.8
15–64	477	68.7	22,383	70.7
65+	68	9.8	3,641	11.5
Total	694	100.0	31,665	100.0

Sources: Survey results (1986); Yūbari City (1987, Sect. 2, item 3.2).

Table 13.3. Age distribution of sample and of Yūbari City, by five-year age group: mid-1980s

Age group	Sample (1986) %	Yūbari (1985) %
0–4	3.0	4.8
5–9	8.4	5.7
10–14	10.1	7.3
15–19	5.9	6.8
20–24	1.7	3.6
25–29	2.6	4.3
30–34	3.9	6.1
35–39	7.9	7.0
40–44	8.6	7.3
45–49	9.1	9.6
50–54	9.1	11.1
55–59	11.4	8.9
60–64	8.5	6.0
65–69	4.2	4.2
70–74	2.9	3.4
75–79	1.6	2.3
80–84	1.0	1.1
85–89	0.3	0.4
90–94	—	0.1
95+	—	—
Total %	100.0	100.0
(No.)	(694)	(31,665)

Sources: Survey results (1986); Yūbari City (1987, Sect. 2, item 3.2).

were less in the sample. After age 35, total percentages for the sample and the city were similar. Thus, although the sample was not randomized, the age and sex distributions were close enough to those of the city population to be considered representative and certainly adequate for the purposes of this study.

The sample was selected by the employment category of the household head, and in most cases it was the household head who was interviewed and supplied the information on other family members. The total sample of household heads consisted of 201 men and 11 women. Only five of these were unemployed, and four of the five were women. Therefore, the interview discussions about the impact of the mine closures for the household and what the household's future plans would entail focused predominately on the male worker's employment or retirement, with the understanding that his wife and young children would accompany him if he chose to leave the city.

Since it was the household head who usually determined the future plans, I examined relevant characteristics of this group first. Although I had requested from city officials a list of names of actively employed residents from which to draw the sample, the quota received for each district resulted in five unemployed and 33 retired employees. The retired workers, however, had been previously related to the requested occupation. For example, 29 of the 33 retirees were former coal-mining company employees. Fifty-eight of the 212 household heads were owners of wholesale, retail, or service establishments; 8 were farmers; 66 were mining company employees; 60 were public employees; and 15 were employed by other private businesses.

With the degree of change that had already occurred in Yūbari and the recent announcement of plans to shut down the remaining mines, many of the household heads in this sample were having to consider whether they would remain in the city or migrate out. In an attempt to understand the principal determinants of their migration decisions, I performed a binary logit regression analysis, using selected variables from the sample survey. A variety of variables was analyzed, but the ones selected were those most suitable for the models presented in the following discussion.

Logit Regression Analysis

Logit regression analysis was chosen because it is appropriate for analyzing the effects of a set of independent variables on a categorical dependent variable (Aldrich and Nelson, 1984). The categorical dependent variable was whether the respondent intended to leave Yūbari or not. Two models were constructed around these responses to demonstrate the "definite migration intention" versus the "potential migration intention." In the first model, which refers to "definite intention," 41 percent of the household heads stated their definite intentions to leave the city. Of the respondents who said they would not leave, however, some qualified their answers with such comments as "if I have work here" or "if conditions in the city don't worsen" or "unless I go when my child leaves." Most of the household heads making these statements were young mining company employees who would need another job when the coal mines closed down completely within the next few years. If the members of this group are recoded into the leaving category, then the second model of "potential migration intention," which includes both definite and potential out-migrants, shows 54 percent intending to leave Yūbari. Using the most relevant set of explanatory variables available with these data, I carried out a logit analysis for each of the two models to clarify the determinants of out-migration for both those who definitely intended to leave and those who wanted to stay in Yūbari but were being pushed out by the loss of jobs and services in the city.

The set of selected determinants and their descriptive statistics are presented in Table 13.4. Given the findings in the previous out-migration calculations with the census data, I selected age for the model to see if a similar bimodal distribution would appear for those in the sample who intended to leave. The age range for the sample was 24 years to 79 years, with a mean age of 50.9 years. The source of employment was introduced into the model by creating four dummy variables: owners of business (the reference category), mining company employees, government or public employees, and employees in privately owned businesses other than mining. The group of owners included owners of businesses engaged in wholesale and retail trade or services and farmers. Because the owners of businesses in Yūbari are closely tied to the community through business networks and property ownership, I hypothesized that they would be less likely than others to leave Yūbari. Mining company employees, on the other hand, are either retired or facing imminent job loss. Public employees, a group including local, prefectural, and national government employees, are predominantly white-collar workers and have a high rate of job transfer that might take them out of the city.

A person who was born in Yūbari might be more likely to remain in the

Table 13.4. Descriptive statistics for the determinants of leaving Yūbari

Variable	Mean	Standard deviation
Age	50.895	10.564
Source of employment		
Mining industry	.316	.466
Public sector	.278	.449
Private sector	.072	.259
Born in Yūbari	.459	.499
Extended-family member	.254	.436
Owns home in Yūbari	.378	.486
Owns home outside Yūbari	.120	.325
Number of household out-migrants	1.431	1.234

Note: Of the 212 households in the sample, 209 were used in the analysis. Statistics on three households with unemployed household heads were omitted.

community than someone who migrated there for work as an adult. In a similar fashion, if the person lived in an extended family, meaning the coresidence of a parent and adult child, the likelihood of his or her leaving would probably be less. At the time of the survey, many of Yūbari's workers were living in company housing, and once they left the job, they also had to leave the housing. Others were living in city rental housing of substandard quality. Even though the rents were cheap, given the decline in other city services, workers who rented might be likely to seek better housing in a more thriving environment. In contrast, given the lack of potential buyers in a depressed economy, those who owned homes might choose to remain. Home ownership outside Yūbari was also a factor, in that some employees had parental homes in other cities or had purchased land and built postretirement homes in other areas.

A final variable included in the model was the number of family members who had left the household and migrated from Yūbari. In the majority of households, these family members were the children of the household head. As the mines have closed in Yūbari and job opportunities have subsequently declined, the young people have left the city either to go to school or to look for employment. If a household head wished to live with or nearby a child, he had to move to where the child was residing. Although some of the households in this sample had no out-migrants, the maximum was five

out-migrants and the mean for the sample was 1.4 persons per household who had left.

Table 13.5 presents the coefficients for the explanatory variables for models 1 and 2. The coefficients reflect the effect of the independent variables on the log-odds of leaving Yūbari or not leaving

Table 13.5. Coefficients and standard errors from the logit estimation of intentions to leave Yūbari

Variable	Model 1: definite migration intention	Model 2: definite + potential migration intention
Constant	1.451 (1.079)	2.252* (1.108)
Age	−.066* (.021)	−.067* (.021)
Mining employee	1.647* (.599)	2.339* (.594)
Public employee	2.112* (.558)	1.906* (.533)
Private employee	.713 (.765)	.383 (.730)
Born in Yūbari	−.746* (.357)	−.508 (.370)
Extended-family member	−.589 (.458)	1.384* (.446)
Owns home in Yūbari	.253 (.520)	−.104 (.510)
Owns home outside Yūbari	1.739* (.592)	1.144** (.658)
Number of household out-migrants	.310** (.166)	.326* (.170)
	N = 209 Leave = 85 Stay = 124	N = 209 Leave = 112 Stay = 97
χ^2	63.49	85.65
d.f.	9	9

* Significant at .05 level.
** Significant at .10 level.

(Retherford and Choe, 1993). For the first model of definite migration intention, all the variables are significant at the .10 level except for whether the respondents lived in an extended family, whether they were an employee of a private company, and whether they owned their home in Yūbari. In the second model of definite plus potential migration intention, whether they were an employee of a privately owned company and whether they owned their home in Yūbari again are not significant. For this model, however, whether they were born in Yūbari or not becomes nonsignificant, whereas membership in an extended family becomes significant.

The dummy variables for the employment category have owners as the reference group. Thus, compared with owners, private employees showed no significant difference in their propensity to leave Yūbari; a majority of both groups intended to remain in Yūbari. The sample, however, contained only 15 household heads who were employed by private companies. Whether a person owned a home in Yūbari appears not to be significant in either model, but this effect is due to the high correlation (.60) between this variable and the employment variable. A majority of the business and farm owners in Yūbari owned their homes, whereas most of the other employees lived in company or city housing. When the employment variable is omitted from the model, the variable of owning a home in Yūbari is significant at the .05 level.

In the first model, whether one lived in an extended family does not make a significant difference in one's intention to remain in the city. Nevertheless, when we consider those who anticipated that they would have to leave whether they wanted to or not (in the second model), the respondents who still expected to remain in Yūbari were more likely to live in extended family units. Likewise, those in Model 2 who were being pushed out included more of those born in Yūbari, and this variable becomes not significant as a result of both those born in Yūbari and those not born in Yūbari leaving the city.

The method used for interpreting the logit regression coefficients is that of adjusted probabilities, which represent the direct effect of the explanatory variables on the probability of intending to leave Yūbari versus not intending to leave (Retherford and Choe, 1993). The results, or adjusted probabilities for the individual variables, which I calculated while controlling for the values of the other explanatory variables at their means, are presented in Table 13.6. For example, the probability of a public employee in Model 1 intending to leave is .73, and for a mining company employee it is .65. In Model 2, with potential migration intention included, these percentages increase to .82 for public employees and .85 for workers in mining. The probability of a person intending to leave who owned a home outside Yūbari is high in both models, .73 in Model 1 and .76 in Model 2. Being born in Yūbari appears to be a holding factor for a person in Model 1 because the probability of his or her intending to leave is only .28, whereas it is .46 for a person not born in Yūbari. But as previously noted, birthplace has no effect in the second model, which includes those born in Yūbari who were being forced to leave.

In both models, as the number of out-migrants from the household increases, so does the probability of the respondent's intention to leave. In Model 1, the probability of intending to leave for a person in a household with no out-migrants is .28, but the probability increases to .57 for a person in a household from which four persons out-migrated. Model 2 shows the same pattern but with an even higher increase in the percentages.

Although being a member of an extended family is not significant in Model 1, it does become significant in Model 2 when an increased number of respondents not in extended families become potential out-migrants. The probability of a person intending to leave who was not in an extended family is then .62.

Again, for both models, the probability of intending to leave is highest for the younger age group. But it is also fairly high for those near retirement age, dropping off after the age of 60.

To summarize, all the variables selected to explain intending to leave Yūbari are significant in the first model except for being a member of an extended family. Thus, considering merely what the respondents intended to do, I found that being born in Yūbari contributed to their desire to remain in the city. But when the reality of the economic decline in the city and the future prospects for employment were included in the deci-

Table 13.6. Adjusted probability of leaving Yūbari, by selected determinants (values of the other determinants controlled at their means)

Determinant	Model 1: definite migration intention	Model 2: definite + potential migration intention
Age (years)		
38	.5834	.7308
50	.3867	.5499
62	.2211	.3548
Source of employment		
Mining industry	.6471	.8508
Public sector	.7322	.8203
Private sector	ns	ns
Place of birth		
Yūbari	.2842	ns
Not Yūbari	.4556	ns
Family composition		
Extended-family member	ns	.2906
Not extended-family member	ns	.6206
Home ownership outside Yūbari		
Owns home outside	.7331	.7592
Does not own home outside	.3255	.5010
Household out-migrants:		
0 out-migrants	.2761	.4194
1 out-migrant	.3421	.5001
2 out-migrants	.4148	.5809
4 out-migrants	.5685	.7267
	N = 209	N = 209
	Leave = 85	Leave = 112
	Stay = 124	Stay = 97

ns = not significant.

sion making, the number of potential out-migrants increased. Model 2 reflects these additions. Having been born in Yūbari is no longer perceived as a deterrent to the probability of leaving. The stronger influence holding a person in the city then appears to change from being born in the city to being a member of an extended family. For both models, other factors that influence a person's intention to leave the city are the source of employment, with high percentages of public employees and mining company employees intending to leave; whether property was owned outside Yūbari; and whether the adult children of the household had migrated out of the city. Whether a person owned his or her home in Yūbari is also significant but does not appear so in the model owing to a high correlation with the employment variable. The cross-tabulation in Table 13.7 therefore clarifies the effect of this determinant. Seventy-three percent of those who owned their homes in Yūbari intended to stay whereas 71 percent of those who lived in company or rental housing planned to leave.

Two other variables considered important in analyzing migration decision making are education and the total number of previous moves. For these models, however, both variables display interaction. Younger household heads are more likely to have a higher level of education than are older household heads. Age also interacts with the variable for total number of moves. If the variable of number of moves is examined outside the model, however, it can be seen that those with a higher number of previous moves are those who intended to leave Yūbari.

Differences by Employment Categories

One encounters limitations in using logit analysis to explain the full set of factors seen as most important in determining whether the household would leave or stay. The following descriptions of the differences found in decision making among the major employment groups present a more complete picture of the family dynamics involved.

Mining company employees After each mine closure in Yūbari over the years, a flurry of movement would occur within the city. Miners would move to other open mines if work was available; in time, however, the larger exodus was out of the city as miners and their family members were pushed to seek employment elsewhere. In this sample of 66 households,

Table 13.7. Intention to leave Yūbari, by home ownership: 1986

Intend to leave	Own home (%)	Rental or company (%)	Total (%)	(No.)
Yes	27.5	70.5	54.2	(115)
No	72.5	29.5	45.8	(97)
Total %	37.7	62.3	100.0	
(No.)	(80)	(132)		(212)

$\chi^2 = 35.3$, $p < .0005$
d.f.= 1

Note: Total of 212 includes unemployed household heads.

80 percent had blue-collar workers. Seventy-three percent of the miners and their wives were born in Yūbari, grew up in Yūbari, or spent all of their adult working lives in Yūbari. Although they were long-term residents of the city and had wide networks of parents, siblings, and friends in the region, most of these workers and their spouses would leave Yūbari within the next few years. In fact, 74 percent of the coal mining employees stated that they intended to leave the city. Families and friends who were once part of a close-knit subculture were now dispersed throughout Hokkaido and Honshu, and the departure of these respondents would further weaken the structure left behind.

The interviews with the mining employees elicited a range of reactions. Older, retired miners seemed less concerned about the situation than those in the middle of their working careers. Their incomes would not be affected and they already knew their future plans. They could afford to live in Yūbari's low-rent public housing, and they were reluctant to leave the familiar environment of Yūbari. Other miners nearing retirement age gave similar responses; postretirement work in Yūbari had been nearly eliminated by this time, and in anticipating the mine closures, they had already planned their next moves. Some would stay whereas others would move out to live with or near their children and look for postretirement employment. The young miners, those in their late 20s to early 30s, had generally entered mining to build up a savings that would enable them to relocate and enter a different career. They tended to view the mine closures as inevitable and expected.

In contrast, the workers most severely affected by the mine closures were blue-collar mining employees in their late 30s to early 50s. They had become too old to retrain easily or to reenter the job market, and still too young to retire. If they had been hired as permanent employees of the company, they would receive assistance in job placement or training but would assuredly take large cuts in salary and benefits. If they had always been temporary laborers, the mine closure meant another move and another job search in a life already disrupted by frequent moves and job changes, with fewer networks and less income to soften the transition. In either case, it would mean a move out of Yūbari to a different city and a different job, as well as a move for their wives into unknown communities and for their children into new schools. And all this redirection generally would be taking place in a metropolitan area, not in the closed coal-mining subculture of Yūbari.

For this age group, the cost of living in a metropolitan area would be an additional strain on the budget. The subsequent long-term effects of these slashes in the household income would be felt when money was needed for the children's education or marriages, for a family member who became ill, or for the couple's retirement. In general, home ownership was less common among these blue-collar workers than among other Yūbari residents, and financial readjustments of this magnitude would most likely make home ownership impossible for these miners. For example, one miner who lost his job but chose to stay in Yūbari took a job as a taxi driver. But the demand for taxi service also declined. As his income dropped, he had to move into cheaper housing and sell his car; his wife had to go to work, and his son had to leave college.

Not only were careers interrupted in mid-life, but also the continuation of a family occupation in mining was disrupted for many of these miner households. More than two-thirds (68 percent) of the families in this sample had two or more generations of coal miners. But among all the households sampled, only four sons were doing this same work, and those four would have to quit when the mines closed. Of the households' 109 adult children, only 23 had remained in Yūbari, and 15 of them were daughters. Among the eight sons who had stayed were the four working as coal miners, three working for the city hall, and one working as a cook. The majority (60 percent) of the children who had left the city did so to take a first job, whereas a third (36 percent) had left to attend a college, junior college, or technical school. Changes in the family life cycle as well as in the city's life cycle had pulled many of these miners' support systems apart, but the survey data also indicate that mining employees planned to migrate out and rejoin the splintered networks of family and friends who had relocated in other parts of Hokkaido.

In summary, miners who intended to stay in Yūbari had strong community ties. The majority had been born in or grew up in Yūbari with their fathers having been coal miners before them. Most had married local women and had brothers and sisters still living in Yūbari. One of the strongest factors for remaining, however, was the presence of a parent or an adult child in the home or nearby. Most of those mining company employees who intended to migrate from Yūbari had a child or another relative at the destination site. The usual circumstance was that of a miner who upon retirement planned to follow a grown child who had previously left the city in search of a job or to go to school. For miners who had moved into the city as adults, the move out of Yūbari would be due to their owning a home in another area or to wanting to rejoin family members in a different location. Potential out-migrants among the mining employees were those who were born in Yūbari, had never left, and did not want to leave but who would be forced to leave by the closure of the mines.

Shopkeepers and small business owners
Patrick and Rohlen (1987) point out that almost one-third of Japan's labor force works as owners and family members of small-scale family enterprises, particu-

larly in agriculture and wholesale and retail trade. They note further that the majority of the retail shops are small, with fewer than four workers. In fact, most are located in the family residence and operated by family members. The expectation in these households is that the business will be passed on to a child, generally the eldest son, and that the stem family, in which the eldest son and his family reside with the parents, is the appropriate social unit for maintaining the family enterprise (Wimberly, 1973). The buying and selling of retail enterprises in Japan is not a common practice, but for the continuation of a business, a successor is necessary (Patrick and Rohlen, 1987). The majority of Yūbari's small shops follow the family business pattern. The owners are therefore concerned over the issue of succession and whether they will be able to continue their businesses in Yūbari's lagging economy.

Fifty-eight owners of retail stores and small businesses located throughout Yūbari's seven districts were interviewed during the survey. The coal mine closures and population decline had indeed affected their businesses, but in contrast to the mining company employees, most of the business owners intended to remain in the city. Owning land or buildings in Yūbari provided a strong motivation for remaining, especially when it was nearly impossible to find a buyer in the city's depressed economic condition. In fact, only seven owners stated that they would definitely leave Yūbari. Regardless of the owner's intention to remain, however, the likelihood of a son or other family member continuing the business appeared to be declining.

Fifty-five percent (32) of the shopkeepers indicated they planned to continue, whereas 45 percent (26) stated that the business would be ended. But the proposed date of closing the business, which was often linked to retirement, varied from five to 20 years in the future, depending on the age of the household head. The ages of the individuals interviewed ranged from 26 to 79 years. An examination of the characteristics of these shops and shopowners, as well as their decisions for the future, must include consideration of the life cycle and transitions of the individual and the household in conjunction with the changes in the city's social structure. Twenty-six of the shopowners were second- or third-generation sons or family members responsible for carrying on the family business. An additional 32 shops had been begun by the present owners, but half of these had an adult child who was also working in the business and could thus be classified as continuing the occupation, bringing the total number of family businesses to 42. The remaining 16 shops that had been started by the present owners did not have a family member or adult child working in them. In fact, 11 of those 16 shopowners had adult children who did not intend to continue the family business.

Including the households planning to have a successor, 83 percent of the shops had been or were now family operations. The tradition of passing on the family business to the eldest son had been continued as long as possible for a majority of the shopkeepers, but the constant erosion of both the city's and the shops' economic foundation had finally begun to interrupt this pattern of succession. Thirty-eight percent of the owners of family-continued businesses had decided to end their businesses upon retirement. Their sons were now being educated for careers that would take them outside Yūbari.

In a review of the characteristics of all the businesses in the sample, several distinct patterns emerged. Those that would be phased out were, in general, the older businesses. Their resources had been depleted over a longer period of time. The children of the owners had left and were not intending to return; thus, for a number of these household businesses, there would be no successor. Similarly, younger household heads who owned family businesses were preparing their children for careers other than retail trade. The future might become even more problematic for those owners whose children had all left Yūbari. The inability to sell their property in a depressed economy prevented them from passing that resource on to a child. Those who rented would eventually move to where their children lived. Those who owned, however, would most likely remain in Yūbari as long as possible without being able to live with their children.

The businesses that were likely to continue, on the other hand, tended to be younger, having begun during boom periods after the war and up to the 1970s. Their resources had not yet been exhausted, and with the decline in similar businesses, they had less competition within the city than before. Having developed with the country's modernization, they had less "catching up" to do than the older businesses. Most of these were one-of-a-kind shops or provided needed services in the more productive districts of Yūbari. All had an eldest son or successor who was either working in the shop or planning to return for that purpose. The owners also had strong ties to Yūbari in the form of land ownership and family relationships. Fifty-three percent had one or more siblings living in Yūbari, and 69 percent had an adult child residing in the home or in Yūbari. In contrast, among the shopkeepers intending to quit, these figures were 35 percent and 46 percent, respectively. The build-up of the replacement tourist industry in Yūbari had benefited a few of these strategically located businesses. But when asked about their futures, 31 percent of the household heads who planned to continue their shops proposed an option that most of those who would quit were financially unable to consider—to move the business out of Yūbari.

Another category of business owner operating within Yūbari is the farmer. As of 1985, only 3.1 percent of Yūbari's 76,166 hectares were designated for agricultural use because 90 percent were covered by forest. In 1987 Yūbari had 372 farm households, with an average of 3.8 persons per household living on an average of 2.52 hectares of land. In contrast with a trend observed across the nation, the number of Yūbari households engaged full-time in farming has increased while the number of part-time farming households has decreased. Only 11 percent of Yūbari's farm households were full-time farmers in 1960, but this figure had increased to 48 percent by 1980 and to 61 percent by 1987. With coal mining being Yūbari's major industry throughout most of the city's history, many farmers were doing both mining and farming. But as the mines have closed, more farmers have had to turn to farming full-time for economic survival. This move into full-time farming is opposite the trend seen in most of Japan.

It is evident that alternative employment opportunities are not available to Yūbari's farmers. But another strong motivating factor for these households to remain in farming has been the city government's decision to promote melon agriculture as part of the city's redevelopment program. Both government and private sources have funded this development project, and most farmers who have joined the venture have been able to improve their production and their living conditions.

Eight farm households were included in the interview sample. All those interviewed owned their land and homes and stated that they intended to remain in Yūbari. All eight farmer households were continuing as family farms. In six of the households a parent and an adult child were working their land together. In the other two households the parents and an adult child had been working teams until the parents died. Only one of the adult children continuing the family's occupation was a woman, the eldest of three daughters. The other seven were eldest sons. This pattern of the eldest son or daughter inheriting the family business was similar to that seen with the shopkeepers; one difference with the shopkeepers' sons, however, was that all the farmers' sons in this sample had finished junior high school or high school in Yūbari and then gone directly into work on the family farm. Some of the shopkeepers' sons had been sent away to college or to apprentice in a similar business before returning to work in the family store.

Income levels and general living conditions had improved for these families. Although three households remained in small, modest homes, the other five households in the sample had built new, two-story Western-style houses and furnished them with a mixture of traditional and modern furniture and appliances. The biggest concern of the farmers in regard to the mine closures was that their primary source of labor would disappear. All these households were employing women workers on their farms, generally the wives of miners. The farmers were concerned that the mine closures would eliminate this cheap source of labor and that replacements would be unavailable.

National policy directed at regional decline due to the coal-mine industry shutdown includes programs of financial assistance for small and medium-size business owners. The shopkeepers who remain in Yūbari, even if intending to close down, may participate in and benefit from such options. Yūbari's farmers are also included in the city's redevelopment schemes and therefore are eligible for financial aid if they participate in the city's melon-based agricultural development project. Nearly all of the shopkeepers and the farmers in Yūbari, because of their land ownership, likelihood of having an adult child in the home or nearby, and long-term social and business networks in the community, intend to remain in Yūbari. As tax-paying land and business owners, they are also the target of the national policy for depressed regions and will therefore be assisted in remaining in Yūbari.

Public employees A range of public employment sectors in Yūbari has been affected by the nation's industry restructuring and by the city's long-term population decline. Coal mines closed, forestry service positions were cut back, and the National Railways began transferring personnel as a result of privatization. With the tremendous outflow of population from the city, the balance between the number of public service employees and residents also shifted. This imbalance precipitated a planned reduction in the number of personnel needed in the fire and police departments, the post office, and the school system; reduction was generally carried out through retirements and transfers. The city government had always functioned as a source of employment for the children of local residents who were unable or chose not to follow in their parents' occupational paths, and in the early stages of the loss of coal-mining employment, the city government also absorbed a number of laid-off coal company employees or their family members. By 1986, however, even the city government had begun to streamline its staff, not by firing or laying off employees, but by encouraging early retirement and not refilling the vacated positions. Thus, both national and local public employment has been affected in Yūbari, but the careers of the individuals in these positions have remained intact and generally unaltered. They are not facing a loss of employment or a dramatic reduction in their salaries. They are not being forced to leave the city unless it is for a routine *tenkin* (job transfer) move. Those who do not hold a prefectural *tenkin* track job may stay in the city until they retire. Nevertheless, the survey results show that a majority of these public employees planned to leave Yūbari in the future.

Of the 60 public employees interviewed, 80 percent were white-collar workers who lived fairly similar lifestyles. Nearly a quarter (22 percent) were living in modern homes that they owned, while the others were residing in company housing that ranged from older wooden housing units to new concrete apartment buildings. Eighteen percent, however, owned homes in other towns or cities while occupying rental units in Yūbari. Seventy-two percent of the government employees had cars and frequently commuted to other cities for shopping and entertainment. Their income levels and the security of their positions had contributed to a gradual improvement in their living conditions, making their lifestyles similar to those of white-collar workers in any metropolitan area.

Because the public employee jobs include city, prefectural, and national positions, it was to be expected that some of these workers had been transferred to the city. In my sample, nearly two-thirds were either born in or grew up in Yūbari. The remainder had come to Yūbari for jobs as adults or been brought to the city on transfer orders. Many of those transferring into Yūbari were in management positions or were upwardly mobile permanent employees within their respective departments.

Half of the public employees had fathers who owned a business or farm, worked as a public employee, or held a white-collar company position. In general, the educational level of the public employee was higher than that of the coal miner, shopkeeper, or farmer in the same age group. This worker had also been receiving salary increases based on a seniority system. The public employees were therefore, in turn, using their resources to assist their sons and daughters in obtaining higher educations to ensure the children's employment success. Of their 71 adult children, 65 percent had left home to attend college, junior college, or technical school whereas only 25 percent had left to take a first job. This pattern was opposite that of the mining company employees, 60 percent of whose children had left Yūbari to take a first job.

Since a third of the 60 public employees had come to Yūbari as adults for employment or on transfer orders, about 20 percent of the adult children had left home before their parents moved to Yūbari. Of the 56 children who had lived in Yūbari, however, only 5 remained in the city, and they were the children of employees who intended to stay in Yūbari.

The public employees had a much higher level of home ownership than did the mining company employees. A total of 40 percent owned homes, with slightly more owning property in Yūbari than owning a home in another Hokkaido town or city. Nevertheless, half of those who owned homes in Yūbari said they would leave, to go to places where children, parents, and siblings are residing. Overall, 75 percent of the public employees intended to migrate out of Yūbari. More than a third were leaving on transfer orders. The remainder stated that they would leave after retirement, and the majority of those planned to move to a place where a child or other family member resided.

In summary, public employees used their job security and financial resources to build an exit route for their children and to pave the way for their own transitions after retirement. Home ownership did not guarantee their remaining in the city, especially if they were financially able to migrate to a place where a child or family member was residing. Even those workers migrating from city to city on transfer orders intended to rejoin family members or move back to homes they owned in other cities after their retirement. Compared with Yūbari-based employees, these workers worried more about the effect of their frequent moves on elderly parents left behind and on their children as the children moved in and out of different schools and neighborhoods. But these worries appeared to be the price paid for the security and status of a permanent job in public employment. That price was perhaps minimal compared with the upheaval in job security and income that shopkeepers and mining company employees in Yūbari were facing.

CONCLUSION

Throughout the period of numerous coal-mine closures and subsequent population decline, the Yūbari city government has received administrative guidance and a variety of government loans and subsidies for restructuring the city's industrial base. The primary industry chosen for this development plan was tourism, and these efforts have been vigorously under way since 1978. A supplemental program is that of promoting melon farming. When respondents in this study were asked their opinions about this conversion to tourism, the majority replied that tourism was not a suitable choice for Yūbari and that it would not provide jobs for Yūbari residents or support an increase in Yūbari's population.

In fact, tourist-facility construction has not provided replacement jobs for this city and is not likely to do so in the future. Unemployed miners are not hired in tourist-industry construction or operation. During the last 10 years of reconstruction, out-migration has steadily continued. The city government is expecting a further decrease in population after the final mine closures but has commented that tourism will support the remaining 10,000 residents.

As has been shown in this study, the remaining residents are primarily owners of land and businesses, who are already the recipients of legislative policy and subsidization. The coal miner is expected to leave the city. Special financial programs will even assist in the relocation process. The government-directed policies and subsidies include assistance to the city, to affected small and medium-size enterprises, and to the coal miners, but that has not meant restructuring the city to provide a place for the miner. It has resulted in the development of an economic base seen as sufficient to provide public facilities and services for those who remain. A consequence of this restructuring, however, has been the outmigration not only of miners and their families but also of laid-off workers in related industries, young people looking for employment or education, residents dissatisfied with the deteriorating services in the city, and residents following their adult children out of Yūbari.

Although the primary reason for out-migration from Yūbari is job related, a second major influence on the decision to leave or stay is the desire to maintain the family unit, particularly the link between parent and eldest child. Itoh (1985) notes that the value of the family in Japan perpetuates a system of succession and a desire for coresidence that may influence workers' and residents' decisions about migration. The traditional family system in Japan involves the *ie*, literally translated as "household," but which has been further described as a "multigenerational property-owning corporate group which continues through time" (Long, 1987:7). The stem family lives and works together, and the eldest son becomes the eventual successor and heir. Although various legislation over time has prompted changes in this system of succession and inheritance, Kumagai (1986) asserts that the *ie* family system persists socially, if not legally, and that the majority of Japanese elderly still prefer to live with their children. The results from the present study, although limited to one rural city, tend to confirm that notion. Shopkeepers, farmers, and retired miners remain in Yūbari with their eldest child in the home or nearby, while retired public employees and unemployed miners move to other places where their children have already relocated.

Although Japan's policies for industry restructuring are indeed comprehensive and have been successful at a macrolevel, the effects at the microlevel appear to be uneven, with more of the social costs being paid by the laid-off worker and his family. The level of assistance in Japan is far greater than that seen in countries without industrial policies; but the results of an unequal distribution of the burden and unanticipated multiplier effects within the community seem to be common consequences, with or without policy directives. Although the Japanese government has been attempting to direct population away from metropolitan areas and back to the hinterland, the situation in Yūbari suggests that the policies and procedures being used have the opposite effect. The policies are actually contributing to the city's decline while adding to the problems of overcrowding in metropolitan areas such as Sapporo, where displaced workers go in search of jobs. These findings therefore point to the need for more research to be done on the social costs of industrial policy, including the effects on workers and families in dependent communities.

REFERENCES

Aldrich, John H., and Forrest D. Nelson. 1984. *Linear Probability, Logit, and Probit Models*. Beverly Hills, Calif.: Sage Publications.

Bluestone, Barry, and Benett Harrison. 1982. *The Deindustrialization of America: Plant Closings, Community Abandonment, and the Dismantling of Basic Industry*. New York: Basic Books.

Flaim, Paul O., and Ellen Sehgal. 1985. "Displaced Workers of 1979–83: How Well Have They Fared?" *Monthly Labor Review* June:3–16.

Gordus, Jeanne, Paul Jarley, and Louis A. Ferman. 1981. *Plant Closings and Economic Dislocation*. Kalamazoo, Mich.: W. E. Upjohn Institute for Employment Research.

Hammerman, Herbert. 1987. "Five case studies." In Paul D. Staudohar and Holly E. Brown (eds.), *De-industrialization and Plant Closure*, pp. 75–88 Lexington, Mass.: Lexington Books.

Higashi Chikara and G. Peter Lauter. 1987. *The Internationalization of the Japanese Economy*. Boston: Kluwer Academic Publications.

Itoh Tatsuya. 1985. "Rural-Urban Demographic Balance." In *Demographic Transitions in Japan and Rural Development*, pp. 123–144. Tokyo: The Asian Population and Development Association.

Kumagai Fumie. 1986. "Modernization and the Family in Japan." *Journal of Family History* 11(4):371–382.

Long, Susan Orpett. 1987. *Family Change and the Life Course in Japan*. The Cornell East Asia Papers, No. 44. Ithaca, N.Y.: Cornell University, China-Japan Program.

Patrick, Hugh T., and Thomas P. Rohlen. 1987. "Small-Scale Family Enterprises." In Kōzō Yamamura and Yasukichi Yasuba (eds.), *The Political Economy of Japan*, Vol. 1, *The Domestic Transformation*. Stanford, Calif.: Stanford University Press.

Perrucci, Carolyn C., Robert Perrucci, Dena B. Targ, and Harry R. Targ. 1988. *Plant Closings: International Context and Social Costs*. New York: Aldine Gruyter.

Retherford, Robert D., and Minja Kim Choe. 1993. "Logit Regression." Chapter 5 in *Statistical Models for Causal Analysis*. New York: John Wiley and Sons.

Saxonhouse, Gary R. 1979. "Industrial Restructuring in Japan." *The Journal of Japanese Studies* 5(2):273–320.

Shaw, R. P. 1975. *Migration Theory and Fact: A Review and Bibliography of Current Literature*. Philadelphia: Regional Science Research Institute.

Wimberley, Howard. 1973. "On Living with Your Past: Style and Structure among Contemporary Japanese Merchant Families." *Economic Development and Cultural Change* 21(3):423–428.

Yūbari City. 1985. *Yūbari Shisei Yoran* (Yūbari municipal government survey). Yūbari City, Hokkaido.

———. 1987. *Yūbari-shi no Tōkei* (Yūbari City statistics). Yūbari City, Hokkaido.

———. 1991. *Yūbari-shi no Tōkei* (Yūbari City statistics). Yūbari City, Hokkaido.

PART III

Family Change in Other
Asian Societies

Rural Family and Community Life in South Korea: Changes in Family Attitudes and Living Arrangements for the Elderly

by Nam-Il Kim, Soon Choi, and Insook Han Park

This chapter reports on a study of 408 Korean households conducted in 1990 to assess changes in rural family and community life in South Korea in recent decades. The study had two objectives. The first was to analyze rural family structure and family life, which have changed as Korea has undergone rapid economic development and urbanization during the last 30 years. In conducting the study, we were interested in comparing the situation in 1990 with that reported in a seminal study on the Korean rural family in 1959 by Ko et al. (1963). Our second objective was to compare our results on the contemporary rural Korean family with those from the Japanese family study conducted by the University Research Center (URC) of Nihon University and the Mainichi Newspapers in 1988 (URC and Mainichi Newspapers, 1989). Our study focused on such family issues as marriage, family and household formation, interfamilial relations (including conjugal and parent-child relations), attitudes and values associated with kinship and the family, and actual conditions and changes in the *dongjok burak* (clan-centered rural village).

STUDY DESIGN

Survey Areas

To do a time-series analysis and maintain comparability with the study by Ko et al., we selected the same areas as those included in the 1959 study. The selected areas are believed to represent typical villages in rural counties (*gun*) of each of South Korea's three subcultural zones: the Youngnam region, comprising the provinces (*do*) of Gyeong Sang Nam and Gyeong Sang Bug; the Honam region, comprising Jeon Ra Nam and Jeon Ra Bug provinces; and the Kiho region, comprising Chung Cheong Nam, Chung Cheong Bug, and Gyeong Gi provinces. (See Figure 14.1 for the location of the selected areas.) The three subcultural zones are considered to have distinctly different cultural practices, particularly in family and community life, and thus were well suited to our research purpose.

The survey areas, like other areas of the country, have undergone major social and economic changes, including the relocation of administrative boundaries, since the early 1960s. These changes, in turn, make our study more interesting because we can trace the changes, compare the contemporary rural situations with one another, and analyze the various factors related to them.

Interview Questionnaires and Respondents

The field survey operation was conducted during 1–7 February 1990. Three types of interview schedules, or questionnaires, were prepared. The first type was for the household interviews with the main respondents to explore questions about the rural family in general. Using this schedule, an interviewer conducted a personal interview with the main respondent of each household, who was chosen by the interviewer. Eligible to be main respondents were the household head, the spouse of the head, and other adults, depending on the household's circumstances. The second type of questionnaire was for the spouse of the main respondent. This questionnaire, which was to be self-administered whenever possible, consisted of a few items eliciting the respondent's values and attitudes. The purpose of having the second questionnaire was to obtain the opinions of an adult of the opposite sex from that of the main respondent so that we could collect male and female views and attitudes about rural family life. (In the 1959 study by Ko et al., all the respondents were male.) The third type of questionnaire was a brief guide designed to be used in the focused interviews with local informants. These focused interviews were conducted to collect qualitative information about life patterns, production activities, the local living environment, and clan (kinship) relations in each survey area. The informants, who were knowl-

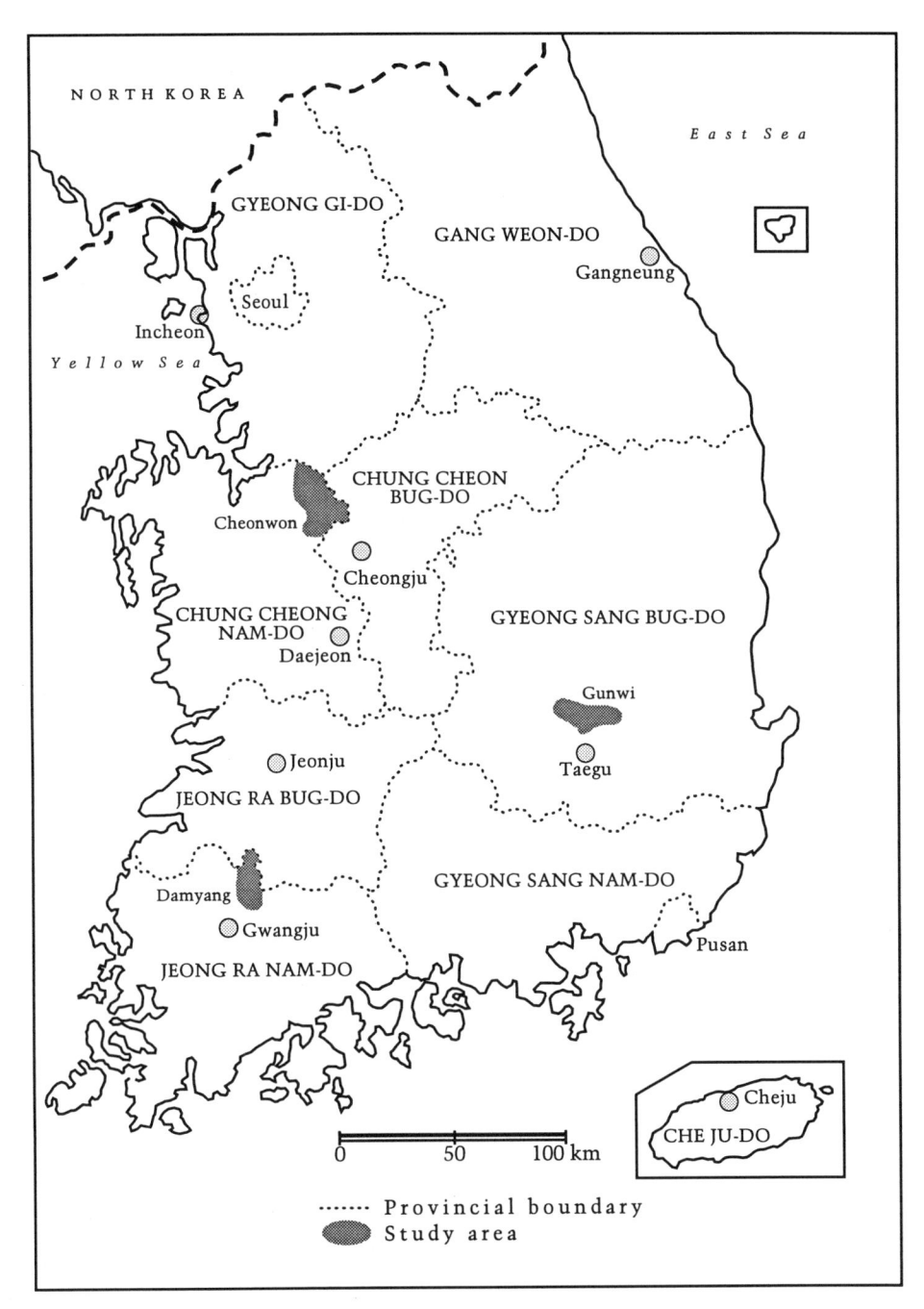

Figure 14.1. The three study areas

edgeable about life in the specific areas or villages, were usually the village chief and a person recommended by him. We selected two informants from each hamlet (*dong* or *ri*). Sometimes we arranged group interviews and discussions in place of person-to-person interviews. The staff members of the research team conducted these focused interviews, whereas our trained interviewers handled the household interviews.

The Sample

In each of the three regions, we initially selected about 160 households for the household interviews, the projected sample size being approximately 150 households in each region. Anticipating the possibility of refusals or the prolonged absence of some prospective respondents, we selected 10 extra households. The purpose of having samples of equal size in the three regions was to ensure that no region was overrepresented or underrepresented in the study.

The sample households were selected from the de jure census household list prepared on 1 November 1989 by each provincial or city government. This household list became our sampling frame for the regions, and from this sampling frame we determined the expected ratio of sampling units, or the sampling fraction, and then applied the systematic sampling method to select the 160 sample households. Summary results of the survey and general characteristics of the respondents and the sample households are presented in Appendix Tables 14.1–14.11 for reference.

FINDINGS: CHANGES IN THE STUDY AREAS

The survey data reveal that the study areas experienced substantial changes in all aspects of family and community life, including their socioeconomic and demographic characteristics. Only those changes that we consider important to family life, however, are summarized in this chapter.

Structural Changes

The study areas—Gunwi-gun in Gyeong Sang Bug Province, Damyang-gun in Jeon Ra Nam Province, and Cheonwon-gun (Cheonan-gun in 1959) in Chung Cheong Nam Province—developed several common characteristics in the process of socioeconomic change. One of the most visible is related to their geographical locations. In 1959 the areas were typical rural, agricultural regions that had limited contact with large cities, mainly because convenient transportation and communication facilities did not exist then. By 1990, however, all the areas were in the vicinity of large cities. Needless to say, this change was due to the profound socioeconomic developments that have taken place in Korea during the last three decades. In particular, the rapid growth of several large cities and the expansion of such social infrastructures as transportation and communication facilities have greatly shortened the distances between the study areas and the cities adjacent to them. In several instances, the expansion of city boundaries has caused the rural areas to be incorporated into the cities.

In 1959 South Korea's transportation system was poorly developed. For example, in Gunwi-gun, Gyeong Sang Bug Province, transportation from the nearest town, or *myun*, then called Gunwi-Myun (now Gunwi-Eup) to Taegu City was either by a regularly scheduled bus, which ran only four to five times a day, or by train.[1] A person who chose to travel by train had to walk about 14 kilometers to the Woobo train station, ride the Central Line to Youngchon, and then transfer to a bus going to Taegu City. At that time, therefore, only a few residents of Gunwi-gun could visit Taegu City, which was the provincial capital, and they could do so only a few times a month. Now, after three decades, the southern parts of Gunwi-gun face the Taegu City boundary line across the Palkong Mountain owing to the expansion of Taegu City's administrative boundaries. The scheduled bus runs every 30 minutes from Gunwi-Eup directly to Taegu City, and the transportation time has been shortened from two hours to only one hour and 20 minutes. As a result, most areas of Gunwi-gun are now becoming Taegu City's adjacent agricultural areas. (The exceptions are the four towns of Sobo-Myun in northwestern Gunwi-Eup and Koro-Myun, Euihung-Myun, and Sansung-Myun in eastern Gunwi-Eup. None of these four towns was a target area for our survey research.)

Among the six *eup* and *myun* in our study, only Sunghwan-Eup in Cheonwon-gun experienced an increase in population during the 1960–85 period, and it grew by 25 percent. The rest of the areas had population decreases ranging from 24 to 48 percent during that period. The number of households increased by 57 percent in Sunghwan-Eup and by 14 percent in Gunwi-Eup, while the other four *myun* registered decreases in household numbers, ranging from 12 to 37 percent. The average number of household members also decreased rather sharply, from 5.9 persons in 1959 to 3.4 persons in 1990. Given that the average number of household members in the rural areas of South Korea was 5.5 persons in 1960 and 3.8 persons in 1990, according to population censuses, the study areas had more household members on average in 1959 than other rural agricultural areas but fewer household members than other areas in 1990.

Decreases in the overall population of most of the study areas have inevitably affected the basic composition of their populations. (See Table 14.1 and Figure

---

1. *Eup* and *myun* are the two lowest levels of self-governing entities in the Korean administrative system. In general, an *eup* has a population of more than 20,000, and a *myun* has a population of less than 20,000. A *gun* (rural county) usually comprises two or three *eup* and more than six *myun*.

Table 14.1. Age distributions: 1959 and 1990 (percentage distributions)

	1959	1990			
Age group	All areas	All areas	Cheonwon	Gunwi	Damyang
0–14	38.8	20.1	24.2	16.8	18.0
15–39	37.5	28.9	32.3	25.4	28.2
40–64	19.2	36.9	32.5	42.0	37.4
65+	4.5	14.1	11.0	15.8	16.8
Total	100.0	100.0	100.0	100.0	100.0
Sample households (no.)	(843)	(408)	(143)	(149)	(116)
Members of sample households (no.)	(4,975)	(1,396)	(555)	(460)	(381)
Sex ratio	101.9	98.6	98.2	101.8	95.4

Notes: Respondents in the 1959 study were all men. Percentages may not sum exactly to 100.0 because of rounding.

14.2.) In 1959, persons under 40 years of age constituted 76 percent of the populations in all the areas, but by 1990 the figure had dropped to 49 percent. This change produced imbalances in the survey areas' age structures that are most visible in Gunwi-gun and Damyang-gun, each of which is located near a large city, Taegu and Gwangju, respectively. Migration from rural to urban areas has been responsible for the age-structure shift.

One of the main reasons for the rural-to-urban migration seems to be the opportunity for education. Taegu and Gwangju have become what are called "direct jurisdiction cities" according to administrative ordinances adopted in the 1980s, and one result of those administrative changes has been to limit the admission eligibility for secondary schools (junior and senior high schools) to students who have completed their primary education within the cities' boundaries. Parents with children in the primary schools, especially in the upper grades, are likely to be in their 30s, and their large-scale migration to the cities has often been justified on the grounds of educational opportunity for their children.[2]

The average age of household heads in the study areas in 1990 was 54.8. Household heads under age 40 accounted for only 12 percent of all study households, compared with 39 percent in 1959.

---

2. In our interviews with the village heads and other residents in Gunwi-gun, we learned that almost all households there face the problem of inadequate educational opportunities for their children. The respondents reported that most parents with children in the upper primary levels were renting a room in Taegu and had transferred their children to a school within the city. At first those children would live with their grandmother, and then a few years later the whole household would move to the city. In other words, if the parents were reasonably well off economically, their children—not only those in middle or high school, but also the primary school children—would be sent to a city (Taegu or nearby Kyungsan or Kumi) for study. Most parents pointed out that the major purpose of providing such education to their children was to enable them to escape from the hard physical labor required in agriculture.

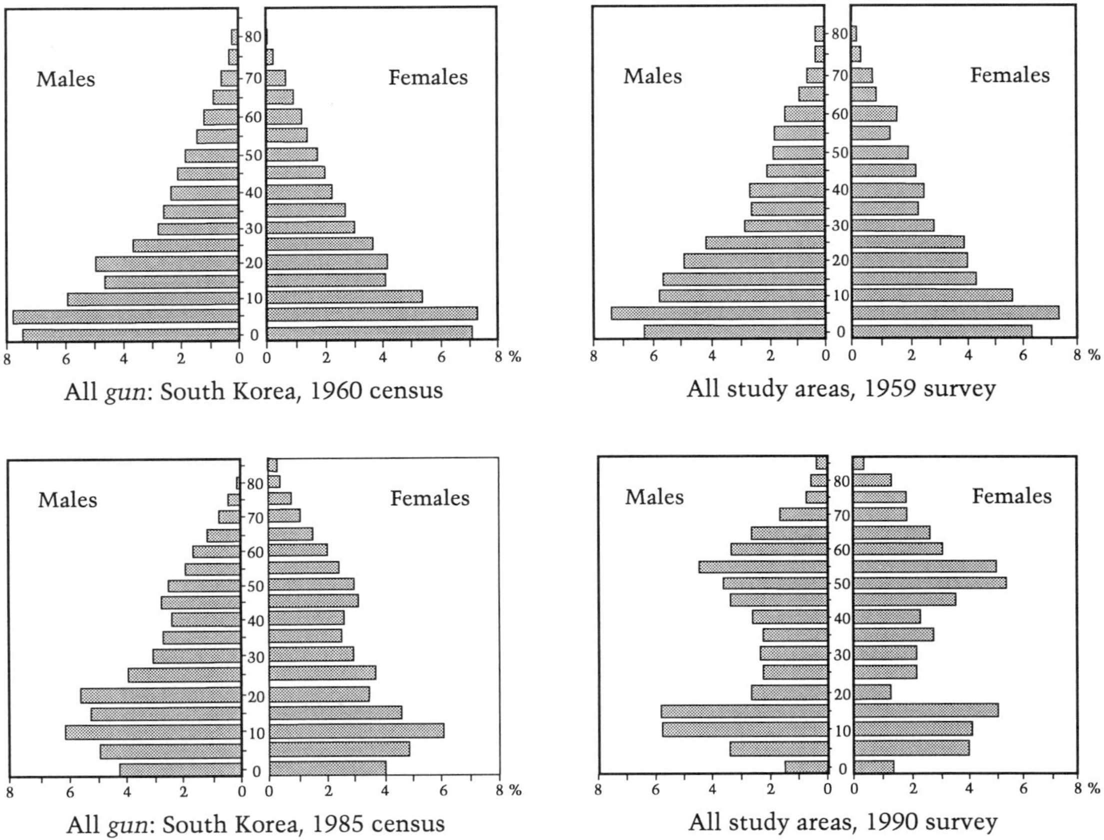

All *gun*: South Korea, 1960 census

All study areas, 1959 survey

All *gun*: South Korea, 1985 census

All study areas, 1990 survey

Figure 14.2. Age and sex distributions of the population: South Korea and the study areas, 1959 and 1990 *(continued on next page)*

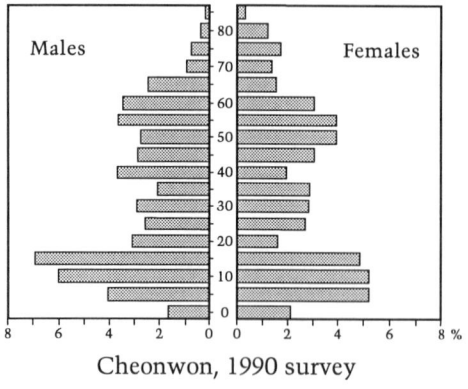

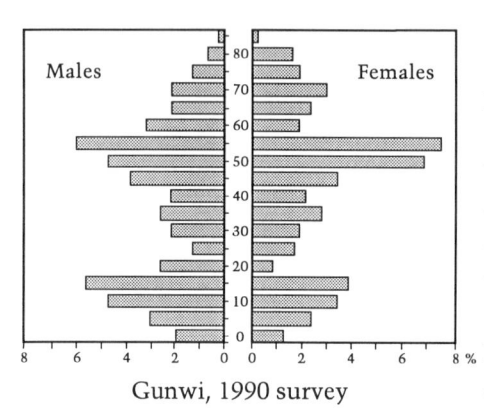

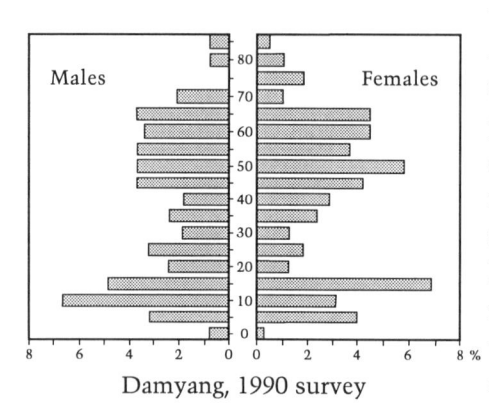

[Population pyramids:
- Cheonwon, 1990 survey (Males / Females, ages 0–80)
- Gunwi, 1990 survey (Males / Females, ages 0–80)
- Damyang, 1990 survey (Males / Females, ages 0–80)]

Figure 14.2 *(continued)*

Those under age 50 in 1990 represented only 33 percent of all household heads. These figures indicate the increasing proportion of older household heads in those areas.

The 1990 survey revealed some improvement in the educational achievement of household heads. In 1959 only 7.8 percent had a middle school education or more, but by 1990 the percentage had risen to 28. Nonetheless, this rate of educational achievement is low when compared with the national average of 65 percent (40 percent in nonurban areas, recorded by the 1985 census). These figures seem to indicate that the educated among the young residents of these rural areas had moved elsewhere, most likely to urban areas.

The changes in the age structure have caused a serious shortage of workers in the rural areas, thereby affecting the roles and life style of most families. Agricultural patterns have also been affected. Agricultural production now depends increasingly on machines. Not a single household in the study areas used farm vehicles in 1959, but in 1990 a large majority (about 71 percent) of the households were using them. Consequently, many of the fields in mountainous areas, which are difficult to till by machine, are neglected. Those families remaining in farming, however, have tended to increase their land holdings; the ratio of households with more than 1 hectare of agricultural fields to all farm households has increased slightly, from 24 percent in

1959 to 33 percent in 1990. Tenant farming rather than owner farming has been increasing; but the traditional, hierarchical landlord-tenant relationship is disappearing. Because many vacated fields are owned by ex-farmers or elderly farmers who are no longer capable of field labor, small groups of younger men form teams to rent the fields and cultivate them. The agricultural products from the rented fields are divided according to the *koksu* system, rather than the *daegali* system. In the *koksu* system, tenants give the landlords only one bag of rice weighing about 80 kilograms per arable field of about 200 *pyong* (660 square meters) and keep the remainder of the products for themselves. In the *daegali* system, tenants and landlords divide the agricultural costs and products in half.

Today, farmers are using vinyl greenhouses to grow fruits, vegetables, and a variety of other crops. They also raise chickens, cows, and pigs and produce dairy products. This pattern of agriculture means that there is no off-season for farming. Farmers have become increasingly busy in their own fields, and therefore *poom-ut-ee* (meaning "to work in turn for each other"), which used to be the major means of labor mobilization and temporary employment in the rural areas, has now almost gone. Women have become increasingly involved in agriculture, so that their child-rearing role and other household duties have become less important.

Other significant changes in family life have been caused by paved roads, an expanded network of unpaved agricultural roads, telephones and television sets, and other developments in transportation and communication. The presence of television and telephone service in more than 90 percent of all rural households makes it easy for urban ways of life to infiltrate into the once-remote rural areas. Finally, since 1989 a regional medical care system has been available to the residents of all rural areas.

Changes in Attitudes and Interactions

Korea is a traditionally Confucianist society, in which great emphasis is placed on the family. The traditional Korean family was patrilineal and patriarchal. It was imperative that the head of the family produce children, especially sons, to continue the family line and perform the rituals of ancestor worship. In our study, we analyzed respondents' attitudes toward such patrilineal values as obedience toward parents, attitudes about family lineage among parents without sons, parents' educational aspirations for their children, and their attitudes toward succession of the family farm and farming careers for their sons. Our objective was to learn more about the changes that have been occurring during Korea's rapid industrialization and the migration to cities from rural areas.

According to traditional Confucian teaching, young people must obey the older generation unconditionally. The

1990 survey, however, revealed that attitudes about children obeying their parents have changed during the past three decades. Asked how adult children should behave if a disagreement arose between them and their parents, only 19 percent of respondents stated that they should obey the parents, compared with nearly 46 percent in 1959, while 19 percent answered that children should do what they deemed best, up from 12 percent in 1959 (Table 14.2).

Among rural Koreans the value of children, especially of sons, as successors of the family line among rural Koreans has also changed substantially from that in 1959, before Korean society became industrialized (Table 14.3). Nearly half (43 percent) of respondents in Ko et al.'s study reported having a need for sons, even if

Table 14.2. Attitudes toward children's obedience to parents: 1959 and 1990 (percentage distributions)

Attitude	All areas 1959	All areas 1990	Cheonwon 1959	Cheonwon 1990	Gunwi 1959	Gunwi 1990	Damyang 1959	Damyang 1990
Children should obey	45.5	18.7	46.0	16.2	38.2	13.4	53.5	28.1
Depends on the situation	40.7	62.4	37.9	65.5	49.4	63.1	34.6	57.9
Children should act according to their own opinion	12.4	18.9	14.2	18.0	11.6	23.5	10.7	14.0
Other	1.4	na	1.7	na	0.8	na	1.2	na
Total	100.0	100.0	100.0	100.0	100.0	100.0	100.0	100.0
(No. in sample)	(1,527)	(402)	(615)	(139)	(490)	(149)	(422)	(114)

Note: Percentages may not sum exactly to 100.0 because of rounding.
na—not applicable.

Table 14.3. Attitudes toward continuing the family lineage in the case of having no sons: 1959 and 1990 (percentage distributions)

Attitude	All areas 1959	All areas 1990	Cheonwon 1959	Cheonwon 1990	Gunwi 1959	Gunwi 1990	Damyang 1959	Damyang 1990
Not necessary to have succession	14.3	25.9	23.9	31.2	5.5	26.2	10.7	19.1
Can be succeeded by daughters	8.3	15.8	9.8	19.9	3.1	16.8	12.3	9.6
Husband may have a concubine	43.4	23.5	34.3	14.2	48.2	24.8	51.4	33.0
Can adopt a son from blood relatives or others	33.2	34.3	31.3	34.0	42.7	32.3	25.1	37.4
Other	0.6	0.5	0.7	0.7	0.6	0.0	0.5	0.9
Total	100.0	100.0	100.0	100.0	100.0	100.0	100.0	100.0
(No. in sample)	(1,522)	(405)	(610)	(141)	(490)	(149)	(422)	(115)

Note: Percentages may not sum exactly to 100.0 because of rounding.

the sons had to be conceived by a concubine of the husband; but in 1990 only about 24 percent of respondents held that view. Many of the respondents in the two studies favored adopting a son (33 and 34 percent, respectively, in 1959 and 1990). Of our respondents, 6 percent indicated they did not need to have children for the purpose of continuing the family lineage and 16 percent could succeed the lineage with daughters; these figures were considerably higher than in the study by Ko et al. (8.3 percent).

Rural residents continued to have strong aspirations for their children's, especially their sons', education, but their attitudes toward differential education for sons and daughters had changed. As shown in Tables 14.4 and 14.5, nearly all respondents (95 percent) in our sample wanted their sons to be educated to the college, university, or higher level, and 81

Table 14.4. Parents' aspirations for sons' education: 1959 and 1990 (percentage distributions)

Aspiration	All areas 1959	All areas 1990	Cheonwon 1959	Cheonwon 1990	Gunwi 1959	Gunwi 1990	Damyang 1959	Damyang 1990
No schooling	0.1	0.0	0.0	0.0	0.0	0.0	0.5	0.0
Elementary school	1.1	0.2	1.8	0.7	0.9	0.0	0.5	0.0
Middle school	3.9	0.2	4.3	0.0	1.8	0.7	6.3	0.0
High school	4.9	4.5	6.0	2.9	4.0	4.7	4.2	6.2
College or university	67.1	56.6	64.8	58.4	69.6	57.0	68.1	54.0
More than university	22.7	38.5	23.4	38.0	23.8	37.6	20.4	39.8
Total	100.0	100.0	100.0	100.0	100.0	100.0	100.0	100.0
(No. in sample)	(700)	(399)	(282)	(137)	(227)	(149)	(191)	(113)

Note: Percentages may not sum exactly to 100.0 because of rounding.

Table 14.5. Parents' aspirations for daughters' education: 1959 and 1990 (percentage distributions)

Aspiration	All areas 1959	All areas 1990	Cheonwon 1959	Cheonwon 1990	Gunwi 1959	Gunwi 1990	Damyang 1959	Damyang 1990
No schooling	0.7	0.0	1.4	0.0	0.4	0.0	0.0	0.0
Elementary school	10.9	0.3	11.7	0.7	5.7	0.0	15.8	0.0
Middle school	25.2	1.0	21.6	0.0	25.6	2.0	30.0	0.9
High school	21.5	17.8	21.6	11.0	24.7	22.2	17.4	20.3
College or university	32.2	53.5	30.9	55.2	35.2	53.0	30.5	52.2
More than university	9.6	27.4	12.8	33.1	8.4	22.8	6.3	26.6
Total	100.0	100.0	100.0	100.0	100.0	100.0	100.0	100.0
(No. in sample)	(699)	(398)	(282)	(136)	(227)	(149)	(190)	(113)

Note: Percentages may not sum exactly to 100.0 because of rounding.

percent had the same aspiration for their daughters. In the study by Ko et al., the result was similar for sons, 90 percent of respondents desiring at least a college education for them; but only 42 percent of Ko et al.'s respondents aspired to a college or higher level of education for their daughters.

A majority of respondents in both studies wanted their eldest sons to have white-collar occupations, but attitudes toward farming and farm-related work were very different among the two groups of respondents (Table 14.6). Only 1.9 percent of respondents in 1990 wanted their eldest sons to go into such work, whereas one-fourth of Ko et al.'s respondents aspired to farming for their sons.

In the past, parents' opinions were decisive in determining marriage partners for their sons and daughters, especially in rural Korean society. Since industrialization began in the 1960s, however, arranged marriages have gradually become less common (Table 14.7). Thirty years ago four-fifths of respondents thought the parents' opinions in the choice of a marriage partner were more important than those of the sons, but by 1990 the same proportion considered the sons' opinions to be more important. Such an abrupt reversal indicates how rapidly traditional attitudes have changed in Korea. The normative change from parent-centered marriage arrangements to child-centered ones appears to come from modernization and the rationalization of moral values under the influence of rapid urbanization

Table 14.6. Parents' aspirations for eldest son's occupation: 1959 and 1990 (percentage distributions)

Aspiration	All areas 1959	All areas 1990	Cheonwon 1959	Cheonwon 1990	Gunwi 1959	Gunwi 1990	Damyang 1959	Damyang 1990
Administrative or government officer[a]	30.2	49.4	26.3	42.1	44.4	49.6	18.2	58.1
Professional	9.7	23.3	9.2	24.6	11.6	21.8	8.0	23.9
Minister or politician	10.4	5.2	8.3	5.6	11.6	5.3	11.9	4.8
Technical worker[b]	10.0	5.6	12.5	7.9	7.4	5.2	9.7	2.8
Self-employed or related worker[c]	14.4	7.7	15.4	7.9	7.4	6.8	21.6	8.6
Farmer or farm-related worker	24.8	1.9	28.3	3.2	16.7	1.5	30.1	0.9
Member of the military	na	1.7	na	2.4	na	2.3	na	0.0
Other	0.5	5.2	0.0	6.3	0.9	7.5	0.6	0.9
Total	100.0	100.0	100.0	100.0	100.0	100.0	100.0	100.0
(No. in sample)	(632)	(364)	(240)	(126)	(216)	(133)	(176)	(105)

Note: Percentages may not sum exactly to 100.0 because of rounding.
na—not applicable.
a. Including clerical worker or social worker.
b. Including craftsman, driver, or related worker.
c. Including merchandiser.

and industrialization. Similar changes have occurred in attitudes toward marriage arrangements for daughters (Table 14.8). In 1959, 89 percent of respondents thought that parents' opinions outweighed those of daughters in the marriage choice, but by 1990 only 22 percent held that view and 78 percent thought that the daughters' opinions were more important. Thus, attitudes toward the choice of children's marriage partners have changed for both sons and daughters. Attitudes also differed by region in 1990. Sons' and daughters' opinions were given most weight in Cheonwon and least weight in Damyang. This outcome was consistent with the respective levels of urbanization and industrialization in the three areas.

Unfavorable attitudes toward divorce seem to have changed little in rural Korea during the past 30 years (Table 14.9). In both 1959 and 1990, a majority of respondents disapproved of divorce; and in the case of couples with children, nine-tenths of the respondents disapproved. For the sample as a whole, about two-thirds of respondents in 1990 disapproved of divorce by couples without children.

Table 14.7. Responsibility for arranging sons' marriages: 1959 and 1990 (percentage distributions)

Who decides	All areas 1959	All areas 1990	Cheonwon 1959	Cheonwon 1990	Gunwi 1959	Gunwi 1990	Damyang 1959	Damyang 1990
Absolutely the parents	20.9	2.7	19.4	0.7	20.7	2.7	23.1	5.3
Parents first and sons later	58.5	18.2	58.8	15.0	56.1	17.4	61.0	23.0
Sons first and parents later	12.4	54.5	13.7	60.7	13.8	53.0	8.9	48.7
Absolutely the sons	8.2	24.6	8.1	23.6	9.4	26.9	7.0	23.0
Total	100.0	100.0	100.0	100.0	100.0	100.0	100.0	100.0
(No. in sample)	(1,509)	(402)	(607)	(140)	(487)	(149)	(415)	(113)

Table 14.8. Responsiblity for arranging daughters' marriages: 1959 and 1990 (percentage distributions)

Who decides	All areas 1959	All areas 1990	Cheonwon 1959	Cheonwon 1990	Gunwi 1959	Gunwi 1990	Damyang 1959	Damyang 1990
Absolutely the parents	28.3	3.2	26.6	1.4	26.5	3.4	33.0	5.3
Parents first and daughters later	60.5	18.4	61.7	15.7	60.0	18.1	59.2	22.1
Daughters first and parents later	6.5	53.5	6.3	60.0	8.6	50.3	4.4	49.6
Absolutely the daughters	4.7	24.9	5.4	22.9	4.9	28.2	3.4	23.0
Total	100.0	100.0	100.0	100.0	100.0	100.0	100.0	100.0
(No. in sample)	(1,505)	(402)	(606)	(140)	(487)	(149)	(412)	(113)

Attitudes toward remarriage by widows, however, continue to be negatively affected by the presence of children (Table 14.10). In 1959 some 85 percent of Ko et al.'s respondents disapproved of remarriage by a widow with children. Although a sizable majority continued to hold that view in 1990, the proportion expressing such disapproval had dropped to about 58 percent. The continued negative view of remarriage by widows with children reveals the importance of women's role in rearing children in contemporary rural Korea. Attitudes to remarriage by widows without children have remained basically unchanged and positive, nearly nine-tenths of respondents in both 1959 and 1990 approving of it.

Table 14.9. Attitudes toward divorce: 1959 and 1990 (percentage distributions)

Attitude	All areas 1959	All areas 1990	Cheonwon 1959	Cheonwon 1990	Gunwi 1959	Gunwi 1990	Damyang 1959	Damyang 1990
If couples have children								
Disapprove	92.4	91.6	89.0	88.8	95.1	91.1	91.4	95.5
Approve	7.6	8.4	11.0	11.2	4.9	8.9	8.6	4.5
Total	100.0	100.0	100.0	100.0	100.0	100.0	100.0	100.0
(No. in sample)	(1,506)	(395)	(501)	(137)	(488)	(149)	(417)	(109)
If couples do not have children								
Disapprove	57.0	64.9	56.3	58.9	63.9	63.9	50.0	73.0
Approve	43.0	35.1	43.7	41.1	36.1	36.1	50.0	27.0
Total	100.0	100.0	100.0	100.0	100.0	100.0	100.0	100.0
(No. in sample)	(1,514)	(395)	(609)	(137)	(485)	(149)	(420)	(109)

Table 14.10. Attitudes toward widows' remarriage: 1959 and 1990 (percentage distributions)

Attitude	All areas 1959	All areas 1990	Cheonwon 1959	Cheonwon 1990	Gunwi 1959	Gunwi 1990	Damyang 1959	Damyang 1990
If widow has children								
Disapprove	85.5	58.4	82.4	58.0	90.8	61.7	83.7	54.3
Approve	14.5	41.6	17.6	42.0	9.2	38.3	16.3	45.7
Total	100.0	100.0	100.0	100.0	100.0	100.0	100.0	100.0
(No. in sample)	(1,477)	(377)	(585)	(131)	(480)	(141)	(412)	(105)
If widow does not have children								
Disapprove	13.0	12.3	9.0	11.3	20.1	13.3	10.2	12.1
Approve	87.0	87.7	91.0	88.7	79.9	86.7	89.8	87.9
Total	100.0	100.0	100.0	100.0	100.0	100.0	100.0	100.0
(No. in sample)	(1,482)	(383)	(589)	(133)	(482)	(143)	(421)	(107)

Interaction among immediate family members and other relatives or friends can be gauged by the observance of traditional family events. As Table 14.11 indicates, respondents in 1990 were more likely to observe family events for worshipping ancestors or honoring parents and older relatives than they were to observe holidays and events adopted recently from other cultures.

Another measure of family interaction is the proportion of households involved in *kye* meetings—that is, social gatherings that are hosted on a cooperative, rotational basis. Such meetings are one of the most prevalent community activities in rural Korean society and a traditional means of gaining cooperation of the local populace for activities of interest to the entire group. At a *kye* meeting, which is usually composed of 10 to 20 members and held once a month, all members contribute the same amount of money (or make a contribution in kind, such as rice, of equivalent value) to a pool, which is given to the host to pay for agreed upon activities. In this way a lump sum can be raised for *kye* purposes. We found that nearly two-thirds (63 percent) of rural households surveyed in 1990 were involved in *kye* meetings, compared with fewer than half (43 percent) of the households surveyed in 1959 by Ko et al. (Table 14.12).

Those participating in *kye* meetings today tend to be older community members left behind when younger family members moved to the cities for education or jobs. The purpose of the majority of *kye* meetings has also changed, from family-centered activities such as ancestor worship and weddings, to nonfamily events such as social gatherings among unrelated members of the same rural community (Table 14.13). In 1959, *kye* meetings were held most commonly for family-centered events such as funerals of family members, ancestor worship, and

Table 14.11. Percentages of respondents observing traditional family events: 1990

Event	All areas	Cheonwon	Gunwi	Damyang
New Year's Day	95.1	95.8	93.3	96.5
Full Moon's Day (*Chusuck*)	94.8	95.1	92.6	97.4
Ancestor Worship Day	92.6	88.1	95.3	94.8
January Full Moon's Day	76.5	76.2	67.1	88.8
Birthdays of elderly family members	74.3	80.7	77.2	62.9
Parents' Day	72.3	84.5	68.7	61.1
Children's Day	24.7	41.9	14.4	15.9
Visiting ancestors' tombs	63.6	44.8	74.3	73.3
Buddha's Birthday	33.1	28.0	47.0	21.5
Caring for Tombs Day (*Hansik*)	30.2	35.2	13.4	45.7
Christmas	17.4	32.2	8.1	11.2
Wedding anniversary	5.7	7.1	4.1	6.1

weddings (64 percent of respondents indicating that they took part in such meetings), and secondarily for social gatherings of friends (32 percent). In 1990, the most common purposes of *kye* meetings in the surveyed communities were social get-togethers among friends (55 percent of respondents reporting their participation in such gatherings); other fairly common nonfamilial purposes of *kye* meetings were sightseeing and savings. Only about half of the respondents reported taking part in family-centered *kye* meetings.

These changes seem to reflect new attitudes toward leisure and a shift in orientation from the family to the individual. They also reflect changes in the economic activities of rural areas during the past three decades of industrialization and farm mechanization.

Household Types

It is generally believed that the traditional family type in Korea has been the extended family and that the extended family is in the process of transforming itself into a nuclear-family structure. The large, extended family, however, has been only

Table 14.12. Households involved in *kye* meetings: 1959 and 1990 (percentage distributions)

Involvement	All areas 1959	All areas 1990	Cheonwon 1959	Cheonwon 1990	Gunwi 1959	Gunwi 1990	Damyang 1959	Damyang 1990
Not involved	57.4	37.1	58.2	39.2	60.6	32.4	52.3	40.5
Involved	42.6	62.9	41.8	60.8	39.4	67.6	47.4	59.5
Total	100.0	100.0	100.0	100.0	100.0	100.0	100.0	100.0
(No. in sample)	(711)	(407)	(228)	(143)	(191)	(148)	(191)	(116)

Note: Percentages may not sum exactly to 100.0 because of rounding.

Table 14.13. Households involved in *kye* meetings, by purpose of meeting: 1959 and 1990

Purpose of meeting	All areas 1959	All areas 1990	Cheonwon 1959	Cheonwon 1990	Gunwi 1959	Gunwi 1990	Damyang 1959	Damyang 1990
Mourning, ancestor worship, marriage of family members	63.7	47.3	60.6	49.4	66.6	38.0	64.9	58.0
Gathering of friends	31.7	54.7	17.1	57.5	36.6	65.0	46.2	36.2
Saving money	8.9	13.2	14.7	24.1	4.4	5.0	6.6	11.6
Sightseeing	na	17.6	na	11.5	na	23.0	na	17.4
For parents	na	2.7	na	3.4	na	2.0	na	2.9
Other	12.2	1.2	21.3	1.1	11.1	2.0	1.1	0.0
(No. of households)	(303)	(256)	(122)	(87)	(90)	(100)	(91)	(69)

na—not applicable.

an ideal because even in the past the size of actual households and the patterns of family composition did not conform to the model of the extended family system. According to the family registry of the seventeenth century, the Korean household contained on average only slightly more than four persons (Kim D.-H., 1986:353). Until very recently, extended or multiple-family households, including the head-family type, represented fewer than 40 percent of all households, whereas nuclear-family households have consistently been in the majority (Table 14.14). The widespread perception that the extended family has been the norm in the past is probably due to the tendency of Korean nuclear families to have a hierarchical order and a sense of family unity that are characteristic of the extended, large-family system.

As can be seen in Table 14.15, since 1966 the proportions of nuclear-family and one-person households in Korea have increased somewhat, whereas the proportion of head-family households has declined. The proportion of nuclear families rose from 65 to 69 percent (or only about 4 percentage points over 20 years), and the proportion of one-person households tripled (growing from 2.3 to 6.9 percent), though still representing only a small fraction of the total. In contrast, the proportion of head-family households fell by half, from 21 to 10 percent; and 70 percent of the total decrease (i.e., 7 percentage points of the decline) occurred during the 1970s. That decade was one of astounding economic growth in Korea—the gross national product grew at an average annual rate of more than 7 percent—and of rapid urbanization due to a huge influx of people from rural areas to the cities. The causes of the change in the distribution of household types, however, cannot be explained simply by Korea's economic boom. Many variables having interactive effects were likely involved, such as rising age at marriage, declining birth and death rates, internal migration, changing housing conditions, and other economic and social changes.

In the study areas, nuclear-family households slightly outnumbered extended-family and multiple-family households in 1959 (53 percent and 47 percent, respectively). (See Table 14.16.) It is noteworthy that Ko et al.'s study did not include data on one-person households. By 1990, nuclear-family households represented about 63 percent of the total and one-person households accounted for 9.1 percent; thus, the two small-family household types together gained about 20 percentage points over the three decades. Conversely, the share of extended-family and multiple-family households declined from 47 to 28 percent.

The three study areas had about the same proportion of nuclear families in 1990, but some differences emerged between them in the proportions of one-person and extended-family households (Table 14.16). Extended- and multiple-family households were more common in Gunwi-gun (30 percent) and Cheon-

Table 14.14. Summary data on households, by family types, from various studies: Korea, 1630–1975

Year	Source of data/ sampling method[a]	Sample size	Study area	One-person	Nuclear	Head[b]	Other extended or multiple	Reference
1630	Family registry	660	Sanum-hyun	25.6	65.5	6.8	2.2	J.-S. Choi (1983)
1756	Family registry	183	Kokseong-hyun	13.7	67.2	14.8	4.4	J.-S. Choi (1983)
1807	Family registry	254	Yangja-dong	–	61.1	31.5	7.4	J.-S. Choi (1983)
1825	Family registry	2,989	Taegu-shi	3.9	65.2	26.8	4.2	J.-S. Choi (1983)
1955	Population census	3,801	South Korea (whole country)					J.-S. Choi (1981)
			(All *shi*)	3.2	63.5	30.7	2.5	
			(All *gun*)	5.2	73.4	19.6	1.8	
				2.6	60.3	34.4	2.7	
1959	Survey method 1	287	Seoul	–	59.2	40.8		H.-C. Lee (1959)
1959	Survey method 1	843	3 rural areas (Cheonan, Gunwi, Damyang)	–		47.2		H.K. Ko et al. (1963)
1964	Survey method 2	na	Andong-gun	–	52.8	32.9	9.7	T.-K. Kim (1964)
1967	Survey method 2	1,182	12 villages from 3 cultural regions	–	57.4			
1969	Survey (method unknown)	600	Seoul, Jincheon, and 3 rural areas (Kyeongsan, Pyeongchang, Jangheung)	–	51.5	34.4	14.1	H.-S. Yang (1967)
1968–72	Survey method 2	933	12 villages	–	69.6	27.6	2.8	K.-K. Lee (1975)
				–	65.1	33.0	1.9	K.-K. Lee (1975)
1975	Population census	6,537	South Korea (whole country)	6.5	67.5	23.5	2.5	J.-S. Choi (1981)
			(All *shi*)	8.0	70.0	18.4	3.6	
			(All *gun*)	4.1	63.7	31.4	0.8	

na—data not available.
a. The two sampling methods were as follows: (1) the survey areas were selected purposefully, but the households or the respondents were selected on the basis of an appropriate sampling, so that the sample represented the selected area; (2) all households in the selected villages were surveyed.
b. "Head family" refers to a household in which a father and his eldest married son live together with their family members.

won-gun (28 percent) than in Damyang-gun (26 percent). One-person households accounted for 11 percent of the total in Damyang-gun, 9.1 percent in Cheonwon-gun, and nearly 7.7 percent in Gunwi-gun. More than half (57 percent) of the one-

Table 14.15. Households, by family type: South Korea, 1966–85 (percentage distributions)

Family type	1966	1970	1975	1980	1985
Whole Korea					
One-person	2.3	4.8	4.2	4.8	6.9
Nuclear-family	64.7	68.1	67.7	68.3	68.8
Head-family	20.6	19.0	11.9	10.9	10.2
Other	12.4	8.1	16.2	16.0	14.1
Total	100.0	100.0	100.0	100.0	100.0
All *shi* (cities)					
One-person	2.8	5.9	4.5	4.7	6.8
Nuclear-family	69.3	72.4	70.5	69.8	70.0
Head-family	13.6	12.7	7.6	7.6	7.7
Other	14.3	9.1	17.4	17.9	15.5
Total	100.0	100.0	100.0	100.0	100.0
All *gun* (rural counties)					
One-person	2.0	4.0	3.9	4.9	7.2
Nuclear-family	62.2	64.8	64.9	66.2	66.4
Head family	24.5	23.7	16.2	15.6	15.1
Other	11.3	7.4	15.0	13.3	11.3
Total	100.0	100.0	100.0	100.0	100.0

Source: Population census reports.
Note: Percentages may not sum exactly to 100.0 because of rounding.
a. Computed from the census tables on the composition and generation of households.

Table 14.16. Households, by family type: 1959 and 1990 (percentage distributions)

	1959 (all areas)		1990							
			All areas		Cheonwon		Gunwi		Damyang	
Type of household	No.	%	No.	%	No.	%	No.	%	No.	%
One-person	0	0.0	37	9.1	13	8.7	11	7.7	13	11.2
Nuclear-family	445	52.8	255	62.5	95	63.8	88	61.5	72	62.1
Extended- or multiple-family	398	47.2	114	27.9	41	27.5	43	30.1	30	25.9
Nonfamily[a]	0	0.0	2	0.4	0	0.0	1	0.7	1	0.8
Total	843	100.0	408	100.0	149	100.0	143	100.0	116	100.0

Note: Percentages may not sum exactly to 100.0 because of rounding.
a. Nonfamily households are those in which the residents have no kin relationships.

person households consisted of individuals who were 65 years of age or older.

It seems that these differences in family types are due more to variations in the specific study areas rather than to differences in the characteristics of the larger cultural regions. For example, according to the national census, the proportions of one-person households in the cultural regions represented by the three areas in 1985 were 5.0 percent in rural Choongnam (Cheonwon-gun), 6.8 percent in rural Jeonnam (Damyang-gun), and 8.7 percent in rural Kyungbuk (Gunwi-gun).

Households with Coresident Parents

One of the most important social functions of families in Korea is to support the elderly. Caring for parents in their old age is considered perhaps the most important duty of children. Traditionally, the eldest son and his immediate family have an obligation to live with his parents and support them. The term "head family" is often used to describe this type of family, consisting of the eldest son, his wife and offspring, and his parents. In recent years, however, an increasing number of households have consisted of elderly parents and adult children other than the eldest son, and the term is sometimes applied to them as well (K.-K. Lee, 1975; K.-O. Lee et al., 1989:40).

The so-called head family is a common household type in Korea, particularly among families in which the children have reached maturity and the parents are still living. After marrying, most sons live with their parents for a short period of time, mainly to show the bride the traditions and customs of the grooms' family. Afterward, the younger sons move from the head-family household and set up their own households, whereas the eldest son is expected to continue living with the parents.

This traditional pattern has been changing along with other social institutions in the face of Korea's economic and industrial development. The older parents may live with younger sons, move around from one son's household to that of another, or live separately from their children, visiting them from time to time (O.-J. Lee, 1980:54). In the cities, an increasing number of parents live with their daughters, although this household arrangement is still deemed undesirable in Korea. These changes are due to a variety of factors, such as an eldest son's occupation that requires him to live in another area from that of his parents, the young wife's occupation and social activities, the unavailability of housing with enough space for head-family households (especially in the cities), lower fertility, and the expansion of Westernized individualistic values.

Among the 398 extended-family and multiple-generation households surveyed by Ko et al. in 1959, 98 percent consisted of the older parents and a son and his family. Similarly, among the 114 multiple-generation households we surveyed in 1990, 97 percent (110 households) contained elderly parents and a son. In 81 of those households, the adult son and his family were living with his parents, whereas in the remaining 29, the elderly parents were living with the son and his family.

Table 14.17 shows the proportions of respondents with living parents who were living with one or both of their own or their spouse's parents. On the assumption that patterns of living with elderly parents have been changing in recent years, we further divided this subsample into six age groups, by the husband's age. Half of the husband respondents with living parents were living with their own parents. Although more wives than husbands had living parents (200 versus 155), only three wife respondents were living with their own parents. Our data show no clear relationship between husbands' ages and husbands with living parents who were living with their own parents.

Factors Affecting Coresidence with Parents

Many social and economic factors influence couples' decisions about coresiding with their parents. We assumed that those factors would be interrelated and deemed a multivariate analysis appropriate for measuring the relative influence of each. Our analysis included the following direct and indirect factors, which we considered important in the decision-making process:

- Characteristics of respondents: whether they were the eldest son or not, their

Table 14.17. Households including one or both parents of the husband or wife, by husband's age: respondents with one or both parents living, 1990

Husband's age[a]	No. of households[b]	One or both of husband's parents alive[c]	Living with husband's parents[d]	One or both of wife's parents alive[c]	Living with wife's parents
20–29	3	3 (1.00)	2 (.67)	3 (1.00)	0
30–39	47	40 (.85)	20 (.50)	41 (.87)	0
40–49	84	54 (.64)	23 (.43)	68 (.81)	0
50–59	129	48 (.37)	26 (.54)	66 (.51)	2
60–69	100	10 (.10)	7 (.70)	20 (.20)	1
70+	43	0 (.00)	0 (.00)	2 (.05)	0
Total	406	155 (.38)	78 (.50)	200 (.49)	3

a. Fifty-seven widowed, divorced, or separated women are classified according to their own age instead of their husbands'.
b. Two households with single heads are excluded.
c. Figures in parentheses refer to the proportion of respondents with one or both parents living.
d. Figures in parentheses refer to the proportion of respondents with living parents who were residing with one or both parents.

age, educational level, occupation, and housing conditions, and the personal characteristics of their spouses, such as age, religion, and urban background
- Characteristics of parents: age, health status, whether both were living, their economic self-sufficiency, their housing conditions, and whether they held traditional values
- Characteristics of the families (types of parent-children relationships)
- Environmental factors, both residential and cultural

It should be noted that our survey questionnaires were not specifically designed to analyze this topic, and as a result our data set does not contain complete information on the above variables. In cases of missing data we substituted proxy variables whenever possible. For example, since information about parents' health status and relationships among family members was not available, we used the variable of parents' age (father's age when both parents were living) as a proxy for parents' health status. We also used the wife's hometown (whether urban or rural) and educational level as a proxy for the type of relationship between parents and children because it is known that the son's wife often plays an important role in a couple's decision not to coreside with his parents. If she has an urban background or higher education, and thus has been exposed to Western culture, she may tend to have more individualistic values—i.e., not to be very obedient—and may wish to avoid conflicts with her mother-in-law that might occur if they were to live together. Such variables as parents' economic self-sufficiency and housing conditions were difficult to measure, especially if the parents lived with their children. Table 14.18 summarizes the variables considered to be related to coresidence with parents.

Perhaps the most difficult problem facing us in analyzing these data was the small number of observations (only 155). This problem was compounded by interaction effects of the variables caused by the wide age range of respondents (from under 30 to over 60), whose life experiences during the rapid changes of the current century varied widely. In particular, given the rapid socioeconomic changes that took place after World War II and the Korean War, the variables can have different meanings for each generation of respondents. For example, having finished secondary school may represent an average level of education for respondents in their 30s, whereas for those in their 50s and 60s it may represent a high educational level. Our cross-tabulation analysis indicated possible interaction effects among the following sets of variables: respondent's status as the eldest son and father's lineage status; respondent's education and father's lineage status; parents' age and father's lineage status; type of marriage (love match versus arranged marriage) and respondent's age; and respondent's status as eldest son and his age. (See Appendix Tables 14.12–14.16.)

For our analysis, we selected male

household heads and husbands of female household heads who had at least one living parent. Whether they lived with their parents or not became the dependent variable, and the variables presented in Table 14.18 became the independent variables. Then we attempted to analyze how much each independent variable affected the dependent variable when we controlled for the other independent variables. Given the special characteristics of the dependent variable, we used logistic regression as our analytic tool.

For our estimation of regression coefficients we used a packaged program for maximum likelihood estimation, testing them at the 5 percent level of significance in a two-tailed t-test. When a variable was shown to be statistically insignificant, we removed it if doing so did not seriously affect the values and directions of the other variables' coefficients. All but

Table 14.18. Definitions and means of variables used in the analysis of data on living with any parents
(no. in sample = 155)

Variable	Mean	Standard deviation
Parents' characteristics		
Father, head family for at least two generations	0.503	0.502
Father's lineage status	1.871	2.660
Father's age	70.123	11.131
Both parents alive	0.194	0.396
Respondent's (or spouse's) characteristics		
Love marriage	0.097	0.297
Spouse's residence in the same *gun* at the time of marriage	0.413	0.494
Using farm vehicle	0.832	0.375
Husband the eldest son	0.529	0.501
Age of the husband	46.168	9.225
Education, high school or more	0.297	0.458
Age of the wife	42.271	9.715
Wife's hometown urban	0.851	0.357
Living with any parents	0.503	0.502
Husband, Buddhist	0.361	0.482
Husband, Catholic or Protestant	0.116	0.321
Wife, Buddhist	0.426	0.496
Wife, Catholic or Protestant	0.155	0.363
Residence, Gunwi	0.335	0.474
Residence, Damyang	0.277	0.449
Currently married	0.935	0.246
Household characteristics: cultivating land area of 330 m², all types	40.490	53.816

one of the variables included in our final equation, presented in Table 14.19, were within the acceptable level of significance, the exception being the respondent's age ($t = 1.89$).

Since the dependent variable is in the log-odds, the meaning of the regression coefficient is not easy to interpret. The adjusted proportions of husband respondents living with their parents were calculated from the estimated equation and are shown with the unadjusted proportions in Table 14.20. The unadjusted proportions were those obtained from simple cross-tabulations of each independent variable with the dependent variable. The adjusted proportions were computed using the method elaborated by Retherford and Choe (1993: Chap. 5). The adjusted proportions in Table 14.20 show the expected proportion of the respondents living with any parents when the independent variable had a specific value and the effect of all other independent variables in the model were controlled.

Our results indicate that being the eldest son was the most important factor influencing coresidence with parents. The adjusted proportion of respondents coresiding with one or both parents was 23 percent for those who were not the eldest son, compared with 74 percent for those who were. If only one parent was alive, the adjusted proportion of sons coresiding with that parent was 55 percent, but if both parents were living the adjusted proportion was only 31 percent. These results indicate that elderly parents tended to maintain separate households from those of their children when both parents were living.

Owning a farm vehicle suggests that a household has achieved a comfortable economic level. As we expected, the presence of such a vehicle increased the probability of coresidence with the respondent's parents. The adjusted pro-

Table 14.19. Results of the logistic regression on living with parent or not, based on the sample of sons with one or both parents alive

Variable	Estimates of coefficient	Standard error	t-ratio
Constant	0.409	1.156	0.35
Father's lineage status	−0.174	0.075	−2.30*
Both parents alive	−1.006	0.509	−1.98*
Eldest son	2.217	0.428	5.17*
Using farm vehicle	1.244	0.535	2.32*
Respondent's age	−0.043	0.023	−1.89
Love marriage	−8.421	4.032	−2.09*
Age × love marriage	0.198	0.100	1.97*

$\chi^2 = 45.2$ d.f. = 7 $p < .000$ (No. in sample = 155)

*Significant at the .05 level, using a two-tailed test.

Rural Family and Community Life in South Korea

Table 14.20. Unadjusted and adjusted proportions of respondents living with any parents, controlling for other predictor variables by holding them at their mean values

Predictor variable		No.	Unadjusted proportion	Adjusted proportion[a]
Father's lineage status				
0		—	—	0.58
1		—	—	0.54
Both parents alive				
0		125	0.54	0.55
1		30	0.37	0.31
Eldest son				
0		73	0.30	0.23
1		82	0.68	0.74
Using farm vehicle				
0		26	0.31	0.26
1		129	0.54	0.55
Love marriage × age				
0	30	—	—	0.68
0	40	—	—	0.58
0	50	—	—	0.47
1	30	—	—	0.15
1	40	—	—	0.46
1	50	—	—	0.80

a. The adjusted proportions are based on the logistic regression shown in Table 14.19.

portion of respondents living with their parents was twice as high (56 versus 26 percent) among those households with a farm vehicle as among those without one.

The type of marriage a person has (whether a love match or an arranged marriage) represents both a characteristic of that person and the type of relationship that exists between that person and his parents. An overwhelming majority of our respondents had arranged marriages; only 9.7 percent had love matches, and among those 50 years old and over the percentage of love matches was just 3.4.[3] Love matches were rare a generation

3. By contrast, in Taegu the figure for love marriage was 13 percent (Han, 1971:115).

ago. We found that among respondents whose marriages had been arranged, the younger were the respondents, the higher was the probability that they lived with their parents, whereas among those who had married partners of their own choice, the younger were the respondents, the lower was the probability of coresidence with parents. We had expected these results because we reasoned that a younger person whose marriage had been arranged probably had more traditional values than did an older person whose marriage had been arranged at a time when arranged marriages were more common.

We also hypothesized that whether the respondent's father was a direct de-

Table 14.21. Summary data on living arrangements of the elderly, from various surveys: South Korea, 1972–88

Survey year	Age definition of the elderly	Sampling method[b]	Sample size	Study areas	Living arrangements[a]						Reference
					Alone	With spouse only	With the eldest ever-married son	With another ever-married son	With an ever-married daughter	With single children	
1972	60	(4)	400	Taegu-shi	0.5	7.3	67.5		1.3	15.6[c]	K.-S. Kwon (1973)
1974	60	(3)	264	Seoul, Taejon, Jeonju, and 3 rural areas		15.5	33.0	29.2	21.6	0	Y.-H. Lee (1975)
1975	60	(2)	279	Seoul and 2 rural areas (Shiheung and Koesan)	5.8	6.1	54.2	10.8	1.8	18.4	D.-E. Hyeon (1976)
1977	60	(2)	983	4 rural areas (Chunseong, Cheongwon, Yechon, and Hwasoon)		17.6	77.2				Y.-S. Lee (1978)
1978	60	(2)	300	Seoul (2 low-income *dong*)	5.0	10.0	48.7		7.7	23.3	H.-C. Lee et al. (1979)
1979	60	u	300	u	2.4	12.1	58.4	19.6	4.7	0	O.-J. Lee (1980)
1981	60	(4)	400	Seoul, Chunan, and rural Okgu-gun		19.8	47.3	18.2	3.5	11.2	T.-H. Kim (1983)
1981	60	u	1,427	South Korea	2.2	u	54.7		u	31.5	Korea Survey (Gallup) (1982)
1981	60	u	225	u		16.8	38.2	13.3	3.7	28.0	S.-N. Choi (1984)
1983	60	(3)	110	Jungwon-gun		4.6	60.0	22.7	0.0	12.7	H.-S. Kim (1983)
1984	60	(4)	2,348	South Korea	3.3	17.3	39.7	14.0	u	10.7	J.-K. Park et al. (1984)

Rural Family and Community Life in South Korea

scendant of the family line (that is, the eldest son of an eldest son) would have a positive effect on coresidence because members of such families might have more traditional attitudes. This variable did not have the expected effect, however, because it decreased rather than increased the probability of coresidence. It is possible that the variable interacted with other variables, such as parents' age and the birth order of offspring. When we included all these interacting variables in our estimation equation, the father's lineage status showed a positive effect on coresidence, but the coefficient had no statistical significance. In the end, we decided to exclude the interaction variables.

In our first trial, we included such variables as the daughter-in-law's personal characteristics (rural or urban hometown, educational level, and religion), the place of residence (which might reveal unique cultural characteristics), and parents' age. The effects of these variables failed to show statistical significance, however, and were thus excluded from the final analysis.

Living Arrangements of the Elderly

General data on the distribution of households by family type alone are not sufficient for analyzing the changing living arrangements of the elderly because there must also be related social, economic, and demographic factors. To explore this subject, it was necessary to consider the el-

1984	60	(1)	3,050	South Korea	8.8	11.7	39.4	12.6	2.8	23.5	J.-K. Lim et al. (1985)
1988	60	(1)	15,632	South Korea	9.6	13.3	53.3		3.6	18.4	K.-O. Lee et al. (1989)
1988	60	(1)	977	South Korea	2.4	11.7		77.5			L. Martin (1989)

u—data unavailable.

a. Percentages do not sum to 100 because other categories are deleted.

b. The sampling methods were as follows: (1) a probability sample representing the whole country or the whole study area was used; (2) the survey areas were selected purposefully, but the respondents were selected on the basis of an appropriate sampling frame, so that the sample represented the selected area; (3) the survey areas were selected purposefully, but the selection of respondents in the designated areas was by a random sampling frame; (4) selection of the sample was based on a list of certain special groups, such as regular attendants of an old folks' meeting house or residents of old people's convalescent homes.

c. Living with a married child plus unmarried children.

derly persons and their spouses as the unit of observation. Table 14.21 summarizes the published data about living arrangements of elderly persons, based on the observations of the elderly themselves. Before 1970 there seems to have been no data dealing with this subject from the viewpoint of the elderly. All of the recent data, except those provided by the Korean Institute for Family Planning (KIFP) surveys of 1984 (J.-K. Lim et al., 1985) and 1988 (K.-O. Lee et al., 1989), have only limited utility for cross-national comparisons. Some of the surveys used unrepresentative samples from selected areas, and the others lacked appropriate sampling methods. The data suggest, implausibly, no significant changes in living arrangements during the 1970s and 1980s.

The 1988 KIFP data, which are based on a nationwide sample, indicate that 9.6 percent of elderly lived alone, 13 percent lived with their spouse only, 53 percent lived with direct male offspring (the eldest son or other sons), only 3.6 percent lived with a married daughter, and 18 percent lived with unmarried children (K.-O. Lee et al., 1989:47). These data thus show that, contrary to the general notion that nuclear families have been increasing rapidly, the traditional living arrangement for elderly—residing with their sons—is still the norm. In rural areas, only a negligible proportion of the elderly live with their daughters and sons-in-law, and in metropolitan areas the proportion is only 5 percent (J.-K. Lim et al., 1985:81).

The most significant change seems to be the increasing numbers of elderly who live only with their spouse or live alone. According to 1984 data (J.-K. Lim et al., 1985:24, 281), the proportion of elderly-only households has risen to 25 percent in nonurban areas and 17 percent in cities. The rapid increase in such households in rural areas can be explained by the migration of adult children to cities in the course of Korea's industrialization and urbanization, coupled with the inability of the parents to follow them for various reasons.

Much of the published literature on this phenomenon indicates that most elderly persons prefer to live with their adult children; the proportion of those expressing that preference in surveys ranged from 71 to 83 percent (K.-S. Kwon, 1973:628; Korea Survey [Gallup] Polls, 1984:79; J.-K. Lim, 1985:317). Among those who wished to live with their children, nearly two-thirds (72 percent) preferred to live with their eldest son and only 1.8 percent preferred to live with a daughter (D.-E. Hyeon, 1976:497). In our own 1990 rural family survey, 80 percent of the elderly men and 84 percent of the elderly women wished to be cared for by their eldest son and daughter-in-law if they became incapable of caring for themselves (Appendix Table 14.10). These findings suggest that the basic living pattern in South Korea is still the traditional patriarchal family.

Y.-H. Lee (1975:205) reports that in a study conducted in Seoul, Daejon, Kongju, and three Korean villages, about one-third of elderly persons who were living alone or with just their spouse reported that they were doing so because their children's workplace was elsewhere (mostly in cities). Others gave as their reasons that they preferred to live on their own (49 percent), that their children did not want to live with them (9.8 percent), or that they either had no children or their children did not have adequate housing for them (9.7 percent).

In our 1990 survey of the three study areas, only 40 percent, or 163, of the households had persons aged 65 and over living in them; the total number of elderly persons was 198. Table 14.22 summarizes the living arrangements of the elderly in those households. About one-third, or 56, of the households were composed of only elderly persons; of those, 21 households consisted of one elderly person living alone and 35 contained couples. One notable pattern was that those elderly who had a spouse tended to live apart from their children (54 percent) but that those who were widowed or divorced tended to live with their children (79 percent).

Among the elderly who lived alone or with their spouse, the average number of male offspring was 2.5. Among elderly who were living with their adult children, the average number of sons was 2.8. Five elderly persons or elderly couples (9.2 percent) did not have a surviving son, however.

Two-thirds of the elderly in our survey had no unmarried children. This figure applies both to elderly who lived alone or with only their spouse and to the elderly who lived with other members of their families.

The average size of agricultural fields for the elderly-only households was 1,720 *pyong* (1 *pyong* equaling 3.3 square meters), compared with an average for all other households of 3,840 *pyong*—about 2.2 times as much. Among elderly persons living in the elderly-only households the rate of employment was 57 percent, whereas for elderly persons living in other households it was about 36 percent. This

Table 14.22. Living arrangements of the elderly, by sex and marital status: 1990 (unit = household)

Living arrangement	Currently married	Currently unmarried Men	Currently unmarried Women	All marital statuses (%)
Alone or with spouse only	35	4	17	56 (34.4)
With the eldest son	9	12	34	55 (33.7)
With other sons	7	1	12	20 (12.3)
With unmarried children	9	0	6	15 (9.2)
With a married daughter	0	1	1	2 (1.2)
With others	5	0	10	15 (9.2)
Total	65	18	80	163 (100.0)

difference was due mainly to the high proportion of elderly women living alone who worked.

Factors Affecting the Establishment of Elderly-Only Households

The characteristics of the elderly and their family members not only affect their patterns of living arrangements but also tend to be interrelated. As in the case of main respondents' coresidence with parents, we therefore used a logistic regression to estimate the effects of the independent variables on the establishment of elderly-only households. Table 14.23 summarizes the definitions and means of the variables used in the analysis. By using every possible variable, we were able to select the most adequate model equation. Table 14.24 presents the regression coefficients and standard errors of the model equation, and Table 14.25 shows the adjusted probability of forming an elderly-only household by values of one predictor variable, holding other predictor variables at their means. Except for the number of living sons, the employment status of the elderly, and elderly males without a spouse, all the explanatory vari-

Table 14.23. Definitions and means of variables used in the analysis of the elderly, living alone or with spouse only (sample size = 163)

Variable	Mean	Standard deviation
Characteristics of the elderly		
Residence in Gunwi	0.361	0.482
Residence in Damyang	0.319	0.467
Head family for at least two generations	0.362	0.482
Male	0.509	0.501
Age 75	0.398	0.491
Age in years	73.632	6.730
Had experience as a public servant	0.116	0.321
Working (employed)	0.423	0.495
Currently married (with spouse)	0.398	0.491
Without spouse, male	0.110	0.314
Living arrangements		
Alone or with spouse only	0.344	0.476
With the eldest son	0.337	0.474
With other sons	0.123	0.329
Other	0.196	0.398
No. of sons alive	2.619	1.736
No. of children single and alive	0.558	0.916
Household characteristics		
Using a farm vehicle	0.681	0.467
Cultivated land area of 330 m^2, all types	31.104	31.994

ables were found to be significant at the 5 percent level in our two-tailed t-test.

Age had negative effects on the establishment of elderly-only households when the effects of other variables were fixed. That is, as the age of elderly individuals rose from 65 to 70 and from 70 to 75, the probability of their establishing elderly-only households decreased from 45 to 33 percent and from 33 to 23 percent, respectively (Table 14.25).

Having a living spouse had the greatest (positive) effect on the establishment of elderly-only households. Among the three groups we observed (elderly men whose wives were no longer living, elderly women whose husbands were no longer living, and elderly individuals [male and female] with living spouses), the adjusted proportion of elderly women without a living spouse was the lowest (14 percent)—that is, this group was the least likely to form an elderly-only household, whereas that of elderly individuals with living spouses was the highest, making them about 3.4 times more likely to form such a household. Contrary to our hypothesis, however, the difference between men and women was not significant, and therefore our analysis has not confirmed the finding reported by S.-D. Choi (1983:27) that adult offspring would prefer to coreside with an elderly mother-in-law who could provide help with housekeeping than with an elderly father, despite possible conflicts between the mother-in-law and the daughter-in-law.

When elderly males were successors of the family line, the adjusted probability of establishing a separate household increased more than twofold, from 19 to 40 percent. This result was somewhat unexpected because we had assumed that direct descendants would be

Table 14.24. Results of the logistic regression on living alone or with spouse only, based on the sample of the elderly

Variable	Estimate of coefficient	Standard error	t-ratio
Constant	6.965	3.117	2.23*
Age	−0.100	0.041	−2.43*
Working (employed)	0.237	0.500	0.47
Currently married (with spouse)	1.710	0.499	3.42*
Without spouse, male	0.254	0.748	0.34
Head family for at least two generations	1.047	0.415	2.52*
Cultivated land area of 330 m²	−0.036	0.009	−3.75*
No. of sons alive	−0.153	0.129	−1.18
No. of children single and alive	−0.577	0.268	−2.14*

$\chi^2 = 62.0$ d.f. = 8 $p < .000$ No. in sample = 163

*Significant at the .05 level, using a two-tailed test.

part of older, more traditional (i.e., extended) families, in which the elderly parents lived with their adult children. Since older traditional Korean families generally are well-off and their children tend to be highly educated, however, there seems to be a tendency for the adult offspring in such families to move to cities for work, and for the elderly parents to remain in the rural areas where they can maintain their family traditions.

Having arable land had the effect of decreasing the probability of establishing an elderly-only household. This finding was expected because the land, if it was to be worked, would require extra help.

Table 14.25. Unadjusted and adjusted proportions of elderly persons living alone or with spouse only, controlling for other predictor variables by holding them at their mean values

Predictor variable	N	Unadjusted proportion	Adjusted proportion[a]
Age of the elderly			
65	—	—	0.45
70	—	—	0.33
75	—	—	0.23
Working			
0	94	0.26	0.24
1	69	0.46	0.28
Marital status			
Currently married	65	0.54	0.48
Without spouse, male	18	0.22	0.18
Without spouse, female	80	0.21	0.14
Head family for at least 2 generations			
0	104	0.23	0.19
1	59	0.54	0.40
Cultivated land area of 330 m²			
20	—	—	0.34
30	—	—	0.26
60	—	—	0.11
No. of sons alive			
0	15	0.47	0.34
1	27	0.37	0.30
2	48	0.31	0.27
3	25	0.44	0.24
4	29	0.28	0.21
No. of children single and alive			
0	109	0.35	0.32
1	28	0.32	0.21
2	15	0.47	0.13
3	11	0.18	0.08

a. The adjusted proportions are based on the logistic regression shown in Table 14.24.

The more unmarried children an elderly individual had, the less likely he or she was to be living alone. The number of married sons, however, was not a significant factor.

CONCLUSION

Our survey has shown that a large proportion of Koreans (71–83 percent of those interviewed) wish to live with their children in their old age, indicating that the ideal family structure in South Korea is still the extended or head family. The actual pattern of residence, however, has been small, nuclear families, and our findings indicate a gradual increase in small families. Perhaps the most important changes that our findings have revealed are in Koreans' perceptions of the family and familial relationships, in particular in their feelings about collective responsibility.

As for the factors influencing respondents' decision to live with their elderly parents, being the eldest son and having the use of a farm vehicle increased the probability of coresiding with parents. Being the eldest son increased the proportion of respondents who coresided with their parents by more than three times when the effect of other variables in the model were controlled. In contrast, the father's lineage status and having a surviving spouse decreased the probability of a respondent's coresiding with his or her parents. For example, if the father was the eldest grandson of the main family in an old family-line succession, his lineage status made him less, not more, likely to reside with his adult children. This finding was unexpected, but it is understandable if one considers that such a father would want to retain the traditional family home, even at the cost of living apart from his children, rather than abandon tradition by moving in with his children in an unfamiliar city.

The respondent's age and whether he or she had an arranged marriage or a love match showed significant interaction effects on coresidence with parents. Among respondents whose marriages had been arranged, the younger were the respondents, the higher was the probability that they lived with their parents; whereas among those who had married partners of their own choice, the younger were the respondents, the lower was the probability of coresidence with parents. These results were expected because we reasoned that a younger person whose marriage had been arranged probably had more traditional values than did an older person whose marriage had been arranged at a time when arranged marriages were more common. Although we had also hypothesized that the daughter-in-law's personal characteristics (rural or urban hometown, educational attainments, and religion) would affect the probability of coresidence with her husband's parents, it was found to be an insignificant factor, probably because the rural study areas are still traditional, male-dominated communities.

One of the most important findings from our survey was the increase in the proportion of households in which elderly persons were living alone or with their spouses only. Thirty-four percent of the households had persons aged 65 and over living in them. The rapid increase in such households in rural areas can be explained by the migration of adult children to cities in the course of Korea's industrialization and urbanization, coupled with the inability of the parents to follow them for various reasons.

Our multivariate analysis of the determinants of elderly-only households has shown that, among characteristics of the elderly themselves, having a living spouse and being a direct descendant of the family line increased the probability of establishing such a household. Being a widow or a widower, however, decreased the probability by more than 30 percentage points, there being no significant difference in the probability between widows and widowers. Age and having unmarried children also decreased the probability. Among household characteristics, the greater the amount of cultivated land, the less was the probability of establishing an elderly-only household. Other variables, however, such as the number of living sons an elderly individual had or his employment status, were not significant factors.

From these findings, we may conclude that elderly Koreans stay in their rural homes rather than live with their adult children elsewhere for various reasons. They stay not because they do not have a living son or cannot find a job, but rather because they are active, are still capable of working, have a living spouse from whom they can seek mutual support, and, finally, wish to keep up the tradition of their family line.

Our analysis of both the living arrangements of the elderly and coresidence of younger adults with their elderly parents has revealed no significant cultural differences among regions. The models used in the analysis may need further refinement, however. For example, since we did not initially intend to analyze the living arrangements of the elderly, our data lack information that would shed light on this topic.

The effects of the variables we used in analyzing the establishment of elderly-only households were rather straightforward. In contrast, the variables we used to analyze coresidence with parents—for example, type of marriage (arranged or love match), educational level, and father's lineage status—interacted with one another and thus showed complex relationships. One reason for these complex interactions may be that the variables had different meanings to each generation owing to the rapid changes that have taken place in Korean society in recent decades.

To gain a better understanding of Korea's changing family structures, a much larger sample is needed, one that can be stratified by age group. Finally, the study of Korea's changing family will not be complete if we simply focus on changes in family patterns. We must also focus on the familial, or kinship, ties and the changing interrelationships among those emotional factors.

Appendix Table 14.1. Summary results of the survey, by region and administrative district: 1990

Province, study area, and village	All households	Sample households	Completed households	Out of town	Refusal	Senility, etc.
CHUNG CHEONG NAM-DO						
Cheonwon	640	161	143	8	5	5
Yulkum 1-gu	136	34	32	1	1	0
Yulkum 2-gu	136	34	28	1	3	2
Yulkum 3-gu	41	11	8	1	1	1
Yangryong 1-gu	47	12	10	1	0	1
Yangryong 2-gu	49	12	8	4	0	0
Yangryong 3-gu	60	15	15	0	0	0
Songyon 1-gu	30	7	7	0	0	1
Songyon 2-gu	43	11	11	0	0	0
Yongdu 1-gu	26	7	7	0	0	0
Yongdu 2-gu	35	9	8	0	0	1
Yongdu 3-gu	37	9	9	0	0	0
GYEONG SANG BUG-DO						
Gunwi	425	160	149	6	4	1
Oenyang 1-ri	43	16	15	1	0	0
Oenyang 2-ri	30	10	10	0	0	0
Oenyang 3-ri	29	11	11	0	0	0
Taepuk 1-ri	74	26	26	0	0	0
Taepuk 2-ri	26	11	10	0	1	0
Ogok-ri	73	27	26	0	1	0
Tupuk-ri	49	21	17	3	0	1
Talsan 1-ri	45	16	15	0	1	0
Talsan 2-ri	56	22	19	2	1	0
JEON RA NAM-DO						
Damyang	454	151	116	24	0	11
Unkyo 1-dong	33	11	7	2	0	2
Doksong 1-dong	75	25	23	1	0	1
Doksong 2-dong	51	16	13	3	0	0
Doksong 3-dong	18	6	3	2	0	1
Taegok 1-dong	44	15	14	0	0	1
Taegok 2-dong	85	28	23	3	0	2
Hwabang 1-dong	42	14	8	5	0	1
Hwabang 2-dong	52	18	12	4	0	2
Hwabang 3-dong	54	18	13	4	0	1
Total	1,519	472	408	38	9	17

Appendix Table 14.2. Age-sex distribution of respondents: study areas, 1990

Age	All respondents Men No.	%	Women No.	%	Both No.	%	Main respondent Men No.	%	Women No.	%	Spouse of main respondent Men No.	%	Women No.	%
Cheonwon	112	100.1	111	99.9	223	100.0	89	99.9	54	100.0	23	100.0	57	100.0
≤39	17	15.2	30	27.0	47	21.1	11	12.4	16	29.6	6	26.1	14	24.6
40–49	28	25.0	25	22.5	53	23.8	22	24.7	7	13.0	6	26.1	18	31.6
50–59	33	29.5	28	25.2	61	27.4	27	30.3	15	27.8	6	26.1	13	22.8
60–69	27	24.1	21	18.9	48	21.5	23	25.8	10	18.5	4	17.4	11	19.3
70+	7	6.3	7	6.3	14	6.3	6	6.7	6	11.1	1	4.4	1	1.8
Kunwi	117	100.0	130	100.0	247	100.0	77	100.1	72	100.0	40	100.0	58	100.0
≤39	18	15.4	25	19.2	43	17.4	10	13.0	17	23.6	8	20.0	8	13.8
40–49	25	21.4	23	17.7	48	19.4	17	22.1	7	9.7	8	20.0	16	27.6
50–59	44	37.6	56	43.1	100	40.5	30	39.0	28	38.9	14	35.0	28	48.3
60–69	21	17.9	15	11.5	36	14.6	17	22.1	10	13.9	4	10.0	5	8.6
70+	9	7.7	11	8.5	20	8.1	3	3.9	10	13.9	6	15.0	1	1.7
Damyang	93	100.0	98	100.0	191	100.0	90	100.0	26	100.0	3	99.9	72	100.0
≤39	10	10.8	14	14.3	24	12.6	10	11.1	0	0.0	0	0.0	14	19.4
40–49	21	22.6	24	24.5	45	23.6	20	22.2	4	15.4	1	33.3	20	27.8
50–59	28	30.1	29	29.6	57	29.8	27	30.0	5	19.2	1	33.3	24	33.3
60–69	25	26.9	27	27.6	52	27.2	25	27.8	14	53.9	0	0.0	13	18.1
70+	9	9.7	4	4.1	13	6.8	8	8.9	3	11.5	1	33.3	1	1.4
All study areas	322	100.0	339	100.0	661	100.0	256	99.9	152	100.0	66	99.9	187	100.0
≤39	45	14.0	69	20.4	114	17.2	31	12.1	33	21.7	14	21.2	36	19.3
40–49	74	23.0	72	21.2	146	22.1	59	23.0	18	11.8	15	22.7	54	28.9
50–59	105	32.6	113	33.3	218	33.0	84	32.8	48	31.6	21	31.8	65	34.8
60–69	73	22.7	63	18.6	136	20.6	65	25.4	34	22.4	8	12.1	29	15.5
70+	25	7.8	22	6.5	47	7.1	17	6.6	19	12.5	8	12.1	3	1.6

Note: In this and subsequent appendix tables, percentages may not sum exactly to 100.0 because of rounding.

Rural Family and Community Life in South Korea

Appendix Table 14.3. Distribution of households, by size of household: study areas, 1959 and 1990

Persons in household	1959, all areas No.	%	1990 All areas No.	%	Cheonwon No.	%	Gunwi No.	%	Damyang No.	%
1–2	42	5.0	149	36.5	36	25.2	66	44.3	47	40.5
3–4	186	22.0	146	35.8	54	37.8	51	34.2	41	35.3
5–6	301	35.7	98	24.0	43	30.1	30	20.1	25	21.6
7+	314	37.2	15	3.7	10	7.0	2	1.3	3	2.6
Total	843	100.0	408	100.0	143	100.0	149	100.0	116	100.0
Mean size	6.0		3.4		3.9		3.1		3.3	

Appendix Table 14.4. Distribution of households, by generational composition: study areas, 1959 and 1990

No. of generations in the household	1959, all areas No.	%	1990 All areas No.	%	Cheonwon No.	%	Gunwi No.	%	Damyang No.	%
1	24	2.9	136	33.3	34	23.8	57	38.3	45	38.8
2	479	56.8	185	45.3	75	52.5	60	40.3	50	43.1
3	311	36.9	82	20.1	33	23.1	28	18.8	21	18.1
4+	29	3.4	5	1.2	1	0.7	4	2.7	0	0.0
Total	843	100.0	408	100.0	143	100.0	149	100.0	116	100.0

Appendix Table 14.5. Distribution of households, by the size of farmland owned: study areas, 1959 and 1990

Size	1959, all areas No.	%	1990 All areas No.	%	Cheonwon No.	%	Gunwi No.	%	Damyang No.	%
None	102	12.8	94	23.0	47	32.9	23	15.4	24	20.7
< 1 hectare	502	62.8	174	42.7	46	32.2	62	41.6	66	56.9
≥ 1 hectare	195	24.4	140	34.3	50	35.0	64	43.0	26	22.4
Total	779	100.0	408	100.0	143	100.0	149	100.0	116	100.0
Mean land size (unit: 330 m^2)	u		29.55		27.16		39.12		20.22	

u—data unavailable.

Appendix Table 14.6. Age distribution of the heads of household: study areas, 1959 and 1990

	1959, all areas		1990							
			All areas		Cheonwon		Gunwi		Damyang	
Age	No.	%	No.	%	No.	%	No.	%	No.	%
< 30	116	13.8	4	1.0	2	1.4	2	1.3	0	0.0
30–39	212	25.1	46	11.3	19	14.3	17	11.4	10	8.6
40–49	219	26.0	84	20.6	34	23.8	26	17.4	24	20.7
50+	296	35.1	274	67.2	88	61.5	104	69.8	82	70.7
Total	843	100.0	408	100.0	143	100.0	149	100.0	116	100.0
Mean age	u		54.8		53.5		54.8		56.4	

u—data unavailable.

Appendix Table 14.7. Educational attainment of the heads of household: study areas, 1959 and 1960

	1959, all areas		1990							
			All areas		Cheonwon		Gunwi		Damyang	
Level attained[a]	No.	%	No.	%	No.	%	No.	%	No.	%
No education	517	64.3	114	27.9	26	18.2	46	30.9	42	36.2
Primary school	225	28.0	178	43.6	67	46.9	59	39.6	52	44.8
Middle school or higher	62	7.7	116	28.4	50	35.0	44	29.5	22	19.0
Total	804	100.0	408	100.0	143	100.0	149	100.0	116	100.0

a. Includes those who attended and those who completed specified level.

Rural Family and Community Life in South Korea

Appendix Table 14.8. Religion of the respondents and their spouses: study areas, 1959 and 1990

	1959, all areas		1990							
			All areas		Cheonwon		Gunwi		Damyang	
Size	No.	%	No.	%	No.	%	No.	%	No.	%
Men	339	100.0	328	100.0	114	100.0	121	100.0	93	100.0
None	189	55.8	177	53.4	50	43.9	58	47.9	69	74.2
Catholicism	0	0.0	4	1.2	4	3.5	0	0.0	0	0.0
Other Christianity	6	1.7	23	7.0	11	9.6	5	4.1	7	7.5
Confucianism	5	1.5	18	5.5	7	6.1	5	4.1	6	6.5
Buddhism	21	6.2	104	31.7	42	36.8	51	42.1	11	11.8
Others	2	0.6	2	0.6	0	0.0	2	1.7	0	6.0
Unknown	116	34.2	0	0.0	0	0.0	0	0.0	0	0.0
Women	333	100.0	345	100.0	112	100.0	135	100.0	98	100.0
None	280	84.1	148	42.9	39	34.8	46	34.1	63	64.3
Catholicism	0	0.0	5	1.4	5	4.5	0	0.0	0	0.0
Other Christianity	14	4.2	40	11.6	22	19.6	6	4.4	12	12.2
Confucianism	2	0.6	7	2.0	3	2.7	3	2.2	1	1.0
Buddhism	32	9.6	141	40.9	41	36.6	78	57.8	22	22.4
Others	5	1.5	3	0.9	1	0.9	2	1.5	0	0.0
Unknown	0	0.0	1	0.3	1	0.9	0	0.0	0	0.0

Appendix Table 14.9. Patterns of respondents' residence, current versus childhood residence: study areas, 1990

	All areas		Cheonwon		Gunwi		Damyang	
Residence	No.	%	No.	%	No.	%	No.	%
Within the same *eup* (*myun*)	315	46.8	84	37.2	125	49.0	106	55.5
Other *eup* (*myun*) within the same *gun*	98	14.6	23	10.2	40	15.6	35	18.3
Other *gun* (rural) within the same province	126	18.7	35	15.5	68	26.6	23	12.0
Other *shi* (city) within the same province	17	2.5	10	4.4	7	2.7	0	0.0
Other rural area outside the province	80	11.9	53	23.5	7	2.7	20	10.5
Other city outside the province	25	3.7	20	8.8	1	0.4	4	2.1
Other	12	1.7	1	0.4	8	3.1	3	1.6
Total	673		226		256		191	

Appendix Table 14.10. Percentage distribution of preferred care-givers in case of becoming old and ill: study areas, 1990

Preference	All areas Men	All areas Women	Cheonwon Men	Cheonwon Women	Gunwi Men	Gunwi Women	Damyang Men	Damyang Women
First choice								
Spouse	75.3	56.8	74.6	59.8	82.6	66.7	66.7	39.8
Eldest son (and his wife)	21.0	36.2	19.3	29.5	15.7	31.9	30.1	50.0
Other sons (and their wives)	1.5	1.2	3.5	1.8	0.8	0.0	0.0	2.0
Daughter (and son-in-law)	0.0	2.0	0.0	3.6	0.0	0.7	0.0	2.0
Sibling	0.6	0.3	0.0	0.0	0.0	0.0	2.2	1.0
Institution	0.0	0.3	0.0	0.9	0.0	0.0	0.0	0.0
Other	1.5	3.2	2.6	4.5	0.8	0.7	1.1	5.1
Total	100.0	100.0	100.0	100.0	100.0	100.0	100.0	100.0
No. of respondents	(328)	(345)	(114)	(112)	(121)	(135)	(93)	(98)
Second Choice								
Spouse	6.7	8.4	3.5	7.1	5.8	8.1	11.8	10.2
Eldest son (and his wife)	59.1	47.0	51.8	42.9	71.9	57.8	51.6	36.7
Other sons (and their wives)	12.8	23.5	19.3	23.2	3.3	21.5	17.2	26.5
Daughter (and son-in-law)	6.4	10.1	8.8	12.5	3.3	3.7	7.5	16.3
Sibling	6.1	2.6	7.0	4.5	5.8	1.5	5.4	2.0
Institution	2.1	0.6	1.8	0.0	4.1	1.5	0.0	0.0
Other	6.7	7.8	7.9	9.8	5.8	5.9	6.5	8.2
Total	100.0	100.0	100.0	100.0	100.0	100.0	100.0	100.0
No. of respondents	(328)	(345)	(114)	(112)	(121)	(135)	(93)	(98)

Appendix Table 14.11. Percentages of respondents who would consider specified relatives as members of their own family, by sex and coresidence: study areas, 1990

Coresidence status and relative specified	All areas Men	All areas Women	Cheonwon Men	Cheonwon Women	Gunwi Men	Gunwi Women	Damyang Men	Damyang Women
Specified relative lives with the respondent								
Eldest married son	100.0	99.1	100.0	99.1	100.0	99.3	100.0	99.0
Other married sons	97.0	97.4	96.5	98.2	98.4	96.3	95.7	98.0
Married daughters	58.5	57.4	57.0	60.7	54.6	53.3	65.6	59.2
Eldest daughter-in-law	98.9	98.0	98.3	98.2	100.0	98.5	98.9	96.9
Other daughters-in-law	95.4	94.5	93.0	95.5	96.7	94.1	96.8	93.9
Sons-in-law	47.6	51.0	50.0	57.1	48.8	46.7	43.0	50.0
Children of the eldest son	97.9	99.4	98.3	99.1	97.5	100.0	97.9	99.0
Children of other sons	95.7	96.2	95.6	98.2	95.9	96.3	95.7	93.9
Parents	98.8	77.1	99.1	81.3	97.5	68.2	100.0	84.7
Parents of the spouse	61.9	97.4	68.4	97.3	62.0	97.0	53.8	98.0
Married sibling	75.6	51.3	74.6	53.6	72.7	37.8	80.7	67.4
Brother-in-law, sister-in-law	67.7	42.9	68.4	43.8	65.3	28.9	69.9	61.2
Children of the daughter	45.1	45.5	56.1	50.0	41.3	39.3	36.6	49.0
Specified relative does not live with the respondent								
Eldest married son	96.6	97.1	97.4	95.5	95.9	98.5	96.8	96.9
Other married sons	91.2	89.9	89.5	90.2	91.7	91.9	92.5	86.7
Married daughters	32.0	30.8	33.3	36.6	28.1	26.7	35.5	30.6
Eldest daughter-in-law	95.1	94.5	92.1	93.8	95.9	98.5	97.8	89.9
Other daughters-in-law	88.4	87.8	84.2	90.2	89.3	88.1	92.5	84.7
Sons-in-law	25.0	29.3	26.3	35.7	24.8	23.7	23.7	29.6
Children of the eldest son	93.0	95.7	91.2	93.8	92.6	97.0	95.7	95.9
Children of the other sons	89.0	89.9	86.8	91.1	87.6	89.6	93.5	88.8
Parents	95.1	53.6	94.7	49.1	95.9	43.0	94.6	73.5
Parents of the spouse	33.8	92.8	36.0	92.9	32.2	91.1	33.3	94.9
Married sibling	55.2	34.2	54.4	38.4	53.7	20.0	58.1	49.0
Brother-in-law, sister-in-law	50.3	28.4	51.8	31.3	47.1	16.3	52.7	41.8
Children of the daughter	27.7	25.5	35.1	29.5	23.1	20.7	24.7	27.6
No. of respondents	328	345	114	112	121	135	93	98

Appendix Table 14.12. Percentage of respondents living with any parents, by age of parents and survivorship of parents: study areas, 1990

	Parents' age < 75		Parents' age ≥ 75	
Living arrangement	One parent alive	Both parents alive	One parent alive	Both parents alive
Without parents	29	13	29	6
With parents	42	8	25	3
Total	71	21	54	9
% living with parents	59.2	38.1	46.3	33.3
$\chi^2 = 4.86$ d.f. = 3 $p = .182$				

Appendix Table 14.13. Percentage of respondents living with parents, by age and birth order of respondents: study areas, 1990

	Respondent's age < 50		Respondent's age ≥ 50	
Living arrangement	Eldest son	Other son	Eldest son	Other son
Without parents	16	35	10	16
With parents	5	17	28	28
Total	21	52	38	44
% living with parents	23.8	32.7	73.7	63.6
$\chi^2 = 23.79$ d.f. = 3 $p < .000$				

Appendix Table 14.14. Percentage of respondents living with parents, by birth order and father's status as a member of the head family for at least two generations: study areas, 1990

	Eldest son		Other sons	
Living arrangement	Head family	Branch family	Head family	Branch family
Without parents	18	8	22	29
With parents	28	28	10	12
Total	46	36	32	41
Proportion living with parents	60.9	77.8	31.2	29.3
$\chi^2 = 24.82$ d.f. = 3 $p < .000$				

Rural Family and Community Life in South Korea

Appendix Table 14.15. Percentage of respondents living with parents, by educational attainment and father's status as a member of the head family for at least two generations: study areas, 1990

	High school +		< high school	
Living Arrangement	Branch family	Head family	Branch family	Head family
Without parents	31	27	6	13
With parents	27	24	13	14
Total	58	51	19	27
Proportion living with parents	46.6	47.1	68.4	51.9

$\chi^2 = 3.06$ d.f. = 3 $p = .380$

Note: Level attained includes those who attended and those who completed specified level.

Appendix Table 14.16. Percentage of respondents living with parents, by age and type of marriage: study areas, 1990

	Arranged marriage		Love marriage	
Living arrangement	< 50	≥ 50	< 50	≥ 50
Without parents	41	26	10	0
With parents	42	31	3	2
Total	83	57	13	2
% living with parents	50.6	54.4	23.1	100.0

$\chi^2 = 6.21$ d.f. = 3 $p = .102$

Appendix Table 14.17. Percentage of elderly persons, by sex, marital status, and age: study areas, 1990

	Men		Women		Total		
Age	Currently married	Others	Currently married	Others	Currently married	Others	Sex ratio
65–69	29	8	18	19	47	27	100.0
70–74	20	3	7	19	27	22	88.5
75–79	9	1	8	19	17	20	37.0
80–84	4	4	1	18	5	22	42.1
85+	3	2	1	5	4	7	83.3
Total	65	18	35	80	100	98	72.2

Appendix Table 14.18. Working status of elderly persons, by sex and living arrangements (%): study areas, 1990

Living arrangement	Alone or with spouse only		Other	
	Men	Women	Men	Women
Not working	13	19	19	61
Working	26	16	25	19
Total	39	35	44	80
% working	66.7	45.7	56.8	23.7

$\chi^2 = 24.47$ d.f. = 3 $p < .000$

REFERENCES

Choi Jae-Seuk. 1981. "Industrialization and Changes in the Types of Family in Korea" (in Korean). *Journal of Korean Studies* 7(3):2–31.

———. 1983. *A Historical Study of the Korean Family System* (in Korean). Seoul: Ilji-Sa Publishing Co.

Choi Soon-Nam. 1984. *Modern Society and the Welfare of the Elderly* (in Korean). Seoul: Hongikje Publishing Co.

Choi Syn-Duk. 1983. "The Support of the Aged People and the Establishment of Norms," in *The Nuclear Family and the Welfare of the Aged: The Report of the Seminar Held in 1982 by the Korea Institute for Population and Health*, pp. 19–33 (in Korean). Seoul: Korea Institute for Population and Health.

Han Nam-Jae. 1971. "A Study of the Problems of the Urban Family of Korea" (in Korean with an English summary). *Research Review of Kyungpook University* (Humanities and Social Sciences) 15:107–120.

Hyeon Du-El. 1976. "A Sociological Study of Living Arrangements of the Elderly in Korea" (in Korean with an English summary). Kon Kuk University, *Journal of the Academic Research Centre* 20(1):463–531.

Kim Du-Heon. 1968. *A Study of the Korean Family System* (in Korean). Seoul: National University Press.

Kim Hyung-Sik. 1983. "A Study on the Living Conditions of the Elderly in Rural Areas and the Development of Programs to Utilize Their Spare Time" (in Korean with an English abstract). M.A. thesis, Graduate School of Social Development, Jungang University.

Kim Tae-Hyeon. 1983. "The Increase of Nuclear Families and the Support of the Elderly," in *The Nuclear Family and the Welfare of the Aged: The Report of the Seminar Held in 1982 by the Korea Institute for Population and Health*, pp. 3–18 (in Korean). Seoul: Korea Institute for Population and Health.

Kim Taek-Kyu. 1964. *A Study on Living in Consanguinity Villages* (in Korean). Taegu: Institute of Culture of Sila-Kaya.

Ko Hwang-Kyeong, Man-Gap Lee, Hyo-Chae Lee, and Hae-Young Lee. 1963. *A Study on the Rural Family in Korea* (in Korean with an English abstract). Seoul: Seoul National University Press.

Korea Survey (Gallup) Polls Ltd. 1984. *Life Style and Value System of the Aged in Korea* (in Korean). Seoul.

Kwon Kyu-Sik. 1973. "Nuclear Families and the Problems of Aged People" (in Korean). *Journal of the Sungkok Academic Culture Foundation* 4:615–666.

Lee Hyo-Chae. 1959. "A Sociological Study of Families in Seoul" (in Korean). Ehwa Woman's University, *Journal of the Korean Cultural Research Institute* 1:9–71.

Lee Hyo-Chae, Soon Chee, and Min-Ja Park. 1979. "A Study on the Socio-economic and Spatial Environments of the Urban Low-income Elderly." Ehwa Woman's University, *Journal of the Korean Cultural Research Institute* 34:239–287.

Lee Ka-Ok, J.-D. Kwon, S.-J. Kwon, H.-Y. Ahn, and Y.-J. Chung. 1989. *A Study of the Structural Characteristics of Elderly Households* (in Korean). Seoul: Korea Institute for Population and Health.

Lee Kwang-Kyu. 1975. *An Analysis on Family Structure in Korea* (in Korean). Seoul: Ilji-Sa Publishing Co.

Lee Ok-Jae. 1980. "A Study of the Elderly in Urban Korea" (in Korean). M.A. thesis, Graduate School of Education, Ehwa Woman's University.

Lee Yoon-Sook. 1978. "A Sociomedical Investigation of the Aged in Rural Areas" (in Korean with an English abstract). *Journal of Dongduk Women's College* 8:199–220.

Lee Young-Ha. 1975. "The Problems of the Aged and General Plans for Solving Them in Korean Society" (in Korean with an English summary). *Research Review of the Kongju College* 13:199–220.

Lim Jong-Kwon, Sae-Kwon Kong, Jin-Sook Kim, Jung-Ja Nam, and Ho-Shin Ryu. 1985. *A Study on the Aged Population of Korea* (in Korean with an English abstract). Seoul: Korea Institute for Population and Health.

Martin, Linda G. 1989. "Living Arrangements of the Elderly in Fiji, Korea, Malaysia, and the Philippines." *Demography* 26(4):627–743.

Park Jae-Kan, Jung-Sook Lee, and Tae-Hyeon Kim. 1984. "A Survey Report on the Recreational Facilities and Programs for the Aged" (in Korean). *Journal of the Korean Institute of Gerontology* 7:1 ff.

Retherford, Robert D., and Minja Kim Choe. 1993. *Statistical Models for Causal Analysis*. New York: John Wiley & Sons.

University Research Center (URC) of Nihon University and Mainichi Newspapers. 1989. Questionnaire for the Survey on the Contemporary Japanese Family: Values and Behavior (mimeo.). Tokyo.

Yang Hoei-Soo. 1967. *The Structure of the Korean Village* (in Korean). Seoul: Korea University Press.

CHAPTER 15

Changes in Intergenerational Relations in the Chinese Family: Taiwan's Experience

by Te-Hsiung Sun and Yin-Hsing Liu

The population of Taiwan has already completed the first stage of its demographic transition from high to low mortality and fertility (Sun, 1984; Freedman, Sun, Liu, and Chang, 1985). The net reproduction rate (the average number of daughters born to a cohort of 1,000 women, given the mortality of the women from the time of birth) was reduced to below replacement level (0.98) by 1984, and by 1990 it was only 0.83. It is projected that the population will reach a growth rate of zero in about the year 2030 and then turn to negative growth (Wang, 1990). Thus, Taiwan seems to have solved its problem of population size, but now it faces a new problem of population aging.

The proportion of the population over age 65 was only about 6.1 percent in 1990, but Wang (1990:49–68) projects that it will reach 11.8 percent by the year 2010 and rise to 22.9 percent by 2030. It might even go up to 30 percent or higher by 2050. The ratio of population in the productive age groups (15–64) to ages 65 and over was 10.9 to 1 in 1990 but will decline to 2.76 to 1 by 2030 and then to 1.84 to 1 by 2050. These figures indicate a rapid increase of the elderly population in the future. Providing for this rapidly growing elderly population will pose a major challenge.

In traditional Chinese society, the elderly were cared for mostly by their own family members. The social norm built on the Confucian teaching of filial piety required that children not only provide for their elderly parents' subsistence but also pay them respect and treat them with love so that they could live happily during their old age. Since the elderly were cared for by their children, the government did not have to worry about them much but simply encouraged children to be dutiful toward their parents by rewarding the children for their filial deeds. Besides, only a few people survived to old age when mortality was high, so that there was little need for public programs or institutions to support the elderly population.

In Taiwan today, however, filial piety is adapting to the contemporary demographic and social situation by assuming a new form. According to K.-S. Yang (1986), the new form is limited rather than extended, emotion-oriented rather than role-oriented, self-controlled rather than controlled by others, diversified rather than unified, and self-beneficial rather than mutually beneficial. In other words, it has changed from being collectivistic to individualistic, from socially oriented to individually oriented, and from altruistic to egoistic. Therefore, it is no longer a set of enforced attitudes and behaviors toward parents, but instead an important means of ego realization. Yang's argument is not universally accepted, but it does describe how parent-child relations have changed in modern-day Taiwan.

Most of the emphasis in studies of Western families has been on the relations between spouses because those families are centered on the husband and wife. Most of the literature on parent-child relations in the West focuses on the erosion of parental authority (Hutter, 1981:333). By contrast, the parent-child relation is the core of the Chinese family, and therefore it has received more attention in the literature on Chinese societies. Wen (1991), for example, used survey data on the quality of life in Taipei City to analyze parent-child relations in families of various social and economic strata. Examining living arrangements after marriage, forms of support for parents, forms of inheritance, and communication between parents and children who were not living together, he found that parents and children were gradually moving from traditional relations to more modern ones, that those with higher status were more modern than those with lower status (that is, their parent-child relations were much weaker), and that all familial relations were in transition. Wen concluded that traditional parent-child relations (e.g., coresidence, support for parents, and inheritance) were undergoing a major change from son-centered obligations and privileges to equal emphasis on sons and daughters, and that this shift was more pronounced among higher-status families. Noting that some aspects of traditional family relations were being preserved, he characterized traditional and modern relations as coexisting rather than in opposition.

Using data from a 1973 knowledge, attitudes, and family planning practices (KAP) survey, Freedman, Moots, Sun, and Weinberger (1978) calculated the net cumulative rate of couples who had stopped living with their parents in Taiwan and found that 92 percent of the couples still lived with their parents one year after marrying but that the percentages of coresiding couples declined to 81 percent, 72 percent, and 59 percent 3, 5, and 10 years, respectively, after marriage. Among more recently married couples the rate of coresidence was lower, indicating greater independence among younger couples. Even so, 78 percent of newlyweds began married life in the home of one set of parents.

Thornton, Chang, and Sun (1984) analyzed the relationship between socioeconomic change and intergenerational relations and family formation in Taiwan, using 1973 and 1980 KAP survey data. They found that rapid changes in family structure and family relations were accompanied by other social changes, including increases in outside work, more independence on the part of children, and increased premarital sexual activity and premarital pregnancies. They also found that the family's social status affected the interaction between parents and children and the formation of families: women with educated fathers had more nonfamilial experiences than others, and farm origins tended to exert a traditional influence on the life course.

Many other studies have examined social change and family structure in Taiwan (e.g., Chen and Lai, 1979; Chu, 1981; Lai and Chen, 1985; Lavely, 1982; Li, 1984; L.-H. Shu and Lin, 1984; Sun 1972, 1991), but few of them discuss intergenerational relations. Other studies examine the welfare of the elderly (e.g., Chan, 1979; Hsiao, 1991; Hsiao, Chang, and Chen, 1983; Lee and Ellitherpe, 1982; L.-C. Shu, 1984), but most focus on the welfare system and social policies affecting the elderly population; few discuss the relations between the elderly and their families. There have also been studies on intergenerational relations from a psychological perspective (e.g., Chang, 1980; Hwang, 1984; Tsai, 1966; S.-J. Yang, 1980; Yen, 1980).

The purpose of this chapter is to analyze from a sociological viewpoint the changes in intergenerational relations of Chinese families during the modernization of Taiwan. The relations investigated include living arrangements, economic exchanges, mutual visiting, marriage arrangements, and parents' expectations for their children's education.

DATA AND METHOD

The data used in this study are from a series of fertility (KAP) surveys conducted by the Taiwan Provincial Institute of Family Planning. Six KAP surveys were conducted by the institute between 1965 and 1986; so as to compare the results of surveys having intervals of six to seven years and few missing data, we have selected for analysis those of 1967, 1973, 1980, and 1986. All of the surveys were based on probability samples of currently married women of childbearing ages (20–39) living in Taiwan Province, excluding the 20 so-called mountain townships (which contain only about 1 percent of the total population and are settled mostly by aborigines, who are Proto-Malay). Sample sizes ranged from 3,145 in the 1986 survey to 5,540 in the 1973 survey (Table 15.1).

Because the households surveyed excluded those with single, divorced, widowed, or older married women, they were not representative of all Taiwanese families. Most of the excluded households were single-parent families, of which there are few in Taiwan, and households consisting of elderly people living alone. Households with elderly people were included if the elderly individuals lived with married children. These limitations of the samples may pose some problems for generalizing the research findings, but the problems should not be serious.

The surveys asked the respondents about their family composition and related matters. The analysis covers a 19-year period, long enough to detect some changes and to foresee others. Since not all questions were identical in the various surveys, some comparisons over time are difficult to make, as will be noted in the findings section.

We employed 15 dependent variables to model the five types of intergenerational relations—that is, living arrangements, economic exchanges, mutual visiting, marriage arrangements, and parents' expectations for their children's education—between the respondents and their parents and children. The relations with parents represent past experience, whereas those with children represent expectations. Figure 15.1 identifies the 15

Table 15.1. Sample size for each KAP survey: Taiwan, 1967–86

Sample characteristics (currently married women)	1967 (KAP 2)	1973 (KAP 4)	1980 (KAP 5)	1986 (KAP 6)
Number in sample	4,989	5,588	3,859	4,312
Analysis sample (ages 20–39)	4,158	5,540	3,821	3,145
Husband's parents available at the time of marriage	3,441	5,193	3,617	2,907
Husband's parents available at the time of survey	3,096	4,030	3,046	2,721
Not living with husband's parents at the time of survey	2,312	3,283	2,273	2,014
Husband's parents living in Taiwan but not living with respondent	1,250	1,744	1,498	1,595

Source: Taiwan Provincial Institute of Family Planning.

Changes in Intergenerational Relations in the
Chinese Family: Taiwan's Experience

variables and shows their arrangement in the model.

Altogether, we selected 38 independent variables to represent the background characteristics of the respondent, her husband, her own parents and her husband's parents, the couple's marital situation, living environment, and family income and facilities. These 38 independent variables are listed in Exhibit 15.A.

Some pairs of the independent variables were found to have high contingency coefficients, since they were reclassifications of the same variable, and therefore we did not use them in the same analysis simultaneously. (We calculated the contingency coefficients of the pairs of these independent variables separately for each sample but do not show them here for lack of space.) Other pairs of independent variables, not surprisingly, also

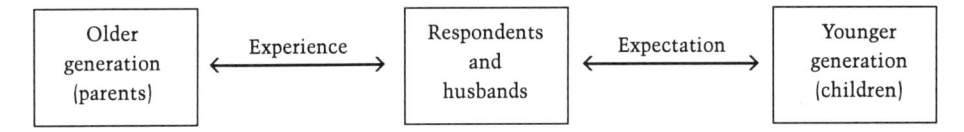

```
┌────────────┐              ┌────────────┐               ┌────────────┐
│   Older    │              │ Respondents│               │  Younger   │
│ generation │ ←Experience→ │    and     │ ←Expectation→ │ generation │
│  (parents) │              │  husbands  │               │ (children) │
└────────────┘              └────────────┘               └────────────┘
```

1. Living arrangement
   1-1 Living with husband's parents at time of first marriage
   1-2 Living arrangement of husband's parents at time of survey
   1-3 Whether living with husband's parents at time of survey

   1-4 Newlyweds should live with husband's parents
   1-5 Plan to live with children after their marriage

2. Economic exchange
   2-1 Sharing meals with husband's parents at time of survey
   2-2 Sharing meals with respondent's (wife's) parents at time of survey
   2-3 Exchange of money with husband's parents
   2-4 Exchange of money with wife's parents

   2-5 Expect children to contribute to family economy before marriage
   2-6 Will depend on children economically when old
   2-7 Source of living expenses when old

3. Mutual visits with husband's parents

4. Arrangement of respondent's marriage

5. Expected education of first child

Figure 15.1. The 15 dependent variables and their arrangement in the model of intergenerational relations: Taiwan

Te-Hsiung Sun and Yin-Hsing Liu

Exhibit 15.A. The 38 independent variables representing background characteristics of KAP respondent families: Taiwan

Age of respondent (wife) at time of survey
Respondent's age at first marriage
Respondent's year of first marriage
Duration of marriage (in months, years)
Respondent's age at most recent marriage
Year of most recent marriage
Respondent's education
Husband's education
Respondent's father's education
Husband's father's education
Respondent's frequency of newspaper reading
Husband's occupation
Respondent's father's occupation when the respondent was growing up
Husband's father's occupation when the husband was growing up
Respondent's work status at time of survey
Respondent's work experience before marriage
Respondent's work experience after marriage
Change of respondent's work status before and after marriage
Caretaker of children while respondent works outside
Relative index of total family income, (for comparability over time)
Relative index of per capita average family income (for comparability over time)
Relative index of modern durables owned
Ownership of home (own, dormitory, rented, other)
Owner of home (respondent and husband or husband's parents)
Respondent's ethnic background
Husband's ethnic background
Cross-classification of respondent's and husband's ethnic background
Religion of respondent
Ancestor worship
Traditional index of husband-wife relationship
Classification of sample township by urbanization
Respondent's rural experience (yes or no)
Respondent's rural experience (currently in rural township, ever, never)
Husband's rural experience (same as respondent's rural experience)
Whether respondent lives in the same township as husband's parents
Whether husband's parents live with respondent
Whether husband's parents live in Taiwan: (both in Taiwan, only one in Taiwan, neither)
Should newlyweds live with husband's parents?

had significantly high contingency coefficients. Examples are the respondent's age at the time of the survey and the duration of her marriage, the respondent's education and her husband's education, the husband's education and the husband's father's education, whether the husband's parents lived in Taiwan and the husband's ethnic background, the respondent's ethnic background and her husband's ethnic background, the husband's father's education when the husband was growing up and the husband's occupation, the respondent's education and the husband's occupation, the husband's education and his occupation, the respondent's education and a change in the respondent's work status before and after marriage, the respondent's religion and her ethnic background, the respondent's religion and her husband's ethnic background, whether the respondent practiced ancestor worship and her husband's ethnic background, the relative index of per capita family income and the respondent's education, and the relative index for per capita family income and husband's education. We have taken these into account when interpreting the results of the analysis. Their effects were found to persist even after the effect of the pairing was controlled. In most of the analyses, we included only those respondents whose husbands' parents were available (i.e., living in Taiwan).

We used multiple classification analysis (MCA) to analyze the effects of background characteristics and social change on intergenerational relations. MCA shows the relative importance of a factor after the factor is adjusted for the effects of other variables, and the results are shown as the deviation from the grand mean for each category before and after the adjustment.

FINDINGS

Changes in Living Arrangements and Attitudes toward Coresidence

In the traditional Chinese family, family members, especially parents and their children, lived together as long as objective conditions would permit. It was therefore common for three generations of family members to live in the same household. In an agricultural society, this arrangement was economical and one way to ensure the continuity of the family line. Coresidence also made it easier for the younger generation to take care of the elderly members of the family. The traditional view was that children should not live far from their parental home while their parents were still living, in part to spare their parents worry about the children's well-being.

This requirement can hardly be expected to be met in a modern society. With the transfer of family functions to other institutions, many activities today—education and work, for example—take place away from the home. Some adult children are thus unable to live with their elderly parents. Living apart would have been considered unfilial in the past, but recent changes in Taiwanese society have forced parents to accept the fact.

Living arrangements immediately after marriage In most Chinese families, when a son marries it is his parents' responsibility to prepare a room for the newlywed couple. Many parents yield the main bedroom to the eldest son upon his marriage and prepare new rooms for other sons when they marry. This custom indicates the strong desire that parents have for their sons to stay at home even after they marry. The expectation is especially strong in the case of the eldest son, who is expected to inherit the family's property and to support the parents in their old age.

Among the currently married women interviewed in the four KAP surveys, the great majority had had living parents-in-law when the respondents married, the percentages ranging from 83 to 95 percent, depending upon the survey. Of those who had once had living in-laws, 90 percent of respondents interviewed in 1967 had lived with them at some time during their own marriage. It is not known, however, how many of those respondents began their married life with the husband's parents because the 1967 survey did not ask respondents specifically about their living arrangements at the time of marriage. As for respondents to the later three surveys, the proportion of those who reported living with their in-laws immediately after marriage ranged from 78 percent in 1973 to 73 percent in 1980 and 1986. Although the proportion decreased over time, it was still quite high. Given the high housing prices in Taiwan, this result is not surprising; it is more economical for young couples to live with parents and commute to work than it is to live separately. Not only did many newly married couples live with the husband's parents at the time of marriage, but also many of them continued to coreside (Freedman et al., 1982:403). The proportion of couples living with the husband's parents immediately after marriage also decreased among later marriage cohorts (Table 15.2).

The proportion of couples living with parents can be affected by modernization or social change in three ways: (1) it may be lower among more modern social strata (strata effects, or differentials by strata); (2) it may decrease because of an increasing proportion of couples in the modern strata (compositional effects, or effects due to changes in composition); and (3) it may change within a stratum over time (substantive change, or effects due to changes within a stratum). These three kinds of effect can be seen in Table 15.3.

For example, the proportion was

Table 15.2. Newly married couples living with the husband's parents immediately after marriage, by marriage cohort (%): Taiwan 1952–86

Year of marriage	No. in sample	% living with husband's parents after marriage	Year of survey
1952–56	673	86.6	1973
1957–61	1,183	79.0	1973
1962–66	1,433	74.6	1973
1967–71	907	72.5	1980
1972–76	1,099	70.7	1980
1977–81	923	70.5	1986
1982–86	699	68.8	1986

Source: Taiwan KAP surveys, Taiwan Provincial Institute of Family Planning.

Changes in Intergenerational Relations in the
Chinese Family: Taiwan's Experience

Table 15.3. Newly married couples living with the husband's parents immediately after marriage, by survey year and selected characteristics (%): Taiwan 1973–86

Characteristics	1973 survey No.	1973 survey %	1980 survey No.	1980 survey %	1986 survey No.	1986 survey %
Husband's ethnicity/origin						
Fukenese	3,567	90.8	2,651	79.1	2,227	73.4
Hakka	638	89.7	437	76.0	415	72.0
Mainlander	868	18.4	400	25.8	148	62.2
Other/u	102	78.4	124	77.4	117	75.2
Wife's religion						
Buddhism/folk religion	4,694	81.9	3,256	75.4	2,625	73.1
Christianity	251	53.0	179	59.8	145	59.3
None/u	230	33.0	177	37.3	137	79.6
Ancestor worship						
The date of birth/death	2,719	88.6	2,028	82.3	1,506	79.0
Only in the spring	1,437	78.7	1,139	68.5	1,140	69.3
No	986	48.6	435	39.5	243	50.2
u	33	—	10	—	13	—
Rural experience						
Current	3,047	87.2	1,977	81.1	1,472	79.8
Ever	1,161	67.5	904	65.3	804	69.8
Never	967	63.3	731	59.5	631	60.0
Husband's education						
No schooling	359	89.4	103	84.5	29	79.3
Literate/primary (attended)	525	79.2	251	75.7	101	72.3
Primary (completed)	2,359	86.7	1,471	78.1	924	78.8
Junior high	704	73.9	512	73.8	578	73.0
Senior high	802	67.6	762	72.3	780	72.3
College+	426	48.6	513	53.2	495	61.4
Total	5,175	78.3	3,612	72.8	2,907	72.7

Source: Taiwan KAP surveys, Taiwan Provincial Institute of Family Planning.
u—data unavailable.

much higher among respondents who regularly worshipped their ancestors on the anniversary of the ancestors' birth or death than among those who did not practice ancestor worship. Whether the change over time was due to compositional or substantive effects is not clear, however, in this case. The compositional effect is clearer when we consider the change in the proportions reporting rural living experience between 1973 and 1980. But the compositional effect is compensated for by the rise in the proportion who lived with parents in cities (the modern strata). This is also the case with the husband's education, the net result of which is that changes in the proportion of newlyweds living with parents were small but the differences among social strata decreased over time, in part because the proportion of more-educated newlywed husbands living with parents rose while that of less-educated newlywed husbands living with parents fell. Similarly, differences in coresidence right after marriage by the husband's ethnicity were great, 91 percent among Fukenese but only 18 percent among mainlanders; but by 1986 the differences were reduced in the case of Fukenese and mainlanders to 73 percent and 62 percent, respectively. This convergence was due largely to modernization among the Fukenese but also to changes in mainlanders' attitudes about coresidence and improvements in their living conditions that enabled families to accommodate newlyweds. A lower proportion of Christian than of Buddhist respondents lived with their husbands' parents after marrying, possibly in part because the Bible prescribes that a husband leave his parents and live with his wife; Christians also have a more modern life style.

Our MCA analysis has revealed that, except for the level of urbanization, net effects were much smaller than gross effects. The wife's education and work experience and the husband's rural living experience had no significant effect on coresidence with the husband's parents immediately after marriage; but the effect of the wife's age, after being controlled for the effects of other variables, increased. Taken together, 11 factors—availability of the husband's parents for coresidence, husband's education, husband's ethnicity, forms of marriage arrangement, urbanization, husband's rural experience, husband's father's education, wife's age at marriage, wife's education, wife's work experience, and wife's age—explained 45 percent of the variance in immediate coresidence in 1973 and 28 percent in 1980.

Living arrangements at the time of the survey
Our analysis of current living arrangements focused on couples living with the husband's parents, husband's parents who lived alone, and couples living with the wife's parents.

Couples who were living with the husband's parents As expected, the proportion of respondents whose husbands' parents were still living, living in Taiwan, and living with the couple decreased over the survey years. Moreover, the decrease in coresidence seems to be accelerating. Thirteen independent variables representing the personal background and current (contextual) situation of the couples explained 12 to 19 percent of the variance in coresidence at the time of the surveys (Table 15.4). When the effects of each variable were adjusted for the effects of other variables, the net effect (R^2) was reduced somewhat but still remained within the range of 11 percent in 1967 to 18 percent in 1980. The Eta values of these independent variables for the four surveys were all significant at the 1 percent level. The relative importance of the variables, however, varied over the survey period (Table 15.5).

As expected, age and duration of

Changes in Intergenerational Relations in the
Chinese Family: Taiwan's Experience

Table 15.4. Couples living with the husband's parents at the time of the survey and the results of MCA for those whose husband's parents were available in Taiwan at the time of the survey, by survey year and selected variables (%): Taiwan, 1967–86

Independent variables	1967 Mean (%)	1967 Adjusted deviation[a]	1973 Mean (%)	1973 Adjusted deviation[a]	1980 Mean (%)	1980 Adjusted deviation[a]	1986 Mean (%)	1986 Adjusted deviation[a]
Wife's age								
20–24	70.6	6.4	61.5	2.5	60.4	5.0	54.7	8.3
25–29	64.3	3.0	55.8	.2	50.6	1.5	45.6	3.2
30–34	56.7	–.0	54.6	–2.2	46.6	–2.1	37.7	–1.7
35–39	48.5	–9.1	56.0	–.3	46.8	–5.4	31.4	–8.2
Eta or Beta value[b]	.1532	.1075	.0525	.0331	.1016	.0707	.1545	.1089
Duration of marriage								
< 2 years	77.9	11.0	62.4	5.3	59.5	5.6	56.6	8.4
2–4 years	66.5	1.8	58.3	1.4	53.9	2.4	44.7	–2.0
5–9 years	60.5	–.7	54.9	.3	48.0	–1.6	42.1	.1
10–14 years	56.4	–1.5	55.5	–1.2	47.0	–2.2	34.8	–2.0
15+ years	50.0	–2.5	56.8	–3.5	50.1	–2.2	36.1	.7
Eta or Beta value[b]	.1490	.0682	.0452	.0487	.0827	.0559	.1270	.0597
Husband's rural experience								
Current	62.4	.3	64.2	5.0	61.6	7.8	49.2	5.1
Ever	42.5	–12.2	31.6	–20.1	26.1	–20.7	27.0	–9.8
Never	61.8	5.1	57.6	3.4	48.4	.8	40.6	–.1
Eta or Beta value[b]	.1372	.1016	.2507	.1955	.2822	.2250	.1868	.1254
Wife's current work status								
Outside home	60.3	6.8	54.4	–.3	53.0	3.4	43.8	3.6
At home	62.6	–1.1	58.8	–1.8	45.1	–4.5	34.9	–5.9
Not working	56.3	–1.4	56.8	.9	51.8	–.3	43.0	.4
Eta or Beta value[b]	.0600	.0587	.0295	.0234	.0582	.0547	.0722	.0706
Husband's occupation								
Specialist/management	54.9	–8.1	48.3	–8.4	43.0	–5.3	36.4	–4.2
Sales/service	54.9	–5.8	49.7	–5.1	42.7	–6.2	31.3	–8.1
Technical/nontechnical	54.5	–2.2	51.5	–4.0	52.4	.8	43.5	1.3
Farming/fishing/forestry	68.5	9.1	76.5	17.5	73.9	16.4	62.7	19.2
None/u	(35.3)	(–23.4)	51.0	–10.3	58.6	4.8	40.3	–1.0
Eta or Beta value[b]	.1398	.1500	.2361	.2115	.2018	.1419	.1658	.1450
Availability of husband's married brothers								
No	62.3	3.8	68.7	11.7	66.1	14.2	59.6	15.9
Yes	58.4	–1.8	52.0	–4.8	45.8	–4.7	36.1	–4.6
Eta or Beta value[b]	.0371	.0542	.1529	.1508	.1750	.1628	.1992	.1741
Availability of husband's parents								
Both	62.3	.2	53.6	–4.1	49.1	–3.3	40.9	–1.7
Only one	56.6	–.3	61.1	5.5	53.9	5.6	42.3	3.2
Eta or Beta value[b]	.0578	.0053	.0748	.0952	.0463	.0864	.0140	.0475

Table 15.4. *(continued)*

Independent variables	1967 Mean (%)	1967 Adjusted deviation[a]	1973 Mean (%)	1973 Adjusted deviation[a]	1980 Mean (%)	1980 Adjusted deviation[a]	1986 Mean (%)	1986 Adjusted deviation[a]
Relative index of family income								
< 20 < m − 1 sd	59.9	−2.5	66.4	−1.5	66.3	2.5	47.4	1.6
20–24 < m − .5 sd	56.4	−6.0	59.3	−1.6	50.2	−1.2	46.4	3.4
25–29 < m	54.4	−5.8	52.0	−2.3	43.2	−6.6	42.0	1.5
30–34 > m	53.7	−4.1	44.3	−7.9	46.1	−3.2	36.2	−4.2
35–39 > m + .5 sd	59.5	2.1	48.2	−1.6	37.6	−8.6	36.1	−4.2
40–44 > m + 1 sd	63.4	6.5	57.8	6.7	57.6	6.7	37.4	−2.2
45+ > m + 1.5 sd	79.0	22.5	56.4	5.2	45.7	1.6	35.3	−2.3
u	82.9	17.4	70.7	9.6	66.1	11.4	46.0	3.4
Eta or Beta value[b]	.1715	.1877	.1655	.1057	.2033	.1409	.0944	.0627
Relative index of modern durables								
< 20 < m − 1 sd	40.0	−15.9	47.3	−20.1	54.9	−12.4	34.3	−15.1
20–24 < m − .5 sd	55.4	−6.6	55.5	−9.7	53.0	−7.9	38.2	−7.3
25–29 < m	62.2	.8	58.7	−1.4	48.3	−2.2	44.4	1.7
30–34 > m	65.1	7.2	55.7	3.9	52.0	4.3	40.9	2.5
35–39 > m + .5 sd	66.4	8.9	54.0	8.5	48.2	3.7	43.4	4.0
40–44 > m + 1 sd	57.1	2.8	59.0	17.1	45.9	6.4	40.1	5.8
45+ > m + 1.5 sd	61.3	8.0	59.0	15.3	54.3	17.2	44.6	10.3
Eta or Beta value[b]	.0988	.1290	.0487	.1720	.0553	.1592	.0596	.1242
Wife's education								
No schooling	62.3	4.3	65.7	7.6	58.2	4.8	48.1	5.1
Literate/primary (attended)	58.9	.5	53.8	−.9	63.3	9.1	36.7	−4.7
Primary (completed)	57.5	−3.5	56.0	−.8	51.2	1.7	41.1	1.5
Junior high	56.0	−3.5	49.0	−6.7	50.8	.0	43.4	−.9
Senior high	62.3	−6.1	49.8	−7.7	42.2	−9.8	41.8	−.7
College+	(44.4)	(−29.9)	39.0	−18.7	40.9	−9.7	36.0	−2.4
Eta or Beta value[b]	.0507	.0823	.1186	.1069	.1187	.1099	.0491	.0386
Wife's newspaper reading								
Every day	55.0	−11.2	46.7	−6.9	44.5	−3.6	39.3	−1.2
Often	51.7	−13.2	54.7	−.2	45.8	−1.0	39.9	.6
Weekly/less often	60.4	−.1	54.2	−.6	56.6	3.3	44.5	1.5
Never	61.6	4.6	60.4	4.6	58.5	2.1	47.3	2.6
Illiterate	60.6	2.6	63.3	1.1	59.4	7.6	47.1	2.2
Eta or Beta value[b]	.0504	.1081	.1302	.0874	.1350	.0784	.0596	.0289
Wife's ethnicity/origin								
Fukenese	59.2	.1	58.2	1.5	50.7	.4	42.0	.5
Hakka	66.1	1.7	52.7	−4.9	53.5	.8	43.2	1.5
Mainlander	58.1	−.7	47.9	−10.1	35.1	−8.2	33.1	−5.8
Other/u	30.5	−15.3	30.8	−25.2	62.6	−2.3	35.3	−5.9
Eta or Beta value[b]	.0966	.0450	.0819	.0843	.0775	.0341	.0497	.0394

Changes in Intergenerational Relations in the
Chinese Family: Taiwan's Experience

Table 15.4. *(continued)*

	1967		1973		1980		1986	
Independent variables	Mean (%)	Adjusted deviation[a]	Mean (%)	Adjusted deviation[a]	Mean (%)	Adjusted deviation[a]	Mean (%)	Adjusted deviation[a]
Husband's ethnicity/origin								
Fukenese	59.1	−.5	57.9	.0	50.6	.1	41.9	.8
Hakka	66.4	3.9	53.8	−1.1	53.3	−2.2	42.4	−2.5
Mainlander	56.9	3.8	56.2	8.3	38.7	−2.4	37.1	−1.2
Other/u	28.6	−15.3	36.8	−9.7	64.9	7.6	34.3	−4.6
Eta or Beta value[b]	.0964	.0515	.0632	.0432	.0771	.0347	.0360	.0300
Grand mean	59.6		56.8		50.9		41.4	
R^2	.1215	.1085	.1790	.1697	.1900	.1778	.1267	.1119

Source: Taiwan KAP surveys, Taiwan Provincial Institute of Family Planning.
Note: Numbers in parentheses indicate a base number less than 20.
u—data unavailable.
m—mean.
sd—standard deviation.
a. Adjusted deviation from grand mean in percentage points; adjusted for the effect of the other 12 variables.
b. Eta value for unadjusted mean; Beta value for adjusted deviation from grand mean.

Table 15.5. Relative importance of selected independent variables in explaining the proportion living with husband's parents at the time of the survey, by survey year, expressed in Eta and Beta values in an MCA: Taiwan, 1967–86

	Eta values				Beta values			
Independent variables	1967	1973	1980	1986	1967	1973	1980	1986
Wife's age	.15	.05	.10	.15	.11	.03	.07	.11
Duration of marriage	.15	.05	.08	.13	.07	.05	.06	.06
Wife's education	.05	.12	.12	.05	.08	.11	.11	.04
Wife's newspaper reading	.05	.13	.14	.06	.11	.09	.08	.03
Husband's rural experience	.14	.25	.28	.19	.10	.20	.23	.13
Wife's ethnicity/origin	.10	.08	.08	.05	.05	.08	.03	.04
Husband's ethnicity/origin	.10	.06	.08	.04	.05	.04	.03	.03
Wife's current work	.06	.03	.06	.07	.06	.02	.05	.07
Husband's occupation	.14	.24	.20	.17	.15	.21	.14	.15
Relative income index	.17	.17	.20	.09	.11	.11	.14	.06
Relative index for modern durables	.10	.05	.06	.06	.13	.17	.16	.12
Availability of husband's married brothers	.04	.15	.18	.20	.05	.15	.16	.17
Availability of husband's parents	.06	.07	.05	.01	.01	.10	.09	.05
R^2	.12	.18	.19	.13	.11	.17	.18	.11

Source: Taiwan KAP surveys, Taiwan Provincial Institute of Family Planning.

marriage were found to be negatively related to the proportion of coresiding couples; that is, the proportion declined as the wife's age and the number of years she had been married increased (Table 15.4). It had seemed likely that older couples would be not only more independent than younger ones, but also more likely to have other married brothers of the husband who could live with the elderly parents.

The husband's rural experience and occupation were very important in explaining whether the couple were coresiding with his parents at the time of each survey. The proportion of coresiding couples was especially low among those in which the husband had once lived in a rural area but now lived in an urban area. Apparently many parents did not follow their sons to the cities. On the other hand, the proportion of coresiding couples was especially high among those in which the husband was engaged in a primary industry, such as farming; these were the couples who remained in rural areas. It is noteworthy, however, that among couples in which the husband had no rural experience, the proportion of those who were coresiding at the time of the 1967 survey was almost as high as that among couples in which the husband had always lived in a rural area; but among that group the decrease in coresidence was faster than for those remaining in rural areas, widening the margin between the rural and urban couples.

Whether a husband had married brothers grew in importance in explaining recent coresidence with the husband's parents, reflecting the effect of Taiwan's fertility decline. Before 1970 or so, it was common for men to have brothers as a result of past high fertility, and therefore the effect of this factor on coresidence was minimal. The decline in fertility, however, reduced the availability of married brothers with whom parents could live and increased the importance of this factor in explaining differences in the proportion of coresiding respondent couples.

The availability of the husband's parents (both parents or one parent) proved to be a less important factor in determining coresidence, and its importance tended to decline over time because of parents' increasing longevity. Coresidence was more likely, though, if only one parent was available. Parents' ages also affected the proportion of coresiding couples (not shown in Table 15.4); in 1986 the proportion coresiding was 38 percent among couples in which the husband's father was 60–64 but nearly 47 percent among those in which the husband's father was 80 or older, after the effects of 10 other variables were taken into account.

In 1967 coresidence with the husband's parents was more common among couples with higher incomes than among those with lower incomes, and the proportion was particularly high among the highest-income couples ($N = 338$). This finding seems to support the argument that only the well-to-do can afford to maintain an extended family. The proportion of better-off couples who were coresiding, however, was much lower by 1973, and by 1986 the trend was reversed; that is, among couples with higher incomes, smaller proportions were living with the husband's parents than was the case among lower-income couples.

Rising living standards may have also contributed to the changing patterns of coresidence. According to the KAP surveys, absolute total family income increased in the sample households by 187 percent over the 1976–86 period, from NT$90,600 to NT$260,500 (all in 1986 values). The proportion of couples owning houses rose from 40 percent in 1980 to 45 percent in 1986 (Council for Economic Planning and Development, 1988). In Taiwan as a whole the proportion of families who owned their homes rose from 67 percent in 1976 to 78 percent in 1986. In 1986 the proportion of couples living with the husband's parents was as high as 82 percent if the husband's parents owned the house but only 31 percent if the couple were the homeowners. These findings suggest that coresidence among higher-income couples declined over the period of the surveys because such couples could afford to buy their own homes and live independently.

On the other hand, we found a high positive correlation, especially in 1973 and 1980, between the proportion of couples living with the husband's parents and their ownership of modern durables. This finding is contrary to our hypothesis that families owning more modern durables would be more modern themselves than other families and therefore less likely to live with the husband's parents. It is not clear, however, which variable is the cause and which is the effect. It may be that coresiding families need more modern durables than do other families, or that coresiding families can afford more durables because they have more discretionary income as a result of sharing housing costs.

We hypothesized that the direction of causality might be clarified by considering the relationship between coresidence on the one hand and education and frequency of newspaper reading on the other. Coresidence was significantly less common among couples in which the wife had a better education or read a newspaper frequently than it was among other couples, especially in 1973 and 1980. The effects of education and newspaper reading became much weaker, however, especially in 1986, when they were adjusted for the effects of other variables. Literacy is becoming less of a marker of modernization in Taiwan as more of the population becomes educated.

The proportions coresiding also differed somewhat by ethnicity but declined over time, especially in 1980 and 1986, in all groups except the residual category. When its effects were adjusted for the effects of other variables, the effect of the wife's ethnicity remained but that of the husband was reduced. Our interpretation is that mainlander wives had more difficulty living with their husbands' parents than did wives of other ethnic groups, owing to differences in custom and possibly other factors.

Couples in which the wife worked outside the home were more likely to be coresiding when the effects of other factors were held constant. Unfortunately, a question about couples' childcare arrangements was asked only in the 1986 survey. Responses to that question revealed that 71 percent of couples whose children were cared for by the husband's parents were coresiding, compared with only 39 percent of couples who had to take care of their children themselves. Thus, the willingness of parents to take care of their grandchildren affects coresidence in Taiwan and appears to be an important factor in sustaining the extended family.

In sum, these results indicate that the proportion of coresiding couples has been decreasing faster during recent years than earlier and that the proportions were lower among migrants from rural to urban areas, couples in which the husband had married brothers who could share the responsibility of caring for the elderly parents, those with higher incomes and better education and who read newspapers more often, and couples in which the wife was a mainlander; but for couples in which the wife worked outside the home and the husband's parents were helping with childcare the proportion was higher. The effects of these variables on the proportions of couples who were coresiding increased in 1973 and 1980 but declined in 1986.

Husbands' parents who were living alone In the traditional Chinese family it was unusual for a couple with married children to live alone. The 1973 Taiwan KAP survey, however, revealed that 20 percent of husbands' parents were living alone even though they had at least one married son. This proportion increased to 31 percent in 1986 (Table 15.6).

The proportions of such parents were higher among couples with modern characteristics—that is, with higher education, more frequent newspaper reading, and more modern occupations. The parents-in-law of wives from the Chinese mainland were much more likely to be living alone, but the parents of farmers and fishermen and of couples who lived in a house owned by the parents were much less likely to be living by themselves. Nevertheless, the proportions of respondents who reported that their in-laws lived alone generally increased from 1973 to 1986. This trend indicates that older parents are becoming more independent and their children have more freedom than in the past.

The change is probably related to the economic development of Taiwan and the democratization of the Chinese family. It is also related to Taiwan's growing urbanization, which makes it more difficult for parents to live with their married children. The proportion of husbands' parents currently living in rural areas who were living alone was only 16 percent, but

Table 15.6. Husband's parents living alone, by survey year and selected variables (%): Taiwan, 1973–86

Independent variable	1973	1980	1986
Wife's education			
No schooling	15.3	14.1	26.0
Literate/primary (attended)	19.3	17.7	26.6
Primary (completed)	20.3	23.1	28.4
Junior high	23.3	25.7	34.9
Senior high	26.5	32.6	33.7
College+	42.9	31.5	36.9
Wife's newspaper reading			
Every day	26.8	27.4	33.8
Often	20.0	30.3	31.1
Weekly/less often	22.9	24.1	29.4
Never	17.3	20.0	23.9
Illiterate	16.0	13.2	24.4
Wife's ethnicity/origin			
Fukenese	19.1	23.2	31.1
Hakka	21.8	22.7	28.8
Mainlander	42.5	50.0	40.7
Other/u	29.2	18.7	33.6
Husband's rural experience			
Current	16.1	19.2	28.2
Ever	32.0	33.5	38.0
Never	21.3	26.6	31.1
Husband's occupation			
Specialist/management	23.4	28.7	35.1
Sales/service	23.4	26.7	34.4
Technical/nontechnical	24.1	23.3	30.6
Farming/fishing/forestry	10.0	10.3	18.3
None/u	15.7	27.6	26.4
Availability of husband's parents			
Both	23.5	27.8	35.7
Only one	15.4	17.7	23.5
Ownership of home			
Husband's parents	u	4.6	10.6
Couple	u	24.0	34.7
Dormitory (free)	u	32.5	41.7
Rented by couple	u	47.4	50.4
Other/u	u	32.1	39.6
Grand mean	20.1	24.0	31.4

Source: Taiwan KAP surveys, Taiwan Provincial Institute of Family Planning.
u—data unavailable.

among those who had moved from rural to urban areas (those who had ever lived in a rural area) the proportion living alone was twice as high. The difference between the two groups was somewhat smaller in 1986 but still substantial (28 percent and 38 percent, respectively).

When we controlled the effects of the 13 variables listed in Table 15.4 by means of the MCA method, the effects of most variables in Table 15.6 were reduced greatly. The two exceptions were home ownership and the husband's rural experience, which continued to have strong effects on whether parents lived alone. Urbanization will inevitably increase in Taiwan, and more young people will move from rural to urban areas. This process will increase the proportion of elderly parents who live alone. Since the elderly population is growing and so is life expectancy, the living conditions of the elderly in Taiwan may become a social problem requiring serious attention unless their economic situation improves greatly.

The 1986 survey results show that the proportion of parents living alone differed by age group. Among parents 60–64 years of age, the proportion was 37 percent, but even among those aged 70–74 it was 21 percent. It is difficult for many people of ages 70 and older to live alone. They need to be cared for by someone. If their children will not or cannot accept this responsibility, then the government may be required to provide the necessary care.

Couples who were living with the wife's parents For traditional Chinese parents it used to be a source of embarrassment to live with their married daughters because it meant that their sons were either unfilial or did not have the economic means to support them. The custom of patrilocal coresidence appears to have been stronger on the Chinese mainland than in Taiwan, however, where there were few women during the island's early stage of development and opportunities for men to marry were limited. As Barclay (1954:229) has noted, matrilocal marriages were common during the colonial era but gradually became less so; 21 percent of registered marriages in Taiwan were matrilocal in 1906, but by 1943 only 6.2 percent were matrilocal. When the first Taiwan KAP survey was conducted in 1967, only 5.1 percent of sampled couples who could reside with the wife's parents (because the wife's parents were living in Taiwan) were doing so. Not all of those couples had lived matrilocally as newlyweds. The proportion of surveyed couples who were currently living with the wife's parents declined further over the survey period, to 4.9 percent in 1973, 4.0 percent in 1980, and 3.4 percent in 1986. Among couples in which the wife's parents were living in Taiwan and the couples were not living with the husband's parents, the proportion living with the wife's parents was somewhat higher (8.3 percent) in 1967, but it too decreased gradually, to 5.3 percent by 1986 (Table 15.7).

Those most likely to be coresiding with the wife's parents were young couples, especially those in which the wife was in her early 20s; those in which the husband was illiterate; those in which the wife had never lived in a rural area; and those in which the wife worked outside the home. This combination of characteristics is puzzling, and it is difficult to imagine a family that would have all of them. One possibility is that some of the couples who were living with the wife's parents consisted of retired soldiers from the mainland who were married to young Taiwanese women. Many soldiers who had left the mainland for Taiwan after the Communists took over mainland China were illiterate but managed to save some money and eventually married Taiwanese women much younger than themselves; they naturally lived with their wives' parents since their own parents were either no longer living or lived on the mainland. A different profile can be assumed for those matrilocally coresiding couples in which the wife worked outside the home and had never lived in a rural area; such couples were likely to be less tradition-bound than others.

Attitudes toward Coresidence

The KAP surveys also probed respondents' attitudes toward traditional coresidential living arrangements. In particular, respondents were asked whether they preferred to live with their married sons and whether they thought newlywed

Changes in Intergenerational Relations in the
Chinese Family: Taiwan's Experience

Table 15.7. Couples living with the wife's parents at the time of the survey, among those with the wife's parents living in Taiwan and who were not living with the husband's parents, by survey year and selected variables (%): Taiwan, 1967–86

Independent variable	1967 No.	1967 %	1973 No.	1973 %	1980 No.	1980 %	1986 No.	1986 %
Wife's age at interview								
20–24	267	15.0	554	11.7	295	10.2	200	8.5
25–29	606	9.4	829	9.5	688	7.1	503	7.2
30–34	714	8.4	910	6.3	599	5.7	630	3.5
35–39	721	4.9	915	6.3	527	4.9	518	4.4
Husband's education								
No schooling	301	15.3	227	11.0	69	11.6	28	17.9
Literate/primary (attended)	253	7.9	350	8.0	171	7.0	70	4.3
Primary (completed)	1,000	6.9	1,276	8.9	795	6.8	602	4.7
Junior high	308	5.8	438	7.3	314	4.8	362	4.7
Senior high	308	7.1	581	5.3	409	6.1	456	5.0
College+	138	12.3	336	8.9	351	7.1	333	6.6
Wife's rural experience								
Current	1,470	8.5	1,617	9.1	989	8.1	826	5.6
Ever	478	6.3	893	3.8	643	4.2	580	3.1
Never	360	10.3	698	11.2	477	6.7	445	7.4
Wife's current work status								
Outside home	359	12.8	668	12.0	655	9.9	566	7.1
At home	777	8.2	719	6.7	431	3.9	469	3.0
Not working	1,172	7.0	1,821	7.2	1,023	5.6	816	5.4
Grand mean	2,308	8.3	3,208	8.1	2,109	6.6	1,851	5.3

Source: Taiwan KAP surveys, Taiwan Provincial Institute of Family Planning.

couples should live with the husband's parents.

Preference for living with married sons The question about respondents' preference for living with their married sons was worded somewhat differently in each survey. In the 1967 survey all respondents were asked "Do you want to live with your children and grandchildren when you are old?" Similarly, in the 1973 and 1980 surveys all respondents were asked "Do you want to live with your children when they are grown up and married?" In the 1986 survey, however, the question was asked somewhat differently of respondents with no sons, those with unmarried sons, and those with married sons but whose sons were not living with them. Because of this difference, we expected the proportion of respondents wanting to live with their married sons would be higher in the 1986 survey results than in the earlier surveys because the number of "uncertain" cases was reduced.

The proportion of respondents who wanted to live with their married sons in the future decreased from 87 percent to 41 percent between 1967 and 1980 but rose slightly (and possibly artifactually), to 46 percent, in 1986 (Table 15.8). Conversely, the proportion of couples who did *not* want to live with their married sons in the future rose sharply over the period, from 4.4 percent to 32 percent. The proportion answering "uncertain" also rose, from 8.7 percent in 1967 to nearly 47 percent in 1980 (not shown in Table 15.8). Although the proportion answering "uncertain" fell to 22 percent in 1986, this was likely due to a difference in the wording of the questions. With the "uncertain" cases excluded from the sample, the proportions wanting to live with married sons in the future were 95 percent in 1967, 86 percent in 1973, 76 percent in 1980, and 59 percent in 1986, indicating a significant decrease having important policy implications over the 19-year period. The high proportions of respondents who were uncertain about their attitudes toward coresidence in 1973 and 1980 may be indicative of a period of normative transition.

The proportion of couples wanting or not wanting to live with married sons in the future was strongly associated with modernization factors (Table 15.8). Differences in responses by degree of modernization were especially pronounced in 1967. For example, in that year 94 percent of illiterate respondents wanted eventually to live with their married sons, whereas only 30 percent of college-educated women wanted to do so. The proportion of respondents who did *not* want to live with their married sons was even more strongly (and positively) associated with the wife's educational level. That proportion decreased somewhat among better-educated women in 1973 and 1980 but rose substantially again in 1986, and among every educational group the rise was pronounced over the period of the surveys. The same trend was found in the case of newspaper reading.

The desire to live with married sons was also inversely associated with the degree of urbanization, but proportions of respondents having that desire declined in every residential area between 1967 and 1986. In contrast, the proportions of respondents who did not want to live with their married sons rose substantially in every residential group, and by 1986 the proportion not wanting to live with their sons exceeded the proportion wanting to do so among respondents living in large cities.

Similarly, the association between the desire to live with sons on one hand and husband's occupational level and personal income on the other showed a negative and salient trend. By 1986, substantially more wives of specialists or managers (40 percent) and respondents with the highest per capita family income, indexed at 45 or higher, (55 percent), preferred not to reside with their married sons than wished to reside with them (36 percent and 23 percent, respectively).

Changes in Intergenerational Relations in the
Chinese Family: Taiwan's Experience

Table 15.8. Couples wanting and not wanting to live with their married sons in the future, by survey year and selected variables (%): Taiwan, 1967–86

Independent variables	% wanting to live with married sons				% not wanting to live with married sons			
	1967	1973	1980	1986	1967	1973	1980	1986
Wife's education								
No schooling	93.8	72.2	58.5	74.7	.4	2.3	2.7	11.0
Literate/primary (attended)	91.7	61.9	45.7	65.7	1.4	4.8	4.3	18.8
Primary (completed)	87.3	55.5	43.5	54.5	3.5	8.8	8.7	24.3
Junior high	63.7	38.2	37.3	42.6	17.6	20.6	16.2	34.1
Senior high	47.1	22.8	24.5	30.4	33.1	27.9	28.2	43.6
College+	30.0	17.0	15.4	21.6	50.0	31.1	37.0	56.8
Eta value	.3491	.2748	.2207	.2765	.3895	.2536	.2918	.2442
Frequency of newspaper reading								
Every day	60.8	36.9	31.7	35.7	21.0	20.7	20.1	40.4
Often	82.9	46.5	36.5	44.3	7.3	9.9	13.2	30.7
Weekly/less often	86.9	50.6	43.2	55.8	4.2	11.3	7.9	23.8
Never	90.7	62.0	49.0	74.7	.8	5.6	5.2	11.2
Illiterate	93.2	71.4	57.6	74.4	.6	2.1	3.0	10.1
Eta value	.3243	.2659	.1947	.2723	.3388	.2473	.2191	.2266
Type of sample area								
Large city	80.4	51.0	27.6	36.5	8.5	13.7	21.7	42.2
Small city	83.8	42.9	36.6	43.6	4.8	12.2	16.2	35.4
Urban township	84.7	59.5	47.0	52.9	5.8	8.3	4.5	26.3
Rural township	92.8	64.1	50.0	52.7	.9	4.8	8.2	23.3
Eta value	.1492	.1497	.1916	.1429	.1480	.1290	.2053	.1709
Husband's occupation								
Specialist/management	72.1	43.2	31.5	35.9	12.8	17.1	20.2	40.2
Sales/service	88.7	51.8	46.0	45.9	3.0	9.1	9.0	33.7
Technical/nontechnical	91.7	60.3	43.6	50.7	1.6	6.6	8.9	27.0
Farming/fishing/forestry	94.2	71.6	55.9	69.5	.5	1.7	2.2	14.1
None/u	(84.2)	56.7	43.5	51.5	(5.3)	8.9	21.7	31.3
Eta value	.2673	.2177	.1687	.2114	.2491	.2061	.2009	.1819
Relative index of per capita family income								
< 20 < m – 1 sd	100.0	65.9	59.0	66.2	.0	1.6	5.2	20.4
20–24 < m – .5 sd	93.6	69.7	49.8	55.5	.6	3.9	5.2	22.0
25–29 < m	91.0	62.2	43.2	48.0	1.8	5.8	10.2	29.7
30–34 > m	86.8	49.5	32.6	37.9	2.9	11.8	16.5	37.5
35–39 > m + .5 sd	78.0	41.8	32.4	37.2	11.5	17.8	18.3	41.7
40–44 > m + 1 sd	69.6	40.1	21.4	29.3	16.5	15.9	27.9	44.4
45+ > m + 1.5 sd	59.8	29.1	22.4	23.4	21.7	27.6	35.8	55.0
u	94.2	57.0	42.4	51.3	1.2	7.3	10.1	28.2
Eta value	.2718	.2306	.1822	.2067	.2908	.2231	.2386	.2002
Wife's religion								
None	71.1	35.6	22.3	38.1	10.1	25.9	31.0	39.9
Buddhism/folk religion	88.2	58.3	42.5	46.6	3.7	7.8	11.1	31.1

Table 15.8. *(continued)*

	% wanting to live with married sons				% not wanting to live with married sons			
Independent variables	1967	1973	1980	1986	1967	1973	1980	1986
Christianity	73.8	42.6	27.2	45.1	12.9	18.4	21.5	37.0
Eta value	.1319	.1139	.1087	.0389	.1120	.1491	.1429	.0500
Wife's ethnicity/origin								
Fukenese	87.1	57.1	41.1	46.6	4.1	8.8	12.3	31.9
Hakka	90.2	58.1	46.6	49.8	3.2	7.7	7.7	26.0
Mainlander	58.6	26.4	16.2	24.4	21.9	28.9	35.8	50.6
Other/u	95.7	63.0	41.6	51.0	1.1	3.7	7.5	26.8
Eta value	.1566	.1062	.1147	.1061	.1539	.1221	.1616	.1061
Should newlyweds live with husband's parents?								
Yes	u	74.3	62.4	66.0	u	3.7	5.5	17.4
Depends/u	u	30.4	25.3	36.7	u	8.5	7.1	26.0
No	u	37.0	29.6	29.0	u	25.9	31.3	56.9
Eta value	u	.4118	.3518	.3307	u	.2935	.3281	.3601
Grand mean	86.8	56.5	40.7	46.1	4.4	9.1	12.6	31.8

Source: Taiwan KAP surveys, Taiwan Provincial Institute of Family Planning.
Note: Numbers in parentheses indicate a base number less than 20.
u—data unavailable.
m—mean.
sd—standard deviation.

Women of Buddhist or traditional (folk) religious beliefs were more likely to want to live with their married sons than were Christian women or women with no religious belief. Moreover, the proportions not wanting to live with their sons in the future rose substantially in every religious group over the period of the four surveys. As for ethnicity, Hakkas were most likely and mainlanders least likely to express a desire to live with their married sons in each survey year, but the proportions not wishing to live with married sons rose sharply in each group over the survey period.

All of the relationships discussed above remained quite strong even after we controlled for the effects of other variables. In sum, even taking into consideration the differences in the wording of the questions, the results suggest that fewer Taiwanese parents, especially more modern parents, will want to live with their married sons in the future than has been the case in the past.

Attitudes toward the living arrangements of newlywed couples Attitudes toward living with married sons in the future were strongly and positively associated with another attitudinal variable, whether newlywed couples should live with the husband's parents immediately after marriage or not. It should be noted that not

Changes in Intergenerational Relations in the
Chinese Family: Taiwan's Experience

Table 15.9. Couples believing that newlywed couples should live alone immediately after marriage, by survey year and selected variables: Taiwan, 1973–86

	1973		1980		1986	
Independent variable	Mean (%)	Adj. dev.[a]	Mean (%)	Adj. dev.[a]	Mean (%)	Adj. dev.[a]
Wife's education						
No schooling	9.6	−4.7	15.7	−4.9	15.9	−7.4
Literate/primary (attended)	18.0	.8	16.3	−4.8	20.3	−7.2
Primary (completed)	19.4	.6	22.3	−.5	24.7	−3.1
Junior high	29.3	3.6	28.6	2.6	33.5	2.5
Senior high	41.3	7.0	39.8	7.5	37.4	4.7
College+	50.5	6.9	42.7	−.0	42.8	7.2
Eta or Beta value[b]	.2216	.0823	.1921	.0834	.1577	.0957
Husband's occupation						
Specialist/management	27.9	1.7	32.3	2.3	33.1	−.6
Sales/service	17.5	−2.4	23.5	−.5	31.0	1.0
Technical/nontechnical	17.3	−1.0	22.0	−.8	28.0	.5
Farming/fishing/forestry	10.8	−.5	13.6	−4.9	20.4	−2.2
None/u	24.4	4.7	31.1	5.5	36.4	7.3
Eta or Beta value[b]	.1650	.0375	.1490	.0556	.0898	.0345
Wife's religion						
None/u	41.7	10.3	45.1	7.2	32.0	−2.0
Buddhism/folk religion	17.6	−.7	23.3	−.7	28.9	−.5
Christianity	32.7	4.0	38.1	4.8	44.4	11.1
Eta or Beta value[b]	.1478	.0620	.1281	.0466	.0760	.0572
Wife's ethnicity/origin						
Fukenese	18.2	−.2	24.4	.3	28.7	−.4
Hakka	19.6	−1.2	21.0	−5.4	28.3	−2.6
Mainlander	50.3	10.6	46.2	5.2	44.8	6.3
Other/u	20.7	−.4	27.8	5.7	35.4	6.0
Eta or Beta value[b]	.1358	.0472	.1107	.0576	.0838	.0486
Living arrangement of husband's parents						
With respondent	13.0	−3.7	19.0	−3.9	23.5	−5.6
With husband's married brother	22.9	2.2	29.1	1.9	33.1	2.8
Alone	23.7	1.4	31.6	2.0	37.0	4.9
u	24.7	3.4	27.3	4.0	26.2	.1
Eta or Beta value[b]	.1373	.0800	.1207	.0755	.1250	.0974
Grand mean		19.4		25.1		29.8

Source: Taiwan KAP surveys, Taiwan Provincial Institute of Family Planning.
a. Adjusted deviation from grand mean. Adjustment was made for other four variables listed in this table plus wife's age, husband's education, per capita family income, and traditional relationship index, which are not included in this table due to their small effects, and for simplification of the table.
b. Eta for unadjusted mean; Beta for adjusted deviation.
u—data unavailable.

all of those who thought that newlyweds should live with the husband's parents wanted to live with their own married sons in the future, and some of those who thought that newlyweds should *not* live with the husband's parents did nevertheless want to live with their married sons in the future.

The 1986 survey found that although more than 73 percent of our sample couples lived with the husbands' parents immediately after marriage, only 40 percent of them thought that newlywed couples should do so. (The proportions holding that view were 56 percent in 1973 and 39 percent in 1980.) In contrast, the proportion of couples who thought that newlywed couples should live alone increased steadily over the survey period, from 19 percent to 30 percent (Table 15.9). This proportion was positively associated with the wife's education and the husband's occupational level, and the positive association remained even after the effects of other variables were controlled.

The proportion holding this view increased in all educational and occupational categories between 1973 and 1986, with the exception of senior high school and college graduates, indicating that the custom for couples to start married life with the husbands' parents has begun to change quite rapidly in the process of Taiwan's modernization and is likely to continue in the future. Young people will therefore have more freedom to choose where to live after marrying. If they start their married life elsewhere than in the home of the husband's parents, they are less likely to coreside with the husband's parents later on. But it is possible that the husband's parents will move in with the children when the parents reach old age.

The proportion of respondents expressing the view that newlyweds should live alone was especially low among Buddhists and those holding traditional religious beliefs, and especially high among mainlanders. As might be expected, relatively few wives who were currently living with their husbands' parents thought that newlyweds should live alone, and relatively more wives were who not coresiding approved of newlyweds living on their own. These relationships were maintained even after we adjusted for the effects of other variables (Table 15.9).

Changes in Economic Relations

Another important relationship between two generations is economic. It includes such things as the sharing of meals, money flows, and old-age support. In the traditional Chinese family, two adult generations not only lived together but also ate together and shared their properties. We have seen in the previous section that this arrangement has become less common in recent years among Taiwanese families, especially the more modern families. The question we address in this section is, Will the economic relations between generations be strengthened to compensate for this social change?

Sharing of meals It is common for Chinese parents to share meals with their married sons, especially when they live together. Even when the two generations live separately, the parents may arrange to come to the eldest son's house for meals if they live nearby. It is also common for parents to rotate sharing meals among their married sons' homes.

Our survey data show that most parents who were living with their married sons also ate with them. Of those couples who were living with the husband's parents, only 7.2 percent in 1967, 7.5 percent in 1973, 5.9 percent in 1980, and 1.5 percent in 1986 were eating separately. The decrease in separate eating arrangements may be related to the fact that over time parents in Taiwan have had fewer sons to share meals with, owing to the country's fertility decline; it may also be related to an improvement in living standards.

The proportion of all couples who regularly ate together with the husband's parents fell from 52 percent in 1967 to 49 percent in 1973, 45 percent in 1980, and 40 percent in 1986. Since the differences in proportions living together and eating together were small in each survey year, the differentials in proportions living together and the proportions eating together by social stratum were quite similar. Therefore, a discussion of findings about the sharing of meals is omitted. We should note, however, that the association (either positive or negative) between the proportion eating together and several independent variables was much stronger than the association observed between the proportion living together and the same independent variables. Those variables included family income, number of modern durables owned, availability of the husband's married brothers, and duration of marriage. That is, couples who were economically well-to-do, owned more modern durables, had no married brothers available, and had married more recently were more likely than others to share meals with the husband's parents. We should also note that the proportion of respondent couples sharing meals with the wife's parents was almost the same as the proportion living with the wife's parents.

Money flow In an agricultural society, child rearing is relatively inexpensive and children usually work, contributing to the family's economy. Thus there is a net flow of wealth from children to their parents as the children are growing up. In contemporary Taiwanese society, in contrast, it is quite expensive to raise children, and few children can contribute significantly to the family's economy before reaching adulthood. Therefore wealth flows mainly from parents to children. After the children marry, however, the direction of the wealth flow is mainly from children to parents. The wealth flow represents a bond that can strengthen a parent-child relationship weakened by separate living arrangements.

Our analysis of the survey data has

focused on four types of money flow after children's marriage: (1) the proportion of married couples who constantly gave money to the husband's parents or who shared their meals with them, (2) the proportion of couples who ever received money from the husband's parents, (3) the proportion who ever gave money to the wife's parents or shared their meals with them, and (4) the proportion who ever received money from the wife's parents. Our analysis, summarized in Table 15.10, is limited to couples whose parents were currently living in Taiwan in 1973, 1980, and 1986.

The proportion of couples who frequently gave money to the husband's parents or shared meals with them remained fairly consistent, at 65–67 percent. The slight decrease in the proportion sharing meals was compensated by the increase in the proportion (shown in parentheses) who frequently gave money to the husband's parents. We are not sure whether the respondent couples paid for all the meals shared with the husband's parents, though it is customary for the married son to pay for meals shared with his parents. This point needs further investigation.

Only 12–15 percent of the married couples surveyed ever received money from the husbands' parents after marriage. The proportion receiving money from the wife's parents was also low (8.4–16 percent) but increased slightly over the 13-year period.

The proportion of respondent couples who ever gave money to the wife's parents or shared meals with them rose sharply, from 19 to 53 percent, between 1973 and 1986. As discussed earlier, the proportion of couples who were

Table 15.10. Changes in four types of money flow between married children and their parents, by survey year: Taiwan, 1973–86

	1973		1980		1986	
Type of money flow	Sample size	%	Sample size	%	Sample size	%
Constantly giving money to husband's parents (or sharing meals with them)	4,003	64.9 (15.6)	3,038	67.1 (22.1)	2,685	64.5 (24.6)
Ever received money from husband's parents	4,003	12.5	3,038	14.9	2,685	13.3
Ever gave money to husband's parents (or shared meals with them)	5,508	18.9 (14.8)	3,600	43.0 (39.7)	3,012	53.1 (49.4)
Ever received money from wife's parents	5,508	8.4	3,600	14.6	3,012	15.8

Source: Taiwan KAP surveys, Taiwan Provincial Institute of Family Planning.

Note: Percentages in parentheses are the balance after percentages of respondents sharing meals have been subtracted.

Changes in Intergenerational Relations in the Chinese Family: Taiwan's Experience

living with the wife's parents was small (less than 5 percent) and stable. But Table 15.10 shows a significant rise over the 13-year period in the proportion who ever gave money to the wife's parents, indicating important changes in women's status. In the traditional Chinese family system, such behavior was regarded as unfaithful to the husband's family because once a daughter married, she belonged to her husband's family and was not expected to visit her own parents often or to send them money.

As mentioned earlier, the proportions of couples currently living with the husband's parents were significantly lower among older couples, those with higher income, those who had migrated from rural to urban areas, and those with married brothers available. As Table 15.11 shows, however, socioeconomic differences made little difference in the proportions who were supporting the husband's parents by frequently giving them money or by sharing meals with them. That is, the decline over time in proportions living together or eating meals together were made up for by higher proportions who were giving money to the parents. The proportions providing such support for the husband's parents were higher among older couples, those married for longer periods, those with higher incomes, those who had moved from rural to urban areas, and those in which the husband had married brothers. Such couples were less likely than others to live or eat with the husband's parents, but they compensated for their unfilial social behavior by giving the parents monetary support. This behavioral change is related to economic development and urbanization, and it is likely to continue and even be accelerated. Who will take care of the daily needs of elderly parents in the future is an important question in this context, especially given the prospect of a rapidly increasing elderly population.

Younger, more recently married, and lower-income couples were more likely than other couples to be receiving money from the husband's or wife's parents or from both sets of parents (data not shown). But the differentials were not substantial except in the case of the wife's age. For example, in 1986 the proportions receiving such support ranged from 20 percent among couples in which the wife was in her early 20s to 7 percent among those in which the wife was 35–39.

More modern couples (those in which the wife frequently read a newspaper or worked outside the home) and those with higher incomes were more likely than others to have ever given money to the wife's parents or to share meals with them (Table 15.12). Nevertheless, the proportions of couples giving such support to the wife's parents rose substantially in all strata between 1973 and 1986, indicating that this behavior is becoming universally accepted. The change may be related to growing equality between men and women and to the increased participation of women in the economic sphere.

Table 15.11. Couples frequently giving money to the husband's parents or sharing meals with them, by selected variables and survey year (%): Taiwan, 1973–86

	% frequently giving money to husband's parents or sharing meals with them			% frequently giving money to husband's parents		
Independent variables	1973	1980	1986	1973	1980	1986
Wife's age						
20–24	70.9	74.2	71.4	14.5	18.4	15.7
25–29	64.1	66.0	65.4	14.8	21.3	22.0
30–34	63.1	66.2	63.8	16.8	25.8	27.4
35–39	61.7	63.1	59.4	15.9	23.1	30.5
Duration of marriage						
< 2 years	75.9	76.1	73.9	16.2	18.2	17.3
2–4 years	69.5	71.9	68.0	17.4	22.8	22.6
5–9 years	62.4	64.3	63.3	14.5	22.8	23.6
10–14 years	62.2	62.5	63.3	15.5	23.4	30.4
15+ years	61.1	64.3	57.9	14.9	21.2	25.0
Relative index of total family income						
< 20 < m – 1 sd	58.9	62.1	62.0	7.5	11.8	19.4
20–24 < m – .5 sd	58.6	62.9	63.2	12.4	21.5	18.4
25–29 < m	61.4	62.3	64.8	16.1	26.2	25.0
30–34 > m	59.9	64.4	61.9	19.7	21.9	27.4
35–39 > m + .5 sd	68.8	62.7	65.2	22.4	26.6	28.7
40–44 > m + 1 sd	72.3	82.0	71.0	14.5	25.7	33.0
45+ > m + 1.5 sd	78.8	73.7	73.7	24.1	29.5	38.5
Husband's rural experience						
Current	67.6	72.8	68.9	13.5	20.0	23.3
Ever	55.8	57.5	59.5	27.6	32.3	31.9
Never	66.1	63.3	61.0	11.5	18.3	19.6
Availability of husband's married brothers						
No	75.8	77.6	72.7	9.0	13.1	13.8
Yes	60.5	63.7	62.2	18.3	25.1	27.8
Grand mean	64.9	67.1	64.5	15.6	22.1	24.6

Source: Taiwan KAP surveys, Taiwan Provincial Institute of Family Planning.

In sum, the flow of financial support between parents and children before the children's marriage has changed from one favoring the parents to one favoring the children, whereas after the children's marriage it continues to favor the parents. In recent years the flow of money to husbands' parents has intensified to compensate for the inability or unwillingness of younger couples to live or share meals with them. The flow of financial support to wives' parents has also increased, chal-

Changes in Intergenerational Relations in the Chinese Family: Taiwan's Experience

Table 15.12. Couples ever giving money to the wife's parents or sharing meals with them, by selected variables and survey year (%): Taiwan, 1973–86

Independent variable	1973	1980	1986
Wife's newspaper reading			
Every day	27.2	49.3	57.4
Often	20.7	49.4	55.2
Weekly/less often	23.9	42.7	47.3
Never	16.5	31.9	47.5
Illiterate	11.9	34.5	36.3
Wife's current work status			
Outside home	22.2	48.8	58.1
At home	18.8	45.6	53.7
Not working	17.8	38.3	49.2
Relative index of per capita family income			
< 20 < m − 1 sd	12.1	29.9	40.7
20–24 < m − .5 sd	15.0	32.7	49.9
25–29 < m	16.5	43.7	51.9
30–34 > m	21.9	53.0	56.4
35–39 > m + .5 sd	25.5	58.2	55.6
40–44 > m + 1 sd	31.4	54.3	63.3
45+ > m + 1.5 sd	34.0	66.1	67.4
u	13.2	33.8	48.4
Grand mean	18.9	43.0	53.1

Source: Taiwan KAP surveys, Taiwan Provincial Institute of Family Planning.
u—data unavailable.
m—mean.
sd—standard deviation.

lenging the tradition of weak economic ties between married couples and wives' parents.

Expectations for Children to Contribute to the Family Economy

In rural societies children are an important source of economic support for a family, and their economic utility is one reason why large families are common in rural areas. As a society modernizes or industrializes, however, children's education is prolonged and the children can no longer perform many kinds of work. This change reduces the value of young children to parents; but when children complete their education and begin working, many parents expect them to contribute to the family economy before marrying.

Our survey data reveal that large majorities of respondents in 1973, 1980, and 1986 expected their unmarried sons to contribute to the family economy by working outside the family business or on the family farm, but that the proportion having such an expectation declined steadily over the survey period, from nearly 90 percent to 75 percent (Table 15.13). The proportion of couples who reported having no such expectation from their sons rose from 9.9 percent in 1973 to 15 percent in 1986. Parental expectations for unmarried daughters were similar to those for sons (data not shown).

Expectations of support from unmarried sons were lower among better-educated respondents, those with higher incomes, urbanites, mainlanders, and those whose husbands had specialist or management occupations than among other respondents (Table 15.13). When we controlled the effects of other variables, the effects of these variables were reduced but the pattern remained, indicating a tendency for more modern parents not to rely upon their unmarried children economically.

Table 15.13. Wives expecting their sons to contribute to the family economy before marriage by working in the family business or on the family farm, by selected variables and survey year (%): Taiwan, 1973–86

Independent variables	1973	1980	1986
Wife's education			
No schooling	94.3	92.5	92.4
Literate/primary (attended)	93.2	86.6	89.0
Primary (completed)	90.5	85.7	83.9
Junior high	82.8	81.0	71.8
Senior high	72.5	73.5	65.1
College+	58.1	65.2	44.7
Husband's occupation			
Specialist/management	83.0	76.2	66.0
Sales/service	90.0	83.9	75.4
Technical/nontechnical	91.4	86.8	82.5
Farming/fishing/forestry	96.1	94.2	88.0
None/u	86.7	77.8	75.8
Relative index of per capita family income			
< 20 < m − 1 sd	97.2	92.5	89.4
20–24 < m − .5 sd	95.0	89.3	84.4
25–29 < m	92.6	86.3	79.8
30–34 > m	86.7	78.3	71.8
35–39 > m + .5 sd	85.6	77.5	65.7
40–44 > m + 1 sd	75.5	75.5	59.4
45+ > m + 1.5 sd	71.7	69.7	50.9
u	90.9	82.7	74.0
Wife's ethnicity/origin			
Fukenese	90.1	83.7	76.6
Hakka	91.2	84.2	75.6
Mainlander	61.6	71.1	55.2
Other/u	95.5	86.7	77.2
Husband's rural experience			
Current	93.4	87.4	79.2
Ever	84.5	78.6	73.3
Never	83.6	78.2	69.0
Grand mean	89.5	83.3	75.3

Source: Taiwan KAP surveys, Taiwan Provincial Institute of Family Planning.
u—data unavailable.
m—mean.
sd—standard deviation.

Arrangements for Old-age Support

Although it used to be customary for Chinese sons to support their parents in old age, we have seen from the survey data that fewer than 70 percent of couples in contemporary Taiwan society provide economic support to their parents. In an effort to learn whom or what respondents planned to depend upon in their old age, the KAP surveys included two questions on this topic: (1) "Do you want to depend on your sons for your old-age livelihood?" and (2) "What will be your main source of income in your old age?"

Dependency on sons for livelihood in old age Sizable majorities of women in the 1973, 1980, and 1986 surveys responded that they wanted to depend economically on their sons in old age; but the proportions giving this response declined precipitously between 1973 and 1980, from 81 percent to 65 percent, and fell slightly again, to 61 percent, in 1986 (Table 15.14). Conversely, the proportions of respondents who said they did not want to depend upon their sons for their own livelihood in old age rose, from 8.7 percent in 1973 to 15 percent in 1980 and 18 percent in 1986. Interestingly, the proportions of women whose attitudes toward this issue were uncertain doubled, rising from 10 percent in 1973 to 20 and 21 percent in 1980 and 1986, respectively.

Not surprisingly, those less inclined to depend upon their sons in old age were younger, more educated, mainlanders,

Changes in Intergenerational Relations in the
Chinese Family: Taiwan's Experience

Table 15.14. Wives wanting to depend on their sons economically in old age, by selected variables and survey year: Taiwan, 1973–86

	1973		1980		1986	
Independent variable	Mean (%)	Adj. dev.[a]	Mean (%)	Adj. dev.[a]	Mean (%)	Adj. dev.[a]
Wife's age						
20–24	78.0	−1.2	63.8	−.8	52.1	−7.2
25–29	77.3	−.3	61.7	−1.3	56.5	−.6
30–34	80.9	−1.0	62.7	−1.6	62.7	1.3
35–39	86.7	2.4	74.1	4.4	69.3	3.1
Eta or Beta value[b]	.0953	.0366	.1039	.0508	.1211	.0653
Wife's education						
No schooling	93.2	3.0	85.2	4.8	83.4	6.3
Literate/primary (attended)	90.4	2.6	78.8	3.0	82.4	11.6
Primary (completed)	82.3	1.3	70.3	.9	74.5	6.3
Junior high	59.3	−7.0	58.7	−.8	57.7	−1.9
Senior high	42.3	−13.5	42.9	−4.7	41.5	−8.4
College+	26.7	−19.3	22.5	−10.3	22.3	−18.1
Eta or Beta value[b]	.3824	.1273	.3360	.0767	.3656	.1660
Wife's ethnicity/origin						
Fukenese	84.6	1.8	66.6	.5	61.9	−.4
Hakka	81.5	−.7	66.4	−.3	66.1	5.9
Mainlander	65.3	−6.0	52.8	−3.1	43.9	−7.1
Other/u	82.1	−5.0	75.4	.8	61.9	−.2
Eta or Beta value[b]	.1813	.0755	.1019	.0248	.1068	.0615
Husband's occupation						
Specialist/management	66.3	−1.9	49.9	−4.1	49.2	−.8
Sales/service	80.2	−.9	70.3	2.5	62.5	.9
Technical/nontechnical	84.8	.2	73.9	3.4	68.5	−.1
Farming/fishing/forestry	95.9	2.7	81.2	−.2	80.2	1.7
None/u	77.8	.2	71.1	5.9	66.7	4.3
Eta or Beta value[b]	.2856	.0436	.2630	.0727	.2242	.0227
Relative index of total family income						
< 20 < m − 1 sd	95.5	1.0	88.8	12.2	82.3	8.3
20–24 < m − .5 sd	93.0	3.1	77.8	3.5	76.3	7.2
25–29 < m	87.0	3.3	69.7	2.1	64.9	1.7
30–34 > m	74.8	−1.3	57.8	−2.6	53.1	−4.9
35–39 > m + .5 sd	69.7	−1.7	53.9	−.9	44.4	−6.4
40–44 > m + 1 sd	60.4	−5.0	43.9	−4.6	42.1	−3.0
45+ > m + 1.5 sd	44.9	−8.9	26.8	−15.2	26.1	−13.3
u	82.1	−3.3	66.7	−.9	63.8	−1.1
Eta or Beta value[b]	.3236	.0908	.2841	.1049	.2959	.1241

Table 15.14. *(continued)*

	1973		1980		1986	
Independent variable	Mean (%)	Adj. dev.[a]	Mean (%)	Adj. dev.[a]	Mean (%)	Adj. dev.[a]
Relative index of modern durables owned						
< 20 < m − 1 sd	96.2	3.2	85.5	4.9	72.7	−1.4
20–24 < m − .5 sd	91.3	1.4	78.6	2.9	72.2	3.2
25–29 < m	85.7	.6	66.7	.4	63.2	.5
30–34 > m	77.4	.6	59.0	.2	55.4	−.3
35–39 > m + .5 sd	66.5	−1.1	54.4	−2.6	47.1	−7.4
40–44 > m + 1 sd	62.2	−.6	46.1	−4.4	52.2	.4
45+ > m + 1.5 sd	49.5	−10.9	40.3	−7.8	43.7	−2.7
Eta or Beta value[b]	.2949	.0688	.2750	.0705	.1983	.0604
Grand mean	80.9		65.2		61.1	
R^2 [c]	.2249	.2177	.1801	.1689	.1938	.1805

Source: Taiwan KAP surveys, Taiwan Provincial Institute of Family Planning.
a. Adjusted deviation from grand mean.
b. Eta for unadjusted mean; Beta for adjusted deviation.
c. Proportion of variance explained by the six variables listed in this table and the seven variables not listed here, including type of sample area, wife's rural experience, husband's education, frequency of wife's newspaper reading, wife's religion, home ownership, and index of husband-wife traditional relation. These seven variables were omitted here for simplicity.

those with husbands in specialist or management occupations, and those with higher family incomes and more modern durables. This negative association was especially strong in the case of the wife's (and husband's) education. But in most of the socioeconomic categories, the proportions hoping to depend upon their sons in old age diminished over the 13 years. The decline in the grand mean was therefore a combined effect of compositional effects and substantive effects. Most of the differentials just observed were maintained when the effects of 12 other variables were held constant, as noted in Table 15.14. This indicates that in the future even fewer parents will want or, perhaps more accurately, expect to depend upon their sons for a livelihood in old age.

Sources of support in old age The answer to the question about the main source of the respondent's income in old age can be divided into three categories: (1) her sons; (2) her own income, including savings, interest, and rents from agriculture, business, and property; and (3) pensions. Because respondents were allowed to mention more than one source, the total percentage for each exceeded 100.

In 1973, 64 percent of the women respondents selected sons as their main source of support in old age and only about 48 percent chose own income. In

1980, though, 66 percent of respondents chose own income, compared with 40 percent who chose sons. By 1986 the gap between the two expected sources had become even larger: 82 percent mentioned own income whereas only 39 percent mentioned sons as a source of income. This result, suggesting that the great majority of wives realized it would be unrealistic to rely upon their sons for support in old age, is related to Taiwan's rapid economic development in recent years and the large growth in personal income.

It is noteworthy that the proportion of respondents who mentioned their sons as the main source of expected old-age support was smaller than the proportion who indicated that they *wanted* to depend upon their sons in old age. The discrepancy may be due in part to the way the two questions were phrased. In response to the first question, the only choice was sons, whereas in response to the second question respondents could mention several sources. Nonetheless, the responses indicate that dependency upon sons for old-age support is eroding in Taiwan. Those who are better-off economically will not be in difficulty if their children are unwilling to support them in old age, but elderly people with low incomes will suffer if their children refuse support or if they have no surviving children. It will be necessary for the government to share responsibility for this less fortunate group, through some form of welfare or insurance.

Changes in Other Relations

The surveys also asked respondents about three other kinds of parent-child relations: expectations for their children's education, decisions about their children's marriages, and mutual visits.

Expectations for children's education Children's education is valued highly in Chinese families. In the past, studying hard and passing the national examination was a sure way for sons to get ahead in China—for example, to be appointed a government official with high status and wealth; and there were many examples of children from poor families who achieved success through hard study. To some extent education is still an important route to success in Taiwan, a college education being one way to secure a well-paid job. Most parents, therefore, consider it their duty to encourage their children to study hard for the college entrance examinations.

The first-born son, as the male heir, used to receive priority in education, but this custom seems to be changing with Taiwan's growing modernization and democratization. As shown in Table 15.15, the educational levels expected for respondents' first and second child were similar. More than half of all respondents expected their first and second child to receive at least a college education, the proportion increasing over time.

It should be noted that even though parents' dependency on their grown children has been decreasing, educational

Table 15.15. Wife's educational aspirations for the first and second child, by survey year (%): Taiwan, 1973–86

Expected level of education	First child			Second child[a]		
	1973	1980	1986	1973	1980	1986
No education necessary	.3	.2	.0	.3		.1
Primary	7.8	1.7	.4	7.5	1.6	.2
Junior high	14.4	8.5	4.9	14.9	9.4	5.0
Senior high/vocational	12.8	19.8	15.1	13.3	21.4	16.4
College+	61.2	63.0	75.5	60.3	61.0	74.4
Depends	2.7	6.4	3.3	2.9	6.2	3.3
u	.8	.4	.8	.8	.4	.6
Total	100.0	100.0	100.0	100.0	100.0	100.0

Source: Taiwan KAP surveys, Taiwan Provincial Institute of Family Planning.
u—data unavailable.
a. Excluding those without a second child.

aspirations for children have increased. This means that parents' motivation for educating their children is not entirely self-serving. Many parents in our surveys wanted their children to receive a better education because they wanted them to have a better life in the future.

The proportion of respondents expecting their children to attain a college or higher level of education varied by the respondents' socioeconomic characteristics (Table 15.16). The expectation was highly and positively associated with modern characteristics (higher education, husbands in specialist or management occupations, higher per capita income, urban and mainland origin). The socioeconomic differentials in educational aspirations were statistically significant even after we held the effects of 11 other variables constant (each of the other four shown in Table 15.16, plus seven other variables: wife's age, wife's education, frequency of newspaper reading, wife's current working status, the relative index of modern durables, husband's ethnicity, and participation in clubs).

Forms of marriage arrangement Traditionally, Chinese parents arranged their children's marriages through match-makers. Arranged marriages have become less common as families have grown more democratic and parental authority has weakened. Increasingly, marriage partners are chosen by the children in consultation with their parents or by the children alone.

The 1973 KAP survey revealed that half of the women respondents had had their husbands chosen for them by their parents, and only about 19 percent had chosen their husbands themselves (Table 15.17). The proportion of marriages reported to have been arranged fell to 28 percent in 1980 and to 25 percent in 1986,

Changes in Intergenerational Relations in the Chinese Family: Taiwan's Experience

Table 15.16. Wives expecting their first child to receive a college or better education, by selected variables and survey year (%): Taiwan, 1973–86

Independent variable	1973	1980	1986
Husband's education			
No schooling	24.2	24.1	31.0
Literate/primary (attended)	38.8	43.3	42.7
Primary (completed)	52.5	50.7	62.1
Junior high	76.1	67.3	77.7
Senior high	89.1	78.8	86.9
College+	96.0	92.8	94.0
Husband's occupation			
Specialist/management	83.6	80.7	87.8
Sales/service	62.3	57.8	71.2
Technical/nontechnical	56.9	55.8	68.8
Farming/fishing/forestry	35.9	37.4	57.3
None/u	61.4	50.0	64.9
Relative index of per capita family income			
< 20 < m – 1 sd	25.0	31.3	55.1
20–24 < m – .5 sd	44.4	49.5	66.7
25–29 < m	58.2	63.8	75.7
30–34 > m	76.0	73.3	81.5
35–39 > m + .5 sd	84.3	79.8	89.2
40–44 > m + 1 sd	87.4	88.5	90.2
45+ > m + 1.5 sd	94.6	91.7	95.5
u	53.9	58.9	70.4
Wife's ethnicity/origin			
Fukenese	60.8	61.5	75.0
Hakka	64.0	73.5	78.9
Mainlander	89.6	89.4	86.4
Other/u	27.4	32.9	62.8
Wife's rural experience			
Current	52.9	55.7	70.7
Ever	67.2	68.0	76.4
Never	79.1	76.7	85.4
Grand mean	61.2	63.0	75.5

Source: Taiwan KAP surveys, Taiwan Provincial Institute of Family Planning.
u—data unavailable.
m—mean.
sd—standard deviation.

whereas the proportion of marriages reported to have been decided by the couple alone rose to 27 percent in 1980, remaining at about that level in 1986. The proportion of respondents who indicated that they and their parents had made their marriage choice in collaboration rose from 32 percent in 1973 to 45 percent in 1980, and to 49 percent in 1986.

As Table 15.17 shows, there was a strong negative association between the proportion of marriages decided by the parents alone and marriage cohort, degree of urbanization, wife's education, frequency of newspaper reading, and education of the wife's father. Although some discrepancies emerged in the relationship between cohort and marriage decision (especially in the 1980 survey), the proportion of marriages decided solely by the parents was much lower for recently married couples than for those married earlier. The proportion was especially low for wives who had married at ages 23 and above. It was higher in rural than in urban areas and among wives whose fathers had been engaged in a primary industry such as farming. Among women who had worked outside the home before marriage, not more than one-third had had their marriages decided solely by the parents. The differentials by independent variable in the proportions of marriages decided by the couple alone and by the couple and their parents in collaboration were quite similar to those in the proportions of marriages decided by the couples alone, but they were weaker.

Table 15.17. Marriages decided by the couple alone, by parents alone, or collaboratively, by selected variables and survey year (%): Taiwan, 1973–86

Independent variables	% decided by the couple alone 1973	1980	1986	% decided by the parents alone 1973	1980	1986	% decided collaboratively 1973	1980	1986
Year of first marriage									
1947–51	14.3			61.9			22.2		
1952–56	15.2	(.0)		64.1	(50.0)		20.4	(50.0)	
1957–61	15.0	20.2	(.0)	58.8	43.1	(66.7)	26.0	35.9	(33.3)
1962–66	19.1	18.6	20.9	48.4	40.4	41.7	32.2	40.4	36.5
1967–71	22.2	22.7	16.7	40.2	34.9	43.2	37.4	42.1	39.7
1972–76	20.8	30.9	22.4	29.2	20.9	30.2	49.7	47.7	46.9
1977–81		35.8	30.1		12.6	17.0		51.5	52.9
1982–86			32.0			11.8			55.8
Wife's age at first marriage									
≤16	25.2	33.2	20.9	45.1	31.6	28.0	29.3	34.8	48.9
17–18	21.2	27.2	27.0	50.5	30.9	27.3	27.9	41.4	45.7
19–20	17.7	22.6	26.8	51.4	30.3	26.5	30.8	46.4	46.5
21–22	15.3	23.2	25.3	51.4	29.2	26.0	33.1	47.4	48.4
23–25	15.6	29.7	25.3	48.9	22.9	22.0	35.3	46.9	52.6
26+	28.9	37.2	27.6	36.2	22.9	19.6	34.5	39.9	52.5
u		(5.9)			(52.9)			(41.2)	
Type of sample area									
Large city	24.8	33.4	26.9	34.3	20.2	17.9	40.7	46.0	55.0
Small city	24.9	31.8	36.7	36.8	24.9	20.5	37.7	43.1	41.9
Urban township	15.5	20.9	20.2	52.6	31.6	28.6	31.8	47.0	51.2
Rural township	13.1	21.7	21.3	64.8	34.7	31.5	21.8	43.0	47.1
Wife's education									
No schooling	11.3	10.3	8.9	70.0	54.6	54.1	18.4	34.5	34.9
Literate/primary (attended)	16.0	20.9	18.7	57.0	35.9	36.3	26.9	43.2	44.5
Primary (completed)	18.9	23.9	20.8	46.0	30.3	33.4	34.9	45.3	45.5
Junior high	25.3	30.5	29.3	30.5	19.0	19.4	43.8	50.2	51.2
Senior high	33.9	42.2	33.8	16.1	8.8	10.0	50.0	48.8	55.9
College+	48.1	49.8	37.2	3.8	4.8	7.0	48.1	44.5	55.8
Husband's first job									
Specialist/management	24.9	34.2	28.3	36.6	17.0	18.0	38.3	48.5	53.1
Sales/service	20.2	33.6	28.6	39.3	21.8	22.3	40.4	43.6	49.1
Technical/nontechnical	22.7	28.3	26.6	42.3	28.4	24.0	34.8	42.9	49.1
Farming/fishing/forestry	8.2	10.7	13.6	71.3	44.9	43.8	20.2	43.9	42.6
None/u	22.0	27.3	36.3	42.7	26.1	25.3	34.9	45.9	38.5
Wife's newspaper reading									
Every day	30.1	35.7	30.1	24.3	18.1	18.9	45.2	46.0	50.9
Often	21.4	33.9	24.1	34.6	23.3	21.6	43.6	42.9	53.9
Weekly/less often	18.1	22.2	24.1	41.4	25.8	28.5	40.2	50.7	47.2
Never	15.9	17.5	13.3	56.1	37.9	42.5	27.8	44.3	43.8
Illiterate	11.2	11.3	10.1	70.1	53.0	50.6	18.5	34.9	37.5

Changes in Intergenerational Relations in the
Chinese Family: Taiwan's Experience

Table 15.17. *(continued)*

Independent variables	% decided by the couple alone			% decided by the parents alone			% decided collaboratively		
	1973	1980	1986	1973	1980	1986	1973	1980	1986
Education of wife's father									
No schooling	13.5	18.9	22.2	62.2	39.6	34.9	24.1	40.9	42.5
Literate	18.3	28.1	24.1	48.8	24.9	27.2	32.8	46.5	48.7
Primary	21.5	28.5	26.0	41.5	25.3	19.9	36.8	46.1	53.8
Secondary	28.7	41.3	34.2	24.8	10.2	12.3	46.5	47.7	53.2
u	16.9	29.0	28.4	57.1	23.4	24.2	25.3	47.7	46.6
Occupation of wife's father									
Specialist/management	26.8	35.8	30.5	31.7	17.5	14.7	41.2	46.3	54.7
Sales/service	25.0	31.7	22.2	39.0	26.8	24.6	36.1	40.8	53.3
Technical/nontechnical	22.5	31.9	32.8	45.4	24.2	15.3	31.8	43.3	51.3
Farming/fishing/forestry	13.9	21.1	22.0	58.4	33.7	31.0	27.4	44.8	46.8
Not working	14.9	30.0	(9.1)	51.7	26.7	(36.3)	32.2	43.3	54.5
u	26.9	22.5	29.8	35.0	35.2	38.5	38.0	42.3	29.8
Wife's outside work before marriage									
Never	13.0	17.5	16.9	61.0	39.3	42.1	25.7	42.5	40.3
Ever	26.5	32.4	28.5	33.1	21.1	19.6	40.1	46.2	51.7
Grand mean	18.5	26.6	25.8	49.6	28.2	24.8	31.6	44.7	49.1

Source: Taiwan KAP surveys, Taiwan Provincial Institute of Family Planning.
Note: Numbers in parentheses indicate a base number less than 20.

Mutual visits As we have seen, fewer couples have been living with their parents in recent years, but to some extent they have compensated for this decline in traditional filial piety by giving money to the parents. But money does not solve all the problems of elderly parents, who also need personal concern and care. Children who care deeply about their parents are more likely than others to visit them often if they are not living with them.

The proportion of couples living with the husband's parents decreased between 1973 and 1986, but the proportion of non-coresiding couples who visited the husband's parents at least once a month increased (Table 15.18). Taken together, those coresiding with and those regularly visiting the husband's parents accounted for about 80 percent of all couples in each survey year. This pattern suggests that a new form of parent-child relationship has evolved in Taiwan, that of living separately but maintaining closeness through mutual visits. In fact, the 1986 survey indicates an increase in the proportion of husbands' parents who visited their sons' families at least once a month. Although the surveys did not include a question about frequency of telephone contact with parents, telephone contact among those not coresiding in all probability rose over the survey period because, according to statistics compiled by the Ministry of Transportation and Communications, the number of telephones per 1,000 population rose from 47.6 in 1973, to 177.8 in 1980 and to 332.9 in 1987, resulting in an average of 1.3 telephones per household (Council for Economic Planning and Development, 1988).

Frequency of visits is also affected by the distance between parents' and children's homes. Among couples living in the same city or township as the husband's parents, 87–88 percent visited the husband's parents at least once a month; but among those living in a different city or township, only 41–43 percent of them did so. The same was true of parents' visiting patterns: 70–80 percent of the parents visited their married sons and daughters-in-law at least once a month if both were living in the same city or township, but only 21–31 percent visited if they lived in different cities or townships. But parents whose married sons had not lived with them in the previous 13 years tended to visit them less frequently than other parents, possibly in part because of the availability of telephone communication.

SUMMARY AND DISCUSSION

Taiwan has experienced rapid social and economic development over the period of the four KAP surveys discussed in this chapter. The per capita GNP rose from US$250 in 1967 to more than US$6,000 by 1986; the proportion of the labor force employed in primary industries (farming, fishing, and forestry) declined from about 43 percent in 1967 to 17 percent by 1986, whereas the proportion employed in secondary industries (manufacturing, construction, etc.) grew from 25 percent to about 42 percent; the proportion of the population living in urban planned districts reached 74 percent in 1986; the proportion of female students among college and university students increased from 29 percent in 1967 to 42 percent in 1986; the number of automobiles per 1,000 population rose from 4 in 1967 to 77 in 1986; the number of television sets per 1,000

Table 15.18. Frequency of mutual visiting between the couple and the husband's parents, by survey year (%): Taiwan, 1973–86

Frequency	1973	1980	1986
Couple visits husband's parents			
Couple living with parents	56.8	50.9	41.4
Not living together			
Couple visits parents at least once a month	25.3	28.1	37.4
Couple visits parents less often than once a month	17.9	21.0	21.2
Total	100.0	100.0	100.0
Husband's parents visit couple			
Couple living with parents	56.8	50.9	41.4
Not living together			
Parents visit couple at least once a month	20.7	19.6	26.2
Parents visit couple less often than once a month	22.5	29.5	32.4
Total	100.0	100.0	100.0

Source: Taiwan KAP surveys, Taiwan Provincial Institute of Family Planning.

households rose from 49 in 1966 to 1,067 in 1986; the proportion of Taiwan residents 6 years old or older who were illiterate fell from 19 percent in 1967 to 8 percent in 1986; and the proportion of the population covered by social insurance grew from 7.4 percent in 1967 to 29 percent in 1987 (Council for Economic Planning and Development, 1988). All these changes worked to affect Taiwan's families, which have inherited the traditional characteristics of the Chinese family.

This chapter has analyzed the changes in intergenerational relations in Taiwan's families, using data from a series of KAP surveys conducted between 1967 and 1986 by the Taiwan Provincial Institute of Family Planning. The relations investigated included living arrangements between married couples and their parents, their economic relations, mutual visits, marriage arrangements, and expectations for children's education. These relations were analyzed separately for past experience (respondents' relations with their parents and parents-in-law) and future expectations (their hopes and expectations about relations with their own children when the respondents reached old age).

In the traditional Chinese family, marriage is patrilocal; that is, the bride marries into the bridegroom's home and lives with her husband's parents. In the families surveyed in Taiwan, however, not all couples started their married life with the husband's parents; although 90 percent of those interviewed in 1967 had begun their marriages patrilocally, by 1986 only 73 percent had done so. Among couples recently married, the proportion was much lower: 87 percent for the marriage cohort of 1952–56 but only 69 percent for the marriage cohort of 1982–86. The change is related to various modernization factors.

Although the majority of couples who had begun their married life with the husband's parents remained with them, not all did so. The 1973 survey found that 59 percent of such couples were still living with the husband's parents 10 years after marrying (Freedman et al., 1982).

The proportion of couples living with the husband's parents at the time of the surveys decreased from 60 percent in 1967 to 41 percent in 1986. The proportion was especially high for couples who had always lived in rural areas but very low among those who had moved from rural to urban areas, indicating that migration is one important cause of the separation of married children from their parents. The proportion of coresiding couples was also lower among those in which the husband had married brothers living in Taiwan, those with higher income, those with higher education and the habit of frequent newspaper reading, those in which the wife was from the Chinese mainland, and those in which the wife worked outside the home and whose parents helped with childcare.

The proportion of parents who had married sons but were living alone rose from 20 to 31 percent between 1973 and

1986. Increased migration and home ownership had a major influence on this trend.

In traditional Chinese families it is unusual for a couple to live with the wife's parents, and in 1967 only 8.3 percent of the sample couples were doing so. That proportion decreased to 5.3 percent in 1986, although it was higher among couples in which the wife had never lived in a rural area or was working outside the home.

Respondents' expectations of living with their married sons in old age declined rapidly over most of the survey period, from 87 percent in 1967 to 41 percent in 1980, but rose slightly, to 46 percent, in 1986. Conversely, the proportion of respondents who did not want to live with their married sons in the future rose from 4.4 percent in 1967 and 32 percent in 1986. These trends were strongly associated with such modernization factors as education, frequency of newspaper reading, urbanization, and modern employment.

Although 70 percent of the couples interviewed in 1986 had begun their married lives with the husband's parents, only 40 percent of respondents thought that newlywed couples should do so in the future. Their attitude may reflect a realization that children today are growing up in a new social environment with more freedom to organize their lives as they wish.

In traditional Chinese families, the older and younger generations not only live together but also eat together and share property. An indication that Taiwan is rapidly moving away from these traditional arrangements is the finding that only 52 percent of couples interviewed in 1967 were sharing their meals with the husband's parents and that by 1986 the proportion doing so had decreased to 40 percent.

The net flow of money between parents and children before the children marry has changed from one benefiting the husband's parents to one favoring children in Taiwan. After the children marry, however, the parents are the net recipients of the money flow, and our survey findings indicate that married children have increased their support to the husband's parents to compensate for not coresiding or sharing meals with them. They have also provided increased financial support to the wife's parents, breaking with Chinese custom.

Parents still expect their unmarried children to work and contribute to the family economy after completing their studies. The majority (75 percent) of unmarried children were doing so in 1986, but this figure was down from nearly 90 percent in 1973.

A substantial but declining proportion of Taiwanese couples wanted to depend upon their children economically for old-age support. The figure was 81 percent in 1973 but had decreased to 61 percent by 1986. Hopes for children's support in old age were negatively associated with the wife's age, education, and mainland origin; the husband's occupational level; and the family's per capita income. The survey data indicate an increasing tendency for couples to depend upon their own incomes and saving for their livelihood in old age.

In Chinese society, children's education has traditionally been regarded as an important parental duty, and most of the surveyed parents wanted their children to receive a higher education. Their motivation was not entirely utilitarian, however; many parents stated that they wanted their children to have a good education so that the children would enjoy a better life in the future.

Increasingly, marriage partners were selected by the couples themselves or in collaboration with their parents. This means that parents' authority over their children's marriage decisions has been sharply reduced, especially in more modern families.

The decrease in shared living arrangements between the older and younger generations was compensated for, in part, by increased visiting and very likely by more reliance on telephone contact. A new pattern of parent-child relations has thus emerged, that of living separately but maintaining close contact through visits and telephone conversations. Not surprisingly, the frequency of visiting was greatest among families who lived in close proximity.

To conclude, intergenerational relations in Taiwanese families are changing rapidly in many respects, owing to the social and economic forces of modernization, urbanization, and industrialization. These trends are likely to continue. An important question is whether elderly Taiwanese will be able to support themselves financially and take care of their own personal needs in the future. And if they cannot, who should take responsibility for them? Given Taiwan's rapid population aging, these important policy questions require serious attention.

ACKNOWLEDGMENTS

We wish to thank Dr. Jack M.-C. Chang for his generous permission to use the KAP survey data collected by the Taiwan Provincial Institute of Family Planning. We also appreciate the valuable comments of Dr. Maxine Weinstein on an earlier draft of this chapter. The research reported here was supported by a National Science Council grant.

REFERENCES

Barclay, George W. 1954. *Colonial Development and Population in Taiwan*. Princeton: Princeton University Press.

Chan Hou-Sheng. 1979. "An Empirical Study of Social Adaptation and Needs of the Elderly in Taipei City" (in Chinese). *Social Development Quarterly* (in Chinese), No. 8:92–103. Taipei.

Chang Hui-Yung. 1980. "The Importance of Family Environment and the Familial Roles of Modern Parents" (in Chinese). *The Renaissance* (in Chinese) 113:57–64. Taipei.

Chen Kuan-Jeng and Jeh-Hang Lai. 1979. *Changes in the Chinese Family System* (in Chinese). Selected Publications of the Institute of the Three Principles of the People (in Chinese), No. 26. Taipei.

Chu Chin-Low. 1981. "Changes in Chinese Family Structure" (in Chinese). In Chu Chin-Low (ed.), *Social Change and Development in the Republic of China* (in Chinese), pp. 255–287. Taipei: Tung-ta Book Co.

Council for Economic Planning and Development. 1988. *Social Welfare Indicators, Republic of China*. Taipei.

Freedman, R., M. C. Chang, and T.-H. Sun. 1982. "Household Composition, Extended Kinship, and Reproduction in Taiwan:1973–1980." *Population Studies* 36:395–411.

Freedman, R., T.-H. Sun, K.-C. Liu, and M.-C. Chang. 1985. "Policy Options in the Second Stage of the Demographic Transition: The Case of Taiwan" (in Chinese). *Economic Papers* (in Chinese) 13(2):201–231. Taipei: Economic Institute, Academia Sinica.

Hsiao Hsin-Huang. 1991. "Reevaluation of Taiwan's Elderly Welfare and Family Welfare Functions" (in Chinese). In Chien Chiao (ed.), *The Chinese Family and Its Changes* (in Chinese), pp. 347–356. Hong Kong: Chinese University of Hong Kong.

Hsiao Hsin-Huang, Ly-Yun Chang, and Kuan-Jeng Chen. 1983. *A Study on Elderly Welfare in the Republic of China: Structural Analysis of the Service Network* (in Chinese). Taipei: Research, Development and Evaluation Commission, Executive Yuan.

Hutter, Mark. 1981. *The Changing Family: Comparative Perspectives*. New York: John Wiley & Sons.

Hwang Kwo-Yann. 1984. "A Study on Value Differentials among Three Generations in Contemporary Taiwanese Society" (in Chinese). *Journal of National Chen-chi University* (in Chinese) 50:139–185. Taipei.

Lai Jeh-Hang, and Kuan-Jeng Chen. 1985. "Social Change and the Family System in Taiwan" (in Chinese). In *Proceedings of the Seminar on the Promotion of Social Harmony through Strengthening of Family Education* (in Chinese), pp. 15–42. Taipei: Research, Development and Evaluation Commission and Chinese Sociological Association.

Lavely, William Roger. 1982. "Industrialization and Household Structure in Rural Taiwan." Ph.D. dissertation, Department of Sociology, University of Michigan, Ann Arbor.

Lee, Gary R., and Eugene Ellitherpe. 1982. "Intergenerational Exchange and Subjective Well-being among the Elderly." *Journal of Marriage and the Family* 44(1):217–224.

Li Yih-Yuan. 1984. "Changes in the Modern Chinese Family: An Anthropological Observation" (in Chinese). *Bulletin of the Institute of Ethnology* (in Chinese), No. 54:7–23. Taipei: Academia Sinica.

Shu Li-Chung. 1984. "A Discussion on Familialization of the Elderly's Life and Socialization of the Elderly's Welfare" (in Chinese). *Community Development Quarterly* (in Chinese), No. 25:83–85. Taipei.

Shu Leung-Hay, and Chung-Cheng Lin. 1984. "Family Structure and Social Change" (in Chinese). *Chinese Journal of Sociology* (in Chinese), No. 8:1–22. Taipei.

Sun Te-Hsiung. 1972. "Changes in Taiwan's Family and Household Structure." Paper presented at the Organization for Demographic Association Conference, Hong Kong, January 10–14.

———. 1984. "Changes in Fertility Attitudes and Behavior, Taiwan Area" (in Chinese). In H.-Y. Chiu and Y.-H. Chang (eds.), *Changes in Taiwanese Society and Culture* (in Chinese), Monograph Series B, No. 16:133–178. Taipei: Institute of Ethnology, Academia Sinica.

———. 1991. "Chinese Family in Social Change: An Experience in Taiwan." In *Proceedings of the National Science Council* 1(2):133–150. Taipei.

Thornton, Arland, M.-C. Chang, and T.-H. Sun. 1984. "Social and Economic Change, Intergenerational Relationships, and Family Formation in Taiwan." *Demography* 21(4):475–499.

Tsai W.-H. 1966. "A Study on the Relationships among Family Members" (in Chinese). *Contemplation and Dialect* (in Chinese) 4(2):28–33. Taipei.

Wang Te-Mu. 1990. "A Few Possible Trends of Future Population Growth in Taiwan" (in Chinese). In *Proceedings of the Conference on the Phases and Analysis of the Post-transitional Demography of Taiwan* (in Chinese), pp. 49–68. Taipei: Population Association of China (in Taiwan).

Wen Chung-I. 1991. "Changes in the Relationship between Industrialization and Family in Taiwan" (in Chinese). In Chien Chiao (ed.), *The Chinese Family and Its Changes* (in Chinese), pp. 171–184. Hong Kong: Chinese University of Hong Kong.

Yang Kuo-Shu. 1986. "The New Filial Piety in Modern Society" (in Chinese). *The Chinese Renaissance Monthly* (in Chinese) 19(1):51–67. Taipei.

Yang Shou-Jung. 1980. "An Analysis of the Father's Role in Modern Society" (in Chinese). *The University* (in Chinese) 137:8–9. Taipei.

Yen Han-Wen. 1980. "The Chinese Elderly and Family in Social Change" (in Chinese). *Health Education* (in Chinese) 46:12–15. Taipei.

CHAPTER 16

Coresidence and the Transition to Adulthood in the Rural Thai Family

by Chai Podhisita

Regardless of how it is defined, the family is an important social unit for at least two reasons. First, its structure and form, which represent the ways in which individuals are incorporated into groups, are essential elements for understanding the organization of human society. Indeed, in anthropology the term "social structure" is sometimes used to mean the family and kinship structure. Second, the family performs certain functions that contribute to the society. These functions include reproduction, the physical maintenance of family members, the rearing of children, socialization, and social control. Although some of these functions may be separated from the family, there is general agreement that the family is the social institution best suited to perform them. Thus, despite changes that are taking place in contemporary societies, the family still retains its significance as a fundamental unit of the larger social structure (Goode 1964:5).

Studies of the family by anthropologists have focused on its form, structure, and other aspects of its functions, including changes brought about by socioeconomic modernization. Social demographers and population scientists, on the other hand, have turned their attention to those aspects of the family that directly or indirectly bear upon population behavior. Marriage, fertility, and life course events are among the issues often investigated by social scientists who work in this field.

In Thailand, early studies of the family were limited in scope and number. Western anthropologists who studied Thai villages during the 1950s and 1960s placed emphasis on kinship and family formation, including the patterns and structure that are believed to have a bearing on individuals' rights and obligations. Studies drawing upon demographic perspectives and methodologies have been rare, except for those on marriage and related topics (e.g., Bhassorn, 1976, 1983, 1987; Aphichat, 1980; Cherlin and Aphichat, 1987; Aphichat, Morgan, and Rindfuss, 1988; Knodel et al., 1984; Chai, 1984; Jawalaksana, 1984).

This chapter is part of an attempt to understand more about the rural Thai family. It begins with a brief examination of Thai concepts of the family, then discusses practices related to coresidence at selected stages of an individual's life, the transfer of material inheritance, and the transition between ages 10 and 30. The final section suggests some areas for future research. I have drawn upon existing knowledge of the traditional Thai family documented in previous studies and on quantitative and qualitative data from fieldwork I conducted with the assistance of my colleagues at the Institute of Population Studies, Chulalongkorn University, in late 1989. The aim of the chapter is to present Thai views and practices regarding the family and to suggest issues in the rural Thai family that need more research attention.

The fieldwork was conducted in two regions of the country, the Northeast and the South. In each region we purposively selected two provinces. From each province, we chose two districts, and from each district we selected two villages. Altogether, 16 villages were covered. Eligible respondents were males and females between the ages of 15 and 55, married and unmarried. Approximately 42 respondents were randomly selected from each village, for a total of 677 individuals, of whom 401 were females and 276 were males. A majority of the respondents (628 cases) had ever married. In addition to the survey interviews, in-depth interviews of 27 key informants were also conducted to provide qualitative data. The selection of the key informants was made purposively with the help of the village headmen. The in-depth interviews proceeded in an informal and comfortable setting in which the interviewers asked open-ended questions according to the discussion guidelines. The interviews were tape-recorded and later transcribed for use in analysis.

THAI CONCEPTS OF THE FAMILY

For academic purposes, social scientists usually distinguish between the family and the household. The term "family" conventionally refers to a group of people who are related to each other through kinship ties, especially blood ties, and who may or may not share the same residence. The smallest and commonest group of this type consists of parents and their unmarried children and is typically known as the nuclear, elementary, or conjugal family (Fox, 1967:36). The term "household" refers to a group whose members may or may not be related but who share the same residence and often cooperate in a number of day-to-day activities. The two concepts can and actually do overlap since most households contain people who belong to one or more families. Members of the same family may or may not live in the same household, and members of the same household may include persons who are not family members.

What is a family and whom does a family include? When asked this question, respondents in the in-depth interviews gave broad definitions that in many cases encompassed conventional characteristics of both the family and the household. To most respondents, the word *krob krua* (family) meant a kin group consisting of persons related mainly, but not exclusively, through blood ties who lived in the same house and shared many day-to-day activities. The types of kin often mentioned by respondents as members of the family included parents and children, grandparents of both sides, uncles and aunts, and grandchildren. Some respondents also consider sons-in-law and daughters-in-law as family members. A few informants even held the view that family members included unrelated individuals, such as workers or maids, who had lived in the house for an extended period of time.

To some respondents, the word *krob krua* also seemed to imply the legal coresidence of a group of people regardless of their relationship. According to that view, family members include those individuals who are registered as legal residents of the same house. Thailand's population registration law requires that permanent residents of a dwelling register their residential status. The law also requires that a change of residence for a period longer than 15 days be registered at both the place of origin and the place of destination. According to this legal residential concept, family fission takes place only when family members legally take separate residences.

The broad concept of the family just described indicates that some Thais do not make a distinction between the family and the household. It may be possible that such a distinction does not exist or is not cognitively meaningful to them.

When does a family begin to exist? Respondents in the in-depth interviews had different opinions. Some thought that marriage marked the beginning of a family, saying that when a man and a woman marry, they form a family regardless of whether or not they have children or have a residence of their own. Others expressed the view that a family does not begin until the married couple and their children (if they have any) separate from their parental family to set up a household of their own; in other words, as long as a couple are not independent, they do not form a family. A third group of respondents regarded the beginning of a family as a process, starting with the marriage of a couple but not reaching its completion until children are born or the couple separates from the wife's parental family.

Among our respondents, therefore, a consensus did not emerge about when a family begins. Perhaps this lack of consensus reflects the various experiences of the respondents. Important among those experiences was their own postnuptial residence. It is likely that respondents who had moved into their own residence when they first married considered the family to begin immediately after marriage, whereas those who had lived with the parents of the bride or the groom consider the family to begin some time after marriage, typically when the couple became independent. Indeed, the Thai word for "having a family" and "beginning family life" can mean either the act of marriage or the setting up of a household and having children.

Who has the jural authority in the family? Respondents generally agreed that authority typically lies with the male head of the family, but that when the male head is absent the female head usually exercises that authority. Where more than one couple reside in the same house, authority typically rests with the most senior man. Despite this general principle, the respondents recognized that husbands and wives share authority in many aspects of family life, especially when important matters are concerned, such as buying or selling valuables and the education and marriage of their children. They also recognized a general division of authority within the family, with the husband representing the family and its business interests outside the home and the wife controlling household activities. Nonetheless, respondents did not regard this division as rigid; they stated that the husband and wife could replace each other in their respective roles and that in many circumstances spouses consulted each other before making a decision.[1]

CORESIDENCE AT SELECTED LIFE STAGES

Coresidence represents a dynamic aspect of the family. The number and combina-

---

1. Previous ethnographic studies have found that, among rural families of North and Northeast Thailand, the women form the core of a matrilocal group through which all or most of the family's material property (mainly land) is transferred. Even in such families, however, it is the husbands, not the wives, who possess jural authority. In those two regions succession of the authority is not from father to son, but rather from the wife's father to his son-in-law. This practice differs from the classical matrilineal custom, in which land and jural authority pass from the mother's brother to the sister's son. It also differs from the classical patrilineal custom, in which jural authority and land pass from father to eldest son (Potter, 1977; Chai, 1984).

tion of persons who live together in the same household change over time as individual members move in and out for various reasons. The rural Thai family is characterized by a cycle of expansion and contraction over the lifetime of the couple, resulting in different forms at different periods. Usually expansion and contraction are the outcome of demographic events and cultural practices of postnuptial residence.

The traditional model of coresidence among members of rural Thai families has to be understood in conjunction with the developmental cycle of the domestic group. The practice of postnuptial residence requires that husbands leave their parents to live with their wives. The young couple stay at the wife's parental home for a certain period of time before moving out to establish their own independent household. After marrying, the youngest grown child of the family (preferably the daughter) stays permanently with the parents to look after them in their old age and to inherit the house. This residence pattern produces a simple family cycle, making the family a two- and three-generation domestic group. A nuclear family becomes a three-generation stem family when the children marry and join the group, reverting again to a nuclear family when the old parents have died (Foster, 1975:37). Ethnographic studies indicate that this residence practice is generally followed in most lowland areas of Thailand, especially in the Central Region, the Northern Region, and the Northeast (de Young, 1955; Kingshill, 1965; Tambiah, 1970).

The residence rule mentioned above provides a framework for understanding coresidence at particular stages of the family cycle and at selected points of an individual's life course. One can generally predict that in rural Thailand old couples will be found in three-generation households whereas young couples with preadolescent children will be found in independent two-generation households. Demographic events can also influence the coresidence of family members.[2]

Quantitative data from our survey are available on the types of family members who shared the same residence with respondents at two points in their lives, around age 10 and in the first year after marriage. Those two points were arbitrarily selected to represent, first, the earliest time when a person begins the transition to adulthood, and, second, the beginning of a couple's family life.

Table 16.1 indicates a great deal of similarity among the respondents with regard to the types of family members who lived with them when the respondents were about 10 years old. Regardless of sex, more than 90 percent of the respondents lived with their mothers and their siblings. A slightly smaller proportion (85 percent for males and 86 percent for females) had their fathers living in the

---

2. Limited space here precludes a discussion of demographic influences on coresidence. For an examination of the subject, see Foster (1978, 1982) and Foster and Seidman (1976).

same house. The difference in the proportions of households with mothers and those with fathers indicates both a higher mortality rate among fathers and the tendency for children to live with their mothers when the parents divorced or separated.

As for the other family members, only about one-fifth of the respondents had one or both grandparents sharing the same residence when the respondents were about 10 years old, indicating that three-generation households were fairly uncommon. Sharing the same residence with the parents' siblings was even less common (12 percent for males and 8.2 percent for females). Our data do not allow us to distinguish between the father's siblings and those of the mother, but from the common pattern of postnuptial residence in Thailand we suppose that the majority of them were maternal siblings.

Table 16.1 also shows that nearly three out of four respondents (about 70 percent for males and 72 percent for females) had uncles or aunts (i.e., parents' siblings) living in the same community.

Focusing still on coresidence around age 10, Table 16.2 shows generally the same pattern of coresidence among various cohorts of respondents. Regardless of their age, nearly all informants had shared the same residence with their immediate family members (mother, father, and full siblings). But two patterns may be noted from this table. First, the percentages of respondents whose fathers and mothers lived in the same residence with them increase somewhat systematically among the younger respondents. This may indicate lower mortality levels in the recent past than in the more distant past. Second, the percentages of respondents whose grandparents lived in the house-

Table 16.1. Respondents who had specified family members living in the same residence or in the same community with them when they were about 10 years old, by sex of respondents (%): rural Thailand, 1989

Family members	Men (no. = 276)			Women (no. = 401)		
	Same house	Same community	Other responses[a]	Same house	Same community	Other responses[a]
Father	85.1	1.1	13.8	86.0	1.7	12.2
Mother	91.6	0.4	8.0	92.0	1.2	6.7
Stepparents	4.3	1.4	94.2	7.5	0.5	92.0
Grandparents	19.2	35.1	45.7	21.9	33.2	44.9
Parents' siblings	12.0	69.9	18.1	8.2	72.1	19.6
Respondent's full siblings	94.2	1.4	4.3	93.5	2.7	3.7
Respondent's half siblings	4.2	1.1	94.9	6.0	0.7	93.3
Other relatives	4.7	65.9	29.4	1.5	64.1	34.4

a. Other responses included: "Lived elsewhere," "Died," "Don't know," and "No members of that type" (not applicable).

hold decreases among younger cohorts (from 23 percent in the age group above 40 to 13 percent in the age group under 20). This pattern supports the general observation that three-generational households are becoming less common in contemporary Thailand.

Overall, Tables 16.1 and 16.2 indicate that in their childhood rural Thais are typically surrounded by various types of family members. Where the immediate family members (parents and siblings) are not found in the same residence, they are almost always found in the same community. Coresidence with grandparents, aunts, and uncles is less common, but those relatives typically reside in the same community. Thus, the conditions under which most rural Thais grow up is conducive to close relationships among family members and relatives.

As can be seen in Table 16.3, respondents' patterns of coresidence in the first year of marriage were different from those experienced in childhood. As expected, the presence of the spouse was practically universal. Although parents and siblings still formed the core coresidence group, there were smaller proportions of them, especially among the male respondents. The greater proportions of own parents and siblings reported by female respondents (56 percent and 49 percent, respectively) indicate the prevalence of matrilocal residence among married couples in rural Thailand. Matrilocality can also be inferred from the fact that more married men than women (38 percent compared with 19 percent) lived with their spouse's parents during the first year of marriage. Other relatives (grandparents, stepparents, and parents' siblings) were also reported to have lived with the newlyweds, but in very small proportions.

Table 16.4 focuses on coresidence during the first year of marriage, by age

Table 16.2. Respondents who had specified family members sharing the same residence with them when they were about 10 years old, by current age of respondents (%): rural Thailand, 1989

Type of family member	Current age of respondents			
	<20	21–30	31–40	41+
Father	94.7	83.8	88.5	82.7
Mother	100.0	94.2	92.7	87.4
Stepparents	2.6	5.8	5.2	8.4
Grandparents	13.2	18.3	21.8	23.4
Parents' siblings	7.9	6.8	10.3	12.1
Respondent's full siblings	97.4	91.1	94.0	95.3
Respondent's half siblings	0.0	5.8	5.6	5.1
Other relatives	2.6	3.1	1.7	3.7
(No. of respondents)	(38)	(191)	(234)	(214)

cohort. Of interest in this table are the higher percentages of younger respondents who lived with their parents and siblings after marrying. It is likely that the majority of those who shared the same residence with their parents and siblings were women, who formed the larger part of our sample (401 women versus 276 men). In other words, I am describing matrilocal residence there. But why matrilocality has become more common among younger people remains unclear. Our survey data do not provide an answer to this question.

Table 16.3. Ever-married respondents who had specified family members living in the same residence or in the same community with them during the first year of their marriage, by sex of respondents (%): rural Thailand, 1989

Type of family member	Men (No. = 249)			Women (No. = 376)		
	Same house	Same community	Other responses[a]	Same house	Same community	Other responses[a]
Spouse	99.6	0.0	0.4	100.0	0.0	0.0
Spouse's parents	37.8	24.5	37.7	18.7	29.6	51.7
Respondent's parents	28.3	26.1	40.1	56.2	13.7	30.1
Respondent's stepparents	2.4	3.2	94.4	4.2	2.1	93.7
Respondent's grandparents	2.8	18.5	78.7	7.4	21.4	71.2
Respondent's parents' siblings	0.8	53.0	46.2	2.9	57.0	40.1
Respondent's siblings	30.5	34.5	34.9	48.8	22.7	28.5
Other relatives	4.4	49.4	46.2	2.6	51.2	46.2

a. Other responses included: "Lived elsewhere," "Died," "Don't know," and "No members of that type" (not applicable).

Table 16.4. Ever-married respondents who had specified family members sharing the same residence with them during the first year of their marriage, by current age of respondents (%): rural Thailand, 1989

Type of family member	Current age of respondents			
	<20	21–30	31–40	41+
Spouse	100.0	99.4	100.0	100.0
Spouse's parents	14.3	24.1	28.0	26.9
Respondent's parents	78.6	49.4	47.0	43.9
Respondent's stepparents	0.0	3.5	2.6	4.7
Respondent's grandparents	7.1	4.7	5.6	6.1
Respondent's parents' siblings	0.0	2.4	2.2	1.9
Respondent's siblings	71.4	43.5	40.9	38.7
Other relatives	14.3	4.1	1.7	3.8
(No. of respondents)	(14)	(170)	(232)	(212)

Coresidence and the Transition to Adulthood in the Rural Thai Family

TRANSFERS OF INHERITANCE

Because agriculture is the main livelihood of the vast majority of rural Thai families, land is not only a crucial means of production but also a family's most valuable property. Possession of agricultural land is typically an important index of family wealth in rural areas. Although the increasing shortage of land due to population growth and the growing importance of Thailand's market economy in recent decades have caused other family assets to acquire significance, the discussion here focuses exclusively on the inheritance of land.

The traditional pattern of inheritance among ethnic Thais follows the partible system. Family property, especially land, is divided equally among all children regardless of birth order or gender. There are few exceptions to this norm; one of them is the common practice of favoring the child who stays with the elderly parents and looks after them in their old age.

Data from our survey generally support the traditional pattern of inheritance. As shown in Table 16.5, the most common means of dividing family property was for parents to give all children equal shares. This practice was reported by nearly three-fourths of those whose parents had already divided their property. About 19 percent of respondents reported that their parents had given the largest share of the property to only one daughter or son (presumably the one who was taking care of the parents), while giving smaller but equal shares to the other children. In about 3 percent of the families, only some (not all) children were given property, which was equally divided. In the rest, the property had been divided by other methods.

The practice of transferring property through inheritance was also discussed in the in-depth interviews. Among our informants' families the norm was for parents to give equal shares to all children, with the exception of giving a slightly larger share to the child who took care of the parents in their old age. In dividing the family property, parents typically reserved a share for themselves which may or may not have been equal to the shares given to their children. It was this share that, after the parents' death, was bequeathed to the child who cared for them.

Information from the in-depth in-

Table 16.5. Respondents whose family property had been divided, by the method of division: rural Thailand, 1989

Method of division	No.	%
Equal shares to all children	210	72.9
Largest share to a daughter or son; smaller, equal shares to other children	54	18.8
Equal shares to some children only	9	3.1
Equal shares to daughters or sons only	5	1.7
Other means	8	2.8
Don't know	2	0.7
Total	288	100.0

terviews indicates roughly equal treatment of daughters and sons. Only a few informants believed that daughters were usually given a larger share than sons because they were closer to parents. Earlier studies in the rural Northeast, however, suggest that where succession of material property (particularly land) is concerned, the common practice is for daughters to receive larger shares. This tendency is indicated by the difference in the mean size of farmland inherited by wives and husbands, which was 15.4 and 11.0 *rai* (2.5 and 1.8 hectares), respectively (Chai, 1985:125). The explanation for the tendency to favor daughters is believed to be found in the custom of matrilocal postnuptial residence, which requires that daughters live with or be emotionally closer to their parents than are sons (Keyes, 1976; Chai, 1985).

Economic and social developments in Thailand lately have provided more opportunities for the rural population to engage in nonfarm employment, which often requires additional education and training. As a result, increasing numbers of rural Thais have received education beyond the compulsory level. A recent study reveals that nearly one-third of those between the ages of 15 and 19 in 1987 went to secondary school (Knodel and Malinee, 1989). This development raises a question, explored in our study, about the division of family property in a hypothetical situation: whether a share of the family land should be given to a child who has been given the opportunity for higher education at the expense of other children or with the support of other family members. Qualitative data from the in-depth interviews reveal that the common practice in this case was to give no farmland, or only a small piece of it, to the child who had been given an opportunity for education. The parents' rationale was that the amount of money spent to support the child's education was equivalent to a share of the inheritance of family land.

A study conducted in the rural Northeast has revealed that some Thais consider providing educational opportunities to their children to be the same as giving them a "rice field" upon which they can establish their families (Chai, 1985:306). For this reason, the educated child often forfeits his or her right to the family land, especially when that child can find a secure occupation outside agriculture.

Information from our in-depth interviews also reveals similarities between the two study regions in the timing of the transfer of inherited property. In the initial stage, a right to use part of the family land is granted to each married child who, after spending a period of time with the parents (which varies according to individual circumstances), moves out to set up a household of his or her own. Children typically work on the land without legal rights to it for varying lengths of time, often many years. When the parents become old, they grant legal ownership to all the children, and this completes the process of inheritance. The time lapse between the granting of the right to use the land and the transfer of its legal ownership sometimes becomes a source of tension between married children and their parents, or among the children themselves. In cases where parents die before the property is divided, children usually settle the matter among themselves.

TRANSITION BETWEEN AGES 10 AND 30

Of interest to us in conducting our study of rural families was to examine significant life-course events that most individuals pass through in the process of becoming adults. Since the meaning of "adult" and "adulthood" can be best understood within a cultural context, we thought it worthwhile to examine our respondents' concepts of adulthood.

In the in-depth interviews we asked the informants to tell us at what stage of life they considered an individual to become an adult and what for them characterized adulthood. In answering the first question, the respondents split into two groups. A majority expressed the view that men and women reached adulthood after experiencing certain events of social and cultural significance, such as reaching the age of 20 or older, ordination into the monkhood (for men), and marriage and starting a family. A few people in this group considered military service as one of the important events for men that lead into adulthood. A number of informants, however, held a different view. They believed that having experienced such events as reaching the age of 20, being ordained, or marrying did not automatically result in a person's becoming an adult. For those respondents, age meant little unless one had learned to think and behave like an adult. Ordination into monkhood also did not necessarily signify adulthood to them either, especially since they believed that a majority of Thai men today observed it just for the sake of following custom rather than for serious study and spiritual training. Military service they considered even less valid as a mark of adulthood because only a small number of men and no women experience it and its main purpose is not to initiate men into adulthood. For this group, marriage too did not always imply that a couple had reached adulthood because some rural people marry at young ages, before they have matured mentally and behaviorally. Thus, according to this view, when a person becomes an adult depends on his or her behavior.

We compared the opinions about the timing of adulthood expressed during the in-depth interviews with those obtained from the survey. When asked to state the age or stage of their lives when they realized that they had become adults, three out of four of the survey respondents mentioned a chronological age, whereas the rest referred to events that had marked their entrance into adulthood (Table 16.6). On average, women recognized their adulthood at a slightly younger age than men. For those who mentioned life-course events rather than age, the salient markers of adulthood were marriage, starting a family, and childbirth.

In the in-depth interviews nearly all respondents mentioned acceptance of responsibility as a characteristic of adulthood. Other important characteristics mentioned by them included reasonableness, patience, thoughtfulness, appropriate behavior in various situations, and the adoption of high moral principles and religious values.

The following paragraphs are concerned with important life-course events that the survey respondents reported having experienced between the ages of 10 and 30. In presenting this information, I assume that adulthood is the outcome of a long process in which a person experiences multiple events leading toward economic, social, and psychological self-reliance. The discussion will focus on the prevalence and timing of formal education, work, migration, monkhood and military service (among males), and marriage and parenthood. Table 16.7 summarizes the life-course events.

The data show the same median ages at entry to and exit from school for men and women (ages 7 and 11, respectively). Three-fourths of the men (74 percent) and a slightly higher proportion of the women (78 percent) had only four years or less of formal schooling. Those with five or more years of education accounted for only a small fraction, with men being slightly better educated than women.

Because most respondents had spent only a short period of time in school, they had entered the work force early, the majority before their teen years. On average, women had begun working at age 11, the men at age 12. This is partly because a higher proportion of the men had received more education (i.e., five or more years of schooling), which delayed their entry into the work force. Similarly, the women had started earning an income at a younger age (15 years) than the men (age 17), on average. As expected, the first job of the majority of rural boys and girls was in agriculture (74 percent and 68 percent, respectively). Fewer than 15 percent had wage employment as their first job.

Most respondents had spent at least

Table 16.6. Responses to the question about the age or stage of their lives when respondents realized that they had become adults: rural Thailand, 1989

Response	Men	Women
Responses mentioning a specific age: median age (yrs.)	21.0	20.0
(No.)	(211)	(293)
Other responses (%)		
(No.)	(65)	(108)
Upon marriage, setting up a household, childbirth	17.0	22.7
Upon graduation, ordination/beginning military service, work	4.0	1.5
Other events	2.2	2.2
Don't know	0.4	0.5
Total	276	401

Coresidence and the Transition to Adulthood in the Rural Thai Family

some time away from their home villages between the ages of 10 and 30. More men than women had moved, but on average the women had experienced their first move a year earlier than the men, at the median age of 19. Information on where they moved to is not available, but I assume that the majority of them moved to urban areas to find temporary employment.

Table 16.7. Timing and prevalence of important life-course events experienced by respondents between ages 10 and 30, by sex: rural Thailand, 1989

Timing and prevalence of specified event	Men	Women
Education		
Median age when respondents began schooling	7.0	7.0
Median age when respondents stopped schooling	11.0	11.0
% of those who had		
≤4 years of schooling	74.2	77.8
5–10 years of schooling	18.9	16.7
11+ years of schooling	6.9	5.5
Work		
Median age when respondents first worked	12.0	11.0
Median age at first paid employment	17.0	15.0
% of respondents, by type of first job		
Agriculture	73.9	67.6
Family enterprise	3.6	9.5
Wage employment	14.9	13.7
Agriculture + family enterprise	7.2	6.7
Mixed activities	0.4	1.0
Never worked	0.0	1.5
Migration		
Median age when respondents first moved	20.0	19.0
% of respondents, by number of moves		
1–2 moves	43.1	56.6
3–4 moves	30.1	14.0
5+ moves	10.9	4.5
Never moved	15.9	24.9
Marriage and parenthood (ever-married only)		
Median age at first marriage	23.0	19.0
Median age at birth of first child	24.0	21.0
% who had experienced marital changes	7.1	11.7
Ordination and military service (males only)		
% who were ever ordained as a novice	18.8	0.0
% who were ever ordained as a monk	46.0	0.0
% who ever had military service	10.5	0.0
(Total no. of cases)	(276)	(401)

The survey respondents had married early. The median age at first marriage was 23 for men and 19 for women. This was younger than the ages at first marriage—24 for men and 22 for women living in nonmunicipal areas—recorded by the 1980 census (Chintana and Aphichat, 1985:6).[3] Like most rural Thais, the respondents had not made much effort to delay parenthood after marrying. Married women in our sample had their first births, on average, around the age of 21, and married men had their first child at the age of 24. The median number of children born before the couple had passed the age of 30 was 2.3 (not shown in Table 16.7). During the period under consideration about 11 percent of the women and 7 percent of the men had experienced marital changes, including separation, divorce, widowhood, and remarriage.

Social scientists who have studied Thai society and culture have generally observed that ordination is an important custom among male Buddhists. It is practiced both as a rite of passage in which a man is believed to repay his parents with merit acquired through the honor of ordination, and as a means of obtaining education and training necessary for improving his social status. In the past a man who never entered the monkhood was considered an "unripe person" (*kon dib*)

---

3. The measure of age at first marriage cited by Chintana and Aphichat was the singulate mean age at marriage (SMAM). The difference between the two sources may be due in part to the different methods of calculation.

whereas the one who did was regarded as a "ripe person" (*kon suk*) (Phya, 1968: 259). The term *suk* (to be ripe) has the same meaning in the current context as adulthood (*pen phuu yai*). It implies that the person is mature enough to assume the role of an adult and to bear responsibilities related to family life. According to popular practice, a man can be ordained as a monk only when he reaches the age of 20 or older; those who are younger can be ordained as novices.

Despite the traditional significance of ordination, fewer than half (46 percent) of the men in our survey had entered monkhood before the age of 31. The proportion who had served as novices was even smaller (19 percent). Interestingly, about one-third of males surveyed in the Northeast had ever been ordained as novices, whereas only 8 percent of those in the South had been. In contrast, a larger proportion of males in the South (58 percent) than in the Northeast (41 percent) had been ordained as monks (data not shown). It is noteworthy that the percentage of men in our survey who entered the monkhood was much lower than the proportions reported in earlier studies. Aphichat (1984:244), for example, reports that about four out of five men in rural communities of a Central Region province had been ordained before they married. (Aphichat's data were collected in 1979, 10 years before the present study.)

If military service can be regarded as one of the events that men pass through in the process of becoming adults, its importance is not confirmed by our findings since only one in 10 men was found to have experienced it. Thailand is different from countries in which military service is required of nearly all young men. The Thai government recruits its servicemen through a process of random selection in which men who have passed a physical examination draw lots. Usually only a small proportion is selected.

From the data in Table 16.7 a general picture of the transition to adulthood in the rural Northeast and South of Thailand can be drawn. Boys and girls leave school at a young age, typically around 11 or 12, after which the majority never have formal education again. Only a small proportion, usually children of well-to-do families, can make their way to secondary school and beyond. The rest stay home with their parents, siblings, and other relatives to work on the family farm. They enter the work force soon after leaving school. Typically the work they do is unpaid labor on the family farm. In very few cases do they find wage employment outside the farm. In their late adolescence, around the age of 17 or 18 and after spending some years helping parents on the farm, most of them move from their home villages to look for work, usually in urban areas where they earn cash income for the first time. For many, their income contributes significantly to the family economy as well as to their own future independence.

Many young people make several moves before finding their marital partners, marrying, and settling down either in their home villages or elsewhere. By this time the girls are close to the age of 20 and the boys are slightly older. Before marriage, nearly half of the men are ordained, typically for a period of three months or less. By the age of 30 those who have married have two or three children. About one in 10 women experiences some kind of marital disruption. The process of becoming an adult seems to reach its completion when a person establishes his or her own family.

RESEARCH NEEDS

A discussion of needed research on the Thai family must include reference to current social, economic, and demographic conditions affecting the family. A brief description of those conditions is offered here to suggest topics needing further research.

In recent decades a number of programs aimed at economic development have resulted in changes in many aspects of rural family life. The increasing importance of the industrial sector has forced rural families, which constitute the majority of Thai families, to adjust to the changes. Although agriculture remains the principal means of subsistence in most rural communities, it is no longer the only source of family income. Recent technological changes and the monetization of the rural economy have made agricultural families, the vast majority of which are small production units, more dependent on the market and middlemen for subsistence and hence less secure. At the same time agricultural land has become increasingly fragmented because of population growth in rural areas and also because of the partible system of inheritance practiced widely in the country.

The demographic response to these changes has been rapid and pronounced. Within the last two decades or so, average family size in rural areas has been reduced by more than one-half, from more than six children per family to fewer than three children on average (Napaporn, Knodel, and Peerasit, 1988:87). This revolutionary change has been made possible by the well-organized National Family Planning Program and by Thailand's unique social and cultural environment (Knodel, Aphichat, and Nibhon, 1987). Other demographic changes in recent decades have been increased migration from rural to urban areas and, lately, international migration of the rural labor force. These changes have also had an impact on the family.

Within this socioeconomic and demographic context several topics for future research can be identified.

One is family support for the younger generation. This research theme is related to the concept of transitions to adulthood, but its focus is on the kinds of material support and the pattern of support that parents give to their children to help them establish their independence. Land has traditionally been the most important form of material support for children attempting to establish themselves in family life. But with land's increasing scarcity and fragmentation, it has become difficult for rural families to provide all their children with enough land to make a living. Other mechanisms need to be sought. Some children have had to seek employment outside the family farm. Formal education is desirable and even necessary for that purpose, but only a small proportion of rural families can afford to provide it. Research is needed on family strategies for allocating resources to children as they grow into adults. Such questions as the following need to be addressed: Who gets the family land, and who continues in school? How do families of different economic classes support their children's education? Who stays home (settles down in the same community) with the parents, and who leaves? What are the differences in family support given to daughters and that given to sons? Research on these issues should contribute to an understanding of social trends in rural areas.

Another topic needing more study concerns family roles and obligations. The so-called loose-structure paradigm views Thai behavior and the Thai personality as less governed by standard rules and regulations than is the case in some other Asian societies (Embree, 1950; Phillips, 1965). In other words, Thai society as a whole exhibits considerable tolerance toward variations in behavior. According to this perspective, interpersonal relationships, including those among family members, are characterized by a lack of strict rules and the strong sanctions usually associated with them. Research on this topic is needed not to support or falsify the loose-structure paradigm but rather to suggest what might be considered standard roles and obligations among family members in Thailand and how they are observed or enforced. Such research issues may include the division of labor, the economic contributions of daughters and sons to the family, and decision making and power within the family. Studies on these topics can enhance comparisons of the Thai family with, for example, the Chinese, Korean, and Japanese families. If it is possible to identify a set of standard roles and obligations, these can serve as benchmarks for studies of family change.

A third topic for research is marital stability. A number of studies have been conducted on nuptiality in Thailand, and we now have a fairly good knowledge of the timing, prevalence, and pattern of Thai marriage. But we know relatively little about marital stability. To my knowledge, only a few master's theses by Thai students have examined the topic of divorce, and limited data constrained those analyses. Conservative views about this issue seem to be that marriages are generally stable in rural areas; that is, marital disruption due to separation, divorce, or death of a spouse happens, but the incidence is insignificant. This view needs to be tested empirically with a nationally representative sample survey. Scattered evidence from some field experiences suggests that there is much to be learned about marital instability, including remarriage, in rural Thailand.

Family support to the elderly is another topic that deserves attention. The Thai population has nearly completed its demographic transition from high to low rates of mortality and fertility. The profound effects of the transition on the population's composition are only now beginning to be felt. Currently about 7 percent of the population is in the elderly age group (60 and above). Given the current rate of population growth, it will take about two decades or so before the Thai population becomes "old," with the elderly constituting 10 percent or more of the total (Napaporn, Malinee, and Chanpen, 1988:2). Nevertheless, rural Thailand has begun to face problems related to the elderly segment of its population. The problems stem not from the population's age structure per se but rather from the out-migration of working-age people, which in many families leaves behind only the old and the very young. One problem is a lack of sufficient welfare programs for the elderly in rural areas. More research is needed on the problems faced by the elderly and on alternative interventions.

Finally, more research attention needs to be paid to adolescents and youth in rural areas. Most studies of this age group have been conducted on a small scale. Given the rapid changes in rural areas caused by the expansion of mass communication and education, there is much to be learned about the behavior of rural adolescents and young adults. Research might address such questions as: How do rural adolescents and youth spend their time—pursuing their families' or their own interests? What is happening to their sexuality? To what extent is their sexual behavior at risk of sexually transmitted diseases such as HIV, the deadly virus that causes AIDS? Is the notion of adolescent dependence on the family undergoing a change? What are the differences between rural and urban adolescents' problems?

CONCLUSION

The study of families is a new area in Thailand's social sciences. Earlier work by anthropologists and ethnographers has tended to focus on form and structure of the Thai household rather than on the family. Issues addressed by those studies have included kinship, marriage, residence, and the succession of material property and power. Ethnographic studies of cultural norms affecting family and household have been descriptive rather than analytical. Few large-scale studies focusing on the family and its various dimensions have been undertaken. A need exists, therefore, for more research, and new kinds of research, on the Thai family. Except for marriage, which has received a fair amount of research attention, many aspects of family life need to be better understood. Investigation of the research topics suggested above should increase the level of understanding of the Thai family.

REFERENCES

Aphichat Chamratrithirong. 1980. *Nuptiality in Thailand: A Cross-sectional Analysis of the 1970 Census*. Papers of the East-West Population Institute, No. 69. Honolulu: East-West Center.

———. 1984. "Loosely-Structured Thailand: The Evidence from Marriage Culture." In Aphichat Chamratrithirong (ed.), *Perspectives on the Thai Marriage*. Bangkok: Institute for Population and Social Research, Mahidol University.

Aphichat Chamratrithirong, S. Phillip Morgan, and Ronald R. Rindfuss. 1988. "Living Arrangements and Family Formation." *Social Forces*, 66(4):926–950.

Bhassorn Limanonda. 1976. "Pattern of Mate Selection and Post-nuptial Residence in Thailand." Master's thesis, Department of Sociology, Cornell University.

———. 1983. *Marriage Patterns in Thailand: Rural-Urban Differentials*. Paper No. 44. Bangkok: Institute of Population Studies, Chulalongkorn University.

———. 1987. *Analysis of Thai Marriage: Attitudes and Behavior (A Case Study of Women in Bangkok Metropolis)*. Paper No. 56. Bangkok: Institute of Population Studies, Chulalongkorn University.

Chai Podhisita. 1984. "Marriage in Rural Northeast Thailand: A Household Perspective." In Aphichat Chamratrithirong (ed.), *Perspectives on the Thai Marriage*, pp. 71–110. Bangkok: Institute for Population and Social Research, Mahidol University.

———. 1985. "Peasant Household Strategies: A Study of Production and Reproduction in a Northeastern Thai Village." Ph.D. dissertation, Department of Anthropology, University of Hawaii.

Cherlin, Andrew, and Aphichat Chamratrithirong. 1987. *Variations in Marriage Patterns in Central Thailand.* Publication No. 109. Bangkok: Institute for Population and Social Research, Mahidol University.

Chintana Pejaranonda and Aphichat Chamratrithirong. 1985. *Nuptiality: 1980 Population and Housing Census.* Bangkok: National Statistical Office.

de Young, John. 1955. *Village Life in Modern Thailand.* Berkeley: University of California Press.

Embree, John F. 1950. "Thailand—A Loosely Structured Social System." *American Anthropologist* 52:181-193.

Foster, Brian L. 1975. "Continuity and Change in Rural Thai Family Structure." *Journal of Anthropological Research* 31:34-50.

———. 1978. "Socio-economic Consequences of Stem Family Composition in a Thai Village." *Ethnography* 17(2):139-156.

———. 1982. "Microdemograhic Variation and Family Composition in Four Thai Villages." *Human Ecology* 10(4):439-453.

Foster, Brian L., and S. B. Seidman. 1976. "Structural Variability in Stem Family Development Cycles: A Simulation Approach." *Behavioral Science Research* 11(4):263-276.

Fox, Robin. 1967. *Kinship and Marriage: An Anthropological Perspective.* Harmondsworth, England: Penguin Books.

Goode, William J. 1964. *The Family.* Englewood Cliffs, N.J.: Prentice-Hall.

Jawalaksana Rachapaetayakom. 1984. "Nuptiality Patterns of the Southern Thai Muslims." In Aphichat Chamratrithirong (ed.), *Perspectives on the Thai Marriage*, pp. 113-129. Bangkok: Institute for Population and Social Research, Mahidol University.

Keyes, Charles F. 1976. "In Search of Land: Village Formation in the Central Chi River Valley, Northeast Thailand." *Contributions to Asian Studies* 9:45-63.

Kingshill, Konrad. 1965. *Ku Daeng: The Red Tomb.* Bangkok: Bangkok Christian College.

Knodel, John E., Aphichat Chamratrithirong, and Nibhon Debavalya. 1987. *Thailand's Reproductive Revolution: Rapid Fertility Decline in a Third-World Setting.* Madison: University of Wisconsin Press.

Knodel, John E., and Malinee Wongsith. 1989. "Monitoring the Educational Gap in Thailand: Trends and Differentials in Lower and Upper Secondary Schooling." *Asian and Pacific Population Forum*, 3(4):1-10, 25-30.

Knodel, John E., Nibhon Debavalya, Napaporn Chayovan, and Aphichat Chamratrithirong. 1984. "Marriage Patterns in Thailand: A Review of Demographic Evidence." In Aphichat Chamratrithirong (ed.), *Perspectives on the Thai Marriage*, pp. 31-68. Bangkok: Institute for Population and Social Research, Mahidol University.

Napaporn Chayovan, John E. Knodel, and Peerasit Kamnuansilpa. 1988. "Approaching Replacement Fertility in Thailand: Results of the 1987 Demographic and Health Survey." *International Family Planning Perspectives* 14(3):86-93.

Napaporn Chayovan, Malinee Wongsith, and Chanpen Saengtienchai. 1988. *Socio-economic Consequences of the Ageing of the Population in Thailand: Survey Findings.* Bangkok: Institute of Population Studies, Chulalongkorn University.

Phillips, Herbert P. 1965. *Thai Peasant Personality.* Berkeley: University of California Press.

Phya Anumanrajadhon. 1968. *Essays on Thai Folklore.* Bangkok: Social Science Press of Thailand.

Potter, Sulamith Heins. 1977. *Family Life in a Northern Thai Village: A Study in the Structural Significance of Women.* Berkeley: University of California Press.

Tambiah, Stanley Jeyaraja. 1970. *Buddhism and the Spirit Cults in North-East Thailand.* Cambridge: Cambridge University Press.

CHAPTER 17

Family Formation in Rural Thailand: Evidence from the 1989–90 Family and Household Survey

by Bhassorn Limanonda

BACKGROUND OF THE STUDY

Early anthropological and sociological studies of Thai families generally focused on the kinship system, family types and structures, family functions, marriage customs and practices, and residence after marriage. Using an anthropological approach that required in-depth information, most of the studies were restricted to the village level and limited to a few localities in certain regions; thus, they were not representative of the population at large. They also tended to be more qualitative than quantitative. Although quantitative demographic data were available on a national scale (e.g., from censuses), the generality of such data inhibited in-depth analyses of the family. Moreover, a majority of these studies were carried out during the 1950s and 1960s.

Only a few nationally representative studies were conducted during the 1970s. One of them was the National Longitudinal Study on Demographic, Social, and Economic Change, fielded during 1969–73 by the Institute of Population Studies, Chulalongkorn University. The study gathered information on families and households in both rural and urban areas. An in-depth analysis of Thai families based on the data from that survey is not possible because its major focus was on assessing changes in demographic behavior in relation to changes in Thailand's social and economic structure.

During the 1980s other large-scale and longitudinal surveys were attempted, but only a few analyses of Thai families were conducted, most of them based on existing data. The economic changes that have occurred in Thailand during the last decade or so are generally believed to have affected many aspects of Thai family life, including people's attitudes about the family. For that reason, up-to-date information on Thai families was needed.

To address this need, the Institute of Population Studies, Chulalongkorn University, and the Institute for Population and Social Research, Mahidol University, jointly conducted a study entitled the Thai Family and Household Survey from December 1989 to December 1990, with the financial support of the University Research Center, Nihon University. Our objective was to apply demographic research methodology to collect a new set of data on household composition, marriage, divorce, decision making in the household, the transition to adulthood, values associated with the family, and attitudes toward the family. By itself, the survey was not expected to yield information that could be used to assess changes occurring over time. By comparing its results with findings from the previous studies, however, we hoped to be able to infer some changes.

SAMPLE SELECTION AND TARGET POPULATION

The sample areas and target population were not intended to be nationally representative. Rather, we were interested in comparing rural samples from two regions of Thailand, the Northeast and the South, which have traditionally had different demographic, economic, social, and cultural characteristics.

The Thai population is fairly homogeneous. Buddhism is the state religion and Thai, the dialect of the Central Region, is the national language, which is spoken and understood everywhere (Knodel, Aphichat, and Nibhon, 1987:49). Nevertheless, cultural and socioeconomic differences characterize, to varying degrees, the four major regions (Central, North, Northeast, and South). The most obvious difference is in the dialects spoken. In the Northeast the Thai Lao dialect is spoken, whereas in the South the Southern Thai dialect and Malay (among Muslims) are common. Many cultural differences are attached to these dialects, resulting in observably different ways of life. The selection of the Northeastern and Southern regions in the present study was based mainly on their cultural differences. In addition, the two regions have different levels of economic development. The Northeast is the poorest and least developed region of the country, owing to its unfavorable geography and other physical characteristics such as infertile soils and a poor water supply, while the South is more prosperous. We expected these two major differences to be reflected in some interesting differences in family formation and structure.

Since the two regions were not intended to be representative of Thailand as a whole, we purposely selected two provinces from each region for the convenience of travel to the field, so as to reduce the costs of fieldwork. From each province we selected two districts, and in each district we randomly selected two villages. Altogether, 16 villages were included in the survey. To insure that the samples covered fairly equal distributions of male and female respondents in each 10-year age group ranging from 15 to 55, we based our selection of respondents on the age criterion and a quota system. Approximately equal numbers of respondents were randomly selected from the 16 villages. Eligible respondents were males and females, married or unmarried. The majority of respondents (628 out of a total of 677) were currently married or had been married. Because men tended to be working away from home during the time of the interviews, slightly more than half (59 percent) of the respondents were women. Of the 333 respondents in the Northeast, approximately 62 percent were females and 38 percent were males.

In the Southern sample, out of 344 respondents, 55 percent were females and 45 percent were males.

OBJECTIVES OF THE PRESENT ANALYSIS

This chapter investigates three main aspects of family formation in the two regions: nuptiality patterns, coresidence at the time of marriage and the establishment of a household, and the assistance that couples receive both when they establish a household and at the time of the first child's birth.

Nuptiality Patterns

Nuptiality patterns include spouse selection, timing of marriage, differentials in husbands' and wives' ages at marriage, the number of times married, and the satisfactions of married life and attitudes toward divorce and remarriage.

Spouse selection Previous studies have consistently indicated that the most prevalent pattern of spouse selection among Thais has been self-selection. Arranged marriages, in which parents alone make the choice and without the young couple's approval, are rare (Kaufman, 1960). The 1969–70 National Longitudinal Study, for example, found that a majority of female respondents had chosen their husbands with the approval of their parents. This pattern was similar in rural and urban areas (Bhassorn, 1979).

Data from the Family and Household Survey indicate that the predominant pattern of spouse selection has not changed over time. More than 80 percent of respondents of both sexes in the South and the Northeast had selected their spouses themselves or concurred with their parents' choice (Table 17.1). Fewer than 10 percent of both males and females in the Northeast and of males in the South (but about 20 percent of southern females) reported that a parent had chosen their spouses without their own consent, or that they themselves had chosen a spouse whom the parents disapproved of or disliked. In the National Longitudinal Study, large proportions of the rural respondents in all regions reported having selected their own spouses. But approximately 44 percent of respondents in the rural South reported that the selection had been made by their parents. This persistent pattern in the South is difficult to explain (Bhassorn, 1979).

Timing of marriage The early socioanthropological and demographic research on Thai marriage patterns found similar patterns of delayed and virtually universal marriage among both men and women. The average age at marriage for men was about 24–25 and for women about 21–22. A comparison of census and survey data covering almost a 40-year period from 1947 to 1984 has revealed only a moderate increase in the proportions remaining single and a stable singulate mean age at marriage for both men and women. The previous studies also indicated regional and rural-urban differences in marriage timing. The earliest average age at marriage was found in the Northeast, a later age at marriage was found in the Central Region, and the latest age was found in

Table 17.1. Percentage distribution of respondents by region, method of spouse selection, and sex: Thai Family and Household Survey, 1989–90

Region and method of spouse selection	Respondents Women	Men
Northeast		
Parental choice without respondent's consent or parent disagreed	9.4	9.1
Self-selection or parental choice with respondent's approval	90.6	90.9
Total %	100.0	100.0
(No.)	(191)	(99)
South		
Parental choice without respondent's consent or parent disagreed	19.7	8.8
Self-selection or parental choice with respondent's approval	80.3	91.2
Total %	100.0	100.0
(No.)	(188)	(147)

Note: In this and subsequent tables, percentages may not sum exactly to 100.0 because of rounding.

the Bangkok Metropolis (Aphichat, 1978: 27; Chintana and Aphichat, 1985:6, cited in Bhassorn, 1987:5).

Findings from the Family and Household Survey indicate lower than the national average ages at marriage for respondents of both sexes in the two regions. This was particularly true of women in the Northeast. Overall patterns of marriage timing practiced in the two regions were similar, however (Table 17.2). More than half of the female respondents had married between the ages of 15 and 19, followed by those who had married between ages 20 and 24. In contrast, more than half of the male respondents had married in their early 20s and about 30 percent in both regions had married at ages 25–29. The mean age at marriage and the proportions married in specific age groups indicate that both men and women in the Northeastern Region tended to marry at younger ages than those in the South. This pattern of regional marriage-age differentials is consistent with the national pattern. Nationally, the lowest age at marriage recorded in the 1980 census was found among the population of the Northeast, the poorest region in Thailand (Chintana and Aphichat, 1985:6).

Husband-wife differentials in age at marriage Differentials between husbands and wives in age at marriage reflect norms and also the status relationship between the sexes. A previous study by Visid et al. (1972) reported that the average age at first marriage for the total male population of Thailand was just three years older than that for women, and the comparable difference in the ages of men and women for provincial urban areas and Bangkok was more than four years (Visid et al., 1972). The Thai Family and Household Survey found that respondents of both sexes had generally tended to marry a spouse in their same five-year age group, although women had also tended to marry men older than themselves and

Table 17.2. Percentage distribution of respondents by age at marriage, sex, and region: Thailand, 1989–90

	Women		Men	
Age at marriage	Northeast	South	Northeast	South
12–14	2.1	1.1	0.0	0.0
15–19	55.0	51.3	9.1	12.0
20–24	35.6	34.8	56.6	51.3
25–29	6.8	8.6	32.3	30.0
30–39	0.5	4.3	2.0	6.7
All ages	100.0	100.0	100.0	100.0
(No.)	(191)	(187)	(99)	(150)
Mean age	19.4	20.4	23.2	23.7

men had tended to marry younger women (Table 17.3). For example, about 48 percent of women married at ages 15–19 had married men 20–24 years of age and about 20 percent of them had married men 25–29. Half of the men married at ages 20–24 and 55 percent of those married at 25–29 had married younger women. But modest proportions of male respondents had wives who were older than themselves. This practice is not uncommon among Thais, even though husbands are traditionally older than their wives and expected to be the head of the family.

Number of times married Marital separation, dissolution, widowhood, and remarriage are not unusual among Thais. Most marriages and divorces, in fact, are unregistered. Evidence from both socio-anthropological and demographic studies indicates high rates of marital dissolution and remarriage (Institute of Population Studies and Population Survey Division, 1977:1; Knodel, Aphichat, and Nibhon, 1987:76). The Family and Household Survey found that 7.2 percent of female respondents and 8.3 percent of male respondents had married more than once. Among those whose marriages had been dissolved, approximately 83 percent of both men and women had married twice and about 14 percent of women and 17 percent of men had married three times. One women in the sample had married six times, behavior considered very unusual in Thai society.

Satisfaction with married life and attitudes toward divorce and remarriage To explore fur-

Table 17.3. Percentage distribution of respondents' age at first marriage by sex and spouse's age at same marriage: Thai Family and Household Survey, 1989–90

Repondent's age at first marriage	Spouse's age at same marriage							
	12–14	15–19	20–24	25–29	30+	All ages	(No.)
Women							
12–14	0.0	50.0	33.0	16.7	0.0	100.0	(6)
15–19	0.0	20.9	47.8	20.4	10.9	100.0	(201)
20–24	0.0	3.8	52.6	30.8	12.8	100.0	(133)
25–29	0.0	0.0	20.7	55.2	24.1	100.0	(29)
30+	0.0	0.0	0.0	12.5	87.5	100.0	(8)
(No. of r's)	(0)	(50)	(174)	(100)	(53)	(377)	
Men							
12–14	0.0	0.0	0.0	0.0	0.0	0.0	(0)
15–19	0.0	85.2	14.8	0.0	0.0	100.0	(27)
20–24	2.3	49.6	39.8	8.3	0.0	100.0	(133)
25–29	0.0	33.8	39.0	20.8	6.5	100.0	(77)
30+	8.3	8.3	33.3	50.0	0.0	100.0	(12)
(No. of r's)	(4)	(16)	(91)	(33)	(5)	(249)	

Family Formation in Rural Thailand

ther the issues of marital dissolution and remarriage, respondents were asked a series of questions about their satisfaction with married life and their attitudes toward divorce and remarriage. Their responses are summarized in Table 17.4.

Only 24 percent of female respondents reported unqualified satisfaction with their married lives, as compared with 43 percent of male respondents. About 71 percent of female and 52 percent of male respondents expressed moderate satisfaction with married life, while 3 percent of both sexes were neither satisfied nor dissatisfied. This pattern of responses may be interpreted as indicating that most Thais do not express their feelings on this subject.

When the respondents were asked whether they had ever thought of divorce, 72 percent of female and 86 percent of male respondents said they had never thought of it. Surprisingly, however, 25 percent of the women, as compared with 13 percent of the men, reported having thought once in a while of divorcing their present spouse. I interpret this response to be a complaint rather than a statement of serious intent. The women who chose this answer had probably thought about the burdens of "being a wife"—that is, one who is expected to serve the husband and assume much of the responsibility for the family. Fewer than 1 percent of the

Table 17.4. Percentage distribution of respondents by attitudes toward marriage, divorce, and remarriage and by sex: Thai Family and Household Survey, 1989–90

Attitudes toward marriage, divorce, and remarriage	Women	Men
Satisfaction with married life		
Very satisfied	24.3	43.3
Moderately satisfied	71.1	52.9
Neither satisfied nor dissatisfied	3.4	3.3
Dissatisfied	1.2	0.4
Total %	100.0	100.0
(No.)	(325)	(240)
Have ever thought of divorce?		
Yes, often	3.1	0.8
Yes, once in a while	25.2	12.9
Never	71.7	86.3
Total %	100.0	100.0
(No.)	(325)	(207)
Would consider remarriage in old age?		
If suitable partner found, will remarry	22.1	33.5
Prefer not to remarry	76.6	64.8
Other responses	1.2	1.7
Total %	100.0	100.0
(No.)	(321)	(236)

men and about 1 percent of the women reported that they were dissatisfied with their married lives, specifying no reasons.

Respondents were also asked, "If you were to become single in your old age, do you think you would remarry?" The interviewer did not define "old age," and therefore the responses to this question probably varied according to each respondent's perception of old age. Approximately 77 percent of female respondents and 65 percent of male respondents answered that they would prefer not to remarry if they were to become single in old age. But about 22 percent of female and 34 percent of male respondents replied that they would remarry regardless of age if they found a suitable partner.

Coresidence at the Time of Marriage and the Establishment of a Household after Marriage

Previous studies have documented that patterns of postnuptial residence and of the establishment of households after marriage differ between rural and urban populations (Bhassorn, 1979:42). The majority of urban couples live on their own (neolocally) after marriage, whereas far lower proportions of couples in rural areas do so. Moreover, patterns of postnuptial residence generally differ among regions. Living with the wife's parents (matrilocal residence) is most prevalent in the Northeast and the North, whereas the majority of couples in the Central Region, particularly in Bangkok, and in the urban South, prefer to live neolocally or with the husband's family (virilocal residence). This last pattern reflects the larger proportions of Chinese people in those areas (Bhassorn, 1979:42). These patterns are determined mainly by cultural differences and practices in each area. The latest findings from the analysis of postnuptial residence patterns of Thai women (Bhassorn, 1989) indicate no major changes, despite the rapid social and economic changes that have occurred in Thailand in recent decades.

Coresidence at the time of marriage In the Family and Household Survey, information on coresidence at the time of marriage was obtained from answers to the questions, "Now think back to the *first year* after your *first* marriage. Who lived with you in the same household or in the same locality then?" More than half (56 percent) of female respondents reported having coresided with their own parents, and about 14 percent had had parents living in the same locality (Table 17.5). With these two categories combined, more than two-thirds of female respondents had had their parents living in the same house or nearby. Nearly half (49 percent) of female respondents had had siblings living in the same house, and nearly one-fourth had had siblings living in the same locality during the first year of marriage. Fewer than one-fifth of the female respondents had lived with their spouse's parents. This pattern reflects the traditional practice among northeastern rural couples of living with the wife's parents. Moreover, about 46 percent reported that their husbands' parents had not lived in the same locality at that time. On the other hand, 38 percent of male respondents had lived with their wives' parents, while a smaller percentage (34 percent) had lived in the same house with their own parents. About 37 percent had not lived in the same locality with their own parents during the first year of marriage. Nearly one-third of them had lived with siblings in the same house, whereas slightly more than one-third had siblings living elsewhere.

The larger percentage of female respondents who had lived with their own parents after marrying, combined with the large percentage of male respondents who had lived with their wives' parents, indicates the predominance of matrilocal residence among Thais in rural areas, especially in the Northeast. This custom can be described as a temporary form of the extended family, created when a married daughter brings her husband to live with her own parents for a short period of time before the couple establish their own residence. In our sample, apart from those who had lived with their parents, parents-in-law, and siblings, only small percentages of both male and female respondents had lived with other relatives during the first year of marriage. But sizable proportions of male and female respondents had had relatives living in the same locality. Moreover, about 50–60 percent of respondents reported that their

Table 17.5. Percentage distribution of respondents by sex and type of relatives who resided in the same house or same locality during the first year of their first marriage: Thai Family and Household Survey, 1989–90

Sex and type of relative	Same house Yes	Same locality Yes	Same locality No	Relative had died	Did not have relative	Total %	Total (No.)
Women							
Own parents	56.2	13.7	26.1	4.0	0.0	100.0	(379)
Spouse's parents	18.9	29.8	45.5	5.9	0.0	100.0	(379)
Step-parents	4.2	2.1	5.5	1.1	87.1	100.0	(379)
Grandparents	7.4	21.4	23.0	48.3	0.0	100.0	(379)
Parents' siblings	2.9	57.1	38.6	0.5	0.8	100.0	(379)
Own siblings	48.8	22.7	26.4	0.5	1.6	100.0	(379)
Other relatives	2.7	51.6	25.8	0.0	19.9	100.0	(379)
Men							
Own parents	33.7	26.1	36.5	3.6	0.0	100.0	(249)
Spouse's parents	38.1	24.7	35.2	2.0	0.0	100.0	(249)
Step-parents	2.4	3.2	6.4	0.4	87.6	100.0	(249)
Grandparents	2.8	18.5	20.5	58.2	0.0	100.0	(249)
Parents' siblings	0.8	53.4	44.5	0.4	0.8	100.0	(249)
Own siblings	30.6	34.7	32.7	0.0	2.0	100.0	(249)
Other relatives	4.4	49.6	30.2	0.0	15.7	100.0	(249)

grandparents had been deceased by the time the respondents married, a reflection of the high mortality rate and shorter life expectancy among older generations of Thais.

When the respondents are classified by region (Table 17.6), the regional differences in postnuptial residential patterns become more obvious. Among respondents in the rural Northeast, matrilocal residence or uxorilocal residence (with the wife's family) was the most prevalent type of household. Fifty-six percent of the respondents had coresided with their parents during the first year of marriage, and 53 percent of them had also coresided with siblings. Although few of them had lived with other relatives in the same house, majorities reported having lived in the same locality with their parents' siblings (61 percent) and with other relatives (51 percent). Only 29 percent of respondents reported that they had lived in the same household with their spouses' parents, and about 31 percent of them reported that their spouses' parents had lived in the same locality.

In the Southern sample, we found a mixture of patterns of postnuptial coresidence. Neolocal and virilocal residence were as common as matrilocal residence. About 40 percent of the respondents had coresided with their own parents, whereas only 24 percent had lived with their spouses' parents. Large proportions of respondents, however, had not lived in the same locality with either their own parents (37 percent) or their spouses'

Table 17.6. Percentage distribution of respondents by region and type of relatives who resided in the same house or same locality during the first year of their first marriage: Thai Family and Household Survey, 1989–90

Region and type of relative	Same house Yes	Same locality Yes	Same locality No	Relative had died	Did not have relative	Total %	Total (No.)
Northeast							
Own parents	56.2	16.9	22.4	4.5	0.0	100.0	(290)
Spouse's parents	29.4	30.8	35.0	4.9	0.0	100.0	(290)
Step-parents	4.5	1.0	5.2	0.7	88.6	100.0	(290)
Grandparents	8.3	27.6	19.0	45.2	0.0	100.0	(290)
Parents' siblings	3.1	60.8	34.7	1.0	0.3	100.0	(290)
Own siblings	53.3	23.2	21.5	0.3	1.7	100.0	(290)
Other relatives	3.8	51.0	23.3	0.0	21.9	100.0	(288)
South							
Own parents	39.6	20.1	37.0	3.3	0.0	100.0	(338)
Spouse's parents	24.0	25.2	46.9	3.9	0.0	100.0	(338)
Step-parents	2.7	3.8	6.5	0.9	86.1	100.0	(338)
Grandparents	3.3	13.9	24.6	58.3	0.0	100.0	(338)
Parents' siblings	1.2	51.3	46.3	0.0	1.2	100.0	(338)
Own siblings	31.7	31.1	35.2	0.3	1.8	100.0	(338)
Other relatives	3.0	50.6	31.3	0.0	15.2	100.0	(338)

parents (47 percent), although about half of the respondents reported that their parents' siblings and other relatives had lived in the same locality.

Establishment of a household after marriage
After being asked about their living arrangement at the time of marriage, respondents were next asked whether they had established a residence of their own after marriage. The question was worded as follows: "Many people establish their own independent households some time after their first marriage. We are interested in knowing more about you. Did you and your spouse establish an independent household of your own at any time after your first marriage?" Their responses (not shown here) indicated that both male and female respondents had gradually established their own households as time went by, the percentage increasing with the respondents' age. About the same proportions of men and women (77 and 78 percent, respectively) aged 50–55 had already established their own households.

Amount of time before establishing a household Respondents were also asked how long after marrying had they established their own household. Their responses reveal different patterns related to age and region (Table 17.7). Respondents from the

Table 17.7. Percentage distribution of respondents by region, amount of time after marriage before establishing their own household, and current age: Thai Family and Household Survey, 1989–90

Region and amount of time before establishing own household	Current age					
	15–19	20–24	25–29	30–39	40–49	50–55
Northeast						
Immediately	0.0	10.8	8.3	12.4	13.9	17.1
< 1 year	0.0	0.0	5.6	1.9	4.2	2.9
1 year	0.0	5.4	5.6	4.8	8.3	11.4
1.5–2 years	0.0	0.0	16.7	6.7	4.2	2.9
3–6 years	20.0	10.8	5.6	21.0	18.1	17.1
7+ years	0.0	2.7	2.8	16.2	26.4	31.4
Did not establish own household	80.0	70.3	55.6	37.1	25.0	17.1
Total %	100.0	100.0	100.0	100.0	100.0	100.0
(No.)	(5)	(37)	(36)	(105)	(72)	(35)
South						
Immediately	0.0	36.7	17.2	32.5	29.5	36.7
< 1 year	0.0	13.3	3.4	7.5	1.3	0.0
1 year	33.3	6.7	17.2	11.7	15.4	10.2
1.5–2 years	0.0	6.7	12.1	11.7	5.1	8.2
3–6 years	0.0	13.3	12.1	6.7	10.3	10.2
7+ years	0.0	3.3	3.4	7.5	7.7	8.2
Did not establish own household	66.7	20.0	34.5	22.5	30.8	26.5
Total %	100.0	100.0	100.0	100.0	100.0	100.0
(No.)	(3)	(30)	(58)	(120)	(78)	(49)

Northeastern Region had lived with their parents for much longer periods of time than those from the South, a finding that indicates the persistence of matrilocal residence in the Northeast. Fewer than 15 percent of respondents of every age group except the 50–55-year-old group had set up their own household immediately after marriage. In contrast, in the South much higher proportions of respondents had lived with their parents for only one year or else had set up their own households immediately after marriage. Another difference is that respondents in the Northeast had waited much longer after marriage to establish their own households (78 months, on the average) than had respondents in the South (38 months). These findings again indicate that patterns of coresidence are more mixed in the South, whereas matrilocal residence is more prevalent in the Northeast.

Within each region, no obvious differences emerged between male and female respondents with regard to the amount of time it had taken them to establish their own households, nor between the sexes in the proportions who had not established their own households after marriage. But between the two regions clear differences did surface (Table 17.8). In the Northeast, larger proportions of respondents of both sexes had stayed permanently, or stayed for longer periods, in their parental homes than left immediately, again confirming the prevalence of matrilocal postnuptial residence among the population of the rural Northeast. By contrast, in the South the pro-

Table 17.8. Percentage distribution of respondents by region, amount of time after marriage before establishing their own household, and sex: Thai Family and Household Survey, 1989–90

Region and amount of time before establishing own household	Women	Men
Northeast		
Immediately	11.0	15.2
< 1 year	3.1	2.0
1–2 years	14.1	9.1
3–6 years	14.7	20.2
7+ years	18.3	14.1
Did not establish own household	38.7	39.4
Total %	100.0	100.0
(No.)	(191)	(99)
South		
Immediately	30.3	29.3
< 1 year	3.2	6.7
1–2 years	20.7	24.0
3–6 years	11.7	6.7
7+ years	4.8	8.7
Did not establish own household	29.3	24.7
Total %	100.0	100.0
(No.)	(188)	(150)

portions of male and female respondents who had left their parental homes immediately after marriage were slightly higher than the proportions of those who had not established their own households after marriage. In addition, the proportions of both male and female respondents who had lived with their parents or in-laws only one or two years were quite large by Thai standards (24 percent for men and 21 percent for women). These findings tend to confirm the higher rate of neolocal residence among southerners. Since this was a rural sample, however, we also found sizable proportions of respondents who had not established their own households since marrying (29 percent among the women, 25 percent among the men). The different patterns of postnuptial residence found in these two regions reflect some of the cultural differences between the two populations.

Help Received in Establishing a Household

Another aspect of family life investigated in the survey was the support that couples receive from relatives and friends upon setting up their independent households. Respondents were asked who had helped them to buy or rent their own house, build the house, move, or purchase the household appliances and furniture. Their responses are summarized in Table 17.9.

Table 17.9. Percentage distribution of respondents by sex and source of assistance received in buying or building a house, moving, and purchasing household appliances and furniture: Thai Family and Household Survey, 1989–90

Sex and source of assistance	Buying or renting house	Building house	Moving	Purchasing household appliances	Purchasing furniture
Women					
No one	17.4	38.0	31.9	53.6	56.5
Parents	5.3	10.6	5.0	7.4	6.1
Siblings	0.3	2.6	6.6	0.3	0.5
Friends	0.5	2.9	3.4	0.8	0.3
More than 1 source	0.3	6.3	17.7	2.1	1.8
Did not do this	42.2	5.5	1.3	1.8	0.8
Did not move	34.0	34.0	34.0	34.0	34.0
Total (379)	100.0	100.0	100.0	100.0	100.0
Men					
No one	21.4	40.3	36.3	61.7	62.1
Parents	3.2	8.9	2.4	3.6	5.6
Siblings	0.4	3.2	4.8	0.8	0.4
Friends	1.2	2.4	4.8	0.0	0.0
More than 1 source	2.0	7.7	17.7	1.6	0.8
Did not do this	41.1	6.9	3.2	1.6	0.4
Did not move	30.6	30.6	30.6	30.6	30.6
Total (248)	100.0	100.0	100.0	100.0	100.0

Help in buying or renting a house With regard to buying or renting a house, most respondents, both male and female, reported that they had not established a new residence after marriage or had not bought or rented a house. Among those who had bought or rented a house of their own, approximately one-fifth of both men and women reported that no one had helped them. Much smaller proportions had received help from relatives or friends. Among those who had received some help, their parents were the main source of assistance. Respondents who had built a house or moved reported similar experiences, except that even larger proportions of them had received no assistance. Majorities of both men and women had purchased their household appliances and furniture without assistance from anyone.

Help around the house at the time of the first child's birth The last two questions explored in the current analysis are the place where the first child of the respondent was born and whether the respondent had received help at the time of the child's birth. With regard to the birthplace of the first child, respondents from the Northeast and the South had had very different experiences. A substantial majority (65 percent) of the first children of respondents in the South were reported to have been born in a hospital, clinic, or health center, compared with only 17 percent of the firstborn children of respondents in the Northeast. Nearly half (42 percent) of northeastern respondents reported that their first child had been born at their own home, and 27 percent reported that the child had been born at their parents' home (data not shown). A much smaller proportion of respondents in the South reported having had the first child born at home (15 percent), and even fewer had arranged for the child to be born at the parental home (13 percent). These findings seem to reflect the greater prevalence of matrilocal residence and possibly a longer period of coresidence with parents in the Northeast Region.

Table 17.10. Percentage distribution of female respondents by place where the first child was born and current age: Thai Family and Household Survey, 1989–90

Place where the first child was born	Respondent's current age				
	15–19	20–29	30–39	40–49	50–55
Hospital, clinic, or health center	100.0	70.0	37.1	26.8	11.9
Own home	0.0	13.0	28.8	31.7	45.2
Parental home	0.0	13.0	22.7	34.1	42.9
Spouse's parents' home	0.0	2.0	8.3	3.7	0.0
Other place	0.0	2.0	3.0	3.7	0.9
Total %	100.0	100.0	100.0	100.0	100.0
(No.)	(7)	(100)	(132)	(82)	(42)

When we classified female respondents by age (Table 17.10), we found differences between age groups in their reports of the birthplace of their first child. Larger proportions of younger than of older women had delivered their first child in a hospital, clinic, or health center. For instance, only 12 percent of women 50–55 years old had given birth to their first child in a hospital, clinic, or health center, whereas about 70 percent of women 20–29 years old had done so. Conversely, much larger percentages of older than of younger women had delivered their first child in their own home or their parental home. These patterns suggest increased levels of modernization and use of health facilities among younger generations.

Few respondents of all age groups had delivered their first child at their spouse's parents' home. This is not particularly surprising. The preference may be due to a new mother's need for physical and psychological help during or after childbirth and her closer attachment to her own parents.

Finally, respondents were asked, "During the first month after the birth of your first child, did anybody give you significant help with work or services? [If so,] who were they?" At least four-fifths of respondents in both regions said they had received some assistance during that period (Table 17.11). The proportion was slightly higher in the Northeast (88 percent versus 81 percent). Assistance came mainly from the parents on either side. Siblings of both sides also contributed assistance during this difficult time. Substantial percentages of the respondents reported that they had received assistance

Table 17.11. Percentage distribution of respondents by region, whether assistance was received, and source of assistance during the first months after the first child was born: Thai Family and Household Survey, 1989–90

Whether assistance was received and source	Northeast	South
Assistance received?		
Yes	87.5	80.8
No	12.5	19.2
Total %	100.0	100.0
(No.)	(273)	(318)
Source of assistance		
No one	12.5	19.2
Own or spouse's parents	43.6	47.5
Own or spouse's siblings	12.5	15.4
Others (friends or relatives)	7.0	6.0
More than 1 source	24.5	11.9
Total	100.0	100.0
(No.)	(273)	(318)

from more than one source, including parents, siblings, relatives, and friends.

SUMMARY

This chapter has analyzed various aspects of marriage and family formation in rural Thailand, using data based on the Thai Family and Household Survey involving interviews of 677 female and male respondents in the Northeastern and Southern region in December 1989 and January 1990. Approximately equal numbers of male and female respondents, both married and unmarried, were randomly selected from each village. Contrary to expectation, the findings reveal no major changes from those reported in earlier studies despite rapid socioeconomic changes in Thai society during recent decades.

In accordance with the national pattern established from previous studies, large majorities of respondents from both regions had selected their spouses themselves or had approved their parents' choices. With regard to marriage timing, the mean age at marriage of both males and females in the sample was slightly lower than the national average, probably because this was a rural sample. Both women and men in the Northeast married at younger ages than did their counterparts in the South.

As in previous studies, our survey revealed age differentials between spouses, men tending to marry women about four or five years younger than themselves, whereas women tended to marry men about five to 10 years older. Nevertheless, a majority of respondents had married spouses of approximately the same age as themselves.

Most respondents were fairly satisfied with their married life and had never thought of getting divorced. Nearly 80 percent of women and 65 percent of men said that they would prefer not to remarry if they were to become single in their old age. Nevertheless, large percentages of both men and women stated that if they found a suitable partner, they would remarry regardless of their age. Among respondents who had experienced marriage dissolution of any kind (separation, divorce, or widowhood), a majority of them had remarried. Because most Thais do not register their marriages, both divorce and remarriage are often de facto.

Differences in coresidence at the time of marriage emerged between respondents in the Northeast and the South and also between male and female respondents. As expected, matrilocal residence was still prevalent in the Northeast, while in the South patterns of residence were quite mixed, including matrilocal, virilocal, and neolocal residence. Immediately after marriage, a majority of female respondents had lived in the same house or in the same locality as their parents. On the other hand, quite a large proportion of male respondents had lived with their wives' families and not in the same locality as their own parents. This pattern of matrilocal residence is common among rural Thais, particularly in the North and Northeast. In addition, much larger proportions of respondents in the Northeast than in the South had coresided with their parental family for three to six years or longer before establishing their own households, and larger proportions of them had continued to live with their parents since marriage and did not intend to establish their own households. Conversely, larger proportions of southern respondents had left their parental homes immediately or almost immediately after marriage to set up their own independent households.

Most respondents had received no assistance in establishing a new residence after marriage. Among those who had received help, their parents were the main source of assistance.

Younger cohorts had usually delivered their first child at a hospital, clinic, or health center, whereas older respondents had done so in their own homes or at their parental homes. Much smaller proportions of respondents in the South than in the Northeast reported having the first child born at home and fewer of them had given birth at the parental home. Again, these findings reflect the greater prevalence of matrilocal residence and longer duration of coresidence with parents among the Northeastern population. A majority of respondents had received some kind of help from their own parents or their in-laws and siblings at the time of their first child's birth, and only a small percentage of respondents had received no assistance from relatives or friends.

REFERENCES

Aphichat Chamratrithirong. 1978. *Thai Marriage Patterns: An Analysis of the 1970 Census Data.* Bangkok: Institute for Population and Social Research, Mahidol University.

Bhassorn Limanonda. 1979. *Mate Selection and Post Nuptial Residence in Thailand.* Paper No. 28. Bangkok: Institute of Population Studies, Chulalongkorn University.

―――. 1987. "Analysis of Thai Marriage: Attitudes and Behavior. A Case Study of Women in Bangkok Metropolis" PSTC Working Paper Series, No. 87-11 (September). Providence: Population Studies and Training Center, Brown University.

―――. 1989. "Analysis of Postnuptial Residence Patterns of Thai women." In *Health and Population Studies Based on the 1987 Thailand Demographic and Health Survey,* pp. 223-252. New York: Population Council.

Chintana Pejaranonda and Aphichat Chamratrithirong. 1985. *Nuptiality: 1980 Population and Housing Census.* Subject Report No. 5. Bangkok: National Statistical Office, Office of the Prime Minister.

Institute of Population Studies, Chulalongkorn University, and Population Survey Division, National Statistical Office. 1977. *The Survey of Fertility in Thailand: Country Report.* World Fertility Survey Report No. 1. Bangkok: Allied Printers.

Kaufman, Howard K. 1960. *Bangkuad: A Community Study in Thailand.* Locus Valley, N.Y.: J. J. Augustin Incorporated Publisher.

Knodel, John, Aphichat Chamratrithirong, and Nibhon Debavalya. 1987. *Thailand's Reproductive Revolution: Rapid Fertility Decline in a*

Third World Setting. Madison: University of Wisconsin Press.

Visid Prachuabmoh, John Knodel, Suchart Prasitrathsin, and Nibhon Debavalya. 1972. *The Rural and Urban Population of Thailand: Comparative Profiles.* Institute of Population Studies, Chulalongkorn University Research Report No. 8. Bangkok: Thai Watana Panich Press Co., Ltd.

CHAPTER 18

Attitudes toward Family Values in Rural Thailand

by Malinee Wongsith

In Thailand, where rapid socioeconomic development in the past decade has been accompanied by an effective family planning program, the impact of social and economic change can be observed on the structure of the family and its functions. As Thailand gradually becomes less an agricultural society and more an urbanized and industrialized one, the family is undergoing a transformation from an extended to a nuclear structure. Even though the family is a fundamental unit of the society, its meaning to the society is changing drastically (Carter and McGoldrick, 1988:10–11). Thais who used to spend their entire adult life span rearing children are now spending less than half that amount of time discharging their parental responsibilities. Owing to a low birth rate, family size is decreasing, causing the roles of women to change. Social exposure offers women better status, but divorce and remarriage rates are rising. Such changes, which are characteristic of modern economic development, are affecting family values and traditions.

The term "modernization" usually carries with it the implication of cultural change, one that moves a society away from traditional practices (Korson,

1978:170). For instance, the traditional value placed on marriage seems to have eroded as Thai society has modernized and surrounding conditions have changed. With increasing modernization and education, discrimination against females can no longer be maintained. Parents' control over their children's choice of marriage partners has weakened, the choice being made more and more by the children themselves (Bhassorn, 1979:2).

This chapter focuses on a study of the attitudes of rural Thais toward family values and their opinions about social life. Because it is reasonable to assume that attitudes reflect existing family conditions, they may serve as crude predictors of future trends in the family.

THE DATA

The data for the study are from the Thai Family Survey, conducted in December 1989 by the Institute of Population Studies, Chulalongkorn University, in collaboration with the Institute for Population and Social Research, Mahidol University. The survey was sponsored by Nihon University and the Program on Population of the East-West Center. The sample consisted of 677 rural persons aged 15–55 (401 females and 276 males) in the Northeastern and Southern regions, most of whom were engaged in agriculture and had at least a primary education. The sampled population was purposively selected to provide contrast between the rural samples of the Northeast and the South. Four provinces were selected, Nongkhai and Udornthani provinces in the Northeast and Suratthani and Phang-Nga provinces in the South. The survey questions were posed to the respondents in interviews conducted in their homes by trained interviewers.

The questions concerned both family life and values and respondents' broader social experiences and attitudes. A section of the questionnaire on family values included questions about marriage, women's roles, children's upbringing, and elderly persons in the household. Each item was read as a statement with which respondents were asked to agree or disagree. In the analysis that follows, the responses of the sample as a whole to those statements are first examined. Because the results indicate differences in attitudes according to respondents' demographic, social, and economic characteristics, the analysis also considers the influence of age, sex, educational background, occupation, and region of residence on attitudes and values. The second part of the chapter analyzes respondents' opinions about their social experiences. Percentage distributions of response categories exclude "don't know" responses and nonresponses. The most noticeable limitation of the survey data is that they deal with only some aspects of respondents' family values and social experiences.

THE THAI RURAL FAMILY AND ITS VALUES

To provide a context for the study, it is necessary to describe the Thai rural family. Thai kinship and marriage units perform a variety of functions. The family, whatever its form, is the fundamental social unit in rural areas. In rural families all able-bodied members are expected to contribute their labor to farm production, whereas nonable-bodied members are consumers. In addition, the family socializes its members, training the young for careers in farming and homemaking, launching them on those careers when they reach adulthood, and caring for the aged until their death. The family is obligated to finance marriages of offspring, the cremation of the deceased, and other religious and social ceremonies (Smith, 1973:136).

Almost all marriages in rural Thailand are monogamous (Smith, 1978:22). A Thai youth of marriageable age seeks a bride among the young women of his acquaintance. Before their marriage occurs, the young Thai generally secures the approval of both sets of parents. After the initial approach, the parents discuss financial matters. Bargaining usually focuses on the amount of the young man's gift to the young woman (*khongman*) and his gift to her parents (*sin sord*). If the two sides reach a satisfactory agreement, the couple proceeds to marry (Supatra, 1985:55–57). A large majority of newlyweds start their married lives in the bride's parental household (Smith, 1978:29) and eventually establish their new household near that of her parents.

Within the Thai family, the father is regarded as the head of the household, to whom his wife and children show due respect. Chores are performed interchangeably by men and women, and in general the division of labor between the sexes is flexible (Smith, 1978:31). Heavy physical farm labor is usually done by men, however, whereas most cleaning, cooking, and child rearing are done by women. The elderly, who serve as a cornerstone of the family, have high status. Younger family members respect and support them, and the elderly contribute to the effective functioning of the family unit by performing household duties and assuming the role of advisor on important matters (Napaporn, Malinee, and Chanpen, 1988:74). When the elderly die, it is the duty of the younger family members to hold traditional ceremonies making merit for the deceased.[1]

Thai society has numerous social values (Supatra, 1985:23–28; Chaweewan, 1979: 42–51). This study focuses on those

---

1. To make merit in the Thai sense is to perform deeds or take actions that benefit the individual in this life or the next. It covers a wide range of activities—e.g., providing food for the monks, cleaning and caring for the temple, entering the monkhood, and making donations in cash or in kind to the temple or to poor people.

related to the family, and specifically on the following:

1. *Buddhism.* Virtually all Thai people believe in the Buddhist concepts of merit and demerit. To quote Kingshill (1976:189), "These words [merit and demerit] are constantly on the lips of the villagers. At frequent intervals, they will do something or other to make merit."

2. *Children's obligation to parents.* It is a common belief that children owe something to their parents, especially in the parents' old age. When the parents die, the children are expected to make merit for them.

3. *Respect and rank.* Every individual, regardless of his or her position in the hierarchy, deserves respect. Seniority is revered. Accordingly, the head of the family exercises more power over other members, and the entire structure of the family is predicated on a system of superordination and subordination. The family instills in its members respect for the superior-subordinate relationships that exist among relatives, teachers, monks, government officials, and others.

4. *Women's central role.* The Thai family system is conceptually centered on women, who perform various functions in the family. For example, most women combine child rearing, care for the elderly, and housework with income-generating activities. But women are not more powerful or influential than men (Potters, 1977:21).

FINDINGS

Attitudes toward Family Values

I have classified the values attached by rural Thais to the family into four categories: values associated with marriage, with sex roles, with children, and with the elderly, as shown in Table 18.1.

Although several studies (e.g., Bencha et al., 1992:17; Amara, Uraiwan, and Sirinan, 1987:23–24) have shown a tendency among Thais to favor equality of the sexes, two-thirds of the respondents in the Thai Family Survey agreed with a statement asserting the authority of the husband over the wife. Nevertheless, only one-fourth agreed that a wife should overlook occasional infidelity on the part of her husband.

Results from the Thailand Demographic and Health Survey of 1987 indicate that very few Thai women have never married by the end of their reproductive age span (Napaporn, Peerasit, and Knodel, 1988:25). Our attitudinal data revealed broad support for marriage, only one-fifth of the respondents agreeing with the proposition of single lives for young people. This result is likely due in part to the Thai belief that marriage makes life more complete.

The dramatic social, demographic, and economic changes in Thailand in recent years have resulted in conflicts within families, in some cases leading to eventual marital dissolution. Even though no precise figures are available on

Attitudes toward Family Values in Rural Thailand

the divorce or separation rate in Thailand—many marriages and divorces are not legally registered in the government rolls, and many separations seem to follow an on-again, off-again pattern (Phillips, 1965:26)—the number of divorces seems to be increasing. As was reported by the Office of the National Economic and Social Development Board (NESDB, 1989:145), the rate of legal divorces in Thailand is increasing and the highest rate is found in Bangkok. This trend is reflected in changing attitudes of rural Thais toward the remarriage of divorced women. Three-quarters of those surveyed in late 1989 were not opposed to their remarriage.

Like other societies, Thailand has its own precepts regarding the appropriate behavior of women. Women's roles have been traditionally confined to the family, as daughter, wife, and mother

Table 18.1. Percentages agreeing with family-value items: Thai Family Survey, 1989

Item	%
Marriage	
Some equality in marriage is a good thing, but by and large the husband ought to have the main say-so in family matters	67.6
A wife ought to overlook isolated instances of sexual infidelity on the part of her husband	25.3
It is good that more young people today prefer to lead single lives on their own instead of getting married	20.7
Divorced women should not remarry	26.0
Sex role	
It is better for the family if the husband is the main breadwinner and the wife takes care of the home and the family	82.1
Almost any woman is better off in the home than in a job or profession	70.0
Both husband and wife should take care of the children when both are at home	94.4
It is a good thing for a man to do kitchen work	22.2
Children	
Children today have too little respect for their parents	64.1
A teenager should be allowed to decide most things for himself or herself	32.6
Parents should encourage just as much independence in their daughters as in their sons	53.6
Elderly	
Younger people should not disagree with elders, even when an elderly person is wrong	50.4
It is the children's responsibility to take care of their parents when the parents get old	99.6
A woman's duty to her parents and parents-in-law comes before her duty to her husband	85.9
In the future the government will have to play a bigger role in providing for the elderly	95.4
It is necessary to hold traditional ceremonies of merit-making for the deceased	96.6
(No. of cases)	(677)

(Holmstrom, 1973:546). Although formal authority is vested in men, women have always been central to the running of the household. Not surprisingly, therefore, four-fifths of the respondents agreed that the wife should take care of the home and the family, and 70 percent agreed that most women were better off in the home than in a job or a profession. Nearly all respondents (94 percent) agreed that both the husband and the wife should care for the children when both spouses were at home, reinforcing findings from other studies (e.g., Smith, 1978:31) of a generally flexible division of labor between the sexes within the Thai home. While each sex has control in certain areas, consultation and cooperation occur regarding family affairs.

Nonetheless, only one-fifth of the respondents agreed with the proposition that "it is a good thing for a man to do kitchen work." Meal preparation is considered a woman's or girl's task and is not thought to be masculine. A Thai man will cook only if he desires to or is forced to do so by necessity (de Young, 1966:37).

As for children's role in the family, young people are expected to show reverence to older family members and family leaders (Japan Research Institute, 1987:25). Although that is the normative expectation, nearly two-thirds of the survey respondents expressed the view that children today have too little respect for their parents.

The teen years mark the beginning of self-assertion and independence from parental authority, but the degree of independence varies among societies. In the case of rural Thailand, parents retain a certain amount of authority over their adolescent children. And this authority continues to be valued; only one-third of respondents agreed that teenagers should be allowed to make most decisions for themselves. As for equality of independence for daughters and sons, slightly more than half (54 percent) of the respondents endorsed that value.

Although the elderly are highly regarded in Thai society, age alone is no guarantee of respect. To maintain respect, elders must behave in a manner befitting their role (Kaufman, 1960:32). Today, as a result of education and greater economic independence, young people are more modern minded than in the past, and their obedience to elders tends to be conditional. Only half of the survey respondents agreed with the idea that young people should submit to elderly people's opinions even when those opinions are wrong.

An earlier study (Napaporn, Malinee, and Chanpen, 1988:68) has found that most elderly Thais live with their children. That practice received approval by virtually all respondents to the 1989 survey, who agreed that it is children's responsibility to take care of their parents in old age. Similarly, 86 percent of the respondents agreed that a woman's duty to please her parents and parents-in-law comes before her duty to her husband.

Even though the older generation

is obligated to take care of the young and the young in turn owe the aged gratitude and care to the best of their ability (Potters, 1977:105), 95 percent of the respondents believed that in the future the government would have to play a larger role in the welfare of the elderly. A similarly high percentage agreed on the importance of observing traditional ceremonies to make merit for the deceased.

Table 18.2, which presents reactions to the family-value items according to respondents' age and sex, indicates little difference among age groups in attitudes toward the family. In general, younger respondents were slightly less traditional in their views than older respondents. For example, somewhat smaller proportions of younger respondents (though still the majority) agreed that the husband should have authority in family matters, that women are better off at home than in a job, and that children have too little respect for their parents; and somewhat smaller proportions of younger respondents agreed that divorced women should not marry. On several items, though, the youngest group appeared to be more traditional than the eldest group. For example, fewer of them agreed that teenagers should be allowed to decide most things for themselves. But nearly twice as many 15–24-year-olds as those 45 and over (29 versus 15 percent) agreed with the statement that it is good that more young people today prefer to remain single rather than marry.

It is reasonable to assume that men and women would differ somewhat in their attitudes toward some of the family values expressed in the survey items. As it turned out, men's attitudes tended to be more modern than women's. Higher percentages of male respondents agreed with the statement that it is good for young people to lead single lives and that teenagers should be allowed to decide most things for themselves. Male respondents also seemed to be self-centered in their attitudes toward marriage and sex roles. A larger proportion of men than of women opposed the remarriage of divorced women and fewer of them agreed with the statement that is a good thing for a man to work in the kitchen.

The survey results revealed a strong association between education and attitudinal differences (Table 18.3). The more educated were respondents, the less likely were they to agree with traditional family-value propositions. More-educated respondents, for instance, were more inclined than less educated ones to endorse young people's remaining single; they were also more inclined to help with household tasks and the family's financial support according to need rather than according to gender-specific roles. The explanation seems to be that education leads to less gender differentiation and more similarity in definitions of masculinity and femininity.

Conversely, larger proportions of less educated respondents agreed with such traditional statements as the husband ought to have the main say in the

Malinee Wongsith

Table 18.2. Percentages agreeing with family-value items, by age and sex: Thai Family Survey, 1989

Item	15–24	25–34	35–44	45+	Males	Females
Marriage						
Some equality in marriage is a good thing, but by and large the husband ought to have the main say-so in family matters	65.1	68.9	64.6	71.2	68.0	67.0
A wife ought to overlook isolated instances of sexual infidelity on the part of her husband	28.4	27.0	18.8	28.8	24.5	26.4
It is good that more young people today prefer to lead single lives on their own instead of getting married	29.4	22.7	18.1	15.0	24.5	15.3
Divorced women should not remarry	23.4	25.7	28.7	28.6	33.1	18.0
Sex role						
It is better for the family if the husband is the main breadwinner and the wife takes care of the home and the family	81.7	83.3	81.3	81.7	84.0	79.3
Almost any woman is better off in the home than in a job or profession	68.8	68.5	70.2	73.0	71.1	67.5
Both husband and wife should take care of the children when both are at home	95.4	95.0	92.7	94.8	93.5	95.7
It is a good thing for a man to do kitchen work	27.8	23.9	17.7	21.6	20.3	25.0
Children						
Children today have too little respect for their parents	63.3	61.5	63.7	68.6	66.3	60.9
A teenager should be allowed to decide most things for himself or herself	33.0	29.7	28.5	41.8	35.4	28.6
Parents should encourage just as much independence in their daughters as in their sons	48.6	54.5	54.4	54.9	55.6	50.7
Elderly						
Younger people should not disagree with elders, even when an elderly person is wrong	49.5	44.1	48.7	62.1	54.1	44.9
It is the children's responsibility to take care of their parents when the parents get old	100.0	98.6	100.0	100.0	99.5	99.6
A woman's duty to her parents and parents-in-law comes before her duty to her husband	85.3	86.5	89.1	81.6	87.3	84.0

Table 18.2. *(continued)*

Item	Age group				Males	Females
	15–24	25–34	35–44	45+		
In the future the government will have to play a bigger role in providing for the elderly	96.3	95.0	94.3	96.7	95.0	96.0
It is necessary to hold traditional ceremonies of merit-making for the deceased	93.6	96.4	98.4	96.7	98.5	93.8
(No. of cases)	(109)	(222)	(193)	(153)	(276)	(401)

family, divorced women should not remarry, women are better off at home than in a job, and it is best for the family if the husband is the main breadwinner and the wife takes care of the home and family. Interestingly, however, a larger proportion of less educated respondents also thought that parents should encourage as much independence in daughters as in sons. This result may reflect the greater number of female than of male respondents in this study. Most rural Thai women have experienced little freedom and few privileges; therefore, they do not want their daughters to suffer as they have.

A similar pattern emerged in the relationship between occupational levels and attitudes, probably because of the interrelationship between education and occupation (less educated respondents tending to work in agriculture and more-educated ones tending to work in non-agricultural occupations).

One interesting feature of Table 18.3 is the clear relationship between region and respondents' attitudes. Northeastern Thailand is the poorest region of the country, with high population density, whereas the South is the most economically developed region and much less highly populated. The northeastern respondents tended to be more traditional than their southern counterparts, larger proportions of them agreeing that the husband should have the main say in family matters, that he should be the main source of support for the family while the wife should take care of the home, and that women are better off at home than in a job. Conversely, smaller proportions of northeastern respondents endorsed the single life for young people. But a smaller proportion of them also agreed with the proposition that divorced women should not remarry. Divorce and remarriage have traditionally been more common in the North. In the northeastern village of Na-asadorn, for example, Suthep (1968:72) reports that many women married more than twice.

Table 18.3. Percentages agreeing with family-value items, by education, occupation, and region: Thai Family Survey, 1989

Item	Education: No education/primary 1–4	Education: Primary 5–middle school 3	Education: Middle school 4+	Occupation: Agriculture	Occupation: Nonagriculture	Occupation: Homemaker/not working	Region: Northeast	Region: South
Marriage								
Some equality in marriage is a good thing, but by and large the husband ought to have the main say-so in family matters	71.6	57.1	48.8	70.0	63.6	65.6	77.8	57.7
A wife ought to overlook isolated instances of sexual infidelity on the part of her husband	24.6	26.1	32.5	22.9	29.3	28.1	27.3	23.3
It is good that more young people today prefer to lead single lives on their own instead of getting married	18.8	24.8	34.1	18.0	22.3	33.3	18.0	23.4
Divorced women should not remarry	29.0	22.2	14.6	27.4	27.1	22.2	22.4	31.2
Sex role								
It is better for the family if the husband is the main breadwinner and the wife takes care of the home and the family	84.1	79.7	63.4	84.0	80.0	76.6	87.1	77.3
Almost any woman is better off in the home than in a job or profession	74.2	67.5	26.8	73.9	65.2	60.9	74.8	65.4
Both husband and wife should take care of the children when both are at home	98.4	94.1	100.0	95.8	93.7	87.5	95.5	93.3
It is a good thing for a man to do kitchen work	20.2	27.1	34.1	24.0	19.4	20.3	25.6	19.0

Children

Children today have too little respect for their parents	64.7	62.2	63.4	60.2	68.3	75.0	60.8	67.2
A teenager should be allowed to decide most things for himself or herself	34.3	26.1	31.7	33.2	31.1	34.4	35.1	30.2
Parents should encourage just as much independence in their daughters as in their sons	55.6	48.7	46.3	56.0	48.1	56.3	53.5	53.8

Elderly

Younger people should not disagree with elders, even when an elderly person is wrong	52.9	49.6	22.0	49.9	50.0	54.7	51.7	49.1
It is the children's responsibility to take care of their parents when the parents get old	99.8	100.0	97.6	99.5	99.5	100.0	99.4	99.7
A woman's duty to her parents and parents-in-law comes before her duty to her husband	87.2	80.7	85.4	87.9	85.4	75.0	84.0	87.8
In the future the government will have to play a bigger role in providing for the elderly	96.0	92.4	97.6	95.8	95.1	93.8	95.8	95.0
It is necessary to hold traditional ceremonies of merit-making for the deceased	98.4	93.3	82.9	96.6	96.1	98.4	96.4	96.8
(No. of cases)	(516)	(119)	(42)	(407)	(260)	(10)	(333)	(344)

Malinee Wongsith

Multivariate Analysis

Given that all the background variables we have been examining in connection with attitudinal differences are interrelated to varying degrees, it is useful to reexamine their effects within a multivariate framework. For this purpose I have chosen multiple classification analysis (MCA). For the dependent variable, I constructed a modernity index from the family-value items. Because not all of the items indicated modernity, and also because some of them received virtually universal agreement from respondents, I chose only 10 items for the index. The index was the sum of points scored by the 10 items in the scheme shown in Table 18.4.

Table 18.5 presents the correlation matrix of the 10 items. Although most of the items appear to be independent, some—such as 1 and 5 (the husband should have authority in family matters, the husband should be the chief breadwinner), 2 and 4 (divorced women should not remarry, a woman is better off in the home than in a job), 4 and 5 (the man's role is that of breadwinner, the woman's is in the home), 4 and 6 (the woman's place is in the home, her first duty is to her parents), 4 and 10 (the woman's place is in the home, young people should not disagree with their elders), and 8 and 9

Table 18.4. Scoring scheme for the 10 family-value items selected for the modernity index

	How scored in the index[a]	
Item	Agree	Disagree
1. Some equality in marriage is a good thing, but by and large the husband ought to have the main say-so in the family	0	1
2. Divorced women should not remarry	0	1
3. It is good that more young people today prefer to lead single lives on their own instead of getting married	1	0
4. Almost any woman is better off in the home than in a job or profession	0	1
5. It is better for the family if the husband is the main breadwinner and the wife takes care of the home and the family	0	1
6. A woman's duty to her parents and parents-in-law comes before her duty to her husband	0	1
7. It is a good thing for a man to do kitchen work	1	0
8. A teenager should be allowed to decide most things for himself or herself	1	0
9. Parents should encourage just as much independence in their daughters as in their sons	1	0
10. Younger people should not disagree with elders, even when an elderly person is wrong	0	1

a. Scores of 1 and 0 represent more modern and more traditional values, respectively.

Attitudes toward Family Values in Rural Thailand

(teenagers should be allowed to make decisions, parents should encourage equal independence in daughters and sons)—proved to be significantly correlated at the 1 percent level and in the hypothesized positive direction. Several hypothesized negative relationships also proved to be significant, in particular that between items 5 and 8 (the man should be the breadwinner, teenagers should be allowed to make decisions).

Given the validation of these hypothesized relationships, I combined the significantly correlated items into a single measure for the purpose of analysis, constructing the modernity index by using the appropriate SPSSX commands. Table 18.6 shows the frequency of scores on the modernity index, and Table 18.7 presents the MCA results for the means by background characteristics of respondents—namely, age, sex, education, occupation, and region.

The adjusted results indicate the net influence of each independent, or background, variable after the influence of all the other variables was taken into account. As indicated by the squared value of the multiple correlation coefficient (.07), the variables included in the MCA together account statistically for less than one-tenth of the total variance.

The degree of association between each of the independent variables and the modernity index, as measured by the mean of the modernity index, remains mostly constant after adjustment in the MCA. This can be seen by comparing the Eta and Beta statistics, which respectively summarize the degree of association between each particular independent variable and the dependent variable before and after the other independent variables are adjusted for. After the other independent variables are controlled, the educational background of the respondents shows substantial influence on the mean of the modernity index. As expected, re-

Table 18.5. Correlation matrix of the 10 modernity-index items

	Item 1	Item 2	Item 3	Item 4	Item 5	Item 6	Item 7	Item 8	Item 9	Item 10
Item 1	1.0000									
Item 2	.0661									
Item 3	−.0584	.0383								
Item 4	.3199*	.1375**	−.0649							
Item 5	.1670**	.0588	−.0548	.2978**						
Item 6	.0977*	.0865	−.0225	.1622**	.3162*					
Item 7	.0208	−.0324	.0525	−.1091*	−.0367	−.0890				
Item 8	.9229*	.0470	.0490	−.1202**	.1625**	.1114*	.0154			
Item 9	.0756	.0110	.0215	−.0771	.0304	.0210	.0611	.2116**		
Item 10	.1313**	.1169*	−.0402	.1941**	.0803	.0284	−.0466	.1177*	.0839	1.0000

* Significant at .05.
** Significant at .01.

spondents with higher education were more modern minded than those with less education.

Much of the influence of age, sex, occupation, and region can be accounted for by the other factors included in the analysis. In some cases, the pattern of difference remains evident in the adjusted results even if attenuated. Males tended to be more modern in their attitudes than females, and respondents in the Northeast less modern in outlook than those in the South; but the association of sex or region with the modernity index is not statistically significant. Before adjustment, younger age is associated with more modern attitudes, but after adjustment the association disappears. Differences between working and nonworking respondents persist after adjustment, however. A possible explanation is that those not working had higher economic status and for that reason were more modern in their thinking than those who were working, but the number of nonworking respondents was small.

Opinions about Social Life

As mentioned earlier in the chapter, when a Thai couple marries, the bridegroom usually presents a gift (*khongman*) to the bride and another gift (*sin sord*) to her parents. Traditionally the *khongman* consists of such articles as a gold necklace or bracelet or a diamond ring, whereas the *sin sord* is usually an amount of money agreed upon by both sets of parents at the time of the engagement. Nearly all (90 percent) of respondents to the Thai Family Survey approved of this practice, whereas only 10 percent considered it old-fashioned. Asked about the appropriate amount of cash to be spent on weddings, three-fourths responded that the amount should not exceed what a family could afford, and nearly all others said the amount should be minimal; fewer than 1 percent answered that a family should spend whatever was needed, even if it meant going into debt or selling property.

Another study has found that the proportion of Thai children completing higher education is associated with household wealth (Knodel and Malinee, 1989:178). When the respondents to the Thai Family Survey were asked which one of their children should receive a better education than the others, given a lack of means to educate them all equally well, 85 percent chose the most gifted child rather than the eldest son or another

Table 18.6. Frequency of scores on modernity-index items: Thai Family Survey, 1989

Value	%	No.
0	2.7	18
1	8.9	60
2	18.3	124
3	25.1	170
4	19.9	135
5	13.1	89
6	6.8	46
7	4.3	29
8	.6	4
9	.3	2
Total	100.0	677

child, and only 11 percent chose the eldest son.

Respondents were asked who should be more responsible for teaching values to children—schools, parents, or both. Forty-three percent answered that schools should be responsible, 39 percent chose parents, and only 18 percent chose both.

Respondents were also asked their opinion about having elderly people live in the household. Responses strongly favored coresidence (92 percent in favor, only 6.6 percent against). The widespread desire to provide moral support to elderly parents and to remain psychologically close to them may explain this result.

Another study, of elderly Thais, has found that spouses, children, and relatives

Table 18.7. Multiple classification analysis of the mean of the modernity index, by selected characteristics of respondents: Thai Family Survey, 1989

Characteristic (independent variable)	No.	Modernity index Unadjusted	Adjusted
Grand mean	676	3.4	3.4
Age			
15–24	109	3.6	3.4
25–34	222	3.5	3.4
35–44	193	3.3	3.5
45+	152	3.3	3.4
Eta/Beta		.07	.01
Sex			
Female	401	3.4	3.3
Male	275	3.6	3.6
Eta/Beta		.06	.07
Education			
No education			
Primary 1–4	516	3.3	3.3
Primary 5–middle school 3	119	3.7	3.7
Middle school 4+	41	4.9	4.9
Eta/Beta		.23	.23**
Current occupation			
Agriculture	406	3.4	3.4
Nonagriculture	206	3.5	3.4
Not working	64	3.9	3.9
Eta/Beta		.09	.09
Region			
Northeastern	333	3.3	3.3
Southern	343	3.5	3.6
Eta/Beta		.06	.07
R^2		—	.07

** Significant at .001.

assumed most of the responsibility for caring for the elderly when the elderly were ill or in need of help (Napaporn, Malinee, and Chanpen, 1988:103). Findings from the Thai Family Survey confirm that the family, and particularly spouses and daughters, are the preferred source of care for the elderly (Table 18.8). Nearly one-third of respondents said they would wish to be cared for in old age or during a prolonged illness by their daughters (30 percent) or spouses (29 percent), 16 percent mentioned their children, and only 8 percent mentioned their sons.

Respondents were also asked with whom they expected to live when they reached old age (Table 18.9). A substantial plurality (35 percent) mentioned a daughter, whereas only about 14 percent mentioned a son. The respondent's spouse was the second most favored choice (18 percent), and "any child" was the third (16 percent). Not surprisingly, the least frequently mentioned was a home for the

Table 18.8. Respondents' choice of caretaker in old age or long-term illness (%): Thai Family Survey, 1989

Caretaker	%
Spouse	29.1
Son	8.1
Daughter	30.3
Children	16.1
Home for the aged	.4
Other	15.9
Total %	100.0
(No.)	(677)

Note: Percentages do not sum exactly to 100.0 because of rounding.

Table 18.9. Person with whom respondents expected to live when old (%): Thai Family Survey, 1989

Person	%
Any child	16.1
Son	13.5
Daughter	35.1
Spouse	18.4
All children	6.7
Home for the aged	.6
Other	9.6
Total %	100.0
(No.)	(658)

Table 18.10. Person to inherit the parents' properties after their demise (%): Thai Family Survey, 1989

Inheritor	%
Eldest son	5.5
Eldest daughter	1.8
Youngest son	1.5
Youngest daughter	2.7
All children with equal shares	68.9
Whoever takes care of the parents	13.1
Other	6.5
Total %	100.0
(No.)	(677)

aged, which in Thailand is regarded as a recourse for those in need of charity.

As for patterns of inheritance, Kaufman (1960:22) found in his study of a Thai village that it was customary for the father to control the division of property and for each child to receive an equal share of land, but for the youngest son or daughter to receive the house and its contents. Results from the Thai Family Survey likewise reveal that a majority (69 percent) of respondents planned to divide their family property equally among their children (Table 18.10). Thirteen percent said they would give their property to whoever took care of them in old age. Only 6 percent favored the eldest son and only 3 percent planned to give all their property to the youngest daughter.

SUMMARY AND CONCLUSION

The results of the Thai Family Survey indicate that despite Thailand's rapid demographic and socioeconomic changes during the past decade or so, a number of traditional family values still persist, at least in rural areas. Support for the traditional role of women and acceptance of the family's responsibility for caring for its elderly members remain strong. Although more modern attitudes surfaced in responses to several questions—for example, whether parents should encourage equal independence for daughters and sons and whether younger people should refrain from disagreeing with their elders even when the elders were wrong—for the most part the respondents espoused traditional views about the family.

Attitudes were correlated in expected directions with nearly all socioeconomic and demographic characteristics of the respondents, but most correlations did not reach statistical significance. A modernity index constructed of 10 family-value items did establish some significant relationships in expected directions. Education showed the strongest modernizing effect on values.

The results from the questions about respondents' social attitudes were similar to those obtained from the questions about their family values: most respondents subscribed to generally traditional views. Although it is more modern for respondents to expect school rather than parents to teach children values and for the most gifted child, rather than the eldest son, to be given preference in educational opportunity, responses to only two out of eight questions on social issues reflected a modern view.

Given that education proved to be a strong and significant predictor of modern attitudes, as education becomes more widely available to the Thai population at least some traditional values may weaken. It should be borne in mind, though, that the survey measured only the respondents' expressed values. It is possible that their actions might diverge from those expressed values. For example, nearly all respondents stated a preference for having elderly family members live in their households. Nevertheless, according to Napaporn, Malinee, and Chapen (1988:69), a substantial proportion of elderly Thais live alone, and that proportion is higher in rural areas (4.6 percent) than in urban areas (3.6 percent); moreover, the proportion living alone increases with age. Further study is therefore needed to determine the degree of compatibility between stated values and actual practice.

REFERENCES

Amara Soonthorndhada, Uraiwan Kanungsukkasem, and Sirinan Saiprasert. 1987. *A Time-Allocation Study on Rural Women: An Analysis of Productive and Reproductive Roles.* IPSR Publication No. 105. Bangkok: Institute for Population and Social Research, Mahidol University.

Bencha Yoddumnern-Attig, Kerry Richter, Amara Soonthorndhada, Chanya Sethaput, and Anthony Pramualratana. 1992. *Changing Roles and Statuses of Women in Thailand: A Documentary Assessment.* IPSR Publication No. 161. Bangkok: Institute for Population and Social Research, Mahidol University.

Bhassorn Limanonda. 1979. *Mate Selection and Post Nuptial Residence in Thailand.* Paper No. 28. Bangkok: Institute of Population Studies, Chulalongkorn University.

Carter, Betty, and Monica McGoldrick. 1978. *The Changing Family Life Cycle: A Framework for Family Therapy,* 2nd. ed. London: Gardner Press.

Chaweewan Wannaprasert. 1979. *Thai Society* (in Thai). Pattanee: Department of Social Sciences, Prince Songkla Nakarindra University.

de Young, John E. 1966. *Village Life in Modern Thailand.* Berkeley and Los Angeles: Institute of East Asiatic Studies, University of California.

Hill, Reuben, and René Konig, eds. 1970. *Family in East and West: Socialization Process and Kinship Ties.* Paris: Mouton.

Holmstrom, Engin Inel. 1973. "Changing Sex Role in a Developing Country." *Journal of Marriage and the Family* 35(3):546–553.

Japan Research Institute. 1987. *The Asian Family: Changes in Structure and Function.* Tokyo.

Kaufman, Howard Keva. 1960. *Bangkhuad: A Community Study in Thailand.* New York: J. J. Augustin.

Kingshill, Konrad. 1976. Ku Daeng, *The Red Tomb: A Village Study in Northern Thailand, 1954–1974,* 3d ed. Bangkok: Suriyaban Publishers.

Knodel, John, and Malinee Wongsith. 1989. "Educational Expectations and Attainment Patterns for Thai Children." In *Health and Population Studies Based on the 1987 Thailand Demographic and Health Survey.* DHS Further Analysis Series, No. 1. New York: The Population Council.

Korson, J. Henry. 1978. "Modernization and Social Change: The Family in Pakistan." In Man Singh Das and Panos D. Bardis (eds.), *The Family in Asia,* pp. 169–207. New Delhi: Vikas Publishing House.

Napaporn Chayovan, Malinee Wongsith, and Chanpen Saengtienchai. 1988. *Socio-Economic Consequences of the Aging of the Population: Thailand.* Bangkok: Institute of Population Studies, Chulalongkorn University.

Napaporn Chayovan, Peerasit Kamnuansilpa, and John Knodel. 1988. *Thailand Demographic and Health Survey, 1987.* Bangkok: Institute of Population Studies, Chulalongkorn University.

Office of the National Economic and Social Development Board (NESDB). 1989. *Social Indicators: 1989.* Bangkok.

Phillips, Herbert P. 1965. *Thai Peasant Personality.* Berkeley and Los Angeles: University of California Press.

Potters, Sulamith Hein. 1977. *Family Life in a Northern Thai Village.* Berkeley and Los Angeles: University of California Press.

Smith, Harold E. 1973. "The Thai Family: Nuclear or Extended." *Journal of Marriage and the Family* 35(1):136–141.

———. 1978 "The Thai Rural Family." In Man Singh Das and Panos D. Bardis (eds.), *The Family in Asia,* pp. 16–46. New Delhi: Vikas Publishing House.

Suthep Soonthornphasuch. 1968. *Sociology of the Village in the Northeastern Region.* Bangkok: Faculty of Political Sciences, Chulalongkorn University.

Supatra Suphab. 1985. *Thai Society and Culture, Values, Family, Religion, Tradition* (in Thai). Bangkok: Thai Wattana Panich Publisher.

PART IV

Conclusion

CHAPTER 19

The Japanese Family in Comparative Perspective

by Andrew Cherlin

Over the past few decades, scholars have created two lines of inquiry into the comparative study of the family. One set of studies is historical. Its objective has been to understand the families of the past and to discover the changes that have occurred over time. Since its inception, the field of historical demography has expanded greatly in both the East and the West. In Japan, as many readers of this volume know, important insights into the past have come from the study of population registers during the Tokugawa Period (1600–1868), the *Shūmon Aratame Chō*, by scholars such as Hayami (Cornell and Hayami, 1986). These studies have provided a picture of how the *ie*, or household, system worked in everyday life.

In Europe, parish registers provided the data for a generation of historical demographers who reconstructed the European families and households of the past. Their work contradicted the widely held belief that most families were extended, with married children and older parents and other kin sharing a residence. In fact, most households proved to contain nuclear families. As Kuroda (in Chapter 4 of this volume) and others have reminded us, the same myth has now been contradicted for the Japanese family.

Nevertheless, the historical studies have unearthed differences between families of the past and contemporary families. The most striking difference is the most obvious: birth and death rates were much higher than they are today. The decline in births, which accelerated in Japan after World War II, has raised questions of whether we are likely to see further declines in the twenty-first century. In some countries, this concern is explicit. In France, for instance, where the decline has been a long-term reality, government anxieties led to payments to families with children, as well as to generous support for that nation's pioneering historical demographers. In other countries, concern about low birth rates is present but not as explicit. I sense that in both Japan and the United States there is now substantial concern under the surface about low fertility. In the United States, where immigration has been a long-standing method of achieving population growth, concerns about fertility quickly shade into concerns about legal and illegal immigration. In Japan, however, immigration provides a much smaller component of population growth. It is clear that one of the major underlying questions of the 1991 Nihon University International Symposium on the Family and Contemporary Japanese Culture and of this volume is the consequences of living in a low-fertility society in which the elderly make up a large proportion of the population.

The second line of inquiry of comparative research on the family has been to understand the ways in which families and households have changed during the twentieth-century process of national development. Here the major perspective has been that of modernization theory. This perspective views development as following a fixed sequence that is similar in all societies. As wage labor replaces agricultural and home production, it is argued, fertility falls, the nuclear family replaces the extended family as the dominant unit, ties between parents and children weaken, and adults become more individualistic and less family-oriented. A sophisticated version of this approach can be found in William J. Goode's influential book (Goode, 1963), in which he argues that, regardless of their starting point, families in all countries have been converging toward the Western-style, nuclear family unit.

There is some validity to the predictions of the modernization theorists. In general, the trends in most developing nations have been toward a greater emphasis on the husband-wife bond as compared with the parent-child bond. For example, in many East and Southeast Asian societies, young adults now have more influence in choosing a marriage partner than was the case a generation or two ago. That is certainly true in Taiwan, one of the countries represented in this volume, where a series of surveys has shown increasing influence of young adults in the marriage process (Sun and Liu, in Chapter 15 of this volume) and in the Republic of Korea, where a follow-up study of a rural area also shows increasing young-adult involvement (Kim, Choi, and Park, in Chapter 14).

I nevertheless argue that it is a mistake to accept modernization theory uncritically. Cultural continuities remain that link a country's family patterns of the past and of the present, and substantial differences remain among countries and regions today. For example, the same surveys that show increasing young-adult involvement in spouse choice in Asian nations also show that parents continue to influence the process far more than in the West.[1] In many Asian countries, including ones described in this volume, parents and adult children continue to report that they participate jointly in the decision about whom their children should marry. Even though children may now initiate the process and find partners themselves, parents are usually consulted about whether the partner is satisfactory. Similarly, patterns of coresidence of older parents and their adult children show that same mix of persistence and change, as I will describe below.

THE JAPANESE FAMILY

What, then, can we learn from comparisons of the contemporary Japanese family with family systems elsewhere in East and Southeast Asia and in the West? No one who has read the chapters in this volume can fail to be impressed with the great changes that have occurred in the Japanese family during the second half of the twentieth century. The 1991 symposium made it clear that Japanese experts are looking outward for clues about what the future of the Japanese family might be. As a Westerner attending the symposium, I received the clear impression that an unstated question underlying the conference was, Will the Japanese family become just like the Western family?

Indeed the changes in the West have been dramatic too. In the United States, for example, about half of all young adults now live with a partner prior to marrying.[2] About one out of four children is born to an unmarried mother. At current rates, one out of two American marriages will end in divorce—the highest rate of divorce in the West, with the possible exception of Sweden. It is not uncommon for an American's life course to include growing up in a family split by a divorce, then living with a partner while still unmarried, then marrying in the mid-20s, then divorcing in the 30s, and then remarrying. Of course, most people still do not have family histories this complex, but many have histories only a bit less complex.

Moreover, the roles of American

---

1. I use the term "West" to mean the developed nations of Western and Central Europe and the overseas English-speaking countries of Australia, Canada, the United States, and New Zealand.

2. I have not cited detailed references for the social and demographic overview of the United States that follows. The information is drawn from Cherlin (1992).

women have changed markedly. At midcentury, about one out of seven married women was working outside the home, whereas now more than half are. During the 1980s, work outside the home increased greatly even among new mothers. Currently, half of all mothers return to work outside the home within 12 months of giving birth. There is much research and discussion in the United States about the consequences for children of having a mother who works outside the home. In general, the research literature has not found negative effects on children whose mothers work. Recent national studies suggest that it may be detrimental to some children to have their mothers work full-time outside the home during the first 12 months of the children's lives, but the same studies find little or no negative effects of mothers' work after a child's first year (Desai, Chase-Lansdale, and Michel, 1989; Baydar and Brooks-Gunn, 1991).

I sensed that many participants in the symposium feared that the answer to the question of whether the Japanese family would become just like the Western family would be yes. But I argue that the correct answer is instead partially, but certainly not completely. I believe that there will continue to be substantial differences between the Japanese family and the Western family. I also believe that differences will continue between Western families and families in developing Asian nations, such as the ones that are represented in this volume: Korea, Taiwan, and Thailand. My argument is as follows.

Japan already has experienced the fertility and mortality transitions that have occurred in the West. The total fertility rate (TFR)—the average number of children that a woman would have during her lifetime if current fertility rates remained unchanged—plummeted in Japan during the late 1940s and early 1950s from about 4.5 to about 2.0 (Tsuya, Chapter 6 in this volume). The rapidity of the fertility decline in Japan during the decade following World War II is unprecedented in world history. In the mid-1970s, the Japanese TFR began to decline again. The current TFR of about 1.5 is lower than in the United States, the United Kingdom, France, or Sweden. It approaches the levels of about 1.4 in Central Europe, from Germany to Italy, which are the world's lowest.

One cannot say with any certainty, of course, what will happen to the TFR in the years ahead. U.S. demographers have a poor record of forecasting fertility trends; for example, no prominent American demographer of the 1940s foresaw the 1950s' baby boom. But I think it is unlikely that the Japanese TFR will drop much further. In the West, there have been signs of a small upturn in some countries in the last few years. For instance, in the United States in the 1980s, there was a modest increase in the TFR, from about 1.8 to 2.1. One reason for the increase was that the women born during the baby-boom years of 1945–65 were reaching the biological ages at which they could no longer postpone childbirth. As more and more couples heard the ticking of the biological clock, they turned their attention to having a child, or possibly two. Consequently, birth rates for women over 30 increased substantially. The Swedish TFR showed a similar rise during the same period. Some Swedish demographers have attributed the rise to government programs that provide generous support to working parents, such as childcare centers and paid leaves of absence from work. This argument may be correct, but the fact is that the United States, which experienced a parallel rise, has little public support for working parents.

As is well known, Japanese men and women have postponed marriage more than previous generations and even more than couples in the West. It is possible that a modest rise in fertility could occur as Japanese couples reach the ages at which they no longer can postpone childbearing.

Perhaps the major potential problem on the minds of those who attended the symposium and who have contributed to this volume is the care of the elderly. Because the Japanese fertility decline was so swift and because of impressive advances in adult life expectancy, Japan's age structure has changed more rapidly than in the West. The Japanese are coping with an elderly population whose relative size will soon exceed that of the United States. By the year 2000, 17 percent of the Japanese population is projected to be age 65 or older (Martin, 1989), compared with a projected 13 percent of the U.S. population (U.S., Bureau of the Census, 1982). Asian societies in general, including Japanese society, have relied on family members to care for the elderly by living with them. The ideal in Japan was that the eldest son and his wife would live with his parents, caring for them and then, when the father died, inheriting the property and headship of the *ie*, or corporate household. This stem-family phase of family life does seem to have occurred in most families in which parents survived to old age. Still, Kuroda (in Chapter 4) and Sun and Liu (in Chapter 15) have reminded us that the extended family was an ideal form, not the statistical norm.

There is now apprehension that coresidence among the generations will decline severely and that the quality of care for the elderly will suffer. It is feared that the state will then have to provide the care, at great financial cost, further eroding cultural ideals. Evidence does show a moderate decline in the proportion of elderly persons who are living with their children. For example, census data show that the proportion of Japanese aged 65 and over who were living with children decreased from 77 percent in 1970 to 65 percent in 1985 (Martin, 1989). Friedman, Chang, and Sun (1982) report that in Taiwan only a modest decline occurred between 1973 and 1980 in the proportion of older parents who were living with a son.

Because the TFR had already fallen to about 2.0 by the mid-1950s in Japan, the first cohort of adults born since then are already approaching middle age. Information on their behavior and attitudes toward intergenerational living arrangements is presented in several chapters in this volume. In 1988, when the National Family Survey conducted by Mainichi Newspapers and Nihon University that is analyzed throughout this volume was conducted, persons who had been born between 1954 and 1963 were 25–34 years old. Let us take them as representative of the first small birth cohort. Among those in that age range in 1988 who were married and had a living parent, 35 percent of the men and 9 percent of the women were living with one or both of their parents. The comparable percentage in the United States was 1 percent for both men and women (Bumpass, in Chapter 12).

In Chapter 7, Kawabe and Shimizu report responses in a 1986 national survey in Japan to the question, "Generally speaking, what do you think about elderly people living with their married children?" The proportions responding that the elderly should live separately were 16 percent among those aged 20–29 and 21 percent among those aged 30–39. The proportion responding similarly was no lower among those in their 40s and 50s. In fact, the major difference between those under 40 and those between 40 and 59 was that fewer of the younger respondents thought that elderly parents should live with a married son and more of them thought that elderly parents should live with a married daughter. Thus, the major difference in attitudes between young adults and middle-aged adults was a shift toward bilateral kinship preferences among the former—not a shift away from supporting coresidence. In Chapter 15, Sun and Liu also remark on a shift to bilaterality in kinship obligations in Taiwan.

Whether these figures show that the remaining support for coresidence is substantial depends on the eye of the beholder. As the well-known English saying goes, one can view the water glass as half full or half empty—or perhaps, in this case, whether the glass is 80 percent full or 20 percent empty. Kawabe and Shimizu remark that the approximately 20 percent of Japanese who support separate residences is "rather high," and perhaps it *is* high relative to the cultural ideal. But a Western reader inspects the same set of figures and notices that about 60 percent of even the most recent cohorts of young adults still favor coresidence. (The remaining 20 percent gave other responses.) When similar questions are asked in Western surveys, few young adults, and also few of the elderly themselves, favor coresidence.

Thus, although there may be some deterioration of support for coresidence compared with the cultural ideal, there continues to be sentiment in favor of it on the part of a majority of young Japanese adults. And more than one-third of young adults were living with their parents in 1988. Coresidence is occurring even though young adults have grown up in an industrialized economy—even though much of the transition to what some scholars characterize as "modernity" has already occurred. It does not appear that coresidence is in danger of disappearing in Japan.

Still, I must admit that more erosion of the traditional norms and practices is possible. Today's young adults were raised by parents still steeped in traditional family values; it may be that today's children will not carry with them as much of the cultural ideal. It is also true that the trends in fertility and mortality mask, to some extent, changes in coresidence. Because fertility is low, there are fewer children per elderly parent, a fact that would tend to inflate the proportion of young adults living with their parents even if preferences stayed the same. And because life expectancy is higher, there are more elderly parents alive.

THE LIMITS OF MODERNIZATION THEORY

More change may also be likely if the many contributors to this volume who cite modernization theory are correct. In numerous chapters, the reader is presented with the argument that as societies modernize, nuclear families become dominant and the obligations of children to parents weaken in relationship to the bonds between husbands and wives. Modernization is usually taken to mean industrialization, with the concomitant phenomena of urbanization, education, and rising incomes. The sometimes implicit model is that modernization proceeds similarly in all societies and produces a uniform set of outcomes. But even as modernization theory is being propounded by some scholars in the newly industrializing nations of East Asia, it is coming under attack by scholars in the West. The attackers argue that there is no proof that all societies will develop in the same way. Some of them argue that non-Western societies that have recently developed or are in the process of development will not become identical to Western nations that developed under the dominance of Western capitalism and culture in the nineteenth and early twentieth centuries.

As I stated earlier, I do not deny that much evidence supports, in a general way, the modernization model. Several chapters in this volume present data showing that people with more education, or who live in cities, or who work for wages, appear more "modern" in their attitudes and behaviors concerning family life. Data on trends over time show moderate declines in the proportion of the elderly who are living with children. And, of course, all of the countries represented in this volume have seen great declines in fertility.

Moreover, attitudinal data often show that although people still hold to the old cultural ideals about filial piety, they think the values will weaken in the future. For example, Malinee (in Chapter 18) presents data from a survey conducted in 1989 in rural Northeast and Southern Thailand. Virtually all respondents, whether better educated or not, and whether they worked in the agricultural or nonagricultural sector, agreed with the statement that "It is the children's responsibility to take care of their parents when the parents get old." Yet nearly all also agreed that "In the future, the government will have to play a bigger role in providing for the elderly."

But not all of the changes toward a more "modern" society necessarily lead to a decline in the obligations that children feel toward parents. When parents and children have more financial resources, they may choose to expend some on coresidence. Kurosu (in Chapter 10) reports that coresidence was more common among the households in the 1988 National Family Survey when the younger or older generation's income was higher. This finding parallels those of many studies in other countries demonstrating that when more resources are at stake, the extended family's influence is greater. For example, in a Northeast Thai village studied by Chai (1984), the larger the size of the parents' farm, the more likely were parents to influence their daughters' choices of marriage partners. About two-thirds of married women from wealthier land-owning families said that they and their parents jointly made the decision or that their parents made the decision for them. Among the poorest families only about one-third of married women reported any parental influence. Villagers often described wealthier families as "choosy" or "demanding" concerning marriage partners for their children. They were choosy because they had more to lose from a bad match. It is reasonable to assume that when Japanese parents have more assets to bequeath to their children, their children are more likely to reside with them.

Kurosu also found that coresidence was more common when the size of the residence was larger. There may be some circularity in this finding: families that wish to coreside may find larger housing units. But it is also possible that wealthier families with larger housing units will use some of their space to coreside. More generally, Kurosu's findings suggest that higher levels of assets and income may have two effects, what economists call income and substitution effects. The income effect would lead a family that has more financial resources to expend some of its resources on consumption it values highly—in this case, the coresidence of older parents and adult children. The substitution effect would lead some family members to expend resources on alternative kinds of consumption, such as independent living. As long as coresidence remains a desired status among many Japanese, it is an empirical question whether the income effect or the substitution effect will dominate. It is thus possible, although not necessarily probable, that rising affluence, in some contexts, could result in more rather than less coresidence.

CONDITIONAL CORESIDENCE

Nevertheless, even when one finds extended families in Japan today, the reasons for the extension may be different from those in the past. This is perhaps the most striking lesson I learned from the symposium: several speakers spoke of the *conditional* nature of extended family residence today. Three-generational households are often formed in response to a specific condition, such as the illness or frailty of an elderly parent. More and more three-generational households come into being because of an economic or health-care obligation, it is argued; fewer come together because children feel a diffuse obligation to repay an infinite debt to their parents. Kawabe and Shimizu note the movement toward what they call *eventual coresidence.* A large proportion of respondents in a study they cite agreed with the statement, "As long as our parents are healthy, they can live separately; but if their condition weakens and they are alone, we will coreside." Steinhoff (in Chapter 3) comments that this belief may be stronger when respondents think about caring for older males rather than for older females because of a common perception that older men cannot take care of themselves as well.

Other conditions for favoring coresidence exist that received less attention at the symposium, such as housing shortages that force younger families and parents to double up and the need for childcare while the mother works outside the home. Conditional coresidence, Kurosu suggests, may even spur the development of living arrangements unlike those of either the traditional extended family or the nuclear family, such as semiseparate housing units for parents and children. In addition, the shift to conditional coresidence makes the three-generational family in Japan more similar to the kind of coresidence found in the United States, which is undertaken to fulfill a specific need or obligation, such as when elderly parents fall ill.

In fact, the arrangements for caring for the most frail elderly already may be more similar in the United States and Japan than many realize. About 5 percent of the U.S. elderly reside in nursing homes or similar institutions. In Japan, the figure is only 1.6 percent. But the average length of a hospital stay for elderly Japanese is much higher than in the United States; these long stays have been labeled "social hospitalization" (Martin, 1989). On any given day, 2.6 percent of elderly Japanese are in a hospital (Martin, 1989:14), as compared with just 0.8 percent in the United States (U.S., Bureau of the Census, 1991:108). Some of the long stays in Japan may be a culturally acceptable alternative to nursing home care.

Japanese adult children may continue to care for their elderly parents in large numbers even if a trend toward separate living arrangements continues. It is often mistakenly thought that most frail elderly in the United States are cared for in institutions such as nursing homes rather than by family members. This belief seems to be based on the fact that few elderly persons reside with their children, but it is incorrect. Two to four times as many disabled elderly, depending on the criteria, are living in the community (that is, in private homes or apartments, not in institutions) as are living in nursing homes, and most of those living in the community are cared for by relatives. To measure disability, gerontologists have developed standard questions about the activities a person needs help with. The most common set, "activities of daily living," or ADLs, refers to personal care, including bathing, dressing, eating, getting in and out of bed, walking indoors, and using the toilet. These questions have been asked of national samples of elderly persons in the community (Liu, Manton, and Liu, 1985) and in nursing homes (U.S., National Center for Health Statistics, 1979), allowing us to make a comparison of their degrees of disability. Even among the most seriously disabled elderly persons—those with five or six limitations—more are living in the community than are in nursing homes. Among the less disabled, even larger majorities are living in the community. Clearly, coresidence is not a necessary condition for large numbers of frail elderly to receive primary care from family members.

ROAD BLOCKS

I think it is important to acknowledge another limitation of the simple modernization model, one that becomes evident from a discussion of several road blocks along the path of modernization that different nations handle in different ways. First, there are the limits to the ability of the welfare state to provide all services. The growth of the welfare state plays a major role in the modernization models that predict the convergence of all societies. And yet we see now in the West that the welfare state cannot assume all of the caretaking functions that the family has provided without drowning in debt or raising taxes to levels that evoke strong public protest. The United States is replacing some of the services previously provided by the family with paid services, and we are coming to realize just how valuable were these services, provided primarily by women without any compensation. Throughout the West there is a sense that the welfare state is in crisis, that great fiscal deficits must be reduced, and that there are limits to how much the welfare state can do. Even in Sweden, where the welfare state is most developed and where individuals already pay about 40 percent of their gross incomes in taxes to the state, there is unease about the welfare state.

A second road block is industrial restructuring or "deindustrialization." Its effects on the economy clearly are profound. Its effect on families are difficult to predict, but I think they too will be profound. At the symposium, Mason and Bauer (1991) provided a thought-provoking discussion of deindustrialization, which is being debated continually in the United States. I see some attention to it in Japan, and its relevance may increase in the future. Mason and Bauer argued that women's authority and independence might be undermined by the loss of jobs in textile plants and other manufacturing plants where the labor force has been largely female. Although I think this is possible, I think it is also possible that women's economic independence may increase if men lose manufacturing jobs while women are protected by virtue of their disproportionate employment in the expanding service sector. For example, in the United States the wages of male workers (controlled for inflation) have declined slightly since 1973, the year of the first oil-price shock. But women's wages have not declined, in large part because women have been working in the service sector, which has been hurt less by the industrial restructuring. Consequently, the ratio of women's earnings to men's earnings has gone up.

Moreover, industrial restructuring may affect the relations between the young and the old, although here again it is difficult to predict just how. On the one hand, older workers have seniority and may be able to retain their jobs even as manufacturing firms cut employment. Younger adults, who are just entering the work force, may find jobs tougher to find.

Thus, young adults may be dependent on their parents economically for a longer period of time owing to the effects of deindustrialization. On the other hand, deindustrialization may induce large migration flows, as Culter (in Chapter 13) shows in her study of Yubari, Hokkaido. When the coal industry collapsed, a large outflow of population occurred in the area. Demographers who study migration patterns know that in any great economic migration, it is young adults who tend to have the highest migration rates because they have their lives ahead of them and can expect to reap the benefits of moving to a new area and training for a new job. Older people, however, do not move nearly as much. Consequently, we may see elsewhere what we have seen in Yubari, namely, that the age structure of the communities affected by the restructuring may become progressively older and it may be increasingly difficult for aging parents to rely on adult children for care.

THE RIVER

In sum, I think it is simplistic for Japan to look to the West and to assume that the Japanese future family lies there. Americans make a similar mistake: we look to Sweden and other European countries much the way Japan may look to us. We see new social trends developing in Sweden, and we think that somehow they are transported directly to Los Angeles and San Francisco and then slowly work their way back toward the East Coast (Popenoe, 1988). But Sweden is a small country of only about 8 million people, with family traditions very different from those in the United States. Swedes have a much greater faith in the ability of government to provide for children and the elderly than do Americans. Sweden, unlike the United States, is also a quite secular country, perhaps the least religious country in the world. The welfare state is much more developed there than in the United States.

I think that Japan is different from the United States in two crucial ways. First, it differs in its culture: there is less emphasis on individual rights in Japan and more emphasis on responsibility to the family and community. This is a longstanding cultural difference that is quite well known. Second, Japan differs from the United States in its style of national development. There is a much greater reliance in Japan on the provision of social services, such as support for the elderly and for the care of young children, by family members outside the market economy. The unpaid work of wives and daughters and sons subsidizes the labor force and has been important to Japan's rapid economic development. It seems to me that without a major reorganization of the relationship of the state and the family in Japan, this difference is unlikely to fade away.

In my opinion, then, the Japanese family will never look just like the American family, any more than the American family will look like the Swedish family. Rather, there will be lasting differences between Japan and the West, although the differences may diminish somewhat. Rindfuss (1991) has aptly summarized this perspective through the metaphor of a river. He describes two philosophers with different views of the river. The first stands close to its banks, observes the flow of water, and concludes that the river is constantly changing. The second stands back, notices that the river is always in the same place and its banks are always at the same height, and announces that the river is always the same. Each philosopher captures a part of the essence of the river. Like the family in the East and the West, it is a mixture of persistence and change.

REFERENCES

Baydar, Nazli, and Jeanne Brooks-Gunn. 1991. "Effects of Maternal Employment and Child-care Arrangements on Preschoolers' Cognitive and Behavioral Outcomes: Evidence from the Children of the National Longitudinal Survey of Youth." *Developmental Psychology* 27(6):932–945.

Chai Podhisita. 1984. "Marriage in Rural Northeast Thailand: A Household Perspective." In Aphichat Chamratrithirong (ed.), *Perspectives on the Thai Marriage*. Publication No. 81. Salaya, Thailand: Institute for Population and Research, Mahidol University.

Cherlin, Andrew J. 1992. *Marriage, Divorce, Remarriage*. Revised and enlarged ed. Cambridge Mass.: Harvard University Press.

Cornell, Laurel L., and Akira Hayami. 1986. "The *Shūmon Aratame Chō:* Japan's Population Registers." *Journal of Family History* 11(4):311–328.

Desai, Sonalde, P. Lindsay Chase-Lansdale, and Robert T. Michael. 1989. "Mother or Market? Effects of Maternal Employment on the Intellectual Ability of 4-year-old Children." *Demography* 26(4):545–561.

Friedman, Ronald, Ming-Cheng Chang, and Te-Hsiung Sun. 1982. "Household Composition, Extended Kinship, and Reproduction in Taiwan: 1973–1980." *Population Studies* 36(3):395–411.

Goode, William J. 1963. *World Revolution and Family Patterns*. New York: Free Press.

Liu, Korbin, Kenneth G. Manton, and Barbara Marzetta Liu. 1985. "Home Care Expenses for the Disabled Elderly." *Health Care Financing Review* 7(2):51–59.

Martin, Linda G. 1989. "The Graying of Japan." *Population Bulletin* 44(2).

Mason, Karen O., and John Bauer. 1991. "The Impact of Industrial Restructuring on Women and the Family: The Asian Experience." In *Proceedings of the Nihon University International Symposium on Family and the Contemporary Japanese Culture: An International Perspective*, Vol. 2, pp. 583–596. Tokyo: University Research Center, Nihon University.

Popenoe, David. 1988. *Disturbing the Nest: Family Change and Decline in Modern Societies.* New York: Aldine de Gruyter.

Rindfuss, Ronald R. 1991. "Comment on Session 1: Social Change and the Family." In *Proceedings of the Nihon University International Symposium on Family and the Contemporary Japanese Culture: An International Perspective*, Vol. 1, pp. 177–184. Tokyo: University Research Center, Nihon University.

United States, Bureau of the Census. 1982. "America in Transition: An Aging Society." *Current Population Reports*, Special Studies. Series P-23, No. 128. Washington, D.C.: U.S. Government Printing Office.

———. 1991. *Statistical Abstract of the United States, 1990*. Washington, D.C.: U.S. Government Printing Office.

United States, National Center for Health Statistics. 1979. *The National Nursing Home Survey: 1977 Summary for the United States*. Vital and Health Statistics, Series 13, No. 43. Washington, D.C.: U.S. Government Printing Office.

APPENDIX

Origin and Design of Japan's 1988 National Family Survey

Michio Ozaki

The family has been described as "an irreplaceable magnifying glass on the structure of a race or society (Japan, Council on Population Problems, *Dictionary of Population*). As the most basic unit of a society, the family might be alternatively described as one cell of the social organism, in which all the cultural and religious traditions and customs of a society are present. Considered in this way it is the ideal material for research on the characteristics of a culture. For this reason the family was selected as the topic for a study entitled The Characteristics of Modern Japanese Culture, one of several research projects commissioned by the president of Nihon University. The Population Institute (now the Program on Population) of the East-West Center, having earlier conducted cross-cultural studies on the value of children to parents and recognizing the importance of the family as a microcosm of society, agreed to participate in the project and showed strong interest in an international comparison of the family in Japan, other Asian societies, and the United States.

Although the family encapsulates the traditional values of a people or society, it is constantly changing in response to events within and even beyond that society. In recent years science and technology have brought about rapid developments in transportation, lowering national boundaries and promoting cross-cultural contact and interaction on a global scale. Such cultural contact leads to change in each society through the processes of collision, adjustment, and fusion of values.

It has been more than a century since the Japanese, whose culture was infused with Confucian values, encountered Western values with their emphasis on rational thought, individualism, and contractual obligations. Those early contacts with the West, however, were limited and confined to the intellectual elite. It was not until after World War II that the Japanese people at large were introduced to Western democracy, and this baptism was performed by U.S. occupational forces. Because, in contrast with the United States, Japan had not experienced a revolution of individualism, it is not surprising that its democratic institutions consisted initially more of form than of substance. Even today, despite reforms in the family system, such as the abolition of the family headship, the granting of equal rights to women, and the equal distribution of property to heirs of both sexes, a few practices remain that are founded in values nurtured through centuries of Confucian tradition.

Western advanced democracies are also experiencing major social changes today. Some countries are witnessing a breakdown of the family as evidenced by increased divorce rates, a trend toward cohabitation that does not lead to marriage, and a rising proportion of single parents. Ironically, the increased income that has come with the development of the industrial society has created diversified values, placing at risk the system of monogamy that has been the basis of that society. The division of labor, in which the husband went to work in a factory while the wife stayed at home to look after their children, has broken down. Liberated from their familial bonds, women in droves have moved into the workplace.

So how should one characterize the family in Japan, a Confucian society that has achieved modernization by embracing Western civilization during the current century? Now that Japan has joined the advanced industrial nations of the West, it is facing changes in the family similar to those taking place in Western countries. For example, in the past few years a novel about single living has become a best seller in Japan, and expressions such as DINK (double income, no kids) now regularly appear in the pages of Japanese newspapers and magazines.

Where is the Japanese family, which lies geopolitically at the crossroads of Eastern and Western cultures, going? Exploring the characteristics of culture through the family is not only an academic pursuit; for those who are involved in the mass media, the changes occurring in the modern Japanese family are also of great interest. Because Japan's population

Appendix

is rapidly aging, some of that interest is due to concern about the family's diminishing role in caring for the elderly.

The Mainichi Newspapers Opinion Research Department, in cooperation with the University Research Center of Nihon University and the Population Institute of the East-West Center, decided to explore modern Japanese familial attitudes and behavior. As part of their joint study, in 1988 the Mainichi Newspapers conducted a National Opinion Survey on the Family (referred to in this volume as the 1988 National Family Survey). It is hoped that the results of this survey will be used as the foundation for case studies and research comparing the Japanese with people in other societies.

In July 1987 the president of Nihon University officially endorsed the research plan. Planning for the full-scale survey took place in August 1987 at a workshop held at the East-West Center in Honolulu. Participants in the workshop included Dr. Lee-Jay Cho of the East-West Center's Population Institute; Professor Ronald R. Rindfuss of the Carolina Population Center, University of North Carolina; and Professor Toshio Kuroda, honorary director of the Population Research Institute of Nihon University. Discussion at that first workshop produced useful suggestions for designing the framework of the questionnaire that was subsequently prepared by the Mainichi Newspapers and Nihon University.

The University Research Center of Nihon University collected, collated, and classified information about previous Japanese surveys on the family; and during a second planning workshop held in Tokyo in January 1988 the Mainichi Newspapers Opinion Research Department presented a draft questionnaire for the nationwide survey. The questionnaire was discussed and revised. In addition to 10 basic demographic and socioeconomic questions (on respondents' gender, date of birth, age, academic background, area where raised, birth order, occupation, number of years employed, working hours, and annual income, the final questionnaire included 28 questions about respondents' attitudes toward the family (e.g., questions about *ie* consciousness), their families' internal structure (e.g., about the selection of their spouse, whether they had a traditional or modern marriage, and the children's socialization), their life structure (e.g., their attitudes toward life in general, how they spent their personal time), and how they handled family problems.

The survey was fielded during the first four days of April 1988. Thirty-four hundred male and female respondents of 20 years of age and older were selected throughout the country by stratified multi-stage random sampling. Using the Mainichi Newspapers survey network, fieldworkers left copies of the questionnaire with respondents for later collection. Altogether, 2,406 valid responses were obtained, for a recovery rate of 71 percent. Slightly more women (53 percent) than men (47 percent) responded.

Appendix

By age group, the sample was distributed as follows:

20–29	15%
30–39	22
40–49	23
50–59	19
60+	21

Thirteen percent of the sample were single, 76 percent were married, 1 percent was divorced, and 8 percent were widowed (2 percent gave no response to this question).

A summary of the survey results was published in the Mainichi Newspapers on 4 May 1988. As this survey was one of the few national polls about family behavior and attitudes ever conducted in Japan, it attracted considerable attention, generating many letters and questions from readers and researchers.

A translation of the questionnaire used in the survey follows.

Appendix

A National Opinion Survey about the Family
April 1988

The Mainichi Newspapers
Nihon University

Address   :
Prefecture   :
City/Ward/District :
Town/Village   :

District code	Individual code

Note: Please fill in the blanks with numbers or circle the number of the most appropriate answer.

Please answer for both you and your spouse. For single respondents, please answer for yourself only.

	You	Your spouse
Sex	1. Male 2. Female	1. Male 2. Female
Date of birth	1. Meiji 2. Taisho 3. Showa Year _____ Month _____ Age _____ (as of April 30)	1. Meiji 2. Taisho 3. Showa Year _____ Month _____ Age _____ (as of April 30)
Academic background (If you are still a student or left school in mid-course, please answer as well.)	1. Elementary school, advanced elementary under old system, junior high school under new system 2. Junior high school under old system, advanced women's school under old system, high school under new system 3. Professional school, advanced professional school, junior college 4. University, graduate school	1. Elementary school, advanced elementary under old system, junior high school under new system 2. Junior high school under old system, advanced women's school under old system, high school under new system 3. Professional school, advanced professional school, junior college 4. University, graduate school
	You / Your father	Your spouse / Your spouse's father
Place where you/your spouse was brought up until graduating from elementary school	1. Urban area 2. Farming or fishing village	1. Urban area 2. Farming or fishing village
Relation to parents	1. Eldest son/daughter 2. Second son/daughter 3. Third son/daughter 4. Fourth son/daughter 5. Fifth son/daughter 6. Sixth son/daughter 7. Seventh son/daughter 8. Eighth son/daughter 9. Ninth son/daughter	1. Eldest son/daughter 2. Second son/daughter 3. Third son/daughter 4. Fourth son/daughter 5. Fifth son/daughter 6. Sixth son/daughter 7. Seventh son/daughter 8. Eighth son/daughter 9. Ninth son/daughter

Appendix

Q 4 (a). Recently the number of young people who prefer to lead single lives on their own, rather than to marry, has been increasing. What do you think about this tendency?

     1. I agree.   2. I do not agree.

For those who chose answer 1 above	For those who chose answer 2 above
(b) Choose only one reason from the following:	(c) Choose only one reason from the following:
1. Because one can live freely without being restricted by one's family. 2. Because it encourages economic independence. 3. Because married life is not the only way to live. 4. Because one can concentrate on work or hobbies. 5. Other (specify).	1. Because happiness lies in marriage. 2. Because it does not look good in other people's eyes. 3. Because it encourages sexual immorality. 4. Because the number of children will decrease. 5. Other (specify).

Q 5. If you become single in your old age, do you think you will remarry? (Choose only one answer.)

    1. I would definitely like to look for a suitable partner and remarry.
    2. If I found a suitable partner, I would like to remarry.
    3. I prefer to live alone.
    4. I definitely want never to remarry.

Q 6. The Supreme Court ruled to permit a person to divorce a spouse who has destroyed their marriage through infidelity, etc., on condition that there be a prolonged separation and the couple have no young children. What do you think about this ruling? (Choose only one answer.)

    1. I agree with it because it opens up a new life to a couple married in form only. It also reflects the current trend.
    2. I do not agree with it because it favors the one who caused the divorce and it is likely to put women (usually the weaker party) at a disadvantage.
    3. I don't know.

Q 7. Choose one answer to express your opinion on each of the following subjects.

	1. Yes, I think so	2. No, I don't think so.	3. I don't know
(A) It is the eldest son's duty to look after his parents.	1	2	3
(B) The family's name must be continued even if that requires adopting a child.	1	2	3
(C) The tomb of one's ancestors must be treasured and should be passed on to posterity.	1	2	3

Appendix

Q 8. When parents die, who do you think should inherit their property?

    1. The eldest son.
    2. The property should be divided equally among the children.
    3. The person in the family, if it is not the eldest son, who takes care of the parents.
    4. The person, if it is not a family member, who looks after the parents in their old age.
    5. The hospital or welfare facility that looks after the parents in their old age.
    6. Other (specify).

Q 9. The family has many roles. Which of the following do you think is the most important? (Choose only one answer.)

    1. Providing economic support for daily life
    2. Providing a place to express marital affection
    3. A place for rest and comfort
    4. A place to raise a family
    5. A place for mutual growth and respect among family members
    6. Other (specify)

Q 10. How often does your family usually do the following things together? Choose one answer for items (A) through (E).

	1 Several times a week	2 Approx. once a week	3 Approx. once a month	4 Several times a year	5 Approx. once a year	6 Seldom
(A) Go to movies, sports events, concerts, etc.	1	2	3	4	5	6
(B) Play sports	1	2	3	4	5	6
(C) Eat out or do some shopping	1	2	3	4	5	6
(D) Go on an overnight or longer trip	1	2	3	4	5	6
(E) Visit friends, acquaintances, and relatives	1	2	3	4	5	6

Q 11 (a). Are you married or not? (Choose only one answer.)

    1. Yes, I am married. (I have a spouse.)
    2. I am divorced and living with my family [parents?] at present.
    3. I am divorced and living alone at present.
    4. I am widowed and living with my family [parents?] at present.
    5. I am widowed and living alone at present.
    6. No, I am not yet married and am living with my family [parents?] at present.
    7. No, I am not yet married and am living alone at present.
    8. Other (specify).

Appendix

If you chose answer 1 to question 11 (a), please also answer the questions 11 (b) to 14 (c).

Q 11 (b). When you married your present spouse, how old were both you and your spouse?

        1. You _____   2. Your spouse _____

Q 11 (c). Was it through an arranged marriage or a love match? (Choose only one answer.)

    1. An arranged marriage   2. A love match   3. Other

Q 11 (d). Was it your first marriage or a remarriage? (Please answer for your spouse as well. Choose only one answer.)

You	Your spouse
1. First marriage	1. First marriage
2. Second marriage	2. Second marriage
3. Third or later marriage	3. Third or later marriage

Q 11 (e). Have you ever thought of divorcing your present spouse? (Choose only one answer.)

    1. Yes, often.   2. Yes, once in a while.   3. No.

If you chose answer 1 or 2 to the above question:

Q 11 (f). What is your main reason for not getting divorced? (Choose one or two answers.)

    1. Because we have a child/children.
    2. Because it would cause economic difficulties.
    3. Because it would hurt my parent(s).
    4. Because it would not look good in other people's eyes.
    5. Because the situation has improved.
    6. Because I realized that I have to be patient.
    7. Other (please specify).

Q 12 (a). Is/Are your parent(s) and your spouse's parent(s) living?

Your parent(s)	Your spouse's parent(s)
[1] 1. Both parents are living. 2. Only my father is living. 3. Only my mother is living. 4. Both parents are dead.	[2] 1. Both parents are living. 2. Only my spouse's father is living. 3. Only my spouse's mother is living. 4. Both parents are dead.

Q 12 (b). Where do they, or does he/she, live now? (Choose only one answer.)

Your parent(s)	Your spouse's parent(s)
[3] If you chose answer 1, 2, or 3 in column [1] above	[3] If you chose answer 1, 2, or 3 in column [2] above
1. With us (in the same house) 2. Next door or on the same land 3. 5–6 minutes away on foot 4. In the same village, town, ward, or city (but not the above) 5. In the next village, town, ward, or city 6. In the same prefecture except the above 7. In another prefecture	1. With us (in the same house) 2. Next door or on the same land 3. 5–6 minutes away on foot 4. In the same village, town, ward, or city (but not the above) 5. In the next village, town, ward, or city 6. In the same prefecture except the above 7. In another prefecture

Appendix

If you chose answer 1 in column [3] above, please also answer questions from 12 (c) to 12 (g).

Q 12 (c). How many parents or parents-in-law live with you? (Choose as many answers as apply.)

1. Your father
2. Your mother
3. Your parents
4. Your spouse's father
5. Your spouse's mother
6. Your spouse's parents
7. Others (specify)

Q 12 (d). When did they/he/she start to live with you? (Choose only one answer.)

1. Since we got married.
2. When we got married they/he/she lived separately and later they/he/she came to live with us.
3. When we got married, we lived with them/him/her. Then we lived separately, and now we live together again.
4. Other (specify).

Q 12 (e). When you started living together, who moved where? (Choose only one answer.)

1. Parents/father/mother moved into our house.
2. We moved into their/his/her house.
3. Parents/father/mother moved into a new house with us.

Q 12 (f). Who is in charge of the family finances? (Choose only one answer.)

1. Parents/father/mother take(s) care of most of them.
2. They/he/she pay(s) more than we.
3. We pay most of the bills.
4. We pay more than they/he/she.
5. We share almost equally.
6. We pay separately.

Q 12 (g). Which of the following is the main reason for your living together? (Choose only one answer.)

1. To help them/him/her financially.
2. To look after them/him/her.
3. We wish to stay close to them/him/her.
4. It's my/my spouse's obligation as the eldest son/daughter.
5. It's the parents'/parent's wish.
6. Parent(s) take(s) care of housekeeping work and the grandchildren.
7. Parent(s) offer(s) us a house.
8. Other (specify).

If you chose answers 2–7 to question 12 (b), please also answer questions 13 (a) to 13 (c):

Q 13 (a). With whom does/do your parent(s) live? (Choose only one answer.)

Your parent(s)	Your spouse's parent(s)
1. With my sister/brother or my spouse's sister/brother. 2. With a relative. 3. With somebody other than the above. 4. My parent(s) live(s) alone.	1. With my sister/brother or my spouse's sister/brother. 2. With a relative. 3. With somebody other than the above. 4. My parent(s) live(s) alone.

Q 13 (b). How often have you met with your parent(s) during the last one or two years? (Choose only one answer from column [4]. Your spouse should choose only one answer from column [5].)

Your parent(s)	Your spouse's parent(s)
[4] 1. Almost every day. 2. Approximately once a week. 3. Approximately once a month. 4. Several times a year. 5. Approximately once a year. 6. We seldom see them/him/her.	[5] 1. Almost every day. 2. Approximately once a week. 3. Approximately once a month. 4. Several times a year. 5. Approximately once a year. 6. We seldom see them/him/her.

Appendix

Q 13 (c). How often do you contact them/him/her? (Choose only one answer from column [6]. Your spouse should choose only answer from column [7].)

Your parent(s)	Your spouse's parent(s)
[6] 1. Almost every day. 2. Approximately once a week. 3. Approximately once a month. 4. Several times a year. 5. Approximately once a year. 6. We seldom see them/him/her.	[7] 1. Almost every day. 2. Approximately once a week. 3. Approximately once a month. 4. Several times a year. 5. Approximately once a year. 6. We seldom see them/him/her.

If you chose answer 2 or 3 (divorced) to question 11 (a), please answer questions 14 (a) through 14 (c).

Q 14 (a). How old were you when you got married? _____ years old.

Q 14 (b). How long were you married? _____ years.

Q 14 (c). Why did you divorce? (Choose as many reasons from among the following as apply.)

1. Husband's/wife's infidelity.
2. Husband's/wife's violence, violence related to alcohol abuse.
3. Financial problems.
4. Incompatibility of personalities.
5. Incompatible sex life.
6. We did not share the same hobbies.
7. I did not get along with my in-laws.
8. We could not have a child (childlessness).
9. Husband's/wife's poor health.
0. Other (specify).

If you chose answer 6 or 7 (unmarried) to question 11 (a), please answer question 15.

Q 15. At about what age did you or do you wish to get married? (Choose only one answer.)

1. At age 20–24.
2. At age 25–29.
3. At age 30–34.
4. At age 35–39.
5. At age 40 or later.
6. Timing has nothing to do with age.
7. I wish to remain single all my life.

Q 16. What kind of person would you like your child to become? (Please choose three answers from the following, answering separately for a son and a daughter. If you do not have a son or daughter, assume that you do.)

1. A gentle and obedient person
2. An independent person
3. A competitive, hard-working person
4. A person with leadership qualities
5. A popular person among friends
6. A thoughtful person
7. A responsible person
8. A tough, vital person
9. A dutiful person
0. A person who can enjoy his/her life

Son			
Daughter			

Q 17. What do you think are good reasons for having a child? (Choose one or two.)

1. Family life is brightened by a child/children.
2. It is enjoyable to raise a child.
3. A child will become a wage earner.
4. A child can be relied upon when one gets old.
5. A child can succeed to the family business.
6. A child can succeed to the family name and property.
7. A child ensures the continuation of the family line.
8. Other (specify).

Appendix

Q 18. How many children do you have? Your answer should include children who live apart from you.

	No.
1. In preschool	
2. In elementary school	
3. In junior high school	
4. In high school	
5. At university	
6. Adult (unmarried)	
7. Adult (married)	
8. No children	

Q 19. By whom do you want to be looked after when you become old or are bedridden for a long time? (Choose only one answer.)

1. My spouse
2. My son
3. My daughter
4. My son's wife (daughter-in-law)
5. My brother/sister
6. Another relative
7. A home helper
8. A welfare institution such as a home for the aged
9. A hospital
0. Other (specify)

Q 20. If one of the following happens to you, on whom or what would you depend the most? (Choose one from each of the following, (A) through (E).)

	Parent(s) (including those of my spouse)	Other relatives	Neighbors	Friends, acquaintances	Colleagues	Government offices or organizations such as welfare offices	Nobody to rely upon
(A) When I am not familiar with the respective formalities such as funerals or weddings	1	2	3	4	5	6	7
(B) When I have problems concerning my child's entry into a higher educational institution or employment	1	2	3	4	5	6	7
(C) When I need a guarantor	1	2	3	4	5	6	7
(D) When I cannot look after bedridden parent(s)	1	2	3	4	5	6	7
(E) When there are marital problems	1	2	3	4	5	6	7

Q 21. What kind of work did you do before your marriage? (Choose only one answer.)

1. Skilled white-collar work (management above section chief, teacher, researcher, skilled worker such as engineer)
2. Unskilled white-collar work (clerk, salesperson, shopkeeper, etc.)
3. Blue-collar work (factory worker, artisan, driver, etc.)
4. Self-employed (proprietor of a shop, office, factory, etc.)
5. Agriculture, forestry, or fishery
6. Profession (lawyer, physician, writer, etc.)
7. Family business (shop attendant, laborer working for a family factory, agricultural helper, etc.)
8. Part-time work
9. Homemaking (engaged in housekeeping work only)
0. Student
Y. Unemployed

Appendix

Q 22. Do you think you would like to live in this area all your life? Or would you prefer to live somewhere else? (Choose only one.)
1. I wish to live here permanently.
2. I wish to live here as long as possible.
3. I prefer to move.
4. I wish to move as soon as possible.
5. Other (specify).

Q 23. Are your family members healthy? (Choose as many responses as you wish.)
1. All members are healthy.
2. Some are outpatients and under medical treatment.
3. Some are hospitalized and under medical treatment.
4. Some are under medical treatment at home.
5. Other (specify).

Q 24. Since when have you lived at your present residence? (Choose only one.)
1. Since my grandfather's generation.
2. Since my father's generation.
3. Since my own generation.

Q 25. In which of the following do you currently live?
1. An urban area
2. An agricultural or fishing village

Q 26. Which of the following applies to your residence? (Choose only one answer.)
1. Detached house (homeowner)
2. Condominium unit (homeowner)
3. Rented house
4. Rented condominium unit
5. Apartment
6. Public housing
7. Housing provided by a company or the government for its workers
8. Dormitory
9. Other (specify)

Q 27. How many family members live in your residence, including yourself?
1. One
2. Two
3. Three
4. Four
5. Five
6. Six
7. Seven
8. Eight
9. Nine
0. Ten or more

Q 28. Which of the following applies to your household? (Choose only one answer.)
1. Single-member household
2. A couple (conjugal household)
3. A couple and a child/children (nuclear household)
4. Single-parent household
5. Two generation family with no minors
6. Grandparent(s), parents, and a child/children
7. Great-grandparent(s), grandparent(s), paren(s), and a child/children (four-generation family)
8. Brother(s) and sister(s) alone
9. Other (specify)

Thank you very much for your cooperation.

INDEX

adolescence in Thailand, 379–80
adoption in Japan and family succession, 200
adulthood, transition to, in Thailand, 373–77, 374t, 375t
age: and attitudes toward family in Japan, 101t, 102t, 106–11, 110t, 112t, 113t, 200–218, 211t, 212t, 214t, 215t; and attitudes toward family values in Thailand, 407, 408t; and attitudes toward marriage in Japan, 101t, 102t, 106–17, 110t, 112t; and coresidence in Japan, 155–56, 159t, 159–60, 163t, 164, 164n 4, 223, 224t, 227t; and coresidence in Korea, 293t, 296t, 297t, 305; and coresidence in Taiwan, 328–32, 329t, 331t, 336, 337t; and coresidence in U.S., 223–25, 224t; and establishment of household in Thailand, 393, 393t; and family type in Japan, 184, 188, 192t, 192–95, 193t; at first birth in Thailand, 375t, 376; in Japan, on survey questionnaire, 439; and living arrangements of elderly in Korea, 303, 303t, 304t, 306; and marriage, type of, in Japan, 143, 143f; and migration intentions in Yūbari, 256, 257t, 259, 259t, 261–63; and modernity in Thailand, 414, 415t; and parental contact in Japan, 159t, 169, 172t, 231t, 232t, 233t, 234–35, 235f, 238t, 239t, 240t, 243; and parental contact in U.S., 231t, 232t, 233t, 234–35, 235f, 238t, 239t, 240t, 243; and parental residence in Taiwan, 335; and parental survival in Japan, 222–23; and parental survival in U.S., 222–23; of parents and coresidence in Taiwan, 332; and place of birth of child in Thailand, 396t, 397; of spouse and coresidence in Japan, 159t, 161–62, 163t; of spouse and parental contact in Japan, 159t, 169, 172t; and spouse selection, criteria for, in Japan, 146–50, 147t; and support from sons in Taiwan, 348–50, 349t, 358; and wealth flows in Taiwan, 345, 346t
age at marriage: and attitudes toward family in Japan, 102t, 106–17, 112t, 113t, 208–18, 211t, 212t, 214t, 215t; and attitudes toward marriage in Japan, 102t, 112t, 114–15; and birth rate in Japan, 139; of bride and groom compared, in Thailand, 387–88, 388t, 398; changes in, in Japan, 95–96, 96t, 141, 151; and fertility in Japan, 96–98; in Japan, on survey questionnaire, 444, 446; and marriage arrangements in Taiwan, 354t; pre-

ferred, in Japan, 103n; in Scandinavia, compared to Japan, 96; in Thailand, 375t, 376; variation in, by region, in Thailand, 386–87, 387t, 398t; in West, 21
age distribution (*see* age structure)
age structure: in Korea, 278t, 308t, 310t A14.6; and migration in Korea, 278; and supply of labor in agriculture in Korea, 280; in Yūbari, 254tt, 254–55
aging (*see also* elderly as proportion of total population); and care for elderly in Japan, 425; and care for elderly in Taiwan, 319–20; and migration in Yūbari, 253; and social welfare in Japan, 130, 154; in U.S., compared to Japan, 425
aging and fertility in Japan, 51
agricultural employment in Japan, 60
agriculture: and age structure in Korea, 280–81; and family in Thailand, 377–78; loss of importance of, in Ōgaito, 88; in Yūbari, 265, 268; in Yuzurihara, 67–68, 68n
American family (*see* family in U.S.)
analysis, cultural (*see* cultural analysis)
ancestors: attitudes toward in Japan, on survey questionnaire, 442; honor and reverence for, in Japan, 9, 11, 30; worship of, and coresidence in Taiwan, 327, 327t; worship of, and *ie* in Japan, 62, 183; worship of, in Korea, 15, 281, 287
arranged marriage (*see* marriage, arranged)
assistance (*see* financial assistance; mutual assistance; support)
assumptions about family: Japan and U.S. compared, 31–35
attitudes (*see also under specific topics*); and behavior, 202–3; toward family in Korea (*see under* family in Korea); toward family in Korea, survey on (*see* rural family and community life in South Korea survey); toward marriage and family in Japan (*see under* family in Japan; marriage in Japan); toward marriage and family in Japan, survey on (*see* National Family Survey of Japan)
authority (*see* hierarchy); in family in Thailand, 366, 366n, 403, 404 (*see also* marriage)

baby boom and household size in Japan, 50, 53
behavior and attitudes, 202–3
belief structure (*see* idealized family morality)
birth order: and attitudes toward family in Japan, 101t, 102t, 106–17, 110t, 112t, 113t, 209–17, 211t, 212t, 214t, 215t; and attitudes toward marriage in Japan, 101t, 102t, 106–17, 110t, 112t, 113t; and coresidence in Japan, 155–56, 159t, 160, 163t, 164, 227t, 227–29; and coresidence in U.S., 225t, 226; in Japan, on survey questionnaire, 439; and parental contact in Japan, 157, 169, 171–73, 172t, 183, 231t, 232t, 233t, 237–43, 238t, 239t, 240t; and parental contact in U.S., 231t, 232t, 233t, 237–43, 238t, 239t, 240t; of spouse and coresidence in Japan, 155–56, 159t, 162, 163t, 164; of spouse and parental contact in Japan, 159t, 169, 171–73, 172t
birthplace: by age and region in Thailand, 396t, 396–97, 399; and migration intentions in Yūbari, 256–60, 257t, 259t; in Taiwan (*see* ethnicity in Taiwan)
birth rate (*see also* fertility); and attitudes toward marriage and family in Japan, 91; and family size in China, 52; and household size in Japan, 50, 51t
births, timing of, in Japan, 93, 95
branch families (*see* families in Ōgaito, main)
breadwinner model of nuclear family, 12, 20
brothers, availability of, in Taiwan: and coresidence, 329t, 331t, 332, 334, 357; and sharing of meals, 343; and wealth flows, 345, 346t
Buddhism: and making merit in Thailand, 404; and stem family in Japan, 183
business owners (*see* shopkeepers)

care, availability of, and family type in Japan, 182, 185–86, 189, 192t, 193t, 193–95
caregiver, desired, in Japan, on survey questionnaire, 447
CBR (crude birth rate) (*see* birth rate)
CDR (crude death rate) (*see* death rate)
childcare: and coresidence, 429; and coresidence in Taiwan, 334; responsibility for, in Japan, 37, 202, 432
child-rearing practices in Japan, 34, 37 (*see also* socialization)
children: availability of, and family type in Japan, 184, 188, 191–92, 192t, 193t, 194–95; desires for, in Japan, on survey questionnaire, 446; education of, parents' aspirations for in Korea, 283tt, 283–84; marital status of, and living arrangements of elderly in Korea, 303t, 304t, 305–6; number of, and

Index

coresidence in Japan, 159–60; number of, and living arrangements of elderly in Korea, 303t, 304t, 305; number of, in Japan, on survey questionnaire, 446; obligations of, in Thailand, 404; parental expectations of, in Japan, 37; preferred traits of, in Japan, 14, 207t, 207–8, 213–16; reasons for having, in Japan, 92, 101t, 102t, 105, 109–11, 110t, 112t, 113t, 114–17; reasons for having, in Japan, on survey questionnaire, 446; support from, and family type in Japan, 184, 189, 192, 192t; support from, in Japan, on survey questionnaire, 442; values about, in Thailand, 405t, 406–13, 408t, 410t, 412t, 417

China *(see under specific topics)*

Chinese cultural sphere *(see also* Confucianism); and family, 4, 54

city size: and coresidence in Japan, 227t; and parental contact in Japan, 231t, 232t, 233t, 237–43, 238t, 239t, 240t; and parental contact in U.S., 231t, 232t, 233t, 237–43, 238t, 239t, 240t

civil codes in Japan, 9, 183–84

coal industry: in Japan, 248–50; and national policy in Japan, 266; in Yūbari, 249–53 *(see also* mine closures)

Coal Plans in Japan, 250

cohort model of social change, 200

collectivity *(see* group)

communal assistance *(see* mutual assistance)

communication and urban-rural relationships: in Japan, 63, 88; in Korea, 276, 281

community life, tradition and change in, in Japan, 59–89

community ties and migration intentions in Yūbari, 262, 264, 266

compositional effects: on coresidence in Taiwan, 326; on expectations of support from sons in Taiwan, 350

conflict, family *(see* family conflict)

conflict management in Japan, 33, 37

Confucianism and the family, 4, 9–10; in China, 320; in Japan, 54, 183; in Korea, 10, 281

conjugal family *(see also* family, nuclear); defined, 7

contact with parents *(see* parental contact)

contextual determinants of family type, 179–80, 185–86, 189–94, 191tt, 192t, 193t; in Japan *(see* family type in Japan)

convergence theory of family structure, 45, 179, 422

cooperative groups *(kye)* and family interactions in Korea, 287–88, 288tt

coresidence *(see also* living arrangements; matrilocal residence; patrilocal residence); and age in Korea, 293t, 293–94, 295t; attitudes toward, in Japan, 11, 128t, 128–29, 426–27; availability of kin for *(see* demographic determinants of family type); bilateral, in U.S., 223; and birth order in Korea, 314t A14.13; and care for elderly in Japan, 425–26; changes in, in Korea, 292; and childcare, 429; conditional, 429; data and methods used for study of, in Taiwan, 321–25, 322t, 323f, 324e; desirability of *(see* normative determinants of family type); desirability of, in Japan, 123, 128; differences in, between men and women in Japan, 165–67; and economic development in Korea, 292; and economic development in Taiwan, 334; and economic development in Thailand, 372, 377, 401; of elderly with children in Japan, 52, 156; factors affecting, in Japan, 154–56, 159–67, 163t, 164nn, 174, 222–28, 224t, 227t; factors affecting, in Korea, 292–99, 295t, 296t, 297t, 305–6; factors affecting, in Taiwan, 326–36, 327t, 329t, 331t, 335t, 357–58; factors affecting, in U.S., 222–26, 224t, 225t; feasibility of *(see* economic determinants of family type); and fertility in Japan, 159–60; and financial arrangements in Japan, 166, 166t; as fundamental family system in Japan, 132; future of, in Japan, 425; and housing shortages in Japan, 429; and income in Japan, 428; in Japan, 153–67, 165t 9.3, 174–75, 223–28, 224t, 227t, 242–45 *(see also* elderly; living arrangements in Japan); in Japan, compared with West, 125t, 126–27; in Japan, on survey questionnaire, 445; in Japan, survey on *(see* National Family Survey of Japan); in Korea, 292–306, 293t *(see also* elderly); in Korea, survey on *(see* rural family and community life in South Korea survey); and labor force status of women in Japan, 160; length of, in Japan, 131; and life-cycle in Thailand, 366–70; and lineage status of father in Korea, 314t A14.14, 314t A14.15; of middle-aged in Japan, 14, 155–77; and migration in Japan,

269; and modernization in Taiwan, 326, 338–40, 339t, 358–59; and mortality, 164, 174, 222; and number of children in Japan,159–60; opinions about, and family type in Japan, 189, 192–93, 192t, 193t, 194–96; and parental contact in Japan, 159t, 169, 171–73, 172t; and parental survival in Japan, 156, 159t, 162, 163t, 164; and parental survival in Korea, 314t A14.12; and parental survival in U.S., 222; patterns and trends of, in Japan, 154–56, 158–59, 165, 165t 9.3; postnuptial (see matrilocal residence; patrilocal residence); postnuptial, attitudes toward, in Taiwan, 340–42, 341t; postnuptial, in Japan, 155, 165t 9.4, 165–66; postnuptial, in Taiwan, 236t, 326; postnuptial, in Thailand, 366–70, 370t 16.4, 372, 390–95, 391t, 392t, 393t, 394t; preferences for, in Japan, 11, 129–31; preferred, in old age in Thailand, 416, 416t; reasons for, in Japan, 132, 166t, 166–67; reasons for, in Japan, on survey questionnaire, 445; and region in Thailand, 15; and self-employment in Japan, 160; and size of house in Japan, 428; in Taiwan, 183, 320–42; in Taiwan, survey on, 321–22; in Thailand, 398–99 (see also matrilocal residence); in Thailand, survey on (see Thai Family and Household Survey); timing of, in Japan, 165, 165t 9.4; traditional model of, in Thailand, 367; and type of marriage in Korea, 294, 295t, 297, 297t, 305–6, 315t A14.16; in U.S. (see also living arrangements in U.S.); in U.S., compared to Japan, 221–45; variables used for analysis of, in Japan, 159t; who moves in with whom in Japan, 165–66, 166t 9.5; with wife's parents in Taiwan, 336, 337t, 358
correlation analysis: of extended family in Japan, 190–92, 191tt; of modernity indicators in Thailand, 412–14, 413t
crowding (see size of house)
crude birth rate (CBR) (see birth rate)
crude death rate (CDR) (see death rate)
cultural analysis of family, 29–30
culture: defined, 31, 41; effects of, on family change, 30–31; and family, 423; and family in Japan and U.S., 31–35; importance of, to family, 7, 12, 16
culture, spiritual, 7, 12

daegali system of tenancy in Korea, 281
data availability for study of the family (see family surveys)
daycare in Japan, 37
death rate: before demographic transition in China, 52; and household size in Japan, 50–51, 51t
decision making in family: in Japan, 32–33, 92; in U.S., 33
deconstruction and family theory, 21
deindustrialization (see industrial restructuring)
demographic determinants of family type, 180–84, 190–92, 191tt, 192t, 193t, 195–96 (see also family type in Japan)
demographic transition: and aging in Taiwan, 319; and aging in Thailand, 379; and family, 5
Denmark, age at marriage in, compared to Japan, 96
depopulation, rural, effects of, in Japan, 63–64, 67–68
development (see economic development; modernization)
development style in Japan, 432
dissolution, marital (see divorce)
distance and parental contact: in Japan, 170–74, 172t, 230, 231t, 232t, 238t, 239t, 240t, 243; in Taiwan, 356; in U.S., 230, 231t, 232t, 233t, 238t, 239t, 240t, 243
division of labor in family: in Thailand, 403; in U.S., 436
divorce: attitudes toward, in Japan, 103; attitudes toward, in Japan, on survey questionnaire, 444; attitudes toward, in Korea, 285, 286t 14.9; attitudes toward, in Thailand, 389t, 389–90, 398; attitudes toward, in U.S., 103; and changes within family in U.S., 42; in East Asia, 4–5; effects of, on family composition in U.S., 16; in Japan, 92, 97t, 97–98, 98t; in Japan, on survey questionnaire, 446; in Sweden, 423; in Thailand, 375t, 376, 404–5; in U.S., 97–98, 423, 436; in West, 4–5, 22, 436
dongjok burak (clan-centered rural village) in Korea, 274
durables, modern (see possessions, modern)
duration of marriage (see marital duration)
duty of children to parents in Thailand, 404
duty of eldest son in Japan: attitudes toward,

206, 209t, 210, 211t, 212; attitudes toward, on survey questionnaire, 439

East-West Center Program on Population (see National Family Survey of Japan)
economic determinants of family type, 180–84, 189–92, 191tt, 192t, 193t, 195 (see also family type in Japan)
economic development: and change, 19–20; and coresidence in Korea, 292; and coresidence in Taiwan, 334; and family, 12, 16, 21, 23, 26, 179, 422; and family in Japan, 13, 202; and family in Korea, 15, 273; and family in Taiwan, 356–57; and family in Thailand, 372, 377–78, 401; regional differences in, in Thailand, 385; and social change in Ōgaito, 88; and social development, 19; and social welfare in East Asia, 16; take-off point in, 20; and urban-rural distinction in Japan, 63
economic factors and family type (see economic determinants of family type)
economic growth (see also economic development); and coal industry in Japan, 247–48, 250; and family type in Korea, 289; and parental residence in Taiwan, 334; in Taiwan, 356–57
education: and attitudes toward family in Japan, 102t, 106–17, 110t, 112t, 113t, 201t, 210–17, 211t, 212t, 214t, 215t; and attitudes toward marriage in Japan, 101t, 102t, 106–17, 107n, 110t, 112t; and children's education in Taiwan, 352, 353t; and coresidence in Japan, 156, 159t, 160, 163t, 164n 4, 227t, 228; and coresidence in Taiwan, 327t, 327–28, 330t, 331t, 333, 337t, 338, 339t, 341t, 357–58; and coresidence in U.S., 225t, 226; and employment in Japan, 35–36; and family in Japan, 37; and family type in Japan, 189, 192–93, 192t, 193t; and family values, attitudes toward, in Thailand, 407–9, 410t; favored child for, in Thailand, 414–15; in Japan, on survey questionnaire, 439; and marriage arrangements in Taiwan, 353, 354t; and migration intentions in Yūbari, 260; and modernity in Thailand, 413–14, 415t; and nonfarm employment in Thailand, 372, 378; parental aspirations for, in Korea, 283tt, 283–84; and parental contact in Japan, 157, 159t, 169, 172t, 231t, 232t, 233t, 236, 238t, 239t, 240t, 243; and paren-

tal contact in U.S., 231t, 232t, 233t, 236, 238t, 239t, 240t, 243; parental expectations for, in Taiwan, 351–52, 352t, 359; and parental residence in Taiwan, 334, 335t; and spouse selection in Japan, 146–48, 147tt, 150; and support from sons in Taiwan, 347–50, 348t, 349t, 358; timing of in Thailand, 374, 375t
educational level: of community and family type in Japan, 189, 192–94, 192t, 193t; and economic development in Taiwan, 356; in Korea, 280, 310t A14.7
educational opportunities in Korea, 278, 278n
education of father: and attitudes toward family in Japan, 101t, 102t, 106–17, 110t, 113t; and attitudes toward marriage in Japan, 101t, 102t, 106–17, 110t, 113t; and coresidence in Japan, 227t, 228; and coresidence in U.S., 225t, 226; and marriage arrangements in Taiwan, 353, 354t, 355t; and parental contact in Japan, 231t, 232t, 233t, 235–36, 238t, 239t, 240t, 242–43; and parental contact in U.S., 231t, 232t, 233t, 235–36, 238t, 239t, 240t, 242–43
education of spouse in Japan: and coresidence, 155, 159t, 161–62, 163t 9.2, 164; and parental contact, 159t, 172t, 173
egalitarianism: in family in U.S., 33–35, 40–41; within marriages in Japan, 104; and spouse selection in Japan, 144, 151
elderly: activities of daily life and coresidence in U.S., 430; by age, sex, and marital status in Korea, 315t A14.17; care for, and aging of population in Taiwan, 319–20; care for, by government in China, 320; care for, by government in Japan, 52, 154, 425; care for, by government in Thailand, 407, 408t, 428; care for, in China, 182–83, 320, 325; care for, in East Asia, 7, 16; care for, in Japan, 14, 37, 43, 202, 425, 429–30, 432, 437; care for, in Korea, 15, 292; care for, in Taiwan, and aging of population (see support); care for, in Thailand, 407, 415–16; care for, in U.S., 16, 40, 429–30; contact of, with children in Japan, 157; contact of, with children in U.S., 157; coresidence with, attitudes toward, in Thailand, 415, 417; employment rates of, in Korea, 301–2; family support for, in Thailand, 379; in Japan, 51–52, 422; living arrangements of, attitudes toward, in Japan,

129, 129t; living arrangements of, factors affecting, in Korea, 302t, 302–7, 303t, 304t; living arrangements of, in Japan, 51–52, 126–27, 127t, 156, 425 (*see also* coresidence); living arrangements of, in Korea, 298t, 299–306, 301t, 302t, 303t, 304t (*see also under* coresidence); living arrangements of, in Korea, preferences for, 300, 305; living arrangements of, in Thailand, 417 (*see also* coresidence); preference of, for caregivers, in Japan, 153, 212; preference of, for caregivers, in Korea, 300, 312t; preferred caregivers for, in Thailand, 416, 416t; proportion of, living with children in Japan, 180–81, 202, 208–9; proportion of, living with children in Taiwan, 181, 183; proportion of, living with children in U.S., 209; proportion of, living with children in West, 180; proportion of total population in Japan, 422, 425; proportion of total population in Taiwan, 319–20, 425; proportion of total population in U.S., 425; proportion of total population in Yūbari, 253; status of, in Thailand, 403; surveys of, in Japan, 124, 131; values about, in Thailand, attitudes toward, 405t, 406–7, 408t, 410t, 412, 412t, 417; work status of, in Korea, 316t

eldest son (*see also* birth order); and coresidence in Korea, 296, 296t, 297t, 305; and coresidence in Taiwan, 326; duties of, attitudes toward, in Japan, 206, 209t, 210, 211t, 212; duties of, attitudes toward, in Japan, on survey questionnaire, 439; parents' aspirations for, in Korea, 284, 284t

employee benefits, 36, 38, 40

employment: and decline of coal industry in Yūbari, 250–53, 256; and education in Japan, 35–36; and family type in Japan, 188; in Japan (*see* self-employment in Japan); in Ōgaito, 82–83, 83t; by sector in Japan, 60, 60t; by sector in Taiwan, 356; source of, and migration intentions in Yūbari, 256, 257t, 258, 259t, 260; in Yūbari, 256

employment security (*see also* unemployment); in Japan, 37; in U.S., 39–40

employment status (*see* work status)

endogamy, village, in Japan, 62 (*see also* marriage partners)

equality in U.S. families (*see* family in U.S., egalitarianism in)

ethnicity in Taiwan: and children's education, 352, 353t; and coresidence, 327t, 328, 330t, 331tt, 333–34, 340t, 340–42, 341t, 357; and parental residence, 334, 335t; and support from sons, 347–50, 348t, 349t, 358

evolution: of family structure, 45, 179, 422; of social systems, 11–12, 19, 21

exogamy in Ōgaito (*see* marriage partners)

extended family (*see* family, extended)

extended family associations in Japan, 61–62

families, branch (*see* families in Ōgaito, main)

families in Ōgaito: extended, and family lines, 69–70, 81, 88;main, 68–70, 89; main, and go-between, 79–82; main, and *kumi*, 86–87; relationships among, 76, 77f

family: assumptions about, Japan and U.S. compared, 31–35; attitudes toward, 202–18, 204f; comparative studies of, 421–22; in Confucian cultures (*see* Confucianism); and culture, 7, 31–35, 423; definition of, contrasted with household, 7, 365; and fertility, 422; functions of, 3–4, 364; future of, 16; historical approach to, 421–22; history of, in West, 3–4; ideals about (*see* family values; normative determinants of family type); and migration, 4, 16; and modernization theory, 422; and mortality, 15–16, 46; past and present, differences between, 422; perspectives on, 7, 12; types of, 7

family, American (*see* family in U.S.)

family, complex: defined, 9

family, conjugal (*see also* family, nuclear); defined, 7

family, extended (*see also* household composition); in China (*see* family type in China); defined, 7, 45, 180; determinants of, 180–86; and economic burden, 181–82; and family size, 47, 49; in Japan (*see under* family type in Japan); in Korea (*see under* family type in Korea); measurement of, 187; product of early marriage and high fertility, 45–46; reasons for, 429; theories about, 180–81; in West, 179–82, 195

family, joint, in Japan, 187, 196

family, multigenerational (*see* family, extended)

family, nuclear, 3, 5 (*see also* household composition); advantages of, in modernizing society, 12, 20; breadwinner model of, 12, 20; in China (*see* family in China); defined, 7; as

Index

endpoint in industrialization process, 20; in Europe, 421; as foundation of human society, 8; in France and England, 124–27, 132; in Japan (see under family type in Japan); in Korea (see under family type in Korea); in Ōgaito, 82, 82t 5.10; prevalence of, 16; U.N. definition of, 187; in U.S., 29, 124–27, 132; in West, 4

family, stem: defined, 7, 181; and family cycle in Thailand, 367; in Japan (see under family type in Japan); as norm in Korea and Singapore, 54

family, traditional: in China (see under family in China); in East Asia, 7–11; in Japan, 8, 10, 122, 200–201; in Korea, 10–11, 281, 288

family associations in Japan, 61–62 (see also ie)

family change: and culture, 30–31; and economic development in Korea, 15; and economic development in Thailand, 401; future of, in Japan, 42–44; future of, in U.S., 41–42; lack of, in Japan, 46; and modernization, 433; theories of, 19–26

family composition (see family type; household composition)

family conflict: avoidance of, in Japan, 33–35; effects of, in U.S., 42; expression of, in U.S., 33–35

family convergence theory, 5, 45, 422 (see also evolution)

family creed (see also family law); in Japan, 9–10

family cycle: and family type, 181, 194

family decision making: equality in, in U.S., 33; hierarchical in Japan, 32–33

family dissolution (see divorce)

family division of labor: in Thailand, 403; in West, 436

family formation in Thailand, 384–99; survey on (see Thai Family and Household Survey)

family goals: collective in Japan, 31–32; individual-oriented in U.S., 32, 41

family ideals (see family values; normative determinants of family type)

family in China, 54–55 (see also family in Taiwan); elderly in, care for, 182–83, 320, 325; extended (see family type in China); inheritance in, 10; intergenerational relations in, 15; and migration, 53–55; nuclear, 13, 48–50, 54–55; stereotype of, 7; traditional, 7–8, 15, 320, 325, 336, 342, 345, 357–58; upper-class, 8; values about, 183

family in East Asia, 7–11, 16; attitudes toward, 92

family in Europe: historical, 3–4, 421

family in Japan (see also ie; National Family Survey of Japan); activities together, on survey questionnaire, 443; attitudes toward (see family in Japan, attitudes toward); change in, 42–44, 46; compared to family in China, 13, 45–55; compared to family in U.S., 12–13, 29–44, 423–24; compared to family in West, 424, 432; conflict in, 33–35; as conservative force, 199–201; coresidence in (see coresidence; living arrangements); creed in, 9–10; cultural approaches to, 29–44; cultural assumptions about, 31–35; cultural dimensions of, 7; decision making in, 32–33, 92; defined, 7; economic and social responsibilities of, 38; and economic development, 13, 202; expectations of, 37; extended (see under family type in Japan); finances of, on survey questionnaire, 445; functions of, attitudes toward, on survey questionnaire, 443; future of, 16, 42–44, 51, 423, 431–32, 436–37; goals of, 31–32; as a group, 13, 30, 32, 42; head of, obligations and rights of, 9; hierarchy in, 32–33; history of, 8–10; ideal, 425; and ie and mura, 13; individualism in, 54; interpersonal relationships in, 14; joint, 187, 196; kin network of, 29–30; law regarding, 10; limitation of, 98; lineage in, 9, 29–30, 150; living arrangements in (see coresidence; living arrangements); main, 68; in Meiji civil code, 183; members' health, on survey questionnaire, 448; and migration, 51, 54–55; and modernization, 8; and mortality, 51; name, succession of, 206, 209t, 212t, 212–13; nuclear (see under family type in Japan); nuclearization of, 8; perceptions of, 131–32; positive and negative outcomes of, 42–43; size of, 47t (see also family type in Japan, extended); size of, on survey questionnaire, 448; spouse selection in (see under spouse selection); stem (see under family type in Japan); stereotype of, 29–30; succession of, 92, 115–16; survey on (see National Family Survey of Japan); traditional, 8, 10, 122, 200–201; tradition and change in, 59–89; types of (see family type in Japan); values about (see

under family values); and Western influence, 436
family in Japan, attitudes toward, 11, 13–14, 91–117, 200–218 (*see also* children; eldest son; family name in Japan; gender roles; home); becoming less traditional, 111, 115–17; factors affecting, 91–94, 100–117, 101t, 102t, 110t, 112t, 113t, 200–218, 204f, 209t, 211t, 212t, 214t, 215t; methods of analysis of, 9; traditional, 92; variables used to measure, 101t, 102t, 104–5
family in Korea, 273–307 (*see also* rural family and community life in South Korea survey); attitudes toward, 281–307; celebrations of, 287, 287t; change in, 15; cohesion of, 15; Confucian influences on, 10, 281; coresidence in (*see* coresidence); and economic development, 15, 273; extended, 10, 288–89, 290t, 291t 14.15; inheritance in, 10; interaction, frequency of, 287, 287t; and intergenerational relationships, 10–11; interpersonal relationships in, 10–11; law regarding, 10; lineage (*see* family lineage; family line); living arrangements in (*see* coresidence in Korea); and modernization, 15; norms about, 289, 300; nuclear, 289, 290t, 291tt, 305; nuclearization of, 11; perceptions of, 313t; stem, 54; survey on (*see* rural family and community life in South Korea survey); traditional, 10–11, 281, 288; types of (*see* family type in Korea); values about (*see under* family values)
family in Taiwan, 319–59; coresidence in (*see* coresidence); and economic development, 357; economic relations in, 342–51; extended, 181–83; intergenerational relationships in, 319–51; living arrangements in (*see* coresidence); norms about, 320–21; survey on, 321–22; traditional (*see* family in China, traditional); values about, 15, 183
family in Thailand, 15, 364–417; and adulthood, transition to, 15, 364–80; attitudes toward, 15, 401–17; authority in, 366, 366n, 403–4; change in, 401; and changes in agriculture, 377–78; concepts of, 364–66; coresidence in (*see* coresidence; living arrangements); definitions of, 365; division of labor in, 403; early studies of, 364, 384; and economic development, 377–78; elderly in, 403; extended, 367–68; formation of, 15, 384–99;

functions of, 403; inheritance in (*see under* inheritance); and life course, 367, 373–77, 374t, 375t; living arrangements in (*see* coresidence; living arrangements); loose-structure paradigm of, 378–79; needed research on, 377–80; norms about, 403, 415–16; residence of members, at respondents' age 10, 367–69, 368t, 369t; residence of members during first year of respondent's marriage, 390–93, 391t, 392t; residence rule in, 367; roles and obligations, 378–79; stem, 367; survey of (*see* Thai Family and Household Survey)
family in U.S.: change in, 41–42; class differences in, 42; compared to Japan, 12–13, 29–44; conflict in, 33–35, 41–42; cultural assumptions about, 31–35, 41; decision making in, 33; egalitarianism in, 33–35, 40–41; extended, 181–82, 195; future of, 41–42; goals of, 32, 41; hierarchy in, 33; individualism in, 32, 41; intergenerational relationships in, 14; kin network of, 29; living arrangements in, 11, 14; nuclear, 29, 124–27, 132; positive and negative outcomes of, 42; stability of, 41–42; stereotype of, 29; values about, 16
family in West: breakdown of, 436; division of labor in, 436; history of, 3–4; as model for Japan, 423–24; norms about, 9, 132
family law: in ancient Rome, and family type, 3–4; and traditional family values in Korea and Japan, 10
family life cycle (*see also* life-course events in Thailand); and changes in family and marriage in Japan, 46, 51, 54–55; and migration intentions in Yūbari, 262–63
family limitation and fertility decline in Japan, 98
family lineage: in Confucian ideal, 4; in Japan, 9, 29–30; in Korea, 10; and status of father and coresidence in Korea, 296t, 297t, 297–99, 303–6
family line in Korea, attitudes toward succession of, 282t 14.3, 282–83
family lines in Ōgaito, 69, 69t, 71, 79–82
family name in Japan: attitudes toward succession of, 206, 209t, 212t, 212–13; attitudes toward succession of, on survey questionnaire, 442
family norms (*see* normative determinants of

Index

family type; norms *under* family *in specific countries*)
family policy in West and family values, 23–24
family properties *(kasan)* and family type in Japan, 184
family size *(see* household size)
family stability in U.S.: factors affecting, 41–42
family structure *(see* family type)
family support *(see also* support); models of, 183
family surveys *(see* KAP surveys in Korea; National Family Survey of Japan; National Survey of Families and Households in U.S.; Ōgaito, surveys of; rural family and community life in South Korea survey; Survey of Changes in Life Structure of the Population in Relation to Aging in Japan; Thai Family and Household Survey; Yūbari, survey of)
family systems *(see also* family type); factors affecting, 22–26
family theory, 21–26 *(see also* family change)
family ties and migration intentions in Yūbari, 262, 264, 269
family type *(see also* household size); convergence theory of, 45, 422; evolution of, 179; factors affecting, 9, 15, 180–86, 189–94, 190e *(see also* family type in Japan); and family cycle, 181, 194; and fertility, mortality, and migration, 51; ideals regarding, 183; incidence of, 46; and mortality, 181; and Victorian family, 182
family type in China, 7–8, 48–50, 49tt, 50t, 54–55, 183, 325
family type in Chinese cultural sphere, 54
family type in Japan, 127t *(see also* coresidence; living arrangements); attitudes toward, 128t, 128–31; changes in, 121; cultural assumptions about, 32–33; and elderly, 125t; extended, 14, 47, 54–55, 179–96, 188t *(see also ie)*; extended, definition of, 180; extended, factors affecting, 188–96, 192t, 193t; extended, measuring, 187; factors affecting, 8–9, 179–96, 190e, 191tt, 192t, 193t; fundamental, 122; and *ie*, 14, 180, 183–85, 193, 195–96; and income *(see* income); and individualism, 185; joint, 187, 196; and land *(see* land); and living arrangements, 123t; and migration, 269; nuclear, 46t, 46–47, 51, 54–55, 122t, 122–24, 123t, 125t, 127t, 132, 188t; nuclear, attitudes toward, 128t, 129,

129t, 130, 130t; perceptions of, 122t; stem, 8, 106, 121–23, 122t, 123t, 127, 127t, 130, 132, 153, 181, 183, 185, 195, 263, 269, 425; stem, attitudes toward, 128t, 128–29, 130t; on survey questionnaire, 448; three-generation, 8, 32, 46, 46t, 124, 132, 161, 429; three-generation, attitudes toward, 129, 130t
family type in Korea, 288–92, 290t, 291tt *(see also* coresidence); extended, 10, 288–89, 290t, 291t 14.15; factors affecting, 289; head-family type of, 289, 290tn, 291t 14.15, 292; ideal, 289, 305; nuclear, 289, 290t, 291tt, 305; stem, 54
family type in Taiwan, 321; extended, 181–83
family type in Thailand and family cycle, 367–68
family type in U.S., 41–42; extended, 181–82, 195; nuclear, 29, 124–27, 132
family type in Yūbari and migration intentions, 257t, 257–60, 259t
family values: attitudes toward, in Thailand, 402, 404–17, 405t, 408t, 410t *(see also* children; elderly; marriage; norms *under* family in specific countries; women's roles); and attitudes toward marriage and the family in Japan, 199–218; changes in, in Japan, 92–93; and children's traits in Japan, 14; in China, 182–83; Confucian *(see* Confucianism); and coresidence in Korea, 294; cultural differences in, 16; and economic development in Korea, 15; factors affecting, 204f; and family creed in Japan, 9–10; future of, 428; future of, in Japan, 427; ideals and practice of, in Korea, 288–89; in Japan, 31–35; in Meiji era of Japan, 183; and modernity in Thailand, 412t; in new family system in Japan, 54, 185; and socialization, 200; in Taiwan, 15, 183; in Thailand, 401–17, 416ttt; in Thailand, survey on *(see* Thai Family and Household Survey); traditional in Korea, 10–11, 281; in U.S., 16
farmers in Yūbari and migration intentions, 264–66
farming *(see* agriculture)
feedback model of family support, 183
fertility *(see also* birth rate; total fertility rate); by age 30 in Thailand, 376
fertility, low, concerns about, 422
fertility, marital: and total fertility, 98, 99t

Index

fertility and family, 8-9, 45-46, 51, 54-55
fertility and government programs: in France, 422; in Sweden, 425
fertility decline, 4-5; age-patterns of, in Japan, 94-95, 95t; in China, 52-53; and coresidence in Japan, 164, 174; effects on family of, 4, 15-16; and elderly as proportion of total population in Japan, 422; explanation of, in Japan, 91-93, 98, 99t; and family in China, 53; and family in France, 422; and family in Japan, 47, 51; and household size in China, 48-49; and household size in Japan, 50-52, 54; in Japan, 94-95, 95t, 98
fertility in Japan: age-specific rates of, 94-95, 95t; and attitudes toward marriage and the family, 91; compared with West, 424; components of change in, 98, 99t; and coresidence, 159-60; differentials in, 93; and family, 50-51; and household size, 50-51; norms and values, 98; patterns of, 93; replacement level of, 91-94, 98
fertility policies in Asia, successes and failures of, 24
fertility transition (see fertility decline)
filial piety, 427-28 (see also Confucianism); and individualism in Taiwan, 320; in Meiji era of Japan, 183
financial assistance: and coresidence in Japan, 174; and displaced workers in U.S., 248-49; in Japan, 269; for small businesses in Yūbari, 265-66; and unemployment in Yūbari, 252; in Yūbari, 268-69
follower (see master-follower relationship)
functional differentiation of social structure, 12, 20, 182, 186, 195
functionalism (see structural-functionalism)
functions of family (see family, functions of)

gender: and age at marriage in Thailand, 375t, 376, 387t, 387-88, 388t; and attitudes toward family in Japan, 101t, 102t, 106-17, 110t, 112t, 113t, 211t, 211-18, 212t, 214t, 215t; and attitudes toward family values in Thailand, 407, 408t; and attitudes toward marriage in Japan, 101t, 102t, 106-17, 110t, 112t; and coresidence in Japan, 227t; and coresidence in Thailand, 390-91, 391t, 398-99; and coresidence in U.S., 225t, 226; and establishment of household in Thailand, 394t, 394-95, 395t; in Japan, on survey questionnaire, 439; and modernity, 414, 415t; and number of times married in Thailand, 388; and parental contact in Japan, 228-29, 229t, 231t, 232t, 233t, 235f, 238t, 239t, 240t, 242, 244f, 244t; and parental contact in U.S., 228-29, 229t, 231t, 232t, 233t, 235f, 238t, 239t, 240t, 242, 244f, 244t; and preferred traits for children, 14; and satisfaction with marriage, 388-89, 389t, 398; segregation by, in Japanese family, 183; and spouse selection, 386, 386t; and spouse selection in Japan, 146-50, 147tt
gender gap and family cohesion in Japan, 43
gender roles: attitudes toward, in Japan, 206-7, 207t, 209t, 213-16, 214t; attitudes toward, in Japan, on survey questionnaire, 441; attitudes toward, in U.S., 207; in Japan (see children); persistence of, in Japan, 14, 149; values about, attitudes toward, in Thailand, 405t, 405-13, 408t, 410t, 412t, 417 (see also women's roles)
gifts at weddings in Thailand, 403-4, 414
goals, family (see family goals)
go-between: and attitudes toward marriage and family in Japan, 109; and family importance in Ōgaito, 70, 79-81
government and care for elderly: in China, 320; in Japan, 425; in Thailand, 407, 408t, 428
group: family as, in Japan, 13, 30, 32, 42; in mura in Japan, 62; priority of, in Japan, 13, 32, 36-37, 144, 151-52; socialization toward, in Japan, 34; in society, emphasis on, 16, 22; and spouse selection in Japan, 144-46, 145t

Hachiōji, Japan, 64, 65f, 66f, 83, 85t
head-family family type (see under family type in Korea)
health insurance in U.S., 39-40
heterological approach in sociology, 61
hierarchy: family, in Japan, 32-33, 42; family, in U.S., 33; social, in Japan, 35-37, 40; social, in U.S., 40; social and family in Thailand, 404
Hinoeuma (Year of the Fire Horse) and fertility in Japan, 91
historical demography and study of the family, 421-22
Hokkaido prefecture, Japan, 249-50 (see also Yūbari)

Index

home in Japan: attitudes toward functions of, 101t, 102t, 104; attitudes toward functions of Japan, factors affecting, 109–11, 110t, 112t, 113t, 114–15
home ownership: and migration intentions in Yūbari, 257t, 257–58, 259t, 260, 260t, 267–68; outside Yūbari and migration intentions, 257, 257t, 259t, 260, 262; and parental residence in Taiwan, 334–35, 335t
homological approach in sociology, 61
household (see also family); contrasted with family, 364–65; defined, 7
household composition: in China, 49–50; dual structure of, in Japan, 51–52; and fertility and mortality, 45–46; and fertility decline in China, 53; during first year of marriage in Thailand, 369–70, 370tt, 390–93, 391t, 392t; in Japan, on survey questionnaire, 445; at respondents' age 10 in Thailand, 367–69, 368t, 369t
households (see also family type in Japan); continuity of, in Ōgaito, 71, 75t, 76; establishment of, in Thailand, 393–96, 394t, 395t, 399; farmland owned by, in Korea, 309t A14.5; number of generations in, in Korea, 309t A14.4
household size: in China, 48t, 48–49, 49tt, 52t, 52–53; and economic development in Thailand, 401; factors affecting, 45–46, 48–49, 53–54; and fertility and mortality in Japan, 47, 50–51, 51t, 53–54; and fertility decline in Thailand, 401; in Japan, 47t; in Japan, on survey questionnaire, 448; in Korea, 277, 309t A14.3; in Ōgaito, 82, 82tt
household type (see also family type; living arrangements); in Japan, compared to West, 125t, 126–27; in Japan, on survey questionnaire, 448; in Ōgaito, 82, 82tt; in West, compared to Japan, 124–27, 125t
housing shortages and coresidence, 429
housing type in Japan, on survey questionnaire, 448

idealized family morality, 22–26
ideals (see family values; values)
identity, sense of, 32
ie (family) in Japan (see also family in Japan, extended; family in Japan, stem); changes in, 63–64; characteristics of, 62; defined, 54; and family size, 53; and family type, 14, 180, 183–85, 193, 195–96; and migration, 269; and mura, 13; in Ōgaito, 68–89; and spouse selection, 150–51; studies of, 61
illegitimacy: in U.S., 423; in West, 25
immigration: to Japan, 422; to Japan and Koreans in Japan, 37; to Japan and labor supply, 37; to U.S. and family reunion, 39; to U.S. and fertility, 422
income: and children's education in Taiwan, 352, 353t; and coresidence in Japan, 161n, 428–29; and coresidence in Korea, 296t, 296–97, 297t, 305; and coresidence in Taiwan, 330t, 331t, 332–34, 338, 339t, 357; and coresidence in Thailand, 428; and family type in Japan, 184, 188, 192, 192t, 193t, 195; and family type in U.S., 195; growth of, in Taiwan, 356; hypothetical, of housewife in Japan, on survey questionnaire, 441; in Japan, on survey questionnaire, 440; in old age in Taiwan, 350–51; and sharing of meals in Taiwan, 343; and spouse selection in Japan, 147tt, 149; and support from sons in Taiwan, 347–50, 348t, 349t, 359; and wealth flows in Taiwan, 345, 346t, 347t
independence in Japan: of household, 64, 88; of individuals, 88; of women, 151
individual, importance of, in U.S., 22, 32
individual achievement and modernization, 20
individualism: and coresidence in Korea, 294; and the family, 9, 16; and family conflict in U.S., 34–35; and family in Japan, 54, 92, 115, 151–52, 432, 436; and family in U.S., 13, 41; and family in West, 22; and family type in Japan, 185; and fertility in Japan, 98; and filial piety in Taiwan, 320; in U.S., 40
Indonesia, marriage law in, and family change, 24–25
industrialization (see also economic development; modernization); and family, 20; and family in Japan, 179, 195; and family in Korea, 15; and family in West, 9
industrial policy in Japan (see also industrial restructuring); and decline of coal industry, 266; effects of, at individual level, 269; and outmigration, 248–49, 269; and outmigration in Yūbari, 252, 269
industrial restructuring, 430–31; effects on family in Japan, 14–16; impacts of, in Japan, 247–49, 266, 269; in Japan, 247–69 (see also mine closures); and migration in Japan, 431;

460

Index

and rural life in Japan, 61, 63; and unemployment in U.S., 39; in Yūbari, 249–69
industrial transition and family, 4–5
inheritance: attitudes toward, in Japan, on survey questionnaire, 443; attitudes toward, in Thailand, 416t, 416–17; in Korea and China, 10; in Meiji era of Japan, 200; opinions about, and family type in Japan, 189; in Thailand, 15, 371t, 371–73, 378
Institute of Population Problems (see National Fertility Surveys of Japan; Survey of Changes in Life Structure of the Population in Relation to Aging in Japan)
Institute of Population Studies (see Thai Family and Household Survey)
institutions and structural-functionalism, 26, 29–31
insurance and support for family in U.S., 39–40
intentions to marry in Japan, 141–42, 142t, 151 (see also universal marriage)
interaction: family, in Korea, 287t, 287–88; social, in Ōgaito, changes in, 88
intergenerational relationships (see also elderly, care for; filial piety; parental contact); attitudes toward, in Japan, 206; changes in, in Taiwan, 320–21; data and methods used for study of, in Taiwan, 321–25, 322t, 323f, 324e; in Japan, 14, 154, 174; in Korea, 10–11; and parental survival in Japan, 222–23, 223t; and parental survival in U.S., 222–23, 223t; in Taiwan, 15, 319–51 (see also coresidence; parental contact; support); in U.S., 14
intergenerational support (see support)
International Comparative Survey on the Lives and Attitudes of Elderly People, 124
International Symposium on Family and Contemporary Japanese Culture in International Perspective, 6
intimacy at a distance: Western model of, 154, 174

Japan (see under specific topics); civil codes, 9, 183; differences with U.S., 432; family and community life, 59–89
jia (Chinese extended family) (see family type in China)
job transfer: in Japan, 36; and migration in Yūbari, 266; in U.S., 38

KAP surveys in Korea, 321–22

kasan (family properties) and family type in Japan, 184
khongman (groom's gift to bride) in Thailand, 403, 414
kin (see also family, extended); assistance to family, 181–82; availability of, and family type in Japan, 182, 184; in Japan, 29–30
kinship, bilateral: in Japan, 201, 426; in Taiwan, 320–21, 426; in U.S., 423
koksu system of tenancy in Korea, 281
Korea (see under specific topics)
Koreans in Japan, rights of, 37
krob krua (family) in Thailand, 365
kumi (community group): in Ōgaito, 13, 69, 86t, 86–88
kye (cooperative groups) in Korea, 287–88, 288tt

labor: availability of, in Yūbari, 265–66; demand for, in Japan, 36–37, 63, 68; seasonal, in Japan, 63; shortage of, in Korea, 280
labor force participation of women (see women, labor force status of)
land: and family type in Japan, 184, 188, 192, 192t, 193t, 194–95; inheritance of, in Thailand (see under inheritance); in Korea, 309t A14.5; and living arrangements in Korea, 301, 304, 306; and migration intentions in Yūbari, 263–64, 266, 268; and spouse selection in Thailand, 428
life-course events in Thailand, 373–77, 374t, 375t
life cycle (see age; family life cycle)
lineage, family (see family lineage)
literacy (measured by newspaper reading) in Taiwan: and coresidence, 330t, 333–34, 336, 338, 339t, 357–58; and marriage arrangements, 353, 354t; and parental residence, 334, 335t; and wealth flows, 345, 347t
living arrangements (see also coresidence; family type); of African Americans, 8; attitudes toward, in Japan, 11, 128t, 128–30, 129t; changes in, in Japan, 121; differences in, between East and West, 11; in England and France, compared to Japan and U.S., 125t, 125–26, 128, 128t; establishment of a separate household in Thailand, 393t, 393–95, 394t, 395t, 399; during first year of marriage in Thailand, 369–70, 370tt, 390–93, 391t, 392t; of husband's parents in

Index

Taiwan and coresidence, 341t; ideal type of, in Japan, 123–24; intentions about, in Japan, 123t, 123–24; in Japan (see also coresidence; elderly; family type in Japan); in Japan, compared to West, 124–27, 125t; in Korea (see coresidence); and migration intentions in Yūbari, 257t, 257–60, 259t; new versions of, in Japan, 196, 429; norms regarding, in Japan, 123–24; and parental contact in Japan, 170–71, 172t; of parents in Taiwan, 334–36, 335t, 357–58; preferred, in Japan, 129–30, 130t; at respondent's age 10 in Thailand, 367–69, 368t, 369t; in Taiwan (see coresidence); in Thailand (see coresidence in Thailand); in U.S., 423, 436; in U.S., compared with England, France, and Japan, 124–27, 125t, 128, 128t; in West, 11, 25

logit analysis: of attitudes toward marriage and family in Japan, 100–115, 110t, 111n, 112t, 113t; compared with regression analysis, 188n; of coresidence in Japan, 162–65, 163t; of coresidence in Korea, 295t, 295–99, 296t, 297t; of living arrangements of elderly in Korea, 302t, 302–5, 303t, 304t; of migration intentions in Yūbari, 255–60, 257t, 259t; of nonresponse to survey, 168, 175–77, 176t; of parental contact in Japan, 206–16, 209t, 211t, 212t, 214t, 215t; of parental contact in Japan and U.S., 225t, 225–42, 227t, 232t, 233t, 238t, 239t, 240t

loose-structure paradigm: of family in Thailand, 378–79

love marriage (see marriage, arranged; marriage, love)

Maekawa report on coal industry in Japan, 249
main families in Ōgaito (see under families in Ōgaito, main)
Mainichi Newspapers (see also National Family Survey of Japan); National Opinion Survey on Family Planning in Japan, 6
Malaysia: fertility policy in, 24
marital disruption in Thailand, 375t, 376, 404–5
marital duration: and coresidence in Taiwan, 328–32, 329t, 331t; in Japan, on survey questionnaire, 446; and sharing of meals in Taiwan, 343; and wealth flows in Taiwan, 345, 346t
marital stability in Thailand: lack of knowledge about, 379

marital status in Japan, on survey questionnaire, 443

marriage (see also remarriage); age at (see age at marriage); arranged (see marriage, arranged); arrangements for, in Thailand, 403; attitudes toward, in East Asia, 92; attitudes toward, in Japan, 13, 91–117 (see also singlehood, attitudes toward); attitudes toward in Japan, factors affecting, 93, 101t, 102t, 105–15, 110t, 112t; attitudes toward in Japan, on survey questionnaire, 442; attitudes toward in Japan, variables used tomeasure, 100–104, 101t, 102t; decisions about, in Japan, 92; delayed (see age at marriage); delayed, in Japan, 425; duration of, in Japan, on survey questionnaire, 446; and family life cycle in Japan, 46; and fertility in Japan, 96–97; frequency of, in Japan, 136t, 136–37; intentions of, in Japan, 141–42, 142t, 151 (see also universal marriage); in Japan, 92–96, 100, 110; law, in Indonesia, 24–25; love (ren'ai), in Japan, 143f, 143–44, 151; morality, 25; norms about, in Thailand, 414; norms about, in U.S., 103; norms regarding, in Japan, 103, 106, 116; number of times married in Thailand, 388; opportunities for, in Japan, 144–46, 145t; partners, attitudes toward choosing, in Korea, 284–85, 285tt; partners in Japan mura, 62; patterns of, in Japan, 136t, 136–41, 137f, 138f, 139tt, 140f, 151; prevalence of, in Thailand, 386; rate of (see proportions single); rate of, in Japan, 137f; remarriage, attitudes toward, in Thailand, 389t, 390, 398; satisfaction with married life in Thailand, 388–89, 389t, 398; spouse selection (see spouse selection); in Thailand, 385–90; timing of, 386–88, 398; universal (see proportions married; universal marriage); value about, attitudes toward, in Thailand, 404–13, 405t, 408t, 410t, 412t; values about, 92–93, 106; values about, in East Asia, 92; values about, in Thailand, 404–13, 405t, 408t, 410t, 412t

marriage, arranged: attitudes toward, in Korea, 284–85, 285tt; and coresidence in Korea, 296t, 297, 297t, 305–6; data and analysis of, in Taiwan, 321–25, 322t, 323f, 324e; factors affecting, in Taiwan, 353, 354t; and family relationships in Ōgaito, 70; and parental authority in Taiwan, 359; prevalence of, in

Taiwan, 352–53; in Thailand, 385–86, 386t, 398 (*see also* spouse selection)
marriage, arranged *(miai)* in Japan: and attitudes toward family, 109, 112t, 113t, 210–17, 211t, 212t, 214t, 215t; and attitudes toward marriage, 109, 112t; and coresidence, 227t; and parental contact, 231t, 232t, 233t, 237, 238t, 239t, 240t, 242; and patrilineal descent, 201; prevalence of, 13, 143f, 143–44, 151; on survey questionnaire, 444
marriage, love (*see also* marriage, arranged); and coresidence in Korea, 294, 295t, 297, 297t, 305–6; prevalence of, in Japan, 13, 143, 143f, 151; *(ren'ai)* in Japan, 143f, 143–44, 151 (*see also* spouse selection)
marriage cohort in Taiwan: and arranged marriage, 353, 354t
marriage partners: origins of, in Ōgaito, 76–79, 78t, 79t, 88
marriage type in Japan, 13, 142–44, 143f, 151; and attitudes toward marriage and family, 102t, 109, 111, 112t, 113t, 115–16; and coresidence, 155, 159t, 162, 163t 9.2, 164n 4, 164–65; effect on fertility, 116; and parental contact, 159t, 169, 172t
master-follower relationship: in Ōgaito, 70, 79–82, 86–89; in rural Japan, 68, 70
mate selection (*see* spouse selection)
matrilineal descent, 366n
matrilocal residence: declining prevalence of, in Taiwan, 336, 337t, 358; and family authority in Thailand, 366n; and inheritance in Thailand, 366n, 372; prevalence of, in Thailand, 369–70, 370tt, 391t, 403; regional patterns of, in Thailand, 390–95, 392t, 393t, 398–99; traditional form of, in Thailand, 367
MCA (multiple classification analysis): of attitudes toward family values in Thailand, 412–15, 413t, 415t; of family relationships in Taiwan, 249t, 328–50, 329t, 331t, 339t, 341t
Meiji government of Japan: civil code of, 9–10, 183; and family system, 9–10, 183, 200
merit making in Thailand, 403n, 404, 407 (*see also* elderly)
methods of analysis (*see* correlation analysis; logit analysis; MCA; probit analysis; regression analysis)

MHU (minimal housing unit) in Japan: defined, 187–88, 188t
miai (*see* marriage, arranged *(miai)* in Japan)
Middle East, family systems in, enforcement of, 23
migration: change in character of, from Ōgaito, 83, 88; and contacts with parents in Japan, 174; decision making in Japan, 248–49; decision making in Yūbari, 255–69, 257t, 259t, 260t; and economic development in Japan, 63; and family, 4, 16, 46, 51, 53–55; and family in China, 53–55; and family in Japan, 51, 54–55; and family in Thailand, 378–79; and family in Yūbari, 258–69; household history of, and migration in Yūbari, 257, 257t, 259t, 259–60, 262; impacts of, in Japan, 249, 269; and industrial restructuring in Japan, 248–49, 431; intentions in Yūbari, 255–69, 257t, 259t, 260t; intentions in Yūbari, factors affecting, 256–69, 257t, 259t, 260t; intentions in Yūbari, measurement of, 255; intentions in Yūbari, probabilities of, 258–60, 259t; intentions of, in Japan, on survey questionnaire, 448; intentions of coal mining employees in Yūbari, 257t, 259t, 261–62, 268; intentions of public employees in Yūbari, 257t, 259t, 266–68; intentions of shopkeepers in Yūbari, 257t, 259t, 263–64, 268; reasons for, in Japan, 248–49; reasons for, in Korea, 278, 278n, 280; reasons for, in Yūbari, 255–69, 257t, 259, 260t; timing of, in Thailand, 374–75, 375t; from Yūbari, 14, 255–69; from Yūbari, survey for analysis of, 253–55
military service in Thailand, timing of, 375t, 376–77
mine closures: effects of, in Yūbari, 249, 251–53, 260–68; reasons for, in Japan, 250; in Yūbari, 250–51
minimal housing unit (*see* MHU)
mining employees in Yūbari, 256t, 257t, 259t, 260–62
mobility, geographic (*see* migration)
mobility, interfirm: in Japan, 36; and migration in Yūbari, 266; in U.S., 38
mobility, social (*see* social mobility)
modernity (*see also* modernization; possessions, modern); and attitudes toward family, 427–29; and attitudes toward family in Japan, 102t, 107–8, 112t, 113t, 114; and

Index

coresidence in Japan, 160, 165; index of, in Thailand, 412t, 412–14, 413t, 414t, 415t, 417; in Taiwan, 328, 333–34, 338, 345, 352; in Thailand, 406–7, 415t, 417

modernization (*see also* economic development; industrialization; urbanization); and coresidence in Taiwan, 326, 338–40, 339t, 358–59; and education of children in Taiwan, 351–52; and family, 11, 12, 16, 20, 401; and family in Japan, 8; and family in Korea, 15; and family support from children in Taiwan, 347; and individual achievement, 20; measurement of, 108, 161; and parental contact in Taiwan, 15; and parental residence in Taiwan, 334; and spouse selection in Korea, 284–85; in Thailand, 401–2

modernization theory, 422–23; and family, 427–30

money flows in Taiwan (*see* wealth flows in Taiwan)

monkhood in Thailand, timing of, 375t, 376

mortality (*see also* death rate); in China, 52; and coresidence, 222; and family, 15–16, 46; and family in Japan, 51; and family type, 181; and parental contact, 222

mortality decline and coresidence in Japan, 164, 174

multiple classification analysis (*see* MCA)

mura (rural community) in Japan, 13; changes in, 62–64; features of, 61–64; in Ōgaito, 68–82

mutual assistance: and *kumi* in Ōgaito, 86–88; and *mura* in Japan, 62; and *mura* in Ōgaito, 68–69

nakoda-oya (*see* go-between)

National Family Survey of Japan, 13, 14, 93, 124, 136, 141–43, 146, 148, 151, 153, 154, 156, 174, 216, 221, 426; design, sample, and procedures, 99, 131, 158, 205, 437–38; origins of, 435–37; questionnaire for, 439–48; sample population characteristics, 438

National Fertility Surveys of Japan, 100n, 141–42, 144

National Land Development Plan (Japan), 63

National Survey of Families and Households in U.S., 221

natural village (see also *mura*); theory of, in Japan, 61

neighborhood association *(kumi)*: in Japan, 13; in Ōgaito, 69, 86t, 86–88

neolocal residence: prevalence of, in Thailand, 393t, 398–99; in Thailand, 390–95; trend toward, 11

Net Reproduction Rate (NRR), decline in, in Taiwan, 319

newspaper reading (*see* literacy)

Nihon University (*see* National Family Survey of Japan; Ōgaito, surveys of)

nonresponse to survey questions, 167–68, 176t

normative determinants of family type, 180, 182–83, 185, 190–96, 191tt, 192t, 193t (*see also* family type in Japan, factors affecting)

norms (*see* norms *under* family in *specific countries*; socialization; values)

NRR (*see* Net Reproduction Rate)

nuclear family (*see* family, nuclear)

nuptiality (*see also* age at marriage; marriage; spouse selection); in Thailand, 385–90

obedience to parents, attitudes toward, in Korea, 281–82, 282t 14.2

occupation: and attitudes toward family in Japan, 102t, 106–17, 112t, 113t; and attitudes toward marriage in Japan, 102t, 106–7, 112t; and children's education in Taiwan, 352, 353t; and coresidence in Japan, 159t, 160, 163t 9.2, 164–65, 227t; and coresidence in Taiwan, 329t, 331t, 332, 338, 339t, 341t, 358; and coresidence in U.S., 225t; and family type in Japan, 188–89, 192, 193t; and family values in Thailand, attitudes toward, 409, 410t; in Japan, on survey questionnaire, 440, 447; and marriage arrangements in Taiwan, 354t; measurement of, in U.S., 246; and modernity in Thailand, 414, 415t; and parental contact in Japan, 159t, 169, 171–73, 172t, 231t, 232t, 233t, 236, 238t, 239t, 240t, 243; and parental contact in U.S., 231t, 232t, 233t, 236, 238t, 239t, 240t, 243; and parental residence in Taiwan, 334, 335t; and spouse selection in Japan, 147tt, 148; and support from sons in Taiwan, 347, 348t, 348–50, 349t, 358

occupation of eldest son: parents' aspirations for, in Korea, 284, 284t

occupation of father: and marriage arrangements in Taiwan, 353, 354t, 355t

occupation of spouse in Japan: and coresidence

Index

in, 155–56, 159t, 160–61, 163t 9.2; and parental contact, 159t, 169, 172t; on survey questionnaire, 440
occupations: in Ōgaito, 83, 84t, 88; in Yuzurihara, 67–68
Ōgaito, Japan, 64–89; agriculture in, 88; changes in family in, 86–88; commuting in, 88; daily activities, areas for in, 83, 85t; employment in, 83, 83t; families in, relationships among, 76, 77f; family, extended in, 69–70, 81, 88; family, nuclear in, 82, 82tt; family lines in, 69, 69t, 71, 79–82; go-betweens in, 70, 79–81; households in, 71, 75t, 76; household size and type in, 82, 82t; *ie* in, 68–69; *kumi* in, 69, 86t, 86–88; main families in, 69–70, 79–82, 86–87, 89; marriage in, arranged, 70; marriage partners in, origins of, 76–79, 78t, 79t, 88; master-follower relationship in, 70, 79–82, 86–89; migration from, 83, 88; *mura* in, 68–89; mutual assistance in, 68–69, 86–88; occupations in, 83, 84t, 88; *ōkata*, role of, in village life, 70, 80; population of, 71; shopping areas for residents of, 83, 85t; social interaction in, 88; social mobility in, 83; surveys of, 68, 71; women in, labor force status of, 83, 84t
oil shocks in Japan: effects of, 247–48, 250
ōkata (most powerful family) (*see* Ōgaito)
old-age income in Taiwan, 350–51 (*see also* support)
old-age security: in Japan, 37 (*see also* elderly, care for; social security); responsibility for, in Japan, 42; responsibility for, in U.S., 39–40
ordination in Thailand, timing of, 375t, 376
origins (Mainland) in Taiwan (*see* ethnicity in Taiwan)
oyabun-kobun relationship (*see* master-follower relationship)

parental availability: and coresidence in Taiwan, 329t, 331t, 332; and coresidence in U.S., 225t, 225–26; and family type in Japan, 181–82, 184, 188, 191–92, 193t, 194–95; and parental residence in Taiwan, 335t
parental contact: and attitudes toward family in Japan, 201–17, 204t, 211t, 212t, 214t, 215t; and attitudes toward family in U.S., 217; differences in, for men and women in Japan, 171–73; factors affecting, in Japan, 157–77, 159t, 163t, 165tt, 166ttt, 168t, 17, 222–46, 223t, 224t, 227t, 229t, 231t, 232t, 233t, 235f, 238t, 239t, 240t, 244f, 244t; factors affecting, in Taiwan, 356, 359; factors affecting, in U.S., 223t, 224t, 225t, 229t, 231t, 232t, 233t, 235f, 238t, 239t, 240t, 244f, 244t; frequency of, in Japan, 167–68, 168t; in Japan, 153–77, 199–218, 221–46, 224t; in Japan, nonresponse to questions about, 167–68, 176t; in Japan, on survey questionnaire, 445–46; in Japan, survey on (*see* National Family Survey of Japan); measurement of, in Japan, 208, 245–46; measurement of, in U.S., 245–46; of middle-aged in Japan, 157–58, 167–74; and modernization in Taiwan, 15; and mortality, 222; and parent-child relationships in Taiwan, 355–56, 356t, 359; patterns of, in Japan, 157, 208–9, 209t; in Taiwan, data and methods used for study of, 321–25, 322t, 323f, 324e; in Taiwan, survey on, 321–22; in U.S., 221–46
parental residence: with another child in Japan, and parental contact, 230, 231t, 232t, 233t, 234, 238t, 239t, 240t, 242–43; with another child in U.S., and parental contact, 230, 231t, 232t, 233t, 234, 238t, 239t, 240t, 242–43; factors affecting, in Taiwan, 334–36, 335t, 357–58; in Japan, on survey questionnaire, 444, 445; and parental contact in Japan, 170–71, 172t, 173–74; in Taiwan (*see* coresidence)
parental survival: and age in Japan, 222–23; and age in U.S., 222–23; and coresidence in Japan, 156, 159t, 162, 163t, 164, 227, 227t; and coresidence in Korea, 296, 296t, 297t; and coresidence in U.S., 227, 227t; and intergenerational relationships in Japan, 222–23, 223t; and intergenerational relationships in U.S., 222–23, 223t; in Japan, on survey questionnaire, 444; and parental contact in Japan, 159t, 169, 171–73, 172t, 230, 231t, 232t, 233t, 238t, 239t, 240t, 243–44, 244f, 244t; and parental contact in U.S., 230, 231t, 232t, 233t, 238t, 239t, 240t, 243–44, 244f, 244t
parent-child relationships (*see* intergenerational relationships)
parents: duties to, in Thailand, 404; obedience

Index

to, in Korea, attitudes toward, 281–82, 282t 14.2; responsibility for, and coresidence in Japan, 164n; responsibility for, in Japan, 14
parents, contact with (*see* parental contact)
parish registers (*see* population registers)
partible inheritance of land in Thailand, 371t, 371–72
patriarchy (*see also* Confucianism; patrilineal descent; patrilocal residence); in Meiji era of Japan, 9–10, 183, 200; persistence of, in Korea, 300; traditional, in Korea, 281
patrilineal descent (*see also* Confucianism; family lineage; patriarchy; patrilocal residence); in Confucianism, 4; in Japan, 9–10, 29, 200–201; in Korea, 10–11, 281; in Sub-Saharan Africa, 23; in Thailand, 366n
patrilocal residence (*see also* patriarchy; patrilineal descent); in China, compared to Taiwan, 336, 357; in Japan, 200; in Taiwan, compared to China, 336, 357
percent married (*see* proportions married)
percent never-married (*see* proportions married)
percent single (*see* proportions single)
Philippines, fertility in, and government policy, 24
place of birth: and assistance to new parents in Thailand, 396t, 396–97, 399; in Taiwan (*see* ethnicity in Taiwan)
plant closures in Japan (*see* industrial restructuring in Japan)
policy, family, and idealized family morality, 23–24
policy in Japan (*see* financial assistance; industrial policy in Japan)
Policy Office of the Aged: surveys on the elderly, 124, 131
population registers and study of the family, 421
possessions, modern, in Taiwan: and coresidence, 330t, 331t, 333; and sharing of meals, 343; and support from sons, 348–50, 350t
postnuptial residence (*see under* coresidence)
primogeniture, 181; in Japan, 200 (*see also* birth order in Japan; family type in Japan, stem)
probit analysis, 168n; of parental contact in Japan, 168–74, 172t
pronatalism and government programs in Europe, 422, 425
property (*see* land)
property, family (*kasan*) in Japan, 184

proportions married (*see also* universal marriage); age-specific, in Japan, 95–96, 96t; changes in, in Japan, 93; in Chinese cultural sphere, 4; effect on fertility in Japan, 98, 99t; in West, 4–5, 25
proportions never-married (*see* proportions married; proportions single)
proportions single (*see also* proportions married); in Japan, 137–41, 138f, 139tt, 140f, 141
public assistance in Yūbari, 265–68; and unemployment, 252
public employees in Yūbari, 256t, 257t, 259t, 266–68
public sector in Yūbari: effects of industrial restructuring on, 252, 266

region in Thailand: and age at marriage, 386–87, 387t; and assistance after birth, 397, 397t; and coresidence, 392t, 392–93, 398–99; and establishment of household, 393t, 393–94, 394t; and family values, attitudes toward, 409, 410t; and language, 384; and modernity, 414, 415t; and place of birth of child, 399; and spouse selection, 386, 386t
regression analysis (*see also* logit analysis; probit analysis); compared with logit analysis, 188n; of extended family in Japan, 188–94, 192t, 193t
relationships, intergenerational (*see* intergenerational relationships; parental contact)
religion: and coresidence in Taiwan, 327t, 328, 339t, 340–42, 341t; in Korea, 311t A14.8; and spouse selection in Japan, 147tt, 149–50
remarriage: attitudes toward, in Japan, on survey questionnaire, 442; attitudes toward, in Korea, 286, 286t 14.10; attitudes toward, in Thailand, 389t, 390, 398; in Japan, on survey questionnaire, 444; in old age in Japan, attitudes toward, 101–4, 102t; in old age in Japan, attitudes toward, factors affecting, 110t, 111–16, 112t
ren'ai (love marriage in Japan), 143, 143f, 151
replacement level of fertility in Japan, 91–94, 98
Republic of Korea (*see* Korea *under specific topics*)
residence (*see also* matrilocal residence; neolocal residence; patrilocal residence); and attitudes toward family in Japan, 101t, 102t, 108–16, 110t, 112t, 113t; and attitudes toward marriage in Japan, 101t, 102t, 108–

16, 110t, 112t; and coresidence in Japan, 155–56, 159t, 161, 163t 9.2, 164–65; and coresidence in Taiwan, 339t; duration of, in Japan, on survey questionnaire, 448; in Korea, 311t A14.9; and marriage arrangements in Taiwan, 353, 354t; and marriage decisions in Taiwan, 354t; and parental contact in Japan, 157, 159t, 169, 171–73, 172t; time at, in Japan, on survey questionnaire, 448; urban-rural, in Japan, on survey questionnaire, 448
restructuring, industrial (*see* industrial restructuring)
roles of women (*see* women's roles)
rural background in Taiwan: and children's education, 352, 353t; and coresidence, 327t, 327–33, 329t, 331t, 334, 336, 337t, 357; and parental residence, 335, 335t; and support from sons, 347, 348t; and wealth flows, 345, 346t
rural depopulation in Japan, effects of, 63–64, 67–68
rural family and community life in South Korea survey, 273; areas sampled, 274, 275f, 277–80, 279f; sample characteristics of, 307–16tt A14.1–A14.18; study design and procedures, 274–76, 307t

sector, economic, and changes in employment in Japan, 60, 60t
security, employment (*see also* unemployment); in Japan, 37; in U.S., 39–40
self-employment in Japan: and coresidence, 160; and family type, 184–85, 188–89, 192, 193t; and *ie* ideology, 185; and stem family, 263; in Yūbari (*see* shopkeepers in Yūbari)
sense of identity and view of family, 32
sex (*see* gender)
sex roles (*see* gender roles; women's roles)
sharing of meals in Taiwan (*see* wealth flows); and coresidence, 343–47, 344t, 358; factors affecting, 343–47, 346t, 347t
shopkeepers in Yūbari, 256t, 257t, 259t, 262–66 (*see also* farmers in Yūbari); succession of businesses of, 263–65
Singapore, stem family in, 54
singlehood in Japan: by age, 137–41, 138t, 139tt; attitudes toward, 100–101, 101t, 102t, 109, 110t, 111–12, 112t, 115–16; attitudes toward, on survey questionnaire, 442

singulate mean age at marriage (SMAM) (*see* age at marriage)
sin sord (groom's gift to bride's parents) in Thailand, 403, 414
size of house: and child care in Hong Kong, 182; and coresidence in Japan, 428; and family type in Japan, 184, 186, 189, 192t, 193t, 193–95
small business owners in Yūbari (*see* shopkeepers in Yūbari)
SMAM (singulate mean age at marriage) (*see* age at marriage)
social change: cohort model of, 200; and coresidence in Taiwan, 334; evolutionary, 11–12, 19, 21; explaining, 26; and parental residence in Taiwan, 338; predicting, 23, 30, 41; theories of, 21 (*see also* family change; family theory)
social Darwinism: and family, 11–12, 19
social group (*see* group)
social interaction in Ōgaito, changes in, 88
socialization: at different ages in Japan, 199–200; in Japan, 34, 43; and traditional values in Japan, 216; in U.S., 34–35, 40
social life in Thailand, attitudes about, 414–17
social mobility in Ōgaito, 83
social security (*see also* old-age security); and individualism in U.S., 39; in Taiwan, 357
social status in Japan: factors affecting, 149; and spouse selection, 147tt, 150
social structure: and family in Japan, 35–38, 92, 150–52; and family in U.S., 38–41; functional differentiation of, 182, 186, 195
social welfare: and aging in Japan, 130, 154; and family type in Japan, 182, 184, 188; and individualism in U.S., 39–40; in Japan (*see* elderly, care for); in Taiwan, 357
Society for the Study of Folklore: survey of Ōgaito, 71, 74f, 78t, 79–80
South Korea (*see* Korea *under specific topics*)
space in Japan: availability of, and family type, 186 (*see also* size of house)
spiritual culture (social morality), 7, 12
spousal availability in Japan: and family type, 188, 191
spousal presence in Japan, 135–52; and egalitarianism, 144, 151; and family type, 184, 191, 192t, 193, 193t, 194–95
spousal survival in Korea: and living arrangements of elderly, 303, 303t, 304t, 305

Index

spouse selection: criteria for, in Japan, 146–51, 147tt; criteria for, in Japan, on survey questionnaire, 441; in Japan, 13–14, 103n, 135–52, 147tt (*see also* marriage); in Japan, survey on (*see* National Family Survey of Japan); and land in Thailand, 428; and modernization in Asia, 422–23; and modernization in Korean, 284–85, 423; and modernization in Taiwan, 422; types of, in Thailand, 385–86, 386t, 398
spouses in Ōgaito, origins of, 76–79, 78t, 79t, 88
stability, family, in U.S., 41–42
status (*see* social status)
status of women: and parental support in Taiwan, 345; and women's roles in East Asia, 92
stem family (*see* family, stem)
strategy, survival (*see* survival strategy)
structural adjustment in Japan (*see* industrial restructuring)
structural factors in Japan: and marriage, 145–46; and spouse selection, 135–52
structural-functionalism, 12, 20–21, 23, 30
Sub-Saharan Africa, family in, 23
succession of family line in Korea, 10–11; attitudes toward, 282t 14.3, 282–83
succession of family name in Japan: attitudes toward, 206, 209t, 212t, 212–13; attitudes toward, on survey questionnaire, 442
succession of small businesses in Yūbari, 263–65
support: from children in Japan, and family type, 184, 189, 192, 192t; from children in Japan, attitudes toward, on survey questionnaire, 442; for elderly in Thailand, by family, 379; in establishing new household in Thailand, 395t, 395–96, 399; intergenerational, in Japan, 154, 174; preferred source of, in Japan, on survey questionnaire, 447; from sons in Taiwan, 320, 347–51, 358–59; from sons in Taiwan, factors affecting, 347–51, 348t, 349t, 358–59; at time of birth in Thailand, 396t, 397t, 397–98; for younger generation in Thailand, 378
Survey of Changes in Life Structure of the Population in Relation to Aging in Japan, 186
surveys (*see* family surveys)
survival and coresidence, 222
survival of parents (*see* parental survival)

survival strategy in Japan and family type, 181–82, 196
Sweden: age at marriage in, 96; divorce in, 423; as model for U.S., 431–32; welfare state in, compared with U.S., 432
systems of families, 22–26 (*see also* family type)

Taiwan (*see under specific topics*)
telephoning parents: in Japan (*see* parental contact); in Taiwan, and coresidence, 355–56, 359
tenkin (job transfer) in Yūbari and migration, 266
TFR (*See* total fertility rate)
Thai Family and Household Survey: design and procedures of, 364, 384–85, 402
Thailand *(see under specific topics)*; language and religion of, 384–85; surveys in, 383–84
three-generation household: in Japan (*see under* family type in Japan); in Thailand, and family cycle, 367
Tokyo Liberal Arts University (*see* Ōgaito, Japan, surveys of)
tonari kumi (neighborhood association) (*see* kumi)
total fertility rate (*see also* fertility); components of, in Japan, 98, 98t; and family in Japan, 91; future of, in West, 424–25; and household size in China, 52–53; and household size in Japan, 50, 51t; in Japan, 94, 94f, 95t, 424, 426
tourist industry in Yūbari, 264, 268
training, employee, 36, 38
transfer, job: in Japan, 36; and migration in Yūbari, 266; in U.S., 38
transportation: effects of, in Japan, 63–64; effects of, in Yuzurihara, 68, 88; and urban-rural relationships in Korea, 276–77

Uenohara, Japan, 64–67, 65f, 66f; as area for Ōgaito residents shopping and daily activities, 83, 85t
ultimogeniture, 181 (*see also* family type in Japan, stem)
unemployment: government policies to combat, in Japan, 248–49; insurance in U.S., and government support of family, 39; in U.S., 39
United States *(see also* U.S. *under specific topics)*; differences with Japan, 432

Index

universal marriage: and coresidence in Japan, 128; erosion of, in Japan, 136, 151; and fertility in Chinese cultural sphere, 4; and fertility in Japan, 93; in Japan (see also under proportions married); and marriage type in Japan, 13; as norm in Japan, 100; persistence of, in Japan, 141–42; in Thailand, 386
University Research Center (see National Family Survey of Japan; Ōgaito, Japan, surveys of)
upbringing, urban (see urban upbringing)
urbanization (see also city size; urban upbringing); and coresidence in Taiwan, 328, 338, 339t, 358; effects of, in Japan, 9, 59, 63; effects on family, in Korea, 15; and family in Taiwan, 356 (see also residence); and family type in Japan, 179, 186; and marriage arrangements in Taiwan, 353, 354t; and parental residence in Taiwan, 334–35; spread of, in Japan, 60–61, 61t
urban penetration of rural areas in Japan: and economic growth, 60; and urban-rural distinction, 63–64
urban-rural distinction in Japan, 63; blurring of, 59–60
urban upbringing: and attitudes toward family in Japan, 101t, 102t, 106–16, 110t, 112t, 113t; and attitudes toward marriage in Japan, 101t, 102t, 106–16, 110t, 112t; in Japan, on survey questionnaire, 439; and values in Korea, 294

values: and socialization, 199–200 (see also family values; values under family in specific countries)
visits with parents (see parental contact)

waraji-oya (sponsor) in Japan, 86
Waseda University (see Ōgaito, Japan, surveys of)
wealth flows in Taiwan, 342–47, 344t, 358; and coresidence, 15; data and methods used for study of, 321–25, 322t, 323f, 324e; factors affecting, 345–57, 346t, 347t; survey on, 321–22
weddings in Thailand: gifts at, 403–4, 414
welfare (see social welfare)
welfare rate in Yūbari, 252

welfare state: limitations of, 430; in Sweden and U.S., 432
widowhood (see also remarriage); in Korea (see spousal survival in Korea); probability of, in Japan, 103
widow remarriage in Korea: attitudes toward, 286, 286t 14.10
women: criteria of, for spouse selection in Japan, 150–51; dependence of, on men in Japan, 149–50; education and employment of, in Japan, 36–37; education and employment of, in U.S., 39; growing independence of, in Japan, 151; individualism of, in Japan, 92; inheritance rights of, in Korea, 10; problems for, in Japan, 43; social status of, in Japan, 92
women, labor-force status of: and attitudes toward marriage and family in Japan, 102t, 107–8, 112t, 113t, 114, 116; and childrearing in U.S., 40, 424; and coresidence in Japan, 160; and coresidence in Taiwan, 328, 329t, 331t, 334, 336, 337t; and family roles in West, 436; and fertility in Japan, 108n; in Japan, 36–37, 43; and marriage arrangements in Taiwan, 355t; in Ōgaito, 83, 84t; in U.S., 39–41, 424; and wealth flows in Taiwan, 345, 347t; and women's roles, 216
women's roles (see also gender roles); attitudes toward values about, in Thailand, 405t, 405–6, 408t, 409, 410t, 412t, 417; changing, in Korea, 281; changing, in U.S., 423–24; and family type in Japan, 182; in Japan, 216; in Thailand, 401, 404–6 (see also gender roles)
women's status: changes in, in Taiwan, 345; in Singapore, 24
work in Thailand, timing of, 374, 375t
work status: and attitudes toward family in Japan, 102t, 107–8, 112t, 113t; and attitudes toward marriage in Japan, 102t, 107–8, 112t; of elderly in Korea (see elderly); and living arrangements of elderly in Korea, 303t, 304t; and parental contact in Japan, 169–70, 172t
World Fertility Survey, 6

Yamanashi Prefecture, Japan, 64, 65f, 66f
year of marriage and marriage arrangements in Taiwan, 354t

yōshi (adoption) system and family succession in Japan, 200

youth in Thailand: lack of studies on, 379–80

Yūbari, Japan, 249–69; agriculture in, 265, 268; coal industry in, 249–53; decline of industries and services in, 252; employment in, 250–53, 266; employment types in, 256, 260–68; farmers in, 264–66; financial assistance in, 252, 266–68; history of, 250–53; migration from, 251–53, 255–69; migration intentions in (*see* migration); mine closures in, 250–51; mine closures in, impacts of, 249, 251–53, 260–68; mining employees in, 256t, 257, 259t, 260–62; population composition of, 252–55, 254tt; population of, 250–53, 251t, 268; public assistance in, 252, 265–68; public employees in, 256t, 257t, 259t, 266–68; public sector in, 252, 266; shopkeepers in, 256t, 257t, 259t, 262–66; survey of, sample design and characteristics, 253–55, 254tt; tourist industry in, 264, 268; unemployment in, 252–53; welfare rate in, 252

Yuzurihara, Japan, 64, 67t, 67–68, 68n